D1482785

In the fourteenth century the Old World witnessed a series of profound and abrupt changes in the trajectory of long-established historical trends. Trans-continental networks of exchange fractured and an era of economic contraction and demographic decline dawned from which Latin Christendom would not begin to emerge until its voyages of discovery at the end of the fifteenth century. In a major new study of this 'Great Transition', Bruce Campbell assesses the contributions of commercial recession, war, climate change, and eruption of the Black Death to a far-reaching reversal of fortunes which spared no part of Eurasia. The book synthesizes a wealth of new historical, palaeoecological and biological evidence, including estimates of national income, reconstructions of past climates, and genetic analysis of DNA extracted from the teeth of plague victims, to provide a fresh account of the creation, collapse and realignment of western Europe's late-medieval commercial economy.

BRUCE M. S. CAMPBELL is Emeritus Professor of Medieval Economic History at the School of Geography, Archaeology and Palaeoecology, The Queen's University of Belfast.

The Great Transition

Climate, Disease and Society in the Late-Medieval World

The 2013 Ellen McArthur Lectures

Bruce M. S. Campbell

The Queen's University of Belfast

CAMBRIDGE
UNIVERSITY PRESS

CAMBRIDGE
UNIVERSITY PRESS

University Printing House, Cambridge CB2 8BS, United Kingdom

One Liberty Plaza, 20th Floor, New York, NY 10006, USA

477 Williamstown Road, Port Melbourne, VIC 3207, Australia

4843/24, 2nd Floor, Ansari Road, Daryaganj, Delhi - 110002, India

79 Anson Road, #06-04/06, Singapore 079906

Cambridge University Press is part of the University of Cambridge.

It furthers the University's mission by disseminating knowledge in the pursuit of education, learning and research at the highest international levels of excellence.

www.cambridge.org
Information on this title: www.cambridge.org/9780521144438

First published 2016

A catalogue record for this publication is available from the British Library

Library of Congress Cataloging in Publication data
Campbell, B. M. S., author.
The great transition : climate, disease and society in the late medieval world / Bruce M.S. Campbell (The Queen's University of Belfast).
Cambridge, United Kingdom ; New York, New York : Cambridge University Press, 2016.
"The 2013 Ellen McArthur lectures."
Includes bibliographical references and index.
LCCN 2016006578   ISBN 9780521195881 (hardback)
LCSH: Europe – History – 476–1492.   Social change – Europe – History – To 1500.   Climatic changes – Social aspects – Europe – History – To 1500.   Climatic changes – Economic aspects – Europe – History – To 1500.   Human ecology – Europe – History – To 1500.   Black Death – Europe – History.   Diseases – Social aspects – Europe – History – To 1500.   War and society – Europe – History – To 1500.   Europe – Social conditions – To 1492.   Europe – Economic conditions – To 1492.   BISAC: NATURE / General.
LCC D202.C33 2016   DDC 940.1/92 – dc23
LC record available at https://lccn.loc.gov/2016006578

ISBN 978-0-521-19588-1 Hardback
ISBN 978-0-521-14443-8 Paperback

For Anthony,
committed post-medievalist,
who in Berlin, Belfast and Mulroy kept company
with this book throughout its long gestation

Contents

In retrospect I can see that this book marks the final stage of an academic journey which began when, aged 16 and on the recommendation of Mr Stow, deputy headmaster and head of geography at Rickmansworth Grammar School, I opted to study Geography, Economics, and Pure Mathematics with Statistics at Advanced Level. From that decision, so lightly taken, springs this book's focus upon economic progress or the want of it across a wide geographical area, the attention paid to climate and disease as agents of socio-ecological change, and the reliance upon the quantification and graphical representation of key variables and developments. In the 1960s regional geography was a core component of the geography curriculum and always began with a study of the physical environment before proceeding to a consideration of the relevant country or region's human geography. This was because, self-evidently, temperature, rainfall, terrain, geology, vegetation and ecology shape where people live, the natural resources available to them, how they make a living, their methods and routes of transport, and the kinds of physical and biological hazards to which they are exposed. Environmental history shares the same premises.

Including nature among the protagonists of historical change risks incurring the stigma of environmental determinism. As a geography undergraduate at Liverpool University I was taught about the environmental determinism of Elsworth Huntington and warned that this was something to avoid. Instead, I learned that, because people have choices and create institutions and technology, environmental conditions powerfully influence but rarely determine human outcomes. The existence of important interactions, both direct and indirect and either positive or negative, between nature and society was taken as axiomatic, as was the idea that natural processes operate in parallel with human processes and are equally worthy of study. The then comparatively young subject of ecology was introduced to us as, perhaps, the most effective and comprehensive theoretical framework for analysing, explaining and understanding environmental and human interactions at a hierarchy of nested scales from a single field to the entire world. The appeal of this holistic approach, with its capacity to accommodate and explain a wider range of variables and inter-relationships than neoclassical, institutional or Marxist economics, has stayed with me ever since. Moreover, without the requirement at this formative stage of my education to read extensively across the sub-disciplines of physical geography, I could not have engaged with the fast-growing modern scientific literatures on palaeoclimatology and the biology of plague upon which this book draws so extensively. What often seemed a chore and was certainly a challenge at the time has many years later stood me in good stead. So, in a very real sense, in this book I have returned to my academic roots.

It was in the early 1970s, as a postgraduate student at Cambridge undertaking detailed case studies of three late-medieval Norfolk manors under the wise supervision of Alan Baker, that the massive economic and demographic impacts of the Great European Famine of 1315–22 and Black Death of 1348–9 were first brought home to me. So far as I could see, neither catastrophe could be convincingly accommodated within the rival, but economically equally deterministic, Malthusian and Marxist interpretations of medieval economic history then in vogue. Nor, given my earlier training, was it satisfying to dismiss these catastrophes as providential exogenous shocks and enquire little further about why two once-in-half-a-millennium events should have occurred within the narrow space of a single generation. At that time, however, it was difficult to explore the environmental dimensions and contexts of these disasters in more detail for the relevant palaeoecological research had scarcely begun. Notwithstanding the compelling advocacy of Emmanuel Le Roy Ladurie's pioneering *Times of feast and times of famine*, historians could safely disregard historical climate change because so little was known about it.[1] Progress on this front has had to await the upsurge of research funding generated by contemporary anxieties about 'global warming', the arrival of laptop computers, and the advent of the World Wide Web, with the facility the last provides for storing, seeking and accessing the growing number of palaeoclimatic datasets so ingeniously derived from tree rings, ice cores, speleothems, lake varves, ocean sediments and much else. Here, the website managed by the United States National Oceanic and Atmospheric Administration (NOAA), at the National Climatic Data Center, has proved invaluable and deserves to be far better known by historians.[2] Would that it had existed when I was researching and writing my doctoral thesis.

[1] Le Roy Ladurie (1971).
[2] www.ncdc.noaa.gov/data-access/paleoclimatology-data

It was as a postgraduate that I began to calculate and gather data on crop yields from what I was beginning to discover was a veritable gold-mine of manorial accounts, extending in time from the mid-thirteenth to the late fifteenth centuries. This exercise started with Norfolk and was funded from 1983 to 1984 by an Economic and Social Research Council (ESRC) personal research fellowship. The two Feeding the City Projects, undertaken in collaboration with Derek Keene, Jim Galloway and Margaret Murphy between 1988 and 1994 with funding provided by the Leverhulme Trust and ESRC, then extended the task to the ten counties closest to London. Subsequently it grew to become a project in itself, in the form of the ESRC-funded project 'Crops yields, environmental conditions, and historical change, 1270–1430', which ran from 2005 to 2007. Additional financial support was provided by the British Academy and a Margary Grant from the Sussex Archaeological Society, and invaluable research assistance was provided by Anne Drewery, David Hardy, Marilyn Livingstone, Christopher Whittick and Elaine Yeates. To the existing yield datasets on Norfolk and the ten Feeding the City counties were added the extensive yield calculations of Jan Titow and David Farmer for the estates of the bishopric of Winchester and Westminster Abbey, plus fresh series for demesnes belonging to Battle Abbey, Canterbury Cathedral Priory, Glastonbury Abbey and an assortment of other estates. The results, at both manorial and aggregated national level, are available online at www.cropyields.ac.uk and are referred to repeatedly in the following pages.

The whole idea for this crop-yields project arose from conversations I had been having with Queen's University dendrochronologist Mike Baillie and the realization that tree rings and grain yields provide complementary but contrasting measures of past growing conditions. Two joint applications to the Natural Environment Research Council were unsuccessful before the ESRC eventually came up with the funding to create a matching 225-year dataset of English crop yields. The results proved more intriguing than I could have hoped, highlighting the paramount influence of weather conditions upon agricultural output and setting both the notorious harvest failures of 1256–7, 1292–5, 1315–16 and 1436–7 and the abundant harvests of 1325–7, 1376–8 and 1386–8 in a clearer environmental context. Especially striking was the indubitable evidence provided by both the grain-yield and oak-ring chronologies, together with an array of other dendrochronologies from around the world, of a major growth downturn in the late 1340s at the very time when the Black Death was carving its destructive path through the populations of western Asia, North Africa and Europe. For the first time it became apparent that a clear association existed between extreme weather, ecological stress and the eruption and spread of plague. Equally clear was the shared origin of both the Great European Famine and the Black Death in a common era of heightened climatic instability. This offered a whole new perspective on a familiar and much debated period. Mike Baillie's own thoughts about this complex episode are set out in his provocative short book *New light on the Black Death*, which is brim full of ideas and evidence and suggested to me several new directions in which I might take my own work. Without this fruitful dialogue with Mike Baillie, and without the tree-ring chronologies with which he plied me, this book, in its current form, could not have been written.

A further spin-off from my crop yields project was an ambitious collaborative project undertaken with Steve Broadberry, Mark Overton, Alex Klein and Bas van Leeuwen to reconstruct the national income of England from 1270 to 1700 and of Britain from 1700 to 1870. This began in 2007 with funding from the Leverhulme Trust and was finally completed in March 2014 when the manuscript of *British economic growth 1270–1870* was delivered to Cambridge University Press. My considerable debt to this project will be apparent from the many citations to it, for it has provided more soundly based quantitative estimates of population, agricultural, industrial and service-sector output, gross domestic product (GDP) and GDP per head than any hitherto available. Further, through meetings convened by Steve Broadberry and Kevin O'Rourke in conjunction with the project 'Historical patterns of development' (HI-POD), funded by the European Commission's 7th Framework Programme for Research (Contract Number SSH7-CT-2008-225342), I became better acquainted with the work of Paolo Malanima, Leandro Prados de la Escosura, Jan Luiten van Zanden and other historical national income accountants (all of whom have been generous in sharing data). Their estimates have enabled me to place England's exceptionally well-documented late-medieval economic development within a broader comparative context. The copious detailed publications on the Flemish textile industry by John Munro, who sadly died before this book could be completed but with whom I have shared many stimulating conversations, have also enabled me to integrate Flanders into the narrative. To him, along with the late Larry Epstein, I also owe the connection made between warfare, rising transaction costs and commercial recession in the early fourteenth century. As a monetarist, John would, I trust, have approved of the emphasis placed in Section 5 upon scarce bullion as a contributory factor to the prolonged post-Black Death economic and commercial contraction.

Meanwhile, in 2004, after sixteen years spent teaching medieval and early modern British and Irish economic history, I had joined the newly established School of Geography, Archaeology and Palaeoecology in the

Queen's University of Belfast, where I offered what proved to be a popular final-year module entitled 'Hazards, humans and history: human–environment interactions during the last millennium'. With reference to Britain and Ireland, this module set out to explore the influence and impact of environmental risks and hazards upon human populations, societies and economies over the last millennium. Due attention was paid both to extreme events, exemplified by famines, livestock epidemics, plagues and other disasters (always a hit with students), and more subtle shifts in human environment relations, such as changes in growing conditions and human morbidity. Students were asked to reflect upon why some societies were particularly vulnerable to natural hazards and others more resilient. The contents and approach of this module informed both my original book proposal to Cambridge University Press (which had the working title 'The anatomy of a crisis: Britain and Ireland 1290–1377') and the successful fellowship application I made at about the same time to the Wissenschaftskolleg zu Berlin (familiarly known as Wiko). The timing of these initiatives, of course, meant that if the British national income project overran, which it did, I would be left with two books to submit to CUP at more-or-less the same time (one co-authored, the other solo authored). This has delayed delivery of both but with the compensation that each has benefited from being closely informed by the other.

Work on *The Great Transition* commenced in earnest in the almost ideal working environment provided at Wiko in October 2010. I am grateful to Gregory Clark for nominating me, to the Rector and governing body for electing me and to the Kolleg for funding me. Here, in an interdisciplinary and collegial environment and with first-class library support, I discovered the NOAA website, came to appreciate the global dimensions of the climate reorganization that occurred between c.1270 and c.1420, and as a result swiftly began to reconceive my original narrowly-British book proposal. Almost immediately, in October 2010, further momentum was lent to this task by publication of the breakthrough paper by Haensch and others that finally confirmed beyond doubt that *Yersinia pestis* was indeed the pathogen responsible for the Black Death. It quickly became clear that I needed to engage with this fast-moving field of biological research, in which teams of plague researchers at Marseille, Mainz and now Oslo appear to be vying with each other. For me as an economic historian this has meant entering hitherto uncharted academic territory. At Wiko I was helped and encouraged by biologists Janis Antonovics and Mike Boots. More recently, comments and leads offered by a lively group of biologically aware medievalists and historians of disease led by Michelle Ziegler, Monica Green and Ann Carmichael have helped keep me up to speed. I am particularly indebted to Ann Carmichael for her informed and constructive comments on an earlier draft of those sections that deal with the Black Death. Responsibility for the views contained, both here and elsewhere in the book, nevertheless remains my own.

At a plague workshop convened by Richard Hoyle at the University of Reading in September 2013 I had the pleasure of hearing and meeting prominent aDNA researcher Barbara Bramanti, who led the Mainz plague team but has now transferred to Oslo, where a radical rethinking of all three plague pandemics is taking place.[3] Leading Norwegian plague historian Ole Benedictow was also at that meeting and kindly offered some helpful responses to my own paper. While I have not heeded all his recommendations his intervention has nonetheless saved me from claiming more than the available evidence will currently allow. His own views, informed by a close reading of the reports of the Indian Plague Commission and the extensive medical literature generated by the Third Pandemic, also served as a reminder that almost everything about the Black Death – its geographical origin, activation, hosts and vectors, mechanisms of transmission and spread, and case fatality rate – remains controversial. This is not a subject about which any prudent historian can afford to be dogmatic.

In a field where new datasets and papers are proliferating so fast, it is difficult to resist the temptation to privilege data gathering and the tracking of the latest publications over analysis, synthesis and writing. Invitations to present conference and seminar papers have therefore been invaluable in spurring me to make sense of the material I have been collecting and providing opportunities to test reactions to it. Participation in the following conferences, workshops and meetings has been material to advancing my thinking and understanding: the Mellon Foundation's Sawyer Seminar Series 2010, 'Crisis, what crisis? Collapses and Dark Ages in comparative perspective', held at Cambridge in May 2010; 'Historical climatology: past and future', held at the German Historical Institute, Paris, in September 2011; 'Climate change and big history', a panel convened at the 2013 meeting of the American Historical Association in New Orleans (with follow-up lecture and seminar presentations at Columbus Ohio and Pittsburgh); 'The coldest decade of the millennium? The Spörer Minimum, the climate during the 1430s, and its economic, social and cultural impact', held at the Historical Institute,

---

[3] European Research Council project: 'MedPlag: The medieval plagues: ecology, transmission modalities and routes of the infections', Centre for Ecological and Evolutionary Synthesis, University of Oslo. Scientific conference, 'The past plague pandemics (Justinian, Black Death, Third) in light of modern molecular life science insights', Oslo, 19–20 November 2014: http://english.dnva.no/kalender/vis.html?tid=63069.

University of Bern in December 2014; and 'Famines during the "Little Ice Age" (1300–1800): socio-natural entanglements in premodern societies', at the Centre for Interdisciplinary Research, University of Bielfeld in February 2015. I am indebted to John Hatcher, Franz Mauelshagen, Gregory Quenet, John Brooke, Patrick Manning, Chantal Camenisch and Dominik Collet for their invitations to speak at these meetings and to the other participants for their instructive contributions. Thanks are also due to Bernd Herrmann, Michael North, Mathieu Arnoux, Bob Allen, John Watts, Paul Slack, Negley Harte and Leandro Prados de la Escosura for invitations to present papers at the universities of Göttingen, Greifswald, Paris 7, Oxford, the Institute of Historical Research, London, and the Fundación Ramón Areces, Madrid.

In April 2009 the Datini Institute at Prato, of which I was then a committee member, devoted its 41st study week to 'Economic and biological interactions in pre-industrial Europe from the 13th to the 18th centuries'. Wim Blockmans wisely presided over this pioneering meeting which revealed just how resistant some historians can be to venturing off what they consider to be piste. It was therefore a pleasure to hear eloquent advocacy of an environmental approach to history from Bernd Herrmann and Richard Hoffmann. The latter's splendid introductory *Environmental history of medieval Europe* was published in the nick of time for me to draw upon it in the final stages of revising this volume. It was narrowly preceded by John Brooke's *A rough journey* and Geoffrey Parker's *Global crisis*, which have sat on my desk reminding and inspiring me to press on and get my own very different treatment of an earlier global crisis completed. Reassuringly, both books have been as long in gestation as my own, testifying to the time that it takes to research and write mature environmental history.

The invitation to present the 2012/13 Ellen McArthur Lectures at the University of Cambridge (delivered in February 2013: podcasts available at www.econsoc.hist.cam.ac.uk/podcasts.html) galvanized me into bringing together and synthesizing the mass of historical, palaeoclimatic and biological evidence I had been assembling and which by then threatened to overwhelm me. Writing these four lectures also provided me with a more effective structure for integrating the environmental and human sides of my story. Given the academic stature of previous Ellen McArthur lecturers, delivering these lectures was a daunting enough commission in itself. In the Mill Lane lecture theatre I was given sterling practical assistance by Chris Briggs and Leigh Shaw-Taylor, while at Trinity Hall I was accommodated and hosted in great comfort by Martin and Claire Daunton. Further hospitality, encouragement and feedback were provided by David Abulafia, Alan Baker, Judith Bennett, John Hatcher and Richard Smith. Revising these PowerPoint-supported lectures for the very different medium of the written word has taken the greater part of two-and-a-half years (including time out to finish *British economic growth*). Readers who watch the podcasts before delving into the text will discover that the latter is a greatly expanded, updated and revised version of the lectures. They will also find that the podcasts provide the most effective introduction to the book.

All academics stand on the shoulders of others. I am in awe of the patience with which generations of historians have painstakingly extracted systematic information from the archives and amazed at the ingenuity and tenacity with which scientists have derived meaningful information from the most unexpected and often intractable sources, including algae deposited on the ocean shelf and the dental pulp of skeletons. My debt to a legion of scholars working individually and in teams will be apparent from the citations. I am especially grateful to all those who have placed their datasets online and whose journal articles are available on open access. Among historical works, Janet Abu-Lughod's *Before European hegemony*, which transcends conventional historical boundaries and chronologies, has been a particular inspiration. Frank Ludlow read and commented upon the greater part of the text and kept me up to date respecting current dating of the eruptions of Quilotoa and Kuwae. Others who have either shared ideas and materials or rendered help include Martin Allen, Lorraine Barry, Ken Bartley, Steve Broadberry, John Brooke, Jan Esper, Bas van Leeuwen, Scott Levi, Marilyn Livingstone, Tim Newfield, Cormac Ó Gráda, Richard Oram, Terry Pinkard, Larry Poos, Leandro Prados de la Escosura, David Reher, Steve Rigby, Ben Sadd, Philip Slavin, Jacob Weisdorf and Ting Xu. Gill Alexander, with whom I have worked for over four decades, drew Figures 1.2, 2.1, 2.9, 2.15, 3.19, 3.22, 3.25, 3.27, 4.9 and 4.10 with her customary eye for cartographic veracity and then uncomplainingly converted all the other figures into the CMYK TIF format required by the Press. At CUP Michael Watson has sent timely email reminders to prick my conscience and then waited like patience on a monument for the finished manuscript. Richard Hoffmann was the well-chosen anonymous referee who read the entire manuscript in draft and whose wise and constructive comments have been of great assistance in helping me sharpen the volume's focus and improve its presentation. The published version is the better for his recommendations, as it is for the eagle-eyed copy-editing by Ken Moxham. This is a great publishing house to work with and its production team have done a magnificent job.

Publication might have occurred sooner had I not, in September 2010, taken on renovation of the then derelict Agent's House on the Mulroy

Estate, Co. Donegal, and with it the complete replanting of its extensive windswept and long-abandoned cliff-top garden. Fortunately, in February 2012 an early-retirement package from the Queen's University of Belfast, my employer of over thirty-eight years, gave me the time to combine gardening and writing. Thus, in the final stages of writing it is here in my first-floor study overlooking the twice-daily tidal race through the narrow and newly bridged neck of Mulroy Bay that this book has taken final shape and the whole of it been written, re-written or revised. As pressure to finish it has mounted, Martin McGroddy, Shaun Boyce and Willie Caldwell have successively taken the strain of developing and maintaining the garden and thereby freed me up to stay indoors plugging away at my computer, although many's the day when blue Donegal skies, fresh air and the sparkling sea have made me wish I could exchange tasks with them. Diana's devoted company has made the long hours at the keyboard less lonely and Sampson and, more recently, Freia have insisted that I occasionally take a break and give them and myself some fresh air and exercise. Whether this has helped or hindered me from finishing the book I cannot quite decide.

At Mulroy, the powerful ebb and flow of Atlantic tides, winter alternation between maritime mildness and bitter Arctic cold, spells of incessant rain, fierce gale-force and sometimes hurricane-force winds, irrepressible germination of weeds, invasive growth of Japanese Knotweed, and seasonal progression from short winter days to brief summer nights have served as constant reminders of the independent and sometimes relentless power of nature. Back in Belfast, flags, marches and protests testify to the determined human pursuit of other agendas, of which some of the most irreconcilable were set in train in this remote northwest corner of Eurasia during Parker's seventeenth-century *Global crisis*. Here, in the north of Ireland, nature and culture clash and co-exist as in few other places. What elsewhere is tacit is here explicit. The same, I hope, is true of this book.

Mulroy, 7 June 2015

ACA	Arid Central Asia
aDNA	ancient deoxyribonucleic acid
DSI	Drought Severity Index
ENSO	El Niño Southern Oscillation
GDP	gross domestic product
LIA	Little Ice Age
MCA	Medieval Climate Anomaly
NAO	North Atlantic Oscillation
Poly.	Polynomial
SNPs	single nucleotide polymorphisms
TSI	Total Solar Irradiance
VEI	Volcanic Explosivity Index (range 1–8)

The Great Transition spanned the late thirteenth to the late fifteenth centuries. It ended one sustained phase of European expansion, cultural efflorescence and trans-Eurasian commercial integration and defined the baseline from which the next eventually sprang. Unique combinations of environmental and human factors triggered the Great Transition and then shaped and determined its course. These included, on the one hand, global climate change and the re-emergence of deadly plagues of livestock and humans and, on the other, mounting warfare, commercial recession, economic contraction, bullion scarcity and a massive implosion of Old World populations. The full ecological and geographical dimensions of these developments are only now coming to light thanks to detailed scientific research into past climates, biological decoding of the *Yersinia pestis* genome, the application of aDNA analysis to Black Death burials, the emergence of global history as a significant field of scholarly enquiry, and the extension of historical national income analysis back to the fourteenth and fifteenth centuries. There have been many attempts to describe and explain the changes in historical trajectory that took place between the 1270s and 1470s but this is the first to take advantage of these new insights and to integrate the role of physical and biological processes and developments fully into the narrative.[1] To do so has required broadening the scale of enquiry to encompass, as appropriate, Latin Christendom, the whole of Eurasia and, in the case of climate, the northern hemisphere and, on occasion, the world.

The Great Transition followed an extended period when in both western Europe and eastern Asia favourable climatic conditions, relative freedom from major epidemics, technical progress and a raft of institutional innovations underscored sustained increases in population and economic output. The resurgence of Latin Christendom in the West was paralleled

---

[1] For reviews of the relevant historiography see Hybel (1989); Hatcher and Bailey (2001). For an almost exclusively anthropocentric interpretation of the transition see Aston and Philpin (1985), and for an environmentally informed view, Hoffmann (2014), 342–51.

in the East by the rise of Song China, the Champa, Dai Viet, Angkor and Pagan states of Southeast Asia, and the Chola Empire of south India.[2] All experienced a flowering of domestic and overseas trade and benefited from the enhanced opportunities for market specialization which this bestowed. One of the greatest achievements of the age was the progressive growth and widening of these independent orbits of exchange until, as documented by Janet Abu-Lughod, they coalesced into an integrated world system of trade that connected the commerce of the Orient with that of the Occident.[3] This was when European elites acquired their cravings for the spices, silks and ceramics of the East which they mostly paid for with bullion produced by Europe's booming silver mines. These developments are the subject of Section 2 (Efflorescence: the enabling environment and the rise of Latin Christendom) and are of fundamental importance to understanding the changes which then ensued as the environmental and societal foundations upon which the era's prosperity had been founded shifted and fractured. Whether the expansion and prosperity of this era of efflorescence was sustainable in the long term can be debated but that it powerfully shaped and influenced the contraction that followed is indisputable.[4]

The first indications of impending change become apparent in the 1260s and 1270s. From then until the 1340s forms the first stage of the Great Transition (Section 3: A precarious balance: mounting economic vulnerability in an era of increasing climatic instability and re-emergent pathogens), when the climatic, biological, military and commercial developments were initiated from which a major socio-ecological regime shift would in due course spring. That critical transition took place between the 1340s and 1370s during the second and most dramatic stage of the Great Transition (Section 4: Tipping point: war, climate change and plague shift the balance). During this short watershed period profound and irreversible changes occurred in both environmental and human conditions. Over the course of the next hundred years, during the third and final stage of the Great Transition (Section 5: Recession: the inhibiting environment and Latin Christendom's late-medieval demographic and economic contraction), the socio-ecological processes then set in train worked themselves out until the point was eventually reached during the last quarter of the fifteenth century when, under significantly altered environmental and commercial circumstances and within the context of

---

[2]   Lieberman (2009), 687–9; Lieberman and Buckley (2012), 1053–68; Tana (2014), 324–32; Abu-Lughod (1989), 263.

[3]   Abu-Lughod (1989); below, Figure 2.1.

[4]   For arguments in favour of the inevitability of some form of crisis see Aston and Philpin (1985).

an enlarged and redefined world, economic and demographic renewal and regrowth began. As outlined in Section 1.02, this eventually led to the Great Divergence between the revitalized and aggressively competitive maritime economies of the West and the more anciently commercialized and technologically advanced but stagnating economies of the East.[5]

Before considering the character of the interactions between nature and society that characterized the Great Transition (Section 1.03) and the practical issues of how best to analyse and describe it given the nature of the available evidence (Section 1.04), it is useful to rehearse in outline the essential features of each of the Great Transition's three stages. As this account of events is unfolded it will be plain that there was nothing pre-ordained about what transpired. At any given juncture several different outcomes were possible depending upon the precise configuration of human and environmental forces. Contingency therefore mattered and so, too, did fortuitous conjunctures of natural and human processes. Because there was so much that was unique about the Great Transition, the Epilogue (Theory, contingency, conjuncture and the Great Transition) will argue that it was in almost all essential respects an intrinsically historical phenomenon.

1.01   The Great Transition: an outline chronology

1.01.1   1260s/70s–1330s: the Great Transition begins

Until onset of the Wolf Solar Minimum in the final decades of the thirteenth century, relatively high levels of solar irradiance had sustained above-average global and northern hemisphere temperatures (Figure 1.1A) and correspondingly settled atmospheric circulation patterns across both hemispheres.[6] This was the last extended phase of the Medieval Climate Anomaly (MCA). Its salient features, which were especially well developed around 1250, are summarized in Figures 1.1B and 1.1C. The dry conditions verging on mega-drought in the North and South American West, in combination with heavy monsoon rainfall across South Asia, are diagnostic of a strongly positive El Niño Southern Oscillation (ENSO) over the Pacific Ocean.[7] The corresponding configuration of monsoon circulation over the Indian Ocean favoured India

---

[5] Pomeranz (2000) coined the term the 'Great Divergence' to describe the point when the leading Asian economies were overtaken by those of Europe.

[6] Delaygue and Bard (2010a); Vieira and others (2011); below, Section 2.02.

[7] Cook and others (2004c); Rein and others (2004); below, Section 2.02.1.

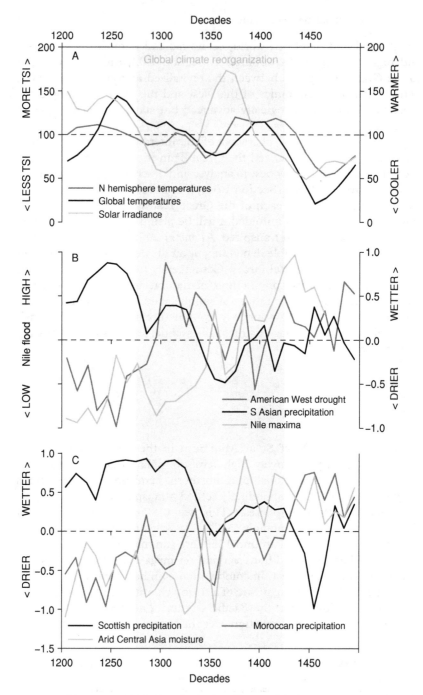

Figure 1.1 **(A)** Indexed solar irradiance, global temperatures and north-ern hemisphere temperatures, 1200–1500. **(B)** Indexed precipitation

and Pakistan over East Africa, with the result that monsoon-fed flood discharge of the River Nile at Cairo remained well below its potential maximum. Long-distance teleconnections between the Indian and Pacific Oceans and the North Atlantic maintained the North Atlantic Oscillation (NAO) in equally positive mode.[8] A strong westerly air-stream kept winters over northwest Europe mild and wet, as exemplified by the regular heavy rainfall experienced by western Scotland, at the expense of precipitation levels over much of Mediterranean Europe and North Africa (Figure 1.1C).[9] Low winter rainfall in these southerly regions meant that the westerly air-stream over Arid Central Asia was equally deficient in moisture, with the result that Eurasia's continental interior remained locked in a state of perpetual drought, never more severe than in the 1190s and early 1200s.[10] Marginal variations in precipitation had potentially big ecological consequences across this vast parched region, with wider human and biological repercussions which would play a big role in the Great Transition.[11]

It was from the 1270s, as solar irradiance diminished and global and northern hemisphere temperatures cooled (Figure 1.1A), that these long-established circulation patterns began to change. El Niño events, when warm water and air replaced cold in the eastern Pacific, now began to occur with increased frequency. Accordingly, precipitation levels rose over the North and South American West, culminating in a major wet

---

Figure 1.1 (cont.) in the North and South American West and in South Asia and the maximum height of the Nile flood, 1200–1500. (C) Indexed precipitation in Scotland and Morocco and moisture levels in Arid Central Asia, 1200–1500.
Sources: (A) Delaygue and Bard (2010b); Vieira and others (2011); Loehle and McCulloch (2008); Mann and others (2008): 100 = mean of the period 1250–1450. (B) Cook and others (2004c); Rein and others (2004); Rad and others (1999); Berkelhammer and others (2010b); Zhang and others (2008); Wang and others (2006); Popper (1951), 221–3. (C) Proctor and others (2002b); Esper and others (2009); Chen and others (2012)

---

[8] A teleconnection pattern is 'a recurring and persistent, large-scale pattern of pressure and circulation anomalies that spans vast geographical areas': United States National Weather Service, Climate Prediction Center, http://www.cpc.ncep.noaa.gov/data/teledoc/teleintro.shtml. Below, Section 2.02.2.
[9] Proctor and others (2002a).   [10] Chen and others (2010); below, Section 2.02.3.
[11] Below, Sections 3.03.1b and 4.02.2.

event *c*.1300.[12] Thereafter, although droughts periodically recurred they would never again be as extreme as in the 1250s.[13] Concurrently, the South Asian monsoon started to weaken (Figure 1.1B) and India's first systemic monsoon failures followed in the 1280s.[14] With a lag, the NAO, in turn, began to weaken. From the 1320s rainfall over Scotland declined and northern Europe began to experience some notably 'arctic' winters, when polar high pressure spilled south and Atlantic cyclones were deflected to a more southerly track.[15] The latter brought bouts of wetter weather to southern Europe and North Africa and penetration of Arid Central Asia by a moister westerly airflow, so that here, too, humidity levels began fitfully to rise (Figure 1.1C).[16] Established circulation patterns were destabilizing almost everywhere and, as they did so, extreme weather events and major back-to-back harvest failures caused economic havoc across Eurasia.[17]

Great as were the dangers posed by extreme weather to agrarian-based economies, disease had the potential to inflict the greater damage. In 1279, for instance, English flocks succumbed to a debilitating outbreak of sheep scab which halved national wool output at a time when the country was Europe's premier producer of fine wool.[18] Scab's causal agent is the mite *Psoroptes ovis*, which lives on the skin of sheep and whose faeces cause an acute or chronic form of allergic dermatitis in the animals. In the 1279 outbreak many of the sheep thus stricken died or were slaughtered, the fleece weights of those that could be shorn plummeted and so inferior was the quality of the wool clip that the unit sale price slumped.[19] For the economy at large the ramifications of the massive shortfall in national wool output were considerable: agricultural incomes were squeezed, want of raw wool depressed English textile output, export earnings contracted, GDP per head took a direct hit, and overseas cloth producers reliant upon fine English wool were starved of vital raw materials, sparking riots among industrial workers in Flanders.[20]

England's commercial specialization in wool production, the sheer size of the national flock and the geographical extent of associated movements of stock, fleeces and wool had left the country's 15 million sheep wide

---

[12] Below, Section 3.02; Magilligan and Goldstein (2001); Mohtadi and others (2007), 1062–3.

[13] Rein and others (2004); Cook and others (2004c).   [14] Cook and others (2004b).

[15] Proctor and others (2002a); Trouet and others (2009a); below, Section 3.02.

[16] Below, Section 2.02.3.   [17] Below, Section 3.02; Figures 3.3 and 3.8B.

[18] Sheep numbers fell by approximately 30 per cent and fleece weights were down by 20–25 per cent: below, Figure 3.4. Lloyd (1977), 63; Stephenson (1988), 372–3, 381, 385.

[19] Below, Figure 3.4.

[20] Broadberry and others (2015), 206–7, 227; below, Section 3.01.2.

open to an infection which, in its early stages, was as difficult to detect as it was easy to spread. Commerce, in effect, amplified a vector-spread epizootic infection of ovines into a national agronomic disaster. In the decades that followed commercial exchange, in combination with high densities of bovines and humans, would similarly aid dissemination of both cattle plague and human plague, with repercussions in the latter case that would be felt across Europe for centuries.

Cattle plague (alias rinderpest) had last posed a major threat to European livestock producers in the mid-tenth century.[21] For over 300 years farmers apparently had little to fear from this most virulent and contagious of viral infections. In the 1290s and early 1300s, however, after unification of the Eurasian interior under the Mongols and the increased latitudinal movement that followed, chroniclers across eastern and central Europe again began to report heavy mortalities of cattle, although from what cause is unclear.[22] Then, between 1316 and 1321 and under conditions of extreme weather and acute ecological stress, rinderpest erupted in Bohemia and thence swiftly spread westwards, devastating herds and destroying vital draught oxen across northern Europe as far as the Atlantic coast of pastoral-farming Ireland.[23] A disease which had long remained effectively dormant as an enzootic infection among the native cattle of Eurasia's continental interior had been amplified by the combination of ecological stress and commercial exchange into a fast-spreading and deadly panzootic against which biologically naïve stock further to the west had little resistance.[24]

Meanwhile, microbiologists and geneticists have inferred that sometime after *c.*1268 *Yersinia pestis*, the causative agent of bubonic plague, entered a more active phase within its reservoir regions in Arid Central Asia.[25] Plague's sudden advance from an enzootic to an epizootic state appears to have been marked by the proliferation of new branches or polytomies in what has been described as a biological 'big bang'.[26] Biologists believe that these developments took place in the semi-arid Tibetan–Qinghai Plateau of western China, where plague had long persisted as an enzootic infection of the region's ground-burrowing gerbils and marmots.[27] Partly responsible may have been a trophic cascade set in

[21] In AD 809–10 outbreaks of cattle plague, possibly rinderpest, are noted in well over a dozen surviving chronicles from Austria to northern England and Ireland: Newfield (2012). For the AD 939–42 cattle plague see Newfield (2012).

[22] Below, Figures 3.25, 3.29 and 3.30 and Section 3.03.1b; McNeill (1977), 134; Abu-Lughod (1989), 154–84.

[23] Newfield (2009); below, Figure 3.25.

[24] Spinage (2003), 51; below, Section 3.03.1b.

[25] Bos and others (2011), 509; Cui and others (2013), 579–80; below, Section 4.04.

[26] Cui and others (2013).　　[27] Below, Section 3.03.2c.

motion by the stimulus given by incursions of a moister westerly airstream to vegetation growth, sylvatic rodent numbers, their burdens of flea parasites and the overall pathogen load. Once amplified in volume and escalated in activity, caravan traffic along the trade routes that traversed this reservoir region may then have transmitted the pathogen and its insect vectors to communities of sylvatic rodents ever further west along the Silk Road, until by 1338 it had reached Issyk-Kul in Kirgizia, at the eastern extremity of the steppe grasslands that extended westwards almost without interruption as far as the Great Hungarian Plain.[28] Here, if not before, it appears to have crossed over and as a zoonotic inflicted significant human fatalities. Plague's full destructive potential would not, however, be revealed until it had crossed the Caspian Basin, reached the lands of the Kipchak Khanate of the Golden Horde and, thence, the busy Genoese-controlled ports of Kaffa, Pera and Trebizond on the Black Sea, with their extensive maritime connections throughout the Mediterranean world and beyond.[29]

As plague was insidiously spreading by one means or another along the caravan routes that traversed the interior of Eurasia, other more vital commercial links between East and West were closing. Mongol and Mamluk conquests in the Middle East, commencing with the sack of Baghdad in 1258 and ending with the fall of Acre in 1291, started the process by obstructing and deterring traffic along the once busy trans-Syrian routes that linked the Persian Gulf with the eastern Mediterranean.[30] Defeat of the crusader states dispossessed the Italian maritime republics of Genoa and Venice of their former commercial privileges; retaliatory papal embargoes upon continuing trade with Muslims further constricted this once thriving forum of Italian commerce and source of sought-after Oriental luxuries. At the same time the Kārimīs cartel of merchants tightened its control of the Indian spice trade reaching the Mediterranean via the Red Sea and extracted the maximum tolls these commodities would bear.[31] Under the circumstances, it is hardly surprising that Venice and more especially Genoa refocused their attention on the alternative commercial opportunities offered by the Black Sea, terminus of the trans-Asian caravan route to Sarai Batu and Tana via Qinghai from Beijing that had prospered following creation of the Mongol Empire, as also of the trade from the Persian Gulf re-routed via Tabriz in Persia to Trebizond.[32] This, however, did nothing to prevent Europe's already negative trade balance with Asia from deteriorating further or to staunch the reciprocal

---

[28] Below, Figure 4.9.   [29] Below, Section 4.03.3 and Figure 4.9.
[30] Abu-Lughod (1989); below, Section 2.05.1.   [31] Munro (1991), 122.
[32] Below, Section 3.01 and Figure 3.1.

outflow of silver and gold. The one-sidedness of this trade was affordable while output from Europe's silver mines was buoyant but not once, from the 1330s, it was falling.[33]

Meanwhile, Italy's trans-Alpine trade with northern Europe suffered a serious setback due to political interference by the French Crown in operation of the hitherto neutral Champagne fairs, at that time the northern hub of European commerce. Following overt discrimination by Philip IV (r. 1285–1314) against both the Italian and Flemish merchants, the volume of trade handled by the fairs started to wither.[34] The Genoese responded by developing their recently established direct maritime link with Bruges via the Straits of Gibraltar, using convoys of heavily armed galleys to counter the threat posed by corsairs and Barbary pirates. This, however, had the effect of raising freight rates by at least a fifth.[35] Brigandage, banditry and predatory lords were similarly posing a mounting threat to merchants plying the old overland routes, rendering trade both riskier and costlier. Rising transaction costs proved especially detrimental to the bulk trade in low-value commodities with narrow profit margins, obliging manufacturers and merchants to switch to high-value products better able to bear these costs.[36] This explains the substitution by Flemish producers of fine woollens for cheap light *says*.[37] With problems mounting in both its North Sea and Mediterranean orbits of exchange, it is hardly surprising that from the 1290s Europe found itself in the grip of a worsening commercial recession from which there was little immediate prospect of relief.[38]

As expansion of the manufacturing and service sectors stalled, the agricultural sector was left to bear the brunt of any further increases in population. The upshot was mounting rural congestion as manifest in the extreme morcellation of holdings, rent seeking via the subdivision and subletting of land, and the piecemeal reclamation and colonization of much environmentally marginal land.[39] The more that this progressed the more that poor rural households multiplied and the greater the exodus of landless migrants to the towns, where they added to the spiralling problem of urban poverty.[40] Recurrent harvest shortfalls exacerbated these trends by sparking the surges of distress land sales that drove the relentless reduction in holding sizes.[41] By the opening of the fourteenth century two out of five English households could afford little more than a bare-bones standard of subsistence.[42] With so little to live on, such

---

[33] Below, Section 3.01.   [34] Edwards and Ogilvie (2012); below, Figure 3.1.
[35] Munro (1991), 124–30.   [36] Munro (1991), 111–14, 133–8.
[37] Below, Section 3.01.2; Munro (1991).   [38] Below, Section 3.01.
[39] Below, Section 3.01.3d.   [40] Below, Sections 3.01.3b and 3.01.3d.
[41] Below, Figures 3.16 and 3.18.   [42] Below, Table 3.2 and Figure 3.10.

economically marginalized households were cruelly exposed to the recessions of trade and failures of harvest that began to recur with increasing frequency and severity as the international recession bit deeper, extremes of weather and panzootics of livestock became more frequent and wars were waged for ever higher stakes. The buoyancy of the preceding era of efflorescence had given way to a precarious balance.

1.01.2   1340s–1370s: from one socio-ecological regime to another

During the 1340s the series of environmental and human crises that had been looming finally materialized: global climate reorganization accelerated and entered a highly unstable phase, warfare escalated and drove international commerce and economic output deeper into recession, and plague reached the shores of the Black Sea and within seven years had spread throughout the European trading system. This trio of crises cohered into a perfect storm, each component of which compounded and amplified the actions of the others. It was the magnitude and comprehensiveness of this composite event, and the fallout from it, that precipitated the abrupt shift from one socio-ecological regime to another. The years from the 1340s to the 1370s thus constitute the pivotal episode within the Great Transition.

The destabilization of climatic conditions was evident almost everywhere as the circulation patterns formerly sustained by high levels of solar irradiance were undermined by the cumulative effect of six decades of significantly diminished irradiance. Global cooling reduced northern hemisphere temperatures to their lowest level in over eight centuries (Figure 1.1A), with significant consequences for ocean–atmosphere interactions, pressure gradients, circulation patterns, wind force and direction and, of course, growing conditions. The negative impact upon temperate tree growth is evident in a marked narrowing of ring widths between 1342 and 1354, which was at its most pronounced in 1348.[43] For this ring pattern to show up so clearly in so many independent dendrochronologies and in both hemispheres implies powerful climate forcing at a global scale. Long-established circulation patterns were thrown into disarray, delivering weather that swung from one extreme to another (Figures 1.1B and 1.1C), as the altered climate regime that would characterize the Little Ice Age (LIA) began to make itself felt.[44]

---

[43] Below, Figure 4.2B.

[44] Grove (2004); Wang and others (2005); Sinha and others (2011). Although sceptics continue to doubt whether a LIA with discernibly colder temperatures ever existed, this misses the essential point that what differentiated this climatic era from the preceding Medieval Climate Anomaly was less average annual temperatures than patterns of

Asia bore the brunt of these developments, as the weakening ENSO undermined the strength and reliability of the South Asian monsoon (Figure 1.1B).[45] Drought may have eased in the North and South American West but this was at the expense of rainfall levels across South Asia. Thus between 1342 and 1346 China experienced mega-drought on a scale unprecedented during the MCA.[46] Here, as elsewhere across Asia, this was a disaster for a society heavily dependent upon wet-rice cultivation. The shock was the greater because the monsoon failed not once but for several consecutive years. In a clear example of climate teleconnections, as monsoon circulation weakened over South Asia it strengthened over East Africa, bringing heavier rainfall to Ethiopia and boosting discharge of the Blue Nile and Atbara which, together, were responsible for the annual Nile flood. In 1341/2 the height of that flood, as measured by the nilometer at Old Cairo, made its single greatest step gain on record.[47] During the 1350s, recorded flood levels then rose further and eclipsed those of any decade during the previous 700 years (Figure 1.1B).[48]

Europe was also visited by extreme weather in 1342, in the form of a rare Genoan low-pressure system which veered north and brought torrential summer rain to much of central Europe, raising river levels to unprecedented heights and causing massive soil erosion.[49] Shortly afterwards, storm surges caused extensive coastal flooding around the North Sea.[50] To blame was the reconfiguration of circulation patterns over the North Atlantic consequent upon a dramatic weakening of the NAO (Figure 1.1B). As the westerlies veered from a northerly to a southerly course and then back again, excessive rainfall ruined harvests, first, in southern Europe in 1346–7 and then in northern Europe in 1349–51.[51] The latter stands out as the only double back-to-back harvest failure on English medieval record.[52] Contemporaries were well aware that the weather they were experiencing was both unseasonable and unsettled.[53]

---

atmospheric circulation: Kelly and Ó Gráda (2014); Brooke (2014), 380–4; Mann and others (2009).

[45] Below, Figures 2.4 and 2.5 and Section 4.02.

[46] Lieberman (2009), 554–9; Brook (2010), 72; Sinha and others (2011); Lieberman and Buckley (2012), 1073; Tana (2014), 335.

[47] From 641 until 1469 the height of the Nile's floodwaters can be tracked from the preserved record of the measurements taken each year at the Rhoda Island nilometer located at the head of the Nile delta at Old Cairo: Popper (1951). For other extreme events in 1341/2 see Fraedrich and others (1997); Hoffmann (2014), 325–6.

[48] Below, Figure 5.3.

[49] Fraedrich and others (1997); Dotterweich (2008); Hoffmann (2014), 325–6.

[50] Britton (1937), 139–41; Bailey (1991), 189–94.

[51] Below, Figures 3.3 and 3.8B.

[52] Campbell (2011a), 144–7; Campbell and Ó Gráda (2011), 869.

[53] Below, Section 4.02.1.

What they had no means of comprehending was that this was a manifestation of climate systems on the cusp of change. These developments placed ecosystems under acute stress and jeopardized agricultural production at a time when pathogens were resurgent and war and commercial recession were placing economic output under great strain.

By the 1340s the international political and military situations were becoming increasingly grave and hitting European trade with Asia particularly hard.[54] Italian relations with the now Islamicized Il-Khanate and Kipchak Khanate were deteriorating fast, obliging abandonment of their bases at Tabriz in Persia and Tana at the mouth of the River Don, and in 1343 a Mongol army laid siege to the important Genoese port of Kaffa.[55] Feuding between the rival Mongol Kipchak and Il-Khanates also rendered unsafe the hitherto trouble-free overland caravan route between China and the Black Sea. Then in 1347 the Egyptian Mamluks conquered the Lesser Armenian kingdom of Cilicia and severed the sole remaining trans-shipment route between the Persian Gulf and the Mediterranean. Apart from the trickle of trade that continued to reach Trebizond on the Black Sea, this left the sultan of Egypt in virtual control of the Indian spice trade. Europeans were thereby obliged to pay significantly inflated prices at a time when the dwindling output from European silver mines meant they were becoming less able to afford to do so.[56] Moreover, Christian trade with Muslim Egypt was undertaken in the teeth of papal disapproval and at the risk of forfeiture or fine. Trade between Asia and Europe consequently shrank to a fraction of its former level and, since the Italians were at the forefront of that trade, it was the Italian economy that was squeezed hardest.[57]

Escalating warfare was also adding to Latin Christendom's own internal problems. Between Italy's rival city-states warfare had become endemic and a growing drain upon state finances. Outbreak of hostilities between England and France, but also involving Flanders and Scotland, had even more damaging economic repercussions.[58] The military campaigns themselves, the counter raids which they inevitably engendered and the brigandage and piracy they spawned, proved massively destructive of capital stock and, more importantly, of the peace and order upon which commerce depended.[59] Tax demands weighed heavily upon all combatants. Provisions were purveyed and merchant vessels impressed

---

[54] Below, Section 4.01.
[55] Lopez (1987), 387; Phillips (1988), 119; Wheelis (2002); Di Cosmo (2005), 403, 413–14, 418.
[56] Spufford (1988), 419; Allen (2012), 344; below, Figure 5.11.
[57] Below, Section 3.01.1 and Figure 3.2.   [58] Below, Section 4.01.
[59] Munro (1991), 124–6, 130; Bois (1984), 277–88.

for naval use.[60] Trade was subjected to heavier duties and manipulated to political ends.[61] The international wool trade was thrown into disarray.[62] Currencies were destabilized, by deflation in England's case and debasement in that of France. The exceptional credit requirements of all the belligerent parties contributed to an international credit crisis which brought down the last of the great Florentine banking houses.[63] Suppliers of military provisions fared well and ransom, plunder and booty boosted the fortunes of a few, but the lot of most non-combatants grew harder. At a time of mounting climatic instability, war with all its negative ramifications was eroding societies' resilience to harvest failure.[64]

Europe's economic prospects were poor. Production of silver was falling fast, lucrative overseas markets had been lost for good, trade with Asia was in decline and had become limited to a single artery, international credit facilities were exhausted, and the bad military and political situation looked set to deteriorate further. Within Europe, higher taxes and tolls and increased costs of defence, protection and insurance had raised transaction costs and were cutting into profit margins. With few exceptions, European overseas commerce was in retreat, its geographical orbit was narrowing and a serious loss of business confidence had set in among merchants trading internationally.[65] Even agricultural output was suffering due to the depredations of war and adverse effects of bad weather.

These were the challenging circumstances prevailing when plague finally completed its tortuous journey across the semi-arid and sparsely populated interior of Eurasia and in 1346 reached the Crimean shore of the Black Sea. Possibly it was hastened on its final leg by the impact of climate change upon the ecology of the steppe grasslands where it had presumably been establishing itself as an enzootic infection of sylvatic rodents. Contemporaries reported that plague had already left a trail of human deaths behind it in the lands of the Golden Horde before it broke out among the Mongol besiegers of the busy Genoese port of Kaffa in 1346.[66] From the besiegers it was then spread, probably by insect vectors, to the besieged and to the commensal rodents that must undoubtedly have been present in considerable numbers both in the town and on the ships docked in its port.[67] Plague caused Khan Janibeg (r. 1342–57) to raise the siege but not before *Y. pestis*, its vectors and its hosts had boarded Genoese ships bound for Constantinople and the lesser Genoese colonies

[60] Maddicott (1987).
[61] Carus-Wilson and Coleman (1963), 194–6; Fryde (1988), 57, 59–60, 66–7.
[62] Fryde (1988), 53–86; Nicholas (1987), 3, 48–52, 150–1.
[63] Hunt and Murray (1999), 116–17.   [64] Campbell (1995b), 94–6; Sharp (2000).
[65] Kedar (1976), 118–32.   [66] Below, Section 3.03.2c   [67] Wheelis (2002).

around the Black Sea and beyond. Once seaborne, extensive maritime networks gave *Y. pestis* access to the four corners of Europe's commercial world and its spread became unstoppable. Over the next seven years it assumed the guise of a highly contagious human pandemic and spread with devastating effect throughout Asia Minor, the Middle East, North Africa and the whole of Europe, as far west and north as Ireland and Norway.[68] Approximately a third of Europe's population is likely to have perished in this first outbreak and documented mortality rates in specific communities of 45 per cent or more are not unusual.[69]

The timing of the Black Death's intervention could not have been more decisive. In alliance with climate, war and commerce it achieved what even the Great European Famine of 1315–22 had been unable to bring about, namely a big and enduring positive check to human populations.[70] Because plague was to recur repeatedly over the next 350 years, this first plague outbreak marks a decisive turning point in Latin Christendom's epidemiological environment.[71] The demographic shadow cast by the Black Death was therefore dark and long. Major sequel outbreaks in 1360–3, 1369, 1374–5 and 1382–3 extinguished any prospect of a post-Black Death fertility-driven demographic recovery and instead established a mortality-dominated regime that maintained negative replacement rates for approximately five consecutive generations.[72] By the 1380s the net decline in Europe's population was of the order of 50 per cent.

By killing both producers and consumers, plague simultaneously ratcheted down supply and demand and thereby transformed factor and commodity prices and the ecological relationship between humans and natural resources.[73] Everywhere it stands out in the historical record as a pronounced demographic, economic, cultural and environmental discontinuity. Insofar as the contraction in population boosted money supply per head, the haemorrhaging of population was not without its benefits. Plague mortality also provided a brutal resolution of the intractable problems of rural congestion and structural poverty. Survivors benefited from substantial gains in daily real wage rates, improved access to land, and the potential to enjoy enlarged household incomes. Initially, these positives helped mitigate the worst effects of commercial recession and in populous and commercialized economies, such as England, bore fruit in rising GDP per head.[74] Yet the boom was short-lived and did not long outlast the exceptional demographic circumstances that had brought it

[68] Below, Section 4.03.3 and Figure 4.10.   [69] Below, Section 4.03.4.
[70] Below, Section 3.01.3e; Jordan (1996); Campbell (2009b); Campbell (2010a).
[71] Below, Figure 4.9.   [72] Below, Sections 4.04 and 5.03.2.
[73] Below, Sections 5.04.1 and 5.04.2.   [74] Below, Section 5.05.

into being. Nor was it universal. The magnitude of the population decline left many more sparsely settled regions and countries, like much of Iberia, worse off, with too few people to maintain pre-existing levels of specialization and productivity.[75] The biological shock may have been common to all countries, but the response of each to this pan-European catastrophe was shaped by the socio-ecological context within which the mortality crisis occurred.

1.01.3   1370s–1470s: the long downturn

From the 1370s to the 1470s climatic and epidemiological factors on one hand and commercial and economic forces on the other combined to inhibit any full-scale demographic and economic recovery. Even the immediate post-plague surge in economic growth experienced by some countries proved transitory and by the 1420s had largely run its course to be followed by half a century or more of stasis.[76] These hundred years constitute the third and longest stage of the Great Transition, when climatic conditions continued to deteriorate, disease, often acting in concert with climate, kept mortality levels elevated, population numbers continued to drift down, market demand remained slack, the continued expansion of Mamluk and Ottoman power raised an almost impermeable barrier to any renewal of direct trade between Europe and Asia and encroached yet further on Europe's established trading zone, and the West's persistent trade deficit with the East steadily drained its increasingly silver-deficient commercialized economy of bullion. Silver apart, resources per head were now available in relative abundance but the economic incentives to exploit them more intensively were persistently weak and environmental constraints upon both human and agricultural reproduction remained strong.

The fifteenth century brought the first extended cold phase of the LIA.[77] The second half of the fourteenth century had experienced a brief resurgence of solar irradiance (the Chaucerian Maximum) and, with a lag, a general recovery in global and northern hemisphere temperatures (Figure 1.1A) but this proved insufficiently sustained to reinstate earlier circulation patterns. Instead, from the close of the fourteenth century onset of the Spörer Solar Minimum sealed the transition to the altered circulation patterns of the LIA (Figure 1.1). Conditions within the Pacific Ocean continued to be influential: El Niño events became more common, the American West's liberation from severe drought continued, the

---

[75] Álvarez-Nogal and Prados de la Escosura (2013); Campbell (2013c).
[76] Below, Figure 5.14B.   [77] Below, Figure 2.2 and Section 5.02.1.

South Asian monsoon fluctuated greatly in strength without ever recovering to the peak strength of the MCA, and the annual Nile flood rose in both height and variability as the East African monsoon fitfully grew wetter (Figure 1.1B).[78] Meanwhile, the Siberian high gained in strength and the NAO weakened, exposing northern Europe to a colder and drier winter air-stream while southern Europe and North Africa benefited from increased winter rainfall. The more southerly course taken by the westerlies also allowed regular penetration of Arid Central Asia by a moister air-stream (Figure 1.1C).

By the 1450s, during the lowest point in the Spörer Solar Minimum, global climates had been profoundly reorganized. Note in Figure 1.1 how different are the values of all the variables at this time, during one of the coldest spells of the LIA, from their corresponding values in the 1250s, when the circulation patterns of the MCA were still firmly in the ascendant. The two solar benchmarks of the Medieval Solar Maximum and the Spörer Solar Minimum framed this extended period.[79] By its close, northern hemisphere and global temperatures had become 0.4–0.8°C colder, northwest Europe was experiencing a shortened growing season and heightened frequency of severe winters, in southern Europe winters were wetter and summers cooler, aridity had diminished in central Asia, and across South Asia the monsoon had become both weaker and more erratic.[80]

Climatic teleconnections ensured that no part of Eurasia was untouched by these changes in temperature, precipitation and circulation. Everywhere weather patterns had become more unsettled. A heightened incidence of extreme weather events exposed ecosystems to increased stress and agricultural producers to greater uncertainty. On the evidence of ten northern hemisphere dendrochronologies and three from the southern hemisphere, negative climate forcing was exceptionally strong between 1453 and 1476 and collectively at its most pronounced in the 1460s, when explosive ejection of volcanic aerosols by Mount Kuwae in c.1458 may have reinforced the effects of low solar irradiance.[81] This episode in many respects marks the climax of the climatic component of the Great Transition.

Throughout this extended period plague remained an active component of an epidemiological regime which maintained high levels of background mortality punctuated by periodic mortality crises. Likely

---

[78] Hassan (2011).   [79] Below, Figures 2.8 and 2.9.
[80] Below, Sections 5.02.1 and 5.02.2.
[81] Below, Figure 5.13; Bauch (2016). The ice-core evidence indicates a tropical eruption in c.1453, explosive eruption of Kuwae in the South Pacific in c.1458, and a high-latitude northern hemisphere eruption in c.1462: Frank Ludlow, personal communication.

there may have been renewed introductions of *Y. pestis* from its reservoir regions in central Asia but mostly plague maintained itself by circulation through Europe's villages and towns, unless semi-permanent reservoirs of infection had become established in the larger port cities and conceivably among sylvatic communities of alpine marmots.[82] Irrespective of where the residual pools of infection were located and how they were maintained, plague was now an established fact of life. The responsiveness of its hosts and vectors to prevailing weather and ecological conditions meant that outbreaks commonly flared whenever adverse weather depressed harvests, stoked poverty and fanned cognate infections.[83] For much of this period, therefore, climate and disease acted in concert and locked generations of Europeans into a negative demographic spiral of ill health, unexpected death, elevated mortality and deficient replacement rates which overrode the countervailing effects of better nutrition, clothing and housing. Not until the very end of the fifteenth century did survivor populations slowly evolve a capacity to co-exist with plague, as years of learning how to cope with and contain the disease began to pay off and the cumulative effects of generations of genetic selection may possibly have favoured those who survived.[84] Plague retained its ability to kill but the demographic corner had been turned and deaths no longer exceeded births, with the result that from the final quarter of the fifteenth century western European populations began hesitantly to increase.[85]

It was in the third quarter of the fifteenth century that European economic activity had sunk to its lowest ebb, as the want of population growth depressed domestic demand, bullion scarcity inhibited multilateral forms of exchange, war, piracy and slave raiding blighted Mediterranean maritime commerce, and the Ottomans took Constantinople, gained control of the Black Sea and overran the Balkans. Not in centuries had Europe been so commercially isolated. International trade continued but at a reduced level; its risks were high and unless niche markets could be tapped into there was little to encourage business optimism. In England, for instance, the contribution of exports to national income was only half in the third quarter of the fifteenth century what it had been during the first quarter of the fourteenth century.[86] The harsh

---

[82] Below, Section 4.04.2; Carmichael (2014); Schmid and others (2015).
[83] Below, Section 5.03.1.
[84] Below, Sections 4.04 and 5.03.2; Laayouni and others (2014).
[85] Below, Section 5.03.2 and Figure 5.7.
[86] I am grateful to Bas van Leeuwen for supplying these estimates drawing upon the results of the project 'Reconstructing the National Incomes of Britain and Holland, *c.*1270/1500 to 1850', funded by the Leverhulme Trust, Reference Number F/00215AR.

weather was in part to blame: extremes of rain and cold hindered movement of people and goods and periodically depressed outputs of such fundamental commercial commodities as grain, wine and wool.[87]

Under these adverse circumstances, with the exception of a few enterprising maritime regions, economic growth remained flat and prone to sag.[88] Towns struggled to maintain their own. Consequently, urbanization ratios, one of the clearest barometers of economic vitality or the want of it, either stagnated or fell.[89] Scarce labour may have elevated male daily real wage rates to unprecedented levels but, while market demand remained slack and work scarce, increased consumption of leisure rather than of goods and services perforce became the default option of many.[90] The dynamic that might have generated fuller employment was lacking. The transition to a scaled-down, realigned and altogether more introspective economic world was complete. Intriguingly, for related but not identical reasons, parallel reversals had been taking place at the opposite end of Eurasia. In the East retreat from the boom years of the thirteenth-century world economy was at least as great.[91]

Christendom's contraction was not terminal but the seeds of its recovery were slow in germinating. When the upturn eventually began, in the final decades of the fifteenth century, the legal institutions, property rights, and factor and commodity markets established during the upswing of the twelfth and thirteenth centuries and in many cases tested, refined and improved during the ensuing downturn provided a secure platform for growth.[92] Technology, too, had advanced during the Great Transition, especially in what would prove to be the key areas of ship design and navigation.[93] Scarcity of bullion remained a crippling constraint but was allayed in part by expansion of credit and resort to an array of new financial instruments.[94] Enterprising Europeans had also developed substitute sources of silk, cotton, sugar, spices, ceramics and other high-value Asian commodities closer to home.[95]

As rent-seeking Muslim middlemen tightened their grip on the old trans-Eurasian overland routes, and especially from 1453 when the Ottomans gained control of the Bosphorus, European commerce took increasingly to the high seas where unit costs were lower. Excluded from the Black Sea and forced to play second fiddle to the Ottomans and

---

[87] Below, Sections 5.02.2 and 5.04.1.   [88] Below, Sections 5.04.1 and 5.04.3.
[89] Below, Section 5.04.3 and Table 5.1.   [90] Broadberry and others (2015), 283–5.
[91] Abu-Lughod (1989), 361: 'the "Fall of the East" preceded the "Rise of the West"'.
Lieberman and Buckley (2012), 1068–77; Tana (2014), 332–7.
[92] Below, Section 2.04.   [93] Unger (1980); Hoffmann (2014), 359–64.
[94] Bolton (2012), 270–95.   [95] Phillips (1988), 227–53.

Mamluks in much of the Mediterranean, Europeans made the most of the commercial opportunities available nearer to hand in the Baltic, North Sea and North and South Atlantic. With the benefit of larger and more manoeuvrable ships and better navigational instruments, they also began to probe further south and west into the Atlantic until, in the 1490s, the Americas were discovered and Africa rounded.[96] In direct contrast to the situation in the thirteenth century, European merchants played a prominent role in the revived Eurasian trade that followed, which was lubricated by liberal doses of New World silver and conducted on terms altogether more favourable to Europe.[97] Moreover, in a significant reversal of fortunes within Europe, it was no longer the Italian merchants that led the way but those of the Northern Low Countries. A new era of efflorescence had begun and the Great Transition was over.

1.02   The Great Transition and the Great Divergence

In the eleventh century, when Europe's commercial revolution was slowly beginning to get under way, Song China was the most developed economy of the age. Not even Italy, with its substantial inherited Roman infrastructure of roads, towns and literacy, could match Song China's technological sophistication and level of economic development.[98] China's scale and unity also meant that it enjoyed far lower transaction costs than were achievable in politically fragmented Europe. Between 1235 and 1279, however, the Mongol conquests of, first, the Northern Song and, then, the Southern Song significantly curtailed China's economic lead. Even so, sufficient recovery was achieved during the reign of the first Yuan Emperor, Kublai Khan (r. 1271–94), to greatly impress Marco, Niccolò and Maffeo Polo, when they visited his court from Venice, then near the height of its own commercial prosperity.[99] Yuan China's prosperity did not, however, long outlast Kublai Khan. During the fourteenth century, under the combined impact of environmental instability and dynastic breakdown, the economies of China and its Southeast Asian neighbours suffered a succession of major setbacks.[100] This was at a time when, in terms of GDP per head, the more dynamic of the European economies were either holding their own or making modest gains.[101] The net outcome of waxing economic fortunes in the West but waning economic fortunes in China and the East was that by the end of the Middle Ages

---

[96] Below, Section 5.06.   [97] O'Rourke and Williamson (2002), 143–364.
[98] Broadberry and others (2015), 375, 384–7; Lo Cascio and Malanima (2009).
[99] Yule (1875).
[100] Brook (2010), 71–2; Lieberman (2009), 551–9; Lieberman and Buckley (2012).
[101] Below, Section 5.05.

the most advanced regions of Europe were drawing abreast of those of Asia.

From *c*.1500, following Portuguese discovery of the direct sea route round Africa, a handful of economically dynamic European countries then moved ahead and assumed a leading role in the commerce of the world. The Northern Low Countries was the initial pacesetter in these developments and by the seventeenth century had very likely achieved levels of GDP per head as high as or higher than its Chinese counter-parts.[102] Later that century it was England's turn to commence growing vigorously and the stage was set for the widening divergence between the economic trajectories of East and West that has become known as the Great Divergence.[103] This was not an outcome that could have been fore-seen at the opening of the second millennium, when the East led and the West lagged and Asian rather than European merchants and commodities dominated trans-Eurasian commerce. Nor could it have been predicted that the various reversals of the fourteenth and fifteenth centuries would have enhanced the southern North Sea region's twin comparative advan-tages in commerce and manufacturing to such an extent as to launch its constituent economies on this upward path. Yet for this core region the roots of the Great Divergence lay in the working out of the Great Transition. It was then that Brabant, Holland and England successively embarked upon the growth that led them to overtake, first, long-time European leader Italy and then the most advanced and commercially developed provinces of China.

1.03   Critical transitions in nature and society

It is because the Great Transition brought no return to the socio-ecological status quo ante that it represents a transition and not a cycle. Its advance was neither smooth nor relentlessly unidirectional. Lulls and reversals were intrinsic to its trajectory. So, too, was instability, as mani-fest in the harvest failures and famines, floods, inundations and droughts, surges and lulls in animal and human mortality, rebellions and wars, dynastic breakdowns, credit crises, banking failures and commercial dis-locations for which the fourteenth century in particular is notorious.[104] While each component of the transition was impelled by a powerful dynamic of its own, the striking synchronicities between environmental

---

[102] Broadberry and others (2015), 375–6, 386.
[103] Broadberry and others (2015), 375–6, 384–7; Pomeranz (2000).
[104] Scheffer (2009), 96–105, 282–95; Tuchman (1978).

and human developments imply the existence of important synergies between them.

Climate's influence was over-arching: it changed ecologies, growing conditions, carrying capacities, the viability of marginal environments, sailing conditions and the risks of experiencing extreme weather events. Microbial pathogens, their hosts and vectors are ecologically sensitive and thus responsive to altered climatic conditions. Once unleashed, the great panzootics and pandemics of the age impacted selectively upon population size, structure and dynamics and filtered the genetic legacies of those, both animal and human, that survived. Humans created the density and distributional preconditions for the pan-continental spread of diseases, whose transmission they inadvertently facilitated. They then responded in varying ways to the changes in health, resource balances and relative factor prices that resulted. Through reproduction of foodstuffs, organic raw materials and animate sources of kinetic energy, humans, too, were challenged and influenced by climate, and with varying degrees of success actively sought technological and institutional solutions to the endless uncertainties that it presented.[105] Resort to fossil fuels is one of several solutions by which humans, in turn, through emissions of carbon dioxide (CO_2), then exerted a reciprocal influence upon climate.[106] To understand and explain the history of the late-medieval world therefore requires an appreciation of these interactions between climate, disease and society: nature as much as society needs to be acknowledged as a protagonist of historical change.[107]

The broad array of natural and societal processes and the complex inter-relationships involved in this unfolding historical scenario constituted what may be called a socio-ecological regime. Climate and society, ecology and biology, and microbes and humans comprise the six core components of such a dynamical system (Figure 1.2). Each component should be viewed as a semi-autonomous sub-system in its own right, made up of sub-elements linked by direct and indirect feedbacks, so that each possesses its own independent dynamic. None, however, exists in isolation, hence change in any one of the six core components will elicit change in one or more of the others, with the character of that change in part mediated by the prevailing state of those other components. When such a system exists in balance, that equilibrium is dynamic not static. Any change in human and environmental pressures and potentials can disturb that equilibrium and initiate a system shift from one dynamic socio-ecological regime, balancing and adjusting itself within one set of

---

[105] Mokyr (1992).   [106] Kander and others (2014).
[107] Campbell (2010a); Hoffmann (2014), 1–20.

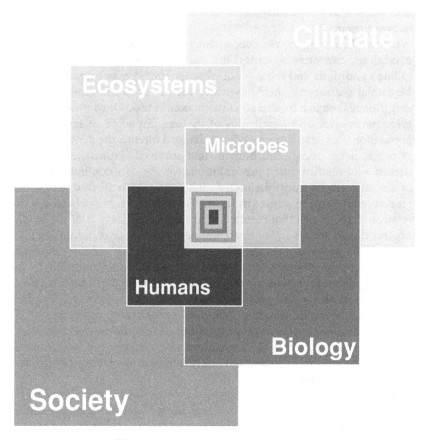

Figure 1.2 The six core components of a dynamic socio-ecological system
Source: based on National Academy of Sciences (2008), figure SA-4, 14

bounds, to an alternative socio-ecological regime varying within a quite different set of bounds. Conceptualizing the human–environment interactions that constituted the Great Transition in this way emphasizes their complex multilateral character and inherent propensity to change. Determinism, be it environmental or economic, climatic or cultural, is inappropriate, since all the component variables are regarded as inter-related in some way and therefore relevant to elucidation of the socio-ecological system as a whole. To privilege endogenous human processes over ostensibly exogenous environmental events is also to create a false dichotomy, since there is nothing in this model that is not endogenous.

Of course, for long periods of time medieval societies were able to take their climatic and epidemiological environments more-or-less for granted. As Section 2 demonstrates, that seems to have been the case during most of the 200-year interval between the end of the Oort Solar Minimum in the late eleventh century and the beginning of the Wolf Solar Minimum in the late thirteenth century. Across these years of consistently high solar irradiance, with the conspicuous exception of bouts of mega-drought in central Asia, environmental events, whether biological or physical, intruded little upon the course of social development, which was shaped above all by religious, political, military, economic and commercial interactions.[108] Those environmental shocks that did throw social change off course, such as the mega-eruption of 1257/8, rarely did so for long and were almost invariably followed by a return to the status quo ante.[109] In this respect, societies at this time were resilient.[110] The more dynamic of them, such as Song China and Latin Christendom, were also lucky in the prevailing conjuncture of mostly benign natural and human circumstances. Nevertheless, such good fortune did not last.

Towards the end of the thirteenth century increasing climatic instability began to impinge more directly upon human activities at a time when population growth, commercial expansion and resource scarcity were rendering societies more environmentally sensitive.[111] From early in the fourteenth century, as politico-economic tensions rose and interstate conflicts multiplied, climatically generated ecological stress came increasingly to the fore. The variance of annual variations in weather conditions, growing conditions, grain and wool harvests and much else was rising and the recovery time after each setback grew longer as recovery itself became more difficult.[112] Repeated exposure to extreme natural and human events was eroding the capacity of the system to cope with such hazards.[113] These are the symptoms of a system that was approaching a critical transition, when a small change arising anywhere in the system could trigger an amplifying sequence of responses with the capacity to overwhelm the system and invoke the transition to an alternative state.[114]

In the case of the Great Transition the critical tipping point occurred in the middle years of the fourteenth century. From that point the Rubicon

---

[108] Below, Section 2.01. [109] Below, Section 2.02.5 and Figure 2.9.
[110] Resilience is here and hereafter defined as 'the ability of a system to recover to the original state upon a disturbance': Scheffer (2009), 11.
[111] Below, Sections 3.01 and 3.02. [112] Below, Figure 4.4.
[113] Below, Section 3.01.3; Scheffer (2009), 282–95; Hoffmann (2014), 342–51.
[114] In systems theory this is called a bifurcation point: Scheffer (2009), 18–22, 96–105.

had been crossed and the momentum and direction of change became mutually reinforcing and irreversible: the MCA finally ended and atmospheric circulation patterns decisively shifted, the Second Pandemic was launched on its deadly path, and established patterns and volumes of international trade and commerce imploded. The upshot was that European populations sustained their greatest and most sustained reversal of the last millennium and established power structures and relations of production were challenged and reshaped almost everywhere.[115] Although this has sometimes been described as the 'crisis' of the fourteenth century, this over-worked term hardly does justice to the magnitude and significance of the changes that were afoot.[116] Instead, the ecological concept of a 'tipping point' more effectively expresses both the transformative character of change and its complex origins.[117]

Tipping points mark major historical turning points and are decidedly rare occurrences.[118] Because they were big, complex, multi-faceted events it could take many years before a new socio-ecological equilibrium established itself and, until that happened, heightened instability tended to prevail on many fronts. In the case of the Great Transition, the lead-up to and fallout from the tipping point of the mid-fourteenth century extended over almost 200 years, over which time climate and society, ecology and biology, and microbes and humans were progressively transformed (Figure 1.2). On all six counts the conditions that prevailed by the 1450s were entirely different from those that had characterized the 1250s. Teasing out how that came about requires combining the approaches of environmental and economic history, integrating the research findings of palaeoclimatologists, microbiologists, geneticists, osteoarchaeologists and historians, and contending with the associated differences of evidence, methods and paradigm.

1.04   Tracking the Great Transition: issues of scale, focus and evidence

Of the changes in climate, disease and society that constituted the Great Transition, those of climate were shaped by the largest forces and unfolded on the greatest geographical scale. Relevant influences upon climate include the output of solar irradiance, the Coriolis force and orbit

---

[115] Russell (1958); McEvedy and Jones (1978), 41–119; Biraben (1979).
[116] Hybel (1989).
[117] Scheffer (2009), 11–25. For the provenance of the term 'tipping point' and a critique of its use in recent debates about climate change, see Russill (2015).
[118] The case for regarding the mid-seventeenth century as such a period is made by Parker (2013).

of the Earth, the character of ocean–atmosphere interactions, the topography of the continents, sporadic ejection of volcanic aerosols and the fallout from extra-terrestrial impacts. Further, climate regimes at widely separate locations are intimately interconnected by what climatologists call teleconnections, so that they rarely change independently of each other.[119] It is via teleconnections that the climatic effects of La Niña and El Niño conditions in the Pacific Ocean are transmitted around the world and, likewise, it is teleconnections that link pressure gradients over the tropical and sub-tropical Indian Ocean with those prevailing at temperate latitudes thousands of miles to the northwest over the North Atlantic Ocean.[120] In the Middle Ages climates separated by vast distances were interconnected to an extent that societies were not, a point not lost on Victor Lieberman, who has invoked it to explain the 'strange parallels' observable in the histories of societies that existed in isolation from each other.[121]

Making sense of the changes in climate conditions that occurred over the course of the late-medieval centuries, when the circulation patterns characteristic of the MCA gave way to those typical of the LIA, therefore requires linking time-series data obtained from the Americas and Eurasia, the northern and southern hemispheres and the Greenland and Antarctic ice caps. Reliance has to be placed upon proxy climate measures derived for the most part from tree rings (dendrochronology), arctic and alpine ice-cores, stalagmites (speleothems), stratified lake and ocean-shelf sediment deposits (varves), and coral growth, and calibrated wherever possible against instrumental climate records for the recent past. The number, geographical coverage, temporal resolution and reliability of these datasets spanning hundreds and sometimes thousands of years are becoming better all the time and many are now in the public domain.[122] As Figure 1.1 exemplifies, it is comparison of meaned time series from around the northern hemisphere that throws the changes that occurred between c.1250 and c.1450 into high relief and provides the global context to the economic and demographic developments taking place in Europe at that time.

Diseases, too, were no respecters of boundaries, although until the overseas discoveries made by European mariners the cordons sanitaires of the Atlantic and Pacific Oceans isolated the New World from the

---

[119] Above, note 8.   [120] Wang and others (2005).
[121] Lieberman (2009), 79–87, 687–91.
[122] A comprehensive palaeoclimatological website is maintained at the United States National Climatic Data Center (NCDC) of the National Oceanic and Atmospheric Administration (NOAA), http://www.ncdc.noaa.gov/data-access/paleoclimatology-data.

pathogens of the Old World and vice versa.[123] Thus, the great fourteenth-century killer diseases of cattle plague and human plague remained essentially Old World events. Both diseases, one a virus, the other a bacterium, originated in inner Asia, whence they spread westwards to the Atlantic rim of Europe.[124] Modern studies of the Second Plague Pandemic link information obtained from climate proxies about growing conditions and precipitation levels in Arid Central Asia, with contemporary genomic information about the strains of *Y. pestis* prevailing at different locations, ancient DNA evidence gathered from victims of past plague outbreaks (all of it, to date, originating from Black Death burials in western Europe), and the substantial body of documentary information that describes and thereby tracks historical plague outbreaks.[125] Eruption and spread of the Black Death in England has received particularly detailed attention due to the quality of the English sources but there are also comprehensive surveys of the epidemic in both Europe and the Middle East.[126] These can be augmented with scientific studies of modern plague outbreaks in central Asia, Africa and North America.[127]

This wealth of information combined with the continental dimensions of the disease both invite and require a pan-Eurasian scale of analysis.[128] In fact, understanding the behaviour of plague in its reservoir regions in central Asia, and especially its putative region of origin in the Tibetan–Qinghai Plateau of western China, is crucial to explaining why plague broke out when it did and how it then succeeded in repeatedly infecting Europe.[129] Necessarily, research into historical plague outbreaks has become a collaborative effort and all the leading teams are alert to the Known World dimensions of the Black Death and the need to improve knowledge and understanding of the disease's emergence and spread within Asia.[130]

Plague reached Europe and North Africa from Asia with relative ease because of the strength of the commercial and political connections which extended across this vast territory following its unification under the

---

[123] Diamond (1999), 210–14, 357–8.   [124] Below, Figures 3.25, 4.9 and 4.10.

[125] For example, Schmid and others (2015); Green (2014).

[126] Shrewsbury (1971); Hatcher (1977); Biraben (1975); Benedictow (2004); Dols (1977).

[127] For example, Stenseth and others (2006); Kausrud and others (2010); Vogler and others (2011).

[128] Green (2014).

[129] Below, Section 3.03.2. Kausrud and others (2010); Cui and others (2013); Schmid and others (2015).

[130] A notable example is the European Research Council-funded project, 'The medieval plagues: ecology, transmission modalities and routes of the infections', at the University of Oslo: http://www.mn.uio.no/cees/english/research/projects/650125/.

Mongols.[131] These are more easily described than quantified due to the fragmentary and diverse character of the written records upon which medieval historians rely for their evidence. Documentary creation and preservation has been uneven and there is a distinct lack of material that allows economic and demographic trends to be reconstructed at a supra-state level over an extended period of time. There are valuable macro-European estimates of population, urbanization, and mint output, but little else.[132] Trust therefore has to be placed in local, regional and national case studies. Here the English evidence is pre-eminent.

For England, prices of staple commodities are available from the late twelfth century, labourers' daily wage rates from the early thirteenth century and real wage rates from much the same time. These price and wage series remain intermittent until the 1260s but are annually continuous thereafter.[133] From the 1270s there are good data on numbers of tenants, a range of agricultural outputs, the yields of crops, the volume of exports, state finances, rural land markets and much else. Moreover, these data have recently been employed to derive annual estimates of population, output-based national income and GDP per head.[134] These are the earliest and most robust time series of this nature currently available for any European economy and, as is evident in Section 2, unavoidably impart a strong Anglocentric bias to the discussions of pre-1300 economic and demographic trends which they inform.[135] For this period England also has the most developed historiography, although the long dominance of anthropocentric analyses grounded in either Marxist theory or neoclassical economics means that scant attention has as yet been paid to the historical roles of environmental processes and forces.[136]

Since no other European economy can be quantified and tracked in such detail through all stages of the Great Transition, or has been the subject of so much debate, England is the default case study in the sections that follow. The country was more populous, urbanized, commercialized and monetized than many parts of late-medieval western Europe but on the same criteria nonetheless consistently lagged far behind the leading economies of the Southern Low Countries and Italy.[137] From the late seventeenth century it would catch up, overtake both, and

---

[131] McNeill (1977), 161–207; below, Figure 2.1.
[132] Russell (1958); McEvedy and Jones (1978); Biraben (1979); Bairoch and others (1988); Spufford (1988), 419.
[133] Most are readily available at Clark (2009): http://www.iisg.nl/hpw/data.php#united.
[134] Broadberry and others (2015).   [135] Campbell (2013c).
[136] Marxist and neoclassical interpretations of the late-medieval crisis clashed in the 'Brenner debate', Aston and Philpin (1985). For a comprehensive review of the relevant English literature see Hatcher and Bailey (2001).
[137] Campbell (2013c).

become the world's leading economy and the first to industrialize and make the full transition to modern economic growth.[138] Given its later economic success there is some merit in singling out its earlier history for special attention, although in the Middle Ages there was nothing to indicate that England was destined for greatness. On the contrary, late-medieval England occupied an intermediate position in Europe's economic league table and for the most part fared neither better nor worse than others.[139]

The quality of the thirteenth- and early-fourteenth-century English evidence highlights the deficiency of that for all other countries, most of which lack as diagnostic an economic measure as an annual wheat price series. Both the Southern and Northern Low Countries are without such a series until well after the Black Death, for Sweden and Spain the available pre-Black Death information is fragmentary, and currently Tuscany alone possesses a reasonably complete annual series, although starting later and by no means as robust and representative as that for England.[140] Nevertheless, from 1310 the availability of daily real wage rate estimates and urbanization estimates for the centre and north of Italy have enabled Paolo Malanima to reconstruct Italian national income and GDP per head and in Sections 3 and 5 full advantage is taken of these estimates to make comparison between England and the leading European economy of the age.[141] For other economies there are qualitative accounts of economic development but quantitative information is at best patchy. Spain has a wealth of extant documentary records upon which a quantitative reconstruction of the various Iberian kingdoms' economic performance might be based but the task of doing so has scarcely begun.[142] Instead reliance has to be placed on some preliminary estimates of national income and GDP per head inferred from the country's incomplete price and wage series in combination with estimates of Spanish urbanization ratios.[143] In these respects, Spain is nonetheless better served than the Southern Low Countries, which for all its economic importance is seriously lacking in quantitative time series. In the Northern Low Countries, however, the tiny and precocious province of Holland has been better served by its economic historians and tentative estimates of Dutch GDP per head from 1348 provide a further basis for comparison, with the merit that Holland emerged from the Great Transition with the fastest-growing economy in Europe and within a century had become

---

[138] Broadberry and others (2015).   [139] Campbell (2013c).
[140] Malanima (no date b).   [141] Malanima (2011).
[142] For a pioneering analysis of the Portuguese evidence see Henriques (2015).
[143] Álvarez-Nogal and Prados de la Escosura (2013).

almost certainly the most successful economy in the world.[144] Together, England, Italy, Spain and the Low Countries provide the cornerstones of the socio-economic component of this description and analysis of the Great Transition and reconstruction of the preceding era of efflorescence from which it sprang.

---

[144] Zanden and Leeuwen (2012). Here and hereafter 'Holland' refers to the province and not the country that became the Netherlands.

For centuries prior to the Great Transition socio-ecological conditions were relatively stable. Atmospheric circulation patterns during
the Medieval Climate Anomaly (MCA) delivered relatively favourable
weather to temperate Europe and Monsoon Asia alike and this provided the environmental preconditions for the great demographic and
economic upswing common to both during the High Middle Ages. Not
since the end of Antiquity had the West experienced such a sustained
period of cultural and economic efflorescence.[1] Given the low base from
which expansion mostly began, much of the initial growth was extensive,
insofar as more output was achieved by deploying more labour on more
land without any radical change in productive technology. In due course,
however, wider adoption of an improved agricultural technology ensured
that rising population continued to be matched by expanding output of
food and organic raw materials.[2] Even so, available agricultural technology was rarely exploited to the full.[3] Instead, it was those institutional
and organizational innovations associated with the commercialization
of economic relations and activity that were the vital achievements of
the age.

Especially important were those institutions that nurtured and protected traders and exchange, especially those participating in high-risk
long-distance trade where the dangers of piracy, confiscation or default
were considerable. Long-distance trade may have been the smallest and
riskiest branch of medieval commerce, far eclipsed in value and volume
by local exchange of staple commodities, but it was the yeast in the economic loaf: its economic multiplier effects were disproportionately great
as were the profits reaped by those successful at engaging in it.[4] Most

---

[1] Goldstone (2002). Other similar periods of efflorescence include Iraq's Golden Age of
Islam, Song China, Golden Age Holland, Tokugawa Japan, the High Qing in China, and
the long eighteenth century in England. For a pessimistically Malthusian interpretation
of pre-industrial economic development see Clark (2007a).
[2] The basis for this view is White Jr (1962).
[3] A point emphasized by Epstein (2000a), 38–9.   [4] Dyer (2011).

of the key business innovations of the age were pioneered by merchants active in long-distance trades: double-entry bookkeeping, profit and loss accounting, bills of exchange, commenda contracts, and substitution of Arabic for Roman numerals. These were the merchants most versed in monetary exchange, with the greatest capital resources and therefore best placed to develop credit banking. Their activities generated much business for the transport sector, production of raw materials for export, and growth of manufacturing activities geared to overseas markets. The leading commercial ports and financial centres became some of the greatest cities of the age, none more so than the maritime republics of Genoa and Venice and inland metropolises of Florence and Milan.

Institutional and organizational innovation bore fruit in a veritable commercial revolution, during which more people became dependent for more of their livelihoods upon engagement with increasingly active commodity, land, labour and capital markets.[5] It helped that a European silver-mining boom was underwriting a steadily expanding supply of money, for this, in turn, facilitated the development of both multilateral and long-distance exchange. Italy was more actively engaged in these developments than any other part of Europe and therefore reaped the greatest returns. Nevertheless, their benefits were suffused to varying degrees throughout Latin Christendom. By the mid-thirteenth century towns almost everywhere were growing, manufacturing was expanding and international trade was booming. Europe's northern and southern internal orbits of exchange had coalesced and were fast becoming integrated into an interlinked system of exchange encompassing the whole of the Known World (Figure 2.1).[6] While commercial opportunities expanded and concomitant enabling environmental conditions lasted, Latin Christendom's general economic outlook was likely to remain bright.

It is this broadly positive set of socio-ecological developments that is the focus of this extended section. Section 2.01 considers the timing of the onset of the revival in economic and commercial activity. Section 2.02 then surveys the atmospheric circulation patterns that characterized the MCA, the relatively benign weather conditions that prevailed over temperate Europe and Monsoon Asia, and the role played by the Medieval Solar Maximum and other climate forcing agents in sustaining these conditions. As Section 2.03 demonstrates, almost the whole of the Known World experienced population growth during the second half of the MCA, although nowhere was the increase more sustained than in Europe. It was predicated upon an economic boom whose institutional

[5] Lopez (1971); Britnell (1993a), 5–154.   [6] Abu-Lughod (1989).

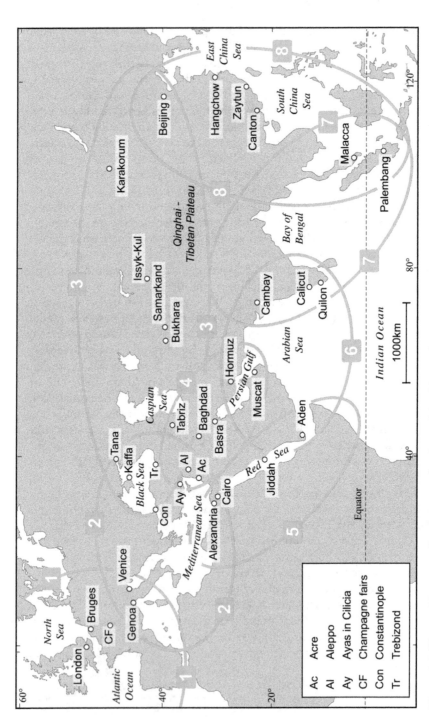

Figure 2.1 The world system of exchange at the close of the thirteenth century
Source: Abu-Lughod (1989), 34

underpinnings – a reformed Church, birth of the Western Legal Tradition, and the establishment of guilds, communes and international fairs – are the subject of Section 2.04. It was these institutions that shaped European development for centuries to come. During the twelfth and thirteenth centuries, however, they bore immediate fruit in the Italian-led commercial revolution described in Section 2.05. It is England, however, for the reasons given in Section 1.04, that furnishes the most detailed case study of the commercial, monetary and agricultural advances made during this formative period.

In both Italy and England demographic and economic expansion proceeded in tandem and without significant erosion of living standards until well into the thirteenth century due to the Smithian gains generated by the expansion of markets and growth of trade.[7] As demonstrated in Section 2.05.3, rising levels of urbanization furnish evidence of the modest but real economic growth then taking place. Unsurprisingly, urbanization ratios peaked in the twin lead economies of Italy and Flanders, with their highly developed commercial and manufacturing sectors. Here, as elsewhere, the greatest cities, with populations in excess of 50,000, were invariably actively engaged in one way or another in international commerce. The pan-European and pan-Eurasian dimensions of that commerce, which are one of the most impressive features of this remarkable era, are described in Section 2.05.4. Finally, Section 2.06 brings the environmental and societal sides of these developments together and reflects on the overall character of this, for a time, remarkably buoyant socio-ecological system.

Of course, Latin Christendom's high-medieval efflorescence was far from unique. This was the golden age of Song China, and, in what Lieberman has called a series of 'strange parallels', the period from the mid-ninth to the late thirteenth centuries witnessed the economic and political rise of the Pagan (Burma), Angkor (Cambodia), Champa and Dai Viet (Vietnam) states of Southeast Asia, along with the Chola civilization of south India.[8] Common to all were processes of territorial consolidation, administrative centralization and cultural integration. Infectious diseases may have eased as a restraint upon population growth, while the extended reach and strengthened force of monsoon flows and concomitant reduction in the incidence and severity of droughts consequent upon a positive El Niño Southern Oscillation (ENSO) undoubtedly benefited

---

[7] Smithian gains are those which stemmed from market growth and a greater division of labour, as elaborated by Adam Smith in Book I of *An inquiry into the nature and causes of the wealth of nations* (1776).

[8] Lieberman (2009); Lieberman and Buckley (2012), 1056–68; Tana (2014); Abu-Lughod (1989), 263.

agricultural output.[9] Greater coordination of water control, improved irrigation systems, and wider adoption of multi-cropping with hardy fast-ripening rice strains further reinforced a sustained rise in agricultural output and, thus, greater food security. Urban growth stimulated production of agricultural surpluses and was itself a function of increased intra-regional and long-distance trade.

Market widening and deepening was therefore as much an Asian as a European phenomenon during these high-medieval centuries and the inter-linkage of these respective orbits of exchange, so compellingly described by Abu-Lughod, was one of the culminating achievements of the age.[10] Lieberman also attaches great importance to the fact that, unlike China, India, western Asia and Russia, the kingdoms of Southeast Asia and western Europe were spared sustained occupation, if not attacks, by nomads from Inner Asia.[11] In contrast, neither the technologically advanced Northern Song Empire of China nor the commercially strategic Abbasid Caliphate of Iraq, with its capital of Baghdad, recovered their former prosperity once conquered by the Mongols. From 1205, repeated eruption of seemingly invincible Mongol armies from their environmentally marginal central Asian homelands was the single most transformative shock of the age. Destructive as in many cases these military excursions proved to be, they did nonetheless redraw the political and military maps of interior Eurasia and, for a time, imposed unity upon a hitherto politically fractured landmass. This created the potential for increased overland transit of personnel and goods as an alternative to the traditional maritime routes, whereby merchandise was shipped either up the Persian Gulf to Basra, and then taken by caravan across the Syrian desert to the eastern Mediterranean ports of Antioch, Tripoli and Acre, or up the Red Sea to Egypt, whence it was trans-shipped to Alexandria. While these fragile trading links endured, the vitality and prosperity of both the Oriental and Occidental commercial zones and their leading entrepôts were assured, provided, of course, that nothing jeopardized the fragile socio-ecological balance upon which their commercial success was founded.

2.01   Latin Christendom's take-off to sustained growth

When did Latin Christendom's own high-medieval efflorescence commence, given the seemingly self-perpetuating post-Roman malaise of endemic military conflict, political fragmentation, de-monetization, commercial implosion, urban decay and depressed population densities?[12]

---

[9] Below, Section 2.02.1.   [10] Abu-Lughod (1989), 352–64.
[11] Lieberman (2009), 85–7, 92–3.   [12] Russell (1958), 88–99.

Michael McCormick detects signs of commercial recovery from the late eighth century and from about the same time there was steady diffusion of the key agricultural innovations of heavy mouldboard ploughs, horse shoes and collars, and regulated common fields, which Lynn White Jr believes made a significant expansion of agricultural output possible.[13] Northwest Europe's distinctive mixed-farming regimes also benefited from milder and wetter winters, warmer summers and generally more settled climatic conditions throughout the greater part of the ninth and tenth centuries, following onset of the MCA.[14]

During this first phase of the MCA, improved sailing conditions in the North Atlantic facilitated Norse colonization of the previously unoccupied Faroes, Iceland and Greenland from, respectively, the 820s, 870s and 890s CE, but also underscored repeated Viking raids on the settled coastal and riverine lowlands of Ireland, Britain and mainland Europe to the south.[15] Partly because of the Viking menace in the north, Muslim advances in the south and encroachments by Magyars and Slavs in the east, these more benign environmental conditions failed to elicit a general re-growth of population and re-expansion of settlement. On the contrary, the dendrochronological record implies that during the tenth and eleventh centuries Ireland, and probably those other European regions most exposed to these threats, experienced a major regeneration of woodland, presumably because agricultural land-uses were in retreat.[16] In England conditions of relative land abundance occasioned a significant reorganization of rural settlement.[17] Evidently, resource abundance, favourable climatic conditions and improved technology were insufficient by themselves within this still politically chaotic world to kick-start a full-scale demographic and economic revival.

Robert Lopez and Jan Luiten van Zanden both date onset of a quickening European dynamic to the mid-tenth century.[18] Michael Mann dates it slightly later, 'once the last marauders – Viking, Muslim, and Hun – were repulsed, say, by AD 1000'.[19] Nevertheless, not until the late eleventh century, as the MCA entered its second and most sustained phase following the Oort Solar Minimum, are there clear signs that population and settlement were belatedly expanding once again and doing so on a pan-European scale. For the next 250 years the dendrochronological, archaeological and historical records bear witness to

---

[13] McCormick (2001), 791: 'The rise of the European commercial economy, indeed the rise of the European economy, period, did not begin in the tenth or eleventh century. It began, decisively, in the concluding decades of the eighth century.' White Jr (1962).

[14] Below, Section 2.02.2.   [15] Marcus (1980), 35–70.

[16] Baillie (2006), frontispiece. See Lagerås (2007), 50–2, for evidence of a contemporary interruption to settlement expansion in southern Sweden.

[17] Oosthuizen (2010).   [18] Lopez (1971); Zanden (2009), 64–8, 89.

[19] Mann (1986), 377.

widespread woodland clearance and a pronounced upsurge in building activity, as Latin Christendom's high-medieval efflorescence got under way.[20] Signs of demographic and economic dynamism show up earlier in some regions than others and the pace and pattern of growth naturally varied a good deal, evidently being stronger in northwestern than southern Europe (where drought was a recurrent problem), and weakest in Iberia (over which Christians and Moors fought for control), but the trajectory of change was almost everywhere the same.[21] Resurgence of the Latin Church, birth of the 'Western legal tradition', state formation, institution of self-regulating urban communes, guilds and commonfield communities, ongoing technological advance, expanding bullion and money supplies, and generally favourable environmental conditions collectively underpinned the palpable socio-economic dynamism of the eleventh to the thirteenth centuries.[22] Growth, once begun, proved almost unstoppable until a punitive combination of war, commercial recession, extreme weather events and infectious diseases finally halted the momentum of expansion in the early fourteenth century.

2.02   The Medieval Climate Anomaly (MCA)

From the ninth to the thirteenth centuries a distinctive configuration of atmospheric circulation patterns prevailed which has become known as the Medieval Climate Anomaly.[23] So dominant were these patterns that, until the fourteenth century, all interruptions to and deviations from them were followed by reversions to the status quo ante. It is consequently easy to take them for granted when, in fact, as Section 2.02.5 shows, they were the product of distinct climatic forcing conditions of their own. Temperature reconstructions show that, globally, the MCA was a period of increased warmth, but the warming was geographically uneven and complex ocean–atmosphere interactions resulted in cooler conditions in some major regions, most notably the eastern Pacific Ocean. Temperatures peaked in the mid-ninth century and, again, during the late

---

[20] Baillie (2006), frontispiece, 21–2; Lagerås (2007), 51–2; Williams (2000), 36–42.

[21] Moreno and others (2012); Russell (1958), 113, 148; McEvedy and Jones (1978), 23, 61–3; Brooke (2014), 363–4; Moreda (1988); Henriques (2015), 150–2, 169.

[22] Berman (1983), 7–10, summarizes the defining characteristics of the 'Western legal tradition'. For the positive institutional legacy of collective action by communes, guilds and groups of commoners see De Moor (2008); Zanden (2009), 50–5.

[23] Bradley and others (2003). The term 'Medieval Climate Anomaly' (MCA) has replaced 'Medieval Warm Period' (MWP) due to the realization that 'this period was characterized not by uniformly warmer temperatures, but rather by a range of temperature, hydroclimate and marine changes with distinct regional and seasonal expressions': Graham and others (2010), 2. For an influential early essay on this era see Lamb (1965).

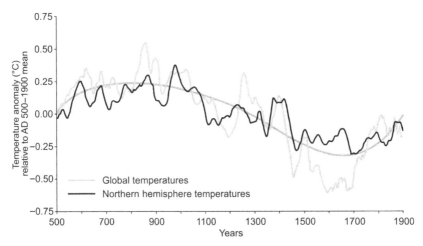

Figure 2.2 Reconstructed global and northern hemisphere temperature anomalies, AD 500–1900
Sources: global – Loehle and McCulloch (2008); northern hemisphere – Mann and others (2008)

tenth and early eleventh centuries (Figure 2.2). In the North Atlantic it was during these two exceptionally warm episodes that, encouraged by relatively ice-free sailing conditions, the northerly migration of fish stocks and favourable growing conditions on land, the Norse established colonies in Iceland and Greenland and then, at the opening of the new millennium, made their discovery of Vinland, alias Newfoundland.[24] Not until the global warming of the late twentieth century would environmental conditions in these most northerly of latitudes again be so benign.

Global and hemispherical temperatures cooled significantly during the latter part of the Oort Solar Minimum (*c*.1010–50) and for most of the twelfth century remained well below the temporal peak attained at the opening of the millennium (Figure 2.2). This decline, which seems to have ended with a particularly sharp downturn in the 1190s, was followed by a partial recovery and by the 1230s temperatures in the northern hemisphere may have risen to a level not experienced since the 1090s.[25] This period of warming represents a late reversion to the conditions and circulation patterns that had prevailed for much of the MCA and

[24] Dugmore and others (2007), 13–17; Patterson and others (2010).
[25] Historical records imply that during the thirteenth century warming was particularly marked in eastern China: Ge and others (2003), 938–9.

coincided with synchronous phases of economic efflorescence in Song China, Southeast Asia and Latin Christendom.

Globally, temperatures may have risen by at least 1°C during the warmest phases of the MCA compared with the coldest years of the LIA at the end of the seventeenth century; in the northern hemisphere the temperature differential may have been somewhat smaller (Figure 2.2). The absolute magnitude of this temperature differential may not seem great but it undoubtedly subsumed far greater changes at smaller geographical scales. It was also quite sufficient to have altered climatic and weather patterns across extensive regions of the Earth in quite fundamental ways, with profound implications for flora, fauna, microbes and humans, and the complex ecological inter-relationships between them.[26] This review of circulation patterns during the MCA considers, first, the El Niño Southern Oscillation (ENSO), second, the North Atlantic Oscillation (NAO) and, third, Arid Central Asia, before finishing with a brief summary of Old World climates as a whole.

2.02.1 The El Niño Southern Oscillation (ENSO)

Any warming or cooling of the Pacific Ocean has particularly far-reaching climatic consequences. The Pacific is a vast and deep water-body which straddles the Equator and is crossed by westward-blowing equatorial trade winds. These cause an east to west movement of surface water across the equatorial Pacific, during which powerful solar warming takes place, thereby raising sea-surface temperatures in the west relative to those in the east and inducing a strong pressure gradient between the eastern Pacific neighbouring the Americas and the western Pacific adjoining Australia and Southeast Asia. The more that sea-surface temperatures cool in the east, the more they push the warmed water to the west. The pronounced thermocline which develops between the warmed surface waters and colder waters of the deep ocean is also shallower in the east than the west. Off the Americas this induces a strong upwelling of cold but nutrient-rich waters from the deep ocean, thus further reinforcing the contrast between a cold eastern and warm western Pacific and strengthening the trade winds. Solar warming can thus have the paradoxical effect of inducing lower temperatures in the eastern Pacific, sometimes by as much as 4°C. These cold offshore waters ensure that most precipitation falls at sea rather than on land, hence

---

[26] Above, Figure 1.2. For a review of the nature and magnitude of these climatic changes see Graham and others (2010).

they are typically associated with dry climatic conditions in mid-latitude South America and western North America, whereas the warm surface temperatures of the western Pacific keep northern Australia and Indonesia wet. These have become known as La Niña conditions and their influence upon global climate is not to be underestimated.[27] For instance, strong La Niñas are associated with strong Asian and Indian monsoons, greater humidity in northern South America, the Sahel and South Africa, and increased aridity in eastern Africa and southern Europe.

During the MCA La Niña conditions appear to have been exceptionally strong, with the result that much of the American West was kept in a state of almost perpetual drought.[28] Dendrochronology provides a precisely dated record of drought-related fire damage to trees and precipitation-related changes in growing conditions across a wide geographical area and over long spans of time. Drawing upon this substantial palaeoecological archive, Edward R. Cook and others (2004c) have constructed a Drought Severity Index (DSI) for the United States west of the 95th meridian west and spanning the last 1,200 years (Figure 2.3A). This highlights a '400-year interval of overall elevated aridity from AD 900 to 1300', a time period 'broadly consistent with the Medieval Warm Period', and 'an abrupt change to persistently less arid conditions after AD 1300'.[29] Extended drought episodes, symptomatic of strongly developed La Niña conditions, centred on AD 936, 1034, 1150 and 1253 (the last and most prolonged of these mega-droughts).

Synchronous episodes of aridity and mega-drought show up in the South American palaeoclimatic record. Thus, an analysis of the stratigraphy of fine-grained lithics eroded by intense El Niño-generated river floods and deposited on the ocean shelf off the coast of Peru has identified a flood-free period of minimal precipitation and runoff from the 940s to 1280s (Figure 2.3B).[30] Thereafter river discharge and erosion rose significantly as witnessed by heightened rates of marine sedimentation. Evidence of a reduction in sea-surface temperatures between c.700 and c.1250 (i.e. consistent with a La Niña-dominated Pacific) has also emerged from comprehensive chemical and mineral analysis of a core taken from the continental slope off the coast of Chile.[31] Across this same period, reduced rates of ice accumulation on the Quelccaya ice cap in Peru bear witness to diminished precipitation levels. These sank to a

[27] Herweijer and others (2007); Seager and others (2007).
[28] Cook and others (2004b); Herweijer and others (2007); Seager and others (2007).
[29] Cook and others (2004b), 2.   [30] Rein and others (2004).
[31] Mohtadi and others (2007).

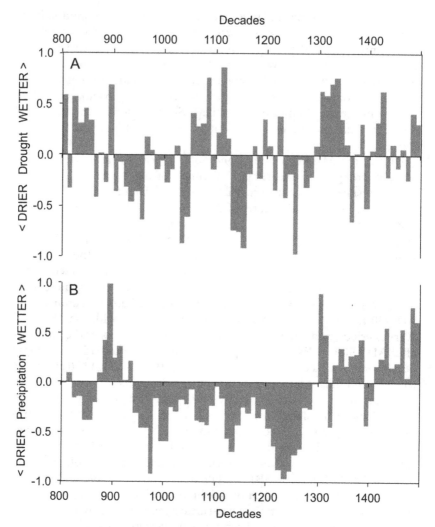

Figure 2.3 (A) North American West: drought index derived from dendrochronology, AD 800–1500. (B) South American Pacific West: precipitation index derived from deposits of fine-grained lithics off the coast of Peru, AD 800–1500

Sources: adapted from Cook and others (2004c); Rein and others (2004)

minimum *c*.1250, contemporaneous with the thirteenth-century mega-drought in the North American West (Figure 2.3A). Together, these testify to an exceptionally strong and positive ENSO event.[32] At Laguna Aculeo in central Chile, sustained high summer temperatures prevailed from the mid-twelfth until the mid-fourteenth century, with a notable peak around 1240.[33] A major flood event in southern Peru around 1300 effectively brought this era of South American mega-droughts to a close (Figure 2.3B). A recent reconstruction of South American tropical temperatures based upon a high-resolution ammonium record from a tephra-dated Bolivian ice-core suggests that the terminal date was, if anything, slightly earlier.[34] Until then, the arid medieval hydro-climate of South America's Pacific littoral remained both intact and entrenched.

Typically, the drier it was in the North and South American Pacific West the wetter it was in the monsoon belt of South Asia and India. A dendrochronologically derived Drought Severity Index (DSI) has been reconstructed by Cook and others (2010) for the greater part of this vast region, along comparable lines to their corresponding DSI for North America. Unfortunately, the difficulty of reconstructing long-run dendrochronologies for trees growing under tropical and sub-tropical conditions means that this DSI extends no further back than the fourteenth and fifteenth centuries, when the South and Southeast Asian monsoons were persistently weak. The mega-drought of 1351 to 1368 shows up particularly clearly in this record.[35] For earlier centuries reliance has to be placed upon a high-resolution varve record of run-off from Pakistan into the Arabian Sea and estimates of precipitation inferred from the dated band widths of speleothems from Dandak Cave, India, Wanxiang Cave, north China, and Dongge Cave, south China (Figures 2.4A to 2.5B). Both individually and collectively (Figure 2.8B), these proxy precipitation measures confirm the dramatic failure of monsoon rainfall in the fourteenth century while highlighting the much wetter conditions that had long prevailed until the end of the thirteenth century (albeit with much annual and regional variation).

The varve record of the ocean shelf in the Arabian Sea is consistent with relatively high levels of precipitation over Pakistan (the source of most run-off) for the greater part of the eleventh, twelfth and thirteenth centuries, punctuated by short episodes of substantially reduced rainfall from the 1190s to 1210s and, again, in the 1280s. Rates of varve deposition peaked in the 1130s, at a time when a pattern of regular and

---

[32] Mohtadi and others (2007), 1061–3.
[33] Gunten and others (2009b).   [34] Thompson and others (2013).
[35] Cook and others (2010), 488. See also Tana (2014), 335.

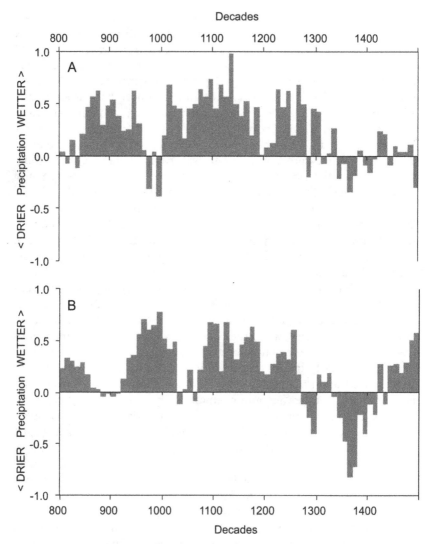

Figure 2.4 (A) Pakistan: precipitation index derived from varves in the Arabian Sea, AD 800–1500. (B) India: precipitation index derived from Dandak Cave speleothem, AD 800–1500
Sources: Rad and others (1999); Berkelhammer and others (2010b)

strong monsoons had long been firmly established, then became more variable during the thirteenth century, and declined to a much reduced level from the 1310s, with a notable downturn from the 1340s to 1400s (Figure 2.4A). In India, levels of precipitation inferred from the Dandak

Cave speleothem indicate the prevalence of regular and strong monsoons from the 930s until the 1020s and, again, from the 1070s to 1250s. There was a temporary weakening of the monsoon during the Oort Solar Minimum, from the 1030s to 1070s, and more pronounced and enduring failure from the 1260s, which was at its most extreme from the 1340s to 1370s (Figure 2.4B).[36] Thus, in both Pakistan and India these two independent chronologies confirm that from the mid-tenth to the late thirteenth centuries strong monsoon rains were the norm.

At Wanxiang Cave, close to the northern limit of the east Asian summer monsoon in northern China, an equivalent speleothem-based index of precipitation documents a broadly synchronous chronology of persistently strong monsoon rains from the mid-tenth to the beginning of the fourteenth centuries, similarly interrupted by a marked weakening of the monsoon during the Oort Solar Minimum from the 1030s to 1080s (Figure 2.5A). Here, the peak in precipitation occurred in the 1100s and was followed by over fifty years of consistently high rainfall. There was some moderation of rainfall levels during the thirteenth century but no decisive and lasting weakening of the monsoon until the 1340s. Thereafter, from the 1350s to 1380s, failure was more-or-less absolute and the monsoon remained greatly weakened for the rest of the Middle Ages. In south China the Dongge Cave speleothem record charts a rather different chronology. Here, rainfall levels rose significantly throughout the first half of the thirteenth century, to reach a medieval peak in c.1254, when flood posed a greater hazard than drought (Figure 2.5B). These strong monsoon conditions persisted into the fourteenth century until, as elsewhere, the onset of serious drought in the 1340s, 1350s and 1360s. A brief but marked recovery then ensued before the era of predominantly strong monsoon rains came to an abrupt end at the opening of the fifteenth century.

Combining these four precipitation indices into one brings out the broad temporal trends in the relative strength of the South Asian monsoon across these seven centuries (Figure 2.8B). Two periods of persistently strong monsoon rainfall stand out, the shorter from the 940s to the 1020s and the longer from the 1070s to 1270s. The 50-year interval of much weakened and geographically more variable monsoon conditions that separated them coincided with the Oort Solar Minimum. Following the prolonged Medieval Solar Maximum, onset of the Wolf Solar Minimum in the closing decades of the thirteenth century brought a progressive weakening of the monsoon, culminating in its near-universal failure and consequent mega-drought of the middle decades of the fourteenth

---

[36] Sinha and others (2007); Sinha and others (2011).

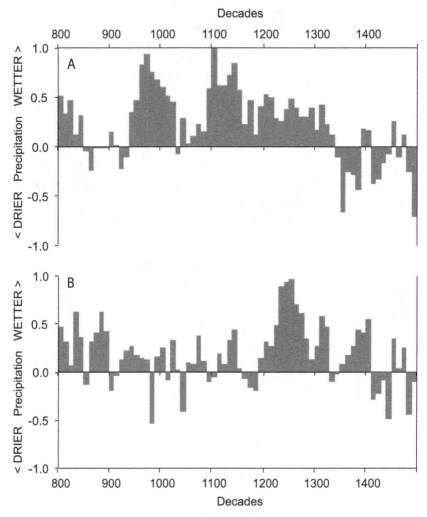

Figure 2.5 (A) Northern China: precipitation index derived from Wanxiang Cave speleothem, AD 800–1500. (B) Southern China: precipitation index derived from Dongge Cave speleothem, AD 800–1500 *Sources*: adapted from Zhang and others (2008); Wang and others (2006)

century. Thereafter, with certain brief and regionally specific exceptions and notwithstanding a late-fourteenth-century revival in solar irradiance, the Asian monsoon failed to recover to its former strength. This switch from strong to weak monsoons was the counterpart of the opposite and synchronous trend from drier to wetter conditions in the North and South American Pacific West. Both arose from a general weakening of the ENSO.

The strong monsoons that were the norm in Asia during the MCA were matched in northwest Europe by the prevalence of strong winter westerlies, the product of a marked pressure difference between Iceland and the Azores, which delivered a warm, moisture-laden, oceanic air-stream.[37] This winter predominance of cyclonic conditions kept cold, dry, anticyclonic polar air at bay and ensured that temperatures remained mild and rainfall levels high. The most notable exception was during and immediately following the Oort Solar Minimum in the mid-eleventh century, when, on the evidence of a speleothem record from Cnoc nan Uamh Cave in northwest Scotland, a significant weakening of the westerlies occurred and winters became drier and colder as Arctic air spilled south (Figure 2.6A). Otherwise, with the exception of some notable short-term perturbations, for the better part of four centuries, from c.900 to c.1300, a strongly cyclonic weather system and mild, moist, westerly Atlantic air-stream predominated.[38]

These cyclonic conditions were particularly well developed in the 1240s, when Northern Europe experienced the wettest weather in more than 200 years. In 1246–7 on the Winchester estates in southern England, year-round predominance of a humid, westerly, cyclonic air-stream depressed grain harvests and inflated grain and salt prices.[39] Oaks,

---

[37] Seager and others (2007); Trouet and others (2009a and b); Graham and others (2010).

[38] For example, drier but colder conditions briefly returned in the 1200s (Figure 2.5A), depressing oak growth and precipitating a major back-to-back harvest failure which, on the evidence of grain prices and the comments of contemporaries, brought England to the brink of famine. The years 1201 and 1202 were notable for storms and unseasonable weather: Britton (1937), 73–9; Cheney (1981), 580–1. Grain and livestock prices more than doubled in 1203 and remained very high the following year: Farmer (1956). In Greenland temperatures plunged during the years 1197–1205 to an extreme of coldness not experienced for centuries and not exceeded in severity until the coldest years of the early fourteenth century: Kobashi and others (2010b). Ring widths of British Isles oaks narrowed significantly from 1197 to 1209 and within this period of depressed growth 1207 stands out as a narrow-ring event: data supplied by M. G. L. Baillie.

[39] On the Winchester estate as a whole the harvests of 1246 and 1247 were 10 per cent below average, while at Highclere, Hants, the wheat harvests of 1246 and 1247 were only half those of 1245 and 1248: Hants R. O., Titow Papers. In 1247 and 1248 wheat and salt prices were respectively over 50 per cent and 100 per cent above normal (grain harvests and solar evaporation of brine both depended upon warm, dry weather):

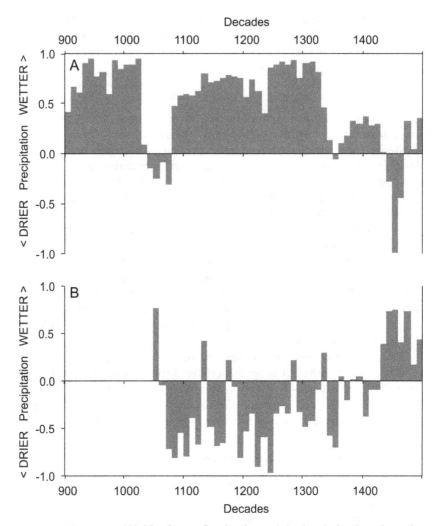

Figure 2.6 (A) Northwest Scotland: precipitation index based on the band widths of a speleothem from Cnoc nan Uamh Cave, AD 900–1500. (B) Morocco: precipitation index based on the ring widths of Atlantic cedar, 1050–1500
Sources: Proctor and others (2002b); Esper and others (2009)

however, thrived under these weather conditions and in the 1240s and 1250s grew some of the widest rings on dendrochronological record.

Clark (2009). English oaks, which thrived on cold winters and mild, wet summers, also exhibited slightly above-average growth in 1246 and 1247: information supplied by M. G. L. Baillie.

Throughout this dynamic growth phase the ring widths of Old and New World trees were positively correlated (with a correlation of +0.46 across the thirteenth century as a whole, rising to +0.85 between 1230 and 1255), which implies that, in temperate zones across the planet, trees were responding to influences of pan-global magnitude.[40] These same climatic conditions sustained moderately warm sea-surface temperatures in the North Atlantic, kept the seas around Iceland largely ice free, and insulated Greenland from the bitterest of cold, thereby ensuring the continuing environmental viability of both the eastern and western Norse settlements.[41] The common denominator of this mostly benign set of climatic circumstances was a strongly positive North Atlantic Oscillation (NAO). In the middle decades of the thirteenth century this was at, or close to, its maximum medieval strength. By the end of that century it was waning fast.

The effect of this +NAO was to draw the westerly winter storm-track north, thereby depriving the countries bordering the Mediterranean of precipitation and creating a pronounced climatic contrast between a mild and moist northwestern Europe and hot and arid southern Europe and North Africa.[42] In Morocco, for instance, a precipitation index reconstructed from the annual growth rings of Atlantic cedars indicates that, following a conspicuously moist interval during the Oort Solar Minimum in the mid-eleventh century, conditions of extreme aridity then prevailed until the early fourteenth century, relieved solely by rare spells of wetter weather in the 1130s, 1170s, 1280s and 1330s (Figure 2.6B). Comparison between this tree-ring based drought reconstruction for Morocco and the Scottish speleothem proxy record of precipitation highlights the wide difference in moisture levels that existed during the twelfth and thirteenth centuries between these two Atlantic-edge locations.[43] In particular, the 1240s stand out as a decade of extreme wetness in Scotland and drought in Morocco (Figures 2.6A and B). Not until the middle

---

[40] The Old World is a composite chronology constructed by M. G. L. Baillie from independent multi-site chronologies for the Polar Urals (pine), Fennoscandia (pine), temperate Europe (oak) and the Aegean (oak, pine, juniper). Within that chronology the years with the widest rings are 1248, 1249 (the widest of all) and 1250.

[41] Jiang and others (2005); Massé and others (2008); Dugmore and others (2007); Kobashi and others (2010b).

[42] The force and direction of westerly winds into Europe are controlled by the relative strengths and positions of low pressure over Iceland and high pressure over the Azores. The bigger the pressure difference between Iceland and the Azores, the more positive the NAO and the greater the strength of the westerlies. A +NAO typically delivers mild, wet winters to Northwest Europe. In contrast, a weak pressure difference and –NAO admits incursions of drier and far colder polar air. When this happens the westerlies are deflected south, toward the Mediterranean, delivering stormy, wet, winter weather to North Africa and southern Europe.

[43] Trouet and others (2009a and b).

years of the fourteenth century did a general and enduring weakening of the NAO lead to a southern shift in the winter westerlies and their accompanying precipitation. Until this point, at the end of the MCA and as the strengths of the ENSO and Asian monsoon both waned, each weakening of the NAO had been followed by a recovery.

2.02.3 Arid Central Asia (ACA)

The trajectory and strength of the mid-latitude westerlies also exercised a powerful influence upon moisture levels in Arid Central Asia, which lay beyond reach of the Asian monsoon and was reliant for such precipitation as it received upon a predominantly westerly airflow.[44] Arid conditions across southern Europe and North Africa, and especially in the eastern Mediterranean, thus tended to replicate equivalent conditions in Eurasia's continental interior. This broad correlation shows up clearly in the close chronological parallel between precipitation levels in Morocco, as reconstructed from the growth rings of Atlantic cedars (Figure 2.6B), and a composite decadal index of moisture levels in Arid Central Asia. The latter has been reconstructed by Fa-Hu Chen and others (2010) from an array of proxy palaeoclimatic records pertaining to the Aral Sea (Kazakhstan/Uzbekistan), Lake Sugan (northwest China), Lake Bosten (Xinjiang, northern China), the Guliya ice cap (Tibetan–Qinghai Plateau, China) and Badain Jaran Desert (Inner Mongolia, China) (Figure 2.7). As in Morocco, the relatively moist conditions that prevailed in Arid Central Asia during the early to mid-eleventh century did not long outlast the Oort Solar Minimum. From the final decades of the eleventh century moisture levels steadily dwindled until an extreme of aridity was reached in the 1190s and early 1200s which provided the Mongols with a powerful incentive to, first, raid and then, from 1209, invade the Western Xia in northern China.[45] The years around 1220 brought some easing of these conditions during the so-called Mongol pluvial of 1211–25 but moisture levels then declined once again in the middle and final decades of the thirteenth century and on this reconstruction the 1300s stand out as only marginally less arid than the 1200s.[46] Thereafter, as the fourteenth century advanced, the NAO weakened, the trajectory of Atlantic westerlies shifted south and, as lower northern hemisphere temperatures helped reduce losses from evaporation, so, fitfully, moisture levels in Arid Central Asia started to rise, with a notable wet phase from the 1310s until 1340 revealed by dendrochronologies from

---

[44] Chen and others (2008); Fang and others (2014).
[45] Lieberman (2009), 185; Brooke (2014), 369.
[46] Hessl and others (2013); Pederson and others (2014).

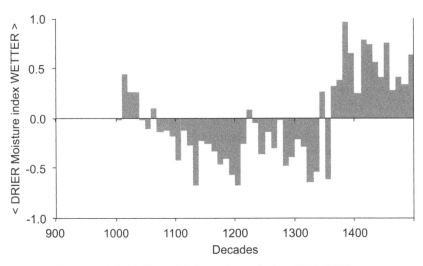

Figure 2.7 Arid Central Asia: moisture index, 1000–1500
Source: adapted from Chen and others (2010)

Mongolia, northeast Tibet and the Tien Shan mountains (but not evident in Figure 2.7).[47]

At these three geographically widely separate locations, Scotland, Morocco and Arid Central Asia, proxy measures of precipitation and moisture reconstructed by independent teams of researchers from diverse types of palaeoclimatic evidence (a speleothem, tree rings, lake cores, ice layers and groundwater recharge rates) at different levels of temporal resolution reveal a remarkably coherent chronology (Figures 2.8C and 2.8D). The Oort Solar Minimum with attendant weakening of the NAO lowered precipitation in Scotland and shifted the winter westerlies south, bringing higher rainfall to Morocco and allowing a moister air-stream to penetrate the Eurasian continental interior. From the 1070s, however, the NAO recovered in strength and the winter westerlies resumed their more northerly course, with the result that precipitation over Scotland bounced back to the levels that had prevailed throughout the tenth century and Morocco and Arid Central Asia were condemned to a state of nearly perpetual aridity. This climatic dichotomy between a mild and moist northern Europe and a hot and dry southern Europe, North Africa and interior Eurasia then endured without serious interruption until the first half of the fourteenth century, when the hitherto strongly positive NAO began to weaken and significantly different patterns of circulation began to make themselves felt.

---

[47] Below, Figure 3.30.

For more than two hundred years, from the late eleventh century until the early fourteenth century, a remarkably stable and resilient global climate regime prevailed. This final and most prolonged phase of the MCA had three closely interlinked and broadly synchronous elements: first, a strongly positive ENSO with a La Niña-dominated Pacific, which entrapped the Pacific Wests of North and South America in a state of drought (Figure 2.8A) and ensured that the Asian and Indian monsoons were both reliable and wet (Figure 2.8B); second, a strongly positive NAO, which raised sea-surface temperatures in the North Atlantic, shielded northwest Europe from major winter incursions of cold, dry, polar air, and created a marked precipitation gradient between northern and southern Europe (Figures 2.6A and 2.6B); and, third, arising from the positive NAO and concomitant strong northwesterly trajectory of the mid-latitude westerlies, the prevalence of conditions of recurrent and sometimes extreme drought in Arid Central Asia (Figure 2.7).

Given the limiting effects of temperature and rainfall upon biological reproduction, these circulation patterns heightened the marginality of some regions while reducing that of others. In particular, the Norse communities of the North Atlantic, mixed-farming societies of northwest Europe, and monsoon-dependent millet- and rice-growing civilizations of China, Southeast and South Asia all benefited from these benign environmental conditions and proved remarkably resilient to the occasional climatic anomalies which inevitably occurred, including those triggered by a notable cluster of major volcanic eruptions in the latter part of the twelfth century and opening years of the thirteenth century (Figure 2.8). Elsewhere in the Old World, deficient rainfall inhibited fuller exploitation of environmental resources, except where irrigation provided an alternative basis for sustaining agricultural production. In interior Eurasia's semi-arid steppe grasslands it maintained ecological conditions unfavourable to build-up of *Yersinia pestis* and its sylvatic rodent host populations beyond enzootic levels. Everywhere, in fact, societies discovered that the relative stability and predictability of prevailing weather patterns was something upon which they could rely. Not until destabilization of these circulation patterns in the fourteenth century did that confidence prove misplaced.

2.02.5   The Medieval Solar Maximum

A case can be made that it was relatively high levels of solar irradiance that maintained the relative stability of circulation patterns during the

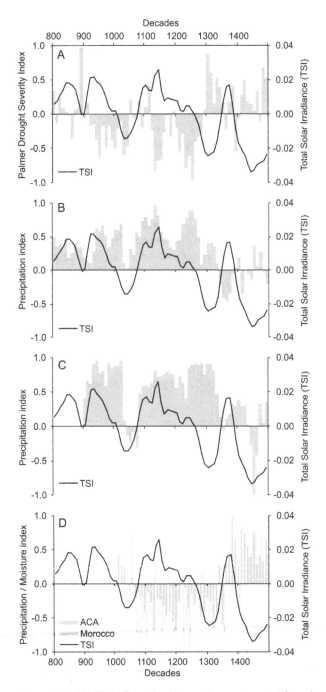

Figure 2.8 (A) Total Solar Irradiance (reconstructed from beryllium-10 and cosmogenic isotopes) and North and South American Pacific West

MCA.[48] Thus, Edouard Bard and Martin Frank claim that 'the weight of evidence suggests that solar changes have contributed to small climatic oscillations occurring on time scales of a few centuries, similar in type to the fluctuations classically described for the last millennium: the so-called Medieval Warm Period (900–1400 A.D.) followed on by the Little Ice Age (1500–1800 A.D.)'.[49] Likewise, Thomas Crowley reckons that 'as much as 41–64 per cent of pre-anthropogenic (pre-1850) decadal-scale temperature variations was due to changes in solar irradiance and volcanism'.[50] At issue is whether the magnitude of the estimated variations in irradiance is sufficient to account for the scale of the observed changes in climate, but certainly the chronology of solar irradiance fits well with those of temperatures and patterns of atmospheric circulation.

Periods of reduced global temperatures (Figure 2.2) tended to coincide with diminished solar irradiance and low or zero sunspot activity, as during the Oort Minimum (*c.*1010–50), Wolf Minimum (*c.*1282–1342), Spörer Minimum (*c.*1416–1534), Maunder Minimum (*c.*1654–1714) and Dalton Minimum (*c.*1790–1830).[51] Conversely, periods when the sun was active and sunspot activity was high, most notably during the Medieval Maximum and the Modern Maximum, were associated with global warming.[52] Increased solar irradiance (the 'Chaucerian Solar Maximum') also appears to have underpinned the brief but marked temperature recovery of the final decades of the fourteenth century. Yet the

---

Figure 2.8 (*cont.*) combined drought index, AD 800–1500. (B) Total Solar Irradiance and Monsoon Asia composite precipitation index, AD 800–1500. (C) Total Solar Irradiance and precipitation in northwest Scotland, AD 800/900–1500. (D) Total Solar Irradiance, Moroccan precipitation index and Arid Central Asia (ACA) moisture index, AD 800/1000–1500

Sources: Delaygue and Bard (2010b) and Vieira and others (2011); Figures 2.3A and B; Figures 2.4A and B and Figures 2.5A and B; Figures 2.6A and B

---

[48] Cook and others (2004a), 2072–3; Graham and others (2010), 13; Jiang and others (2005); Mann and others (2005); Moberg and others (2005), 615–17; Wang and others (2005); Bard and Frank (2006); Seager and others (2007); Zhang and others (2008); Trouet and others (2009a and b); Berkelhammer and others (2010a); Graham and others (2010). For a dissenting view see Cobb and others (2003), 274–5.

[49] Bard and Frank (2006), 1.   [50] Crowley (2000), 270.

[51] The dates are those given by Stuiver and Quay (1980); see also Rogozo and others (2001). The reconstruction of solar irradiance by Delaygue and Bard (2010a and b) supersedes that of Bard and others (2000): the correlation between the two series for the years 868–1936 is +0.897.

[52] Bard and Frank (2006), 1.

fit is neither proportionate nor exact between the Total Solar Irradiance (TSI) curves reconstructed by Gilles Delaygue and Edouard Bard (from the beryllium-10 content of Antarctic ice-cores) and Veiria and others (from measurements of cosmogenic isotopes in Greenland ice-cores calibrated against the carbon-14 content of tree rings for the last thousand years) (Figure 2.8A) and the global and hemispherical temperature series reconstructed respectively by Craig Loehle and J. Huston McCulloch and Michael E. Mann and others (Figure 2.2).[53] This is because, as with most aspects of climate change, the influence of varying solar irradiance upon the Earth's atmosphere and climate, especially as arbitrated by the agency of ocean–atmosphere interaction, was neither simple nor direct.

Four prominent solar minima punctuated the seven centuries from 800 to 1500 (Figure 2.8). The briefest, lasting little more than a couple of decades, was at the end of the ninth and turn of the tenth centuries. This was followed by the much more prolonged reduction in TSI between c.1010 and c.1070, with a minimum value in the 1030s, known as the Oort Minimum. The Wolf Minimum of c.1280 to c.1340 was of broadly similar duration and reached its lowest point in the opening decade of the fourteenth century. After little more than fifty years, the Spörer Minimum then began: TSI was declining from the 1390s, reached a minimum in the 1440s, and remained low for the rest of fifteenth century. The Spörer exceeded in scale and duration the better-known Maunder Minimum of the second half of the seventeenth century and was associated with a major drop in global and northern hemisphere temperatures (Figure 2.2), with a spell of intense cold in the 1430s, which marks onset of the first extended phase of Little Ice Age cold.[54]

Each reduction in TSI tended to weaken the thermocline within the Pacific Ocean and lead to a corresponding weakening of the ENSO, as manifest in an easing of drought conditions in the Pacific West of the Americas (Figure 2.8A) and lessening of the strength of the Asian monsoon (Figure 2.8B). Imprints of the AD 900 Minimum and the Oort Minimum stand out particularly clearly in precipitation chronologies reconstructed from the Dandak Cave (India) and Wanxiang Cave (China) speleothems (Figures 2.4B and 2.5A). At the same time, the NAO weakened and the prevailing winter westerlies shifted to a more southerly trajectory. The Oort Minimum brought drier, colder winter weather to northwest Scotland, wetter weather to North Africa and

---

[53] Delaygue and Bard (2010a and b); Solanki and others (2005). Respective correlations of solar irradiance with global and northern hemisphere temperatures are +0.28 and +0.09. Equivalent correlations of estimated sunspot numbers with temperatures are lower, +0.20 and +0.08.

[54] Below, Section 5.02.2.

allowed a moister westerly air-stream to penetrate Arid Central Asia (Figures 2.8C and 2.8D). The Scottish speleothem record hints that something similar may earlier have occurred during the AD 900 Minimum (Figure 2.6A). Of course, the complexity of atmospheric circulation patterns also meant that they never exactly replicated themselves, with the result that there was much that was unique about each of these episodes.

A solar maximum of varying intensity and duration followed each solar minimum. TSI had been high during the greater part of the ninth century and it recovered quickly after the AD 900 Minimum. With this one short, sharp interval, the first two centuries of the MCA were a time of fairly sustained, high, solar irradiance. This ensured that the ENSO and NAO were both generally strongly positive, bringing drought to the Pacific West of the Americas, regular wet monsoons to South Asia, and mild, wet winters to northwest Europe. The Oort Minimum then destabilized these established climatic patterns and brought the first phase of the MCA to a close. The big bounce-back in TSI which then followed reinstated the status quo ante and initiated the second phase of the MCA throughout which solar irradiance remained at a sustained high level, but with a notable peak from the 1090s to 1140s (Figure 2.8A). No subsequent solar maximum has been as prolonged as this Medieval Solar Maximum (Figure 2.8). The patterns of atmospheric circulation that it underpinned prevailed with little significant interruption for the better part of two hundred years. Throughout the twelfth and thirteenth centuries La Niña conditions dominated the Pacific, consigning the Pacific West of the Americas to a state of more-or-less unremitting drought (Figure 2.8A) while South Asia benefited from reliable and strong monsoons (although India's gain was Ethiopia's loss). At the same time, strong winter westerlies kept northwest Europe mild and wet at the expense of southern Europe and North Africa. The pronounced northwestern trajectory of the westerlies also ensured that conditions in Central Asia became increasingly arid.

It was in the middle decades of the thirteenth century that this particular configuration of circulation patterns appears to have reached its apogee. Rainfall over Peru sank to a temporal low during the 1220s, 1230s and 1240s, while the 1250s mark the climax of one of the greatest of the mega-droughts in the North American West (Figures 2.3A and B and 2.08B). The 1220s–40s had brought strong monsoon rainfall to Pakistan and the 1250s stand out as an exceptionally wet decade in the Indian Dandak Cave speleothem record (Figures 2.4A and B). Precipitation levels were also high over north China from the 1240s to 1260s and increasingly so, according to the Dongge Cave speleothem record, over south China from the 1230s to 1260s (Figures 2.5A and B). A drought severity index derived from the ring widths of the rare Fujian Cypress (*Fokienia hodginsii*) also testifies to heavy monsoon rainfall over Cambodia in the 1250s.[55] In Europe, northwest Scotland became yet wetter during the 1240s while, at the same time, Morocco and presumably much of southern Europe were reduced to a state of mega-drought as the NAO achieved its maximum medieval strength (Figures 2.6A and B and 2.8D).[56] Unsurprisingly, Arid Central Asia experienced a spell of intense drought in the 1250s (Figures 2.6 and 2.8D).[57] Thereafter, these extreme conditions gradually eased and from the 1270s, as the Medieval Solar Maximum drew to a close, so, first the ENSO and then the NAO weakened, as the transition began to the altered circulation patterns of the LIA.

Superimposed upon this solar-generated climate chronology were many more transitory fluctuations triggered by an array of other forcing agents. The impacts of volcanic eruptions stand out particularly clearly in the palaeoclimatic record because of their telltale signature deposits of sulphate and tephra preserved in the Greenland and Antarctic ice sheets. Some of these may be attributed to historically recorded and dated events and linked in turn to precisely dated deviations in tree growth.[58] As will be noted from Figure 2.9A, after the relative absence of any significant stratospheric injection of sulphate aerosols for over 150 years, a marked upturn in volcanic activity appears to have occurred between the eruptions of Kirishima in Japan in 1167 and Etna in Italy in 1284. Across this 120-year period, notable sulphate spikes stand out in *c*.1167 and *c*.1176 (followed by lesser spikes in *c*.1188 and *c*.1196), *c*.1227/32, 1257/8 (the single largest sulphate spike of the entire Holocene), and then in quick succession *c*.1269, *c*.1276 and *c*.1286, of which by far the greatest probably originated from the VEI 6 eruption of Quilotoa in Ecuador sometime around 1280.[59] The scales of their respective sulphate signatures imply that each of these eruptions had the potential to affect weather patterns for several years afterwards.

Further, Chaochao Gao and others estimate that cumulative loading from the 1227 to 1284 eruptions may have been sufficient to have caused 'a clear temperature decrease of several tenths of a degree

[55] Baker and others (2002), 1342; Britton (1937), 99–104; Mohtadi and others (2007), 1061–2.
[56] Moreno and others (2012).   [57] Below, Figures 3.29 and 3.30.
[58] Ludlow and others (2013).
[59] Frank Ludlow, personal communication; Venzke (2013); E. Venzke, ed. (2013), *Volcanoes of the world*, v. 4.3.4, Global Volcanism Program, Smithsonian Institution 2013: http://www.volcano.si.edu/volcano.cfm/vn=352060 (accessed 27 May 2015).

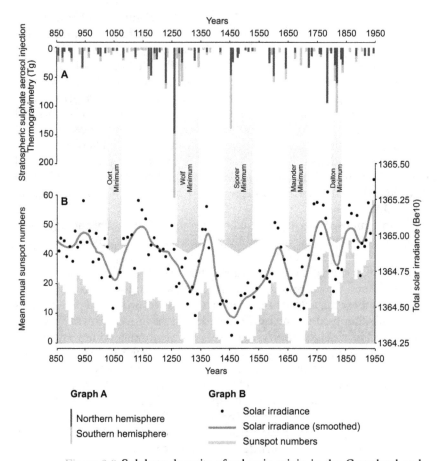

Figure 2.9 Sulphate deposits of volcanic origin in the Greenland and Antarctic ice sheets, Total Solar Irradiance from beryllium-10 and estimated sunspot numbers, AD 850–1950
Sources: Gao and others (2009b); Delaygue and Bard (2010b); Solanki and others (2005)

Celsius' and compounded the effects of the post-1270 downturn in solar irradiance.[60] Indeed, Gifford Miller and others (2012) have proposed that massive atmospheric forcing by the VEI 7 mega-eruption of 1257/8 (since identified as the Samalas volcano, Rinjani Volcanic Complex, Indonesia) may have been responsible for ending the MCA and ushering in the altered atmospheric circulation patterns of the LIA.[61] Impressed

---

[60] Gao and others (2008), 6 of 15.   [61] Lavigne and others (2013).

by the scale of the 1257/8 sulphate signal, A. G. Dawson and others speculate that 'the "unknown" AD 1257/8 eruption may have had a significant, but as yet unknown, impact on northern hemisphere climate', while Mann and others suggest that it may have forced an El Niño-like response in the tropical Pacific, a suggestion recently endorsed by Julian Emile-Geay and others.[62] Considerable claims have also been made for the historical significance of this event.[63]

Recent critical assessments of the available environmental evidence nevertheless cast doubt upon whether the climatic effects of this mega-eruption were either very great or especially enduring.[64] Unless the dating of the eruption to no earlier than late spring 1257 is seriously awry, it clearly cannot have caused the extreme weather of 1256 and early 1257 or the disastrous northern European harvests of 1256 and probably 1257 and consequent high grain and salt prices of 1258.[65] Rather, any volcanic forcing of the climate must have been felt between 1258 and 1261; years, intriguingly, which do not stand out as particularly extreme or unusual in the palaeo-environmental record, since, as some vulcanologists and climatologists are beginning to theorize, the eruption's cooling effect was likely limited by the size and density of the aerosol particles emitted.[66] That it may have so loaded the Earth's atmosphere with volcanic aerosols that it contributed to the ending of the MCA that occurred in its wake now seems unlikely.

In fact, whereas the ice-core evidence implies that the 1257/8 eruption was by far the single most explosive event of the MCA, dendrochronology identifies 1232–6 as having constituted by far the greater environmental downturn. It is possible that the latter was caused by the combined eruption of Reykjanes in Iceland and Zao in Japan in 1227 and repeat eruption of Reykjanes in 1231, although the match between the scale and timing of these eruptions and the subsequent downturn in Eurasian

---

[62] Dawson and others (2007), 431; Mann and others (2005), 450–1; Mann and others (2012). 'We conclude that there was indeed an El Niño event in 1258/59, though perhaps not exceptional in amplitude': Emile-Geay and others (2008), 3144.

[63] Stothers (2000); Connell and others (2012), 228–31.

[64] Zielinski (1995), 20,949–50; Timmreck and others (2009); Brovkin and others (2010).

[65] Oppenheimer (2003); Witze (2012).

[66] New World trees nevertheless displayed reduced growth in 1258 and Old World trees in 1259: dendrochronologies supplied by M. G. L. Baillie. Emile-Geay and others (2008); Brovkin and others (2010). In southern England there was no marked inflation of grain or salt prices during the years immediately following the 1257/8 eruption: Clark (2009). In 1261 at Radstone (N'hants) and 1262 at Froyle (Hants) there may have been a modest reduction in harvest volumes, although neither was of crisis proportions: The National Archives PRO SC6/949/3; British Library Add. Ch. 174. For the situation in London see Keene (2011).

tree growth is poor.[67] More likely, some other forcing agent or combination of agents may have been responsible. This twelve-year perturbation (tree growth did not return to normal until 1244) thus presents an environmental enigma and highlights the difficulty, in the present state of scientific knowledge, of providing convincing explanations for many of the lesser climatic anomalies that stand out in the palaeoclimatic record.[68] Moreover, the human impacts of such anomalies are likely to have been mitigated by the fact that, owing to the over-arching influence of the Medieval Solar Maximum, they occurred at a time otherwise characterized by considerable climatic stability and continuity.

2.03   The growth of Old World populations

The post-Oort second phase of the Medieval Solar Maximum was associated with a marked growth of Old World populations, most conspicuously in those regions and countries (notably Monsoon Asia and temperate Europe) where climatic conditions particularly favoured sustained expansions of agricultural output. Estimating the size of medieval populations is not a task for the faint-hearted, given the lack of comprehensive documentary evidence and the social and demographic biases of most of what survives. Of the available estimates, those advanced by Jean-Noël Biraben in 1979 have gained the most credence (Table 2.1).[69] He reckons that Eurasia supported a population of 329 million by 1300, which is double his estimate for the mid-first-millennium demographic low point at c. AD 600. Including Africa north of the Sahara, which comprised an integral part of the Known World, would raise this total to 337 million. Asia, with well over four times the land area of Europe, accounted for three-quarters of this Known World total.

Before c. AD 900, population growth was slow, sporadic, geographically uneven and prone to reversal (Table 2.1 and Figure 2.10). Thereafter, until the second quarter of the thirteenth century, decline became the exception and growth the norm. Rates of increase were particularly vigorous in technologically advanced China, at that time benefiting

---

[67] According to the Smithsonian Institution's Global Volcanism Program, at least two eruptions – Reykjanes, Iceland, in 1226–7 and Zao, Japan, from late 1227 – were probably responsible for the pronounced sulphate spikes of 1227/8 in the Greenland and Antarctic ice-cores: Gao and others (2008 and 2009b). In England the summer of 1228 was stormy, the winter of 1229 severe, and summer droughts then followed in 1331 and 1332: Britton (1937), 88. Dry summers are consistent with the narrow growth rings of British Isles oaks 1231–3: data supplied by M. G. L. Baillie.

[68] For an effective summary of current thinking see Graham and others (2010).

[69] For example, Biraben's figures are cited by Livi-Bacci (2001), 27. Here, his figures are used in preference to those of McEvedy and Jones (1978).

Table 2.1 *Estimated total Eurasian population, AD 600–1400*

Year		Estimated population (millions)			
	China	Indian subcontinent	Rest of Asia	Europe	Eurasia
600	49.0	37.0	53.5	27.5	167.0
700	44.0	50.0	46.0	27.0	167.0
800	56.0	43.0	52.0	30.0	181.0
900	48.0	38.0	58.5	33.5	178.0
1000	56.0	40.0	62.5	36.5	195.0
1100	83.0	48.0	64.5	42.5	238.0
1200	124.0	69.0	73.5	57.5	324.0
1300	83.0	100.0	68.0	78.0	329.0
1340	70.0	107.0	69.0	82.0	328.0
1400	70.0	74.0	63.5	58.5	266.0

Source: Biraben (1979), 16

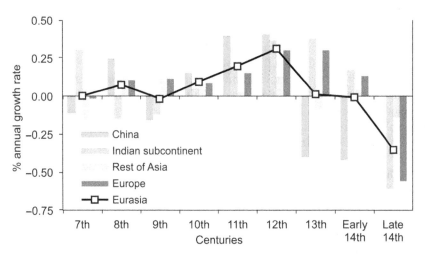

Figure 2.10 Estimated annual Eurasian population growth rates, AD 600–1400
Source: calculated from Table 2.1

from abundant and relatively reliable monsoon rains. China's population appears to have more than doubled over the course of the eleventh and twelfth centuries, growing at rates of at least 0.4 per cent for much of this period. The momentum of growth looked set to continue for some time to come and no doubt would have done so but for the devastating demographic impact of the Mongol invasions, which sent numbers tumbling from the 1230s. The Indian subcontinent's population similarly grew impressively and with gathering impetus from the tenth century, in contrast to drought-stricken western and central Asia, the Middle East and North Africa, where scarce rainfall limited the capacity to expand food production. Europe's population, too, was on an upward trajectory and for much of the second phase of the MCA was increasing at around 0.3 per cent per annum. Numbers continued to rise long after those in Asia had started to fall and by 1300, at approximately 78 million, were more than double what they had been in 1000 (Table 2.1).[70] Across Eurasia as a whole, the twelfth century therefore stands out as having experienced the most vigorous population growth (Figure 2.10), with around 90 per cent of that growth occurring in the climatically favoured zones of Monsoon Asia and temperate Europe.

In Europe, as elsewhere, these gains in population were unequally distributed. Estimates advanced by Josiah Cox Russell for ten major European regions imply that growth was below average in hot, dry southern Europe and Mongol-ravaged Russia, but well above average in the greater North Sea region, comprising the British Isles, France, the Low Countries, Germany and Scandinavia, where numbers may have more than trebled.[71] Colin McEvedy and Richard Jones agree that growth was slower in southern than northern Europe but believe that it was also above average in central and eastern Europe, notwithstanding the latter's exposure to Mongol aggression. On their figures, numbers multiplied fastest in the Low Countries, where the population approximately trebled, thereby becoming possibly the most rapidly reproducing population in the Old World.[72] More cautious estimates of the Iberian population by Vicente Pérez Moreda confirm that demographically this was one of the least dynamic major regions in medieval Europe, with a combined Spanish and Portuguese population which grew from around 4.5 million in 1100 to just 5.5 million two centuries later (substantially less than Russell's estimate of over 9 million and the 8¾ million of McEvedy and Jones).[73] Such tardy growth is consistent with the dryness of the Spanish climate and destructive effects of the *Reconquista*.

---

[70] Biraben is here following Josiah Cox Russell (1958), 148, who proposed a doubling of Europe's population over these three centuries from around 38 million to 75 million in 1340. For 1300, McEvedy and Jones (1978), 18, give an almost identical figure of 79 million. Bairoch and others (1988), 297, have since proposed a higher figure of 88 million, while Livi-Bacci (2000), 6, has suggested an increase from 30–50 million in 1000 to around 100 million in 1300.

[71] Russell (1958), 113, 148.   [72] McEvedy and Jones (1978), 23, 61–3.

[73] Moreda (1988); Russell (1958), 102; McEvedy and Jones (1978): 105. On Iberian exceptionalism see Zanden (2009), 40–1.

Italian population trends are more firmly documented. Here, the figures recently advanced by Giovanni Federico and Malanima suggest that Russell substantially underestimated both the size of country's population and the magnitude of the increase which occurred between 1000 and 1300 during the boom years of Italy's commercial revolution. Across this period they propose a two-and-a-half-fold increase from 5.2 million to 12.5 million, with, somewhat surprisingly, growth rates accelerating from a little over 0.2 per cent per annum between 1000 and 1150, to 0.3 per cent between 1150 and 1250, and then over 0.4 per cent between 1250 and 1300.[74] At this time Italy was the most populous, urbanized and prosperous country in southern Europe, with the Low Countries – where population growth was probably at least as fast – its sole rival in northern Europe.[75]

England was altogether less developed and urbanized and per head barely half as wealthy, yet its population grew by a similar order of magnitude from approximately 1.7 million in 1086 to around 4.75 million in 1290.[76] Thanks to the survival of a remarkable range of cross-sectional and longitudinal evidence, these estimates are better founded than those for most other countries. Time-series data of tenant numbers imply that, in contrast to Italy, initially fast population growth rates gradually subsided over time, slowing from an impressive 0.57 per cent per annum from 1086 to 1190, to 0.52 per cent from 1190 to 1250, and then 0.29 per cent from 1250 to 1290, after which further sustained growth more-or-less ceased.[77] Growth before 1290 was maintained notwithstanding periodic harvest crises, notably those of 1202–4 and 1256–7, and losses of significant numbers of colonists to Wales, Ireland and Scotland.[78] Internal migration in England also redistributed surplus population away from areas of established settlement and into those of new settlement, notably the East Anglian fens, the emptied lands devastated by William I in the north of England, and wherever forests, heaths and hillsides offered scope for assarting and reclamation.[79] Between 1086 and 1290 mean annual growth rates sometimes differed by as much as 0.4–0.5 per cent between non-colonizing and colonizing regions. Growth was slowest in the south and especially the southwest of England and fastest in the north, whose

[74] Federico and Malanima (2004), 446.   [75] Below, Section 2.05.1; Table 2.2.
[76] Broadberry and others (2015), 20–2.
[77] The data are those published by Hallam (1988), 536–93, augmented by additional information and re-worked using a similar index-number method: Broadberry and others (2015), 10–15.
[78] Davies (1990), 11–15.
[79] These changes are reflected in significant shifts in the distribution of recorded wealth: Darby and others (1979).

potential for colonization was never completely exhausted.[80] Such differences between areas of established settlement and new colonization were repeated throughout Europe.

These centrifugal processes of migration and colonization ensured that at the high tide of medieval expansion few localities remained wholly empty of settlement and economically unproductive. Had Europe as a whole supported a population of 80–100 million by 1300 its average population density would have been 8–10 people per square kilometre, equivalent to about 50 hectares of land per household. Excluding Russia with its vast tracts of thinly peopled terrain raises the average density to 14–16 per square kilometre and reduces the amount of land per household to 30 hectares. Spain, Scotland, Poland and Hungary all seem to have supported mean densities of this general order of magnitude and, in each, extensive tracts of sparsely inhabited territory contrasted with pockets of more thickly peopled country.[81] In Scotland, for example, densities ranged from less than 2 persons per square kilometre in the Highlands to over 30 per square kilometre in the eastern Lowlands, which constituted one of the most northerly concentrations of moderately high population density in Europe (Figure 2.11). Here there were at most 16 hectares of land per household.

England, with fewer mountainous tracts and a climate better suited to grain production, was altogether more closely settled and, with a mean of 36 persons per square kilometre, already ranked as one of the most densely populated countries in Europe. In the most thickly peopled parts of the eastern counties (Figure 2.11), where conditions of rural congestion prevailed, densities were double the national average and, at 60–75 per square kilometre, on a par with the highest rural population densities prevailing in parts of Flanders and central and northern Italy, whose mean population densities – boosted by Europe's highest levels of urbanization – were in excess of 40 per square kilometre.[82] At these densities there were less than 8 hectares of land per household. By the early fourteenth century population densities in parts of southern Luxembourg and Lorraine reached 70 per square kilometre, while in 1344, in the countryside around Pistoia in Tuscany, rural densities ranged from a minimum of 10 per square kilometre up in the Apennine hills to a

---

[80] Broadberry and others (2015), 19, 26–7. For the late continuance of colonization in the northeast see Dunsford and Harris (2003).

[81] Population densities in recently reconquered and resettled land-abundant Portugal c.1300 were in the range 4–44 per square kilometre, with a mean density of 11.4 per square kilometre: Henriques (2015), 168–9.

[82] On rural congestion see Campbell (2005).

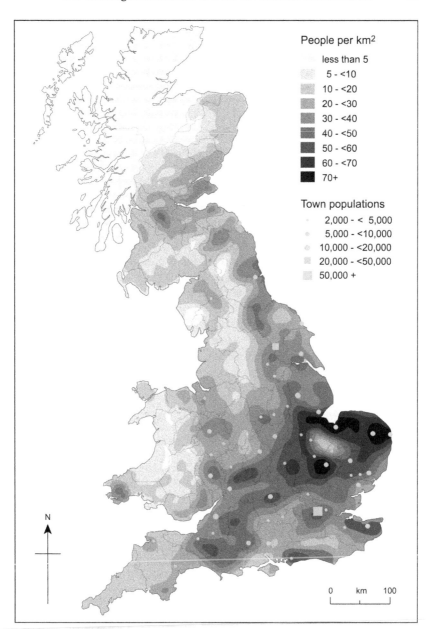

Figure 2.11 The distribution of population in Great Britain in 1290
Source: Campbell and Barry (2014)

maximum of 63 per square kilometre in the intermediate hills above the ill-drained alluvial plain of the River Arno.[83] Maximum densities of 60–70 per square kilometre similarly seem to have prevailed in the environs of Florence, Siena and San Gimignano.[84]

Only the most fertile, intensively cultivated and proto-industrialized parts of the Low Countries sustained higher rural population densities. Thus, by the early fourteenth century in south Brabant, along with much of Liège, Hainaut and the French provinces of Artois and Picardy, population densities sometimes exceeded 100 per square kilometre (an allowance of just 5 hectares per household), levels seemingly unmatched anywhere else in Europe at that time except perhaps Lombardy in northern Italy.[85] These exceptionally high population densities were underpinned by equally impressive levels of land productivity: grain yields obtained by Thierry d'Hireçon on his estate in Artois are the highest recorded for medieval Europe.[86] Without Asian-style multi-cropping, with its heavier labour demands and superior food output per unit area, greater population densities were unsustainable.[87]

What, at some point in the late-eleventh or twelfth centuries, caused reproduction rates across Europe to swing from periodic deficit to recurrent surplus is an enigma. Anticipating Lieberman's verdict on Southeast Asia, Russell believed 'the age was probably the healthiest of the Middle Ages' and a steady lowering of disease mortality as populations acquired a degree of immunity to existing pathogens could undoubtedly have raised survival rates and lengthened life expectancy.[88] The fact that this long period remained plague-free must also have helped, as adverse ecological conditions limited stocks of the bacillus and densities of its natural hosts and vectors in the disease's reservoir regions in the semi-arid interior of Eurasia.[89] Alongside these probable improvements in health went greater political and military security, as the Viking, Magyar, Slav and Muslim menaces retreated and feudal lordship and urban communes developed to provide effective protection at a local level. New household formation may thus have been encouraged. In a land-abundant and labour-scarce age, lords would have had a vested interest in promoting the multiplication of households and tenancies. Seigniorial demand for labour and tenants may therefore have given a positive stimulus to fertility rates, as

---

[83] Pounds (1973), 332, 337.   [84] Pounds (1973), 337.

[85] Pounds (1973), 332; Bavel (2010), 283.   [86] Richard (1892).

[87] Continuous multi-cropping with rice sustained contemporary population densities in the Yangzi Delta of eastern China that were substantially higher, averaging around 160 per square kilometre at the start of the Yuan era c.1290: Yoshinobu (1988), 146, 148 (I am grateful to Dr Ting Xu for this reference).

[88] Russell (1958), 113.   [89] Below, Section 4.02.2.

may improved employment opportunities created by the revival of trade and commerce. Commercial vigour would also certainly help explain why China's population for so long headed the Eurasian league table of growth.

Since population growth became a European-wide and, to some degree, Eurasian-wide phenomenon, the factors responsible were plainly pan-continental in scope. Further, they became so securely established that the impetus of growth proved able to withstand periodically severe short-term shocks without stalling or going into reverse.[90] Across the greater part of western Europe for most of the twelfth and thirteenth centuries natural increase therefore became the norm and thereby greatly reinforced the expansionist tendencies of this climatically favoured age. Demand for the basic necessities of food, clothing and housing grew, as did the supply of labour to produce them. Commercialization advanced and, with it, opportunities for achieving a greater division of labour. For a time at least, population growth was economically beneficial and labour specialization and skill advanced.

2.04   The institutional underpinnings of Latin Christendom's commercial expansion

If effective political and military authority over an extensive geographical area is a precondition for peace and prosperity, it is unsurprising that China under the Song Dynasty should have displayed such demographic and commercial vitality. Until challenged by the usurping power of the Mongols, the Song state had promoted and regulated private enterprise over a wide and diverse geographical area and made heavy investments in a substantial navy and international diplomacy so as to advance and protect its overseas interests. Nor was the Mongol takeover, first of the Northern Song in 1234 then of the Southern Song in 1279, wholly negative in its effects since the vast pan-Asian empire thereby created greatly extended the territorial area over which Chinese commodities could safely be traded and lowered the transaction costs of doing so.[91] For a while it even became possible for adventurous European merchants to contemplate engaging directly in trade with China.

---

[90] Hybel (2002), 788. The disastrous harvests of 1256 and 1257 failed to interrupt the steady increment of adult males paying tithingpenny on the vast manorial complex of Taunton belonging to the bishops of Winchester: numbers rose at a rate of 0.8 per cent per annum from 897 in 1255 to 973 in 1265 (calculated from revised data supplied by Christopher Thornton).

[91] Transaction costs are those involved in making an economic exchange: Williamson (1989).

It is altogether more remarkable that politically divided Europe with its multiplicity of competing and often warring fiefs, principalities and kingdoms, each potentially predatory upon trade and merchants, should have experienced a commercial boom at the same time. Nowhere was the contrast between commercial vigour and political fragmentation more marked than in the centre and north of Italy, where each city was, in effect, a separate state. Yet from at least the eleventh century this region was in the van of Europe's commercial revolution and its merchants engaged in trade over a wider geographical area than any others. To do so, they required institutions that promoted trust, justice, and greater security of persons and merchandise at a supra-state level.

At a macro level no body was better placed to serve such a purpose than the Latin Church (Section 2.04.1), which was the sole over-arching and unifying institution within this politically and culturally fissured continent. From the late eleventh century it became 'the leading agent of trans-local extensive social organisation'.[92] The following century, secular powers (partly in reaction to the Church's codification of Canon Law) developed and enforced legal systems (Section 2.04.2), which further improved the institutional environment within which trade was conducted. Meanwhile, (i) proliferation of self-governing urban communities, (ii) formation of merchant guilds which protected the goods and persons of their members, and (iii) foundation of international fairs which guaranteed swift justice to those frequenting them, collectively created an environment within which trust between strangers was promoted, reputations defended, and rogues and free-riders exposed and penalized (Section 2.04.3). These institutional developments were usually country-specific in character and so, in the accounts that follow, England is taken as the exemplar of trends that prevailed, in one form or another, throughout Christendom.

2.04.1. Revival and reform of the Latin Church

Latin Christendom's efflorescence owed much to the Roman Church. In the eighth century the Church's fortunes and standing had been at a singularly low ebb. At that time the one bright spot was in Europe's extreme northwest, where the insular and monastic Irish Church was experiencing a golden age.[93] Elsewhere, central and northern Europe and all of Scandinavia remained aggressively pagan; in the Middle East, North Africa and Iberia, Islam was in the ascendant; and in the Mediterranean

---

[92] Mann (1986), 337; Zanden (2009), 33.   [93] Ó Cróinín (1995), 196–224.

a rift was opening between Rome and Constantinople. By the eleventh century this parlous situation had been transformed and Latin Christendom was resurgent.[94] The Saxons, Bohemians, Croats, Scandinavians, Poles and Hungarians had all been converted to Roman Christianity. In Britain the Celtic Church had begun to conform to Roman practice while in 1054 internal tensions with Byzantium had been resolved when the Greek Church formally seceded from the Latin Church. Meanwhile, in Spain the Christian *Reconquista* had made great progress and in 1085 the strategically and symbolically important city of Toledo was recaptured. Finally, in 1095, Pope Urban II (p. 1088–99) preached the First Crusade, ostensibly to assist the Byzantine emperor in repelling the invading Seljuk Turks from Anatolia but with the ulterior objective of liberating the Christian holy places of Palestine from Islamic rule. This culminated in the recapture of Jerusalem in 1099, foundation of the crusader states of Jerusalem, Tripoli, Antioch and Edessa and direct engagement by Christian and especially Italian merchants in the commerce of the Levant.

Internally, too, the Latin Church was reinvigorated by radical reforms initiated by Gregory VII (p. 1073–85), first as a papal administrator then as pope. For the first time, the papacy's political and legal supremacy over the entire Church was asserted. This claim was made real by emulating the tenth-century monastic reforms of the Cluniac Order and placing the papacy at the head of a centralized ecclesiastical hierarchy comprising province, diocese, archdeaconry, deanery and parish, now strengthened and extended throughout Latin Christendom.[95] Further, the Church set itself against simony (the buying and selling of ecclesiastical offices), clerical marriage (celibacy was subsequently made mandatory by the Second Lateran Council in 1139) and, most provocatively, the right of lay rulers to choose and install archbishops and bishops.[96] In fact, Pope Gregory VII had declared the clergy to be independent from secular control and, further, claimed the papacy's ultimate supremacy in secular matters, including the authority to depose kings and emperors. According to Harold Berman, the totality of the transformation of Latin Christendom thereby effected was so great and its wider implications so far-reaching as to have constituted a veritable 'Papal Revolution'.[97]

To assert its authority and defend these claims the Church created and systematized its own code of Canon Law, dispensed through its ecclesiastical courts.[98] It was in the Church courts that the clergy were tried but

[94] Compare the maps of Christendom in 737 and 1000 in McEvedy (1992), 36–7, 54–5.
[95] Golding (2001), 136–42, 162–5.   [96] Lepine (2003), 375–6.
[97] Berman (1983), 99–107.
[98] Berman (1983), 199–224, considers Canon Law to have constituted 'the first modern Western legal system'.

also, and more importantly, where cases of a religious (blasphemy, heresy) and moral (defamation, sexual misconduct, breach of contract, marriage, probate) nature were decided. These courts supplied the power by which the Church was able both to transform European marriage rules, and hence family life, and preside over bequests of property.[99]

At a time when Latin Christendom comprised a mosaic of vernacular languages and dialects, the Church was also instrumental in creating a literate culture in a common language – Latin – over which it enjoyed a near monopoly until the thirteenth century.[100] According to van Zanden, book production per head grew almost six-fold in the British Isles and seven-fold in western Europe between 1000 and 1300, while absolute output of books rose twelve-fold over the same period.[101] The store of literate knowledge contained in monastic and other libraries consequently accumulated year on year. Because no book was more important than the Bible and the sole authorized version was the Latin Vulgate, all clerks required basic instruction in Latin grammar. Ecclesiastical schools therefore multiplied along with numbers of literate clerics, so that Latin became more widely adopted as the universal lingua franca, read, spoken and written in every parish of Christendom. The upshot was a communication revolution with far-reaching ramifications for the whole of secular society.

Literate ecclesiastical bureaucracies developed, soon emulated by those of the state, which created, preserved and increasingly ascribed legal authority to written records.[102] The number of extant letters per year rose seven-fold between the pontificates of Alexander II (p. 1061–73) and Alexander III (p. 1159–81) and, in England, more then eleven-fold between the reigns of William I (r. 1066–87) and Henry II (r. 1154–89).[103] An almost nine-fold rise in purchases of sealing wax by the English Chancery over the brief forty-year period 1226/30 to 1265/71 testifies to an explosion in the volume of written business generated by central government at that time.[104] It is hardly a coincidence that the earliest extant English manorial accounts and manor-court rolls date from these same years.[105] The latter testify to the increasing availability of, and reliance upon, practical literary skills at a local level.[106]

In a world politically fragmented into more than two hundred competing polities, the Church's powers were in certain respects mightier than those of any monarch, for, whereas a king's sovereignty was circumscribed

---

[99] Goody (1983).   [100] Mann (1986), 379.   [101] Zanden (2009), 77, 81.

[102] Clanchy (1979).   [103] Clanchy (1979), 44.   [104] Clanchy (1979), 43.

[105] Campbell (2000), 27–8; Razi and Smith (1996).

[106] Razi and Smith (1996), 67: 'England, certainly between 1250 and 1349, contained a larger proportion of its rural population in possession of practical literary skills than was to be found in any of her European neighbours'.

by time and territory, the Church was a supra-national perpetual institution representing both this world and the next. Unquestioning belief
in and fear of God endowed the Church with immense moral authority. From the end of the tenth century the Church ever more actively
promoted the idea that Christians should treat the persons and property of fellow Christians with respect: violating and robbing them carried moral opprobrium and the probability of divine retribution.[107] This
helped establish the trust upon which commerce and trade depended:
deals were typically sealed with an oath and testimonies sworn upon the
Bible. Christian morality pervaded how markets functioned and commerce was conducted, underpinning notions of fair trade and justice.[108]
It also informed treatment of the poor. Yet, at the same time, attitudes
towards non-Christians, especially Jews and Muslims, hardened. The
preaching of crusade was often accompanied by violent anti-Semitism, as
in 1190 when Richard I's (r. 1189–99) imminent departure for the Holy
Land prompted massacres of Jews in London, York and other towns.
The Church's intolerance likewise extended to those it regarded as religious and sexual deviants and, paradoxically, with the rise of the cult of
the Virgin Mary it became more discriminatory in its attitude towards
women, whose subordination to men it justified.[109]

Increasingly, the Church espoused the sentiment that true virtue lay in
productive labour. This was actively embraced by several of the reformed
monastic Orders of the twelfth century, which set an example of absti-
nence, self-discipline, study and manual labour.[110] Although not noted
for the generosity of its own alms giving (the Church probably devoted
less than 5 per cent of its own substantial income to poor relief), charity, according to the Church, was an obligation of the landed and the
wealthy. The deserving poor (i.e. those whose poverty was involuntary
because of sickness, or misfortune, or want of work or land) had a right
to be supported from the surplus wealth of society. Through the giving of alms (the pious Henry III (r. 1216–72) fed five hundred paupers
daily) and the foundation of charitable institutions (hospitals, hospices,
leper houses and almshouses) the propertied should alleviate the lot of
the outcast and propertyless. This new work ethic discouraged indolence
and made little scruple about harnessing the laws of nature to economic
advantage. The Church itself was a significant investor in technological
change – especially drainage, engineering, mills and clocks – the pace of
which steadily quickened.[111]

---

[107] Duby (1974), 162–5; Mann (1986), 381–2.   [108] Davis (2011), 22–31.
[109] Moore (1987); Golding (2001), 136.   [110] Burton (1994), 63–6.
[111] Mokyr (1992). On Christianity's possible legitimization of resource exploitation see
White Jr (1967), and the observations of Hoffmann (2014), 85–94.

The revived and reformed Church of the eleventh century and after, and the greatly extended *Pax Christiana* over which it presided, therefore helped create many of the institutional preconditions for a European-wide economic revival based upon greater circulation of people, goods and information, technological advance (including improved organization), market exchange, and expanding international commerce and trade. It did so by promoting normative rules, beliefs and attitudes across a territorially extensive area that transcended individual lordships, kingdoms, legal jurisdictions, urban hinterlands, market areas and trading networks. Thereby, as Mann observes, it 'enabled more produce to be traded over longer distances than could usually occur between the domains of such a large number of small, often highly predatory, states and rulers'.[112]

The Church also became an increasingly significant economic player in its own right by dint of the accumulating resources of land, labour, capital and enterprise that it owned and controlled and the privileged access to knowledge and information that it enjoyed. Bishops and abbots were active investors in the development of a commercial infrastructure, major producers of foodstuffs and an array of raw materials, and bought and sold commodities on a large scale. Moreover, one effect of Church reform was to attract an even greater share of resources to the Church, as men and some women flocked to join the new religious Orders and the laity showered these Orders with endowments and gifts. By 1300 in pious England the Church controlled half or more of landed resources (Table 3.5). Nevertheless, if the Church was instrumental in fostering economic development based upon market exchange and technological progress, within their territories it was states that were crucial to sustaining it. States had a greater vested interest in changing the rules upon which continued market growth depended and could use their judicial and military clout to impose and enforce such changes.

Certain of the Church's attitudes and teachings, particularly its opposition to the charging of interest for credit, were actually obstructive to the efficient operation of commerce. Because usury was regarded as contrary to natural law and against the teaching of the Bible it was banned in 1139 by the Second Lateran Council and in 1179 the Third Lateran Council imposed further prohibitions against the charging of interest. These rules created a major obstacle to the development of an open and competitive market for capital at a time when capital investment was critical to maintaining the processes of growth.[113] Such rules were not insurmountable,

---

[112] Mann (1986), 383.   [113] Davis (2011), 213–15.

but they were only circumvented with much difficulty and ingenuity and, for a time, with the cooperation of those who were exempt, notably Jews.[114] Even so, the position of Jews within Christian society remained both ambiguous and vulnerable. English kings protected Jews so that they might exploit them and then, having impoverished them, in 1290 expelled them.[115] French Jews suffered a similar fate in 1306. In the long run, progress depended upon the emergence of merchant banking, in which the Italians were to the fore, but this could not thrive until canonists rethought and reformulated the Church's attitude towards money, credit and interest.

The growing numbers of clerics and churches serve as proxy measures of the progress of Church reform. In England, Domesday Book records 1,800 places with a church or churches and a further 500 places with a priest.[116] Their distribution was, however, uneven.[117] In many parts of the realm, and especially the north, large parishes were still served by central minster churches staffed by groups of priests who ministered to the surrounding area via satellite chapelries. The post-Conquest proliferation of manors encouraged subdivision of these large parishes into smaller parishes served by new churches typically built by the local manorial lord. As a result, manor, parish and vill often became coterminous and developed overlapping functions and identities. By 1150 this more localized parish system was well established and by 1200 a total of between 8,500 and 9,500 parishes had come into existence; four times the number that had apparently existed in 1086.[118] Each parish was served by an average of at least three clergy comprising either a rector or, in the case of the third of parishes appropriated to a monastery, a vicar, usually assisted by several members of the un-beneficed clergy.[119]

Additional priests served the secular cathedrals, acted as chaplains in the growing number of private chapels and oratories attached to the more substantial residences of the landed nobility, and staffed the many hospices and hospitals now being founded to succour pilgrims and the needy and prepare those terminally sick for the next world. There was also an expanding population of un-beneficed clergy, often in minor Orders and therefore disqualified from both ministration of the sacrament and the requirement to remain celibate, who supplied the basic literate skills upon which society was increasingly dependent. These clerks, like Robert, whose father, Adam, was the prior of Wallingford's miller, were typically

[114] Hunt and Murray (1999), 70–3. Below, Section 2.05.2b.
[115] Stacey (1995); Mundill (2010).   [116] Darby (1977), 346.
[117] Darby (1977), 52–6.   [118] Blair (1988); Lepine (2003), 361.
[119] Lepine (2003), 361, 369.

of comparatively humble origin, plied their clerical skills wherever they could find employment in a society increasingly dependent upon the written word, and, in brushes with the law, claimed benefit of clergy and the right to be tried in an ecclesiastical court.[120] Very likely, therefore, over the course of the twelfth and thirteenth centuries the number of secular clergy grew at least ten-fold, to a total of perhaps 30–35,000 (equivalent to about one in every forty adult males).[121]

Over the same period there was an even more striking rise in the number of regular clergy – monks, canons, nuns and friars – for the clerical reforms initiated by the papacy were accompanied by a parallel and even more successful programme of monastic reform. The latter was manifest in a revival of the monastic ideal as expressed in the establishment of a succession of new monastic Orders, each with the intention of returning to the pure monasticism, unsullied by material wealth and outward show, that had been so prominent a feature of the original Rule of St Benedict.[122] The mainspring of the reform movement was France. Here, in 910 at Cluny in Burgundy, the first of these reformed monastic Orders, the Cluniacs, had been founded, with the then novel feature that all its houses were subordinate to the jurisdiction of the abbot of Cluny.[123] Following the great success of the Cluniacs, and partly in reaction to them, the Carthusian Order was established in 1084 at La Grande Chartreuse and shortly afterwards the Orders of Cîteaux, Savignac and Tiron, all, again, in France. Thence, these reformed religious Orders spread throughout Latin Christendom.

In England, within a dozen years of the Norman Conquest, the first Cluniac priory was established at Lewes in Sussex in 1077, and others soon followed.[124] Forty years later it was the turn of the new French reformed Orders. First, in about 1120, the Tironensians established themselves at Andwell and Hamble (Hampshire), and St Cross on the Isle of Wight.[125] Next, in 1124, the Savignacs founded a house at Tulketh in Lancashire, relocated in 1127 to Furness in the same county.[126] Then, in 1128, the Cistercians settled at Waverley in Surrey.[127] The Cistercians were the most centralized, hierarchical and successful of all these Orders, with a system of administration and communication that transcended national and ecclesiastical boundaries and by the close of the thirteenth century embraced a family of five hundred houses spread throughout mainland Europe, Britain and Ireland. Meanwhile, the new

[120] Harvey (1965), 144.   [121] Lepine (2003), 368–9; Harvey (2001), 256–7.
[122] Burton (1994), 63–6.   [123] Berman (1983), 88–94.
[124] Burton (1994), 35–9.   [125] Victoria County History (1973), 221–3.
[126] Burton (1994), 67–9.   [127] Burton (1994), 69.

Order of Augustinian Canons had arrived at St Botolph's, Colchester, in the 1090s.[128] It was based upon the letters written by St Augustine, bishop of Hippo in North Africa between 396 and 430, and laid considerable emphasis upon pastoral duties and care. Largely because of this, and because of their adaptability, the Augustinians eventually proved the most popular of all the Orders, with more English houses than any other Order.[129] Last to arrive were the Carthusians, who founded their first English house at Witham, Somerset, in 1178/9.[130] They combined the ascetic ideal of the hermit with the monastic ideal of communal worship but the high spiritual standard they set meant their number of houses always remained small.

The arrival of each of these new religious Orders lent fresh momentum to the process of monastic expansion and widened the options available to prospective founders as the passion for monastic foundation spread rapidly down the social scale. In a chronology which uncannily paralleled the rising level of Total Solar Irradiance, between 1066 and 1100 the number of English religious houses more than doubled to 119 and over the next half-century, as the pace of foundation quickened, it almost trebled (Figure 2.12B). In the 1130s, when this movement was at its height, no fewer than 76 new houses were established. This was when diffusion of the Cistercian Order was at its peak. Much of its appeal and success derived from the opportunity it gave men of genuinely humble origin to pursue a monastic vocation by becoming lay brothers. Even in the following decade of civil war between Stephen and Matilda more new monastic houses were founded than during the whole of the previous century. Thereafter the rate of foundation began to decline as a saturation point was approached and patronage and pious intentions were again diverted, this time to the less costly and more immediately practical enterprise of founding hospitals. Whereas the number of new monastic foundations declined progressively from over 230 in the first half of the twelfth century, to 220 in the second half of the twelfth century, and 77 in the first half of the thirteenth century, the number of hospital foundations rose from 54, to 144, and then 171 over the same period (Figure 2.12A). By the mid-thirteenth century there was approximately one hospital per 10–12,000 people. For a materially poor society this constitutes a significant investment in private welfare provision.

By 1260 in England there were over four hundred hospitals of one sort or another and over six hundred abbeys, priories and nunneries

---

[128] Burton (1994), 43–5.   [129] Knowles and Hadcock (1971); Golding (2001), 151.
[130] Burton (1994), 77–80.

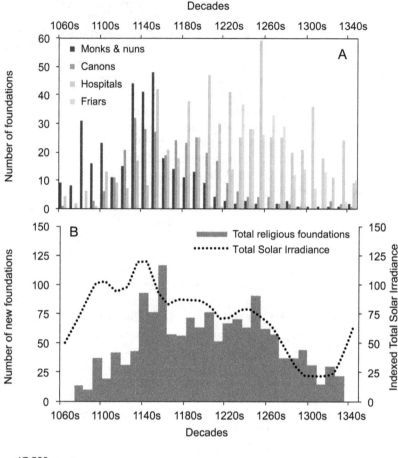

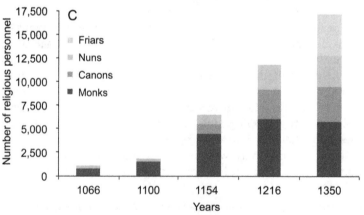

Figure 2.12 (A) Numbers of English foundations of new religious houses, 1060s to 1340s. (B) Total numbers of English foundations of new religious houses and Total Solar Irradiance, 1060s to 1340s. (C) Total numbers of English regular clergy, 1066, 1100, 1154, 1216 and 1350

Note: Total Solar Irradiance is indexed on the range 40–120, where 1140s = 120.

Sources: Knowles and Hadcock (1971); Figure 2.8A

plus substantial numbers of lesser dependent cells.[131] Yet, two hundred years earlier there had been only a handful of hospitals and fewer than fifty monasteries, all of them Benedictine and none located north of the River Trent. This betokens immense economic vitality in the fields of organization and decision taking. Establishing each new conventual community was a major undertaking and involved careful negotiation, planning and implementation. Much could and did go wrong and it was not unknown for a house to be both relocated and refounded but the success rate is remarkable. From 844 monks and 206 nuns in 1066, the number of religious men and women had grown twelve-fold to over 5,500 monks, 3,700 regular canons and 3,250 nuns in 1216 (Figure 2.12C). Indeed, the appeal of the religious life was more powerful even than these figures indicate for, from the 1220s, the arrival of the friars gave a further boost to ecclesiastical recruitment.

The friars rejected the ownership of property and were committed to pastoral care, preaching and teaching. London, other urban centres and especially the university towns of Oxford and Cambridge therefore exercised a particular appeal for them.[132] The Dominican Friars were the first to establish themselves, at Oxford in 1221 and London in 1224. These were followed by the Franciscans at Oxford (where they rapidly assumed intellectual leadership), London and Canterbury in 1224, the Crutched Friars at Colchester by 1235, the Carmelite Friars at Aylesford (Kent) and Hulne (Northumberland) in the early 1240s, the Austin Friars at Clare (Suffolk) in 1248, and the Friars of the Sack at London in 1257. By 1260 over a hundred houses of friars had been established and the number of mendicants, as the friars were known, had grown to over two thousand. In fact, so great was the appeal of the friars that recruitment to the older monastic Orders suffered. Overall, however, there was a net gain (Figure 2.12C) and the number of regular clergy increased to approximately 15–16,000 (12–13,000 of them male).

By this time the religious reform movement had largely run its course and as the thirteenth century drew to a close the numbers of new foundations steadily dwindled. The prestige of the Latin Church was also on the wane as the papacy became increasingly politicized and worldly. In 1291 the fall of Acre had brought the whole crusading project to protect Christian access to the Holy Land to an inglorious end and within twenty years the Order of Knights Templar, founded to protect pilgrims, had

---

[131] In Europe there were over forty thousand monastic houses by the early fourteenth century: Catholic Encyclopaedia, www.newadvent.org/cathen/02443a.htm.

[132] Burton (1994), 112–15.

been disbanded amid accusations of heresy and sorcery. From 1305 election of a succession of French popes also exposed the papacy to undue political interference from the French Crown, especially once Clement V (p. 1305–14), in 1309, had relocated the papal court from Rome to Avignon, where it remained 'in Babylonian captivity' until 1376. By then, and during the twelfth century in particular, the Latin Church had nevertheless helped create the preconditions for a full-scale pan-European revival of trade and commerce.

The changes effected by the Church were considerable. By 1300 there were more clergy per head of population than at the outset of the papal reform movement c.1070, and the new infrastructure of parishes, priories and friaries ensured that pastoral care was closer and more effective. Significant investment had taken place in welfare provision. Monasteries, hospices, bridges (many of them constructed with charitable intent) and a culture of Christian fellowship made travel easier and safer while crusade, pilgrimage and the business of the Church provided many with incentives to journey. Throughout Christendom, Latin, the language of worship, was the language of all educated and literate people as well as of most governments and administrations. Greater national and international exchange of information, ideas and personnel was thus facilitated. The intellectual vigour of the age was reflected in the foundation of new religious Orders, schools and the first universities (Bologna 1088, Paris c.1150, Oxford 1167) and a concomitant sustained rise in book production, as knowledge accumulated.[133] During this cultural and economic efflorescence the arts flourished as never before and the Church became the single greatest patron of a much expanded construction sector. In a poor society where most people could better afford leisure than material goods, the Church rationalized and formalized feast days and fast days, decreed significant numbers of high days and holy days, and promised surest salvation to the meek and humble. Elaborate rituals and grand religious ceremonies were held that gratified the desire for music, spectacle and mystery, in lavish buildings largely paid for by the rich but to which all enjoyed access. In all these largely non-material and non-quantifiable respects, the quality of life and the prospects of the after-life improved.

2.04.2   Secular states and birth of the Western Legal Tradition

The Church's codification of Canon Law engendered a general renewal of interest in the law which bore fruit in the creation of a pluralistic legal

---

[133] Zanden (2009), 69–91.

system (what Berman terms the Western Legal Tradition) within which more sophisticated forms of social and economic relationship could flourish, multilateral patterns of commodity exchange thrive, and factor markets become established.[134] From the twelfth century, monarchs, city-states and other secular authorities began to codify their own systems of civil and criminal law based either on Roman Law, as laid down in the sixth-century Justinian law code, or the Common Law, as in the case of Britain and Ireland. From this diversity of legal initiatives sprang growing interest in the study, teaching, codification, application and enforcement of law and emergence of a class of professional lawyers.[135] Henceforth, all social and economic relationships were bounded within this evolving legal infrastructure, which was itself a by-product of the papal reforms.

In England, although he cannot have realized it, Henry II's (r. 1154–89) creation of the Common Law became a mainspring for fuller development of economic forces. From the time of his grandfather, Henry I (r. 1100–35), there had been a growth in royal justice at the expense of seigniorial justice handled in honorial and manorial courts.[136] The old shire courts, which met every forty days, retained a key role in these developments, for, from 1166, they became the venue of the courts held by the king's itinerant justices when on eyre (i.e. out on circuit).[137] Here criminals were presented before the royal justices by panels of jurors from the hundreds and vills. From this time the volume of criminal business dealt with by the royal courts began to grow. Then in 1176 the Assize of Northampton initiated the process that put in place a system of civil law based upon consistent rules applied by specialized justices appointed by the Crown.[138]

Henceforth, those seeking justice in a case concerning land or property initiated an action by purchasing one of a limited range of writs from the Crown. This instructed the relevant sheriff to empanel a jury of law-worthy men to look into the case and give evidence. The case was then heard before a specialized justice and judgement given irrespective of whether the defendant chose to appear. The bulk of these civil pleas were dealt with alongside the criminal cases heard before itinerant royal justices in the shire courts. As the volume of litigation grew, so the business of shire courts increased and contacts with the central *curia rege* at Westminster grew closer. Already in 1179 it required twenty-one judges touring the country on four circuits to conduct a general eyre.[139] Even

---

[134] Berman (1983).   [135] Berman (1983); Zanden (2009), 43–50.
[136] Chibnall (1986), 161–83.   [137] Chibnall (1986), 192–207.
[138] Palmer (2003), 244–9.   [139] Harding (1973), 54.

within the quasi-autonomous palatinate of Durham it was royal justice that the bishops dispensed, not their own, for their regalian rights did not extend to the enactment of laws.

From an early date, cases unable to be heard before the justices in eyre were tried by the Court of the Exchequer which met at Westminster in Westminster Hall. Establishment of the Court of Common Pleas, where a decision could be obtained at any time during the law terms, followed. The Court of the King's Bench, in contrast, dealt with difficult cases adjourned from the shire courts.[140] The business of all three of these courts grew substantially in the 1240s, thereby confirming Westminster as the gravitational centre of the law and of the legal profession. At Westminster, too, resided the monarch when in the capital, in addition to the royal household, the bureaucracy of royal administration, and members of the royal council.

In contrast to the Roman Law of the continent, which was codified, rational and rigid, the Common Law of England and the Lordship of Ireland was un-codified, reasonable and flexible. It comprised a clear set of legal rules and the principle that judgements should be based upon precedent. The intrinsic simplicity of this legal structure lent it great appeal for it reduced cases to their essentials and ensured that litigation became streamlined. Royal justice thus became cheap and efficient at a time when the judicial rights associated with feudal lordship were becoming increasingly fragmented. As a result, the royal courts experienced a major increase in litigation, the impetus for which came from the litigants rather than the Crown. To cope with this business the Crown appointed a corps of professional judges, schooled in the law. Thereafter, as literacy grew and landowners became more familiar with documents, so any person of reasonable substance found it possible to bring a case before the royal courts, even, if prudence allowed, against their lord. By 1215 the legal revolution was complete, for there was wholehearted acceptance of the king's justice and the Common Law by a broad range of the Crown's subjects.[141] One of the cornerstones upon which the country's subsequent economic development would be founded had thereby been created. Until the end of the Middle Ages the Common Law would co-exist with Canon Law and seigniorial justice but its ultimate ascendancy over both alternative judicial systems was assured.

---

[140] Harding (1973), 53–4, 75, 84.
[141] 'Between 1176 and 1215 England built a legal system and generated a law of property, in the process rendering sufficient benefits to a broad enough sector of subjects that the government apparatus gained their fundamental loyalty': Palmer (2003), 244.

The chief economic effect of these institutional developments was to create secure and defensible property rights in land.[142] The writ of *mort d'ancestor* enabled those who had been wrongfully disinherited to recover their property and the writ of *novel disseisin* gave redress to tenants who had been unlawfully dispossessed by their lords. Whether or not it was Henry II's original intention, legal rights to land took on an existence of their own independently of personal and feudal relationships. Moreover, these individual property rights in land were alienable. As clear legal procedures were gradually established for its transfer and sale, land was transformed into an economic resource and the commercialization of economic and social relations was accelerated. Initially freeholders acquired the right to sell land by substitution, whereby land was surrendered to the lord who in turn granted the land to another. But as the thirteenth century progressed a succession of actions brought in the *curia rege* permitted alienation by substitution between freemen without the mesne lord's permission, thereby rendering land held by freemen freely alienable.[143] Verdicts such as this attracted more and more business from the seigniorial courts to the royal courts and were a major solvent of feudal socio-property relations.

As land became a commodity, basic assumptions about its use and management as an economic resource were changed. For instance, it became possible to realize the full capital value of land by using it as security for loans. Land, thereby, became liquid. Robert Palmer has suggested that this sudden injection of capital into the economy may be why in England advent of the Common Law was closely followed by the single greatest known price inflation of the Middle Ages.[144] Certainly, advent of the Common Law reinforced the legal distinction between freemen and villeins for only the former were entitled to plead their cases in the King's Court.[145] As the manorial lords progressively lost jurisdiction over freemen they also lost control over the fast-proliferating numbers of freeholdings. This had major consequences for rural property structures and agrarian conditions.[146]

Nor was the legal example of the freeholders wasted upon the villein tenants of customary land, dependent though the latter were upon the localized justice dispensed more arbitrarily by lords in their own autonomous manorial courts. By the second half of the thirteenth century, increasing numbers of lords were permitting their villein tenants to use substitution as a method of 'buying' and 'selling' customary land.[147] The

---

[142] Palmer (1985a); Campbell (2009a), 88–92.   [143] Yates (2013).
[144] Palmer (1985b); Palmer (2003), 249; below, Section 2.05.2c.
[145] Hyams (1980).   [146] Campbell (2005); below, Section 3.01.3d.
[147] Razi and Smith (1996), 50–6; Campbell (2009b), 90–2.

lord charged an entry fine for this service and a corresponding entry in the manorial court roll provided a cheap and convenient means of recording the change in title. Once lords had conceded this 'right' to their villein tenants it acquired the force of custom and proved impossible to rescind. Thereafter, lords, like the Crown, contented themselves with profiting from the potentially substantial licence fees that such transactions could generate. Although enterprising lords succeeded in attracting extra business to their courts, overall, royal justice grew at the expense of seigniorial justice and bred a desire by the unfree to enjoy the legal benefits bestowed so exclusively upon the free.[148] The ability to buy and sell land was one of these. The markets that developed first in freehold and then in customary land had far-reaching consequences for the allocation of land and the size and layout of holdings. In particular, under conditions of rising population they tended to promote the morcellation of both holdings and plots.[149]

2.04.3 *Guilds, communes and international fairs*

In parallel with the papal reform movement, a number of institutions developed below the level of the state that promoted and facilitated exchange between third parties and provided speedy and effective redress of disputes between them.[150] Trading with strangers or in strange lands ran obvious risks of fraud, default, breach of contract and confiscation. From at least the eleventh century Italian merchants engaging in long-distance trade were organizing themselves into formal associations or guilds which helped protect their persons and goods against the perils presented by warring armies, arbitrary rulers, brigands and pirates. These merchant guilds also facilitated enforcement of contracts whenever goods or money changed hands. Thus were 'solved' what Avner Greif has defined as two of the 'fundamental problems of exchange'.[151] In northern Europe the Hanse confederation of merchant guilds and trading cities, which grew from modest beginnings in the twelfth century to major significance in the fourteenth century, is the prime exemplar of this phenomenon. In a politically fragmented and uncertain world, the Hanse worked to secure commercial privileges and remove restrictions

---

[148] By the first half of the fourteenth century the most lucrative manorial courts held by lay tenants-in-chief of the Crown yielded upwards of £20 a year; nevertheless, over three-quarters of those recorded by the *Inquisitiones post mortem* were valued at £1 or less: Campbell and Bartley (2006), 269–73.

[149] Campbell (2005); Campbell (2013b); Bekar and Reed (2009).

[150] Greif (2006); De Moor (2008); Zanden (2009), 50–5.   [151] Greif (2006).

to trade for its members. Hanse merchants thereby benefited from lower costs of market information, negotiation and protection than competitor merchants in the same markets. By dint of these lower transaction costs they came to dominate trade in and between the Baltic and North Seas, from Novgorod in the east to Bruges and London in the west.[152]

The self-governing urban communities multiplying at the same time served an analogous function. The twin freedoms of movement and contract so fundamental to commercial activity were enshrined in their civic charters. Their councils enacted by-laws governing the conduct of trade at their markets and fairs and regulated weights and measures, while their borough courts enforced contracts and fair trading. A well-run town was likely to attract traders from elsewhere. Towns typically grew up in close physical association with a castle, monastery or episcopal seat due to the combination of protection and justice initially provided by the latter. Seigniorial power and justice could, however, become restrictive and in the fullness of time most towns endeavoured to assert their own jurisdictional autonomy.[153] Those that achieved this were able to hold their own courts, levy their own taxes and manage their own affairs free from seigniorial interference and, consequently, were better placed to promote long-distance commerce. From the late eleventh century, numbers of Italian, Northern-French and Flemish urban communes won their independence from seigniorial authority so that, henceforth, their citizens assumed responsibility for corporate action. In the commercially precocious centre and north of Italy, Cremona secured full rights of self-government in 1078, Pisa in 1081, Genoa in 1096, Verona in 1107 and Florence, Siena, Bologna and Ferrara shortly after 1115.[154]

As S. R. Epstein has emphasized, most of these towns were motivated to seize control of their own affairs by the quickening tempo of commercial life and the incentive this gave to establish fair and permanent trading relations with like-minded merchant communities elsewhere.[155] That meant respecting the persons and goods of merchants from other towns, upholding property rights, and providing swift and impartial settlement of commercial disputes in courts dedicated to the purpose, although there was a clear temptation for towns to give preferential treatment to their own citizens. In a world hidebound by class and in which opportunities for rent seeking were rife, true free trade was almost impossible to achieve. Instead, mercantilism prevailed, whereby licences or

---

[152] Hunt and Murray (1999), 164–6.   [153] Trenholme (1901).
[154] Epstein (2000b), 6 of 36.   [155] Epstein (2000b), 6–7 of 36.

monopolies to trade or toll-free exemptions were granted to specific merchant guilds or city-states, to the detriment or exclusion of others.

The Venetian Republic experienced a period of unprecedented prosperity after 1082, when it cannily sealed a treaty with Byzantine Emperor Alexios I Komnenos (r. 1081–1118) granting Venice control of the main harbour facilities at Constantinople and the right to trade tax-free throughout the empire. A few years later, in 1098, the small, newly independent but as yet relatively insignificant free commune of Genoa did equally well when, as a reward for supplying ships and men-at-arms to the successful First Crusade, it was granted lucrative trading privileges in the newly captured Levantine ports of Antioch and Acre. These were the twin termini of the ancient trans-Syrian caravan routes which linked the maritime commerce of the Arabian Sea and Persian Gulf with that of the eastern Mediterranean. Over the course of the next two centuries the Levant trade underpinned Genoa's commercial rise to European pre-eminence, in rivalry to the older maritime republic of Venice. Numbers of other Italian cities transformed themselves into city-states and thereby, like Genoa, became masters of their own political destinies and better able, through a combination of war, diplomacy and commercial clout, to promote their economic self-interests.[156] This, however, was at the long-term price of perpetuating political fragmentation, heightening the potential for economically disruptive inter-state conflict and warfare, and limiting the extent to which transaction costs could be lowered.[157]

Established entrepôts like Constantinople, Antioch and Acre had an obvious attraction for European merchants. In their absence, merchants naturally gravitated towards sites where they could congregate with others with complementary wares to trade. Periodic fairs, usually of several days' duration, were obvious magnets. During the eleventh and especially twelfth centuries great numbers of these were founded.[158] They were usually timed to avoid the dark and cold winter months when travel and transport were most difficult and to synchronize with seasonal production of livestock, wool, salt or fish. From modest beginnings, a handful of these fairs grew over the course of the twelfth century into major international marts. Those that did so included the English fairs of St Ives (chartered in 1110), Boston (founded before 1125), Northampton, and St Giles, Winchester (established in 1096); the Flemish fairs of Ypres, Lille, Mesen, Torhout and Bruges (all established in the 1120s); the Rhenish fairs of Utrecht, Duisburg, Aachen and Cologne; and, most

---

[156] Epstein (2000b).   [157] Epstein (2000a), 49–72.   [158] Pounds (1974), 355.

famously, the French Champagne fairs of Lagny, Bar-sur-Aube, Provins (two) and Troyes (two), whose rise to international prominence seems to have begun in the 1140s.[159] The fairs comprising each of these groupings evolved into marts of quite extended duration, to allow merchants time for entry, display, negotiation, sale and payment. They also tended to be held sequentially so that merchants could travel between them, with the coordinated cycle of six Champagne fairs spanning the greater part of a year.[160]

All these fairs owed much of their success to the protection of great magnates with the power and prestige to preserve the security, uphold the property rights, enforce the contracts and generally facilitate the business of those attending the fairs. Patrons of the English fairs included the honour of Richmond (Boston), abbot of Ramsey (St Ives), earl of Northampton (Northampton) and bishop of Winchester (St Giles, Winchester).[161] The Crown, too, became actively involved in several of them (especially, as in the case of the St Giles fair, when they began to over-run the number of days originally granted) and eventually, under Henry III, founded and promoted its own fair at Westminster.[162] The Flemish fairs all came under the single jurisdiction of the counts of Flanders, as did the Champagne fairs under the counts of Champagne. Guarantees of safe passage given by these great lords to merchants travelling within their extensive dominions gave their fairs a competitive edge. Almost uniquely, the counts of Champagne were successful at extending this guarantee beyond their own territories.

Rise of the Champagne fairs to European pre-eminence owed much to the active encouragement given them by the counts of Champagne.[163] Successive counts improved the transport infrastructure of roads and canals, contributed to physical development of the four host towns, regulated weights and measures, used their commercial and political clout to protect loans made by foreign merchants to powerful debtors and ensured that outsiders and locals received parity of treatment under the law. Thus promoted, these fairs rapidly became the principal mart where finished and unfinished cloth and wool supplied by Flemish and northern-French merchants were exchanged for spices, silks and other luxury merchandise supplied by Italians. In due course, too, the Italians adopted these fairs as a base for their money-changing and money-lending activities and the place where balances were struck and settled at the end of a year's

---

[159] Moore (1985), 12–22; Bavel (2010), 221; Edwards and Ogilvie (2012), 131–2.
[160] Pounds (1974), 355–6; Bavel (2010), 221; Edwards and Ogilvie (2012), 135.
[161] Moore (1985), 13–21.   [162] Moore (1985), 17–21.
[163] Edwards and Ogilvie (2012).

trading. It helped, of course, that Champagne was strategically located astride the key trans-Alpine axis of overland movement between Italy in the south and the Low Countries in the north.

How trust was established, reputations made or broken, contracts enforced and swift justice provided at these international fairs has long intrigued economic and legal historians. Considerable interest has attached to the idea that impersonal long-distance exchange developed without the support of a public legal system because the international community of merchants subscribed to an informal code of justice known as the 'law merchant'.[164] It has been proposed that a system of private-order contract enforcement ensured that only those of trustworthy reputation were able to keep trading at the fairs; those found by private judges to be guilty of fraudulent and dishonest dealing were ostracized and excluded. This appealing notion has, however, been discredited by careful re-examination of the justice systems operated at St Ives fair in England and the Champagne fairs in France, where it has been demonstrated that contract enforcement was mainly provided by public institutions with powers of coercion.[165]

At St Ives the fair court was conducted by the abbot of Ramsey's officials acting under the executive control of the abbot and its profits accrued to the abbey. It was essentially a seigniorial court in which merchants participated and whose business was primarily commercial in nature.[166] Likewise, at the Champagne fairs 'the jurisdiction of the various tribunals enforcing contracts at the fairs emanated from the public authorities, not from the merchants, and there is no evidence that any of these tribunals applied a private, merchant-generated law-code'.[167] Visiting merchants seeking justice had access to the four-tier system of public courts operated by the counts or, alternatively, the municipal courts of the fair-towns and the ecclesiastical tribunals of local religious houses. In addition, fair wardens appointed by the counts conducted public tribunals at the fairs where contracts could be judged and enforced.[168] Merchants seeking swift, effective and impartial justice thus had access to a choice of public institutions. It was the combination of mercantile enterprise, enlightened and influential lordship and an advantageous location that made these, and the other great international fairs, the magnets for long-distance commerce and the agents of commercial growth that they duly became.

---

[164] For example, Milgrom and others (1990).
[165] Sachs (2002); Sachs (2006); Kadens (2011); Edwards and Ogilvie (2012).
[166] Sachs (2002).   [167] Edwards and Ogilvie (2012), 146.
[168] Edwards and Ogilvie (2012), 133–5, 146.

2.05   Latin Christendom's commercial revolution

Urbanization constitutes the most conspicuous and mature manifestation of the revival of European trade and commerce, whose beginnings McCormick has now re-dated to the eighth century.[169] Over the ensuing centuries, the institutions, codes of behaviour, mental attitudes, knowledge and trust upon which market exchange depended evolved and became embedded in society. Progressively, and with gathering momentum, a veritable 'commercial revolution' took place, as markets widened and deepened, a greater proportion of net production was traded, and more and more Europeans came to rely upon market transactions for part or all of their livelihoods.[170] In the process, local orbits of exchange became increasingly interlinked into regional, national, international and, eventually, inter-continental orbits of exchange. By the final decades of the thirteenth century Abu-Lughod believes that the world's eight great circuits of exchange – encompassing Europe, Asia and East and North Africa – had at last become interlinked into a single global trading network (Figure 2.1), making possible, at some cost, exchange of bullion and commodities between westernmost Europe and easternmost Asia.[171]

All parts of Europe participated to some degree or other in the new commercial order. For instance, high-prestige furs trapped on the shores of the Arctic Sea by the Sami (alias Lapps) of northern Scandinavia and Finns to the east became from the 1240s the object of an active trade developed by Hanse merchants, in collaboration with Novgorod and other Russian city-states. Some of these furs were shipped down the great Russian rivers which had their outlets in the Black Sea and the Caspian Sea and were destined for markets in Byzantium and the Middle East.[172] Far to the west, in the North Atlantic, the remote Norse colony in Greenland (technically part of North America) also became reliant upon an irregular but lucrative trade in walrus ivory and narwhal tusks, classic low-bulk but high-value commodities, which were exchanged for a range of essential subsistence goods in which Greenlanders were otherwise deficient.[173] Meanwhile, from the eleventh century, Iceland developed as a major supplier of dried stockfish to an increasingly hungry and religious observant European market, consuming fish in greatly increased quantities.[174] Dependence upon these trades helped sustain the viability of these geographically remote and environmentally marginal

---

[169] McCormick (2001).   [170] Lopez (1971); Britnell and Campbell (1995), 1.
[171] Abu-Lughod (1989).   [172] Dugmore, Keller and McGovern (2007), 18.
[173] Dugmore, Keller and McGovern (2007), 16–17.
[174] Dugmore, Keller and McGovern (2007), 18; Woolgar (2010), 7.

communities but also exposed them to the additional risk of commercial dislocation and failure.

Alternatives to commerce included relative self-sufficiency (absolute self-sufficiency was rarely attainable); various forms of reciprocity including hospitality and gift exchange; ransom, tribute, piracy and plunder; and the coercive extraction of labour and produce rents imposed and levied via the institution of serfdom. Since these were not mutually exclusive, they long co-existed with market exchange and, outside the core areas of commercial activity, sometimes remained the dominant socio-property relationships. In this respect, most late-medieval European economies were mixed economies. Nevertheless, once a degree of civil order had been established and population levels had risen to the point that labour had to compete for work and land effectively ceased to be free, commerce offered productivity gains and efficiency savings which none of these alternative and often more predatory systems could match.[175]

Progressively, from the tenth century, production for exchange supplanted production for use, money became more widely adopted as a medium of exchange, measure of value and store of wealth, and prices acquired an ever more powerful influence upon economic behaviour, shaping decisions both to produce and to consume. The consequences for European society were profound. Distinctive institutions and social groups emerged to handle trade. Incentives to invest capital in production strengthened and capital itself became cheaper and more available.[176] Efforts, both public and private, were made to improve transport and communications and thereby reduce the costs of overcoming distance. Practical technology and useful knowledge advanced.[177] In a process described by R. A. Dodgshon as 'taking space to market', economic, geographical and occupational specialization progressed and associated changes took place in the social and geographical distributions of wealth.[178] Finally, until diminishing returns set in and for as long as transaction costs continued to fall, national incomes in aggregate and per head both grew. Italy, in the van of most of these developments, was significantly richer and more urbanized in 1300 than 1000 and by then enjoyed double the GDP per head of England, which, in turn, was economically and commercially more developed than less urbanized Ireland, Scotland and much of Scandinavia (Table 2.2).[179] Progress of the commercial revolution in these two very different economies repays closer investigation.

[175] Domar (1970).   [176] Below, Section 2.05.2b.
[177] Mokyr (1992), 31–56; Landers (2003).   [178] Dodgshon (1987), 287–351.
[179] Malanima (2005), 99–102, 111–12; Broadberry and Campbell (2009); Campbell (2008), 931.

2.05.1   Italy: the vanguard economy

In Italy, as in much of southern Europe, commerce and the urban life it supported were not entirely extinguished by the collapse of the Roman Empire. A foundation therefore existed for the revival of both, stirrings of which become detectable from the eighth century. By the start of the new millennium Malanima estimates that central and northern Italy had an urbanization ratio of, perhaps, 8 per cent and GDP per head of around $1,000.[180] Although both measures were substantially below their respective Roman peaks of 15–20 per cent and $1,400, both were higher than in any other European country at that time.[181] Over the next three centuries the Italian population increased two-and-a-half-fold and the proportion of that population living in towns at least doubled, as the commercial and manufacturing functions of towns grew apace and the formidable spending power of noble elites became concentrated within them.[182] By c.1290 Italy (centre-north) was more populous, urbanized and prosperous, and engaged in commerce over a wider geographical area, than any other part of Latin Christendom. Town dwellers accounted for at least a fifth of the population and GDP per head had risen to around $1,665, having grown at the impressive average annual rate of 0.16 per cent.[183] As in other episodes of pre-modern economic efflorescence, population growth was fast but economic growth was faster.[184]

Initially, much of this growth was generated by the expansion of domestic Italian market demand and opportunities thereby created for a greater division of labour. Limited supplies of good agricultural land also meant that from quite an early date the fast-expanding cities of the hilly centre and north of Italy became dependent upon grain shipments from the more extensive cornlands of southern Italy and Sicily.[185] This maritime bulk trade in grain and other staple commodities became one of the mainstays of Italian commerce, along with the associated trades in wine, oil and salt. Nevertheless, the peninsula's advantageous location at the centre of the Mediterranean meant that it soon became a focus of wider orbits of exchange.

At almost all stages in this commercial revolution the merchants of no other European country were more active than the Italians in promoting

---

[180] Malanima (2005), 101, 108; Malanima (2002), 450.
[181] Malanima (2005), 99; Lo Cascio and Malanima (2009), 396–400.
[182] Malanima (2002), 450; Malanima (2005).
[183] Malanima (2002), 450; Lo Cascio and Malanima (2009); Malanima (2011), 204–5. This compares with a Dutch growth rate of 0.33 per cent per annum in the period 1500–1650 in conjunction with a trebling of population (Zanden and Leeuwen (2012)), and an English growth rate of 0.36 per cent in the period 1680–1800 in conjunction with a 70 per cent growth in population (Broadberry and others (2015), 28–33).
[184] Goldstone (2002).   [185] Abulafia (2005).

long-distance trade and commerce and, among Italians, none were more eminent in developing the risky but potentially highly profitable trade in high-value luxury products from the Orient than the Venetians and Genoese.[186] Venice initially enjoyed the advantage following its 1082 commercial treaty with Byzantium, which gave it privileged access to 'Christendom's largest and most prosperous city and the gateway to Central Asia'.[187] Soon, however, it found itself in direct competition with Genoa, whose active support of the First Crusade paid commercial dividends in terms of the trading privileges Genoese merchants thereby gained in the Levant, until the fall of the crusader ports of Antioch and Acre in 1268 and 1291 brought this episode to an end. In 1204 the Venetians had regained the initiative, through their involvement in the sack of Constantinople, as a result of which they were finally able to break through and trade directly with the ports of the Black Sea. This gave them direct access to the consignments of Asian spices and silks reaching these ports via the various caravan routes that terminated at them.[188]

Given the vast distances involved and obstacles to be overcome, Oriental commodities traded in European markets were perforce high in value, low in bulk and lacking in substitutes. For want of reciprocal commodities, they were largely paid for with bullion. Some reached the Mediterranean, and thence northwestern Europe, via the maritime routes across the Arabian Sea to either the Persian Gulf (and then by caravan to Baghdad and across the Syrian desert to Antioch and Acre) or the Red Sea and Egypt (whence they were trans-shipped to Alexandria). Others were carried via the many-stranded overland route (collectively known as the Silk Road) that terminated at Trebizond on the southern shore of the Black Sea, Tana on the Sea of Azov and Kaffa in the Crimea, to which Constantinople, on the Bosphorus, held the key.[189] The Black Sea's share of the Oriental trade gained in importance from the late 1250s following the Mongol capture and destruction of Baghdad, which diverted much of the maritime trade reaching the Persian Gulf northwards, away from Baghdad, Aleppo, Antioch and the Levant, towards Tabriz in Persia and, thence, Trebizond.[190] Overland trade following the southern caravan route across Eurasia was similarly deflected away from Baghdad towards Tabriz.

In 1261 the Venetian monopoly on European trade with Constantinople had been broken by the Genoese, who then penetrated the Black

[186] Abu-Lughod (1989), 102–34.   [187] Abu-Lughod (1989), 105.
[188] Abu-Lughod (1989), 109–11.   [189] Abu-Lughod (1989), 137–51.
[190] Phillips (1988), 66, 106–7; Abu-Lughod (1989), 145–7; Karpov (2007).

Sea and proceeded to establish themselves at Pera opposite Constantinople, Kaffa in the Crimea, Tana (gateway to the steppes, at the mouth of the River Don on the Sea of Azov), Trebizond and, from the 1280s, Tabriz itself.[191] This was at a time when the trans-Eurasian overland trade in silks and spices had entered an exceptionally active and prosperous phase. Demand from Europe's feudal and urban elites for these high-prestige commodities was stronger than ever and the Mongol conquests of the mid-thirteenth century had effectively unified the Eurasian interior under a single authority and thereby bestowed greater security on the overland caravan routes. For Abu-Lughod this was 'a remarkable moment in world history', for 'never before had so many regions of the Old World come into contact with one another'.[192] Over half a century later, around 1340, Florentine merchant Francesco Balducci Pegolotti in his practical treatise *Pratica della mercatura* described the northern overland route across the interior of Eurasia, from the Sea of Azov in the west to Beijing (alias Peking) in the east, via Astrakhan, Khiva in Uzbekistan, Otrar in Kazakhstan, and Ghulja (alias Kulja) in northwest China, as 'perfectly safe by day and night'.[193]

Foreign trade propelled the maritime republics of Venice and Genoa into the first rank of European cities and by 1300 both supported populations of approximately 100,000, Genoa's population having more than doubled over the course of the thirteenth century under the impetus of this booming long-distance trade.[194] The inland cities of Florence and Milan were of comparable size and their merchants were heavily involved in the fast-developing trans-Alpine trade with northern Europe, which supplied wool and unfinished cloth to manufacturers and processors in the south (the finished textiles were then exported to Levantine and other Mediterranean markets where these cheap, light European cloths were in demand).[195] Italian merchants began visiting the Champagne fairs in the 1170s, from the 1190s were attending in significant numbers, and over the course of the next century became, with the Flemings, the most important group of merchants participating in them.[196] As well as exchanging spices and silks for wool and cloth the Italians became major suppliers of credit and dealers in exchange and thus indispensable to the ongoing success of the fairs. Within Europe a clear axis of commerce emerged linking the commerce of the North Sea via Flanders, the Champagne fairs and Alpine passes, to northern and central Italy and, thus,

---

[191] Lopez (1971), 109–11; Phillips (1988), 108–9; Abu-Lughod (1989), 207.
[192] Abu-Lughod (1989), 3.   [193] Cited in Lopez (1971), 111.
[194] Greif (2006), 243.   [195] Munro (1991).
[196] Edwards and Ogilvie (2012), 131–2, 136.

the far greater commerce of the Mediterranean and Black Seas with their links east to Arabia, India and China.

Throughout the long thirteenth century the thriving mercantile cities of Lombardy and Tuscany were more successful at attracting and accumulating silver and gold bullion than any others. Merchants from these cities had already led the way in the formation of guilds to enforce contracts with third parties and protect traders and their goods from the depredations of lords, buccaneers and thieves. Now they were the pioneers of the key commercial innovations of the age, notably the bill of exchange used for settling accounts in international trade 'without the high cost and hazard of shipping actual specie', double-entry bookkeeping developed in order to keep track of 'multiple transactions executed at multiple locations', and the formation of business partnerships or firms to pool capital and share risks.[197] Equally important was the realization that it made better financial sense to mobilize coins and bullion for investment than hoard them for safety. Once this occurred, commercial loans became an ordinary part of north Italian economic life, allowing credit, and the economic activity which it supported, to expand. This further added to the money supply.

In the evolution of this fledgling financial system the merchant money-changers played a crucial role.[198] By dint of their superior knowledge of bullion prices and the exchange rates of foreign currencies, they became the main suppliers of used coins and bullion to the various Italian mints. This was a business in which professional expertise, integrity and trust were paramount. Those commanding the greatest trust and respect attracted deposits of specie for safekeeping, to the point where depositors began to use them to settle payments. In turn, these merchants used their new-found wealth to fund new enterprises, underwrite the burgeoning volume of their exchange dealings, finance their growing involvement in international trade, and supply loans to monarchs, all at a falling rate of interest. In effect, mercantile banking was born.

As a result of these developments the greater international merchants found it economically and politically disadvantageous to absent themselves from the centre of their business operations for too long. Instead of moving with their goods between the various international fairs, they now entrusted their overseas dealings to professional agents, employed specialist carriers for the despatch and trans-shipment of goods, and used bills of exchange to settle their accounts. London was one of several major European cities where Italian agents were to be found by the

---

[197] Hunt and Murray (1999), 56–7, 65–7.   [198] Hunt and Murray (1999), 64–5.

close of the thirteenth century.[199] By 1299/1304 the Italian Societies of Amanti, Bardi, Bellardi, Boncini, Cerchi Bianchi, Cerchi Neri, Chiarenti, Corone, Frescobaldi, Magelet, Markener, Mozzi, Peruzzi, Portinari, Pulchi-Rimbertini and Spini had all established offices in London. Thirty years later, the Peruzzi Company of Florence maintained major branches at Naples and Barletta (Italy), Palermo (Sicily), Rhodes, Avignon and Paris (France), Bruges (Flanders) and London (England), with further minor branches at Venice and Pisa (Italy), Castel de Castro (Sardinia), Majorca, Tunis (North Africa), Chiarenza (Balkans) and Cyprus, and agencies at Barcelona (Aragon), Ragusa (Balkans) and Constantinople (Byzantium).[200] Italians, in fact, might be encountered wherever commercial prospects beckoned, business acumen was at a premium, and kings and other great lords required large-scale credit. Small wonder, therefore, that Italians were among the first Westerners to visit China in the late thirteenth century.

2.05.2   England: a lagging economy

Where Italy led, England and most of the rest of Latin Christendom followed, with Flanders alone matching the urbanization ratio and, by implication, level of GDP per head achieved in the highly commercialized centre and north of Italy.[201] Demographic growth was, however, at least as strong in England as in Italy. Its population grew from approximately 1.71 million in 1086 to around 4.75 million by 1290, with numbers rising at an annual average rate of 0.58 per cent during the twelfth century, slowing to 0.43 per cent during the thirteenth century, with a marked deceleration during the latter decades of that century.[202] Without Italy's advantages of a substantial and vigorously increasing urban sector, expanding industries, and proactive involvement in foreign trade, the growth of English national income nonetheless successfully kept pace with the expansion of population until at least the mid-thirteenth century: GDP per head grew at an annual rate of 0.15 per cent between 1086 and 1250. This was no mean feat for a poor, insular and predominantly agrarian economy on the commercial periphery of Europe and was partly achieved by a profound restructuring of the economy along more commercialized lines.

English GDP per head may have recovered from a post-Conquest low of probably less than $700 in 1086 to a mid-thirteenth-century high of

---

[199] Lloyd (1982), 7, 172–203; Keene (2000b), 198–9.   [200] Hunt (1994).
[201] Bairoch and others (1988), 259, estimate an urbanization ratio of 25–35 per cent for Flanders c.1300.
[202] Broadberry and others (2015), 12, 20–1, 31.

perhaps $850 in 1253 but then slipped back to $730 at the close of the thirteenth century, following the substantial negative impact of the 1280s sheep scab epizootic upon national wool output and, thus, cloth production and exports.[203] During the boom years of the late twelfth century, contemporaries certainly thought that material conditions were improving. For instance, Richard FitzNigel, Henry II's treasurer, complained that because people were better off, drunkenness and crime were on the increase.[204] Certainly, farm labourers did not need to work as hard to secure a subsistence income at the beginning of the thirteenth century as they would have to by its end. Moreover, the available price and wage evidence implies that labourers' real wage rates held up reasonably well until the harvest crisis of 1256–7, after which real wage rates and GDP per head both slid downwards.[205] Until that point, productivity gains stemming from fuller commercialization of the English economy, in conjunction with expanding overseas demand for English tin, lead, wool and unfinished cloth, appear to have kept output growth abreast of population growth.

Progress was especially marked between 1175 and 1250 when the Crown was actively involved in development of the realm's commercial infrastructure. During these formative years the Common Law came into being, record creation and keeping grew apace, money supply per head surged (Table 2.3), weights and measures were regulated, rules of exchange established, numbers of chartered markets, fairs and boroughs multiplied (Figure 2.13), parish churches proliferated, hospital foundations peaked (Figure 2.12A), the University of Oxford rose to prominence and the University of Cambridge came into being. The first friaries were also founded (Figure 2.12A), bridges were constructed in great numbers and a major ecclesiastical building boom got under way. Key themes in this process of commercialization are the creation of a commercial infrastructure (Section 2.05.2a), the establishment of factor markets in land, labour and capital (Section 2.05.2b), mint output and coin supply (Section 2.05.2c) and the expansion of agricultural output and production of agricultural surpluses (Section 2.05.2d).

2.05.2a Creation of a commercial infrastructure In contrast to Italy's plethora of rival city-states, England was a unified and centralized kingdom with effectively defined and defended borders within which a high degree of peace and order prevailed. By contemporary European

---

[203] Walker (2009). 1253 GDP per head estimate provided by Bas van Leeuwen. On the sheep scab epizootic see Stephenson (1988), 381; above, Section 1.01.
[204] Warren (1973), 355.   [205] Clark (2007b), 99, 130–1.

standards, English kings were therefore in an unusually privileged position when it came to creating an institutional environment conducive to the conduct of trade and exchange.[206] From the late twelfth century the Crown began to take steps towards establishing national uniformity in weights, measures, currency and prices, all of which were instrumental to the ease and efficiency with which trade was conducted.[207] In 1196 new legislation in the form of the Assize of Measures was introduced which promulgated standard weights (volume measures for cereals and liquids, and, in the case of woollen cloth, widths measured by a standard ell) for the whole of England. This did not bring about wholesale adoption of statute measures but did set in train the processes by which that would eventually be brought about. For instance, in 1255, 1257 and 1270 commissions appointed by Henry III enquired into the way in which these regulations were enforced.[208] Subsequently, Edward I and Edward II conducted nationwide scrutinies of weights and measures at the commencement of their reigns: those not using the standard measures were fined. Most well-governed towns also took steps to ensure that traders complied with a uniform set of measures and anyone using false measures was punished. From the 1190s an assize of bread and ale was also introduced to regulate the prices and qualities of these staple foodstuffs by determining how much bread and ale could be purchased for a penny. Further regulations issued from the 1270s (and, from 1307, formally enforced alongside the laws relating to weights and measures) were aimed at ensuring a competitive market price by prohibiting the practice of forestalling (i.e. brokerage activities which deliberately or inadvertently raised the price of goods on sale); thereafter 'forestalling was penalised by local authorities as a statutory offence'.[209]

Rules and regulations governing trade were, of course, most readily enforced and scrutinized at markets that were formally established and thereby entitled to hold courts capable of dealing quickly and effectively with infringements of these regulations along with the many civil and criminal cases which inevitably arose when people congregated to conduct trade. Grant of a charter to establish a borough or hold a weekly market and annual fair was a Crown prerogative. These grants were made to individuals, not places, and entitled the recipient, usually the local manorial lord, to found a borough and/or hold a market or fair on a specified day or date, charge tollage on the goods traded and levy stallage from those who traded them, and profit from fines levied at borough, market

---

[206] For the coordination failures and consequent high transaction costs that could arise when political power was more fragmented see Epstein (2000a).
[207] Britnell (1993a), 90–7; Davis (2011), 141–4.   [208] Britnell (1993a), 91.
[209] Britnell (1993a), 93; Davis (2011), 254–6.

and fair courts. The substantial financial rewards to be reaped from successful borough and market foundations provided lords with a powerful incentive to establish them: in this respect elaboration of a network of formal markets was inseparable from the exercise of lordship.[210] By the early fourteenth century, according to the *Inquisitiones post mortem*, boroughs, markets and fairs had respective average annual values of £6.50, £3.38 and £2.60 and the most successful yielded revenues at least ten times as great.[211] The aggregate net value to their licensees of the 600 boroughs, 1,700 markets and 2,000 fairs granted by the Crown between 1100 and 1350 would therefore have been almost £15,000.[212] This impressive valuation also testifies to high levels of mostly small-scale and localized commercial activity.

In 1086 Domesday Book had recorded only forty-one places with markets, which implies that local trade was less regulated, more informal and involved fewer commercial transactions and smaller volumes of traded commodities.[213] Probably much trade was undertaken on an itinerant basis and conducted by pedlars. Additional exchange undoubtedly occurred at informal markets held on set dates at fixed sites, characteristically when people congregated for some other purpose, as, for instance, on Sundays.[214] The Sabbath had apparently been the most common market day in the twelfth century and in Lancashire Sunday markets survived until the fifteenth century.[215] From the early thirteenth century, however, as rural markets began to proliferate, the Church actively opposed Sabbath trading and many hitherto unlicensed Sunday markets were re-scheduled to other days of the week and legitimized with the grant of a market charter.[216]

The transitions from itinerant to sedentary and from informal to formal marketing were only feasible once significant numbers of local inhabitants had begun to engage in trade on a weekly basis and the physical volume of that trade had become too great for pedlars alone to handle (although weekly markets were often synchronized so that itinerant traders could move between them).[217] Chartering of markets also denoted closer regulation of local trade by central government, which attempted to protect the viability of existing markets by insisting that new foundations be at least 6.67 miles distant from them. To judge from recorded numbers of royal charters (Figure 2.13), this critical transition in the character, volume and frequency of rural marketing occurred between *c.*1175 and *c.*1225. This was when a spatially dense network of boroughs, markets

[210] Britnell (1981); Letters and others (2003); Jamroziak (2005).
[211] Campbell and Bartley (2006), 301–8.   [212] Letters (2010).
[213] Darby (1977), 318–19, 369–70.   [214] Davis (2011), 184–6.
[215] Tupling (1933).   [216] Davis (2011), 184–6.   [217] Unwin (1981).

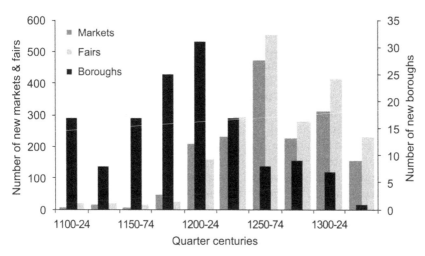

Figure 2.13 Numbers of English royal grants of market, fair and borough charters, 1100–1349
Source: Letters (2010)

and fairs was established throughout the realm and especially in the populous counties of East Anglia and the east midlands. Typically, in the long run it was these pioneering early foundations which proved to be the most profitable and durable, enjoying a clear advantage over most of those (and there were a great many) founded later.[218] The latter nevertheless greatly increased the choice of markets and ensured that most rural inhabitants were within a day's walk of a formally constituted mart. Meanwhile, royal purveyors and many corn-mongers, wool-mongers and other bulk dealers continued to purchase directly from producers, usually at the farm gate or, in the case of wool, at estate headquarters. Likewise, much informal trading took place in most villages, as neighbours exchanged land and labour, housing and clothing, drink and foodstuffs, implements and craft goods. Christopher Dyer has called this the 'hidden trade' of the Middle Ages.[219]

One way or another, by 1300 and throughout the greater part of England, the market nexus had become all-encompassing.[220] By then, as a host of extant manorial and other accounts demonstrate, just about everything, both new and old, could be bought and sold and therefore had its price. Criminal records show that property crime was rife due to the ease with which stolen goods could be made over and sold on.[221]

[218] Masschaele (1994).   [219] Dyer (1992).   [220] Masschaele (1997).
[221] Hanawalt (1979).

Everywhere, the range and volume of available price information can be seen to increase almost exponentially from the late twelfth century in step with the advance of commercialization. In the process, literacy, numeracy and the creation and preservation of written records all gained in importance.[222] Methods of accounting also advanced apace, as exemplified by seigniorial attempts at profit-and-loss accounting.[223] Thanks to the wealth of its preserved medieval archives, England is exceptionally well served by extant price information: annual price series have been reconstructed for a range of staple products extending back continuously to 1268 and then intermittently for a further hundred years.[224] These, of course, are cash prices and consequently testify to the fact that over this period money was becoming more widely adopted and available as a means of exchange.

2.05.2b Factor markets in labour, land and capital Growth of commercial exchange at all levels was accompanied by the more fitful and uneven development of markets in the labour, land and capital upon which commodity production depended. Such markets were fundamental to evolution of a mature commercial economy and eventual establishment of capitalist socio-property relations. Even more than commodity markets, factor markets were shaped and constrained by the legal, tenurial and institutional contexts within which they operated.[225] Labour markets tended to be the first to emerge since they faced the fewest institutional obstacles. Land markets followed, first in freehold land and then, by the late thirteenth century, in villein land. Once land had become a saleable asset it became possible for property owners to use their land as a security against loans and capital markets grew accordingly.

In England labour was already being exchanged for wages paid in cash and in kind by the late twelfth century.[226] Waged labour was the norm in the construction industry (especially on the many large building projects of the period), which experienced a sustained boom from the late eleventh century to the early fourteenth century.[227] Building accounts provide the best and longest available series of task-specific wage rates, for skilled and unskilled male labourers, as famously reconstructed for

---

[222] Clanchy (1979).
[223] Stone (1962); Postles (1986); Bryer (1993); Hunt and Murray (1999), 62–3, 111.
[224] Pioneering compilations of early price data were made by J. E. Thorold Rogers (1866–1902), Beveridge (1939) and Farmer (1988). Beveridge's manuscript tabulations are preserved at the London School of Economics and Farmer's at the University of Saskatchewan Archives. Additional price information preserved in England's copious pre-1300 manuscript sources awaits collection.
[225] Bavel and others (2009).   [226] Latimer (1997).
[227] Morris (1979); Knowles and Hadcock (1971).

the period 1264–1954 by Henry Phelps Brown and Sheila Hopkins.[228] A wage-rate series for farm labourers reconstructed by Gregory Clark starts even earlier, in 1209, while Paul Latimer has assembled all available information contained in the Exchequer Pipe Rolls on wages paid to the king's vintner, chaplains, porters and watchmen and to people in temporary or casual employment, such as sailors, steersmen and foot soldiers, which extends English wage history back to the 1160s.[229] Wage earning was naturally integral to the urban economy and, over the course of the twelfth and thirteenth centuries, expanding urban employment opportunities lured many migrants to towns. Within the economy at large Richard Britnell has estimated that waged labour may have accounted for about a fifth to a quarter of the total labour expended in producing goods and services by 1300.[230]

It was in the countryside that the single greatest volume of waged employment was to be found, both throughout the year and, most conspicuously, at periods of peak labour demand during the hay, wool and grain harvests. Self-employed and family labour may always have accounted for a greater share of agricultural production but by 1300 hired labour had undoubtedly superseded servile labour in importance, notwithstanding that the latter is typically regarded as one of the hallmarks of the English feudal economy and looms large in traditional accounts of the period.[231] The numerous small manors without servile tenants had no alternative but to hire labour and on many demesnes the supply of labour services was inadequate to the requirements of cultivation.[232] The same usually applied to the thousands of modest glebe farms belonging to rectors. Great serf-run estates, such as those operated by the abbot of Glastonbury and bishop of Winchester in southern England, were very much the exception.[233]

Most lords, even when the supply of servile labour was sufficient to their needs, preferred to manage their demesnes with a permanent staff of farm servants or *famuli* (forerunners of the 'servants in husbandry' of later centuries) supervised by salaried serjeants and bailiffs and employed on termly or annual contracts in return for liveries of food and

---

[228] Phelps Brown and Hopkins (1956). For a revised and corrected version of this series see Munro (no date). For a recently constructed wage rate series beginning in the 1260s for females employed on daily and annual contracts see Humphries and Weisdorf (2015).

[229] Farmer (1988) provides much of the evidential base for Clark (2007b); Latimer (1997).

[230] Britnell (1993b), 364.

[231] See the key revisionist arguments advanced by Hatcher (1981) and endorsed by Campbell (2005).

[232] Campbell and Bartley (2006), 251–68.

[233] Keil (1964); Titow (1962a); Campbell (2003a).

accommodation and a fixed money wage.[234] On the vast majority of English manors, these were the workers who ploughed, harrowed, sowed, reaped and carted, managed the working animals, and herded and shepherded livestock. Consequently, the proportion of seigniorial output produced using labour services may have been as little as 8 per cent, whereas the proportion accounted for by hired labour was more than ten times as great.[235] Substantial freeholders and even many 12½-hectare (30-acre) yardlanders (tenants of the largest class of standard villein holding) also undoubtedly hired labour on a casual or annual basis. On serf-run estates, yardlanders owing weekworks often lacked sufficient family labour to manage a 12½-hectare arable holding and fulfil their potentially heavy labouring obligations on the demesne and therefore sent hired workers to perform their services in their stead.[236]

Smallholders, in contrast, mostly had more labour than they could gainfully employ on their own holdings and, over the course of the thirteenth century, constituted an expanding proportion of rural households. Without a well-developed labour market such households could not have survived, although the real value of the wage rates they earned declined as the numbers seeking work rose. Only by working more hours per day and more days per year and by fuller participation by family members in the labour market could they have maintained their incomes, which in turn, in the absence of a concomitant expansion of employment, placed further downward pressure upon real wage rates.[237] Within the countryside, those who lived by their labour alone, unsupported by landholding in any form (including an entitlement to common rights), were as yet a minority. Employment opportunities varied too much from season to season and year to year for wage earning by itself to provide a reliable basis for family formation and household survival. Without at least some land, albeit only a cottage and a garden with a cow or sheep on the commons, it was difficult for labourers to survive slack seasons and poor years. The principal suppliers of live-in servants were therefore young adults from established tenant households – the *garciones* of the documents – and those cottagers and smallholders with labour in excess of their own needs.[238] At Halesowen in Worcestershire Zvi Razi has demonstrated that it was the constant downward social displacement of the surplus

---

[234] Postan (1954); Farmer (1996).   [235] Campbell (2000), 3.

[236] Page (2003), 66–7.

[237] Farmer (1988), 778, estimates that over the course of the thirteenth century farm labourers could only have maintained the same standard of living by increasing the number of days worked by one-third. On the inverse relationship between daily real wage rates and labour supply see Langdon and Masschaele (2006), 69–77; Angeles (2008); Allen and Weisdorf (2011); Broadberry and others (2015), 260–5.

[238] Fox (1996).

children of substantial tenants into the ranks of cottagers, commoners, squatters and sub-tenants that maintained the supply of wage earners on the manor.[239] Those depressed further into true landlessness were always liable to succumb to destitution and vagrancy, becoming beggars and thieves rather than workers. Able-bodied vagrants were the objects of much contemporary social disapproval.[240]

A land market was far slower to develop than the labour market since it had to await the legal reforms instituted by Henry II in the 1170s and 1180s which established legally secure and defensible private property rights in land.[241] Creation of the Common Law, enforced in royal courts by Crown-appointed justices, provided the essential precondition for growth of a genuine market in freehold land over the course of the thirteenth century. Material testimony to the rise of that market is provided by the 'private charters that grant or sell or exchange or quit-claim or lease tiny pieces of land [and] survive in their thousands in the muniment-rooms of estate owners, in local record offices, and in other repositories'.[242] Increased commercial availability of clerical skills lent further momentum to growth of this land market, as did development of cheap and effective legal procedures developed by the royal courts for the conveyance of free land.[243] In particular, from the 1160s a stream of legal reforms extended the efficiency and scope of the writs necessary to initiate litigation in the royal courts.[244] Only freeholders transacting freehold land could avail themselves of this service, but the co-existence of freehold and villein land throughout even the most manorialized parts of lowland England meant that where a market in freehold land led, a local manorial market in villein land often followed.[245]

Sales and leases of villein land between servile tenants lay outside the purview of the royal courts and were subject instead to the jurisdiction of manorial courts, whose rolls provide a more comprehensive register of customary land transfers than anything available for freehold land.[246] Although some lords, such as the abbots of Glastonbury, set themselves firmly against anything which compromised the holding-based allocation and levying of labour and money rents, most lords condoned both the leasing and selling of villein land on condition that sales and leases for more than five years were registered in the manor court and an entry

[239] Razi (1980).   [240] Horrox (1994), 289.   [241] Above, Section 2.04.2.
[242] Harvey (1984a), 19. A 'quitclaim' was a formal renunciation of all existing and residual legal property rights in a piece of land.
[243] Razi and Smith (1996), 57–68.   [244] Above, Section 2.04.2.
[245] Campbell (2005), 36; Hyams (1970); Harvey (1996).
[246] See Maitland (1889) for examples. On the evidence provided by Feet of Fines of the market in freehold land see Yates (2013).

fine was paid. Since custom varied a great deal, even between manors on the same estate, this was a market with much local variation.[247] The pipe rolls of the bishops of Winchester provide the earliest documentary evidence of this market in customary land and it is not until the 1240s that corresponding evidence begins to become available for other estates, by which time these *inter vivos* conveyances of villein land were employing the language and conventions of the royal courts.[248]

Establishment of secure and transferable private property rights in land helped liberate the stored capital value of land and this, in turn, stoked inflation.[249] Over the period 1176–1215, when a law of property effectively came into being, prices doubled on average and thereafter continued to rise steadily to a peak in the second decade of the fourteenth century (Figure 2.14).[250] Land, consequently, became an appreciating asset. Rising land values, in turn, fed the growth of a capital market. Although credit and money lending had prevailed in England long before Henry II's legal innovations, it was only in the wake of those reforms that they grew to significant proportions and became indispensable components of most aspects of economic life.[251]

Growth of an English capital market owed much to Jewish financiers and for long they dominated the English credit market. William I and Henry I had established Jewish communities in England, where they grew wealthy on the opportunities for bullion dealing, money changing and money lending.[252] During the thirteenth century they became much more exclusively dependent upon money lending and for the first half of that century enjoyed a virtual monopoly. English Jews employed a system of lending by bonds against gages (pledges), in which the Jewish exchequer provided a reliable mechanism for registering bonds and collecting debts.[253] In the 1240s, when detailed records survive of their assets (including loans), Robert Stacey estimates that the English Jewish community as a whole was owed between £76,500 and £79,000 on its unpaid bonds, exclusive of any interest charges, equivalent in value to almost a fifth of the total circulating coin in England at that time (Table 2.4) and maybe 2 per cent of national income.[254]

From the 1260s, however, for mainly political reasons, Jewish moneylenders found their activities increasingly restricted and curtailed and their capital assets seriously depleted by royal taxation. They also

---

[247] Page (2003).   [248] Stocks (2003); Razi and Smith (1996), 38–42.
[249] Palmer (1985a), 249; Palmer (1985b).
[250] Farmer (1988); Latimer (1999); Bolton (2012), 148–9, 176–82.
[251] Briggs (2008); Bolton (2012), 191–214.   [252] Stacey (1995), 82–8.
[253] Stacey (1995), 78–101; Mundill (2002).   [254] Stacey (1995), 94.

suffered from the anti-Semitism that was a growing phenomenon throughout Europe but which became particularly acute in England.[255] In the final years before their expulsion by Edward I in 1290 their loans were mostly small-scale, short-term and rural, i.e. they became pawn-brokers and suppliers of capital to the peasantry. As their fortunes waned so those of Christian financiers rose. In fact, once land could be offered as the most usual security for loans, the Italians had a far stronger vested interest than the Jews in advancing credit since foreclosing on debts furnished them with a means of acquiring landed property, an option from which Jews were effectively excluded.[256] This may help to explain why the land market appears to have increased in activity during the final decades of the thirteenth century as Christians became more actively involved in the credit market.[257]

The scale of that credit market following the Statute of Acton Burnell (1283), which in England at last placed Christian lenders on a par with Jewish lenders, can be estimated from the certificates of debt registered under the 1285 Statute of Merchants. Between 1290 and 1309 the annual total of registered certificates ranged between 167 and 864, with a total value of £3,000 to £27,000.[258] Although the average value of debt was an impressive £17 in 1284–9, and thereafter became progressively higher still, large numbers of relatively modest debts were registered, sufficient to cover the purchase price of several acres of average quality land such as many a husbandman must have contracted. Indeed, the creditors and debtors include representatives from most of the principal walks of life: rural and urban, lay and ecclesiastical, and humble and illustrious. Whether the certificates are truly representative of all the relevant debts contracted in the kingdom is a moot point, but, if they are, Pamela Nightingale reckons that they represent an average unpaid debt of at least £10,000 per year.[259] If a fifth of all contracted debts remained unpaid, this represents credit with a total value of £50,000, equivalent to 2.6 per cent of the total taxable wealth of the nation, both lay and ecclesiastical, and maybe 1.0–1.5 per cent of national income. Significantly, as the nation's taxable wealth waned from its medieval peak in 1290–1, so the size of its debt grew, to as much as £150,000 in some years.[260] In all probability, these are minimum estimates of the value of credit. Given

[255] Mundill (2010).
[256] Stacey (1995), 101: Jews 'were not usually interested in acquiring possession of landed property itself. Christians were'. For the situation in the Lordship of Ireland see O'Sullivan (1962), 26–86.
[257] Stacey (1995), 101.   [258] Nightingale (2004b), 15.
[259] Nightingale (2004b), 15.   [260] Jenks (1998); Nightingale (2004b), 12, 15.

annual rates of interest in excess of 10 per cent, most loans were given short term, for months rather than years.[261]

Kings needed credit on a massive scale in order to wage war. Their aristocratic and ecclesiastical elites borrowed in order to pay taxes, build, and finance a lifestyle of largess and conspicuous consumption. Additionally, those directly involved in agricultural production needed credit to help bridge the inevitable lags between sowing and harvesting, rearing and shearing, breeding and culling. Husbandmen bought land, livestock, seed, implements and buildings on credit, which they then counted upon their harvests of wool and grain to repay. At greater risk, they borrowed to expand their operations against the security of their land and livestock.[262] Many monastic houses, in particular, got into serious financial difficulties by making bulk wool sales in advance to Italian merchants, which for one reason or another they were then unable to deliver.[263] Those forced into bankruptcy were put into receivership until their debts were paid off.[264] Their difficulties echoed those of the many small producers, whose precarious credit arrangements were undone by the recurrent harvest failures that punctuated the first half of the fourteenth century, commencing in the 1290s.[265] The more commercialized the economy became, the more dependent it undoubtedly became upon credit.

Those with credit to advance were professional moneylenders, traders and townsmen, and those, notably country rectors, whose incomes greatly exceeded their household expenditure. Pleas of debt in manorial courts, borough courts, county courts and royal courts highlight the scale and extent of these credit operations and who was engaged in them.[266] Yet for all credit's pervasiveness, especially in the most populous and commercialized parts of the country in the south and east, the capital market was not as yet strongly centralized. Analysis of debt litigation as recorded in the Court of Common Pleas during the Michaelmas Term 1329 demonstrates that London may have been the nation's single greatest source of credit but its lending activities nonetheless remained largely confined to proximate counties in the south and east.[267] The city's rise to become the capital of the English credit market lay in the future.[268]

Clark has used perpetual rent charges to infer the cost of capital since 1170. Until the 1330s annual interest rates never fell below 8 per cent,

[261] Bell and others (2009a).   [262] Schofield and Mayhew (2002).
[263] Lloyd (1977), 289–95; Bell and others (2007).
[264] For examples see Lloyd (1977), 289–90.
[265] Schofield (1997); Briggs (2008), 149–75.
[266] On debt cases recorded in manorial courts see Clark (1981); Briggs (2003); Briggs (2004); Briggs (2008).
[267] Centre for Metropolitan History (2000).   [268] Keene (2000a).

mostly exceeded 10 per cent and at their peak in the 1320s exceeded 12 per cent.[269] Interest rates on loans were typically higher due to the risk that debtors might default: the greater the perceived risk of default the costlier the credit, especially when there was little or no collateral to offset the risk. Between 1270 and 1340 English kings, with the tax revenues of the realm available as collateral, were sufficiently creditworthy to be able to borrow at annual interest rates of around 15 per cent.[270] Annual interest rates on short-term loans negotiated during the financial emergencies of 1294–5 and 1340–1 were nevertheless as much as ten times greater.[271] On both occasions war simultaneously increased the need to borrow and dramatically inflated the costs of doing so. In their urgent quest for substantial military finance, it was mostly to the Italian merchant bankers that the three Edwards turned.[272]

The returns that the Ricciardi, Frescobaldi, Bardi, Peruzzi and other major Italian banking houses could secure from lending to the English Crown were higher than those obtainable from the Italian city republics. The latter, as was consistent with their superior wealth, more advanced commercial development and greater institutional stability, appear to have enjoyed the lowest interest rates in Europe.[273] According to Epstein, annual interest rates on long-term loans averaged 8–12 per cent in Venice between 1285 and 1326 and 6–12 per cent in Genoa from 1303 to 1340.[274] In all cases, various devices were employed to ensure that Christian lenders of capital and credit did not fall foul of the Church's prohibition of usury. Thus, interest payments might be disguised as 'gifts' to the lender, compensation for 'delayed' repayment, or by creative accounting which overstated the size of the loan received.[275]

2.05.2: Silver output and money supply In Italy use of coins as a medium of exchange, unit of account and store of value extended back to at least Roman times. Britain, in contrast, along with much of northern Europe, lapsed into coinlessness following collapse of Imperial Roman rule. Not until the early seventh century were coins again minted in England. Several centuries then elapsed before money came into general use, since this was contingent upon the supply of specie expanding and unit value of individual specie declining to the point where a penny would buy

---

[269] Clark (1988).   [270] Bell and others (2009a), 419, 432.
[271] Bell and others (2009a), 417, 419, 432.
[272] Prestwich (1980), 33, 85, 106, 217, 223.
[273] Epstein (2000a), 19–20.   [274] Epstein (2000a), 20.
[275] Hunt and Murray (1999), 70–3; Bell and others (2009a), 422–5; Briggs (2008), 74–9.

a loaf of bread and its fractions – the half-penny and farthing (quarter-penny) – lesser items and quantities. For this to happen required, in turn, a sustained expansion in silver bullion supply. Until then barter remained the normal means of exchange and rents and other payments continued for the most part to be rendered in kind.

Around 1130 silver-bearing ores were discovered in northern England (Cumberland, Northumberland, Durham) and a minor silver rush ensued.[276] Briefly, England became a significant silver producer. Then, in 1168, far richer deposits of silver ore were found at Freiberg in Germany and a boom in European silver production began which was to last the next 160 years.[277] Output from the Freiberg mines rose rapidly to a peak in the opening years of the thirteenth century, when Peter Spufford speculates that these mines may have been producing at least twenty tons of silver a year: colossal quantities by the standards of the day and enough to strike 18 million silver pennies.[278] Un-minted silver from Freiberg quickly entered international trade. In the 1170s it was to be found at Cologne, Flanders and the Champagne fairs of northern France, from the 1180s it was being imported into England, and by the 1190s it had reached the Île de France and Italy. Re-coinages followed almost everywhere.[279] As well as promoting the greater monetization of economies, this underwrote sustained expansion of the European import of luxury commodities from Asia, which was paid for in part 'by the large-scale export of gold and silver in all forms to the Levant'.[280]

From evidence of mint records and coin hoards Martin Allen reckons that during the first forty years of the Freiberg mines' operation (c.1170–1210) the English currency grew approximately five- to six-fold, from around £33,000 to £200,000 (Table 2.2). Since this was faster than the economy could absorb, prices, which previously had remained steady for well-nigh two centuries, registered a dramatic inflation.[281] A contemporaneous growth in credit arising from establishment of private property rights in land further reinforced the price rise.[282] English livestock prices doubled and grain prices trebled during the opening quarter of the thirteenth century (Figure 2.14). The serious harvest crisis of 1203–4 sparked a particularly marked price surge but in its aftermath

---

[276] Claughton (2003) qualifies the account given by Blanchard (1996).

[277] On the mining and refining of silver see Hoffmann (2014), 219–21.

[278] Spufford (1988), 110–13. For the conversion of kilograms of silver to numbers of pennies struck and the amount of ore required to yield that quantity of silver, see Hoffmann (2014), 221.

[279] Spufford (1988), 139–40.   [280] Day (1987), 3–10.

[281] Harvey (1973); Latimer (1999).

[282] Above, Section 2.04.2; Palmer (1985b); Latimer (2011).

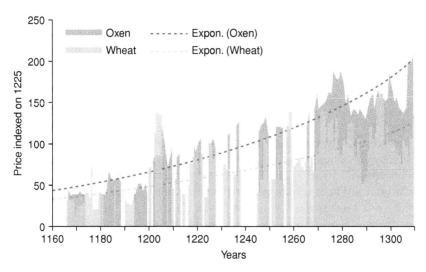

Figure 2.14 The English price inflation, 1160–1309
Source: Clark (2009)

prices failed to return to their pre-crisis level.[283] Instead, they continued to drift upwards, rising, on average, by 0.5 per cent per annum over the course of the next hundred years as the nation's stocks of bullion and credit continued to expand.[284] The sources of England's mounting wealth in silver were its booming export trades in tin, lead and especially wool and cloth.[285]

Freiberg continued to supply silver to the European economy throughout this inflationary period, although probably at a declining rate as the ores accessible using available technology were progressively mined out. From the early thirteenth century substantial quantities of silver were also produced for a time by mines opened up at Friesach, Styria and Carinthia in the Austrian Alps and Montieri in Tuscany. The ores discovered around 1230 at Jihlava on the borders of Bohemia and Moravia proved to be even richer. From mid-century output from mines at Iglesias in Sardinia also became appreciable and remained so until the 1330s. All these mines displayed a characteristic boom-to-bust chronology of production. Meanwhile, prospecting identified lesser deposits at a scatter of

[283] Britton (1937), 73–9; Cheney (1981), 580–1; Keene (2011), 45–6. Grain and livestock prices more than doubled in 1203 and remained very high the following year: Farmer (1956).
[284] But see the observations of Bolton (2012), 182–4.
[285] Miller and Hatcher (1995), 181–97; Mayhew (1999), 24–5.

other European locations, including Beer Alston in Devon, whose output helped offset the now dwindling yield from the Freiberg mines. Finally, 'at the very end of the century, the most prolific mines of the whole period were opened up at Kutná Hora in Bohemia', with a peak annual output in excess of 20–25 tons.[286]

With the sole exception of Flanders (where the peak came in the 1420s), those cities and countries with documented pre-1350 mint output – Florence, Barcelona, Sardinia, Flanders, France and England – struck more silver coins during the first half of the fourteenth century than at any subsequent time before 1500.[287] Almost certainly, this was when, buoyed up by the extended silver-mining boom, minting of the small change used in everyday exchange attained its temporal peak. Maintaining silver output was important to the prosperity of both domestic and international trade because a substantial proportion of new bullion production went immediately to make good the marked trade deficit with Asia.[288] In combination with purchases of African gold and irrecoverable losses from wear and tear and the expenses of pilgrims to the Holy Land, this meant that Latin Christendom's bullion stocks were in constant need of replenishment. Large and especially international payments were obviously more conveniently made in gold than silver, hence, unsurprisingly, it was the Italian city republics that led the way in switching to a bi-metallic currency and minting of gold coins.[289] By 1252 Genoa and Florence had accumulated sufficient gold from their trade with North Africa to commence minting the genovino and florin. Venice followed with the ducat in 1284. English mints, however, did not strike their first gold coins (first the leopard and then the noble) until the 1340s, at a time when Edward III (r. 1327–77) was making very large international payments.[290]

England may never have been a major producer of precious metal but its long-maintained positive trade balance with the continent meant that it was remarkably bullion rich and consequently among the most monetized of European economies. Allen's revised estimates indicate that the nominal value of the English currency increased more than ninety-fold between 1158 and 1319 until it probably exceeded £2 million in value (Tables 2.2 and 2.3). From just 2 pence per head in the 1150s, the supply of currency grew to approximately 90 pence per head on the eve of the Great European Famine and almost 120 pence per head in the immediate aftermath of that demographic disaster. Money supply per head thus grew

[286] Spufford (1988), 124.   [287] Spufford (1988), 415–19.   [288] Day (1987), 4–10.
[289] Spufford (1988), 176–8.   [290] Spufford (1988), 281–2.

Table 2.2 *Estimated volume of the English currency, 1086–1331*

Year	Median currency estimate	Margin of error (£)	Margin of error (%)	Approximate pence per head
1086	£30,000	± £7,500	± 25%	4 ± 1
1158	£22,500	± £7,500	± 33%	2 ± 1
1180	£37,500	± £22,500	± 60%	3 ± 2
1210	£200,000	± £100,000	± 50%	14 ± 7
1247	£475,000	± £15,000	± 3%	27 ± 1
1279	£650,000	± £150,000	± 23%	35 ± 8
1282	£835,000	± £35,000	± 4%	44 ± 2
1290	£1,150,000	± £150,000	± 13%	58 ± 8
1310	£1,700,000	± £200,000	± 12%	88 ± 10
1319	£2,050,000	± £250,000	± 12%	118 ± 14
1331	≥ £1,700,000	± £200,000	± 12%	≥ 92 ± 11

Source: Allen (2012), 344

Table 2.3 *Estimated annual growth rates of the English currency, 1158–1348*

Years	Annual % growth rate Currency	Currency per head
1158–80	2.3	2.2
1180–1210	5.7	5.1
1210–47	2.4	1.9
1247–90	2.1	1.8
1290–1319	2.0	2.5
1319–48	− 3.3	− 3.8

Source: Table 2.4

approximately thirty-fold over the course of the long thirteenth century, at a mean annual rate of 2.6 per cent. Growth was almost twice as rapid (i.e. in excess of 5 per cent) during the inflationary decades between 1180 and 1210 (Table 2.3), as the influx of silver from the Freiberg mines began to swell bullion supplies already boosted by England's own brief silver rush in the 1140s and 1150s. By the mid-thirteenth century, when almost all the metal needed for the London mint had to be obtained from continental sources, it was the London merchants who were most active in supplying it.[291] They exported commodities in exchange for bullion, engrossing an increasing share of the nation's expanding overseas trade in order to do so, to the enrichment of themselves and the metropolis. Above all, it was the sustained export of wool and un-dyed cloths to continental textile producers which drew silver in quantity into England, where the Crown's requirement that 'all transactions in England had to be in English coin' ensured that much of that silver was delivered to the mint.[292]

Inevitably, the cumulative increase in money supply stoked inflation. Prices for a wide range of staple commodities rose steadily over the course of the thirteenth century, culminating in the sky-high prices of the famine years, 1315–18. For instance, by the opening decade of the fourteenth century wheat prices were three times and ox prices four times what they had been 150 years earlier, having risen at mean annual rates of 0.9 and 1.0 per cent (Figure 2.14). As a result, the purchasing power of a silver penny declined to the point where everyday transactions of petty quantities of minor commodities came increasingly within its range. By 1300 a farthing (¼d.), the smallest unit of currency, would buy ¼ loaf of bread, ¼ to ½ pound of butter, ½ pound of cheese, 2 salted herrings, 2 ounces of wax candles, 5 pounds of salt, 6 eggs, 6 ounces of iron nails, or 2 hours of work by an unskilled farm labourer. Inflation also created an expectation of higher prices and thereby served as a stimulus to investment and greater market participation.

Under these conditions of growing bullion abundance it is little wonder that money rapidly established itself as the nation's preferred medium of exchange. The royal monopoly of minting and policy of maintaining the soundness of the coinage also promoted confidence in the currency. Simple bilateral transactions in either labour or kind consequently gave way to more intensive and complex multilateral patterns of exchange in which labour and commodities were sold for money, which was then used to pay rent and purchase goods and services. Market activity consequently grew almost exponentially, as reflected in the contemporaneous proliferation of boroughs, markets and fairs (Figure 2.13), and, with it, the opportunities for greater arbitrage between markets. As liquidity increased so transaction costs fell and specialization grew, increasing the commercial interdependence of individuals, households and communities. Resources, too, came to be judged in terms of the money that they could produce and the more astute accountants began to think in terms of profit and loss and calculate the returns being obtained from stock and land.

---

[291] Mayhew (1999), 22–4; Britnell (2000), 120.   [292] Mayhew (1999), 25.

2.05.2d Expanding agricultural output England's high-medieval demographic and commercial upswing and growing exports of high-quality wool and cheap semi-finished cloths were underpinned by rising agricultural production. The latter, in turn, was underpinned by the Medieval Solar Maximum and, for northwestern Europe, the concomitant relatively benign climatic conditions of the MCA in the form of mild, wet winters and warm summers. In common with farmers across Europe, English husbandmen practised various forms of mixed farming, since this spread risks, helped recycle nutrients, produced a range of arable and livestock products, and was eminently adaptable to a variety of physical environments and market opportunities. Extensive use was made of draught animals to perform the essential tasks of ploughing, harrowing and carting. Thus, in England by 1300 working animals of one sort or another contributed four times as much muscle power to farm work as humans.[293] Maintenance and replacement of adequate numbers of draught animals, a majority of them grass-fed oxen, were therefore vital to the sustainability of crop production. Additionally, most grain was ground mechanically by mills powered by water or, after 1180, by wind.[294]

Because of the heavy reliance upon draught animals, to whose support a substantial share of resources had to be devoted, it required a lot of land to produce the staple foodstuffs upon which the population depended. Further, the large amounts of expensive working and fixed capital that were essential elements of these farming systems, plus the mills that processed the raw grain into meal and flour, meant that the kilocalories each person consumed were comparatively costly to produce and process. The value-added component of each bowl of pottage, loaf of bread, pint of ale, pound of cheese, rasher of bacon and joint of meat was substantial. The development potential of these farming systems was nonetheless the greater for that. The heavy energy subsidy from draught animals was a latent source of higher agricultural labour productivity. Creating and maintaining the considerable stocks of fixed and working capital generated much skilled ancillary work for building workers, smiths, carpenters, and wheel and mill wrights. Millers present in almost all rural communities possessed practical knowledge of cogs and gears. Food processing, brewing and preparing agricultural raw materials (straw, flax and hemp; skins, hides and wool) for industrial production created plenty of spin-off employment opportunities for men and women. Key inputs, such as iron and millstones, usually needed to be purchased, often from a distance, and there were always excess outputs and redundant items of working

[293] Campbell (2003b).   [294] Holt (1988); Langdon (1991); Langdon (2004).

capital to be disposed of. These farming systems consequently thrived on exchange and lent themselves to the growth of manufacturing and commerce.

Livestock represented a large and indispensable source of working capital. So too did the ploughs, harrows, carts and wagons which they drew. Horses, the front hooves of oxen, shares and coulters of ploughs, rims of wheels and tips of spades were shod with iron, forged in furnaces heated with charcoal. Wood, sometimes augmented or replaced with peat or coal, was the all-purpose fuel employed for forging, heating, baking and cooking.[295] Timber was also the single largest component of most farm implements, vehicles and buildings. Of necessity, therefore, woodland comprised a key component of agricultural land use, alongside grassland for the sustenance of livestock (horses, cattle, sheep and swine) and arable land for the cultivation of an array of grain and leguminous crops (wheat, rye, barley, oats, peas, beans and vetches and mixtures of the same). It was from this spectrum of land uses and combined production of crops and livestock that English agriculture derived its predominantly mixed character. These component elements could be configured to create a wide variety of farming systems suited to different soils, terrains, climatic conditions and institutional environments, varying in their intensity and productivity, and attuned to available commercial opportunities.[296]

By c.1300 English agricultural producers were successfully feeding at least 3 million more people than in 1086, including a greatly enlarged urban population which now accounted for approximately an eighth of the total.[297] Of the several major urban centres that had come into being, London was by far the largest. It was at the climax of its medieval growth and contained at least seventy thousand inhabitants, provisioned with food and fuel from an extensive rural hinterland.[298] Had the metropolis been larger it would undoubtedly have drawn forth an increased supply of provisions from an expanded hinterland. Agriculture was also supplying an array of horticultural, arable, pastoral and woodland products to an enlarged and diversified manufacturing sector and exporting large quantities of several of these primary products overseas.[299] Together, wool and hides accounted for over 15 per cent of net agricultural output by value (Table 2.4) and wool and cloth contributed the lion's share of the growing volume of English exports. At the peak of the wool-export boom

---

[295] Galloway and others (1996).   [296] Campbell and Bartley (2006), 209–30.
[297] Campbell (2000), 386–410; Campbell (2008), 922.
[298] Campbell and others (1993); Galloway and others (1996).   [299] Campbell (2002b).

Table 2.4 *Percentage composition of total annual net English agricultural output by value, 1300–9*

Product			% of total agricultural output (net of seed and fodder) by value
Grains	Wheat	25.7	
	Rye/Maslin	3.2	49.9
	Barley/Dredge	12.0	
	Oats	8.9	
Legumes			1.3
ARABLE SUB-TOTAL			51.2
Meat	Beef and veal	2.3	
	Mutton	13.4	20.7
	Pork	5.0	
Milk			11.7
Wool			14.6
Hides			0.7
Hay			1.1
PASTORAL SUB-TOTAL			48.8
AGRICULTURAL TOTAL			100.0

Source: Broadberry and others (2015), 116–17

in the early fourteenth century the equivalent of 8–10 million fleeces were leaving the country annually.[300] Their value far exceeded that of the one net agricultural import of note, namely wine.

The single most immediate source of England's increased agricultural output was exploitation of a greatly enlarged agricultural area.[301] On the evidence of the number and size of holdings enumerated in Domesday Book, there were just under 2.5 million hectares of arable in 1086 plus at least as much grassland, a great deal of woodland and significant quantities of waste.[302] By *c.*1300, notwithstanding that much potential

---

[300] Campbell (2000), 386–9.   [301] Donkin (1973), 98–106.
[302] This figure is a re-computation of the estimate made by Seebohm (1890), 102–3. The relative merits of alternative methods of deriving estimates of the arable area from information contained in Domesday Book are discussed in Campbell (2000), 386–8.

farmland remained in reserve as common pasture and waste, royal forest, and private hunting grounds, reclamation and the conversion of grassland and woodland to tillage had very likely more than doubled the amount of arable to 5.3 million hectares (fractionally less than the record nineteenth-century area of 5.8 million hectares).[303] In many lowland arable-farming regions advance of the plough had been at the expense of permanent pasture of one sort or another, although the need to preserve some grassland for the support of predominantly grass-fed draught animals set limits to this process. Also, at a national scale these lowland pastoral losses were undoubtedly more than offset by pastoral gains elsewhere. Indeed, the national sheep flock of almost 15 million animals and cattle herd of over 2 million beasts are unaccountable unless permanent grassland remained abundant. Likewise, dominance of exports by hides, wool and woollen cloth demonstrates that internationally the country's principal comparative advantage lay in pastoral production.

Pasture rather than arable was the principal beneficiary of the clearance of woodland and forest, drainage of low-lying fenland and marshland, and enclosure and upgrading of upland 'waste'. In fact, most reclamation around England's extensive upland margins, especially that undertaken by the many newly founded Cistercian abbeys which received substantial land grants in these areas, was aimed primarily at the creation of stock farms.[304] Except when strong urban demand for fuel placed a premium upon the preservation of timber stocks, it was woodland rather than grassland which bore the brunt of the expansion of the agricultural area, with the result that timber and wood often became the land-use products in most limited supply.[305] Access to and harvesting of such scarce resources became carefully regulated and trade developed to rectify the worst deficiencies. Live animals could be moved over considerable distances and their products were better able to bear the costs of overland transport than grain, hay, firewood or timber, whose shipment in bulk was heavily dependent upon access to cheap water transport.[306]

Reclamation was a labour-intensive task and typically proceeded via a series of step changes in land use. At Podimore in Somerset, for example, Harold Fox has demonstrated how marshland was upgraded, first, to rough pasture and then, by further ditching and draining, to mowable meadow capable of yielding an annual hay crop.[307] The upshot of this conversion from marsh to meadow was a lasting increase in labour demands per unit area. When arable was substituted for pasture

---

[303] Broadberry and others (2015), 65–73.   [304] Donkin (1978), 104–34.
[305] Galloway and others (1996), 449.   [306] Farmer (1991a and 1991b).
[307] Fox (1986), 544.

labour inputs rose approximately five-fold, hence a significant increase in available labour supply was normally a precondition for this kind of changeover. Arable land could also be cultivated with varying degrees of intensity, depending upon the frequency with which it was fallowed, the choice of crops grown, and the amount of effort expended upon the maintenance and improvement of soil fertility. Rising ratios of labour to land during the twelfth and thirteenth centuries thus engendered more intensive systems of husbandry.

Involution, as it was termed by Clifford Geertz, undoubtedly went furthest on the smallest holdings, since they were usually capital deficient and far better endowed with labour than land. Customary tenants at Martham in Norfolk at the close of the thirteenth century had at least six times the available labour resources per unit of land as the prior of Norwich on his 90-hectare demesne.[308] Even so, the Martham demesne was itself remarkable for the intensity with which it was cultivated and the high yields per unit of arable thereby achieved. Cultivation methods on the bishop of Winchester's demesne at Rimpton in Somerset were significantly less intensive, although labour inputs per hectare on this demesne had increased by 40 per cent over the course of the thirteenth century.[309] Adoption of written accounting here as elsewhere facilitated more careful management and closer supervision of the workers. As labour inputs rose on demesne farms, so tasks became more specialized. Partial or complete substitution of waged for servile labour helped improve the quality of labour inputs while development of a monetized labour market facilitated greater seasonal use of casual labour remunerated by the task for weeding, manuring, mowing, shearing, harvesting, threshing and winnowing.[310]

In the eleventh century low land values and dear capital had deterred investment. Thereafter, rising population, expanding commerce and more clearly defined property rights drove up land values and rendered capital investment more worthwhile (although high interest rates remained an obstacle).[311] By far the most spectacular capital investments of the age were the great drainage schemes, involving cooperation between several communities and the digging of drains and construction of dykes and sluices, which brought vast areas of potentially fertile alluvial marshland into agricultural use. Nowhere was the transformation greater than in the East Anglian silt fens.[312] By the 1330s land that had been

[308] Campbell (1983), 39.   [309] Campbell (2000), 341–5; Thornton (1991), 205.
[310] Stone (1997), 640–56; Farmer (1988), 760–72.   [311] Clark (1998), 265–92.
[312] Hallam (1965).

of little value in 1086 supported the greatest concentrations of taxable wealth and tax-paying population in the country.[313]

Meanwhile, grain storage and the housing of livestock benefited from substantial fixed capital investment in bigger and better farm buildings.[314] Sowing seed more thickly represented a further form of investment and was one of the surest ways of raising yields per unit area provided this was justified by the rental value of land. Seeding rates and land values attained their respective national maxima in eastern Norfolk and eastern Kent, both strongly commercialized areas of fertile soil and high population density.[315] Whereas even smallholders could afford to invest in higher seeding rates, and may have led the way in this regard, lords alone could muster the substantial capital sums required for mill construction. Under seigniorial initiative mills were built and rebuilt in large numbers throughout the twelfth and thirteenth centuries. In particular, invention of the windmill c.1180 allowed mills to be erected where there had been none before.[316] Mills enhanced the processing rather than the production of grain and as such represented an infrastructural improvement. Parallel investment in bridge construction similarly gave all classes of producer better access to markets.[317]

As the population rose and the relative scarcity of land increased, so greater emphasis was placed upon agricultural food-chains with higher productivities of food and energy per unit area. Certain crops and animals were more productive of cash, food and/or energy than others. Industrial and horticultural crops, for instance, yielded particularly high cash returns per unit area and hence gained in favour as holdings shrank in size, commercial dependence grew and the demand from craft-workers rose. Cultivation of flax and hemp appears to have been almost exclusively associated with tenant rather than seigniorial producers.[318] Processing grain into ale is far more extravagant of available kilocalories than milling it and consuming it as bread and/or pottage. Over time, therefore, the baking and stewing grains gained relative to the brewing grains and the cheaper food grains – maslin, dredge and oats – gained relative to those of highest value (i.e. wheat and barley).[319] Such simple production shifts delivered significant gains in the rate of food output per unit area, albeit at

[313] Darby (1940); Darby and others (1979), 249–56; Campbell and Bartley (2006), 320–34.
[314] Hurst (1988); Dyer (1995); Campbell and Bartley (2006), 97–103.
[315] Campbell (2000), 309–17.
[316] Holt (1988), 20–2, 171–5; Langdon (1991); Campbell and Bartley (2006), 279–98.
[317] Britnell (1995), 17–18; Harrison (2004).
[318] Evans (1985), 41–6; Livingstone (2003), 277–81.
[319] Campbell (2000), 238–48, 399–400.

the sacrifice of dietary preferences: ale and meat, especially beef, dwindled in their relative contribution to diets, whereas bread, particularly of the coarser sort, pottage and dairy produce all grew.[320] Substituting legumes for bare fallows was part of this process. They provided a nutritious food source for humans, swine and draught animals alike and had the further merit that they helped vary rotations and fix atmospheric nitrogen within the soil.

Once the decision was taken to cultivate fodder crops, with all the extra drudgery that this involved, it made sense to substitute horses for oxen since horses convert fodder into work with greater efficiency. Over the course of the twelfth and thirteenth centuries horses came into more general use for farm work of all kinds, but especially for carting and harrowing. Their adoption progressed furthest in the more commercialized and urbanized east and southeast of England, particularly on tenant holdings where they served as an all-purpose work animal.[321] Pigs, sty-fed with legumes, were likewise the most efficient producers of meat and were quintessentially a smallholder's animal.[322] Poultry performed a similar role since eggs are one of the most nutritious of all food sources.[323] Milk, which could be processed into butter and cheese, was of comparable food value and producers who substituted horses for oxen often did so with the aim of making more effective use of scarce meadows and pastures by focusing more exclusively upon cattle-based dairying.[324] These herds displayed a strong demographic bias towards mature females in contrast to those kept to reproduce replacement oxen in which male and immature beasts were more prominent. Sheep were the most land-extensive and least food-productive animal of all and, but for the industrial value of their wool, would have lost out to their more food-productive rivals over this period. Instead, rising demand for high-quality English wool from the expanding textile industries of Flanders and Italy ensured that tenants and lords alike stocked sheep in large numbers, with the result that mutton was the meat in greatest supply.

Since grain remained the staple foodstuff, raising crop output in step with population was an obvious priority. Instead of attempting to improve crop yields per se, medieval husbandmen aimed at producing more from a given area of land by lengthening and varying rotations and thereby reducing the frequency of unproductive bare fallows. Within the ostensibly rigid framework set by regular commonfield systems greater rotational diversity and flexibility could be achieved by creating extra field

[320] Dyer (1989), 151–60.   [321] Langdon (1986).
[322] Biddick (1989), 121–5; Campbell (2000), 165–8.
[323] Slavin (2009).   [324] Campbell (1992).

divisions better able to accommodate temporary *inhoks* from the fallow. Formal replacement of two-course with three-course cropping, in contrast, required a more far-reaching structural reorganization and for that reason was less common than has sometimes been supposed.[325] Consequently, it was where institutional obstacles to reform were weakest, in areas of irregular and flexible field systems, that the greatest changes to rotations tended to occur.

In the most advanced farming regions, by the close of the thirteenth century, rotations had evolved in which cropping was virtually continuous and annual fallows were kept to an essential minimum.[326] These developments were supported by wider adoption of a raft of fertility-enhancing measures, including cultivation of nitrogen-fixing legumes, systematic folding of sheep, and regular application of farmyard manure, urban night-soil, marl, lime and any other available fertility-enhancing agents.[327] To counter the weed growth engendered by longer rotations, bare fallows were subject to multiple summer ploughings, seed-beds were thoroughly prepared, seed was sown more thickly especially at the tail end of rotations, and the more valuable crops were systematically weeded. Crucially, the increased draught-power and manure requirements of these intensive cropping systems meant that maintaining high stocking densities was a sine qua non of their development.

Emergence of integrated mixed-farming systems geared towards the intensive production of grain supported by the rapid recycling of nutrients through livestock partially fed on produced fodder (both hay and crops) was an especially striking achievement of the period. In these systems the arable and pastoral components of husbandry were mutually supportive, with the arable supplying fodder and temporary fallow grazing to livestock, upon which the arable, in turn, depended for manure, traction and haulage.[328] Without this functional symbiosis these ecologically demanding arable-based mixed-farming systems were unsustainable in more than the short term.[329] Measures aimed at maintaining sustainability included systematic coppicing of woodland, close regulation and stinting of available grassland, intensive management of hay meadows, tight control of fallow grazing and folding, development of convertible-farming systems in which land alternated between arable and temporary pasture, a greater reliance upon fodder crops (principally legumes and oats) in conjunction with the stall- and sty-feeding of animals (especially in winter), and a more systematic recycling of nitrogen via the collection

[325] Hall (1982), 44–55; Astill (1988), 75–80; Fox (1986).
[326] Campbell (2000), 290–301.   [327] Smith (1943), 135–7; Campbell (1983), 31–6.
[328] Overton and Campbell (1991), 42–3.   [329] Pretty (1990), 1–19.

of animal wastes and their application to the arable fields.[330] In eastern Norfolk, one of the country's most naturally fertile, populous and innovative farming regions, fully fledged integrated mixed-farming systems had already emerged on the estates of St Benet's Abbey by the 1240s.[331] Over the next hundred years they were elaborated further, with the result that mean grain yields displayed a modest upward trend over the period 1275–1349 as methods were refined and labour inputs per unit area were ratcheted ever higher.[332]

The shift to more intensive methods of production inevitably courted diminishing returns, to labour if not to land. This was most effectively countered by greater specialization and exchange.[333] Trade enabled land-deficient areas to draw upon the resources of land-abundant areas and encouraged individual farmers to concentrate upon what they could best produce, thereby maximizing comparative advantage. The extent to which specialization resulted was determined by the size of the market: during the twelfth and thirteenth centuries local, regional, national and international markets for agricultural produce all grew. Demand, to some degree, became more concentrated. Husbandmen almost everywhere were influenced in some way by these expanding commercial opportunities, although their capacity to exploit them was constrained by the often-punitive cost of delivering their produce to market.[334]

Pastoral husbandry was particularly open to specialization due to the ease with which animals and certain of their products – wool, hides, bacon, butter and cheese – could be transported without deterioration over long distances. Moreover, the demand for animals from rural producers far exceeded that from urban consumers. Accordingly, farmers increasingly specialized in different species of livestock, different stages of livestock production and different types of livestock product.[335] It was to accommodate the seasonally specific sales generated by these pastoral activities that so many new fairs were licensed between c.1150 and 1250 (Figure 2.13). To these fairs came upland pastoral farmers with surplus stock to sell and lowland arable farmers seeking replacement draught oxen and horses. Unwanted male calves sold off by dairy farmers were bought up by petty producers who lacked breeding resources of their own; in due course the finished oxen would be sold on and either put to

---

[330] Rackham (1986), 62–118; Witney (1990); Campbell (1995a), 290; Simmons (1974).
[331] Norfolk Record Office (Norwich) Diocesan Est/1 & 2,1.
[332] Boserup (1965); Campbell (1991).   [333] Persson (1988), 71–3; Grantham (1999).
[334] Campbell (1995b), 91–4; Campbell (1997a), 235–42; Campbell and others (1993), 46–75.
[335] Overton and Campbell (1992); Campbell (1996).

the plough or butchered. Quantities of cheese and butter were also mar-keted, output of which varied with the seasonality of milk production.[336] Wool, some of the finest of which was produced in the remotest locations, was even more highly commercialized and was often sold wholesale and in bulk and occasionally, and at some risk, in advance of the wool clip.[337] No agricultural commodity was transported and sold at a profit over a greater distance.

Within the arable sector the opportunities for commercial specializa-tion were equally real but geographically more circumscribed, due to the higher unit transport costs of grain, especially overland. Above a local scale, access to cheap bulk transport by river and sea thus shaped patterns of arable specialization.[338] The concentrated demand of major urban centres was a spur to specialization within their hinterlands, espe-cially on demesnes whose grain output was, on average, well in excess of seigniorial consumption requirements. By the close of the thirteenth cen-tury London's normal grain-provisioning hinterland encompassed well over ten thousand square kilometres. Within that hinterland the choice of grains produced was consistent with the cost-distance of transport-ing them to the metropolis. Thus, the cheapest fodder and bread grains were produced in greatest quantity close to the city, high-quality brewing grains at an intermediate distance, and wheat – the most highly prized bread grain – at the greatest distance of all.[339] Commercial production of hay and of firewood, charcoal and timber bore similar cost-distance relationships to the London market.[340]

Great cities like London were the forcing ground of agricultural change as levels and contours of economic rent within their hinterlands were reconfigured in response to expanding urban demand. North of the Alps, however, with the conspicuous exception of urbanized Flanders, they and the commercial opportunities they presented remained few and far between. Even London's 'von Thünen field of force' embraced, for all commodities, no more than perhaps a fifth of the total national land area, less than half of which was engaged in the regular supply of grain to the city. Moreover, within this area of regular grain supply relatively low levels of economic rent prevailed over high, with the result that exten-sive systems of production prevailed over intensive.[341] This is consistent with the von Thünen model which predicts that, within the provisioning hinterland of a major city, high-yielding intensive systems will occupy

[336] Campbell (1992), 113–14; Campbell (1995a), 172–3; Atkin (1994).
[337] Power (1941); Lloyd (1977).
[338] Campbell (1995b), 81–91; Campbell (1997a); Campbell (2002b).
[339] Campbell and others (1993), 76–7, 111–44.
[340] Galloway and others (1996).   [341] Campbell (2000), 425–6.

6 per cent of the arable, moderately productive and intensive systems a further 54 per cent, and low-yielding extensive systems 40 per cent of the arable.[342] Lesser urban centres had a weaker forcing effect upon economic rent and their grain-provisioning hinterlands were far smaller: Exeter's extended no further than 20 miles from the city, Winchester's to a maximum of 12 miles, and Cambridge's to just 10 miles.[343]

Before 1300 small towns were very much the English norm, as they were in all the least urbanized countries of Europe, with the result that urban demand was more dispersed than concentrated. Low economic rent and extensive farming systems therefore remained very much the order of the day. Low unit land values characterized half of the total agricultural area south of the River Trent and were predominant throughout those southern and western parts of the country at furthest remove from the metropolis and the thriving commercial entrepôts of the east coast (Figure 2.15). For husbandmen in these areas 'the local markets and the communities around them were the more important outlets for the produce of the countryside'.[344] Such markets were, however, incapable of stimulating economic rent and agricultural intensification to the same extent as great cities, which is why evidence drawn from estates located in these regions conveys a powerful impression of technological inertia and low land productivity.[345] Until there was a quantum leap in the scale of English urban centres and major proto-industries took root in the countryside, incentives to rural producers to adopt more intensive and productive farming systems were inevitably selective in nature and geographically circumscribed in impact.

When and where the right economic incentives existed, the uniquely detailed and abundant pre-Black Death English evidence shows that medieval husbandmen were active in upgrading their methods and increasing their output. Contrary to older pessimistic verdicts, they were not wilfully backward, nor was technology deficient. Rather, the problem was that across large parts of the country, as across broad swathes of Europe, the demand incentives were not yet strong enough to justify widespread adoption of the more progressive and intensive methods, with the extra demands these made upon labour and/or capital. While these economic conditions prevailed agriculture remained in a low productivity trap and unable to achieve its full technological potential. The

---

[342] Thünen (1826). South of the Trent, high unit land values accounted for 12 per cent, average unit land values for 35 per cent and low unit land values for 52 per cent of the agricultural area (Figure 2.15).

[343] Campbell and others (1993), 172–4; Campbell (1997), 241–4; Lee (2003), 261.

[344] Farmer (1991a), 329.   [345] Astill and Grant (1988), 213–16.

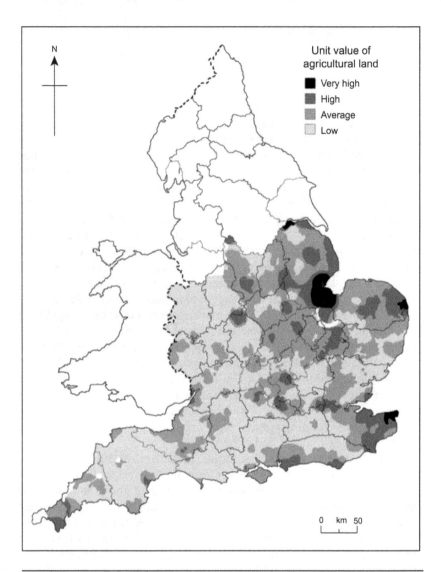

		Mean ratio (unit value : unit value) of		
Land category	Mean unit value of arable (pence)	grassland : arable	meadow : arable	meadow : pasture
Very high	16.2	1.1	1.3	2.9
High	7.0	2.2	2.8	3.3
Average	4.3	3.6	4.3	3.9
Low	2.6	5.7	6.5	5.3
All	3.9	4.5	5.3	4.5

Figure 2.15 The unit value of agricultural land in England, 1300–49, according to the *Inquisitiones post mortem*
Source: Campbell and Bartley (2006): 191–5

intensive extremes of coppiced woodland, enclosed grassland, more-or-less continuously cropped arable, and closely integrated mixed-farming systems exemplify best contemporary practice but were confined in their adoption to relatively limited areas of high population density, resource scarcity and strong market demand in the east midlands, East Anglia and parts of the southeast. Elsewhere, scope for fuller adoption of these methods remained largely unfulfilled and had to await the far-reaching socio-economic changes of the seventeenth and eighteenth centuries. Until then, for inland districts at a distance from major domestic markets, the best commercial prospects lay in the extensive production of high-quality wool for export markets or rearing of replacement animals for onward sale.

In England the story of agricultural change before 1300 is therefore one of uneven development; different regions contributed to the overall increase in agricultural output in different ways and to very different degrees. The country illustrates the variety and latent productivity potential of medieval mixed-farming systems and the entirely valid reasons why so many producers chose not to exploit the full technological potential of those systems. Consequently, although agricultural production increased significantly over the course of the twelfth and thirteenth centuries, output growth barely kept pace with population. As relative prices of the better-quality and higher-status foodstuffs rose, growing numbers of poor households were obliged to sacrifice their dietary preferences and trade down to cheaper sources of kilocalories.[346] Eventually probably at least a third of English households were subsisting on merely a 'bare-bones' basket of consumables. Their dietary poverty arose less from agricultural supply-side constraints than from the inability of the manufacturing and service sectors to generate sufficient well-remunerated employment to raise incomes and provide commercially minded farmers with the demand incentives to take maximum advantage of available technological opportunities.

2.05.3   Urbanization as a proxy indicator of relative economic development

Urbanization ratios (the proportion of the population resident in towns of a given minimum size), of which estimates exist for all major European regions *c*.1300, provide a useful proxy measure of economic development.[347] As Simon Kuznets has enunciated, urbanization represents 'an increasing division of labour within the country, growing specialization, and the shift of many activities from non-market-oriented

---

[346] Campbell (2000), 238–48.   [347] Bairoch and others (1988), 259.

Table 2.5 *Size distribution and estimated populations of European towns,* c. *1300*

Urban population (,000s)	Europe (excluding Russia)		England and Wales	
	% number	% urban population	% number	% urban population
50+	0.9	13.9	1.6	18.3
20 – <50	4.5	17.8	1.6	6.0
10 – <20	11.8	20.5	4.7	10.2
5 – <10	24.0	21.1	29.7	35.1
2 – < 5	58.8	26.6	62.5	30.4
Approximate total	1,484	10,560,000	64	382,000

Source: Europe, estimated from Bairoch and others (1988), 255, 271. England and Wales, from Campbell (2008), 911

pursuit within the family or the village to specialized market-oriented business firms'.[348] Typically, only economies with developed manufacturing and service sectors and actively involved in international trade were able to support major urban centres with 50,000 or more inhabitants and urbanization ratios in excess of 20 per cent. Such economies bear out E. A. Wrigley's maxim that 'a rising level of real income per head and a rising proportion of urban dwellers are likely to be linked phenomena in a pre-industrial economy'.[349] By 1300, after almost 250 years of sustained commercial development, Paul Bairoch, Jean Batou and Pierre Chèvre estimate that 7–9 per cent of Europeans lived in towns with 5,000 or more inhabitants, a proportion that might almost double if the many petty urban places that came into being during this formative quarter-millennium are included. In England, for instance, significantly more people lived in small towns with populations of 2–5,000 than in substantial cities with populations of 20,000 or more and there was a long tail of petty boroughs with even smaller populations. As Table 2.5 indicates, the situation in Europe as a whole was not radically different.

England's urbanization ratio calculated for towns with a minimum population of 5,000 was just under 7 per cent and therefore slightly below the European average. Wales, Ireland, Scotland, Scandinavia, European Russia, Poland, Germany, Switzerland, Austria and Hungary all had urbanization ratios as low or lower. All possessed significantly more towns in 1300 than in 1000 but, since the economies of these countries

[348] Kuznets (1966), 271.   [349] Wrigley (1985), 683.

remained rooted in primary production, few of these towns had grown to a great size. The lifeblood of their many fledgling and as yet petty urban places was the weekly and daily exchange of food and drink, crops and livestock, oil and wine, salt and fish, wool, furs, hides and leather, iron, copper, lead and tin, and an array of craft goods including textiles, metal wares and pottery. It was upon regular exchange of these commodities, in trivial quantities by petty traders as well as substantial consignments by wholesale merchants, that commercial life depended.[350] Across a broad swathe of northwestern, northern and interior Europe it was this small-town phenomenon which over the course of the twelfth and thirteenth centuries had elevated urbanization ratios to new, albeit modest, levels. It denoted economic structures in which commerce had advanced but within which centripetal forces were as yet but weakly developed. Except for a few prominent centres, engagement in great commerce remained decidedly circumscribed.

Because towns with at least 5,000 inhabitants are historically the most conspicuous, it is nevertheless upon these that most systematic analyses of the scale of European urbanization c.1300 have been based. Whereas only two Irish, two Scottish and nineteen English towns meet this size criterion, Malanima (building on the earlier work of K. J. Beloch) reckons that in Italy there were at least 193 cities of this size, containing an estimated 20.6 per cent of the country's population.[351] Including lesser urban places with fewer than 5,000 inhabitants would obviously raise this proportion, to maybe over a third of the total. Patently, Italy was far more urbanized and, by implication, economically developed than the British Isles, where the equivalent urbanization ratio was less than 5 per cent.[352] In fact, Italian cities accounted for almost a third of Europe's urban population and a quarter of the continent's largest cities (24 out of 103) with populations of at least 20,000.[353] So many urban residents aggregated into such large urban centres (seven of them with at least 50,000 inhabitants and at least three, Florence, Venice and Milan, with populations of at least 100,000) could only be supported where agricultural workers regularly produced substantial surpluses and incomes per head were sufficiently high to sustain significant employment in manufacturing and services.[354]

Between 1000 and 1300 Malanima reckons that the proportion of Italians living in substantial towns doubled from a tenth to a fifth of the

[350] Hilton (1985); Masschaele (1997).   [351] Malanima (1998).
[352] Campbell (2008), 911, 931.   [353] Bairoch and others (1988), 259.
[354] Kuznets (1966), 271.

total. Urbanization was especially rapid in the centre and north of Italy; here the proportion of the population living in such towns approximately trebled from 5–8 per cent to 21.4 per cent of the total, increasing at a faster rate than the population as a whole; a clear symptom of economic vigour.[355] The peninsula's political fragmentation into a constellation of rival city-states nevertheless ensured that, unlike London in England (*c.*70–80,000) and Paris in France (150–200,000), no single primate city dominated. Instead, several relatively autonomous urban sub-systems prevailed, each headed by a large city: Tuscany and the Arno valley by Florence, the Veneto by Venice, and Lombardy by Milan. In fact, the extensive seaborne urban systems headed by the great maritime entrepôts of Venice and Genoa were largely external to Italy.

In Italy urban life had survived the fall of the Roman Empire, and the same was true of many parts of southern Europe, so that here the roots of the medieval urban revival went deep. In much of northern Europe, however, there was no such continuity, hence the foundation and growth of towns from the tenth century represent a radical new departure. In this context, the scale and vigour of urban growth in the Low Countries is especially striking, so much so that by 1300 levels of urbanization were broadly comparable, and maybe even superior, to those attained in central and northern Italy (Table 2.5), where growth had begun from a higher base. Bas van Bavel estimates an overall urbanization ratio of 20 per cent for the Low Countries, rising to 27 per cent in Belgian Brabant and 30 per cent in Artois (comparable to the 27.9–30.4 per cent estimated by Malanima for Tuscany at the same date).[356] A concentration of major towns with populations in excess of 25,000, comprising Tournai, Ypres, Bruges and Ghent (the largest, with 60–80,000 inhabitants) in inland Flanders and Lille, Arras, Douai and Saint-Omer in Artois and Walloon Flanders, underpinned these high urban ratios and bears witness to the economic vitality of the preceding centuries. It follows that growth of Flemish GDP per head between 1000 and 1300 is likely to have been at least as impressive as that of Italy.[357] Towns in Holland had also been developing fast, generating an urbanization ratio which grew from approximately 5 per cent in 1200 to 13 per cent by 1300.[358]

[355] Malanima (2002), 375, 380. On the estimates provided by Zanden (2009), 40, the proportion of the Italian population resident in towns with at least 10,000 inhabitants rose from *c.*12 per cent in 1000 to *c.*13.5 per cent in 1300.

[356] Bavel (2010), 281; Malanima (1998), 104.   [357] Bavel (2010), 280–1, 375.

[358] Bavel (2010), 281. Zanden (2009), 40, implies respective urbanization ratios for Flanders and Italy of *c.*20 per cent and *c.*13.5 per cent for towns with 10,000+ inhabitants by 1300. His equivalent rate for the Netherlands is *c.*4.5 per cent.

On the estimates of Bairoch and others, no other countries at this date had urbanization ratios as great and hence, by implication, they must all have been poorer. Iberia, France and the Balkans all had urbanization ratios close to the European average of 9–10 per cent and for Spain Carlos Álvarez-Nogal and Leandro Prados de la Escosura have proposed a GDP per head in 1300 of £1,050.[359] This is 40 per cent below Malanima's estimate of $1,650 for the centre and north of Italy at the same date but consistent with the fact that Spain was only half as urbanized. In England GDP per head at this time was lower still, just $750, and so too was its urbanization ratio of 7 per cent. The latter was broadly on a par with that of Germany, where there had been a similar proliferation of new, small urban centres in conjunction with the eastward extension of German settlement during the twelfth and thirteenth centuries. The urban populations of both countries were more dispersed than concentrated.

Outside the axis of commercial activity that extended across Europe from the Mediterranean to the southern North Sea, urbanization ratios were mostly well below the European average.[360] Maybe in the poorest and least populous of these commercially most peripheral economies – Scandinavia, European Russia and east-central Europe – GDP per head was as low as the $500–600 that Angus Maddison took to be the norm almost everywhere in Europe at this date (and which is the level prevailing in the poorest countries of sub-Saharan Africa today).[361] Their sparse populations were incapable of sustaining the levels of economic specialization and commercial development attained in populous, urbanized and commercially proactive Italy and Flanders. They may have been resource rich but this did not prevent them from remaining economically underdeveloped and consequently in terms of GDP per head, both absolutely and relatively poor. These countries were in a low-productivity trap: limited market demand restricted the division of labour while low labour productivity consequent upon the lack of economic specialization restricted the growth of market demand. For them the challenge was how to initiate Smithian growth, whereas for the leading commercial economies of Italy and Flanders it was how to sustain it.[362] In the latter's case closer integration of Europe's North Sea and Mediterranean orbits of exchange and the forging of closer links with the vibrant commerce of Asia appeared to offer the way forward.

---

[359] The Spanish urbanization ratio excludes rural workers resident in towns: Álvarez-Nogal and Prados de la Escosura (2013), 13–14, 23, 34–6.

[360] Bairoch and others (1988), 258, 259.   [361] Maddison (2007).

[362] Smithian gains are those which stemmed from market growth and a greater division of labour, as elaborated by Adam Smith in Book 1 of *An inquiry into the nature and causes of the wealth of nations* (1976).

Concentrated urban growth was a key engine of this high-medieval phase of Smithian growth through its differentiating effects upon both the functions and hierarchies of central places and associated patterns of economic rent. Great commerce, in turn, underpinned the wealth and populations of the largest cities. By 1300 a dozen European cities had achieved populations of at least fifty thousand. Several of the greatest – Constantinople, Venice, Genoa, Milan and Bruges – owed their superior size and prosperity to their active engagement in international trade. Others, notably Florence and the agglomeration of Flemish textile-producing towns, prospered as suppliers of manufactured goods to international markets. A third group – Rome, Naples, Paris and London – were major ecclesiastical and royal capitals, fashion setters, and conspicuous consumers and distribution centres of the commodities supplied by international commerce. No city in Latin Christendom attained this great size, with all the manifold multiplier effects emanating from such a concentration of demand, without a direct and/or indirect involvement in international trade. Hence, for as long as commercial expansion could be maintained, their fortunes were likely to be assured. Such expansion was contingent upon a continued lowering of transaction costs, improved access to overseas markets and sources of prestigious trade goods, and maintenance of the silver production that paid for Europe's net trade deficit with Asia.

The twelfth and thirteenth centuries witnessed a marked widening and deepening of Europe's own circuits of exchange, as its emergent Mediterranean and North Sea trading networks coalesced into a single, integrated trans-Alpine trading system. This protracted process began in the late eleventh century with a number of formative developments. In the Mediterranean the Byzantine–Venetian Treaty of 1082 bestowed major commercial advantages upon Venice, including tax-free access to trade with the Byzantine Empire. In 1099 the success of the First Crusade endowed Genoa with similar commercial advantages in Syria and Palestine. Italy's two premier maritime republics now enjoyed enhanced access to supplies of Asian silks, spices and ceramics together with greatly expanded marketing opportunities in the Aegean, eastern Mediterranean and Levant. At around the same time, numbers of Italian and southern French cities were repudiating the authority of feudal overlords and transforming themselves into self-governing communes better able to broker reciprocal trading arrangements with other cities and their merchant guilds.

Jewish merchants were prominent participants in this re-emergent market-based socio-economic order, circulating information, advancing credit and, crucially, brokering exchange between the Christian and Muslim worlds.[363] As a dispersed and stateless people, their far-flung international connections stood them in commercial good stead, while Judaism encouraged literacy and placed no proscription upon usury. Social exclusion debarred them from conventional avenues of material advancement through land and office and deflected their energy and enterprise into commerce. These qualities recommended the Jews to William I and Henry I, who invited them to establish communities in England, whose commerce, along with that of much of northern Europe, was at a less advanced stage of development.

In the North Sea region it was during the closing years of the eleventh century and opening decades of the twelfth century that great lords and powerful princes founded the fairs which, under their patronage, subsequently rose to national and international prominence. The English fairs established between 1096 (St Giles, Winchester) and 1125 (Boston) were all conveniently located relative to the east and south coast ports frequented by foreign merchants and were strategically positioned with respect both to sources of wool production (increasingly sought after by foreign buyers) and the urban centres of the country's expanding textile industry, especially York, Beverley, Louth, Lincoln, Leicester, Stamford and Northampton.[364] At around the same time the counts of Flanders founded the great Flemish fairs of Ypres, Lille, Mesen, Torhout and Bruges, their sites possibly chosen in response to the commercial potential presented by a nascent urban wool-textile industry. Here, wool, cloth and other goods were bought and sold and bullion exchanged on an ever-greater scale by merchants attracted from an increasingly wide radius. By the 1180s named cloths from Flanders and northern France (a sure sign of product specialization) were being sold throughout the Mediterranean and Levant and textile output had so outrun local wool supplies that English wool was being imported.[365] Meanwhile, in the 1130s the discovery of silver-bearing ores in northern England initiated a European silver rush that successive discoveries in Germany, Bohemia, Sardinia and the Balkans would sustain for the next two hundred years. Shortly afterwards the Champagne fairs began their rise as the pivotal hinge between the expanding commerce of southern and northern Europe.

Merchants, acting individually and collectively, were the key protagonists of these widening orbits of international exchange. Flemings, with

[363] Lopez (1971), 60–2.   [364] Moore (1985), 10–62; Chorley (1988).
[365] Lloyd (1977), 5.

cloth to sell and wool to buy, were early prominent in the wider North Sea region and by the end of the twelfth century were active throughout England, whose own merchants they eclipsed in energy and enterprise. Merchants from northern France were also active from an early date, followed by Brabanters and Germans. By the middle of the twelfth century these northern merchants were frequenting the Champagne fairs on a regular basis, where, from at least 1174 and increasingly from 1190, they were joined by Italians attracted by the potential of exchanging silks, spices and other exotic wares for cloth and wool under conditions of fast-expanding demand.[366]

Much of the northern cloth was light and un-dyed and would be finished by Italian dyers using dyestuffs imported from Asia and alum from Asia Minor, prior to onward sale in domestic, Byzantine and Levantine markets. The trade was profitable because transaction costs were kept low by effective assurances of safe passage for merchants and their goods by the counts of Champagne, reinforced by the Peace of God movement promoted by the Church. The strength of demand in these southern markets for cheap, light, colourful northern textiles underwrote continued expansion of both the Flemish and English urban cloth industries as well as the Italian finishing trades.[367] The appetite of northern consumers for the luxury goods of the south and Orient was equally as great. Thus was initiated a reciprocal exchange between the North Sea and Mediterranean trading zones, conducted overland via the trans-Alpine passes through which traffic moved at modest cost and with little hindrance. From 1204 it received a further fillip when Venice finally won direct access to the Black Sea, ultimate terminus of several of the most important trans-Asian caravan routes. Henceforth, and until penetration of the Indian Ocean by the Portuguese at the close of the fifteenth century, La Serenissima became the single greatest supplier of spices to European markets.

Throughout the first half of the thirteenth century, although Italian and Provençal merchants made regular appearances in northern markets, the ascendancy in these markets of Flemings and other northerners remained assured. Flanders was England's pre-eminent trading partner and, having outstripped domestic supplies of wool, its export-dependent textile industry had become heavily reliant upon imports of English wool, preferred for both its abundance and quality. From 1226 the rise of the Hanse trading confederation, headed by Lübeck and Hamburg and joined from 1259 by Cologne, Rostock and Wismar, complemented

---

[366] Edwards and Ogilvie (2012).
[367] Munro (1991a); Munro (1991b); Munro (1999c).

rather than challenged the Flemish hegemony, since the Hanse had little interest in wool and dealt mainly in salt, herrings, timber, grain, furs, wax and other Baltic products. Moreover, in 1236 the Flemings had received a perpetual safe conduct from Henry III to trade by land and sea throughout his dominions, which effectively guaranteed their ability to dominate English wool exports.[368] Thus the situation remained until a rupturing of political relations between England and Flanders in 1270–6 gave other merchants their chance.[369]

The Italians were quick to take advantage of the Flemings' misfortune, since they now had their own rapidly expanding urban cloth industry to supply with wool. Merchants from the textile centres of Piacenza, Lucca and especially Florence cornered Cistercian supplies of wool and secured more wool export licences than any other alien group.[370] They consolidated their position by making themselves financially indispensable to Edward I, who from 1275, with their help, began to tax exports of wool, cloth and hides on a regular basis. These substantial and assured revenues provided the security against which Italian financiers supplied credit to the king. By the end of the thirteenth century numbers of the leading Italian super companies had established offices in London, as they annexed their expanded stake in the commerce of the North Sea region to their dominant stakes in the commerce of the Mediterranean and the Black Sea.

By the third quarter of the thirteenth century Italian mercantile enterprise appeared to know no bounds. While Florentines were penetrating the English wool market the Genoese had superseded the Venetians in the Black Sea and were actively establishing commercial colonies around its shores and, from there, pushing west into Persia in response to the more settled conditions for overland trade created by establishment of the *Pax Mongolica*. In effect, Latin Christendom was becoming integrated into what Abu-Lughod believes 'might, with little difficulty, be called a world system'.[371] The merchant-mariner city-states of Venice and Genoa were the principal protagonists of this development. Together they constituted the termini of two alternative routes: a southern sea route, which connected the Mediterranean, via either Egypt and the Red Sea or Palestine/Syria and the Persian Gulf, to India, Malaysia and southern China; and a northern overland route, which extended from Asia Minor's Black Sea ports through the continental interior of the newly established Mongol Empire to northern China. The existence of these rival routes provided a hedge against the volatile political and military

[368] Lloyd (1977), 22.   [369] Nicholas (1992), 176–9.
[370] Lloyd (1977), 40.   [371] Abu-Lughod (1989), 124.

situation in the Holy Land and kept trading costs competitive, with the result that prosperity became 'pandemic'.[372] Although Marco Polo alone has left an account of his travels, numbers of inquisitive and enterprising Italians are known to have availed themselves of these enticing opportunities and ventured east to Cathay during the final expansive decades of the thirteenth century. In their outward and return journeys, the mercantile Polos made use of seven of Abu-Lughod's eight circuits of exchange (Figure 2.1).

2.06   The enabling environment and Latin Christendom's high-medieval efflorescence

From the ninth century, onset of the more benign and settled climatic conditions of the MCA, availability of an improved agricultural technology comprising the heavy mouldboard plough, better harnessing of draught animals and regular two- and three-course rotations, and the gradual revival of commerce and town life, provided the preconditions for a re-growth of European population and re-expansion of economic activity.[373] Take-off to rapid growth, however, seems to have been delayed until the late eleventh century, following the Oort Solar Minimum (*c.*1010–*c.*1050). Only then, in conjunction with resurgent solar irradiance, did Latin Christendom's high-medieval efflorescence truly get under way. Quantifiable aspects of that boom include a doubling to trebling of populations, an almost two-and-a-half-fold increase in the number of monasteries, a thirteen-fold expansion in the annual output of manuscripts, a doubling in the number of cities with populations of at least ten thousand, and a rise of at least 50 per cent in the urbanization ratio.[374] Small towns increased dramatically in number and many were founded where there had been little or no urban life before.[375] Between the opening of silver mines in northern England in the 1130s and depletion of those at Kutná Hora in Bohemia two hundred years later, European output of bullion rose dramatically and, with it, the amount of coinage in circulation: the growth of the English coinage over this period was in excess of fifty-fold and, unsurprisingly, prices registered a sustained inflation (Table 2.2 and Figure 2.14). Most major river crossings were bridged and a host of ambitious military and ecclesiastical construction projects was brought to completion.[376] Literacy rates improved

---

[372] Abu-Lughod (1989), 124.
[373] Above, Section 2.02; White Jr (1962); McCormick (2001).
[374] Table 2.1; Figure 2.12A; Table 2.5; Zanden (2009), 40, 44, 77.
[375] Graham (1979); Britnell (1996).   [376] Harrison (2004); Duby (1976).

to such an extent that reliance upon the written word in administrative, legal and financial affairs became the norm.[377]

Synergies generated by a range of mutually reinforcing factors launched Latin Christendom onto this more dynamic cultural and economic trajectory. Christendom itself had expanded and the threats once posed by Vikings, Magyars, Slavs and Muslims had receded due to the progress made by Christian missionaries, crusaders and conquistadors, so that, with the notable exception between the 1220s and 1280s of the Mongol attacks on Russia, Poland, Hungary, Bulgaria and Croatia, social and economic life especially on Europe's northern and southern margins had at last become more secure.[378] The revival of commerce and diffusion of improved agricultural technology, both under way since the ninth century, had each acquired a self-sustaining momentum. Feudal lords in need of rent-paying tenants may have fostered higher rates of household formation at a time when improved climatic conditions were lowering morbidity, so that fertility rates were elevated above mortality rates and rates of natural increase became consistently positive (Figure 2.10).[379] Lieberman has suggested that populations may also have begun to reap an immunity dividend from wider exposure to once deadly diseases, notably smallpox and measles.[380]

In a politically fragmented world, Gregory VII's papal revolution established the Latin Church as a powerful over-arching institution which regularized behaviour by, and relations between, Christians across a territorially extensive area that transcended Europe's plethora of competing and often predatory and warring states and lordships.[381] This lowered transaction costs and enabled more travel and trade to take place than would otherwise have been possible under conditions of such pronounced political fragmentation. Birth of the Western Legal Tradition in reaction to the Church's codification of Canon Law created a legal environment within which more sophisticated forms of social and economic relationship could flourish, multilateral patterns of commodity exchange thrive, and factor markets become established.[382] Institution of guilds, communes and urban corporations and foundation and promotion of fairs by powerful overlords resulted in better management and allocation of resources, self-government of cities, security of traders and their goods, and contract enforcement.[383] Technological progress was far from unimportant and by no means insignificant, for, as Joel Mokyr has documented, the store of useful knowledge and practical technology available

---

[377] Clanchy (1979).   [378] McEvedy (1992), 36–7, 54–5.
[379] Duby (1974); Russell (1958), 113.   [380] Lieberman (2009), 78–9.
[381] Mann (1986), 337, 383.   [382] Berman (1983).
[383] Greif (2006); De Moor (2008); Zanden (2009), 50–5; Edwards and Ogilvie (2012).

to Europeans continued to advance.[384] Nevertheless, it was 'this sudden wave of institutional gadgets', both macro in the form of the papal revolution and creation of the Western Legal Tradition and micro in the case of individual merchant guilds, which from the eleventh century galvanized western Europe's hitherto latent potential for expansion and growth so that progress became real.[385]

Blessed by enabling environmental conditions, once Latin Christendom's high-medieval boom began, populations grew fast.[386] In fact, with average growth rates of 0.5 per cent per annum for successive generations in the demographically most dynamic regions, the rising numbers might quickly have become economically self-defeating. Within agriculture the mounting pressure to produce more could have undermined fragile ecological balances and initiated a vicious circle of resource degradation.[387] There was also an inherent tendency for the marginal productivities of land and labour to decline as inferior land was brought into production and the intensity of labour inputs was ratcheted ever higher. Yet, insofar as these limitations materialized it was in specific circumstances and at a relatively late stage in the process of expansion. In part this was because growth began from a situation of comparative resource abundance, but it was also because it was transformative as well as extensive in character. Husbandmen devised better systems for managing resources and maintaining land productivity and the growth of commerce and rise of cities provided stronger incentives to invest, innovate and specialize. Further, as markets widened and deepened so non-primary sectors of production were able to expand, creating alternative means of earning a living and adding greater value to farm output by turning hides into leather; flax and wool into cloth; grain into bread and ale; and so forth. Where commercial and urban growth were strongest, and for as long as their expansion could be sustained, the course of economic development was consequently more Smithian and Boserupian than Malthusian or Ricardian.[388]

Of the tangible legacies of this expansive and self-confident age, none are more impressive than Latin Christendom's many Gothic cathedrals.

---

[384] Mokyr (1992), 31–56.   [385] Zanden (2009), 65.

[386] Lieberman (2009), 80–3, 162–4; Brooke (2014), 358–60.

[387] A view elaborated by Abel (1935) and Postan (1966).

[388] Grantham (1999). Smithian growth is defined in note 7, above. Boserup (1965) argued that population growth determined agricultural methods and output. The Rev. T. R. Malthus, *An essay on the principle of population* (1798), had famously argued the opposite. The tendency for increments of land and labour above a critical threshold to incur diminishing returns was formulated by David Ricardo, *The principles of political economy and taxation* (1817).

Indeed, so many were built at once that Georges Duby famously christened these high-medieval centuries the 'age of the cathedrals'.[389] France led the way, pioneering the new Gothic style, pushing its structural potential to the limits and rebuilding cathedral after cathedral. Other countries followed. Between 1066 and 1350 all sixteen of England's pre-Reformation cathedrals were rebuilt and enlarged, often repeatedly. Salisbury was successively enlarged and beautified, most notably in the 1330s, when the church's 123-metre stone spire daringly added a load of 6,397 tons to the earlier crossing.[390] Each rebuilding extended its length – from 53 metres in 1075, to 96 metres in 1120 and, finally, 137 metres in 1220 – and increased its architectural splendour, most spectacularly when, in the early-thirteenth century, the cathedral was relocated to a spacious valley-bottom site and work began on an entirely new structure in conjunction with planning and building of a spacious new town.[391]

By any standard, the creation of such monumental buildings constitutes a major artistic and organizational achievement. Formidable resources had to be mobilized in order to bring each project to completion. Without peace, prosperity and confidence it would not have been possible to build on such a scale and maintain the momentum of construction for decades at a time. The peace emanated in part from the renewed vigour and authority of the Latin Church following its 1054 separation from the Greek Church, aggressive expansion of Christendom's frontiers through processes of conversion and conquest, and growth of the rule of law. The prosperity arose from rising population, increased agricultural output and, especially, the revival of trade and commerce (it was no coincidence that at Salisbury creation of the new cathedral and new town proceeded hand in hand). The confidence sprang from a resurgent Christianity and the gathering momentum of a materially creative age which, in retrospect, stands out as a 'golden age' of stability, prosperity and high cultural achievement.[392] The economic growth that so patently occurred proceeded at pre-industrial rather than modern rates but was nonetheless real, so that during the heyday of this socio-ecological era material conditions for many gradually improved.

---

[389] Duby (1976).
[390] William Golding's novel *The spire* (Golding (1964)) is a vertiginous reconstruction of the raising of the steeple on foundations never intended to bear such a weight: without extra support added in the fifteenth and seventeenth centuries Salisbury's spire would no longer be standing.
[391] Rogers (1969).
[392] Goldstone (2002), 333; De Moor (2008); Zanden (2009), 50–5.

3   A precarious balance
Mounting economic vulnerability in
an era of increasing climatic instability
and re-emergent pathogens

By the close of the thirteenth century, across core regions of western Europe, a commercialized and monetized society with developed
commodity and factor markets, functioning networks and hierarchies
of towns and cities, and established regional, inter-regional and international flows of exchange had been brought into being and connections established with other commercially developed societies elsewhere
in the Old World.[1] For the better part of two centuries economic activity had expanded and become more differentiated and, sustained by
generally favourable environmental conditions and concomitant gains in
food security and public health, populations had grown.[2] Returns to the
macro- and micro-institutional innovations responsible for Latin Christendom's remarkable twelfth- and thirteenth-century efflorescence were,
nevertheless, dwindling fast.[3] Without fresh institutional and technological innovations that would further reduce the risks of exchange, lower
transaction costs, and widen and deepen domestic and overseas markets,
continued expansion along these lines was unsustainable. It also hinged
upon the persistence of stable and benign climatic conditions and a relatively modest epidemiological burden, neither of which looked set to
continue.

Indeed, from the late thirteenth century it is plain that both economic
and environmental conditions were deteriorating and the established
bases of growth foundering.[4] As Sections 3.01.1 and 3.01.2 show, change
for the worse is unmistakable in the hitherto vanguard economies of Italy
and Flanders. In England (the subject of Section 3.01.3), poorer and
less developed than either and consequently with less to lose, stagnation
rather than outright decline prevailed.[5] Other countries, such as Spain,
still catching up and with a more favourable balance between population
resources, fared better but repercussions of the international recession

---

[1] Above, Section 2.05; Abu-Lughod (1989).   [2] Above, Sections 2.02 and 2.03.
[3] Above, Section 2.04.   [4] Below, Sections 3.01 and 3.02.
[5] Below, Section 3.01.3.

and onset of environmental instability were nonetheless felt widely.[6] Even the Norse communities in remote Iceland and Greenland were adversely affected by shifting patterns of trade, as supplies of African elephant ivory began to supplant those of Arctic walrus and narwhal ivory, cooler sea-surface temperatures caused shoals of cod to migrate south and, in the face of worsening sailing conditions, voyages to these remote northern waters dwindled.[7] It was, of course, the Icelanders and Greenlanders who bore the brunt of the rapid onset of harsher winter weather.[8]

Almost everywhere, in fact, maintaining the existing socio-ecological balance was becoming more precarious. Telltale signs that economic and environmental conditions were beginning to destabilize are evident from the 1270s and become increasingly so from the 1290s (Sections 3.01, 3.02, 3.03.1b and 3.03.2d). The 1310s and 1320s brought a major crisis, when anomalous weather, harvest failure, war and devastating livestock murrains threatened to overwhelm the socio-ecological status quo (Sections 3.01.3e and 3.03.1d). Meanwhile, plague was re-emerging within its reservoir regions astride the Silk Road in central Asia (Section 3.03.2) and spreading inexorably westwards. A slow fuse was burning and it is plain that socio-ecological relations were approaching the critical point when the prevailing precarious balance would prove unsustainable (Section 3.04).

3.01   From efflorescence to recession

Marco Polo (born September 1254, died January 1324) lived through the cusp of change, from a socio-ecological system that was close to its apogee to one that was plainly beyond it. He was seventeen in 1271, when, with his father Niccolò and his uncle Maffeo, he famously set out from Venice for the court of Kublai Khan at modern-day Beijing in China. The first leg of their epic journey took them by ship across the eastern Mediterranean to the crusader port of Acre on the Levant coast. Thence, to have reached the Persian Gulf by the shortest and most direct way, they should have taken the ancient caravan route which led inland to Damascus, then east across the Syrian Desert to Baghdad and, finally, down the Tigris Valley to Basra at the head of the Gulf. Alternatively, they could have headed north through the crusader states to Antioch and then travelled inland to Aleppo and across the desert to the Euphrates Valley

---

[6] Álvarez-Nogal and Prados de la Escosura (2013); Kitsikopoulos (2012).
[7] Dugmore and others (2007).   [8] Figure 3.22.

and eventually Baghdad. These, until 1258, had been the key overland links between the thriving maritime commerce of the Arabian Sea and that of the Mediterranean and, when they functioned well, were easier and cheaper than any of the then available alternatives.[9] Overthrow of the Abbasid Caliphate by the Il-Khanate Mongols put paid to that and from the 1260s these once pivotal axes of East–West commerce became a war zone, fought over by rival armies of Il-Khanate Mongols and Egyptian Mamluks and effectively impassable to unescorted traders.[10]

Blocked from following what Abu-Lughod has dubbed 'Sinbad's Way' to the East, the Polos prudently took ship once again and sailed north along the Levant coast to the busy port of Ayas in the Christian kingdom of Cilicia in Lesser Armenia. It had become the principal Mediterranean destination for goods brought overland from the Persian Gulf by a cir-cuitous and rugged route which kept well behind the Mamluk–Il-Khanate battle lines.[11] Traversing this caravan route took the Polos through Ana-tolia to Erzincan in Greater Armenia, past Mount Ararat, and then down the Mongol-controlled Tigris Valley to Baghdad (much reduced since its capture and sack in 1258) and, finally, to the Persian Gulf at Basra and, thence, Hormuz at the head of the Gulf of Oman. Frustrated in their hope of taking ship to China, they instead headed inland and followed various branches of the Silk Road through the heart of the *Pax Mon-golica* to the oasis cities of Balkh and Kasgar (south of Issyk-Kul) deep in Asia's semi-arid interior. Continuing east across the parched Tibetan–Qinghai Plateau to Lanzhou on the Yellow River in northern China, they detoured to the former Mongol capital of Karakorum in Mongolia and then resumed their journey until, after over three years on the road, they reached the Yuan Dynasty's new capital of Beijing.

Following an extended twenty-four-year sojourn at the court of Kublai Khan the three Polos returned to Italy by the southern sea route from Hangzhou in the Yangzi Delta, through the Strait of Malacca and across the Indian Ocean to Ceylon, India and, eventually, back to the vital Arabian intersection between the commerce of Asia and that of Europe. Here, they found their safest way home to Venice was to disembark at Hormuz at the entrance to the Persian Gulf and follow the 2,000-kilometre overland route which led inland and then northwest, by-passing Baghdad, to Tabriz in Persia and then through the mountains of Greater

---

[9] Abu-Lughod (1989), 185–211.   [10] Ashtor (1976), 263.
[11] '. . . all the spicery, and the cloths of silk and gold, and the other valuable wares that come from the interior, are brought to that city. And the merchants of Venice and Genoa, and the other countries, come hither to sell their goods, and to buy what they lack': Yule (1875), 43.

Armenia to Trebizond on the southern coast of the Black Sea, where they took ship for the final leg of their journey to Venice.[12]

Acre, the Polos' outward point of departure and the last crusader foothold in the Holy Land, had fallen to the Mamluks in 1291, who now controlled the entire Levant coast from Antioch in the north round to Egypt and were in a more-or-less perpetual state of war with the Il-Khanate Mongols. The Tigris Valley had become the effective frontier between these two opposing and belligerent power blocs, with the result that trade reaching the Persian Gulf was now diverted northwest to Tabriz and thence either east to Ayas on the Cilician coast of the Mediterranean or north to the Black Sea at Trebizond, along the route taken by the Polos.[13] Without low tolls the greater length and cost of this transshipment would have been prohibitive. Customs levied on the otherwise far cheaper Red Sea route, and the profits reaped by the Kārimīs cartel of Muslim merchants who controlled it, were therefore able to rise commensurately.[14] The upshot was that, whether trading at Alexandria or at Ayas on the Mediterranean, or at Trebizond on the Black Sea, from the 1260s and especially the 1290s European merchants had to pay higher prices for Indian spices and other sought-after Asian luxury goods.

With final defeat of the crusader states, Genoa also forfeited the lucrative trading privileges obtained at the outset of that great venture and the direct access these gave to valuable Levantine markets. Papal sanctions upon Christian trade with Mamluk Egypt imposed in reaction to the loss of Acre compounded these losses and penalized, in particular, Genoese and Venetian trade with Alexandria, whose importance as the ultimate destination for goods shipped across the Indian Ocean and up the Red Sea had been greatly enhanced by closure of the land routes across Syria.[15] For as long as these sanctions prevailed, Italian trade with Egypt would be conducted at a price and at constant risk of confiscation. Purchase of papal trading licences became a further cost to be borne, which rose as the papal stance toughened and anti-Muslim sentiment intensified. At the height of this stand-off, between 1323 and 1344, Venice was forced to close its Alexandrian consulate and trade indirectly with the Mamluks via Cyprus.[16] The lure to the Italians of Alexandria was three-fold: first, within the eastern Mediterranean, it was the sole remaining outlet for European cloth, iron and timber; second, it was the principal market for the slaves mostly delivered from the Genoese Black

---

[12] Ashtor (1976), 264–5.   [13] Ashtor (1976), 298–9; Ashtor (1983), 43–4, 57–61.
[14] Ashtor (1976), 300–1; Ashtor (1983), 57.   [15] Ashtor (1983), 17–57.
[16] Ashtor (1983), 45–6.

Sea entrepôts of Tana and Kaffa for enlistment in the Mamluk armies; and, third, by default it had become the major source of seaborne supplies of Asian spices.[17]

The net effect of these reversals in the Middle East and the eastern Mediterranean was to refocus Italian commercial interest upon the Black Sea. Here were substitute markets to compensate for those lost in the Levant, important termini of an array of Asian caravan routes, and in Scythia and southern Russia the principal sources of the slaves that sustained the valuable multilateral trade with Alexandria. Since 1204 the Venetians had been the dominant maritime power both at Constantinople and in the Black Sea but from 1261, following the Treaty of Nymphaeum, they were ousted by the Genoese who established themselves at Pera across the Golden Horn from Constantinople and at a series of fortified bases and depots around the Black Sea, of which Kaffa in the Crimea and Trebizond on the southern coast were among the most important. From Kaffa the Genoese traded east to Tana at the mouth of the River Don and then east again to the Kipchak Khanate's capital of Sarai Batu, key to the caravan routes that traversed the steppe-land interior of central Asia.[18] From Trebizond they traded south to Sivas and southeast to Tabriz in Persia, capital of the Il-Khanate Mongols and a key hub on the caravan routes that linked the Persian Gulf to the Black Sea.[19]

Final loss of their trading privileges in the Levant in 1291 brought Venetian and Genoese rivalry within the commercially strategic Black Sea region to a head and for the next eight years a bitter and destructive naval war was fought between these two powers. It was in the midst of this conflict that, at some risk, the three Polos finally returned via the Black Sea, Bosphorus, Aegean and Adriatic to Venice. Three years later, in September 1298, Marco Polo commanded one of the Venetian galleys at the decisive battle of Curzola, where Genoa was victorious and Polo himself taken captive. It was while he was in Genoese custody that he dictated the much-embroidered account of his Oriental travels to fellow inmate Rustichello da Pisa that, upon publication, ensured his enduring fame and excited European curiosity about the East for centuries to come.[20] Paradoxically, *Livres des merveilles du monde* appeared and began to circulate at the very time that the West's own commercial vitality was starting to falter and obstacles to trans-Eurasian trade were mounting. In fact, Genoa's victory over Venice proved pyrrhic, for the glory days of

[17] Ashtor (1983), 7–17; Malowist (1987), 588; Abu-Lughod (1989), 124, 214.
[18] Malowist (1987), 584–8; Abu-Lughod (1989), 154–9.
[19] Ashtor (1983), 57–8. Polo reported the presence of 'Latin merchants, especially Genoese' at Tabriz: Yule (1875), 75–6.
[20] Yule (1875).

its international trade were over and by the time of Marco Polo's death in 1324 the volume of the republic's maritime commerce was well past its peak.[21]

Commercial setbacks in northern Europe were as much to blame for the worsening economic situation as those in the eastern Mediterranean. From the mid-twelfth century, under the wise jurisdiction of successive counts of Champagne, the Champagne fairs of north-central France had risen to become 'the most important emporium for European trade'.[22] Their success hinged upon their judicious location, reinforced by effective guarantees of safe passage for the goods and persons of those travelling to the fairs from a distance and the non-discriminatory access of all merchants to a choice of public courts for the speedy and just settlement of disputes.[23] Following absorption of this fief into the kingdom of France upon the accession of Philip IV, who had become count of Champagne by marriage, these beneficial institutional conditions ceased to apply.

Unscrupulously, Philip IV used the economic leverage provided by the fairs to advance his political and territorial ambitions, especially respecting the still semi-autonomous French fief of Flanders. He therefore targeted the activities of Flemish merchants and their main trading partners, the Italians. His tactics included banning Flemish merchants from the fairs, imprisoning them and confiscating their goods, arresting and taxing Italian merchants, and forbidding French exports of raw wool and undyed cloth.[24] Such arbitrary, discriminatory and economically harmful actions deprived the fairs of their principal attraction with the result that international merchants increasingly forsook them. Since the Flemings were one of the mainstays of the fairs, retaliatory and coercive treatment of them following the shock of the French defeat at the battle of Courtrai in July 1302 proved particularly harmful.[25] The incomplete record of tax receipts from four of the six Champagne fairs implies that business conducted at the fairs dropped by 70 per cent between the early 1290s and 1310 and by 1340 had reduced further to barely a fifth of its peak late-thirteenth-century level (Figure 3.1).

Business lost to the fairs was typically taken elsewhere, although usually at a cost. This especially applied to the direct maritime route established between Genoa and Bruges from the late 1270s using convoys of heavily armed galleys to negotiate the Marinid-controlled Strait of Gibraltar

---

[21] Lopez (1987), 381–3; Kedar (1976), 16–19. Munro (1991), 124–7, summarizes evidence of a general decline in Mediterranean commerce at this time.
[22] Abu-Lughod (1989), 70.   [23] Edwards and Ogilvie (2012).
[24] Edwards and Ogilvie (2012), 139.   [25] Nicholas (1992), 186–97.

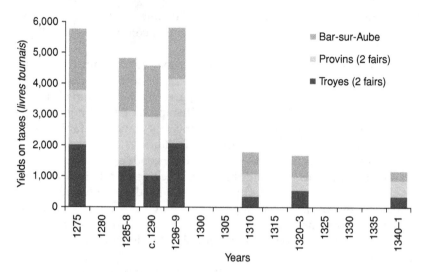

Figure 3.1 Yields on taxes levied at five of the six Champagne fairs, 1275 to 1340–1

Note: at the sixth fair of Lagny-sur-Marne tax revenues declined by 80 per cent from 1,814 *livres* in 1296 to 360 *livres* in 1340–1.
Source: Edwards and Ogilvie (2012), 137

and counter the real threat of pirates and corsairs. Although this effectively by-passed France and Champagne and enabled the Italians to deal directly with the Flemings and their various North Sea neighbours, it was both substantially longer and slower than the trans-Alpine overland route and incurred significantly higher freight costs.[26] Among the more prominent casualties of this increase in unit costs was the long-established bulk trade in cheap, light, undyed northern cloths. Their narrow profit margins meant they were now priced out of Mediterranean markets. Instead, the Flemings concentrated upon supplying luxury woollens capable of bearing the increased transaction costs, while the Italians switched from dyeing and finishing and developed their own textile industry using imports of the fine wools over whose production the English enjoyed a near monopoly.[27]

An additional incentive for establishing direct maritime connections between the Mediterranean and North Sea was that the old trans-Alpine

---

[26] Munro (1991), 129–30; Munro (1999b); Edwards and Ogilvie (2012), 138–9.
[27] This thesis is developed and elaborated in Munro (1991), Munro (1999a), Munro (2001) and Munro (2003a).

overland routes were becoming less secure. The Peace of God movement which had promoted mutual respect between Christians at the onset of Latin Christendom's commercial revolution had by the late thirteenth century largely spent its force.[28] Politicization of the Church, long-running divisions between the Holy Roman Emperor and the pope, ultimate failure of the crusades, and the wealth and worldliness of certain of the religious Orders had all contributed to a general loss of prestige by the Church. From the 1290s, fallout from the multiplying number and escalating scale of feudal disputes, dynastic quarrels and territorial conflicts was also adding greatly to the risks and uncertainties of travel. In a militarily mercenary age, armed free companies were a particularly troublesome legacy of Europe's many wars. Rising brigandage on land was matched by increasing piracy on water as warfare created both the culture and opportunities in which ransom and plunder thrived.[29]

Risk spreading consequently became essential along with adoption of business methods which minimized movement of specie and bullion and the travel of key personnel. The greater Italian merchants now remained in their counting houses, ran their affairs by correspondence, delegated local business dealings to trusted factors and agents, settled international money transfers with bills of exchange, and spread their cargoes between different vessels and carriers.[30] Shippers and hauliers, in turn, invested in a raft of expensive defensive counter measures, of which the armed, high-sided galleys of the Genoese are the costliest example.[31] Whilst these innovative developments undoubtedly bestowed significant efficiency gains, on John Munro's assessment they were insufficient to offset a general European rise in transaction costs, with significant negative consequences for the scale and composition of international trade.[32]

Further, the greater of the new breed of Italian super companies became ensnared in credit operations of mounting scale and complexity which rendered them increasingly vulnerable to the credit crunches that occurred whenever liquidity dried up and nervous depositors rushed to withdraw funds. The major wars between the kingdoms of Sicily and Naples, and between England and Scotland and France, of which these societies became the reluctant financiers, proved particularly disruptive to the international commercial activity upon which their own fragile fortunes rested. In 1298 the Sienese Gran Tavola bank of the Bonsignori was the first of the great Italian merchant banks to go to the wall; the

---

[28] Above, Section 2.04.1.   [29] Lloyd (1982), 5–6; Munro (1991), 121–4.
[30] Hunt and Murray (1999).   [31] Unger (1980), 172–82.
[32] Munro (1991), 120–30; Munro (1999a), 20–5; Munro (2001), 420–6.

Florentine Bardi Company in 1344/5 was the last. In Italy this was an era in which fortunes were lost rather than made.

All these developments undermined the Smithian growth upon which Latin Christendom's commercial revolution and associated economic efflorescence had been founded. Transaction costs were now rising rather than falling and markets stagnating and contracting rather than expanding. Opportunities for specializing and achieving productivity gains through a greater division of labour were therefore diminishing with the result that per head, in the more populous and resource-scarce parts of Europe, output and incomes tended to erode.[33] Downward pressure upon daily real wage rates, household incomes and holding sizes was especially pronounced whenever the momentum of population growth continued but employment growth in services and manufacturing stalled. In the countryside, servanthood, subdivision, subletting and piecemeal colonization of the waste were standard methods by which excess numbers were accommodated on the land.[34] Within towns, dependence upon casual labouring, begging and thieving grew. Either way, structural poverty became entrenched and, as power and wealth became more polarized, crimes against property mounted.[35] The longer that the commercial recession continued, the more intractable became these problems.

With gathering momentum from the 1270s, climate change became a further source of instability in the unfolding scenario.[36] Long-prevalent atmospheric circulation patterns destabilized and, as the extended transition began to the significantly altered circulation patterns of the LIA, the incidence of extreme weather events increased with all the extra problems and uncertainties that this created for agricultural producers. Cruelly, risks of major harvest failures and, worse, of consecutive bad harvests rose at the very time that the proportion of economically vulnerable households was growing. Damaging epizootics of sheep scab, liverfluke and other infections, and a devastating pan-European panzootic of cattle probably triggered by the ecological stresses engendered by these weather extremes, also struck directly at wool, milk and meat production and supplies of vital draught power.[37] Few parts of Europe were entirely spared these environmental problems, although their guise and timing varied a good deal from region to region.[38] Moreover, because of their global

---

[33] Under-populated Spain and Portugal were exceptions: Álvarez-Nogal and Prados de la Escosura (2013); Rodríguez (2012); Henriques (2015). For Scandinavia, central Europe and Russia see Myrdal (2012); Myśliwski (2012); Martin (2012).
[34] Below, Section 3.01.3d.   [35] Hanawalt (1979).   [36] Below, Section 3.02.
[37] Stephenson (1988); Newfield (2009); Campbell (2011b); Slavin (2012).
[38] Kitsikopolous (2012).

dimensions they impacted in one way or another upon the whole of the Old World and thereby affected the peoples, economies and ecosystems with which Europeans were directly or indirectly interacting. Hence the strange parallel that western Europe and eastern Asia, alike, experienced serious environmental difficulties at this time.[39]

Table 3.1 *Italy (centre-north): macro-economic trends, 1300–50*

Variable	1300	1310	1320	1330	1340	1350
Population (1310 = 7.9 million)	98	100	100	101	97	71
Agricultural price index	82	100	116	131	149	206
Non-agricultural price index	100	100	100	100	100	100
Real wage rate		100	93	56	79	131
Gross domestic product (GDP)		100	97	88	85	68
GDP per head (1310 = $1,650)		100	97	87	87	96

Sources: Malanima (2002), 366, 405; Malanima (2003), 289–90; Malanima (2011), 205

3.01.1   Commercial contraction in Italy

As the leading economy of Latin Christendom, wealthier and commercially more enterprising and sophisticated than any other, Italy was particularly hard hit from the 1290s by the deteriorating political and military situation in many of the regions in which its cities and merchants had acquired valuable commercial interests. Additional damage to domestic Italian markets was inflicted by the ongoing conflicts within the peninsula between Guelphs and Ghibellines, Angevins and Aragonese, Venice and Genoa, and one ambitious city-state and another. Trade at all levels became riskier and more expensive and markets more fickle, uncertain and politicized, to the detriment of continued employment and income growth.[40] From 1310, if not before, as transaction costs rose and domestic and overseas markets fractured and shrank, the growth of this hitherto most dynamic and urbanized economy stalled. By the 1340s both Italy and Italian wage earners were poorer than they had been at the opening of the century (Table 3.1). This was a significant reversal of fortunes with negative repercussions which would be felt throughout Christendom.[41]

---

[39] Above, Chapter 1; Brook (2010); Lieberman (2009); Lieberman and Buckley (2012), 1068–78; Tana (2014), 332–7.

[40] Epstein (2000a), 52–72. For symptoms of declining mercantile confidence see Kedar (1976).

[41] Above, Section 2.05.1.

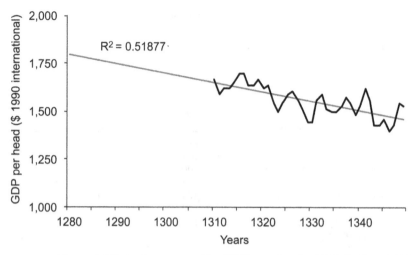

Figure 3.2 Italy (centre-north): GDP per head (1990 Int$), 1280/1310–1350
Source: Malanima (2011), 205

Recent estimates of Italian national income leave no doubt of the impressive level of economic development achieved by the close of the thirteenth century. Malanima's careful demand-based GDP per head estimate of $1,664 (1990 Int$) in 1310 for the populous and highly urbanized centre and north of Italy, including Umbria, Tuscany, Liguria, Piedmont, Lombardy and the Veneto, places this politically fragmented region firmly in the pre-industrial rich league, on a par with the same region during its golden age of peace between 1454 and 1494, Holland during its sixteenth- and seventeenth-century golden age and England on the eve of its industrial revolution.[42] In fact, extrapolating back to the boom years of the third quarter of the thirteenth century, at the point when Marco Polo set forth on his travels to China, suggests that Italian GDP per head might then have exceeded $1,750, close to the maximum attained by any European economy until the advent of modern economic growth in the nineteenth century (Figure 3.2).[43] By 1310, however, the boom was clearly over. Malanima's series of annual estimates indicate that over the course of the next three to four decades wealth in the most developed centre and north of Italy shrank rather than grew so that by the

[42] Malanima (2011); Zanden and Leeuwen (2012); Broadberry and others (2015), 375–6. By convention, all estimates of historical national income are expressed in a common currency, namely 1990 Geary–Khamis (i.e. international) dollars.
[43] Campbell (2013c).

mid-1340s GDP per head had reduced to barely $1,400. Unsurprisingly (since they are a key building block of these GDP estimates), the purchasing power of agricultural and industrial wages diminished by around a fifth over the same period (Table 3.1).

By 1310 industry and services were already contributing half of Italian national income and continued growth was contingent upon expanding yet further that share.[44] Instead, the reverse happened, as warfare, banking failures and commercial contraction took their toll of these hitherto leading sectors of the economy. By default, therefore, agriculture gained in relative importance and, as it did so, the urbanization ratio commenced a downward slide. By 1400 the proportion living in towns of at least 5,000 inhabitants had reduced from 21.4 per cent to 17.6 per cent in the centre-north and from 20.3 per cent to 13.9 per cent in Italy as a whole. Although heavy urban plague mortality obviously lent momentum to this trend from 1348, de-urbanization was plainly already under way before plague struck.[45] This left the economy increasingly dependent upon its least dynamic sector, agriculture.

On Malanima's damning verdict, Italian agricultural technique 'was unable, in the long run, to counterbalance the declining ratios of capital to labour and resources to labour and make capital or resources more productive'.[46] To compound matters, rural population densities were already among the highest in Europe.[47] The inability to shed excess rural labour consequently depressed labour productivity in agriculture, while the inability to improve land productivity drove up agricultural prices relative to those of non-agricultural commodities (Table 3.1), all of which further squeezed disposable incomes. A reverse multiplier–accelerator effect was thereby set in train whereby falling consumption exerted further downward pressure upon investment, aggregate incomes, and demand. Population growth had effectively ceased by 1310 but rural population densities remained at an exceptionally high level. The modest reduction in numbers by 1340 (Table 3.1) reflects the negative demographic impact of the serious Italian famine of 1328–30 (Figure 3.3).[48]

By 1300 the aggregate grain-provisioning needs of the leading Tuscan cities of Lucca (25,000), Pisa (30,000), Siena (50,000) and Florence (110,000) and their lesser satellites were far in excess of the productive capacity of their immediate *contadas*, in whose hilly terrains good arable land had been pushed to its limits. Florence, for example, could satisfy

[44] Malanima (2003), 282.   [45] Malanima (2005), 99–102, 108.
[46] Malanima (2012), 113.   [47] Above, Section 2.03.
[48] Jansen (2009); Alfani and others (2015).

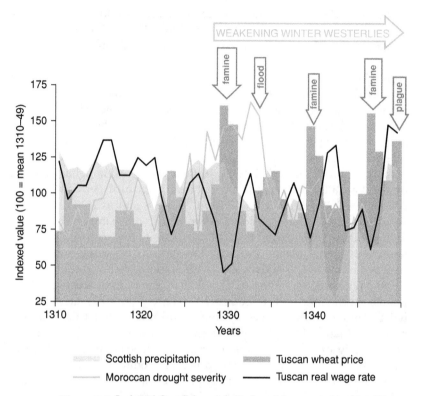

Figure 3.3 Indexed Scottish precipitation, Moroccan drought, Tuscan wheat prices and Tuscan daily real wage rates, 1310–49
Sources: Proctor and others (2002b); Esper and others (2009); Malanima (2008); Malanima (no date a); Malanima (no date b)

less than half its annual grain requirements from its own hinterland and relied therefore upon grain imports from southern Italy and Sicily.[49] Nor were these cities self-sufficient in the fine wool which was the chief raw material of the textile industries upon which their many artisanal households relied for a livelihood. A complex trade had therefore developed whereby merchant companies based in these inland cities, each with a network of agencies in the commercial centres of their principal trading partners, (i) negotiated vital trading privileges to make bulk purchases of English wool and southern Italian and Sicilian grain, (ii) advanced credit to the papacy and to warmongering and cash-needy Plantagenet

---

[49] Abulafia (1981), 385; Hunt and Murray (1999), 101.

and Angevin sovereigns, (iii) oversaw and supplied essential working capital to urban textile workers, and (iv) distributed the finished product via their branches in Italy and abroad and through other Italian merchants active in domestic and Mediterranean markets.[50]

It was the ever increasing hunger of the belligerent rulers of England and Naples for credit and of the Tuscan textile-manufacturing cities for high-quality wheat and wool that fed the rise of the greater merchant banking companies during this period, most notably the Ricciardi of Lucca, Bonsignori of Siena, and the Frescobaldi, Acciaiuoli, Peruzzi and Bardi of Florence. The profits to be made were considerable but dealing with princes was a precarious business since rulers were mortal, trading concessions could be withdrawn, assets confiscated and debts defaulted on. Such political factors contributed to the bankruptcy of the Bonsignori's Gran Tavola bank in 1298, whose collapse heralded the end of Siena as a major banking centre to the benefit of the emerging super companies of Florence. All were pioneers of the new business methods of the age, which included rigorous systems of management and control, high levels of internal communication, elaborate systems of accounting including double-entry bookkeeping, knowledge and use of Arabic numerals, meticulous calculation of interest, and the use of bills of exchange to facilitate international money payments and transfers.[51] Yet, notwithstanding their administrative and financial sophistication, all by 1346 had either failed or crashed. The economic fallout from this disaster is, however, overshadowed by that from the far greater calamity of plague, which reached Florence early in 1348.[52]

A combination of factors progressively undermined the viability of the Italian super companies. Politics was one. In 1294 the Ricciardi of Lucca came unstuck when Philip IV of France moved against them for giving financial support to his enemy, Edward I of England; four years later his confiscation of Sienese assets helped bring down the Gran Tavola.[53] War proved especially perilous. From 1337, following declaration of war between England and France, the Peruzzi and Bardi both discovered to their cost the impossibility of maintaining a working business relationship with the English and French Crowns and the Flemings trapped between them. The greater the credit arrangements to which they became committed the greater their vulnerability to the machinations of monarchs manoeuvring for political and military advantage. Meanwhile, from the

---

[50] See Hunt (1994) for a case study of the Peruzzi Company of Florence. See Lloyd (1977), 60–98, for Italians and the English wool trade and Abulafia (1981) for the Italian grain trade.
[51] Hunt and Murray (1999).   [52] Benedictow (2004), 94–5.
[53] Bell and others (2011).

1330s, as European silver output began to dry up but that of gold rose, the leading companies also found their profit margins eroded by a one-third decline in the gold/silver ratio, which depressed the value of receipts (paid in gold) relative to expenditures (mostly made in silver) and undermined the assets of all gold-based commercial firms.[54]

For Edwin Hunt and James Murray, however, what eventually sank the super companies was 'a fundamental deterioration of the international grain trade on which their prosperity had always been founded'.[55] War, taxation, bad weather, poor harvests and the consequent need of city governments (politically under pressure from hungry and discontented artisans) to become directly involved in urban provisioning collectively eroded the scope of the super companies' activities in this once most lucrative and central component of their business. Ultimately, therefore, they were victims of Italy's general economic contraction and the significantly reduced commodity flows of the 1330s and 1340s, coupled with the need of urban governments to maintain public order when food prices soared. In an age of retrenchment, their size and concomitant high overhead costs counted against them.

Changing weather patterns were a key ingredient of some of the more acute problems of flood and food supply that confronted city governments during the second quarter of the fourteenth century. Comparison of a speleothem-derived index of precipitation over Scotland with a tree-ring based index of drought in Morocco reveals that from the 1320s the North Atlantic Oscillation was weakening and the track of rain-bearing winter westerlies shifting south. Rainfall levels thus tended to decline over northern Europe and increase over southern Europe and North Africa (Figure 3.3). Whereas the years 1327–33 were the driest for a century in Scotland, they brought wetter weather to Morocco than anything experienced since the Oort Solar Minimum of the mid-eleventh century.[56]

Sudden onset of successive years of heavy rainfall proved environmentally damaging for Italy's hilly Tuscan terrain, long stripped of most of its protective woodland by the advance of tillage cultivation. Soil and gully erosion became acute and runoff rates in the Arno basin rose dramatically. The devastating Florentine flood of 4 November 1333 was the result: eyewitness Giovanni Villani reported that three bridges were swept away and parts of the city's centre flooded to a depth of three

---

[54] Hunt and Murray (1999), 118–19; Munro (2001), 419n.
[55] Hunt and Murray (1999), 119. See Abulafia (1981), 379–83, for the scale of Florentine purchases in the Kingdom of Naples.
[56] Proctor and others (2002b); Esper and others (2009). In England, 1333 marks the first of an exceptional run of above-average harvests: Campbell (2007).

metres.[57] The same prolonged climatic deviation probably accounts for the harvest failures and food shortages that were widely reported across Mediterranean Europe at this time.[58] Although transitory in itself, this extreme environmental perturbation was a sign that climatic conditions had taken a turn for the worse, with the potential to cause further havoc in regions, like Tuscany, where much of the land was so ill suited to large-scale grain production and urban demand for essential foodstuffs outran the productive capacity of their immediate hinterlands.[59]

Already in 1328 and 1329 the unprecedented wet weather had caused harvests to fail across southern Europe.[60] 'Famine was widespread throughout Italy' in 1329 and 1330 and these years stand out in Malanima's Tuscan consumer price index as the two dearest on record, the sharp inflation in prices practically halving the purchasing power of agricultural and industrial daily wage rates (Figure 3.3).[61] Giovanni Villani's *Nuova Chronica* reports that famished migrants from the countryside flooded the cities in their quest for relief but were expelled from Perugia, Siena, Lucca and Pistoia. Florence, with a far more substantial population to be fed, acted differently and implemented one of the most effective subsidized food-relief schemes of the age, at great cost to the public purse. The city's government purchased grain in Sicily, shipped it to Talamone (south of Siena) and then, at considerable risk and expense, transported it the 140 kilometres overland to Florence. There, it was baked into bread in the commune's own ovens and sold, under armed supervision, at an affordable and sub-market price to the poor, at an estimated total cost to Florence over the two years of the crisis of 70,000 florins.[62]

Scarcity returned in 1339–41 and again, more seriously, in 1346–7 (Figure 3.3), when livestock murrains greatly exacerbated the dismal harvests.[63] On this occasion the scarcity of foodstuffs was more universal, especially in Florence's *contado*, and the influx of destitute country people

---

[57] Bartlett (1992), 38–40; Hunt (1994), 169; Hoffmann (2014), 326–7.
[58] See Furió (2011) and Furió (2013), for the 1333 crisis in Spain. Catalonia experienced serious harvest failure in 1333–4 and in late winter 1334 Barcelona witnessed significant excess mortality; the same year, shipment of grain from Puigcerdá to Perpignan sparked violent protests: Maltas (2013).
[59] Malanima (2012), 101, 102–3, 116–17.
[60] Italy had escaped unscathed from the Great European Famine of 1315–22, when sky-high prices in the North Sea region had encouraged enterprising Genoese merchants to ship cheap Mediterranean grain north (wheat prices in Tuscany were well below average in both 1315 and 1316: Figure 3.3). Catalan merchants also sent significant shipments of grain to Aigues Mortes and, thence, up the Rhône to northern France: Maltas (2013).
[61] Jansen (2009).   [62] Jansen (2009).
[63] Alfani and others (2015). 1346–7 were also years of scarcity in Catalonia: Furió (2013) and Maltas (2013).

was correspondingly greater. Florence's capacity to cope with the crisis was, however, diminished: the city was encumbered with war debt and its leading merchant companies insolvent. Once more, the city purchased grain at a distance and then sold bread (on this occasion baked from a mixture of wheat, barley and chaff) at a subsidized price, using a voucher system to ration the distribution of loaves among the deserving poor. From the number of vouchers issued, Giovanni Villani reckoned that by April 1347, when the crisis was almost at an end, 94,000 mouths were being fed in this way.[64] That the crisis was contained is a tribute to the resourcefulness and determination of the city's government but, coming on top of the bankruptcy of the Bardi, Peruzzi and other leading merchant companies, it reduced the Florentine and Tuscan economies to their lowest ebb.

For all its misfortunes, fourteenth-century Florence was still a wealthy city and therefore better able than most to afford the measures needed to preserve the food entitlements of a swollen population of needy poor. Yet even in good years securing sufficient grain to provision the city was heavily dependent upon negotiation of trading privileges with the Angevin kings of Naples or their enemies, the Aragonese rulers of Sicily, which in turn hinged upon the provision of credit and political support.[65] More-over, in its quest for grain, and the favour of those who controlled its supply, it was in direct competition with other neighbouring states and principalities, for politically Italy remained a divided country. There was no over-arching central authority with the power to curb the rent-seeking activities of vested-interest groups intent upon taxing, regulating, restricting and even monopolizing trade, or impose jurisdictional uniformity upon a commercially active region fractured into multiple sovereignties. Full market integration at a pan-Italian scale, with the advantages this offered of improved market coordination, lower transaction costs and greater arbitrage of prices, was therefore impossible.

For Epstein, Italy's political fragmentation was the single greatest obstacle to its continued economic growth and progress.[66] Whereas in the ninth, tenth and eleventh centuries the rise in central and north-ern Italy of semi-independent city governments had been a source of economic vitality and strength, metamorphosis of many of these com-munes into self-serving city-states had by the fourteenth century cre-ated a situation in which 'strong . . . urban jurisdiction was incompatible with long-run economic growth'.[67] Manifestations of this sub-optimal situation include the peninsula's polycentric urban structure,

---

[64] Jansen (2009).   [65] Abulafia (1981).   [66] Epstein (2000a), 36, 169–74.
[67] Epstein (2000a), 51; Epstein (2000b), pp. 14–22 of 36.

parcellized jurisdictions, contested boundaries, endless petty inter-state wars, the monopolies claimed by cities over the produce of their hinterlands, the politically conditional nature of so much inter-territorial trade, and the super-company phenomenon.[68] Reducing these multiple sources of market inefficiency and friction was contingent upon processes of political and jurisdictional centralization and state building which were as unimaginable as they were unattainable in the economically and politically fissured circumstances prevailing in Italy during the first half of the fourteenth century.

3.01.2 Industrial crisis in Flanders

Flanders was Italy's closest counterpart in northern Europe, in terms of population density, urbanization ratio, and active involvement in international trade, and by the close of the thirteenth century shared many of the same problems of land scarcity, reliance upon imported foodstuffs and raw materials, shrinking and uncertain overseas markets, rising transaction costs, and political and military disruption of key commercial relations. Although the entire territory of Flanders was no larger than that controlled by a single great Italian mercantile city, the concentration of substantial towns within it was unmatched in Italy.[69] Most had grown from practically nothing over the course of the eleventh, twelfth and thirteenth centuries when Flanders had thrived on the benevolent rule of its counts, who held it as a semi-autonomous fief from the kings of France.[70] Their merchants and manufacturers had profited from developing commercial links with Britain to the north, Italy to the south, and northern Germany and France to the east and west. Flanders's own international fairs early attracted merchants from far and wide and when these were eclipsed by the rise of the Champagne fairs the latter became the favoured mart where the Flemings and Italians, both benefiting from safe conducts, did much of their business.[71] Like their Genoese, Venetian and Florentine counterparts, the Flemish merchants dealt in a wide range of commodities, although grain, wool and cloth bulked largest in value and volume.[72]

The commercial dynamism of its economy ensured that population growth rates in Flanders were well above the European average.[73] As a result, by 1300 it supported a population density of over forty per

---

[68] Epstein (2000b). See Herlihy (1967) for a case study of the Tuscan city of Pistoia.
[69] Bairoch and others (1988), 259; Nicholas (1992), 117; Bavel (2010), 280–1.
[70] Nicholas (1992), 97–139.
[71] Nicholas (1992), 171–2; Edwards and Ogilvie (2012), 132, 136, 139–40.
[72] Lloyd (1982), 108–12.   [73] Above, Section 2.05.3.

square kilometre, with maximum population densities more than twice as great.[74] Consequently it had long since ceased to be self-sufficient in both essential foodstuffs and an array of raw materials, of which the fine wool required by its substantial urban cloth manufacture was by far the most important. Its growth had therefore been founded upon a Smithian process of specialization and exchange coupled with a Boserupian process of agricultural intensification which ensured that, in terms of land productivity, Flemish agriculture was among the most productive in Europe and operated closer to the technological frontier than most others.[75] Processes of land-use substitution resulted in the conversion of pasture to arable so that from the twelfth century the expanding textile industry became increasingly reliant upon wool imported from England.[76] Then, as urban demand for staple foodstuffs began to outrun the capacity of domestic agriculture to supply it, England became one of several countries sending grain and other provisions to Flanders.[77] Flemish shippers and carriers also derived significant profits from handling much of this traffic and thereby made a significant contribution to an economy with a substantial value-added component. In fact, it would be surprising if, at the peak of its thirteenth-century prosperity, Flemish GDP per head was much less than that prevailing in Italy (centre-north) at about the same time (Table 3.1), or in the Southern Low Countries at the end of the Middle Ages, when it has been estimated by Erik Buyst at around $1,600 (1990 Int$).[78]

After 1270 Flanders experienced mounting difficulty sustaining its established growth trajectory.[79] Conditions on the land were becoming increasingly congested. In the twelfth century many lords had made life grants of their properties on generous terms and in return for fixed rents whose real value was subsequently eroded by the combination of monetary inflation and rising land values.[80] This created a powerful incentive for those holding land on these generous terms to subdivide and sublet it to others for the full market rent. Strong rural population growth meant that there was an almost insatiable demand for holdings.

---

[74] Pounds (1973), 332; Bavel (2010), 283. Nicholas (1976), 25–6, reckoned that Flemish rural population densities averaged over sixty per square kilometre in the early fourteenth century.

[75] Nicholas (1976), 7; Thoen (1997), 74–85; Bavel (2010), 133–6, 141.

[76] Lloyd (1977), 2–24.

[77] Lloyd (1982), 108–10; Nicholas (1992), 97–104; Campbell and others (1993), 180–2; Campbell (2002b), 6–7, 15–16, 21–3.

[78] Buyst (2011). A GDP per head double that of England in the early fourteenth century is consistent with Flanders's correspondingly higher urbanization ratio.

[79] Nicholas (1976), 28–9.

[80] Nicholas (1992), 106–7; Thoen (1997), 81, 84–5; Bavel (2010), 171.

In combination with active land markets and customs of partible inheritance, it also resulted in an ever greater morcellation of holdings, a growing proportion of which were incapable of keeping a family fully occupied or providing them with an adequate livelihood (by the fourteenth century most agricultural producers in the Ghent area held only 2–3 hectares of land).[81] The expansion of leasehold from the end of the thirteenth century also created a situation in which townsmen often took land at lease and then sublet it at higher rents to others.[82] In all these ways farm sizes and farm incomes were squeezed. Incentives to occupiers of holdings to raise output per unit of land were high but often this was at the expense of output per unit of labour.[83] Such circumstances fuelled a quest for supplementary sources of income and encouraged migration of excess rural workers to the towns where the textile industry gave employment to many. Indeed, without an abundant supply of relatively cheap labour the Flemish cloth industries could not have risen to the international prominence they had acquired by the 1270s.

Redistribution of excess labour from the countryside to the towns and from agriculture to manufacturing and services was vital if the problems of rural congestion and poverty were not to become overwhelming. Yet, from the 1270s the Flemish urban textile industry experienced a succession of significant setbacks. From 1270 to 1274 a breakdown in Anglo-Flemish relations seriously disrupted the supply of English wool upon which the Flemish industry had become reliant and diverted much of it elsewhere, depriving Flemish shippers of the lucrative carrying trade (a loss from which they never fully recovered).[84] Then, in 1279/80, a devastating sheep scab epizootic dramatically reduced both the volume and quality of English wool output and resulted in a sharp drop in exports (Figure 3.4).[85] This coincided with a first wave of unrest among disaffected Flemish textile workers.[86] Next, in 1294, the outbreak of war between France and England over Gascony (the French fief held by the English king as a vassal of the king of France) placed Flanders in an invidious position, for the counts of Flanders were vassals of the French Crown and yet England was their country's primary trading partner and natural ally in Flemish resistance to the feudal and territorial ambitions of Philip IV of France.[87] Under these difficult political circumstances

[81] Nicholas (1976), 7, 26; Nicholas (1992), 124, 262, 264; Soens and Thoen (2008), 41–5.

[82] Nicholas (1968), 477; Nicholas (1992), 127; Soens and Thoen (2008), 36–7, 46–7; Bavel (2010), 170–8.

[83] Nicholas (1992), 262–3; Bavel (2010), 327, 329, 331.   [84] Lloyd (1977), 25–40.

[85] Lloyd (1977), 63; Stephenson (1988), 372–3, 381, 385.

[86] Nicholas (1968), 461; Nicholas (1992), 181–5; Cohn (2006), 312n.; Bavel (2010), 272.

[87] Lloyd (1977), 75–98; Prestwich (1988), 376–400; Nicholas (1992), 186–92.

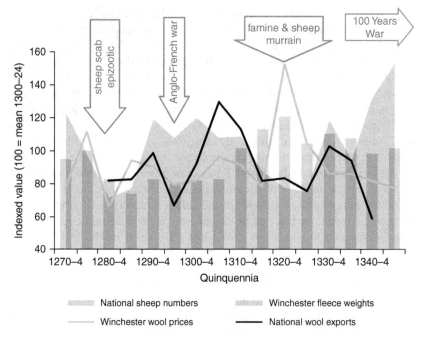

Figure 3.4 English sheep numbers, fleece weights, wool prices and wool exports, 1270s to 1340s
Note: wool prices are deflated.
Sources: Winchester fleece weights and prices: Stephenson (1988), 378, 388; sheep numbers: National Accounts Database; wool exports: Carus-Wilson and Coleman (1963), 36–46

maintaining both a regular supply of wool from England and sales of finished cloth at the Champagne fairs, now under French control, proved to be an impossible balance to strike. Either it was difficult to buy wool (English wool exports shrank by a third between 1290–4 and 1295–9) or to sell cloth (especially when Philip IV rescinded the safe conducts traditionally granted to Flemish merchants attending the Champagne fairs and thereby prevented sales of Flemish cloth to Italian merchants).[88] Such uncertainty was naturally very damaging to the industry.

Both situations eased somewhat after 1297. Blocked from purchasing Flemish cloth at the Champagne fairs, the Genoese exploited to the full their direct maritime connection with Flanders.[89] Bruges, the destination, first, of Genoese convoys, then, from 1314, of Venetian fleets,

[88] Carus-Wilson and Coleman (1963), 38–9; Edwards and Ogilvie (2012), 8–10.
[89] Munro (1999b).

became a centre of international commerce and its bourse, established in 1309, the most important money market in the North Sea region. Meanwhile, with the ending of hostilities with France and encouragement of strong overseas demand from both Flemish and Italian buyers (the latter now taking a greatly enlarged share of the clip), English wool exports recovered and rose to new heights: at their peak in 1304/5 over 45,000 sacks were exported (Figure 3.4), equivalent to the fleeces of between 10.8 million and 13.5 million sheep.[90]

The boom did not last long. Troubled Anglo-French and Franco-Flemish political relations continued to complicate exports to Flanders and then between 1315 and 1330 bad weather and outbreaks of murrain caused heavy mortalities of sheep (Figure 3.4). English wool exports contracted once more while prices rose, aggravating political tensions in Flanders and triggering urban revolts in 1319–20 and 1323–8.[91] Then, on 12 August 1336, in anticipation of his declaration of war against France and with the purpose of coercing the Flemish into entering an alliance with him, Edward III cut off supplies to Flanders altogether, prompting further protests in the Flemish cloth towns.[92] Exports were only resumed in January 1340 after the Flemish had pledged support and acknowledged Edward as king of France. All the while, commencing in 1275, all exports of English wool were liable to the payment of customs duty which was mostly passed on to the foreign purchasers. There was a temporary sharp increase in the duty payable between 1294 and 1297, then in 1303 the basic rate of £⅓ per sack was permanently raised to £½ for wool exported by alien merchants. A further permanent across-the-board rise to £2 to £2½ per sack followed outbreak of the Hundred Years War and greatly increased the cost of English wool to Flemish and other overseas textile manufacturers and, consequently, the price of the finished cloth.[93]

These problems of raw-material supply were compounded by rising transaction costs in international trade and the loss or contraction of several important overseas markets. As Munro has emphasized, during the boom years of the thirteenth century the bulk of the textiles sent for export were 'the cheaper-line *sayetteries* and other *draperies legeres*' produced 'in towns large and small, in both Flanders and Brabant'.[94] Many were sold undyed at the Champagne fairs to Italian merchants,

---

[90] Lloyd (1977), 99. Flock numbers estimated on the basis that each sack contained 364 lb of wool, shorn from 240–300 sheep.
[91] Nicholas (1992), 212–17; Munro (1999a), 9–10; Bavel (2010), 271–3.
[92] Lloyd (1977), 144–6; Fryde (1988), 53–86; Nicholas (1992), 217–24; Bavel (2010), 271.
[93] Carus-Wilson and Coleman (1963), 194–6.   [94] Munro (1999a), 21.

who finished them and then sold them on in Christian and Muslim markets throughout the Mediterranean and Black Sea.[95] This was a bulk trade geared towards consumers at the bottom end of the market and its success depended upon keeping costs down. Some of these cloths were merely coarse woollens, others were full worsteds and yet others were woollen/linen or woollen/cotton unions. All 'sold for only 40 to 60 per cent of prices for the *lowest* grade of Flemish quality woollens; and many for much less (20 to 40 per cent)'.[96]

Collapse of the Levant trade after 1291 deprived these cheap cloths of a significant market; rising transport costs everywhere, as burgeoning warfare on many fronts rendered carriage by land and sea riskier, then priced them out of others. 'As the combined production, transport, and transaction costs in exporting such textiles to the Mediterranean basin rose above the prevailing market prices in those regions, producers of those cheap light textiles were evidently forced out of production'.[97] Mention of these cloths disappears from commercial records from the 1320s. In most of the Flemish textile towns regulations governing production of these fabrics ceased to be revised from early in the fourteenth century, and at Ypres the cloth stalls for *says* were frequently unrented from that time.[98] At Saint-Omer in Artois, which had once exported sixty thousand *says* annually, it became impossible to farm the *say* excise from 1299 and references to the *sayetterie* at Leuven cease from 1298.[99] Insofar as this branch of manufacture survived, it was to supply the domestic rather than international market.

Flemish textile manufacturers had always produced a range of higher-quality and more expensive woollens and from the close of the thirteenth century, as far as the international market was concerned, these alone remained a viable commercial proposition. Woollen output consequently expanded, as manufacturers of *says* converted to producing these more expensive fabrics, which became known as the *nouvelles draperies*. It also became more closely regulated, especially from the 1330s, since export success hinged upon tight control of quality.[100] From the 1320s these cloths feature with increasing frequency in Italian notarial records while mention of *says* virtually disappears.[101] Nevertheless, the Mediterranean market was anything but expanding and Italian manufacturers were in a far better position to supply it, which is why the Italian merchants had been so keen to obtain privileged access to English wool supplies. Unfortunately for their Flemish rivals, production of the finest cloths required

---

[95] Munro (1991), 110.   [96] Munro (1991), 111.   [97] Munro (1999a), 25.
[98] Munro (1991), 112.   [99] Munro (1991), 112–13.   [100] Munro (1999a), 56.
[101] Munro (1991), 117.

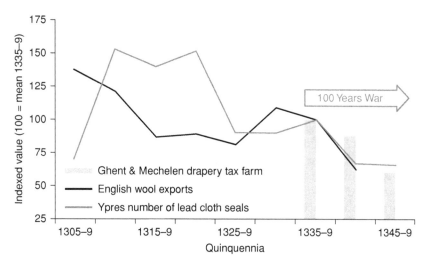

Figure 3.5 Indicators of the output of the Flemish woollen industry, 1305–49

Sources: wool exports: Carus-Wilson and Coleman (1963), 36–46; Ypres cloth seals: Boussemaere, (2000); Ghent and Mechelen drapery tax farms: Munro (1999a), 42

the finest wools, hence this reinforced reliance upon English supplies, to which there was not yet an adequate alternative. On the contrary, efforts at quality control led some Flemish textile towns to ban the use of inferior wools, such as those produced in Ireland.[102] This imposed a major supply-side constraint upon expansion of the Flemish woollen manufacture and rendered it seriously vulnerable to the environmental and political disruptions of supply which affected the English wool-export trade from the 1310s (Figure 3.4).[103]

Reorientation of Flemish textile production from the manufacture of light and cheap to heavy and expensive cloths after *c*.1290 may have saved the export branch of the industry from terminal decline but it did not restore the industry's former dynamism. On the contrary, the available quantitative evidence implies that cloth output was falling from the 1330s and maybe earlier (Figure 3.5). At Ypres the number of cloths sealed fell almost continuously from the 1310s to the 1340s and had halved by the eve of the Black Death.[104] At Ghent and Mechelen revenues

---

[102] Munro (1991), 136; Munro (2003a), 245. The value of Irish exports of wool, woolfells and hides shrank by almost 60 per cent between the 1310s and 1332: estimated from McNeill (1980), 132–5.
[103] Lloyd (1977), 99–203.   [104] Nicholas (1992), 279; Boussemaere (2000).

from drapery tax-farm sales dropped by respectively 20 and 60 per cent between the late 1330s and late 1340s (Figure 3.5).[105] Jealous of their own beleaguered manufactures, the three leading cities of Ghent, Bruges and Ypres – the *drie steden* – redoubled their efforts at this time to prohibit rural cloth producers from imitating their luxurious speciality cloths and under-cutting them in price.[106] They also forbade their citizens from purchasing cloth made elsewhere.[107] Such protective behaviour betokens adversity rather than prosperity.

The first half of the fourteenth century was therefore a time of increasing difficulty for the Flemish textile industry and, consequently, the Flemish economy. The economic slowdown fed mounting tensions between tenants and landlords, countryside and town, weavers and fullers, proletariats and patriciates, one city and another, urban patriciates and the counts of Flanders, and the counts of Flanders and the French king. Social unrest became endemic in the towns while growing inequality and the economic marginalization of many rural households bred discontent in the countryside. Short-term leases, tithes, and taxes and those who imposed or levied them all became objects of growing resentment. Anger and frustration spilled over in 1323. The combined urban and rural revolt that erupted that year has been described as 'the largest and longest revolt in western Europe in the Middle Ages'.[108] It was eventually suppressed with great brutality.

This great Flemish revolt followed in the immediate wake of the Great Famine of 1315–22 and accompanying cattle plague and sheep murrains.[109] The inadequate size of so many holdings, reliance of so many households upon supplementary sources of income, and the country's general lack of self-sufficiency in grain, even in normal years, meant that this Europe-wide famine 'seems to have been more severe in the southern Low Countries than elsewhere'.[110] Urban industrial workers suffered a particularly acute loss of food entitlements as demand for cloth collapsed and that for food soared. Rates of urban price inflation appear to have been greater in highly urbanized Flanders than anywhere else in northern Europe.[111] At Ypres, with an urban population of at least 25,000, municipal records list 2,794 deaths between May and October 1316 when the famine was at its height.[112] Bruges, although larger, coped

[105] Munro (1999a), 42.
[106] Nicholas (1968), 464–5, 467; Nicholas (1992), 281–3.
[107] Nicholas (1992), 206.   [108] Bavel (2010), 272.
[109] The rinderpest panzootic appears to have spread to the Low Countries in 1318: Newfield (2009), 162.
[110] Nicholas (1992), 207; Jordan (1996), 146, 161.   [111] Bavel (2010), 279.
[112] Jordan (1996), 146; Bavel (2010), 279.

better, mainly because of its established direct maritime link with southern Europe, where grain prices were unusually low in 1315 and 1316 (Figure 3.3). The city's magistrates bought 20,000 hectolitres of grain (enough to feed a third of its population for a year) from Italian merchants and sold it at or below cost to licensed bakers.[113] Nonetheless, famine fevers killed many and two thousand bodies were collected from the streets and buried in mass graves.[114] It has been estimated that between 5 and 10 per cent of the population of Flanders may have perished at this time.[115] Meanwhile, shrinkage of peat soils, inundation of low-lying coastal areas and destabilization of dune systems exacerbated the latent tension between population and resources in the most ecologically vulnerable areas.[116]

Flanders stood in the van of providing a literate education to laymen and the region's religious and urban institutions undoubtedly made widespread use of written records. It is therefore disappointing that documentary survival has been too poor to permit construction as yet of annual price and wage series and GDP estimates comparable to those reconstructed by Malanima for equally commercialized and urbanized central and northern Italy.[117] In part, this reflects the absence of an effective central governing authority and associated bureaucracy, which in turn partly explains the country's political volatility and difficult relationship with its two larger and more centralized neighbours, France and England. Nevertheless, the want of such price, wage and GDP series makes it virtually impossible to track the precise course of the Flemish economy between the two great natural disasters of the Great Famine and the Black Death. Plainly, the country's single most prominent industry and foreign exchange earner – woollen textiles – was struggling to maintain earlier levels of output and employment (Figure 3.5). Reliance of the textile towns upon external sources of wool and grain also left them exposed to political and environmental disruption of supplies. From 1337 outbreak of war between England and France left Flanders politically compromised and once again threatened to jeopardize supplies of wool or grain, or both. Meanwhile, agricultural land remained as parcellated as ever, a situation which the spread of short-term leasing by lords and townsmen is more likely to have reinforced than reversed.

No doubt early fourteenth-century Flanders remained per head wealthier than any other country or region of northern Europe. Nevertheless, by the 1340s, like Italy, its wealth is more likely to have been

---

[113] Jordan (1996), 146–7, 161–2.   [114] Nicholas (1992), 207–8.
[115] Nicholas (1992), 207–8; Bavel (2010), 279.
[116] Nicholas (1992), 260; Bavel (2010), 47; Soens (2011); Soens (2013), 161–73.
[117] Bavel (2010), 313–17.

decreasing than increasing. Its open, commercialized, urbanized and industrialized economy had grown on the Peace of God movement of the twelfth century, the capacity of the Flemish and Champagne fairs to attract traders and merchandise from far and wide, the demand for cheap northern textiles in Mediterranean markets, and the capacity of English and northern French producers to make good growing Flemish deficiencies in wool and grain. For a combination of reasons, these happy preconditions no longer prevailed. Instead, overcrowding on the land, mounting ecological problems, shrinking textile employment and output, declining exports, and the fast-escalating political and military crisis in which it was enmeshed were placing its now vulnerable and shrinking economy under duress.

3.01.3   Agricultural stagnation in England

3.01.3a Wage rates and GDP per head England was more centralized and consequently less prone to coordination failures than Italy or Flanders but also substantially less urbanized and developed than either: its GDP per head of around \$750 (1990 Int\$) in the early 1310s was less than half Italy's \$1,650.[118] It was, however, a highly commercialized economy, with well-developed commodity and factor markets and widespread dependence at all social levels upon market exchange of one sort or another. Although insular it was not isolated and exports, mostly of unprocessed primary products, contributed almost a sixth of national income. It was therefore as fully exposed to the effects of the post-1290 international commercial recession as Italy and Flanders but, with smaller manufacturing and service sectors than either, had less to lose. In fact, want of alternative sources of fine wool and quality tin ensured that overseas demand for these twin bastions of England's export trade held up well.[119] Recession even worked to the advantage of native merchants by enabling them to secure a larger share of foreign trade.

Early adoption of record creation and preservation by seigniorial, institutional and governmental administrations and high archival survival rates mean that England is better served from an earlier date by price, wage and a range of economic output data than any other European country. Annually continuous price and wage series are available from the 1260s and output-based estimates of national income and GDP per head have been reconstructed back to 1270 and extrapolated back more tenuously to 1253.[120] Agricultural information for the demesne sector

---

[118] Above, Section 3.01.1.   [119] Below, Section 3.01.3c.
[120] Construction of these GDP estimates is described in Broadberry and others (2015), 1–244. They have been extended back to 1253 by Bas van Leeuwen.

is particularly abundant, detailed and robust and has provided the basis for reconstructions of annual chronologies of crop yields and trends in livestock numbers from the 1270s, thereby capturing fluctuations in harvest quality and the impacts of livestock diseases.[121] In a predominantly agrarian and organic economy reliant upon animate sources of energy, these obviously had a direct bearing upon the outputs of staple foodstuffs and essential raw materials and, thus, prices, purchasing power and national income.[122] Because the output-based national income estimates have been derived independently of the daily real wage rate data, the two series are less obviously correlated and provide a clearer cross-check on each other than those reconstructed from the demand side by Malanima for Italy. England thus provides an exceptionally well-documented example of the experience of a still relatively underdeveloped and poor middle-ranking economy.

Historians of this period of economic slowdown now have a choice of alternative daily real wage rate series. Most useful are the well-known series for master masons and building labourers constructed by Phelps Brown and Hopkins in the 1950s and recently checked, corrected and recalculated with reference to a revised basket of consumables by Munro, and a corresponding series for agricultural labourers constructed by Clark using a somewhat different basket of consumables.[123] Both are plotted in Figure 3.6 (along with a nominal wage rate series for building labourers) and reveal a broadly similar chronology with a positive correlation between them of +0.70. Farm labourers appear to have experienced a reduction in the purchasing power of their daily wages of around one-fifth during the third quarter of the thirteenth century, after which it settled at a fairly constant low level, albeit with wide short-term fluctuations according to the varying price of consumables. Daily real wage rates of building labourers likewise remained effectively trendless from the 1270s until 1348/9, when heavy plague mortality transformed both the supply of and demand for labour. In direct contrast to the experience of their Italian counterparts (Table 3.1), English building labourers suffered no more than a 5 per cent erosion in the purchasing power of their daily wages between 1310 and the mid-1340s, while rates paid to agricultural labourers purchased 15 per cent more by the later date. This divergence in the relative experience of building and agricultural labourers only emerged in the late 1330s (Figure 3.6) and probably reflects the fact that construction workers experienced a major slump in demand for their labour due to a notable contraction in the number of major

---

[121] Campbell (2000), 26–37; Campbell (2007).   [122] Wrigley (1962).
[123] Phelps Brown and Hopkins (1956); Munro (no date); Clark (2007b), 130–4.

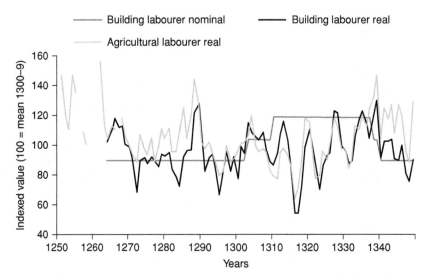

Figure 3.6 Nominal and real daily wage rates of English male labourers: building labourers, 1264–1349, and farm labourers, 1251–1349
Sources: Munro (no date); Clark (2007b), 130–4

new ecclesiastical building projects being initiated, whereas demand for agricultural labour held up well and price deflation worked in their favour.[124]

Across this critical eighty-year period nominal daily wage rates of both groups of workers remained essentially fixed. From 1264 until 1302 a building labourer earned 1½ pence a day, rising to 1¾ pence from 1303–9, and then 2 pence from 1310 to the outbreak of war with France in 1337, after which it quickly returned to 1½ pence until the plague-induced collapse of labour supply in 1348/9.[125] Prior to the Black Death nominal wage rates for all types of workers were in fact decidedly 'sticky' and responded only slowly and fitfully to changes in the demand for labour, price of consumables and value of money.[126] Thus, the higher nominal wages paid from 1302 and especially from 1310 to 1337 and lower nominal wages paid thereafter may be interpreted as adjustments made in

[124] Numbers of major new ecclesiastical building projects declined from 15 in the 1310s, to 13 in the 1320s, 7 in the 1330s and 2 in the 1340s: Morris (1979), 178–81. Corresponding numbers of new hospital foundations were 18, 11, 24, 9 (Figure 2.12A and B).

[125] Munro (no date). Nominal wage rates of agricultural labourers registered a more modest gain from 1¼ to 1½ pence over the same period: Clark (2007b), 131–3.

[126] Munro (2003b).

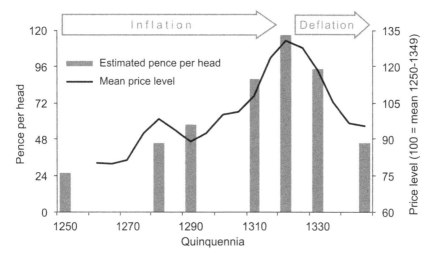

Figure 3.7 Estimated English money supply per head and the mean price level, 1250s to 1340s
Sources: estimated from Allen (2012), 343–5; Broadberry and others (2015), 20, 227–9. Composite price index as described in Broadberry and others (2015), 189–94, and supplied by Bas van Leeuwen

response to concurrent changes in money supply per head as successive re-coinages stoked price inflation, until the trend was abruptly reversed by Edward III's massive export of bullion during the opening stages of the Hundred Years War (Figure 3.7).[127] Scarcity of coin kept prices relatively low during the 1340s, to the advantage of those, like agricultural labourers, paid an effectively fixed nominal wage (Figure 3.6).

These monetary effects apart, what largely determined what and how much a wage labourer could purchase was the price of essential subsistence goods and this, for an array of supply-side factors, varied enormously from season to season and from year to year (Figure 3.8A). In 1290, when an unskilled agricultural labourer earned around 1¼ pence a day, a farm hand would need to have worked for 166 days in order to afford what R. C. Allen has called a 'respectability basket' of consumption goods (costed at current prices) containing ale, bread, legumes, meat, eggs, butter, cheese, soap, cloth, candles, lamp oil, fuel and rent in sufficient quantities to provide a daily diet containing the minimum of 2,000 kilocalories required to satisfy the essential nutritional needs

[127] Allen (2012), 283–5, 329–31, 344–5.

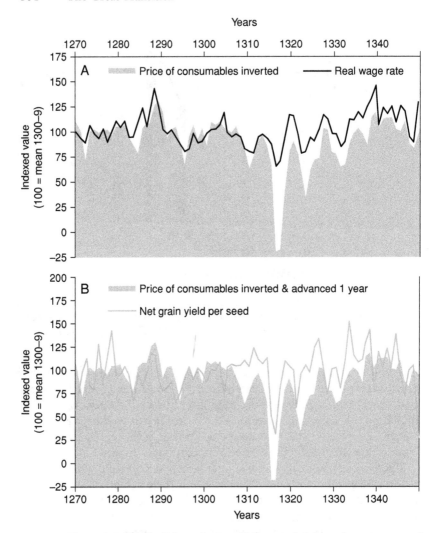

Figure 3.8 (A) English agricultural labourers' daily real wage rates and the price of a basket of consumables (inverted), 1270–1349. (B) English net grain yields per seed and the price of a basket of consumables (inverted and advanced 1 year), 1270–1349
Sources: Clark (2007b), 130–4; Clark (2009); Campbell (2007)

of an adult male.[128] For a single man that was a realistic possibility but his wages would have fallen far short of the income needed to support

---

[128] Allen (2001); Allen (2009), 36–7. Livi-Bacci (1991), 27, considers 2,000 kilocalories to have been the minimum required to satisfy essential nutritional needs, although

a wife and three children. Moreover, that would have remained the case irrespective of whether his wife was earning since women were invariably remunerated at a lower rate.[129] Even to provide a family of five with a coarser and narrower 'bare-bones basket' of oat-meal porridge augmented by limited quantities of legumes, meat and butter and Spartan quantities of soap, cloth, candles, lamp oil, fuel and rent would have required 227 days' waged employment.[130] Since this was barely a living wage, English waged labour at this high tide of medieval population growth was plainly cheap.[131]

Attempting to rear and maintain a family on wages alone was a precarious existence, especially given the seasonally and annually uneven demand for farm labour. Since few wage earners could count upon being fully employed for all of the year it was necessary to supplement waged work with additional income or food sources from smallholding, common rights, fishing, mining or craft working. Contributions made by women and children to the household budget were also important.[132] Simply to get by, and as a hedge against the difficulty of securing sufficient regular paid work, most rural families needed some land of their own, or rights of access to common resources, on which they could grow or rear produce for consumption or sale.[133] Servanthood and landless labouring were viable economic propositions solely for those who remained single, women as well as men.[134] Only skilled workers, such as master masons, paid a premium wage of 3 pence or more a day, could have earned the 56 shillings a year which by 1290 was the annual cost of providing a family of five with a respectability basket of consumables.[135]

The problem for wage earners and others dependent in whole or in part upon the purchase of staple consumption goods was that after 1290 prices became increasingly unstable under the influence of monetary inflation in combination with a succession of major agricultural output shocks arising from extreme weather events and major panzootics of livestock.[136] These problems were most acute during the years of agrarian crisis from 1315

---

substantially higher levels of intake would have been required to sustain hard manual labour on the land in all weathers.

[129] Langdon and Claridge (2014); Humphries and Weisdorf (2015), 25.
[130] Allen (2009), 36–7.   [131] Henriques (2015), 160–1.
[132] Langdon and Masschaele (2006), 69–77.
[133] Britnell (2001), 10–14; Campbell (2005), 60–74.
[134] The terms *anilepimen/anilepiwymen* were used to describe male and female workers, and *garciones* male servants, who were single: Clark (1994); Fox (1996).
[135] Detailed costings of the 'respectability' and 'bare-bones' baskets of consumables *c*.1290 given in Appendix 3.1, Table 3.4 are the work of Alex Klein, undertaken in collaboration with Stephen Broadberry.
[136] Campbell (2010a), 287–93.

to 1322 when the cost of a standard basket of consumables doubled, with disastrous consequences for the wellbeing of families reliant upon the exchange of labour for goods. With less to harvest and fewer animals to shear and tend, demand for labour also shrank, precipitating many into temporary poverty or worse. Earlier, scarcity and high prices had squeezed wage earners' purchasing power hard in the mid-1290s and again in 1310/11, cutting daily real wage rates by a quarter (Figure 3.8A). The famine years of 1315 and 1316 were, however, far worse: farm workers' purchasing power shrank by a third and building workers' by a half. Never again would labourers' daily real wage rates sink as low,[137] although 1322–3, 1331 and 1347–8 were also years of great hardship. In contrast, during the cheap years of 1288–9 and 1338–9 labourers enjoyed a 40 per cent gain in purchasing power. Such bonanzas were, however, exceptional and for over forty years from 1290 to 1333 a decidedly rare occurrence (Figure 3.8A).

These wide price-driven swings in daily real wage rates obscure the latter's long-term stability and highlight the great economic stresses and strains by which this troubled half-century was characterized. Harvest success and failure was a major factor in the equation. Thus the abundant harvests of 1278, 1287–8, 1325–6, 1333–4, 1337–8, 1340 and 1342 all delivered windfall reductions in prices (Figure 3.8B). Conversely, dismal grain harvests in 1283, 1293–4, 1315–16, 1321, 1328, 1331 and 1346 drove prices of staple foodstuffs up and daily real wage rates down. Additionally, the devastating cattle panzootic of 1319–20, from which recovery was much slower, in combination with recurrent murrains of sheep, kept prices high for six consecutive years from 1321 to 1326 (Figure 3.8B). Nevertheless, not all major harvest shortfalls prompted commensurate price rises: 1339 and 1349 were notable exceptions when, first, lack of money and, then, massively reduced demand muted the price response. The effects of variations in the productivities of crops and livestock might thus be mitigated or exacerbated by other factors. It is nonetheless plain from the clear association between harvests, prices and daily real wage rates that this was a harvest-sensitive economy (Figures 3.8A and 3.8B). Wage earners fared well when harvests were abundant and badly when they were deficient and in the absence as yet of any effective public welfare provision, there was little to cushion the impact of harvest shortfalls.[138]

It is therefore all the more impressive that GDP per head held up remarkably well across this period (Figure 3.9). To be sure, there was

---

[137] The year 1316 constitutes the single lowest point on both Munro's (no date) revised building labourers' and Clark's (2007b) farm labourers' daily real wage indexes.

[138] Keene (2011); Sharp (2013).

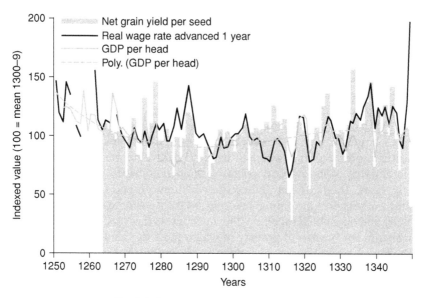

Figure 3.9 English farm labourers' daily real wage rates, net grain yields per seed, and GDP per head, 1250–1349
Sources: Figures 3.8A and B; Clark (2007b), 130–4; Campbell (2007); Broadberry and others (2015), 227–9; pre-1270 GDP per head estimates provided by Bas van Leeuwen

no economic growth and from the 1250s to 1280s, when GDP per head shrank from around $828 to $679 (with an absolute minimum of $637 in 1289), there may have been some economic decline. Yet the latter proved temporary since in large part it arose from the depressing effects of the sheep-scab epizootic of the late 1270s and 1280s upon the volume, quality and value of national wool output, farm incomes, domestic textile employment and production, and export earnings (Figure 3.4).[139] Between 1277 and 1285 national income contracted by approximately a quarter, which illustrates just how prominent production of this single raw material bulked in the value of the nation's economic output and how long it took to restore flock sizes and wool production to their pre-scab levels. Once that crisis had passed, GDP per head recovered to $755 in the 1300s and for the next half-century fluctuated around $763, ranging from minima of $686 in the famine year of 1316 and $682 in the war year of 1339 to maxima of $827 in 1319, and $836 in 1338 and 1344. Paradoxically, given the worsening international economic situation, GDP

[139] Lloyd (1977), 63; Stephenson (1988), 372–3, 381, 385.

per head was higher during the second quarter of the fourteenth than it had been during the last quarter of the thirteenth century (Figure 3.9).

Notwithstanding the conspicuous evidence of instability, the English economy was remarkably resilient. What it lacked was a capacity to grow. On the evidence of daily real wage rates and GDP per head, it held its own but no more. Four things locked it into a low productivity and low income per head trap: first, its inability to expand its modest commercial and manufacturing sectors due to shrinking international trade and low per head domestic demand; second, its consequent over-dependence upon primary production to which little additional value was added; third, the dominance of its overseas trade by alien merchants; fourth, the over-supply of labour within agriculture which entrapped too many families and workers on sub-optimal holdings, to the detriment of labour productivity and household incomes. The upshot was that this was a society with a significant burden of poverty in which mass demand was restricted to the most basic subsistence goods and only a privileged minority possessed significant disposable incomes.

3.01.3b The bottom-heavy socio-economic structure If the poverty line is defined as the income sufficient to provide a household comprising two adults and three children with a 'respectability' basket of consumables, on the evidence of the socio-economic profile reconstructed in Figure 3.10, almost 30 per cent of English households were living on that line and a further 40 per cent below it in 1290 and subsisting on a 'bare-bones' basket of consumables of varying degrees of adequacy.[140] As historians have long recognized and these figures demonstrate, one consequence of the two- to three-fold increase in population during the twelfth and thirteenth centuries was a dramatic expansion in the proportion of families living close to the subsistence minimum.[141] In later centuries, when times were good and poor relief was generally available, the proportion of families thus circumstanced would shrink to 20–25 per cent.[142] Conversely, in the second decade of the fourteenth century, when times were at their worst and the purchasing power of labourers' wages at its historical nadir, that proportion would rise to almost 70 per cent.[143]

At the close of the thirteenth century those leading this hand-to-mouth existence included households of most petty smallholders and cottagers

---

[140] This reconstruction is constrained by the need to accord with a total estimated national population of 4.75 million, arable area of 5.3 million hectares and national income of £4.2 million.

[141] Postan (1966), 563–5.   [142] Lindert and Williamson (1982).

[143] Above, note 137.

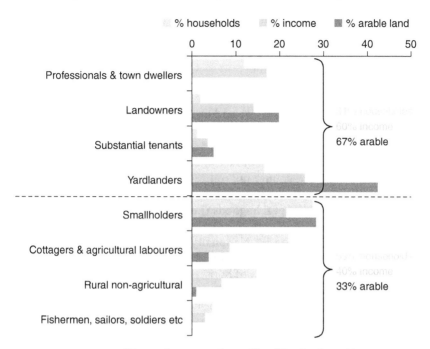

Figure 3.10 The socio-economic profile of England, *c.*1290
Source: Appendix 3.1, Table 3.4

provided with just a garden, a hectare or two of land, and/or common rights, plus many rural and urban artisans, most miners, fishermen and sailors, men-at-arms, all agricultural, non-agricultural and urban labourers, and, of course, paupers and vagrants. None of these groups possessed enough landed resources to be self-sufficient: in one way or another, all therefore depended for their survival upon the market. Proliferation of households with little or no land was in fact a symptom of commercialization. In contrast, the price of a respectability basket of consumables was well within the budget of the king, all lords, better-off townsmen, master craftsmen, the beneficed clergy, a majority of substantial tenants and minority of lesser tenants.

On this analysis, only a tiny minority of households, perhaps 1 per cent of the total, were truly rich and received annual incomes a hundred times greater than the national average of £3.84. A further 2 per cent of households were affluent, with incomes three to five times the national average, which placed them well above the poverty line. These rich and affluent households may have comprised only 3 per cent of the total but they received almost 15 per cent of the national income. A further 42 per cent of national income went to the 24 per cent of middling households, comprising substantial freeholders, villein yardlanders, millers, skilled artisans and substantial tradesmen, well able to afford a respectability basket of consumables (Appendix 3.1, Table 3.4). Collectively, these well-off groups comprised 31 per cent of households, received 60 per cent of income and possessed 67 per cent of arable land (Figure 3.10). The rest of the nation's income and land was shared between the 69 per cent of households living on or below the poverty line. Families in the bottom half of this income group lived in abject poverty and struggled to get by on even a bare-bones basket of consumables.

The sole surviving county tax roll recording individual taxpayer contributions to the lay subsidy levied in 1290 at the rate of a fifteenth of the assessed value of movable goods (i.e. those goods deemed surplus to subsistence) provides a useful cross-check on the credibility of this socio-economic reconstruction.[144] Nationally, this subsidy yielded £114,400, more than any other single tax granted the king.[145] In the case of Hertfordshire, around 40 per cent of households contributed; the bulk of the rest were exempted by poverty from doing so.[146] Individual tax assessments averaged £4.75, which implies that maybe half or more of the county's households were sufficiently well off to have been able to afford a respectability basket of consumables (Appendix 3.1, Table 3.4). Nevertheless, the average tax contribution of £0.32 (equivalent to a quarter of the annual earnings of a farm labourer) will have left many significantly worse off. The range of individual assessments recorded in the Hertfordshire lay subsidy roll demonstrates that differences were often as great within as between social groups, while the fact that so many households were too poor in movable goods to contribute highlights the bottom-heavy socio-economic structure then prevailing.

Such a highly polarized and skewed social distribution of wealth naturally constrained and shaped consumption. The vast majority of families were preoccupied with satisfying basic consumption needs. Over half lacked sufficient land to feed themselves and hence made increasing resort to the market to earn a living and obtain basic subsistence goods. Their need to live frugally sustained the trades in second-hand and stolen goods and a great deal of informal and illicit exchange. They dealt in petty quantities and most of their needs could be met within predominantly local orbits of exchange. Commercialization and urbanization may have

[144] The National Archives, PRO E179/120/2.
[145] Jenks (1998), 31; Ormrod (1991), 153.
[146] Assuming a national population of 4.75 million, a county population of 76,400, a household total of 15,300–17,000 and at least 6,500 taxpayers, each of them the head of a household.

provided the poor with new economic methods of survival but this had been at the price of sapping the means of their subsistence and leaving them increasingly exposed to the vagaries of the market. For them poor harvests carried a double jeopardy since the terms of trade swung against market suppliers of craft wares, services and labour and thereby compounded the adverse income effects of higher food prices.

The better-off tenant producers, in contrast, held more than enough land to satisfy their own subsistence needs and hence were regular suppliers of surpluses to the market. Their flocks produced the greater part of the wool that entered international trade and was paid for in part with the continental silver which stoked the expansion of monetary exchange.[147] Part of the iron used to shoe their horses and repair their ploughs and carts likewise came from abroad, as did numbers of the millstones employed to grind their grain into meal and flour and much of the salt with which some of their staple foodstuffs, most notably herrings, were preserved.[148] Typically, these better-off households bought seed, livestock and implements, hired labour and were regular purchasers of food, drink, clothing and housing. Indeed, they 'found it convenient to buy their bread, ale, joints of meat, pies and puddings from neighbours or from local markets'.[149] Substantial as was their demand for commercialized commodities, it nevertheless remained intrinsically unsophisticated. Their consumption of exotic goods obtained by long-distance trade mostly occurred at one remove, most commonly via attendance at church, where richly ornamented books, vestments, altar vessels, and buildings all incorporated materials obtained internationally.

Only about 5 per cent of households enjoyed significant spending power by the end of the thirteenth century and were therefore in a position to consume on a sufficiently large scale to stimulate production, influence taste and set fashions. Consequently, it was their more discriminating demand which sustained the national and international trades in exotic and luxury goods and high-quality manufactured wares. Further, the great estates of the landed elite were bulk suppliers of grain, livestock, livestock products, and timber and wood to the market.[150] Sales of these staple commodities combined with rents paid by their tenants and the profits of seigniorial jurisdictions and monopolies financed purchase of a luxury basket of consumables comprising wine, fish, meat, game, spices, wax, fine cloth, hawks, riding horses, arms and armour, religious art, and elaborate and prestigious buildings.[151] The Church in particular, which

[147] Campbell (2000), 158–9.   [148] Childs (1981), 26–7; Farmer (1992).
[149] Dyer (1992), 142.   [150] Campbell (1995a).
[151] Dyer (1989), 49–85; Woolgar (1999).

had gained more in lands and wealth than any other social group during the twelfth and thirteenth centuries, built for the glory of God. The services and rituals that it supplied constituted public goods mostly paid for by the rich but intended for the benefit and salvation of all. Religion, in fact, was one of the few staple commodities of the age consumed in approximately equal measure by both rich and poor.

3.01.3c Commerce, towns and industry England, like Flanders and Italy, was profoundly affected by the post-1291 downturn in international trade. Over the course of the thirteenth century it ran a positive trade balance based upon export of unprocessed primary products – wool, woolfells and hides, grain, herrings, tin, lead and coal – and a range of qualities of cloth, much of it light and undyed, in return for imports of a wide array of general merchandise and bullion. The net inflow of silver found expression in a sustained inflation of prices as English monarchs successively expanded the volume of the kingdom's silver currency (Table 2.2). Much of this trade, and the profits to be derived from it, nevertheless remained in the hands of foreign merchants. By the 1270s, for example, although native English merchants were the single largest group of wool exporters, they handled barely one-third of the wool trade. By 1304–11, however, when the wool-export trade was at its peak they had expanded this share to 57 per cent.[152] Londoners, in particular, had upped their participation in North Sea trade mostly at the expense of the Flemings and then, from the 1320s, successfully displaced Gascons in the wine trade.[153] Operating at a greater range was beyond their resources and as far as the long-distance trade in luxury products of Mediterranean and Asian provenance was concerned, 'participation of alien merchants was essential to the country's well-being throughout the period'.[154] Trade in general merchandise thus remained dominated by foreigners – Germans, Brabanters, Flemings, Gascons, Provençals and, above all, Italians – who, as the returns to the 1304 London tallage show, all maintained a strong presence in the capital.[155]

By 1304 London's commercial fortunes were probably at a peak. Derek Keene's reconstructions of rental values and occupancy rates in Cheapside, 'the principal marketing street of the city, if not the kingdom', indicate that both had been pushed to exceptionally high levels (Figure 3.11).[156] Here, in closely packed shops and private covered bazaars (known as selds), were innumerable complementary and competing retail

[152] Lloyd (1982), 204.   [153] Childs (1996), 133.
[154] Lloyd (1982), 206.   [155] Lloyd (1982), 227–33.
[156] Keene (1984a), 13; Keene (1985), 19–20; Schofield and others (1990), 185, cited in Nightingale (1995), 139.

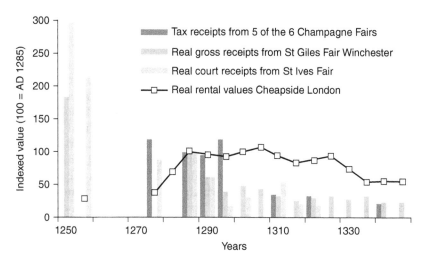

Figure 3.11 Indexed receipts from the fairs of Champagne (France), St Giles, Winchester, and St Ives, Hunts., and rental values in Cheapside, central London, 1250–1345
Sources: Titow (1987), 64–5; Moore (1985), 208; Edwards and Ogilvie (2012), 137; Keene (1984b)

outlets. More permanent establishment of the court at Westminster had brought increased patronage and spending power to the city and encouraged international companies to make it the base of their English operations. It was now the principal English base of the German Hanse and, more importantly, of the Italian societies of Bardi, Cerchi Bianchi, Chiarenti, Corone, Frescobaldi, Mozzi, Peruzzi, Portinari, Pulchi-Rimbertini and Spini, who had located themselves in Candlewick, Cheap and particularly Langbourn wards in the heart of the city.[157] Commercial displacement of the Flemings by the Italians had also drawn an increasing share of the wool trade to London, to the loss of Boston, and likewise enabled the capital to capture much business from the kingdom's once thriving international fairs, whose heyday, already by 1290, was clearly over.[158] Gross receipts to the bishops of Winchester from their fair of St Giles halved between 1250 and 1290 while court fines received by the abbots of Ramsey from their fair at St Ives contracted by two-thirds over the same period (Figure 3.11). At the same time, demand for commercial outlets in Cheapside rose and, with it, rental values.[159] Plainly, traders

---

[157] Lloyd (1982), 227–33.   [158] Nightingale (1996), 93–4; Campbell (2008), 914–15.
[159] Keene (1985), 12–13, 19–20.

were becoming less itinerant and deserting the fairs for permanent bases in the city.

A particularly sharp downturn in receipts at the fairs of St Ives and St Giles during the 1290s, almost exactly paralleling that at the Champagne fairs, nevertheless bears witness to the marked reduction in international commercial activity which set in at that time, following the fall of Acre and, in northern Europe, intensification of Philip IV's political and military aggression towards Guy Dampierre of Flanders and Edward I of England, holders respectively of the French fiefs of Flanders and Gascony. It was this festering feudal squabble that impelled England and France, and their neighbours Scotland and Flanders, on the course of conflict over the next half-century which had such negative ramifications for the multilateral patterns of trade upon which the economies of these realms had become dependent. Direct political interference in the conduct of commerce, first in the 1290s and then more seriously in the 1330s and 1340s, undermined business confidence by creating circumstances in which fortunes were more easily lost than made. Financing costly and destructive military campaigns destabilized both the French and English currencies and contributed to the credit crises which ruined those, like the Ricciardi and later the Bardi, who became drawn into supplying huge loans to the protagonists.[160] Increasingly, merchants, hauliers and shippers had to run the gauntlet of marauding armies and the brigands and pirates who thrived on the lawlessness engendered by war.

Unsurprisingly, business lost to the fairs of St Giles and St Ives during the commercial and political crisis of the 1290s was never wholly recovered. By the 1320s revenues from St Giles fair had settled at barely half their pre-crisis level while court revenues from St Ives fair were down by two-thirds (Figure 3.11). Ellen Wedemeyer Moore's analysis of entries in the St Ives court rolls demonstrates that after 1291, and especially from 1302, numbers attending the fair fell off significantly. Occasional appearances by merchants from southern Europe ceased, Flemings, once present in some numbers, stayed away and were replaced by Brabanters, fewer English fairgoers came from afar and, tellingly, numbers attending from the English cloth towns 'were markedly reduced by the 1290s and continued to fall throughout the early-fourteenth century'.[161] Since St Ives, in common with the other major fairs, had prospered as a wholesale outlet for English cloth, the last of these developments implies a significant falling off of demand for products of the urban textile industry.

---

[160] Nightingale (1995), 114–15, 121, 169–71, 175–6; Hunt and Murray (1999), 116–17; Bell and others (2011).
[161] Moore (1985), 210–13.

High-quality and high-value *scarlets* always found a market overseas and constituted the luxury end of the trade. Additionally, Patrick Chorley and Munro have argued that during the thirteenth century England, like Flanders, became a notable supplier of cheap, light, semi-finished and unfinished cloths to the international market.[162] These comprised the bulk of the cloths shipped abroad. All the country's leading fairs were geographically well placed to broker exchange between native cloth merchants and overseas buyers, many of them Flemish, who sold the English cloths on to Italian merchants at the great fairs of Flanders and Champagne.[163] Dyed and finished in Italy, these lower-grade cloths were eventually destined for sale in an array of southern markets. From the 1290s, however, loss of Levantine trading privileges, higher freight rates and rising transaction costs rendered this branch of commerce unprofitable and the English industry suffered much the same fate as its *say*-producing Flemish counterpart. Small-scale export of luxury *scarlets* continued but references to the cheap, coarse light textiles known as *burels*, *says*, *stamforts* and *wadmals* vanish from the record of English cloth exports and at the same time many of the towns particularly associated with their manufacture complained of industrial decline. Winchester, Oxford, London, Leicester and Lincoln all protested that their textile workers were reduced in both prosperity and numbers and in 1334 Northampton, seeking a lower tax assessment, reported that of the three hundred weavers active in the town in the time of Henry III, none remained.[164]

A steep decline in numbers of un-dyed (un-grained) and semi-finished cloths exported by alien merchants over the first two decades of the fourteenth century (Figure 3.12A) suggests that these claims of 'industrial crisis' were not without substance.[165] Concurrently, exports of English merchandise by aliens contracted by one-third, while imports, always three or four times more valuable, halved (Figure 3.12B). These downward trends continued into the mid-1330s and leave little doubt that overseas traders were becoming less actively engaged in English commerce. This left potential for native merchants with available capacity to extend their activities and capture a larger share of English overseas trade, which is one reason why Wendy Childs is more sanguine than Munro about the fate of the native cloth industry and its ability to adapt and survive.[166] Shrinking cloth imports is another.

By the early 1330s cloth imports by alien merchants were down by a quarter to fewer than 9,000 (and less than 7,000 in 1333–5) from

---

[162] Chorley (1988); Munro (1999a); Munro (1999c).
[163] Moore (1985), 11–12.   [164] Munro (1999c), 118, 119–21.
[165] Munro (1999c), 118.   [166] Childs (1996), 133.

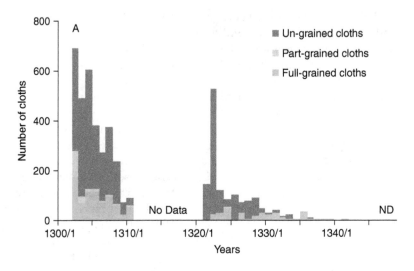

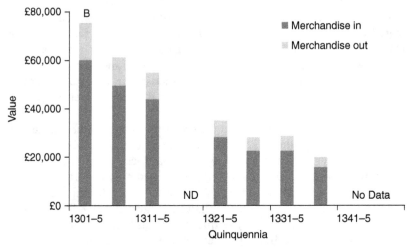

Figure 3.12 (A) English cloth exports by alien merchants, 1303–46. (B) Imports and exports of general merchandise by alien merchants through eight English ports (Boston, Lynn, Yarmouth, Ipswich, London, Sandwich, Winchelsea, Southampton), 1303–36
Sources: Munro (1998), 63–4; Lloyd (1982), 210–24

almost 12,000 a year in the early 1300s and a peak of 16,700 cloths in 1304/5.[167] Since there was no commensurate contraction in the number of English backs to be clothed, this gave native producers a larger

---

[167] Calculated from Lloyd (1982), 210–26.

share of the home market. In Norwich, for example, employment in textile production actually grew at this time and although cloth exports were hardly expanding, a range of English cloths continued to be sent abroad, especially to Iberia.[168] Symptoms of industrial revival are evident from the 1330s as differential duties imposed upon wool exported by alien merchants began to create the tariff protection that shielded native cloth producers from the full force of foreign competition.[169] For the time being, however, the chief mercantile advances made by the English were in the all-important wool and wine trades. These were on a sufficient scale to deprive native traders and shippers of the resources required to make good all the losses sustained by foreigners in other branches of commerce. Imports of general merchandise therefore undoubtedly fell, to the detriment of those dependent upon its sale and distribution. A reduction in spice imports probably explains the faltering fortunes and shrinking numbers of London grocers in the 1320s and 1330s.[170]

By the second quarter of the fourteenth century the volume of business handled by the once great fairs of St Giles and St Ives was well below the levels prevailing at the opening of the century and both emporia were becoming less international and more regional in character. London, too, was feeling the effects of the deepening international commercial recession as imported merchandise became scarcer and dearer. From the second decade of the century Cheapside rents slid inexorably downwards and by the 1340s had halved in real value (Figure 3.11).[171] Competition for retail space had eased substantially and shops and stalls were beginning to fall vacant.[172] Nightingale believes that business activity and employment in the metropolis were both shrinking and that fluctuating exchange rates and periodic scarcities of coin were making a bad situation worse.[173] Popular discontent spilled over into the London riots of October 1326.

The city's loss of economic dynamism was reflected in the waning taxable wealth of much of its hinterland. London and Middlesex's relative contribution to the lay subsidy of 1334 was 15 per cent less than to that of 1290, a magnitude of decline matched by a broad swathe of neighbouring counties comprising Hertfordshire, Buckinghamshire, Northamptonshire, Huntingdonshire, Bedfordshire, Cambridgeshire, Suffolk, Essex and Kent.[174] Complaints in the 1340/1 *Nonae* Returns of land falling

[168] Rutledge (2004), 166, 169, 188; Childs (1996), 133, 135, 146–7.
[169] Bolton (1980), 199–202.
[170] Nightingale (1995), 571; Nightingale (1996), 98–9.   [171] Keene (1985), 20.
[172] Keene (1984b); Keene (1985), 19; Nightingale (1996), 97.
[173] Nightingale (1996), 99.
[174] Calculated from the county totals given in Jenks (1998), 31, 39; Glasscock (1975).

out of cultivation and other economic problems, in tandem with reduced valuations of demesne assets and resources recorded by numbers of *inquisitiones post mortem*, reinforce the impression that all was not well in what, had metropolitan demand continued to serve as an engine of growth, should have been one of the most prosperous parts of the country.[175] These agrarian difficulties ensured that London continued to attract migrants, but this probably had more to do with push factors operating within the towns and countryside of its hinterland than the lure of booming employment opportunities in the city.[176] Bioarchaeological analysis has revealed the truncated and harsh lives and poor nutritional status experienced by many of those interred in the city's cemeteries at this time.[177]

The same was true of a number of other towns and cities, whose shrinking commerce and decaying industries failed to deter a steady influx of needy and often impoverished migrants, displaced from the countryside and lured to the towns by the ostensibly greater availability of casual work and charity. Non-inheriting sons and daughters no doubt were prominent among their number, which increased at times of harvest failure when operation of land and credit markets reduced many of the most marginalized property holders to the ranks of the landless. In Norfolk, England's most densely populated county, these were the processes which sustained the growth of Norwich's population between 1311 and 1333, even though the city's commercial and manufacturing bases were narrowing.[178] The upshot was a growing polarization of wealth. 'Within the leet of Mancroft real wealth became concentrated in the hands of a smaller proportion of the population, while immigration probably increased the number of urban poor', so that 'while Norwich grew in size and population during the early-fourteenth century, it may have declined both in relative wealth and in social cohesion'.[179]

Since most of the newcomers to Norwich lacked capital and were unable to secure regular employment and a reliable income, almost none succeeded in acquiring property. The proportion of non-property

[175] Baker (1966); Livingstone (2003), 320–61; Campbell and Bartley (2006), 44–51.
[176] Kowaleski (2014), 593–6. Migration to London possibly accounts in part for the downward trend in numbers of adult males evident from the 1320s on several Essex manors: Poos (1985).
[177] Dewitte (2010); Connell and others (2012); DeWitte and Slavin (2013); Kowaleski (2014).
[178] 'During the course of the early-fourteenth century Norwich seems to have moved from being a prosperous city with a wide industrial and commercial base to a city with a far greater proportion of urban poor heavily dependent upon a single industry' (textiles): Rutledge (2004), 188.
[179] Rutledge (1988), 28.

owners within Mancroft's tithing population rose from 87 to 94 per cent and, as the growth of population outpaced the supply of habitable properties within the leet, the sharp rise in demand for rented property was largely met by an increase in multiple occupancy, as available space was subdivided and sublet. Property owners exploited the situation by adding to the stock of cheap housing and demanding a full rack rent from its hapless occupants. Even so, by the late 1330s and 1340s rental receipts were falling as shrinking employment and mounting poverty eroded the capacity of many to pay. Here, therefore, continued in-migration 'had had the effect of increasing the proportion of urban poor and reducing living standards in a more densely occupied environment'.[180]

Norwich's economic plight would have been worse but for the revival of its cloth manufactory. The same applied to numbers of other towns, including York, Beverley, Winchester, Salisbury and Bristol, as well as such rural areas as the West Riding of Yorkshire, East Anglia and Wiltshire, all of which, from these early beginnings in the second quarter of the fourteenth century, would develop into important centres of cloth production.[181] In a parallel development, native merchants captured a larger share of wool exports, to the extent that by the early 1330s over three-quarters of the trade was in their hands, equivalent to an annual shipment of over 25,500 sacks (Figure 3.13). This position of dominance and volume of exports proved unsustainable once Edward III decided, in 1336, to use the wool trade to broker foreign alliances and secure massive loans in pursuit of his claim to the French Crown.[182] Given the absence of direct substitutes for English fine wool, his interference was more damaging to foreign buyers and manufacturers, especially the Flemings (Figure 3.5), than English growers and merchants. With the conspicuous exception of Shropshire, all the leading sheep-farming and wool-producing counties, from Sussex west to Dorset and the East Riding of Yorkshire and Lincolnshire southwest to Somerset, increased their relative shares of taxable wealth between 1290 and 1334 (Oxfordshire, Berkshire, Hampshire, Somerset and Dorset, substantially so).[183] Most had made good the losses incurred during the recurrent sheep murrains of 1315–25 and from the 1330s sheep numbers were rising strongly (Figure 3.4). Contracting exports during the opening decade of the Hundred Years War therefore imply that an expanding share of an enlarged wool clip was being diverted to English cloth manufacturers.

---

[180] Rutledge (1995), 23.   [181] Lloyd (1977), 144–92; Bolton (1980), 200–1.
[182] Lloyd (1977), 144–92; Ormrod (1990), 181–3, 188–94.
[183] Calculated from the county totals given in Jenks (1998), 31, 39; Glasscock (1975).

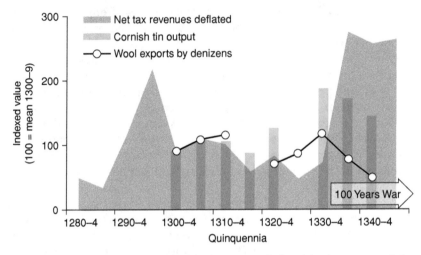

Figure 3.13 England: indexed output of Cornish tin presented for coinage, exports of wool by denizen merchants, and deflated net receipts from direct and indirect taxation (quinquennial means), 1280–4 to 1345–9
Sources: Hatcher (1973), 156; Carus-Wilson and Coleman (1963), 40–6; Ormrod (2010)

No part of the country appears to have fared better during the first half of the fourteenth century than the southwest. In fact, Cornwall's relative tax contribution grew by more than that of any other county between 1290 and 1334, with Devon's not far behind.[184] Much of their prosperity is attributable to the booming output of the stannaries. At the recorded peak of production in the early 1330s the weight of tin presented for coinage, the bulk of it from Cornish mines, was double that presented at the opening of the century (Figure 3.13). This impressive rise in output was sustained by an abundant supply of cheap labour and the strength of overseas and especially Italian demand for English tin. The Peruzzi and Bardi companies were notable purchasers of tin, which they shipped via Southampton and London to Flanders and then Italy, whence, often converted into rod and sheet form, it was traded throughout the Mediterranean and Black Seas, as far as Kaffa in the Crimea and Tana at the mouth of the Don.[185] Their bankruptcy a few years later must therefore have constituted a significant setback to tin production, which had already been adversely affected by the trade downturn that

[184] Calculated from the county totals given in Jenks (1998), 31, 39; Glasscock (1975).
[185] Hatcher (1973), 93–5.

followed Edward III's declaration of war against France in 1337 (Figure 3.13).

The destructive effects of war are writ large in the substantially reduced relative tax contributions of those northern counties – Cumberland and Westmorland, Northumberland, the North and West Ridings of Yorkshire, and Derbyshire – which most bore the brunt of post-Bannockburn Scottish raiding and the depredations of defending English armies.[186] French raids on the south coast had a similar but more localized impact upon the Isle of Wight and towns such as Winchelsea and Southampton.[187] Further, purveyance of provisions and requisitioning of merchant vessels for naval use were disruptive of economic activity and affected some counties and ports repeatedly, prompting much contemporary complaint.[188] Heavy and recurrent taxation, especially in the lead-up to major campaigns, was more general in its impacts and redistributed wealth and spending power to the benefit of the Crown and its military objectives. In an economy otherwise dominated by primary production, the kingdom's involvement in a succession of costly wars against Scotland and France consequently promoted expansion of the state and its tax-raising apparatus. Rising military expenditure ensued. Provided that war was mostly waged abroad rather than at home, this, paradoxically, constituted a source of growth.[189]

As the analogous example of seventeenth-century Sweden shows, large-scale state-funded warfare could raise the GDP per head of an otherwise relatively poor and primary-producing economy.[190] For Sweden to operate as a belligerent 'not only human resources had to be mobilized, but industrial as well, for instance, for weapons, ammunition, and textile goods'.[191] Likewise, in the case of early fourteenth-century England, hiring, equipping, transporting, provisioning and maintaining armies on the scale of those deployed by the three Edwards and keeping them in the field at a considerable distance for sustained periods of time demanded deployment of formidable resources.[192] Although there was an obvious downside to the cost of it all, much paid employment was generated and suppliers and manufacturers of munitions and much else thrived on the upturn in demand for their services and wares. This was especially the case during preparations for the English invasion of France which took place in 1346. Net receipts from direct and indirect taxation

---

[186] Calculated from the county totals given in Jenks (1998), 31, 39; Glasscock (1975).
[187] Livingstone (2003), 347.   [188] Maddicott (1987), 299–318.
[189] Langdon and Masschaele (2006), 75–6.
[190] Stimulated by the 'Military State', Swedish GDP per head rose from $847 in 1600 to $1,251 in 1700: Schön and Krantz (2012), 541–3, 546.
[191] Schön and Krantz (2012), 542.   [192] Hewitt (1966); Allmand (1988), 91–119.

capture both the unprecedented financial demands made by this and earlier episodes of open warfare and the correspondingly substantial injections of military expenditure into the economy that potentially occurred at such times (Figure 3.13). From 1335 to 1349 real tax receipts were consistently three times greater than at the opening of the fourteenth century and at their absolute peak under Edward III from 1339 to 1341 were two-thirds greater than the previous peak from 1294 to 1297, when Edward I was simultaneously fighting a war of defence in Gascony and of aggression in Scotland.[193] In fact, the intensity of the tax demands necessitated by the scale of Edward I's and Edward III's military operations placed the Crown's international creditors under financial duress, begot major domestic constitutional crises and, for many poor people, greatly compounded the adverse effects of the bad harvests of 1293–4 and 1339.[194] Moreover, regardless of whatever ambiguous economic benefits these great conflicts may have bestowed on England, they did irrevocable harm to the peaceful conduct of trade and commerce upon which the general prosperity of Latin Christendom had rested.

3.01.3d Morcellation and the growth of structural poverty The fact that English GDP per head rose by a quarter immediately following the demographic disaster of the Black Death strongly implies that previously pressure of numbers had been weighing the economy down and depressing average output per head.[195] Nor, in later centuries, when population growth eventually resumed was there a return to the depressed GDP per head levels of the late thirteenth and early fourteenth centuries, because rising real output and employment within the manufacturing and service sectors provided both a demand stimulus and an occupational alternative to primary production.[196] During the twelfth and thirteenth centuries, in contrast, the lesser scale and weaker dynamic of the secondary and tertiary sectors meant that it befell agriculture to absorb the bulk of the population growth set in train and sustained by the positive environmental, institutional and economic circumstances then prevailing. This was achieved in part by bringing more land into more productive uses. Thus, between 1086 and 1290 the nation's stock of arable land more than doubled from just under 2.5 million to maybe as much as 5.3 million hectares.[197] Proliferation of rural households nevertheless proceeded

---

[193] Prestwich (1988), 401–35; Ormrod (1990), 10–15.
[194] For a case study see Schofield (1997).   [195] Broadberry and others (2015), 229.
[196] Broadberry and others (2013), 228–38.
[197] For the Domesday area see Campbell (2000), 386–9. For the area in 1290, Broadberry and others (2015), 65–73, revise upwards the estimate of Campbell (2000), 388–90.

faster, trebling over these two centuries, with the inevitable result that holdings, on average, shrank in size.

Had the reduction in holding size proceeded uniformly its consequences for household incomes might not have been too serious. Instead, pre-existing differences in holding size and tenure became magnified so that inequality grew.[198] Especially ominous for living standards and labour productivity was the multiplication of holdings containing five hectares or less of land. By 1290 approximately 700,000 households (over three-quarters of the rural total) subsisted on such petty holdings, 400,000 of them on less than one hectare of land and 240,000 of those dependent upon augmenting their incomes by labouring on the land of others (Appendix 3.1, Table 3.4).[199] The growing cheapness and abundance of the surplus labour they supplied to the minority of larger producers farming two-thirds of the land helped raise and bolster land productivity within the market-orientated sector.[200] On their own sub-optimal holdings they substituted labour, of which they had no shortage, for land and capital, in which they were deficient, with adverse consequences for labour productivity, since too little of their labour was efficiently and effectively deployed for too little of the time.[201] Where returns to their labour were so poor, poverty was inescapable and sprang less, as once supposed, from exploitative and arbitrary feudal lordship than the want of resources and enforcement of effective restrictions on the morcellation of land.[202]

Economic survival for tenants everywhere depended upon possession of family and land, the twin sources of welfare and subsistence. Providing for adult children was therefore a priority. Creating new holdings by piecemeal reclamation from the waste was one way of achieving this. Employing equitable inheritance practices was another. Partible inheritance had an obviously fragmenting effect whenever there were several surviving heirs. Its divisive effects were the more profound because it was normal practice to give each heir an equal share of each component plot.[203] Even primogeniture was likely to result in subdivision since,

---

[198] In 1086, according to Domesday Book, 13,600 free households held on average 16.7 hectares, 23,300 sokeman households and 109,200 villein households each held 9.4 hectares, and 88,800 households of bordars, cottars and coscets held on average 1.3 hectares: recorded household numbers from Darby (1977), 89, 337; mean holding size from Seebohm (1883), 102–3.

[199] For a comparable example of extreme morcellation see Vanhaute (2001).

[200] Campbell and Overton (1993), 74, 97–9; Campbell (2000), 306–85.

[201] For the productivity of smallholders at Oakington, Cambridgeshire, see Sapoznik (2013).

[202] This is contrary to the claims of Brenner (1976) and Brenner (1982).

[203] For example Baker (1964); Campbell (1980).

in default of sons, all daughters inherited equally. Also, parents usually endeavoured to make at least some landed provision for otherwise dispossessed children. A gift of assarted land might be used for this purpose but more commonly younger children were settled on smallholdings either hived off from the main holding or obtained for the purpose by lease or purchase. At Sedgeford in Norfolk, 'a great deal of the fragmentation of holdings that can be traced through the thirteenth century court rolls and surveys was the result of the transfer of land by tenants in order to provide for non-inheriting sons or daughters'.[204] In a demographic situation where each generation was more numerous than its predecessor, the net effect of all forms of inheritance was therefore a progressive division of both parcels and holdings. Of itself, however, as Cliff Bekar and Clyde Reed emphasize, *post mortem* subdivision did not necessarily promote inequality: what drove the latter was concurrent operation of a land market.[205]

Although land markets might be used to counter the divisiveness of inheritance and engross plots and holdings, in thirteenth- and early fourteenth-century England their net effect was the opposite. Indeed, once plots had been detached from a family holding and permanently alienated to non-kin there was little prospect of their being reunited. What recommended such transactions to subsistence producers was the dubious double advantage of being able to acquire additional land when circumstances permitted and sell off plots and capitalize their value when necessity dictated. In this way the risks of harvest failure were mitigated.[206] In order to participate in the market, tenants typically employed credit to finance their purchases and land sales to pay off their debts. This compounded the effects of harvest failure since debt default was more likely at such times, many creditors were themselves adversely affected by crisis years and creditors were more likely to resort to litigation in such years. In fact, 'the coincidence between dearth and increased debt recovery is well attested'.[207] Creditors foreclosing on debts were therefore as likely to trigger distress land sales as the need to acquire cash to buy food.[208]

In the longer term, it was recurrent repetition of this scenario that promoted the progressive attrition of holdings and reduced many households to a state of semi-landlessness. The effects of this process are graphically illustrated by the two east Norfolk manors of Hevingham and Martham, belonging respectively to the bishop of Norwich and prior of Norwich Cathedral Priory (Figure 3.14). Morcellation was already well advanced

---

[204] Williamson (1984), 100.   [205] Bekar and Reed (2013), 298–301.
[206] Bekar and Reed (2013), 300–1, 312.   [207] Briggs (2009), 187.
[208] Schofield (1997).

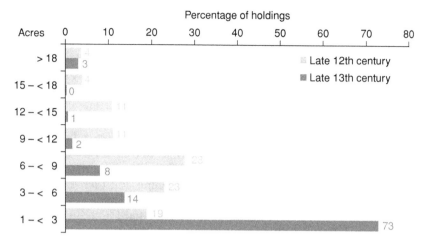

Figure 3.14 Evidence of shrinking holding sizes on the manors of Hevingham and Martham in Norfolk between the late twelfth and late thirteenth centuries
Source: Campbell (1981), 18–26

on these two manors by the late eleventh century, when 70 per cent of all recorded holdings were smaller than nine acres (3.64 hectares) and the modal holding size was six to nine acres (2.43–3.64 hectares). A century later the modal holding size had fallen to less than three acres (1.21 hectares) and 95 per cent of tenants held less than nine acres of land. Undoubtedly, many of these tenants must have held additional land from other lords and by other tenures, yet because that too must have been subject to similar processes of attrition, there is no escaping the fact that a clear majority of tenant households were being relegated to the status of petty smallholders.[209] This was morcellation with a vengeance and on both manors over the next half-century it proceeded further since, until the growth of population was reversed, the process contained its own self-perpetuating momentum.[210]

Once land markets became established, each sale, by reducing a household's landed resources and increasing its exposure to harvest risk, begot another.[211] Runs of good harvests obviously provided some respite but

[209] The corrosive effects of land markets upon holding sizes at Gressenhall and Sedgeford (Norfolk) and Redgrave and Hinderclay (Suffolk) are documented by Williamson (1984); Smith (1984a); Smith (1996); Schofield (1997).
[210] Holdings continued to fragment at neighbouring Coltishall between 1275/1300 and 1349: Figure 3.17.
[211] Bekar and Reed (2013), 301, 308–10.

recouping losses was difficult since sales in bad times were relatively disadvantageous to the seller and purchases in good times disadvantageous
to the buyer. Distress sales therefore favoured those who remained economically strong and able to purchase land on beneficial terms at the
expense of those who were sliding irrevocably into greater poverty. It
was the ability of those who were relatively well off to avail themselves
of the misfortune of others and to establish non-inheriting children on
purchased land that sustained their own superior reproduction rates. As
Razi's case study of Halesowen in Worcestershire demonstrates, the processes of downward social mobility thereby set in train served to swell the
ranks of smallholders whose inferior material wellbeing prevented them
from reproducing as successfully.[212] A widening gulf therefore opened
between, on one hand, a shrinking minority of households with sufficient
land to make ends meet even when times were hard and, on the other,
a growing majority of poor households for whom economic survival was
an increasing struggle. In fact, at Hevingham and Martham this process proceeded so far that substantial holdings virtually disappeared and
almost all tenants were reduced to smallholding status (Figure 3.14).
What had brought this extreme situation to pass had been the unrestrained workings of land and credit markets in conjunction with partible
inheritance practices under conditions of population growth and harvest
variability.

Tenants of these pitifully small villein holdings at Hevingham and
Martham were servile and held their land, in which they enjoyed her-
itable rights, according to terms that were customary rather than con-
tractual. By convention, they 'sold' villein land by surrendering it back
into the lord's hands, who then re-granted it to the 'purchasing' tenant in
return for an entry fine.[213] Record of the transaction in the court roll provided proof of title. Seigniorial approval was therefore fundamental to the
transfer of ownership with the result that the market in villein land was
subject to considerable variation from manor to manor, estate to estate,
and region to region in accordance with custom and estate policy.[214]
In this regard the situation at Hevingham and Martham represents an
extreme. Extant court rolls show that an active market in villein land was
well established on both manors, whose lords had long abandoned any
attempt to preserve the integrity of standard villein *tenementa*.[215] In both
cases individual plots of ¼ to ½ hectare rather than entire holdings were
the objects of exchange, reflecting the limited resources of those who

---

[212] Razi (1980), 94–8. See also Britton (1977), 132–43.
[213] Razi and Smith (1996a), 54–5.   [214] Harvey (1984b); Page (2003).
[215] Campbell (1980), 178–82.

bought and sold them.[216] Elsewhere in densely populated Norfolk it is the market in individual plots that similarly dominates the record on all manors with surviving court rolls.

A parallel market existed in freehold land, freely and actively transacted by private charter (of which many thousands survive) according to the Common Law of the realm. Feet of Fines preserved in The National Archives constitute the single most comprehensive record of these property transactions (Figure 3.18). By the early fourteenth century there was as much freehold as villein land, although it was unequally distributed across the country.[217] It could be acquired and held without any taint of servility and bought and sold with little if any seigniorial interference and hence, in an increasingly land-deficient age, was much sought after.[218] The fixed low assize rents attached to free land were a further attraction as they constituted a significantly lighter rental burden than the customary rents paid for villein land: 9,827 free holdings recorded in the 1279 Hundred Rolls were liable for an average rent of 10.23 pence a hectare compared with the average of 17.54 pence paid by 10,080 villein holdings.[219] The facility with which free land could be transacted and the generally lower rents charged for it therefore meant that it was more susceptible to morcellation than villein land. Although the Hundred Rolls record some very substantial free holdings of 16 hectares or more, two-thirds contained less than 4 hectares and 60 per cent were smaller than 2½ hectares, in contrast, respectively, to 41 per cent and 36 per cent of villein holdings.[220]

Notwithstanding that customary tenants usually paid substantially higher rents for their land and have often been represented as the victims of arbitrary and oppressive lordship, free tenants, in fact, had become the new poor.[221] Their landholdings were so shrunken that self-sufficiency was not an option. Instead, to meet their subsistence needs, they were obliged to become increasingly dependent upon the market, hiring out their labour and producing high-value goods for sale so that they might purchase lower-value goods for consumption. Theirs was a commercial subsistence economy. Yet market forces were turning against them: the multiplying number of land-hungry poor householders bid up land values and competed for employment in an increasingly glutted labour market.[222] Dwindling opportunities for augmenting their incomes from

---

[216] Campbell (1975), 71–9, 124–5, 280–2, 294–5.
[217] Campbell (2005), 24–44; Campbell and Bartley (2006), 253–65.
[218] See the essays contained in Smith (1984b); Harvey (1984b); Razi and Smith (1996b); Britnell (2003).
[219] Kanzaka (2002), 599.   [220] Kanzaka (2002), 599.
[221] Campbell (2005).   [222] Langdon and Claridge (2014).

other sources further eroded their living standards and reinforced their mounting dependence upon their own inadequate holdings. Poor harvests hit them hard and generated further spates of distress land sales and yet further morcellation (Figure 3.18).[223]

As yet very little land, most of it former demesne, was held by leasehold and the property rights of lessees were poorly defined and defended. Informal short-term subletting was however probably rife, although mostly hidden from view in surviving documents.[224] By the end of the thirteenth century most head rents for both free and villein land had long been fixed by custom and were therefore well below the current rental value of the land, as witnessed by the tenth of all villein tenants and half of all free tenants in the Hundred Rolls who paid less than 5 pence a hectare for their land.[225] Low fixed rents and rising prices and land values were an ideal recipe for rent seeking, since by subdividing and subletting their land those paying these sub-market rents could appropriate to themselves the full rack rent. The many freehold tenants were in the strongest position to act in this way. The lowest head rents recorded in the 1279–80 Hundred Rolls were for freehold land, much of which had been acquired by gentry, ecclesiastics, craftsmen and tradesmen, who did not cultivate it themselves but acted as 'middlemen', no doubt subletting it piecemeal for terms of years in return for profit rents.[226] At Bishops Cleeve in Gloucestershire, for example, twenty-one individual sub-tenants held from a single free tenant.[227] Nor, when they could get away with it, can substantial servile tenants have been indifferent to the advantages of subletting, especially as they, too, by the early fourteenth century usually paid sub-economic rents for their yardlands. On manors recorded by the Hundred Rolls, rents paid by villein tenants consistently fell short of the rents paid for recent commercial lettings of freehold and leasehold land.[228] Subletting also offered them a means of recruiting and remunerating farm servants. By 1315 probably at least a quarter of a million immiserated households must have eked out a tenuous and anonymous existence as the tenants and tied labourers of other men.

By the end of the thirteenth century these interconnected processes of partition, subdivision, piecemeal selling and subletting had created the bottom-heavy landholding structure outlined in Figure 3.10.[229] Harvest failure was a key ingredient of the process because it was to mitigate its

[223] Davies and Kissock (2004).   [224] Campbell (2005), 45–60.
[225] Kanzaka (2002), 599.   [226] Kanzaka (2002); Barg (1991).
[227] Dyer (1989), 120.   [228] Kanzaka (2002), 599, 610–12.
[229] Bekar and Reed (2013), 312, attribute morcellation to interactions between inheritance practices, land markets, the relative size of largeholder families, harvest risk, the extent of pooling and storage, on multiple variables.

effects that many small producers availed themselves of the land market in the first place and because of its effects that so many were then pushed into making distress land sales. Such crisis-motivated sales may have enabled these smallholding households to survive harvest shortfalls but this was at a high economic price insofar as so many had to part with a portion or all of the means of their subsistence.[230] As Bekar and Reed point out, it was onto these households therefore that the bulk of society's subsistence risk was shifted and their members consequently suffered the greatest deprivation when harvests failed.[231] Worryingly, a large, economically vulnerable socio-economic group had come into being at the very time that long-established atmospheric circulation patterns were destabilizing and the frequency of extreme weather events increasing.[232] After 1300, even though rates of population growth eased, the severity and incidence of these harvest shocks lent renewed momentum to the morcellation process and made victims of those individuals and families whose holdings had already succumbed to it. An intractable problem of structural poverty had been created which left little prospect of income inequality diminishing, agricultural labour productivity improving or mass demand for non-agricultural goods and services reviving.

For the poorest households grain consumed as pottage, bread and ale contributed over 80 per cent of daily kilocalories.[233] Annual carryovers were small. Dependence upon the annual harvest was therefore absolute and prices typically rose and scarcity mounted during the hungry weeks and months leading up to the next year's harvest. As a hedge against harvest failure most cultivators sowed a mixture of winter and spring crops. This made rotational good sense and experience also showed that growing and harvesting conditions had to be unusually good or bad before the yields of both types of grain were similarly affected.[234] Individually, wheat, barley and oats delivered deficient yields on a regular basis: between 1270 and 1349 each returned a net yield 20 per cent below average about once every six years (Table 3.2).[235] More serious failures of 30 per cent or more might be expected every dozen years or so. For all crops to fail together, however, was exceptional. Between 1280 and 1314 the bumper harvests of 1277–8 and 1288 stand out clearly but 1294 and 1304 alone delivered across-the-board harvest failures (Figure 3.15).

---

[230] Campbell (1984).   [231] Bekar and Reed (2013), 310–12.
[232] Below, Section 3.02.   [233] Broadberry and others (2015), 289.
[234] Campbell and Ó Gráda (2011).
[235] Hoskins (1964), 29–30, reckoned on the evidence of grain prices that one year in six delivered a really bad harvest and cites Elizabethan Dr John Hales, who believed that one harvest in seven was a failure.

Table 3.2 *English net grain yields per seed, 1280–1340: frequency of harvest shortfalls, percentage variance and correlation coefficients*

Magnitude of shortfall	Number of deficient harvests 1270–1349 (N = 80)			
	Wheat (W)	Barley (B)	Oats (O)	W(BO)
≥10%	24	24	23	21
≥20%	12	14	13	8
≥30%	6	9	5	3
≥40%	3	1	0	2

Years	% variance			
	Wheat (W)	Barley (B)	Oats (O)	W(BO)
1280–1314	12.9	14.3	17.4	9.3
1315–40	26.1	21.8	15.9	19.6

	Correlation coefficients		
	Wheat : Barley	Wheat : Oats	Barley : Oats
1280–1314	+0.13	+0.04	+0.13
1315–33	+0.69	+0.55	+0.83
1315–40	+0.58	+0.35	+0.70

Note: W(BO) is the average yield of the principal winter and spring grains ((W × 0.5) + ((B + O) × 0.25)).
Source: calculated from Campbell (2007)

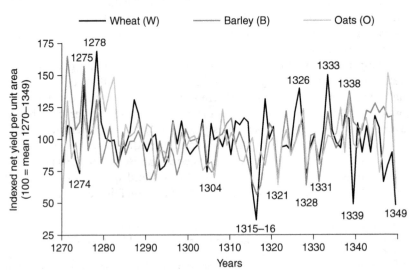

Figure 3.15 Indexed English net grain yields per unit area, 1270–1349
Source: Campbell (2007)

In fact, the most remarkable feature of this fulcrum period is the weakness of the correlations between the yields of the different grains, including, surprisingly, spring-sown barley and oats (Table 3.2). Even when the 1290s brought an extended run of sub-standard harvests, with four out of ten wheat and oats harvests and no less than seven out of ten barley harvests yielding at least 10 per cent below average, almost miraculously, 1294 was the sole year when yields of all three grains were seriously deficient (Figure 3.15). In every other year during this exceptionally difficult decade, spreading risks by growing a mix of crops clearly paid off and helped mitigate the worst effects of the prevailing adverse weather conditions. From 1315 to 1340, however, this strategy proved far less effective as hemispherical patterns of atmospheric circulation and their associated weather conditions changed profoundly.[236]

3.01.3c The effects of the agrarian crisis of 1315–22 and its aftermath In the long-term chronology of harvests, 1315 marks the onset of a distinctive twenty-year episode when harvests failed repeatedly and year-on-year variations in yields of wheat, barley and oats displayed a conspicuous synchronicity, either succeeding or failing together (Figure 3.15 and Table 3.2). The insurance benefits hitherto gained by cultivating a mix of grains ceased to materialize as producers now found the environmental odds stacked against them. Five times within the space of fifteen years, in 1316, 1321, 1324, 1328 and 1331, serious shortfalls occurred in the harvests of all three principal grains (Figure 3.15). At the same time, the heightened variability of yields meant producers faced much greater uncertainty (Table 3.2). Although yields of oats (the hardiest of grains) registered no significant change in variance, the variance of barley yields rose by 50 per cent and that of wheat doubled. Yields of winter and spring grains were now closely tracking each other and varying widely from year to year. In the worst years the amplitude of the harvest shortfalls was also greater than anything experienced in living memory, with net reductions in excess of 25 per cent in 1315, 1316, 1321 and 1328. Not since the back-to-back failure of 1256–7 had harvests failed on such a scale.[237] The harvest of 1316, the second of two ruined by incessant rains, was an outright disaster: yields of oats, barley and wheat (the principal bread grain) were respectively 25 per cent, 40 per cent and 60 per cent below average.

Coming at the climax of two centuries of population growth and mounting income inequality, the timing of this weather-inflicted collapse in output of staple foodstuffs could not have been worse, especially as further damage was inflicted by associated outbreaks of sheep murrain

---

[236] Below, Section 3.02.   [237] Campbell (2013a).

(Figure 3.4), devastating raids by the Scots on northern England, and then the great cattle panzootic of 1319–20.[238] Back-to-back harvest failures on this scale were once-in-250-years events, although the context of global climatic change in which the 1315–16 failure occurred implies that it was anything but a random statistical freak.[239] Agricultural output and employment shrank dramatically and seed corn became scarce and expensive. National income contracted and as food prices soared, building and farming labourers' daily real wage rates plumbed their lowest recorded levels (Figures 3.6 and 3.9). The economic vulnerability of so many households ensured that these were years of genuine famine, when the triple penalty of poverty, malnutrition and disease generated significant excess mortality.[240]

Nor was the 1315–16 harvest failure a passing event. Sequel shortfalls in 1321, 1324, 1328 and 1331 (Figure 3.15) progressively undermined the budgets of many normally solvent households, leaving them deficient in grain and unable to satisfy their subsistence needs and credit obligations. Hardship reached higher up the socio-economic scale than ever before, with the result that more households were obliged to resort to distress land sales in order to make ends meet. On the small lay manor of Hakeford Hall in Coltishall in densely populated east Norfolk the normal steady trickle of petty transactions became a flood, far greater in amplitude and duration than that which had followed the lesser harvest failures and war-induced economic stresses of the 1290s (Figure 3.16).[241] Prevailing circumstances left no room for sentiment, as those in need endeavoured to obtain the best price from whoever would buy.[242] Most transactions were contracted between non-kin and typically involved pathetically small pieces of land, as sellers attempted to minimize their losses and few buyers could afford to purchase large plots.[243]

Waves of crisis selling involving hundreds of individuals prevailed until the bumper harvest of 1333, and the run of above-average harvests that followed it, brought an end to the crisis (Figure 3.16). An initial surge in transactions followed the famine years of 1315 and 1316, another accompanied the devastating cattle plague of 1319, a third was triggered by the disastrous harvest of 1321 and a fourth by the dismal harvests of 1328 and 1331. Each successive output shock with its sequential inflation of prices elicited a disproportionately greater spate of land sales

---

[238] For a detailed examination of this episode see Campbell (2010a), 287–93.
[239] Campbell and Ó Gráda (2011), 865–70.
[240] Postan and Titow (1959); Campbell (2010a), 291–2.   [241] Campbell (1984).
[242] Schofield (2008).   [243] Campbell (1984), 107–15.

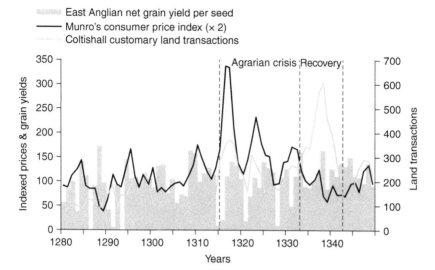

Figure 3.16 Numbers of customary land transactions on the manor of Hakeford Hall in Coltishall, Norfolk, 1280–1349

Notes: price index × 2; East Anglian yield index (wheat × 0.3 + barley × 0.6 + oats × 0.1) × 1.5; number of land transactions is a 3-year moving average.

Sources: Munro (no date); Campbell (1984), 131–2; Campbell (2007)

as the economic plight of this manor's many smallholders progressively worsened.[244] Nevertheless, against all the odds and partly because of the effectiveness of these desperate survival measures, the tenant population of this manor was actually greater on the eve of the Black Death in 1348 than it had been a generation earlier on the eve of the Great Famine.[245] Indeed, during the windfall run of good harvests in the mid-1330s, the land market was busier than ever before as many desperately attempted to make good their earlier losses. During this brief reversal of the earlier crisis situation, buyers, therefore, outnumbered sellers.[246]

So many petty land transactions in such a short space of time inevitably resulted in a further intensive round of morcellation. The holdings of those Coltishall tenants who died in the Black Death of 1349 were, on average, barely half the size of those held by their forebears during the final quarter of the thirteenth century. Largely as a result of distress sales enforced by the mounting agrarian crisis, the privileged minority

[244] Campbell (1984), 118–19.   [245] Campbell (1984), 95–101.
[246] Campbell (1984), 111, 115–17.

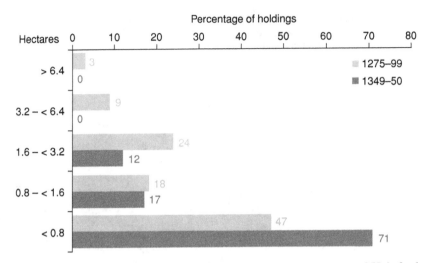

Figure 3.17 The progress of morcellation on the manor of Hakeford Hall in Coltishall, Norfolk, over the first half of the fourteenth century *Source*: Campbell (1984), 105

of tenants who had once held at least 3¼ hectares had vanished, while the proportion holding ¾ hectare or less had grown by over 50 per cent (Figure 3.17). In fact, so extreme was the morcellation of holdings that it is difficult to imagine how it could have progressed further. Efforts by a few enterprising individuals to engross land were not unknown but did not endure beyond their own lifetimes. The economic tide was against them. As holdings were further eroded in size so, too, plots were split and truncated in order to supply the market with the petty parcels in which its impoverished participants now dealt. Fields, therefore, became as fragmented as holdings, which did little to enhance the efficiency and productivity of the labour applied to them.[247]

The massive surge in crisis-related land sales between 1315 and 1332 was repeated elsewhere with mostly similar consequences. The Suffolk manors of Hinderclay and Redgrave had already experienced major surges in distress sales during the subsistence crisis of the 1290s but these were eclipsed by their responses to the Great Famine. Between 1310 and the peak of the crisis in 1316, sales at Redgrave increased two-and-a-half-fold and at Hinderclay five-fold; on the Norfolk manor of Hindolveston the increase in land-market activity was three-fold while on the Winchester estates non-familial land transfers doubled.[248] After a lull

---

[247] Campbell (1980); Campbell (1981).
[248] Smith (1984a), 154–5; Schofield (2008), 46; Hudson (1921), 202–3; Page (2001).

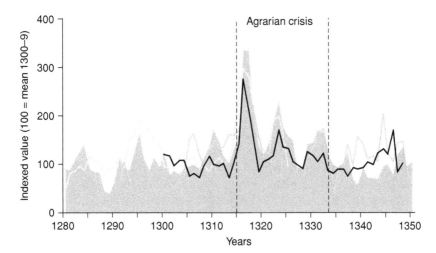

Figure 3.18 Prices, land transactions and crimes in England, 1280–1349

Notes: index of customary transactions derived from manorial chronologies for Coltishall 1280–1325 and Hindolveston 1309–26 (Norfolk) and Hinderclay 1288–1322 and Redgrave 1280–1319 (Suffolk); index of freehold land transactions derived from counts of Feet of Fines for Berkshire, Essex, Gloucestershire, Herefordshire, Shropshire, Somerset, Surrey, Warwickshire and Wiltshire.

Sources: Prices: Munro (no date). Customary land transactions: Campbell (1984), 131–3; Hudson (1921), 202–3; Schofield (2008), augmented by data supplied by the author; Smith (1984a), 154–5. Freehold land transactions: Davies and Kissock (2004), 220, 225, augmented with data on Berkshire and Essex kindly supplied by Dr Margaret Yates. Crimes: Hanawalt (1979), 278–80.

in 1319 and 1320, the return of subsistence problems in 1321 triggered further surges of distress sales at Hinderclay and Hindolveston in 1322 and 1323.

To a remarkable extent the chronology of the freehold land market revealed by numbers of recorded Feet of Fines in nine counties (Berkshire, Essex, Gloucestershire, Herefordshire, Shropshire, Somerset, Surrey, Warwickshire and Wiltshire) spread across central and southern England parallels that of the customary land market on these East Anglian manors (Figure 3.18). Activity of the freehold land market gives little hint of serious problems in the 1290s but leaves no doubt of their severity during the Great Famine when conveyances more than doubled to levels unmatched at any other time before the Black Death (Figure 3.18). Because the baronial war of 1322 put a temporary halt to freehold conveyancing, the harvest crisis of 1321 does not register on this index of hardship whereas the later failures of 1324, 1328 and 1331 clearly do and convey a clear impression of the wide area over which the severity of these after-shocks was felt.[249] Since, as Bekar and Reed have demonstrated, the net effect of medieval land markets was to promote morcellation and greater inequality of landholding, the result of so many distress sales over such a sustained period was to reduce yet more households to small-holder or sub-tenant status.[250] This immiserated class probably bore the brunt of famine mortality and yet its ranks were endlessly refilled by demotion from above.[251] The upshot was that rural poverty was patently more acute and more general by the 1340s than it had been in 1290.

Those squeezed hardest during these crisis years forfeited the land upon which their subsistence depended and were relegated to the ranks of the landless. With labouring employment scarce, and bereft of the economic entitlements that property ownership bestowed, many unable to survive by licit means resorted to crime.[252] When deprivation was greatest the resort to unlawful behaviour by the normally law abiding was so great as to constitute a wholesale breakdown of social order.[253] Seigniorial and Crown courts were swamped with business and the gaol delivery rolls document an avalanche of criminal cases, mostly for thefts of property, whose chronology closely tracks the activity of the customary and freehold land markets and price of essential provisions (Figure 3.18). Undoubtedly, the bulk of these crimes were committed, like a majority of the conveyances contracted, out of dire need. Life for the growing number of economically marginalized households was becoming even more precarious. These were the push factors that drove many to the towns in quest of employment or charity.[254]

It is, however, an ill wind that blows nobody any good. Those able to maintain their economic strength benefited from the scarcity-inflated

---

[249] For the concurrent impact of Scottish raids upon a wide area of northern England see McNamee (1997), 72–122; Dodds (2007), 55–64; Campbell (2010a), 290–1.

[250] Bekar and Reed (2013).   [251] Longden (1959), 413–14.

[252] On entitlements see Sen (1981).

[253] For the situation in Norfolk see Hanawalt (1976), 14–15. Although less extreme, the resort to crime is also evident in Yorkshire, Essex, Northamptonshire and Somerset: Hanawalt (1979), 241–9.

[254] On rural migration to Norwich and the overcrowding that resulted see Rutledge (1995) and Rutledge (2004).

prices, glutted labour market and abundance of land available for purchase. These included cornmongers and other dealers in provisions, townsmen who had bought up rural land for letting, lords whose demesne produce commanded high prices and whose manorial courts profited from the surge in entry fines, glebe owners and rectors and monasteries in receipt of tithes, and substantial tenants with sufficient land, capital and creditworthiness to keep their heads above water. The last included many villeins occupying non-divisible standard yardlands held for rents fixed by custom at sub-economic levels.[255] They showed little inclination to change places with those less well off than themselves and from whom they purchased land upon which to settle their non-inheriting children.[256] Their material security enabled them to maintain higher demographic reproduction rates than their less well-off neighbours and ensured that there was no net easing of demographic pressure.

On the manors of Glastonbury Abbey in Somerset and Dorset the monastery's refusal to allow villein holdings to be divided or sublet displaced many young adults into servanthood, pending acquisition of land by inheritance, gift or marriage.[257] On the bishop of Winchester's great manorial complex of Taunton, widows who had inherited outright their late husbands' virgates were not short of suitors. Here, competition for the limited supply of substantial yardlands drove up the entry fines that the bishop's officials were able to charge for them.[258] Only customary tenants with considerable resources could have afforded to pay these inflated fines. Ramsey Abbey, in fact, deliberately charged high entry fines for standard villein holdings in order to debar capital- and credit-deficient tenants from attempting to take them on, and had no shortage of suitable candidates from whom to choose.[259] These are the individuals who show up most clearly in court-roll based reconstitutions of these manors and who to an impressive extent successfully survived the economic stresses and strains of these climatically challenging years.[260] On the Ramsey Abbey estate and Abbey of Halesowen's large multi-vill manor of Halesowen it was the demographic and economic resilience of this class of substantial villein tenants that enabled manorial populations to recover from the trauma of the Great Famine and its aftermath.[261] Nationally, however, the bottom-heavy socio-economic structure persisted and, with it, the economic dominance of primary production.

---

[255] Hatcher (1981); Kanzaka (2002).
[256] Schofield (2008); Razi (1980), 94–8; Raftis (1996), 19, 31–3.
[257] Fox (1996), 535–6.   [258] Titow (1962b), 4–6.   [259] Raftis (1997), 11–46.
[260] For example, DeWindt (1972); Raftis (1974); Britton (1977).
[261] Razi (1980), 30–98.

Extreme morcellation was by no means unique to England. It prevailed in all populous regions in one form or another, wherever tight enforcement of strict tenurial controls was absent and factor markets operated in conjunction with population growth.[262] Nevertheless, in few parts of Europe can the processes that generated and sustained it be demonstrated as graphically as in England.[263] Harvest shortfalls played a key role in promoting morcellation by setting spates of distress land sales into motion, so that each crisis created the preconditions for the next. These, too, were a Europe-wide phenomenon during the first half of the fourteenth century, as established patterns of atmospheric circulation destabilized and extreme weather events increased in occurrence. Autonomous changes in climatic conditions were therefore an important component of this unfolding scenario. Operation of this conjuncture of processes meant that economic survival for a growing proportion of households became increasingly precarious.

3.02   Increasing climatic instability

3.02.1   Climate forcing and changes in atmospheric circulation patterns

By the 1260s the Medieval Solar Maximum was drawing to a close as the sun entered a quiescent phase and a succession of significant eruptions in c.1269, 1276 and 1286, including the VEI 6 eruption of Quilotoa in Ecuador, cast a veil of volcanic aerosols around Earth, thereby further reducing the amount of solar energy penetrating the atmosphere.[264] By the final decade of the thirteenth century it has been estimated that sunspot activity had effectively ceased and the so-called Wolf Solar Minimum had begun (Figures 2.8A and 2.9).[265] Slowly but ineluctably, global and northern hemisphere temperatures started to trend downwards once again (Figure 2.2) and, as they did so, global circulation patterns began to shift away from those that had reached such an apogee of development in the 1240s and 1250s. As temperatures decreased so oceans cooled, changing sea-surface temperatures, thermoclines, currents, pressure gradients, wind force and direction, atmospheric circulation, precipitation levels and frequency, and much else. After c.1260 the El Niño Southern Oscillation (ENSO), Asian monsoon and North Atlantic Oscillation (NAO) all weakened, with far-reaching consequences for weather

[262] For the situation in Normandy see Bois (1984), 287.
[263] Bekar and Reed (2013).
[264] Gao and others (2008); Salzer and Highes (2007), 62–3; Frank Ludlow, personal communication.
[265] Rogozo and others (2001); Solanki and others (2005).

patterns across the world. Such climatic swings of the pendulum had occurred before but not in many centuries had they swung so far in a contrary direction. Indeed, they may have swung beyond the point of no return. In some major regions changes were abrupt, far-reaching and, in terms of human experience, unprecedented. Via long-distance climatic 'teleconnections', developments in one region were sometimes communicated to localities far removed from the original source. To this day, big La Niña and El Niño events in the Pacific Ocean can be felt worldwide via the disturbance of normal weather patterns.[266] On this occasion, however, there was no return to the status quo ante and palaeoclimatologists are in no doubt that a major reorganization of the global climate system was occurring, although much remains to be learnt about the nature of and reasons for that reorganization.[267]

On the continental shelf off the Pacific coast of South America, dramatically rising rates of sedimentation during the final quarter of the thirteenth century indicate that the centuries-long La Niña-generated drought was finally over (Figure 2.3B).[268] In North America, too, the area affected by serious drought shrank and would never again be as extensive (Figure 2.3A). Across Asia, in contrast, the monsoon started to diminish in strength (Figure 2.8B), leading in the 1270s to the first major drought-induced harvest failures in over a century. Shortly afterwards, a dramatic narrowing of varve thicknesses in the Arabian Sea implies that rainfall and runoff had fallen to levels not experienced since the late tenth century (Figure 2.4A).[269] Ocean–atmosphere interactions in the Indian and Atlantic Oceans were linked by long-distance teleconnections and in the 1270s and 1280s the first symptoms of change also began to manifest themselves in the North Atlantic as a succession of high-amplitude sea-surface cooling events set in, of varying duration and magnitude, that would persist for the next hundred years (Figure 3.19A and B).[270]

For the rice-based agrarian civilizations of Southeast and South Asia the sudden reduction in monsoon rainfall had particularly serious consequences.[271] In south China the years $c.1285-c.1304$ show up as exceptionally dry in the Dongge Cave speleothem record, with $c.1287-8$ the driest years of all (Figure 2.5B). The period $c.1285-c.1298$ also stands

---

[266] The global effects of the 2010–11 La Niña have been widely reported and commented upon. For El Niños see Grove (1998); Grove and Chappell (2000).
[267] Seager and others (2007); Graham and others (2010); Sinha and others (2011).
[268] The Miraflores flood of $c.1300$ brought the drought to a decisive end: Magilligan and Goldstein (2001); Mohtadi and others (2007), 1062–3.
[269] Rad and others (1999).   [270] Graham and others (2010), 18–20.
[271] Sinha and others (2011).

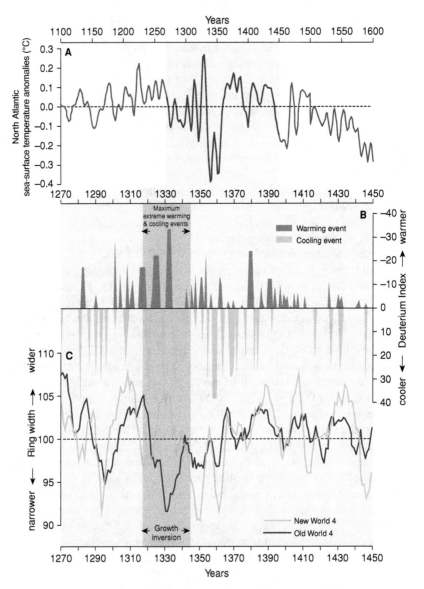

Figure 3.19 (A) Reconstructed North Atlantic sea-surface temperatures, 1100–1599. (B) North Atlantic sea-surface temperatures reconstructed from the deuterium content of Greenland ice, 1270–1450.
(C) Mean ring widths of Old World and New World trees, 1270–1450
Sources: Mann and others (2009); redrawn from Dawson and others
(2007), Figure 3B; dendrochronological data supplied by M. G. L. Baillie. The 'Old World' chronology is derived from independent multi-site
chronologies for the Polar Urals (pine), Fennoscandia (pine), temperate Europe (oak) and the Aegean (oak, pine, juniper); the 'New World'
chronology is derived from equivalent chronologies for North America (bristlecone pine), South America (*Fitzroya*), New Zealand (cedar)
and Tasmania (Huon pine). Both chronologies are five-year moving
averages.

out in the Indian Dandak Cave speleothem record as a time of extreme drought, the worst for at least two hundred years, with $c.1287$ (following the major eruption of $c.1286$) again the single driest year on record since AD 890 (Figure 2.4B).[272] Serious harvest failure, hunger and famine followed.[273] Collectively, available proxy records indicate that across South Asia the 1280s were the driest decade since the 1040s and the Oort Solar Minimum (Figure 2.8B). Maybe short-term climate forcing by the $c.1276$ and $c.1286$ tropical eruptions was partly to blame, but the cooling effects of the Wolf Solar Minimum must also have been starting to bite, as sunspot activity subsided (Figures 2.8A and 2.8B), accelerating the cooling of temperatures, destabilizing established ocean–atmosphere inter-relationships, reducing tree growth, and depressing harvests wherever farmers depended upon the monsoon.

During the closing years of the thirteenth century the mean ring widths of Old World and New World trees narrowed dramatically, a sure sign that environmental conditions had changed suddenly and probably for the worse (Figure 3.19C). In the opinion of dendrochronologist M. G. L. Baillie, 'this short-lived downturn must have affected enormous numbers of trees to show up as clearly as this in a wide grid of chronologies from around the world'.[274] In Siberia, larch ring widths exhibit a pronounced narrowing from 1283 to 1302 and, within this episode, 1287–9, 1293 and 1302 stand out as years of minimal growth (Figure 3.30).[275] In the Mongolian larch chronology the greatest growth reduction occurred from 1291 to 1307, with the narrowest rings dated to 1295–6 and 1299.[276] Reduced precipitation from April to June and cooler temperatures in July were probably responsible.[277] Likewise, 1293 stands out as a narrow-ring event in the northeast Tibet juniper chronology (Figure 3.30) and the Cambodian Drought Severity Index derived from the ring widths of the Fujian Cypress (*Fokienia hodginsii*) identifies 1291–2 and 1295–6 as years of unusually low rainfall.[278]

In England, 1292 and 1293 were evidently unusually wet for, against the prevailing negative trend, the ring widths of oaks widened.[279] Grain harvests during these same years were also seriously deficient, so that by 1294 the country was in the grip of a major subsistence crisis, the worst since 1258.[280] Intriguingly, the years 1292–5 are also marked in the

---

[272] Salzer and Hughes (2007), 62–3; Frank Ludlow, personal communication.
[273] Sinha and others (2007).   [274] Baillie (2006), 135.
[275] Data supplied by M. G. L. Baillie.
[276] Jacoby and others (no date); Figure 3.30.   [277] Velisevich and Kozlov (2006).
[278] Yang and others (2014); Buckley and others (2010).
[279] Data supplied by M. G. L. Baillie.
[280] For six consecutive years, 1289–94, grain yields per seed were below average, and most decisively so in 1290–1 and 1293–4. The worst of these harvests, in 1293, was 25 per

Greenland ice by concentrations of ammonium and nitrate – the telltale signatures of incoming space debris – and coincide with a cluster of contemporary references to meteors reported by chroniclers from China and Russia in the east to England and Ireland in the west.[281] On the strength of this evidence Baillie hypothesizes that Earth may at this time have experienced some form of extra-terrestrial bombardment and that it is because of this extra atmospheric loading that the environmental downturn was so much more pronounced in these years. The 1290s were a harbinger of worse to come and mark the advent of a period of more extreme and unstable weather conditions.

3.02.2 Evidence of increasing annual variability

In Europe reconstructed annual temperature series for Greenland, northern Scandinavia, central Europe, Alpine Switzerland and Slovakia (derived from ice-cores and tree rings) all display increasing year-on-year variability during the second quarter of the fourteenth century, rising to a period of elevated variance during the middle years of that century (Figure 3.20). This trend is even more marked in Mann's series of reconstructed northern hemisphere temperatures derived from an array of proxy measures, albeit with the difference that the peak in variability occurs towards the end of that century. The synchronicity of this rise in variance across all six temperature series is virtually unique, as is the synchronicity of the reduced variance that prevailed during the second quarter of the following century.

In Siberia the variance of the annual ring widths of larch (*Larix Sibirica*) offers an interesting long-term perspective on these developments. Over the last two millennia the variance of larch ring widths has peaked on four separate occasions at intervals of 300–400 years: in the 250s, 550s/580s, 980s and, finally and most prominently, in the 1330s (Figure 3.21). In Siberia, on the evidence of this proxy measure, the years from 1290 to 1340 emerge as the least stable 50-year period of the last 2,000 years. Their instability is all the more conspicuous because the variance of larch growth subsequently diminished dramatically to a temporal minimum in

---

cent below average. Such a run of poor harvests was unparalleled: Campbell (2007). By 1294 grain prices had risen by 40 per cent and by 1295 by over 50 per cent: calculated from Farmer (1988), 790. The adverse economic effects of these weather-induced harvest shortfalls and price rises were further compounded by a sudden increase in taxation to pay for Edward I's military exploits in Gascony and Scotland: Ormrod (1991); Schofield (1997). For contemporary references to these difficulties see Britton (1937), 127–9.

[281] Baillie (2006), 135–41.

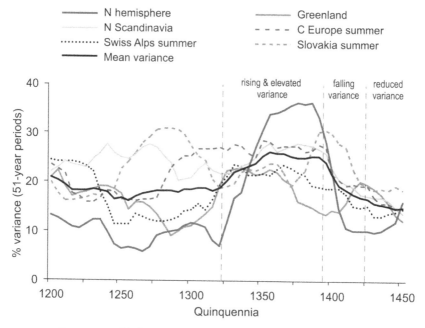

Figure 3.20 Variance of temperatures: northern hemisphere, Greenland, northern Scandinavia, central Europe, Swiss Alps and Slovakia (51-year periods, final-year plotted), 1200–1450
Sources: northern hemisphere – Mann and others (2008); Greenland – Kobashi and others (2010); northern Scandinavia – Grudd (2008 and 2010); central Europe and Swiss Alps – Büntgen and others (2011); Slovakia – Büntgen and others (2013)

the mid-fifteenth century, and ever since has remained well below the peak level of the early fourteenth century.

In Britain synchronous annual variations in Scottish speleothem band widths, oak ring widths and southern English grain yields (each providing different and entirely independent indices of weather-determined growing conditions) shed further light on this chronology, with low variance in all three series at the start of the fourteenth century, rising to high variance in the mid-fourteenth century, and then declining to new minima in the 1370s–90s.[282] Here on the Atlantic rim of northwestern Europe the weather appears to have become increasingly variable during the first half of the fourteenth century, with potentially grave consequences for

[282] Below, Figure 4.4.

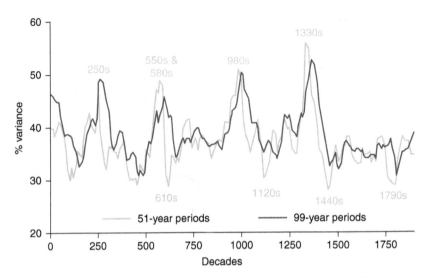

Figure 3.21 Variance (51-year and 99-year periods smoothed) of annual ring widths of Siberian *Larix Sibirica*, AD 0–1900
Source: calculated from data supplied by M. G. L. Baillie

societies whose populations were already pressing hard upon scarce agricultural resources. This bears witness to a profound change in the reliability of the NAO which hitherto had maintained consistently high levels of winter rainfall and relatively unvarying rates of speleothem growth.[283] As the winter westerlies weakened and shifted south, precipitation levels rose across southern Europe and North Africa while incursions of polar high pressure brought bitterly cold, dry weather to northern Europe, first in 1321 and then more persistently from 1330 to 1348.

Fluctuations in sea-surface temperatures in the North Atlantic were a major component of these changing weather conditions across Scotland and much of the rest of northwestern Europe. As recently reconstructed by Mann and others, the years from *c*.1275 to *c*.1375 stand out as a major discontinuity in the mean surface temperature of the North Atlantic, with greater swings from cold to warm than either earlier or later (Figure 3.19A). Confirmation of the unusual character of this period is provided by an alternative reconstruction of sea-surface temperatures made by Dawson and others.[284] They have used the varying amounts of deuterium-10 (heavy isotope hydrogen) preserved in annual

[283] Above, Figure 2.6A; Trouet and others (2009a and b).
[284] Dawson and others (2007).

layers within Greenland ice-cores to infer the surface temperature of the North Atlantic across which the deuterium-bearing winds had passed before reaching Greenland and depositing their chemical signature in the cumulating snow and ice deposits (Figure 3.19B).

A series of high-amplitude ocean cooling events commenced in the 1280s and then grew in scale and duration from the late 1310s until the early 1380s. Strikingly, from $c.1300$ they alternated with warming events of increasing magnitude and duration. Whereas the cool Atlantic surface waters tended to depress rainfall over northern Europe, the warm surface waters typically raised it, occasionally to excess. The first prolonged warming event, from 1315 to 1318, proved to be particularly disastrous, for it seems to have been responsible for the prolonged summer rains and storms which ruined northern European grain harvests in 1315 and 1316 and depressed that of 1317, thereby precipitating the Great European Famine.[285] This alternation between cold and warm sea-surface temperatures was at its most pronounced from $c.1315$ to $c.1345$ (Figure 3.19B), so that precipitation tended to be either deficient or excessive, as reflected in the high variability of the Scottish Cnoc nan Uamh speleothem band widths. This explains the high annual variability of oak growth and grain harvests across this period, since the former responded positively and the latter negatively to incessant summer rain.[286] Thereafter, these warming events tended to abate. Nevertheless, the high-amplitude cooling events continued and in the 1350s and 1360s actually grew in frequency until from the 1380s they, too, subsided and eventually ceased (Figures 3.19A and B).

The period when the see-sawing of North Atlantic sea-surface temperatures was at its most pronounced was environmentally distinctive in a further respect: the normally synchronous relationship between the ring widths of Old World and New World trees became asynchronous, as trees in the two hemispheres responded in opposite ways to prevailing environmental conditions (Figure 3.19C). First, from $c.1314$ until $c.1322$, Old World trees were favoured, then, from $c.1322$ until $c.1342$, New World trees displayed the greater growth.[287] For the normally positive correlation between tree growth in the Old and New Worlds so suddenly and completely to have been inverted implies that something very

---

[285] Dawson and others (2007), 428–30, 431; Kershaw (1976); Jordan (1996).
[286] Below, Figure 4.4.
[287] The statistical correlation between the two composite dendrochronologies across the years 1314–42 is a strongly negative –0.69; this compares with respective positive correlations of +0.46 and +0.39 for the periods 1200–1314 and 1342–1600 (correlations peaked at over +0.8 and +0.9 during the short sub-periods 1230–55 and 1510–35).

unusual had happened at a global scale.[288] The strange fluctuations in sea-surface temperatures within the North Atlantic seem to have formed part of this episode, which began when unusually warm Atlantic surface waters sustained some of the wettest weather with which European agricultural producers have ever had to contend and ended with an even more prolonged spell of ocean cooling which was the prelude to four devastating outbreaks of plague.[289]

Throughout this period it is clear that conditions both in the North Atlantic and more generally were becoming much colder. By c.1300 temperatures over central Greenland, as estimated from nitrogen and argon isotopes contained in air bubbles trapped in annual ice layers, were colder on average by 1°C than they had been c.1100.[290] Thereafter, three successive bouts of intense cooling reduced them by a further ½– 1½°C: in 1303 temperatures plunged to a level not experienced since the early 1200s, in 1320 they sank even lower, extreme cold then returned again in 1353, after which temperatures ameliorated for the rest of the fourteenth century (Figure 3.22).[291] As waters in the North Atlantic cooled, especially once sea-surface temperatures fell to 2°C and less, cod and other fish stocks migrated south.[292] These worsening conditions placed the Norse colonists in Greenland under extreme duress at the very time they were encountering increased competition from Inuit hunters and experiencing declining European demand for the walrus ivory and narwhal tusks which were the commercial mainstay of their economy.[293] Consequently, sometime between 1341 and 1364 the western settlement, which relied in part for its survival upon access to the northern hunting grounds of Nordrsetur, was abandoned.[294] As environmental conditions became both harsher and less predictable, agricultural options available

---

[288] Episodes of significant negative correlation between New World and Old World trees were: 1173±10 −0.67; 1205±10 −0.49; 1325±10 −0.79; 1464±10 −0.41; 1607±10 −0.40; 1635±10 −0.52; 1649±10 −0.66; 1729±10 −0.30; 1745−47±10 −0.67; 1794±10 −0.79; 1803±10 −0.70; 1847±10 −0.76; 1859±10 −0.71; 1924±10 −0.42; 1932±10 −0.64; 1965±10 −0.65. Only 1794±10 therefore matched the negative correlation of −0.79 reached in 1325±10, and in no period was the negative correlation stronger.

[289] Hatcher (1977).   [290] Kobashi and others (2010).

[291] Note that each of these bouts of extreme cold in Greenland was followed within two to three years by an exceptionally severe winter in central Europe. Thus, an index of central European winters based upon historical sources ranks the winters of 1305–6, 1322–3 and 1354–5 as three of the four coldest of the fourteenth century. Moreover, few, if any, since have been more severe: Pfister and others (1996), 100–1, 104. Wiles and others (2004) provide evidence of marked advances in Alaskan glaciers commencing c.1300 and c.1450, which they attribute to significant decreases in solar irradiance.

[292] Grove (2004), 607.   [293] Dugmore and others (2007), 18–22, 29–30.

[294] Grove (2004), 617; Dugmore and others (2007), 18–22.

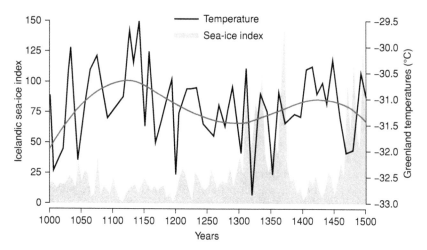

Figure 3.22 Greenland temperatures reconstructed from nitrogen and argon isotopes contained by air bubbles trapped in the ice, and index of sea ice derived from the presence of a biomarker (IP25) produced by sea ice algae within sediments deposited on the ocean shelf off the north coast of Iceland, 1000–1500
Sources: Kobashi and others (2010); redrawn from Massé and others (2008), figure 3

to the mother Norse colony in Iceland also became seriously constrained. Crop production ceased to be viable, over-wintering of animals became a greater challenge and summer biomass output diminished so that fewer stock could be supported.[295] Everywhere in northern Europe's many upland regions, harsher winters and shorter growing seasons were making life for pastoralists more difficult.[296]

In the North Atlantic, incursions of intense polar cold promoted a marked expansion of sea ice. The varying extent of sea ice off the north coast of Iceland has been estimated from the presence in sediments deposited on the ocean shelf of a biomarker (IP25) produced by sea ice algae, calibrated against a range of other environmentally derived proxy measures and contemporary historical evidence.[297] From these estimates it is clear that each bout of extreme cold over Greenland was closely followed by a growth of Icelandic sea ice, which first became extensive in the 1310s and then expanded further in the 1320s and 1330s (Figure 3.22). Sea ice formation was partly promoted by diminished levels of

---

[295] Dugmore and others (2007), 22–6. [296] Oram and Adderley (2008a).
[297] Massé and others (2008).

solar irradiance, but the process was not continuous, for, as with Atlantic sea-surface and Greenland temperatures, there were marked short-term oscillations in the extent of sea ice according to the prevailing strength of the NAO.

Simultaneously, ice was accumulating and glaciers were growing and advancing in the Swiss Alps.[298] For this to have occurred required 'a run of years in which snow accumulation is sufficient to increase volume more than ablation decreases it'.[299] Documentary research by Christian Pfister and others has demonstrated that a run of unusually severe winters provided precisely these conditions from 1303 to 1328 and the same years stand out as exceptionally cold in the Netherlands winter temperature series and central European annual temperature series, both similarly reconstructed from historical evidence. Thereafter, however, as the Atlantic winter westerlies shifted south, bringing milder and wetter weather to southern Europe, these severe winter conditions in central Europe ameliorated. Specifically, Pfister identified an unusual run of fifteen consecutive years from 1339 until 1354 when 'not a single winter was clearly cold compared with the 1901 to 1960 average'.[300] The parallel winter temperature series for the Netherlands shows that here, too, with the exception of 1339, these winters were relatively mild, especially those of 1341, 1343 and 1350. The years 1338–43 also witnessed major storm surges in the North Sea, causing serious marine flooding in both Holland and eastern England.[301] To this period belongs the notorious St Magdalene's Day flood of July 1342 in central Europe and a step gain in the height of the annual Nile flood.[302] Coincidentally, on Minze Stuiver and Paul D. Quay's dating, 1342 marked the end of the Wolf Solar Minimum and estimates of sunspot numbers and solar irradiance certainly suggest that solar activity was increasing again from the 1340s.[303] Yet by this point the die was cast and on this occasion the effect of rising solar irradiance was to add momentum to the changes in global circulation patterns already set in motion.

---

[298] Grove (2004), 153–9.   [299] Grove (2004), 159.
[300] Pfister and others (1996), 101. With the exception of 1339, these winters were also relatively mild in the Netherlands, especially 1341, 1343 and 1350: Engelen and others (2001).
[301] Britton (1937), 139–41; Bailey (1991), 189–94.
[302] Tetzlaff and others (2002); Dotterweich (2003): Kundzewicz (2005), 387; Rohr (2007), 93–4. For a model of the possible weather patterns involved see Böhm and Wetzel (2006). Dotterweich (2008), 204: 'Most of the gully systems in central Europe today are a result of . . . catastrophic occurrences. In the year 1342, for example, events initiated many gully systems and hillslope erosion delivered 50% of the colluvial material'. Fraedrich and others (1997) and above, Section 1.02.
[303] Above, Figures 2.8 and 2.9; Stuiver and Quay (1980), 11, 16.

The ecological repercussions of the changing climatic conditions that unfolded with gathering momentum from the 1270s were profound. Flora, fauna, humans and micro-organisms were all affected in both separate and inter-connected ways as they acted and reacted to successive environmental shocks and hazards.[305] Especially devastating were a series of major diseases of domesticated animals, notably sheep scab (an acute or chronic form of allergic dermatitis caused by faeces of the mite *Psoroptes ovis*), liverfluke (infestation by the parasitic flatworm *Fasciola hepatica*) and, very likely, rinderpest (a highly infectious viral disease of cattle and some other even-toed hoofed animals). Consequent morbidity and mortality of animals depressed outputs of food (meat, lard and milk), quality raw materials (skins, hides and wool) and draught power, destroyed essential working capital, jeopardized the fragile ecological balance upon whose maintenance the productivity of mixed-farming systems depended, and struck at vital sources of farm and export earnings.

Given that the bulk of medieval livestock, especially sheep and cattle, spent much of their time out of doors, they were scarcely less exposed than crops to the extremes of rainfall, cold and drought that were such a feature of this climatically transitional period. Harsh winter weather inevitably elevated livestock mortalities and was especially deadly when it persisted and coincided with spring calving and lambing. Inclement spring and summer weather in turn depressed the nutritional value and stocking capacity of pastures and yields of hay and fodder crops. In years of acute scarcity, oats and legumes normally intended for livestock were diverted to human use. Incessant rain and sodden pastures also provided ideal breeding grounds for the liverfluke flatworm *F. hepatica* and the freshwater snails that were its intermediate host, thereby triggering outbreaks of sheep murrain. Further, altered management in response to extreme weather often resulted in overcrowding of animals and creation of insanitary conditions that were ideal for dissemination of infections, such as the rinderpest virus, spread by direct contact between infected and healthy animals or via contaminated soil, fodder and water. Not unusually, the virus also acted in concert with secondary infections such as pneumonia, which thrived under cold, wet climatic conditions. As eighteenth-century commentators noted, 'outbreaks began when cattle

---

[304] A panzootic is a large, trans-boundary outbreak of disease not afflicting humans: Newfield (2009), 180–8.
[305] Above, Figure 1.2.

were weakened by unseasonable weather, thus rendering them temporarily susceptible to infection'.[306] Rinderpest was temperature sensitive and most virulent in the winter, as was sheep scab. The latter, too, was most readily spread by direct animal-to-animal contact under conditions of close folding or housing of sheep, as well as via shared rubbing posts and contaminated tags of wool or scab attached to brambles and bushes.[307] Because of their relatively simple mechanisms of spread, rinderpest and scab, in fact, were transmitted with alarming ease.

The natural response of most husbandmen at the first sign of sickness was to redeem as much of the stricken beasts' value as they might before the animals became wholly worthless. Such panic selling inevitably helped spread infection further, since livestock were intrinsically mobile and in normal times were driven and traded over considerable distances. The baggage trains of armies and plundered flocks and herds of war bands and rustlers similarly helped spread infection, as did inter-manorial transfers of stock on large landed estates. Stock movements played a major role in dissemination of sheep scab since to this day mite infestation is hard to detect in its early stages. Crucially, murrains and plagues were no respecters of administrative or national boundaries and, in the absence of veterinary science or implementation of remedial and preventive measures learned from long experience, were incapable of being brought under control. Once processes of biological diffusion had been activated they assumed a dynamic of their own. Typically, they ran their course until the diseases had either burnt themselves out or a further change in environmental conditions arrested their advance.

Rinderpest, the most dangerous and contagious of this trio of zootics, would not become the object of damage-limitation measures for some centuries to come.[308] Policing and funding such measures was always problematic because although disease prevention was very much in the public interest there was invariably a strong incentive for private individuals to evade legislation which interfered with their personal business. It was always in the interests of husbandmen to encash the value of animals which might otherwise sicken and die and, when they could get away with it, pass off as healthy stock which they knew to be incubating infection. Contagion stoked mobility, and mobility in turn fanned contagion. Human actions and reactions, the commercial infrastructures and networks they had created, and the extensive trades in live animals upon which the semi-pastoral European commercial economy had grown to

---

[306] Cited in Spinage (2003), 20.
[307] Eradication was only completely achieved between 1952 and 1973 when dipping was compulsory.
[308] Broad (1983).

depend, were therefore material to dissemination of the lethal pathogen. Stocking density also mattered, insofar as the chances of contracting the virus rose as livestock densities increased and the developed mixed-farming systems of early fourteenth-century Europe probably supported more bovines than for many centuries past.[309]

3.03.1a Sheep and cattle murrains during the agrarian crisis of 1315–22 The perils that extreme weather and disease could present to livestock producers are graphically illustrated by the fate of the pastoral economy on the estate of Bolton Priory in the Craven district of west Yorkshire during the agrarian crisis of 1315–22 (Figure 3.23). The demesnes and granges of this modest English Augustinian house were located in an upland area of relatively poor soils and above-average rainfall that was always environmentally marginal for agriculture.[310] The only surprise is that during the fifteen-year period between 1296/7 (when the extant Bolton *Compotus* first records detailed information on crop and livestock production) and 1313/14, so few of the potential risks actually materialized. On the contrary, under the expansionist management of Prior John of Laund, 'by the beginning of the second decade of the fourteenth century Bolton's estate exploitation reached its apogee', with more than 800 acres under crop, 20 working horses and over 240 working oxen, around 530 other cattle, a stud containing 80 horses of varying ages, at least 100 swine and a flock of 3,150 sheep managed to produce wool for sale.[311] Then, in 1315 and 1316, bad weather in the form of torrential rains struck.

The grain harvest of 1315 was down by 25 per cent from that of 1314 and the harvests of 1316 and 1317 were poorer still as waterlogged soils and scarcity of seed reduced the area that could be sown (Figure 3.23). Meanwhile, the hay harvest was a washout. Scarcity of fodder, in combination with the Priory's own pressing provisioning needs, precipitated slaughter of 94 per cent of the swine herd between Michaelmas (29 September) and Martinmas (11 November) 1316.[312] The same year heavy mortality from mostly natural causes shrank the Priory's sheep flock by two-thirds and the following year numbers eroded yet further. For Ian Kershaw, historian of the Bolton Priory estate, 'starving flocks must have proved easy victims for disease such as liver-fluke which the sodden pastures would foster'.[313] Ewes fared worse than wethers, and hogasters (yearling sheep) worst of all.[314] The estate's horses and cattle

[309] Campbell (2000), 102–87.   [310] Kershaw (1973b), 19–21.
[311] Kershaw (1973b), 19–112; Kershaw and Smith (2001).
[312] Kershaw (1973b), 107.   [313] Kershaw (1973b), 84.   [314] Kershaw (1973b), 80.

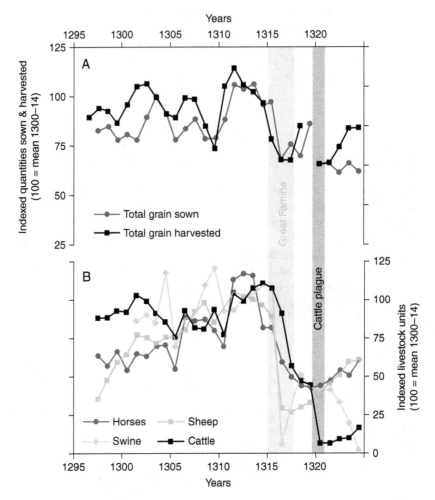

Figure 3.23 Impact of the agrarian crisis of 1315–22 upon the agricultural economy of the Bolton Priory estate, west Yorkshire
Source: calculated from Kershaw and Smith (2001)

initially proved more resilient and at Michaelmas 1316 numbers were respectively 74 per cent and 84 per cent of those enumerated the previous Michaelmas. Thereafter, however, numbers of both continued to contract (Figure 3.23), partly because of the scaling down of arable cultivation and its concomitant draught requirements but more particularly because of losses inflicted by Scottish raiding parties in spring 1318 and September 1319.

By Michaelmas 1319 numbers of horses and cattle (the preferred target of the Scots) on the estate were less than half those present on the eve of the crisis. Then sometime during the winter of 1319/20 cattle plague struck and left the Priory with only fifty-three oxen and thirty-one head of cattle, a drop of 84 per cent within the space of a single year.[315] The loss was all the greater because the fertility and milk yields of any of the twenty surviving cows and heifers that had been exposed to the infection would have been adversely affected. Only the deliberate Martinmas butchering of pigs had been as destructive. By this time numbers of sheep and horses were beginning to recover but an incipient recovery in the cropped area was thwarted by this sudden curtailment of draught resources and the next year, 1321, this was further compounded by renewed bad weather and failures of the barley and oats harvests (Figure 3.23). The rinderpest panzootic, therefore, 'was the last straw which broke the back of the canons' efforts at recovery'.[316] Moreover, disastrous as were these years for crop production, the intervention of disease ensured that their impact upon this estate's pastoral economy was even greater.

The Bolton estate's experience of these disasters was exceptionally severe. The susceptibility of its moorland and valley-bottom grazings to flooding meant that environmentally its flocks were more exposed to the risk of contracting liverfluke than those kept on the porous downland pastures of southern England, where many flocks escaped unscathed. Liverfluke and other weather-related ailments were nevertheless sufficiently widespread at this time to reduce aggregate demesne sheep numbers across East Anglia, southeastern and southern England by 30 per cent between 1314 and 1317 (Figure 3.24). This then translated into a one-third contraction in the volume of wool exported from London and the country's east- and south-coast ports between 1314 and 1319 (Figure 3.24). To blame was the ecological impact of the incessant rains upon the environments in which the parasitic flatworm *Fasciola hepatica* and its water-snail hosts thrived. Yet devastating as were these murrains, losses from the sheep-scab epizootic of the early 1280s appear to have been greater. The mites that caused scab were less dependent upon a specific habitat and therefore more susceptible to general diffusion. The entire national flock was therefore potentially at risk, with the result that across southern England demesne sheep numbers halved between 1277 and 1282. The epizootic struck Canterbury Cathedral Priory's Kent flocks following Michaelmas 1279 and resulted in a net reduction of 47 per cent over the course of that single accounting year.[317] So damaging was

---

[315] Kershaw (1973b), 96–8.   [316] Kershaw (1973b), 16.
[317] Calculated from Canterbury Cathedral Archives, beadles' accounts.

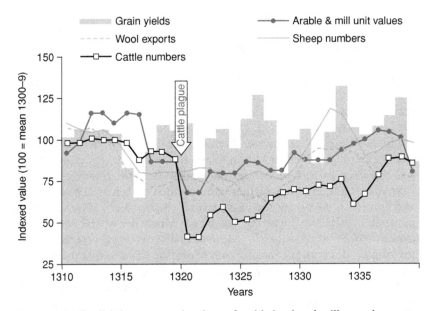

Figure 3.24 English harvests, unit values of arable land and mills, wool exports, sheep numbers and cattle numbers, 1310–39
Sources: grain yields, Campbell (2007); arable and mill unit values, Campbell and Bartley (2006), 167, 207, and IPM Database; wool exports, Carus-Wilson and Coleman (1963); sheep and cattle numbers, Manorial Accounts Database

scab to the weight and quality of fleeces that wool prices slumped and the fleece weights of Winchester sheep fell by a quarter between 1275/9 and 1285/9, reducing wool exports to a low ebb and precipitating several major ecclesiastical wool producers into insolvency (Figure 3.4).[318] Yet although this was undoubtedly the ovine disease event with the greater impact and the multiplication and dissemination of mites undoubtedly benefited from cold, damp winter weather, it was less obviously related to anomalous climatic conditions than the murrains of 1315–25.

Similarly, although cattle plague constituted probably the single most destructive component of the cocktail of natural disasters that struck between 1315 and 1321, it reached the Bolton estate during the winter of 1319/20 after the worst of the bad weather had passed and murrain-induced mortalities of other livestock were over (Figure 3.23). This was an altogether more deadly and contagious infection whose outbreak in

---

[318] Lloyd (1977), 290; Barnes (1984), 43–4; Bell and others (2007b).

west Yorkshire simply formed the latest stage in a pan-European pattern of biological diffusion which had begun some years earlier from an initial source in east-central Europe, whither it had probably been introduced from an ultimate source in the steppes of Arid Central Asia.[319] The Bolton estate lost over 80 per cent of its remaining cattle, which compares with a national decline of approximately 60 per cent (Figure 3.24) and overall bovine mortality rate, as estimated by Philip Slavin, of 62 per cent.[320] Again, however, Bolton Priory was unlucky, for the scale of its losses places it within the upper quartile of the range of observed bovine mortalities. Here, of course, it arrived after Scottish raiders had already taken their pick of the Priory's herd. Thus far Scottish cattle producers had been unaffected but later that same year oxen in the English baggage train at the siege of Berwick fell victim to the disease, and from here Scottish raiders, rievers and rustlers probably took it north of the border where it had the potential to wreak even greater havoc upon the cattle-based Gaelic socio-political order of the Highlands.[321]

3.03.1b The Great Cattle Panzootic's identity, origin and spread

Among modern contagious bovine diseases – anthrax, bovine pleuro-pneumonia, foot-and-mouth disease, and rinderpest – the last has long been the prime suspect as the cause of the panzootic since its epizooti-ology most closely matches the historically recorded and observable characteristics of the early-fourteenth-century outbreak. Unfortunately, rinderpest is a virus that has ribonucleic acid (RNA) as its genetic ma-terial, with the result that clinching aDNA of this diagnosis will never be forthcoming.[322] Now extinct, rinderpest (literally 'cattle plague') was an acute and usually fatal morbillivirus, akin to measles and canine distem-per, which existed in a variety of genetic lineages differing in their symp-toms and virulence.[323] It was susceptible to climatic conditions, insofar as the virus was vulnerable to heat, light and aridity and thrived when temperatures were low and humidity high.[324] Unlike anthrax, humans were unaffected and although it was not exclusive to cattle (other even-toed horned animals could be affected) it is clear from the stock entries in

---

[319] Below, Section 3.03.1b.   [320] Slavin (2012), 1242.
[321] McNamee (1997), 90–6; Oram and Adderley (2008a).
[322] I am grateful to Michelle Ziegler for this information.
[323] In October 2010 the United Nations Food and Agriculture Organization provision-ally announced final elimination of the rinderpest virus following a sustained veteri-nary campaign: http://www.fao.org/news/story/en/item/46383/icode/. The world was declared to be officially free from rinderpest infection at the World Organisation for Animal Health (OIE) General Session in May 2011.
[324] Spinage (2003), 13–14.

manorial accounts that in England in 1319–20 horses, sheep and swine were largely unscathed.[325]

As a respiratory infection, rinderpest was directly communicable from animal to animal via virus-rich aerosol secretions and droplets. Animals that were closely housed or otherwise confined were therefore especially at risk. It was typically spread by introduction of infected animals to healthy herds but the virus could also be transmitted indirectly via the meat and skins of diseased carcasses, the infected clothes and footwear of agricultural workers, contaminated water, and by pigeons, rats, dogs and hares.[326] In fact, until the modern development of vaccines, preventing the disease's contagious spread proved extremely difficult unless all animals exposed to infection were promptly slaughtered and their carcasses destroyed (an extreme measure most farmers were reluctant to accept without assured compensation) and all movement of animals was halted (against the will of many vested interest groups). Without firm government and effective public funding there could be little prospect of enforcing such uncompromising measures.[327]

Once animals became infected, rinderpest usually ran its course, from incubation, to the emergence of symptoms, and finally death, in nine to twenty-one days.[328] During the incubation period animals could be infectious without showing obvious signs of the disease. Following the onset of fever, the output of infectious matter increased dramatically, putting all cattle that came into contact with the sick animal greatly at risk. Consequently, death rates among herds during outbreaks could be as high as 100 per cent, with usually only a small minority of animals recovering.[329] Immunity was acquired by the few that did, although infertility sometimes resulted. Pregnant cows typically aborted naturally and the milk output of cows that recovered was often impaired.[330] Post-plague herds were therefore significantly reduced in size, fertility and productivity (Figure 3.26). Rebuilding them was consequently a protracted process, especially as further losses typically resulted from recurrences of the disease.[331]

Clive Spinage believes that ultimate origin of the various medieval outbreaks of the disease lay outside Europe in inner Asia. Here rinderpest was enzootic and long-distance movements of cattle – looted, traded, or

[325] Slavin (2010), 175–7.   [326] Spinage (2003), 15–19.
[327] Eighteenth-century English governments were more successful: Broad (1983).
[328] Spinage (2003), 5–7.   [329] For examples see Newfield (2009), 185–8.
[330] Slavin (2010), 170–2.
[331] For example, on the Kent estates of Canterbury Cathedral Priory oxen were restored to their pre-plague numbers within ten years, but restocking with cows and their followers took longer; all bovines then suffered a major setback in 1333–4, from which the estate had still not recovered when the Black Death struck in 1349: Campbell (2010b), 48–9.

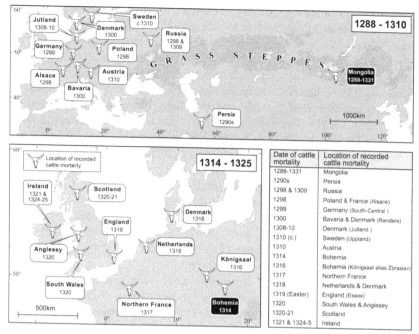

Figure 3.25 The Great Cattle Panzootic of 1314–25 and some possible precursors

Sources: Spinage (2003), 54; Newfield (2009), 160–1; Slavin (2010), 165–6

supplying armies with transport and food – were common.[332] Timothy Newfield suggests that, like *Yersinia pestis*, it was enzootic in the Caspian Basin.[333] On the evidence of an assortment of chronicle references to 'murrains' (the blanket contemporary term for most sorts of livestock disease) and 'mortalities' of cattle, Slavin believes an origin even further east is possible whence 'the pestilence came to Europe through the Russian steppes', following a route which had been taken by previous rinderpest panzootics.[334] It was when animals from these enzootic areas came into contact with cattle lacking much if any prior exposure to the disease that the risk of the infection escalating into a full-scale panzootic was greatest.

---

[332] Enzootic = a disease affecting or peculiar to animals of a specific geographic area. Spinage (2003), 51.

[333] Newfield (2009), 188; Norris (1977), 19.

[334] Slavin (2010), 165–6. For the European panzootic of AD 809–10 see Newfield (2012).

Fourteenth-century Chinese chronicles record repeated outbreaks of cattle disease in Mongolia commencing in 1288.[335] Subsequently, sometime after 1291, two Persian authors reported that 'all the cattle died', then in 1298 pestilential mortalities of cattle are chronicled in Russia and Poland, the following year in south-central Germany and Alsace, and in 1300 in Bavaria, where the chronicle of Ensdorf Abbey states 'the greatest pestilence of animals and especially of cows arose throughout the whole world'. The same year there is a reference to a cattle pestilence in Denmark, which may have been the prelude to a far worse and more general pestilence during the years 1308–10, when heavy losses of cattle are mentioned right across northern Europe in Danish, southern Swedish, Russian and Austrian sources.[336] If any or many of these mortalities constitute manifestations of the same cattle plague, they hint at a disease which spread over a period of twenty years from east to west through the cattle-ranching and -rearing heartland of Eurasia. It is therefore unfortunate that the fate of Hungarian cattle at the western end of Eurasia's steppe grasslands is unknown.

Intriguingly, the disease appears to have been spreading at the very time when an array of proxy measures indicates that climatic conditions were taking a turn for the worse.[337] The first outbreaks in central Asia coincided with a sharp narrowing of the ring widths of Mongolian pines as climatic conditions turned harsher and, to the south, a significant weakening of the Asian monsoon occurred.[338] In mainland Europe 1306–10 were conspicuously cold years. Mean annual temperatures in Germany and central Europe fell almost continuously from 1299 to 1310, while in the Netherlands the winter of 1306 was exceptionally cold and that of 1310 only marginally less so.[339] According to Pfister's index of central European winter temperatures, the winter of 1306 was one of the coldest of the fourteenth century and the winters of 1308 and 1311 were also colder than average.[340] Conceivably, therefore, the cattle fatalities reported at this time may have resulted more from these weather extremes than the ravages of disease. On the other hand, later European rinderpest outbreaks were particularly associated with cold, wet, winter weather, when 'the animals may be herded into shelter, bringing them

---

[335] I am indebted to Newfield (2009), 159–63, Slavin (2010), 165–6, and personal communications from both authors for the examples and references contained in this section.

[336] Janken Myrdal, personal communication, generously supplied the Swedish reference.

[337] Sinha and others (2011).   [338] Jacoby and others (no date); above, Section 3.02.

[339] Glaser and Riemann (2009); Pfister and others (1996); Engelen and others (2001).

[340] Pfister and others (1996).

into closer contact with one another and spreading infection more rapidly, as well as being more susceptible in the winter to secondary infection by pneumonia'.[341]

Whatever the case, within another five years, during a spell of even more extreme weather, it is beyond doubt that a lethal disease most likely to have been rinderpest had broken out in central Europe and within a further six years had spread as far west as Ireland.[342] Bohemia experienced pestilences of 'heavy animals' in 1314 and of 'oxen and all the cattle of the field' in 1316.[343] By the latter year, the worst of the Great European Famine, central Germany was also badly affected.[344] Temperatures in Germany and central Europe also appear to have been unusually cool.[345] Disease became rife among the beleaguered human population and, probably for equivalent reasons of scarce forage and fodder, stress, overcrowding, poor sanitation and malnutrition, cattle seem to have suffered a similar fate. The latter problems were general and ensured that these were difficult years for pastoral producers almost everywhere, yet only in interior Europe did these physical and ecological stresses provide the catalyst that activated rinderpest and set it on its destructive course. To have done so the virus had either to be present already in a latent or dormant state, or introduced from elsewhere at this time, as infectious cattle were brought into close contact with virgin-soil herds of weakened and vulnerable animals.

It mattered not where the initial outbreak occurred, since once the deadly virus had been unleashed its victory was assured. Rinderpest was a highly contagious disease with a simple and therefore efficient mechanism of infection; no vector or intermediate host was required to transmit the virus from victim to victim. This explains how and why the fourteenth-century outbreak so rapidly infected herds across such a wide geographical area. Humans inadvertently contributed to this process and may have been directly responsible for helping it leap the cordons sanitaires of the Channel and Irish Sea. Moreover, oxen were widely used for carting and hauling, and cattle of all sorts (and their skins and hides) were exchanged and traded over sometimes quite considerable distances, as well as being favoured targets of thieves, rustlers and war bands.[346] In the absence of effective preventive measures or any real contemporary understanding or recent empirical experience of how to combat the infection, the disease's spread was therefore unstoppable.

---

[341] Spinage (2003), 19.   [342] Newfield (2009), 161–71.
[343] Newfield (2009), 161.   [344] Jordan (1996).   [345] Glaser and Riemann (2010).
[346] Langdon (1986); Campbell (1995a), 142–3, 148–9, 152–3, 163–74; Hanawalt (1979); McNamee (1997).

By 1317 two French sources imply that the cattle plague had reached the ox-ploughing grainlands of north-central France.[347] The next year (1318), in the pastoral-farming Northern Low Countries, 'so great a mortality thrived among cows that from ten hardly one survived'. Cattle were also a mainstay of the Danish economy and that same year Danish annals likewise testify to 'a mortality of cattle'. Thus far the panzootic had spread overland but by Easter 1319 it had crossed the North Sea and broken out in southeast England, transported there no doubt by the brisk maritime trade in agricultural products and other commodities plied between the Southern Low Countries and eastern England.[348] Here, 'all the cattle died straightaway', bringing fresh economic hardship to a rural economy just beginning to recover from the devastating back-to-back harvest failures of 1315 and 1316 and inferior harvest of 1317.[349] Two years later the panzootic leapt the Irish Sea and continued its prodigies of destruction throughout Ireland.[350]

3.03.1c The Great Cattle Panzootic in Britain and Ireland Nowhere can progress and impact of the Great Cattle Panzootic be tracked with greater precision than in Britain and Ireland. In 1319, on the testimony of St Alban's Abbey annalist John de Trokelowe, 'at Easter the plague began at Essex and continued through the whole year'.[351] Trokelowe describes it as 'a great pestilential mortality of cattle', Robert of Reading (a monk of Westminster Abbey) as an 'invasion' of the 'kingdom of the English people' by a 'great pestilence of animals', and the anonymous Tintern Abbey annalist as 'the greatest mortality of animals, that is oxen and other animals, on account of which people had hardly, or no, oxen to cultivate their lands'. Initially, onset of summer weather slowed the panzootic's progress, with the result that few manorial accounts from the accounting year ending Michaelmas 1319 record significant losses.[352] From autumn 1319, however, with the advent of cooler weather, deaths mounted and consequently it was during the accounting

---

[347] Newfield (2009), 162.   [348] Newfield (2009), 172n.

[349] Dean (1996), lines 409–14: 'Tho com ther another sorwe that spradde over al the lond / A thusent winter ther bifore com nevere non so strong / To binde alle the mene men in mourning and in care / The orf deiede al bidene, and maden the lond al bare / so faste / Com nevere wrecche into Engelond that made men more agaste'. Kershaw (1973a), 14, 24–9; Campbell (2010a), 287–93.

[350] Newfield (2009), 169–70.

[351] See Newfield (2009), 163–71, for this and subsequent British and Irish references to the cattle plague.

[352] An example is the Canterbury Cathedral Priory manor of Ickham in Kent: DCc/Bedels rolls Ickham 23. Slavin (2012), 1241.

year 1319–20 that the bulk of English fatalities occurred.[353] Within the space of these fatal twelve months Canterbury Cathedral Priory's Kent demesnes suffered a 60 per cent reduction in bovine stocks from the combined effects of premature death, culling of sick animals and panic sales.[354] On its demesne of East Farleigh, nine out of thirteen oxen, the sole bull, eight out of nine cows, all four bullocks and heifers, the two yearlings and all five calves perished.[355] Two years later, Prior Henry of Eastry reckoned that the estate's losses amounted to 'more than a thousand oxen, cows and other cattle'.[356] That same year the disease's ravages are reported the length and breadth of the kingdom, from as far north as Berwick and around Carlisle on the Scottish border to as far west as the estate of Newenham Abbey in Devon.[357]

Spread of the virus to the north and west of England augured ill for the prospects of herds in neighbouring Scotland and Wales, both of them major cattle-rearing areas. Very likely Scottish raiding and rustling introduced the panzootic north of the border, although there are neither Scottish manorial accounts to confirm this nor any contemporary reports by Scots chroniclers.[358] The clearest statement that Scotland was not spared the panzootic is the laconic observation contained in John of Fordun's *Chronica gentis Scotorum*, written in the 1370s, to the effect that in 1321 'nearly all the animals were extinguished'. Whether this was true of the whole of Scotland, cattle-farming Highlands as well as mixed-farming Lowlands, awaits investigation.[359] For Wales the documentary evidence is both fuller and more explicit. Thus royal tenants in the Marcher counties of Glamorganshire and Monmouthshire complained in 1320 they could not meet their dues 'because of the great pestilence of cattle'. The handful of contemporary manorial accounts available for southeast Wales show that here, too, herds had become infected. At about the same time, complaint was made of heavy cattle losses on the lands of the bishop of Bangor in Caernarvonshire and Anglesey at the opposite corner of the principality in northwest Wales.[360]

The panzootic had earlier taken approximately two years to cover the 720 kilometres from Bohemia to Brabant, travelling at a rate of almost

---

[353] Spinage (2003), 19–20.   [354] Campbell (2010b), 48–9.
[355] DCc/Bedels rolls East Farleigh 12–13.
[356] Newfield (2009), 155. Accounts of the cattle plague in England include: Kershaw (1973a), 14, 24–9; Spinage (2003), 81–4, 92–4; Newfield (2009); Campbell (2010a), 287–93; Campbell (2010b), 48–9; Slavin (2010); Slavin (2012).
[357] McNamee (1997), 90–6; Newfield (2009), 165, 173n., 185, 187.
[358] In later centuries rinderpest outbreaks tended to follow in the wake of armies: Spinage (2003), 43, 52.
[359] But see the speculations of Oram and Adderley (2010), 262.
[360] Newfield (2009), 168, 185.

1 kilometre a day. To reach Anglesey in Wales by late 1320 starting from Essex in England at Easter 1319 it maintained much the same speed. From Wales, or maybe Scotland or England, it then leapt the Irish Sea and in 1321 began its devastation of herds in Ireland, where the annals of Connacht, Clonmacnoise and Inisfallen all record 'a great murrain of cattle in Ireland this year'.[361] Three years later, in 1324, when demesnes in central and southern England appear to have suffered further heavy mortalities of cattle (Figure 3.24), 'grave cattle plague' again broke out in many parts of Ireland.[362] The annals of Connacht named the murrain 'Mael Domnaigh', the annals of Clonmacnoise 'Moyle Dawine' and the annals of New Ross 'Maldow', and it is also reported by the annals of Ulster, St Mary's Dublin, and Friar John Clyn of Kilkenny.[363] There can therefore be no doubt of the scale of the destruction wrought upon herds throughout the entire island of Ireland. The next year 'the cattle plague continued to rage in Ireland' and the panzootic did not finally abate, its force spent, until 1326, which was the driest year in living memory.[364]

In England passage of the panzootic impacted upon the prices of live cattle and their products, notably butter and cheese (Figure 3.26), in a manner akin to that of the sheep-scab epizootic of the 1280s upon sheep and wool prices (Figure 3.4) but opposite to that of the famine years of atrocious weather and failed harvests. Under the latter circumstances purchase of cows became an inessential cost that fewer could afford, with the result that by 1316, when agrarian conditions were at their worst, the purchase price of cows had fallen by an average of 20–30 per cent. Butter and cheese, in contrast, shared in the price inflation that affected all staple foodstuffs and gained in value by 10–20 per cent. Notwithstanding the sodden pastures and scarcities of hay and fodder, bovine numbers held up comparatively well with the result that by 1318, when this initial bout of extreme weather had passed, prices of cows and dairy produce were more-or-less back to normal (Figure 3.26). The respite proved transitory. The next year, following arrival in England of rinderpest, market conditions for bovines and their products were thrown into chaos as stock everywhere sickened and died. Across this single farming year the national demesne herd shrank by 60 per cent (Figure 3.24) and Slavin's precise calculations of bovine mortality for 7,605 head of stock on 165 manors indicate a median mortality rate in the range 61–70 per cent, a modal mortality rate of 71–80 per cent and

[361] Cited in Lyons (1989), 64.   [362] Newfield (2009), 171.
[363] Cited in Lyons (1989), 64.
[364] For a possible connection between dry weather and reduced rinderpest activity see Spinage (2003), 19. For the drought of 1325–7 in England see Stone (2014), 437–9.

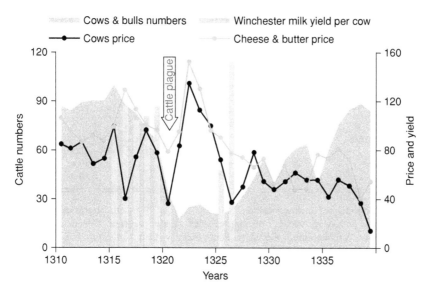

Figure 3.26 Impact of the English cattle plague of 1319–20 upon numbers of cattle, prices of cows and of cheese and butter, and milk yields *Sources*: cattle numbers, Manorial Accounts Database; prices, Clark (2009); milk yields, Slavin (2010), 171

an overall mortality rate of 62 per cent.[365] Nationally, across all classes of producer, probably in excess of ¼ million working oxen were eliminated during the months that the disease raged in England, plus innumerable cows, heifers, bullocks and calves. Since each ox possessed the muscle power of six men, this was equivalent to a manpower loss of at least 1½ million adult males in a society with an adult male population of probably fewer than 1½ million.[366]

Yet in 1319/20, in direct contrast to the inflationary effect of a bad harvest on the price of grain, cattle prices collapsed. It was a rash buyer who in the midst of such a deadly disease outbreak purchased animals that might soon sicken and die or, worse, were already incubating the virus. In this uncertain and risky situation, with a market glutted by panic selling-off of herds but shunned by buyers, the purchase price of cows fell by 30 per cent. Butter and cheese also slumped in value,

---

[365] Slavin (2012), 1242.
[366] Langdon (1983), 397–400; Campbell (2003); Apostolides and others (2008). The national population is unlikely to have numbered more than 4.75 million, of which adult males probably accounted for less than one-third: Broadberry and others (2015), 8–9, 21.

Table 3.3 *Regional impacts of the English cattle plague of 1319/20*

	Percentage change in cattle numbers at Michaelmas	
Region	1317/18 to 1320/1	1317/18 to 1339/40
East Anglia[1]	−28%	−1%
Southeast[2]	−44%	−14%
Midlands[3]	−48%	−24%
West Yorkshire	−60%	
Southern counties[4]	−78%	−44%
Southwest[5]	−84%	−59%
ENGLAND	−56%	−26%

[1] Cambridgeshire, Huntingdonshire, Norfolk, Suffolk. [2] Essex, Hertfordshire, Kent, Middlesex, Surrey, Sussex. [3] Buckinghamshire, Gloucestershire, Northamptonshire, Oxfordshire, Warwickshire. [4] Berkshire, Hampshire, Wiltshire. [5] Devon, Somerset.
Source: Manorial Accounts Database

presumably because these too were regarded as tainted: cows exposed to the virus typically lost their fertility and yielded milk at a much-reduced level.[367] Hollingbourne in Kent lost nineteen out of twenty-five cows and the handful that survived proved sterile, while at Great Chart in the same county five cows aborted their calves while others, along with heifers, bullocks and oxen, were hastily sold off.[368] On the Winchester estate milk yields per cow more than halved in the wake of the plague and were not back to normal until the drought year of 1326 (Figure 3.26). The paradoxical result was that as numbers of cattle declined, prices of cows, butter and cheese also fell. Not until the disease had spent its force in 1324/5 did prices return to a more normal level, although stock numbers remained depleted since breeding replacement animals from such debilitated herds was a protracted process, especially under conditions of recurrent drought.[369] By 1339/40 the national demesne herd was still 26 per cent down on its size of twenty years earlier on the eve of the pathogen's arrival in England (Table 3.3).

Repeat outbreaks of the pestilence also delayed full recovery.[370] Demesnes in central and southern England appear to have suffered further losses in 1324 and ten years later, in 1333–4, widespread mortalities reduced the national demesne herd by approximately one-fifth

---

[367] Slavin (2010).
[368] DCc/Bedels rolls Hollingbourne 29; DCc/Bedels rolls Great Chart 32–3.
[369] Stone (2014).
[370] Eighteenth-century Europe experienced multiple rinderpest outbreaks, since once introduced the disease proved hard to eradicate: Spinage (2003), 103–50.

(Figure 3.24), an event subsequently reported by annalist Henry Knighton.[371] At Great Chart in Kent in 1333–4 no calves were born due to the infirmity of the cows, many cattle died and those that did not were hastily sold off, so that on this demesne the crisis looks very much like a repeat of the 1319–20 disaster.[372] Then in 1345 English herds experienced a further significant setback of about 20 per cent, although it is unclear whether this was a further visitation of the cattle plague or something else altogether. Thereafter, for the remainder of the four-teenth century, nothing of comparable magnitude or synchronicity shows up across the entire demesne sector, which implies that any residual out-breaks of cattle plague were increasingly circumscribed in their geograph-ical scope. Moreover, herds now exposed to the pathogen had lost their biological naïvety.

In all these outbreaks, for reasons that are far from clear, demesne herds in East Anglia proved to be the most resilient and were restocked most quickly (Table 3.3). This is something of a paradox given how populous and commercialized was this region of intensive mixed farming and the demographic bias of many herds towards dairying.[373] Yet the net drop in numbers was only half the national average. Net bovine losses in Norfolk during the accounting year 1319–20 averaged 42 per cent and ranged from a minimum of 13 per cent on the prior of Norwich's demesne at Hindolveston to a maximum of 90 per cent on the de Vallibus demesne at Keswick just outside Norwich, a commercially exposed location where infection must have been unavoidable.[374] In contrast, horse-ploughing Sedgeford on the light soils of geographically isolated northwest Norfolk seems to have been spared the disease altogether.[375] Losses in Kent were altogether greater.[376] Here, herds at Agney in the heart of Romney Marsh and at Barksore on the North Kent marshes were among the few that remained untouched, presumably because they too were suf-ficiently isolated from potential sources of infection.[377] Generally, it was southern, central and southwestern England that repeatedly sustained the heaviest losses and where there was no full recovery to pre-plague stocking levels (Table 3.3). It was also patently the case that capital-rich

---

[371] Cited in Newfield (2009), 171.
[372] DCc/Bedels rolls Great Chart 42 (cf. DCc/Bedels rolls Great Chart 33). Two years later Icelandic sources describe 'a great destruction of cattle' and in 1339 the Annals of Connacht report further losses from 'a great pestilence upon the cattle': Newfield (2009), 171.
[373] Campbell (1996).
[374] Manorial accounts database; Norfolk Record Office DCN 60/18/21–22; Norfolk Record Office NRS 23357 Z 98.
[375] Norfolk Record Office DCN 60/33/18–25.   [376] Campbell (2010b), 48–9.
[377] DCc/Bedels rolls Agney 31–2; DCc/Bedels rolls Barksore 25–7.

seigniorial producers were better placed to restock with purchases from the greatly diminished pool of animals that had survived the plague than their host of smallholding neighbours. Differences of environment, herd management, animal nutrition, natural resistance, exposure to infection and capital resources clearly underlay the panzootic's varying impact and recovery from it.

3.03.1d The Great Cattle Panzootic of 1315–21: some conclusions

The picture currently to hand of this pan-European and possibly pan-Eurasian event is patchy and incomplete. The pathogen most likely originated somewhere in the semi-arid Mongol-dominated interior of central Asia, whence, impelled perhaps by climatically induced ecological shocks and shifts, it spread westwards sometime after 1288 by routes and methods that remain obscure until it reached the steppe lands of southern Russia and neighbouring cattle-ranching regions. Here, it may have been responsible for the heavy bovine mortalities widely reported in the 1290s. Decades earlier the Mongols had taken a broadly similar route in a series of invasions and conquests which for a time opened up the trans-continental caravan routes to more substantial and regular flows of travellers, traders and merchandise.[378] In this way the potential was created for a greater inter-continental exchange of pathogens between Asia and Europe.

It is, however, with the extreme weather of 1314–16 (responsible for the near-universal harvest shortfalls which caused the Great European Famine of those years) that emergence of the main contagion is most closely associated. In this instance the link between successive years of abnormally cool, wet weather and outbreak of a lethal cattle infection seems to have lain in the effects of the weather on animal nutrition and herd management and the almost ideal opportunities that close herding and housing of malnourished animals created for rapid and extensive transmission of the rinderpest virus once biologically naïve herds had come into contact with those indigenous to central Asia that had long been hosts to the infection.

Currently available evidence suggests that the panzootic surfaced in its most virulent and aggressive form in Bohemia between 1314 and 1316 when the impact of physical environmental forcing upon vulnerable ecosystems was exceptionally strong. Thence, it spread rapidly westwards across Europe, at a rate of almost one kilometre a day, to reach Britain in 1319 and, eventually, Ireland in 1321.[379] Only in England is its passage

---

[378] Abu-Lughod (1989).   [379] Newfield (2009).

and demographic impact copiously recorded by extant chronicles, manorial accounts and price evidence. Elsewhere its course is obscure and has attracted little historical attention. Atlantic-edge Ireland obviously represents the maximum western extent of the panzootic but whether it penetrated south of the Alps and beyond the Pyrenees is not known. Certainly, there are no obvious climatic or environmental reasons why Mediterranean Europe should have escaped the contagion. Also, given the panzootic's probable Asian origin, it is *a priori* unlikely that herds on eastern Europe's extensive rangelands were untouched by the disaster, although explicit evidence that this was the case is currently lacking.

In northwestern Europe the populations of bovines struck by the disease lacked any prior exposure to it, since the disease had not occurred since perhaps the widely reported great cattle pestilence of AD 939–42.[380] Antidotes were unknown, individual responses mostly counterproductive, and institutional counter measures non-existent. The plague therefore ran its course more-or-less unchecked until it eventually burnt itself out. Everywhere it devastated herds, destroyed vital working oxen and depressed dairy output, thereby compromising nutritional standards and massively magnifying and prolonging the damage already inflicted by the devastating harvest failures of 1315 and 1316.[381] It ensured that until herds, and especially stocks of draught oxen, had been rebuilt there could be no immediate recovery to pre-famine levels of agricultural output and food production. In England this took at least twenty years to achieve (Figure 3.24) and underlined the precarious balance upon which the country's predominantly agrarian economy rested. Above all, the Great Cattle Panzootic of 1315–21 illustrates the capacity for environmental change in one part of the Old World to activate deadly pathogens which then spread unchecked across the continent with devastating consequences for all populations with which they eventually came into contact. The same would hold true of the human plague that struck Europe a generation later but whose biological reactivation after more than half a millennium of quiescence began during this same episode of climatic and ecological instability.

3.03.2   Yersinia pestis

Sometime during the opening phase of the Great Transition plague reemerged as an epizootic infection of sylvatic rodents within its reservoirs

---

[380] Newfield (2012).

[381] For speculations on the possible negative nutritional consequences of the loss of so many milk cattle see Slavin (2012), 1263; DeWitte and Slavin (2013).

of infection in the semi-arid interior of Asia. More animals became infected over a wider area and, as stocks of the pathogen built up, so the *Yersinia pestis* genome mutated and spawned new branches. From modest and geographically circumscribed beginnings, the disease became successively amplified and transformed until the prospect of a wholesale spillover from sylvatic rodents to commensal rodents and, thence, humans became a real possibility. When, in the 1340s, the latter happened, plague wrought prodigies of destruction upon human populations throughout the greater part of western Asia, Asia Minor, the Middle East, North Africa and most of Europe. Nothing as deadly had happened since the First Pandemic had burnt itself out in the second half of the eighth century. Biological developments between the 1260s and 1340s constitute the essential precursor to this greatest of all Old World demographic disasters, whose origins clearly owed much to the environmental changes then in train. Recent biological, genetic and palaeoclimatic research is shedding fresh light upon the nature, sequence and timing of these developments, upon which the fate of societies throughout the greater part of the Old World would hinge.

Plague is a vector-borne disease and, as such, especially susceptible to changes in climatic and therefore environmental conditions, since the pathogen and its hosts and vectors are all directly and indirectly responsive to ecological influences.[382] In Kazakhstan during Soviet times Kyrre Linné Kausrud and others have shown that milder and wetter weather were the very conditions most likely to promote reproduction of both plague's gerbil hosts and its flea vectors, leading to outbreaks of plague among sylvatic rodents and consequent zoonotic cases among humans.[383] Similarly, since introduction of *Y. pestis* to the southwestern United States during worldwide spread of the Third Pandemic at the beginning of the twentieth century, El Niño pluvial events have shaped plague outbreaks among the ground-burrowing prairie-dog populations that have become the pathogen's sylvatic rodent hosts in this semi-arid region.[384]

In all these areas, interactions between climate and plague are complex since they operate via the effects of temperature and rainfall upon (i) vegetation growth, (ii) threshold densities of plague's sylvatic hosts,

---

[382] Woodruff and Guest (2000), 92. Above, Figure 1.2. Flare-ups of malaria, rift-valley fever in East Africa, hantavirus pulmonary syndrome in southwest America, and cholera in Bangladesh are similarly influenced by environmental conditions (I am grateful to Ben Sadd for alerting me to this parallel): Patz and others (2005), 311.

[383] Kausrud and others (2010); Schmid and others (2015).

[384] Stapp and others (2004).

(iii) the flea burden of those hosts, and (iv) the activity of those fleas. In central and western Asia, for example, higher precipitation increases growth of natural vegetation in the regions' water-limited grasslands and thus enhances the supply of food sources to sylvatic populations of the great gerbil (*Rhombomys opimus*), allowing their numbers to rise. If gerbil densities are too sparse *Y. pestis* can neither become established nor spread. To serve as hosts of *Y. pestis*, gerbil communities therefore need to be of sufficient size to support an initial invasion and then allow it to persist without burning itself out.[385] At the same time, higher soil moisture levels enhance daily survival rates of fleas, while milder springs and wetter weather favour flea reproduction so that flea-infestation rates rise with host population densities.[386] Contact and transmission rates between infectious fleas and susceptible hosts are thus amplified. Moreover, the earlier that spring temperatures rise above a threshold of 10°C the sooner that fleas become active, while the more humid the summer the greater the number of fleas. Provided that host gerbil population densities have risen above the minimum required to sustain an outbreak, it follows that warmer springs and cooler but wetter summers can trigger a cascading effect on the occurrence and level of plague prevalence.[387] In contrast, hot and arid conditions are known to have a harmful effect upon the survival of both immature and adult fleas. Field-study results show that the effects of temperature, rainfall and humidity upon host density and flea survival and reproduction are the two most critical components of this cycle.[388]

That a clear link existed between climatic conditions and plague panzootics and zoonotics is now well established, although consideration of the implications of this finding for historic outbreaks of plague has scarcely begun.[389] It is one thing to demonstrate an association between extreme weather events and plague outbreaks but it is another to elucidate the precise and likely non-stationary nature of the relationship between them. For example, in 1999 Richard Stothers went no further than to draw attention to the 'implied causal connection' between the large volcanic eruptions of AD 536, AD 626 and 1783 and the plague pandemics that subsequently broke out in the Middle East and/or eastern Mediterranean in AD 541–4, AD 627–39, and 1784–7.[390] The greatest of these plagues was the sixth-century Justinianic Plague, long suspected

---

[385] Davis and others (2004).   [386] Kausrud and others (2010).
[387] Eisen and Gage (2012), 64–5.   [388] Ari and others (2011).
[389] Enscore and others (2002); Stapp and others (2004); Stenseth and others (2006); Zhang and others (2007); Mills and others (2010); Kausrud and others (2010).
[390] Stothers (1999), 719–29.

of having been the first trans-continental pandemic of *Y. pestis* and now confirmed as such on the strength of aDNA results obtained from two mid-sixth-century skeletons excavated from the early-medieval cemetery at Aschheim in Bavaria.[391] As Baillie has demonstrated, it provides a clear example of the conjuncture of a devastating human outbreak of *Y. pestis* with a pronounced short-term climatic anomaly of at least hemispherical dimensions, when relationships between ecosystems, pathogens, hosts and vectors may have been disturbed within one of plague's natural reservoir areas, most probably somewhere in Arid Central Asia.[392] Intriguingly, the environmental context within which the Second Pandemic erupted was not dissimilar, for the cue for its re-emergence after centuries of quiescence was onset of the transition from the atmospheric circulation patterns of the MCA to those of the LIA.

3.03.2a Hosts and vectors of Y. pestis As a disease *Y. pestis* is notable for its ability to invade and colonize new territories, adapt to different ecological niches, and adopt alternative hosts. Because the bacterium appears to be capable of surviving and persisting independently in the soil for days, weeks and even months at a time, contaminated soil provides a potential reservoir of infection from which ground-burrowing mammals can become reinfected via inhalation and/or ingestion.[393] Marmots, gerbils and susliks are its sylvatic (i.e. wild) mammalian hosts in Central Asia but ferrets and voles and, in America, black-tailed prairie dogs and ground squirrels can also harbour the infection.[394] As is common in host/parasite relationships, the most long established of these sylvatic (or maintenance) hosts have a relatively high tolerance of *Y. pestis*; it is only when the bacterium spreads to commensal (i.e. domestic) rodents that rapid amplification takes place and human fatalities mount.[395] Contrary to popular belief, commensal rats (notably *Rattus rattus*, the black rat) are rarely a primary host of *Y. pestis*. Instead, their role in plague outbreaks typically derives from their capacity to act 'as "liaison" hosts, carrying plague between the sylvatic reservoir and people'.[396]

---

[391] Wiechmann and Grupe (2005); Harbeck and others (2013); Wagner and others (2014).
[392] Below, Appendix 4.1, Figure 4.15; Baillie (1994); Baillie (2008). On the probable central Asian origin of the First Pandemic see Morelli and others (2010); Wagner and others (2014).
[393] Drancourt and others (2006); Ayyadurai and others (2008). But see also Eisen and others (2008).
[394] Gage and Kosoy (2005), 513–14.
[395] Gage and Kosoy (2005), 509, 513–14; Christakos and others (2007), 701–2.
[396] Stenseth and others (2008), 0010; Gage and Kosoy (2005), 518–20.

Y. pestis is primarily a disease of animals and is typically transmitted via the bites of insects that are parasitic upon the blood of their hosts.[397] Since fleas usually perform the key role in spreading the bacterium, either directly from sylvatic hosts or indirectly via commensal rodents to humans, critical importance has long been attributed to the role of 'blocked fleas' to the transmission process.[398] These are fleas with stomachs 'blocked' with *Y. pestis* following ingestion of high concentrations of the bacillus (typically $\geq 10^6$ colony-forming units per millilitre) in a blood meal taken from an infected rodent.[399] Blocking happens to only a minority of fleas following a blood meal and is heat sensitive, ideally requiring temperatures in the range 16–22°C. It usually has an incubation period of two to three weeks and, since blocking causes fleas to become starved, most die soon after becoming infectious. During this brief period of infectiousness starvation nevertheless drives them to feed voraciously upon rodents or, as a last resort, humans, either regurgitating blood mixed with blockage material bearing *Y. pestis* back into the bite wound or excreting the bacillus in their faeces onto the skin whence it is rubbed by scratching into the wound so that the victim's blood becomes contaminated with *Y. pestis*. In the case of humans,

Within the first week after transmission from the flea, bacteria disseminate from the intradermal bite site to the regional lymph nodes to produce bubonic plague. From there, the bacteria rapidly invade the bloodstream and infect many internal organs. Infected tissues typically contain massive numbers of bacteria, and a high-density, usually fatal septicemia is a hallmark of plague.[400]

When transmitted in this way, fleas usually only switch to feeding on humans following mass mortalities among their rodent hosts.[401] Hence J. F. D. Shrewsbury's claim that 'in every instance of bubonic plague in human history an epizootic of the disease in a domiciliary rat population must have preceded and progressed currently with the human disease'.[402] In other words, 'unless the rodents die, the human population remains untouched'.[403] The two most efficient rat-flea vectors of plague are *Xenopsylla cheopis* and *Nosopsyllus fasciatus*, of which *X. cheopis* (the vector also responsible for transmission of murine typhus) is by far the more dangerous. Dense populations of infected rats and a high

---

[397] See Sun and others (2014) for 'a step-wise evolutionary model in which *Y. pestis* emerged as a flea-borne clone, with each genetic change incrementally reinforcing the transmission cycle'.
[398] Shrewsbury (1971), 2–3, 21–2; Benedictow (2010); Eisen and others (2015).
[399] Eisen and Gage (2012), 65.   [400] Lorange and others (2005), 1907.
[401] Lorange and others (2005), 1908; Prentice and Rahalison (2007), 1200–1; Monecke and others (2009), 587, 590; Eisen and Gage (2012), 65–9.
[402] Shrewsbury (1971), 4.   [403] Herlihy (1997), 26.

flea burden per rodent host are required before a full-scale panzootic can ignite, which in turn is an essential precondition for eruption of a human zoonotic.[404] On this analysis, regions without rats or their sylvatic counterparts, such as much of northern Scandinavia, ought to have been immune to infection.[405]

Ole Benedictow is adamant that such a mechanism of transmission, involving *Rattus rattus* as the principal host and *X. cheopis* as the principal vector, is sufficient to account for the Second Pandemic.[406] Modern biologists are less sure and now concede that 'dissemination of *Y. pestis* by blocked fleas...cannot sufficiently explain the rapid rate of spread that typifies plague epidemics and epizootics'.[407] Plainly, other methods of plague transmission were operative, involving unblocked fleas, other species of rat flea, possibly the human flea (*Pulex irritans*), or even other human ectoparasites, such as lice.[408] Accordingly, increasing attention is now being devoted to scrutiny of the vectors responsible for plague's transmission, the hosts upon which they are parasitic and the precise mechanisms by which transmission takes place.[409]

Plague was introduced to the western United States at the beginning of the twentieth century, where it has since become enzootic among populations of ground-burrowing black-tailed prairie-dog and ground squirrels. Here, *Oropsylla montana* is the flea vector primarily responsible for transferring the infection to humans. These fleas rarely 'block', nor is there a long incubation period before they become infectious. Instead, they become almost immediately infectious after having consumed a blood meal charged with *Y. pestis* and remain so for at least four days thereafter, and significantly longer if they receive a booster infectious blood meal. Moreover, this method of transmission can take place at temperatures significantly below the 16–22°C required by the blocked-flea route.[410] Rebecca Eisen and others consider this 'scenario of efficient early-phase transmission by unblocked fleas' to be sufficient to 'explain the rapid rate of spread that typifies plague epidemics and epizootics'.[411] Numerous flea

---

[404] Lorange and others (2005), 1907; Gage and Kosoy (2005), 506–9. For a robust defence of the classic model of plague and its dependence upon the black rat (*Rattus rattus*) and flea (*X. cheopis*) see Benedictow, 2010, especially 3–22.

[405] Hufthammer and Walløe (2013).   [406] Benedictow (2010).

[407] Eisen and others (2006), 15380; Webb and others (2006); Eisen and Gage (2012), 65–6; Eisen and others (2015).

[408] Gage and Kosoy (2005), 514–17; Ell (1980), 502–3, 510; Walløe (2008), 71–3; McMichael (2010); Houhamdi and others (2006); Leulmi and others (2014); Ratovonjato and others (2014).

[409] Inglesby and others (2000); Prentice and Rahalison (2007); Stenseth and others (2008); Eisen and Gage (2012).

[410] Williams and others (2013); Eisen and others (2015).

[411] Eisen and others (2006), 15380; Eisen and Gage (2012), 66.

species are now known to have been capable of early-phase transmission, including the rat flea, *X. cheopis*.[412] Further, and potentially of far greater significance, given the resemblance of the Second Pandemic's diffusion to diseases spread directly from person to person under conditions of malnutrition and poverty, 'early-phase transmission by *Pulex irritans* [the human flea] could explain the rapid spread of plague observed during the Black Death in regions of Europe where *X. cheopis* was rare or absent'.[413]

The human flea has been dismissed as 'an exceptionally poor biological vector of plague': it does not block and it has also been doubted whether it can harbour bacteria in sufficient numbers to ensure transmission.[414] Nevertheless, suspicion has long fallen on *Pulex irritans* as a vector of plague's transmission since it would better account for the Black Death's ostensible capacity to spread swiftly and directly from person to person.[415] In 1965 it was incriminated in 'a limited outbreak of bubonic plague in the Bolivian Andes' and in 2007 a case study of plague transmission in Tanzania demonstrated a clear positive correlation between the density of *Pulex irritans* and plague frequency,[416] while in 2008 physiologist Lars Walløe felt confident enough to assert:

most (or all) of the historical European plague epidemics did not involve rats as intermediate hosts. The mode of transmission was from human to human via an insect vector. *Pulex irritans* may have been the most important anthropod vector in Europe prior to the late nineteenth century, but other ectoparasites (other fleas, lice, etc.) could also have been involved.[417]

So far, however, conclusive evidence that would confirm the effectiveness of human fleas as an active vector in the pan-continental spread of the Second Pandemic remains wanting.[418]

The same qualification applies to lice, notorious as the vector responsible for transmission of the bacterium *Rickettsia prowazekii* which causes epidemic typhus (a disease which may, or may not, have been present

---

[412] Eisen and others (2006), 15380; Eisen and Gage (2012), 66.
[413] Eisen and others (2006), 15383; Eisen and others (2015).
[414] Eisen and others (2015). The human flea has been proposed as responsible for rapid person-to-person transmission in the Ragusan epidemic of 1526–7 and the Venetian epidemic of 1575–7: Blažina Tomić and Blažina (2015), 162, 301.
[415] Slack (1989), 462–3; Ell (1980), 502–3, 510; Gage and Kosoy (2005), 517. But see the objections of Benedictow (2010), 9–16. To be efficient, flea vectors must (i) become infected after feeding on a bacteremic host, (ii) live long enough for the bacteria to multiply to sufficient numbers to ensure transmission, and (iii) be able to transfer *Y. pestis* to a susceptible host at concentrations adequate to cause infection: Eisen and Gage (2012), 69.
[416] Eisen and others (2015), citing Beasley (1965); Laudisoit and others (2007). For recent detection of *Y. pestis* in human fleas in Madagascar and the Congo see Leulmi and others (2014); Ratovonjato and others (2014).
[417] Walløe (2008), 72–3; Eisen and others (2015).   [418] Eisen and others (2015).

in late-medieval Europe).[419] The case for lice as an effective vector of plague transmission rests on field observations from south Morocco and the Congo and the results of laboratory experiments on rabbits, which demonstrated that the *orientalis* strain of *Y. pestis* was capable of being spread in this way.[420] If the same were true of the more primitive strain of plague responsible for the Black Death, lice would have provided an ideal vector for transforming human populations into both amplifying hosts and victims of *Y. pestis*. Lice infestation of humans is likely to have been widespread in the Middle Ages and lice, like fleas, were capable of being transported in clothes and textiles. They thrived under cooler temperatures than those required by *X. cheopis*, were readily introduced to plague-free areas by humans, and could remain infectious for up to three days after the death of their human host, thereby infecting those who handled the dead. Intriguingly, the Marseille team reports identification of a late-medieval Venetian plague victim who was co-infected with *Bartonella quintana* (transmitted by the human body louse *Pediculus humanus corporis*) and *Y. pestis*, which it claims 'is compatible with the hypothesis that the body louse was a vector driving the Black Death epidemics in Europe'.[421] Extrapolating from these clues, Michel Drancourt and others hypothesize that panzootics among commensal rodents may have sparked localized zoonotics of human plague which then evolved into major pandemics spread by human ectoparasites.[422] It follows that the greater the infestation of human populations with these ectoparasites, the greater the likelihood of such a crossover occurring. It would also help explain the clear association between human plague, bad weather, harvest failure, famine and poverty and the presence of plague in the absence of rats.[423]

Among humans, *Y. pestis* can also enter the human body via the respiratory tract and, in this pneumonic and deadlier form, plague can be spread directly from person to person once the crossover from panzootic to zoonotic has occurred. Yet, despite claims that pneumonic plague may have been the greater killer during the Black Death, 'this form cannot persist as an independent disease in the absence of the bubonic form'.[424]

---

[419] Raoult and others (2004); Bechah and others (2008). Nightingale (2005), 54, 61, speculates that outbreaks of typhus may have occurred in fourteenth-century England.

[420] Blanc and Baltazard (1942); Drancourt and others (2006); Houhamdi, and others (2006); Ayyadurai and others (2010); Piarroux and others (2013).

[421] Tran and others (2011), 3 of 5.

[422] Drancourt and others (2006). Alternatively, as postulated by Shrewsbury (1971), 124–5, the pandemic of *Y. pestis* may have proceeded in tandem with a pandemic of epidemic typhus.

[423] Cohn (2002a), 1.

[424] Morris (1971); Shrewsbury (1971), 2; Benedictow (2010), 7–8, 511–14.

Evidence from modern epidemics shows that the risks of contracting plague by this route are low and that 'persons with plague usually only transmit the infection when the disease is in the end stage, when infected persons cough copious amounts of bloody sputum, and only by means of close contact'.[425] Extensive dissemination of the disease is also impeded by the swiftness with which pneumonic victims sicken and die, as those infected quickly become too ill to travel. Pneumonic plague is thus typically a secondary rather than primary feature of plague pandemics. Primary pneumonic plague spread person to person can take on an existence of its own, as most famously in Manchuria in 1910–11 and 1921–2, but such outbreaks have invariably been circumscribed in both their temporal and geographical extent and their death tolls were modest.[426] In an even smaller minority of cases the disease is contracted by consumption of infectious tissues from animal carcasses.[427]

3.03.2b From enzootic to pandemic: the plague cycle Plague has existed in the wild for millennia as a sporadic enzootic disease of ground-burrowing rodents, responsible for only the occasional human fatality. Yet in the sixth century, the fourteenth century and the nineteenth century it crossed over and became a devastating pan-continental human pandemic. The biological odds were against this happening, for each pandemic required key changes in plague's hosts (between different sylvatic rodents and from sylvatic rodents to commensal rodents) and vectors (from rodent fleas to possibly human fleas and maybe lice), which, in turn, were contingent upon wider ecological developments. With its interactions between a bacterium, the soil, rodent hosts, insect vectors and humans, plague is in fact a profoundly ecological disease. Anthony McMichael, drawing upon the evidence of Kausrud's twelve-strong Oslo team of scientists, has outlined a sequential 'plague cycle' comprising five main stages: enzootic, epizootic, panzootic, zoonotic and pandemic (Figure 3.27).[428] The first four of these are well documented and understood, the last remains hypothetical.

During the initial enzootic stage that prevailed during the long lulls between major pandemics (Stage 1, Figure 3.27), permanent reservoirs of plague existed among the sylvatic ground-burrowing rodents – marmots, susliks and gerbils – indigenous to the semi-arid interior of Asia. Through long exposure to the bacterium, these animals lived in a relatively benign relationship with *Y. pestis* and mortality levels arising from

[425] Kool (2005), 1166.   [426] Benedictow (2010), 8, 511–14.
[427] Eisen and others (2006), 15380.
[428] Kausrud and others (2010); McMichael (2010).

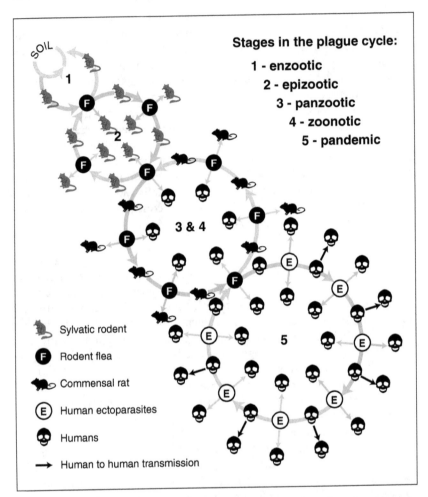

Figure 3.27 The five-stage plague cycle: enzootic, epizootic, panzootic, zoonotic and pandemic
Source: derived from McMichael (2010)

the pathogen were low.[429] *Y. pestis* was able to persist because enough hosts remained sufficiently susceptible to maintain the very high concentrations of bacteria in the bloodstream required for flea-borne transmission and, hence, perpetuation of the transmission cycle.[430] The

---

[429] Gage and Kosoy (2005), 506–9; Stenseth and others (2006); Eisen and Gage (2009); Kausrud and others (2010).
[430] Eisen and Gage (2012), 69.

bacterium's ability to survive for periods at a time in the soil of mammalian burrows is a further reason why *Y. pestis* was unlikely to become extinct. In fact, it is improbable that plague, unlike smallpox and rinderpest, can ever be completely eradicated as a disease. While *Y. pestis* remained in this quiescent state it was rarely present in sufficient concentration in both sylvatic rodent hosts and their flea vectors to pose more than an incidental threat to humans. The sparse vegetation of these semi-arid grasslands kept populations of sylvatic rodents below the densities required to sustain an epizootic outbreak and low humidity acted as a similar constraint upon flea numbers and activity. Prevailing climatic conditions were therefore material to maintenance of *Y. pestis* in this enzootic state.

A shift to increased precipitation and higher moisture levels allowed the productivity of this grassland ecosystem to rise. More rainfall meant more vegetation, increased food supplies for sylvatic rodents, greater survival of young rodents, and a corresponding elevation of population densities to the levels required to maintain natural stocks of *Y. pestis* at more dangerous levels. Survival of flea larvae also increased with humidity. This is what ecologists term a trophic cascade and it allowed the disease to make the transition to a more active epizootic state (Stage 2, Figure 3.27), in which more active transmission by fleas exposed to increased concentrations of the pathogen generated rising mortality among sylvatic rodents.[431] Crucially, more animals now succumbed to the intense bacteremia (the concentration of plague bacteria in the blood), which is essential for effective transmission of plague by flea vectors because their blood meals are so small. Humans directly exposed to sylvatic rodents and their skins, especially hunters, trappers and herders, were now at greater risk of contracting the infection, although while rodent hosts existed in substantial numbers there was little danger of their fleas switching wholesale to humans and thereby amplifying the outbreak into a full-blown human epidemic. In regions with well-established sylvatic reservoirs of plague, infection of humans by this route could be quite common but typically produced sporadic deaths rather than great surges of mortality.

Plague only became a serious threat to humans when it made the crossover from sylvatic to commensal rodent populations and became a panzootic (Stage 3, Figure 3.27). Quite possibly this only occurred after plague had already spread to a variety of other sylvatic rodents and small mammals all of which then served as maintenance hosts of the disease. Spillover of *Y. pestis* to commensal rodents should therefore be regarded as an exceptional development, most likely to occur when a sudden

[431] Eisen and Gage (2012), 69.

contraction in sylvatic populations, either from an abrupt drought-induced reduction in food supplies or abnormally heavy disease mortality, caused their blood-hungry and pathogen-bearing flea vectors to seek alternative hosts. It was at this stage that domestic rats became implicated in spread of the pathogen. As well as living in immediate proximity to humans, rats were far less resistant to *Y. pestis* than their sylvatic counterparts, so that, as fleas rapidly transmitted the pathogen through their colonies, the outbreak assumed the form of a panzootic and rats began to die en masse. Death typically occurred within ten to fourteen days of a rat becoming infected. The consequent collapse of commensal rodent populations had grave consequences for humans. Once again, flea vectors, both blocked and unblocked (the former ravenously hungry), were obliged to seek alternative hosts, this time humans, who proved as susceptible to the infection as the commensal rodents.[432] Among the many species of rat flea, *Xenopsylla cheopis* is considered to have been the most efficient of potential vectors since it is capable of effecting transmission by both early-phase and blocked mechanisms and feeds on commensal rats, sylvatic rodents and, when necessary, humans.[433]

What had begun as a panzootic largely confined to sylvatic and commensal rodents had now spilled over and become a zoonotic (Stage 4, Figure 3.27), killing humans in large numbers. While rodents served as the maintenance hosts of *Y. pestis* and their fleas, notably *X. cheopis* and *Nosopsyllus fasciatus*, were its principal vectors, perpetuation and spread of the zoonotic could not be sustained independently of an accompanying panzootic. As Stefan Monecke and others have demonstrated with respect to the Freiberg plague outbreak of 1613–14, first, populations of commensal rats succumbed to *Y. pestis* and collapsed, next their blood-hungry fleas adopted humans as temporary hosts who, in turn, became infected with *Y. pestis*, then populations of fleas crashed, transmission to humans ceased and the plague outbreak died out.[434] Moreover, so long as plague was mainly transmitted by 'blocked' rat fleas the zoonotic's spread was conditioned by prior infection of rat populations and shaped by human exposure to, and transportation of, those fleas, with the result that it spread fitfully and unevenly and was far from indiscriminate in its human impact.[435] Nor would outbreaks of pneumonic

---

[432] Christakos and others (2007), 702.
[433] Eisen and Gage (2012), 69; Eisen and others (2015). The same vector is responsible for transmission of murine typhus.
[434] Monecke and others (2009).
[435] Lorange and others (2005); Drancourt and others (2006), 235–6; Christakos and others (2007), 716–17; Vogler and others (2011).

plague have significantly altered this pattern, unless allied with some other contagious pneumonic disease such as influenza, for cases were too few and progression from infection to death was too rapid.[436]

Only in the fifth and, as yet, entirely hypothetical final stage, when human ectoparasites replaced rat fleas as the principal vectors of *Y. pestis*, may plague have become unfettered from its dependence upon an accompanying panzootic and acquired an autonomous existence as a deadly disease of humans. To make this final (and, as yet, scientifically unverified) transition from zoonotic to pandemic (Stage 5, Figure 3.27), the human flea (*Pulex irritans*) and, conceivably, louse (*Pediculus humanus corporis*) would need to have become activated as vectors. With this key biological substitution plague would have acquired the potential to spread far and wide through vulnerable human populations, irrespective of whether commensal rodents were present or infected.[437] The disease's passage would now have been shaped by the speeds, directions and distances that humans travelled and the respective incubation periods of infected humans and the relevant insect vectors.[438] Enabling human preconditions included dense populations, integrated networks of communication, high levels of movement, and famine and/or war-induced breakdowns of nutrition, hygiene and public health. Poor, over-crowded and insanitary populations infested with ectoparasites were therefore especially at risk. At this final stage, the pandemic will have assumed the outward appearance of an infectious disease spread contagiously from human to human, notwithstanding that insect vectors of one sort or another remained intrinsic to its transmission.[439] The plague then ran its course until reserves of susceptible vectors were exhausted, at which point it either died out or became dormant, only to be rekindled or reintroduced in the next generation when ecological, biological and demographic circumstances were again ripe. Note that only those very few plague oubreaks with a conspicuously contagious pattern of spread, such as the Black Death, could have been transmitted in this way and it is an open question whether this mechanism of spread could have operated wholly independently of a rodent-based panzootic/zoonotic.

The appeal of the hypothesized fifth stage of this unfolding scenario is that it is consistent with six key features of the Second Pandemic which have long perplexed historians and led some to question whether

---

[436] Kool (2005); Drancourt and others (2006), 235–6.
[437] Wood and others (2003), 427: 'the Black Death spread too rapidly *between* locales to have been a zoonosis such as bubonic plague'.
[438] Ell (1980), 502–3, 510; Drancourt and others (2006).
[439] Welford and Bossak (2010a), 568–70; Welford and Bossak (2010b).

plague could have been *Y. pestis* at all. First, it would account for the widespread contemporary perception that humans were active agents in the plague's dissemination. Second, it fits the Black Death's ostensibly contagious pattern of spread via arteries of human communication from port to port, town to town and settlement to settlement, with a clear summer mortality peak when travel and mobility were greatest and temperatures and humidity levels were most favourable to the bacterium and its insect vectors.[440] This was neither the pattern of spread of an airborne pathogen nor that of one spreading contiguously through sylvatic and commensal rodent populations. Third, it would explain the conspicuous absence from contemporary accounts of any reference to an accompanying rodent panzootic, great though this must otherwise have been, and, more particularly, plague's penetration of regions from which black rats are thought to have been absent.[441] Fourth, it is consistent with plague's ability to invade a wide range of geographical environments, wherever humans were settled, from North Africa to northern Scandinavia and from the shores of the Black Sea to those of the Irish Sea, and thereby highlights how closely interconnected, both commercially and administratively, were most European communities from the Mediterranean to the Baltic and from the Black Sea to the Atlantic by this date. Fifth, the capacity of human ectoparasites to act as vectors would elucidate why entire households tended to succumb, irrespective of wealth or social class, and why mortality was nevertheless highest among those most infested with fleas and lice or exposed to them, notably the poor and the beneficed clergy. Finally, with humans and their ectoparasites acting as hosts and vectors, and with early-phase transmission predominant, it is easier to see how the Black Death was able to spread at double the speed of the railroad-assisted and panzootic-dependent twentieth-century Indian pandemic and five times that of the highly contagious 1316–21 rinderpest panzootic, with its simpler viral mechanism of transmission.[442] Plague travelled over sea and land with the speed of humans, assisted by ships and horses, rather than at the far slower speeds of herded cattle or carts hauled by oxen, let alone the altogether more haphazard movement of black rats and their fleas moving contiguously from settlement to settlement or stowing away on ships and in consignments of grain and bales of merchandise.

---

[440] Benedictow (2010), 396–484.

[441] Herlihy (1997), 26: 'not a single Western chronicler notes the occurrence of an epizootic, the massive mortalities of rats, which ought to have preceded and accompanied the human plague. Humans, in the classic bubonic epidemiology, can contract the disease only from a dying rodent.' Hufthammer and Walløe (2013).

[442] Christakos and others (2007); above, Section 3.03.1b.

3.03.2c The central Asian origin of Y. pestis It was the founding father of medical history, J. F. C. Hecker, who in 1832 proposed that the Second Pandemic originated in China and thence spread west across Eurasia.[443] The idea has lingered ever since and in 1977 was powerfully re-enunciated by William H. McNeill in his influential *Plagues and peoples*.[444] McNeill speculated that the Yunnan province of southwest China (origin, in 1855, of the Third Pandemic), located in the eastern foothills of the Himalayas between China, Burma and India, was one of plague's natural foci. From here, sometime in the thirteenth or early fourteenth century, he proposed that humans inadvertently spread the bacillus north until *Y. pestis* became established among the ground-burrowing mammals of the Eurasian steppe lands, between Manchuria and southern Russia. He identified a deadly but unspecified pandemic in the Hopei province of eastern China in *c.*1331–2 as the earliest recorded major outbreak of the Black Death and proposed that over the next fifteen years plague made the journey of almost 6,500 kilometres west via the interior caravan routes that traversed the *Pax Mongolica* until in 1346 it emerged among the Mongol troops besieging the Black Sea port of Kaffa.

Not all have been convinced by this thesis. From a careful review of the published evidence at that time available to European scholars John Norris (1977) reported that 'historical records are such as to cast strong doubt on the various attributions to China, India or Central Asia as the source of the Black Death in the fourteenth century'.[445] George Sussman (2011), in a more recent comprehensive review of the literature, failed to find any Chinese description of disease symptoms consistent with a diagnosis of plague and therefore concluded that the Black Death 'never reached China'.[446] Sinologist Paul D. Buell (2012) concurs. In his view there is neither convincing medical evidence of plague in the Chinese sources, nor anything in the historical record to suggest that China 'suffered the enormous plague epidemics that the West or the Middle East experienced'.[447] In fact, all three of these scholars believe that the Black Death is more likely to have originated in western than eastern Asia.[448]

Instead of China, Norris located the critical biological event which initiated the Black Death, namely the spillover of *Y. pestis* from sylvatic to commensal rodent hosts, somewhere in the Caspian Basin. This semi-arid continental region of cold winters and very hot summers, dependent

---

[443] Hecker (1832).   [444] McNeill (1977).   [445] Norris (1977), 24.
[446] Sussman (2011), 354.   [447] Buell (2012), 129.
[448] For a dissenting view see Hymes (2014).

upon a westerly air-stream for such moisture as it receives, has long been one of plague's natural foci. Its steppe grasslands are home to hibernating ground-burrowing marmots and susliks which continue to act as sylvatic hosts of the plague bacillus and whose contaminated burrows serve as reservoirs of infection. On Norris's analysis, the infection spread west from the Caspian Basin through the lands of the Kipchak Khanate to the Crimea, east into what is now Kazakhstan, and south into Kurdistan and Iraq. Benedictow (2004) agrees and believes that it is necessary to look no further than the lower reaches of the Rivers Volga and Don, with their respective outlets into the Caspian and Black Seas, for the original plague focus from which the Black Death spread in the mid-1340s.[449]

A western Asian origin is certainly consistent with the statement of Byzantine chronicler Nicephoros Gregoras that plague came from 'Scythia and Maeotis and the mouth of the Tanais [Don]' in the spring of 1346.[450] Similarly, Byzantine Emperor John VI reported that the Black Death first surfaced in Scythia, between the Caspian and Black Seas, in the lands of the Kipchak Khanate of the Golden Horde.[451] According to lawyer and chronicler Gabriel de Mussis, of Piacenza in northern Italy, it was Khan Janibeg's Mongol army which then spread the infection to the inhabitants of the Genoese port of Kaffa, whose mariners in turn spread it to the ports of the Black Sea, Aegean and Mediterranean.[452] Although Baillie (2006) has questioned the veracity of de Mussis's account and in 2001 Susan Scott and Christopher Duncan proposed an East African origin for the plague (which they claimed was a haemorrhagic fever and not *Y. pestis*), most authorities now accept that the disease that ravaged the lands of the Golden Horde in the mid-1340s is the first clearly documented outbreak of the Black Death.[453] All that is lacking is clinching aDNA evidence of *Y. pestis* from fourteenth-century plague burials within this broad region.

But were the steppe lands between the Caspian Basin and the Black Sea the ultimate or merely the proximate origin of the Second Pandemic? When plumping for this region as the Black Death's ultimate origin, Norris did concede the possibility of an outlier and earlier outbreak over three thousand kilometres to the east at Issyk-Kul in Kirgizia, north of the Tien Shan mountains on the northern branch of the east–west caravan

---

[449] Benedictow (2004), 50.
[450] Cited in Norris (1977), 11; Benedictow (2004), 44–54.
[451] Aberth (2005), 15–16.
[452] Schamiloglu (1993); Horrox (1994), 14–26, gives de Mussis's account in full.
[453] Scott and Duncan's proposed East African origin is at variance with recorded dates and directions of the Black Death's spread in 1347–8: Benedictow (2010), 586–7.

route which has become known as the 'Silk Road'.[454] Here, according to the unverifiable results of an 1885 Russian excavation, headstone
inscriptions from two Nestorian cemeteries indicated heavy mortalities in
1338/9 from a mysterious and deadly 'pestilence'.[455] To this day, sylvatic
plague remains enzootic among this region's great gerbil populations,
whose numbers are typically a function of the effect of varying precipitation levels upon vegetation growth and therefore food supplies.[456] Fatalities still occasionally occur when flea vectors transmit plague to human
victims.[457]

Since Norris, historians Michael Dols (1977), Uli Schamiloglu (1993)
and Rosemary Horrox (1994) have all subscribed to an origin of the
Black Death somewhere in central Asia.[458] Historical support for this
view is provided by contemporary commentator Abū Hafs 'Umar Ibn
al-Wardī. Writing at Aleppo in northern Palestine in 1348, Ibn al-Wardī
reported that plague had struck northern India, 'the lands of the Uzbeks',
Transoxiana and Persia before it reached the Crimea.[459] The Oslo plague
team, which has been working with high-quality Soviet-era records of *Y.
pestis* outbreaks and weather for the Kazakh region of eastern Kazakhstan
(immediately to the north of Issyk-Kul), is also of the opinion that the
Second Pandemic 'probably emerged from the interior of Central Asia,
where the plague bacterium seems likely to have evolved after diverging
from its most recent extant relative, *Yersina pseudotuberculosis*, and is also
still endemic in large areas'.[460]

Whereas historians understandably believe that the answer to the question of the ultimate origin of the Black Death 'must lie, if anywhere
at all, in the Central Asian and far-eastern sources', resolution of this
issue appears instead to have been provided by the new genomic evidence assembled by microbiologists and geneticists.[461] This is because
mutation of the *Y. pestis* genome during its geographical spread has created country-specific genealogies whose lineage-specific single nucleotide
polymorphisms (SNPs) provide clues to the routes its spatial diffusion
has taken and the sequence in which they were followed.[462] Thus, initial
phylogenetic reconstruction of the *Y. pestis* genome strongly suggested to

---

[454] Below, Figure 4.9.   [455] Norris (1977), 10–11.
[456] Stenseth and others (2006); Kausrud and others (2010).
[457] On Tuesday 27 August 2013 BBC World News reported the death from bubonic
plague of a fifteen-year-old herder from the small mountain village of Ichke-Zhergez,
in eastern Kyrgyzstan, close to the border with Kazakhstan, the first plague death,
apparently, for thirty years.
[458] Dols (1978); Schamiloglu (1993); Horrox (1994).   [459] Aberth (2005), 17.
[460] Kausrud and others (2010), 2 of 14; Suntsov (2014).   [461] Dols (1978), 113.
[462] See Vogler and others (2011) for detailed application of this approach to the spread
of plague in Madagascar. SNPs are the most common type of genetic variation; each

Giovanna Morelli and others (2010) that the bacillus probably 'evolved in China and spread to other areas on multiple occasions'.[463] Crucially, as microbiologist Mark Achtman (2012) has explained, to nowhere else can so many variant and ancient strains of *Y. pestis* be traced; moreover, the basal populations on the genealogy are found in China, as are multiple other populations from all branches (Figure 3.28).[464]

It is ancient Chinese genotypes to which the newly identified strain of *Y. pestis* from which fourteenth-century French, English and Dutch plague victims perished is most closely related.[465] This aDNA evidence reverses the direction of transmission postulated by Norris, who had proposed 'that the micro-organism was transmitted *eastward* from the Caspian focus' and who had also argued against 'long-range, rapid and covert transmission of the micro-organism' of the sort that phylogenetic analysis now indicates took place.[466] Instead, the new genomic evidence shows that the diversity of *Y. pestis* isolates from central Asia is lower than in China, not all populations on the genealogy are represented in central Asia, and the oldest central Asian populations are more recent than the oldest Chinese population (Figure 3.28). Achtman thus concludes that 'the most parsimonious interpretation of these observations is therefore that sylvatic plague originated in China and spread to other global regions on multiple occasions'.[467]

Yujun Cui and others (2013) have deployed 2,326 SNPs identified from 133 genomes of *Y. pestis* strains isolated in China and elsewhere to bring the Chinese and east Asian component of this phylogenetic tree into sharper focus. Their work points to the northeast Tibetan–Qinghai Plateau in western China as the most likely ultimate origin of the Second Pandemic (Figure 3.28). Here alone the deepest branching lineage of *Y. pestis* has been isolated (designated 0.PE7), with representatives of younger lineages fanning out from it radially. Qinghai is remote and elevated and, crucially, lies north of the reach of the South Asian monsoon within a climate zone dominated by a westerly air-stream.[468] Historically, it was strategically located at the intersection of several ancient overland trade routes and it was through this region in the early 1270s

---

SNP represents a difference in a single DNA building block, called a nucleotide: http://ghr.nlm.nih.gov/handbook/genomicresearch/snp.

[463] Morelli and others (2010), 1141; also Achtman and others (2004), 17842.
[464] Achtman (2012), 864.
[465] Haensch and others (2010), 5 of 8; Bos and others (2011); below, Section 4.03.1.
[466] Norris (1977), 24; Norris (1978). Benedictow (2010), 621n., also expresses the view that 'there are interesting reasons to assume that bubonic plague came to China from Europe'.
[467] Achtman (2012), 864.
[468] I am grateful to John Brooke and Scott Levi for clarifying this crucial climatic point. For the northern limits of the Asian monsoon see Chen and others (2008); Fang and others (2014).

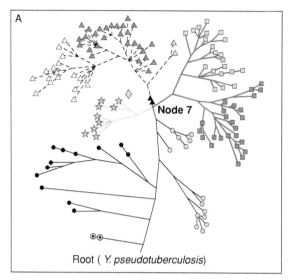

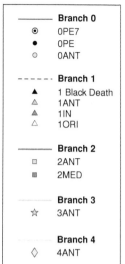

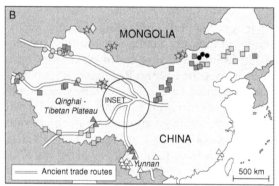

Figure 3.28 The *Yersinia pestis* phylogenetic tree and the distribution of *Y. pestis* genomes in China

Names of genomic sequences: ANT & IN = *antiqua*; MED = *medievalis*; ORI = *orientalis*; PE = *pestoides*; Node 7 = multiple polytomy that preceded the Black Death.

Black Death genomes = specific *Y. pestis* strains identified from aDNA analysis of fourteenth-century plague victims at Saint-Laurent-de-la-Cabrerisse (France), Hereford (England) and Bergen-op-Zoom (Netherlands).

Source: redrawn from Cui and others (2013), 578

that Marco Polo, his father and uncle passed en route to Lanzhou and Beijing. The assumption of the Cui team is that one way or another human travel along these axes of movement transmitted plague between rodent populations, south to Yunnan, northeast to Mongolia, and west to central Asia and, thence, western Asia and Europe (Figure 3.28). This echoes the speculation of Morelli and others (2010) that the westward spread of *Y. pestis* into Kazahkstan and the Caucasus was via 'trade articles that were carried along the Silk Road', one branch of which lay through Issyk-Kul.[469] It is widely assumed that human trans-shipment of infected insect vectors and maybe even rodents permitted plague to leapfrog stretches of barren terrain lacking sufficient sylvatic rodents to sustain invasion by *Y. pestis* and thereby become established among otherwise unconnected virgin populations of sylvatic and commensal rodents along these routes.[470] This is what Benedictow has termed metastatic spread.[471] So far, however, corroborating biological and/or historical evidence that plague did indeed migrate westwards along this route and by this method is lacking.

3.03.2d The environmental context of plague's spread across Asia

McMichael believes that it was 'naturally occurring climatic fluctuations' within Eurasia's semi-arid interior, 'acting through their environmental, ecological and political impacts', that ended plague's five centuries of relative quiescence and set the Second Pandemic in motion.[472] The new biological evidence assembled and scrutinized by Cui and others (2013) implies that this had occurred up to eighty years before the Black Death, when plague's activation from an enzootic to an epizootic state spawned multiple new lineages (Node 7 in Figure 3.28).[473] They attribute this marked increase in diversity to rapid fixing of neutral SNPs under alternating endemic and epidemic conditions and date this 'big bang' to around 1268 but with a possible chronological range between 1142 and 1339 (Figure 3.28).[474] Kirsten I. Bos and others (2011), however, placed this event within the slightly later and narrower time frame 1282–1343.[475] On either dating, it was during this short time period

---

[469] Morelli and others (2010), 1140.
[470] Davis and others (2004); Eisen and Gage (2009); Heier and others (2011).
[471] Benedictow (2010), 151–93.   [472] McMichael (2010), 1 of 3.
[473] Bos and others (2011), 509, prefer a date within sixty years of the Black Death.
[474] Cui and others (2013), 580.
[475] Bos and others (2011), 509: 'Temporal estimates indicate that all *Y. pestis* commonly associated with human infection shared a common ancestor sometime between 668 and 729 years ago (AD 1282–1343, 95% highest probability density, HPD), encompassing a much smaller time interval than recently published estimates and further indicating that all currently circulating branch 1 and branch 2 isolates emerged during the thirteenth century at the earliest, potentially stemming from an Eastern Asian source'.

that the aDNA sequences first emerged that have been retrieved from the dental remains of French, English and Dutch victims of the Black Death.

This new genetic evidence clearly implicates the northeast Tibetan–Qinghai Plateau in western China as the ultimate origin of the Second Pandemic (Figure 3.28). This probably rules out the mystery pestilence that struck the Hopei province of eastern China in *c*.1331–2 as the first major outbreak of the disease but rules in the equally mysterious Issyk-Kul pestilence of 1338–9 as a possible product of the pandemic's westward spread, by which time, to judge from the concentrated number of human fatalities, the disease must clearly have entered is panzootic/zoonotic stage as flea vectors transmitted *Y. pestis* from collapsing populations of rodents to humans (Figure 3.27).[476] It also fits Abū Hafs 'Umar Ibn al-Wardī's observation that plague 'began in the land of darkness' where it had been 'current for fifteen years' (i.e. since *c*.1333) and chimes with the recent estimate of Boris Schmid and others that it took ten to twelve years for plague outbreaks to spread from central Asia to the European ports of the Black Sea.[477]

In this unfolding scenario what first launched and then impelled the Black Death on its ultimately lethal course were changes in ecological conditions in its semi-arid source region in east-central Asia and the steppe lands through which it then spread. The impact of medium- and short-term climatic variations upon vegetation growth and thus the densities and behaviour of the bacterium, its hosts and flea vectors were crucial. These, in turn, were linked to the transition then taking place from the relatively settled atmospheric circulation patterns of the MCA to the less stable conditions of the LIA.

Particular interest naturally attaches to a reconstructed annual precipitation index for the northeast Tibetan–Qinghai Plateau, derived from annually resolved and absolutely dated ring widths of Qilian juniper (*Juniperus przewalskii* Kom.), since this sheds light on climatic, and by implication ecological, conditions in the very region where it has been proposed that plague was first reawakened from its long dormant enzootic state (Figure 3.28).[478] As Figure 3.29 shows, the natural aridity of this elevated continental region tended to increase over the course of the twelfth century, with a succession of dry years of increasing severity in 1108–9, 1112, 1145 and 1152, until the sustained drought of 1191–1201, with 1200 the single driest year since AD 374. Drought returned with a vengeance in 1207 (as Chinggis Khan launched his second raid across the

[476] Cui and others (2013); McNeill (1977), 143; Schamiloglu (1993), 448; Horrox (1994), 9.
[477] Aberth (2005), 17; Schmid and others (2015).   [478] Cui and others (2013).

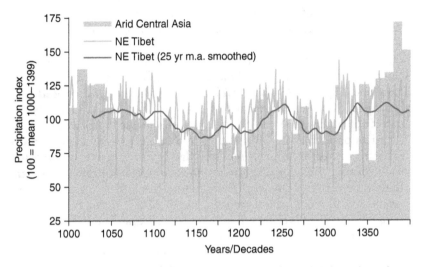

Figure 3.29 Indexed precipitation in Arid Central Asia and northeast Tibet, 1000–1400
Sources: Chen and others (2010); Yang and others (2014)

Gobi Desert against the Western Xia) and did not ease until 1210. The central Asian multi-proxy precipitation index reconstructed at decadal resolution by Chen and others (Figure 3.29) shows that these drought conditions were felt right across the continent's steppe grasslands. It can be inferred that diminished rainfall naturally restricted vegetation growth and, thus, populations of the ground-burrowing sylvatic rodents that were plague's natural hosts. The combination of high temperatures and low humidity ought also to have depressed their flea burdens. Consequently plague is likely to have remained in an enzootic state, posing little threat to humans throughout this long period.

From 1211 to 1253 these conditions eased significantly, both in Qing-hai and more generally, with 1225 and 1242 the only dry years and neither as severe as the worst droughts of the previous century (Figure 3.29). Instead, the period was characterized by a number of wetter than average years, notably 1222, 1230, 1241 (the wettest for over 250 years), 1247 and 1249. From 1215 to 1252 the trend in precipitation was decidedly upwards, with the 1240s the wettest decade since the 1090s (Figure 3.29). To the north, in Mongolia, this pluvial episode began slightly earlier and the years 1211–25 stand out as the most persistently wet of the second millennium, when 'no annual values or their bootstrapped confidence limits drop below the long-term mean of the [warm-season Palmer

Drought Severity Index] reconstruction'.[479] The Tien Shan mountains, two thousand kilometres to the west, do not appear to have shared in these improved precipitation levels but on the Tibetan–Qinghai Plateau and in Mongolia grassland productivity will undoubtedly have been boosted, allowing elevation of sylvatic-rodent densities and build-up of *Y. pestis* infection to the thresholds necessary to sustain a transition from enzootic to epizootic plague (Figure 3.27).

Higher grassland productivity also benefited Chinggis Khan's cavalry-based troops and thus helped sustain the momentum of Mongol military conquest (first partly set in motion by the adverse effects of persistent drought upon the nomadic pastoral peoples of the steppes) with the result that by the middle of the thirteenth century virtually the whole of Eurasia's steppe grasslands had been brought under Mongol control.[480] This opened up this vast and hitherto politically fragmented region to greatly increased latitudinal movement by armies, couriers and caravans, with all the consequences this potentially had for wider human-assisted metastatic diffusion of the plague pathogen via transportation of the insect vectors responsible for its transmission between sylvatic rodents, commensal rodents and humans.

On the Tibetan–Qinghai Plateau six consecutive years of drought from 1255 to 1260, with 1258 the worst of them, brought this prolonged pluvial episode to an abrupt close (Figures 3.29 and 3.30). This was the worst episode of drought for fifty years and was all the more ecologically traumatic because it followed almost forty years of rising moisture levels: 1255 was the driest year since 1207 and 1258 the driest since the mega-drought of 1200. Onset of these drought conditions coincided with a time of climatic extremes throughout the northern hemisphere, when the ENSO, NAO and Asian monsoon were all at mega strength.[481] The marked precipitation failure of 1258 may however be linked to the climatic impact of the VEI 7 eruption of Samalas Volcano, Indonesia, in spring/summer of the previous year.[482] The great claims that have been made of the global climatic impact of this most explosive of eruptions are nevertheless hardly borne out by the rapid easing of drought conditions in Qinghai in 1259 and the absence of any corresponding narrow-ring event in the pine and juniper dendrochronologies for Mongolia and the Tien Shan (Figure 3.30).[483] In fact, in Mongolia the big downturn came a few years later in 1262–4 and in Qinghai the drought year 1271 was far worse than 1258 and was the driest year since AD 360. Nor in either

---

[479] Pederson and others (2014), 4376.   [480] Pederson and others (2014), 4376–8.
[481] Above, Figures 2.2 to 2.7.   [482] Lavigne and others (2013).
[483] Stothers (2000); Oppenheimer (2003). For a recent reassessment of this eruption's effect upon northern hemisphere summer temperatures see Stoffel and others (2015).

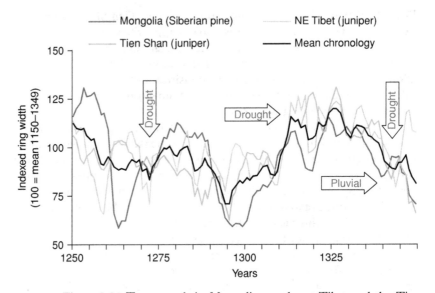

Figure 3.30 Tree growth in Mongolia, northeast Tibet and the Tien Shan (3-year moving averages), 1250–1349
Sources: Mongolia, Jacoby and others (no date); northeast Tibet, Yang and others (2014); Tien Shan, data supplied by Jan Esper

region was there any sustained recovery of precipitation levels until the 1310s.

These drought events must have been ecologically traumatic for fauna which had grown accustomed to the more abundant flora sustained by the wetter conditions previously prevailing. The mega-drought of 1271 is precisely the kind of environmental shock that may have boosted mortality among sylvatic rodents and led flea vectors to migrate and seek alternative hosts, bringing about wider diffusion of the pathogen. Quite possibly this key crossover will have brought humans into increased contact with both the bacterium and its vectors and heightened the likelihood of inadvertent long-distance metastatic movement of the hosts and/or vectors of plague. Note that these climatic and consequent ecological developments coincide closely with the sudden multiplication of *Y. pestis* lineages (Node 7 in Figure 3.28) as dated by Cui and others to around the 1260s, which they interpret as a clear sign that plague had entered a more active phase.[484] Possibly it was at about this time that plague started to spread outwards from the Tibetan–Qinghai Plateau.

---

[484] Cui and others (2013), 579–80.

Alternatively, Bos and others (2011) date the east Asian emergence of the strain of *Y. pestis* responsible for the Black Death and all subsequent plague outbreaks to sometime between 1282 and 1343,[485] in which case a second and far more universal episode of drought in the 1290s (Figure 3.30), manifest in respective growth minima of 1293 for Qinghai (junipers), 1294 for the Tien Shan (junipers) and 1295–6 for Mongolia (Siberian pines) and coinciding with a sharp global downturn in tree growth, may have been the catalyst that set trans-Asian diffusion of the pathogen into motion.[486] If so, its progress may have gained momentum from onset in the 1310s of another pluvial episode (coinciding with onset of the Dantean Anomaly) which lasted until the early 1340s.[487] This fits the date given by Abū Hafs 'Umar Ibn al-Wardī to the first appearance of the Black Death and the timing of the possible plague outbreak among communities of Nestorian Christians at Issyk-Kul, two thousand kilometres to the west of Qinghai.[488] In Qinghai itself, 1316 (a year of weather extremes across Eurasia and incessant rain and acute famine in northwest Europe) was the wettest year since 974.[489] Intriguingly, the juniper dendrochronologies for both Qinghai and the Tien Shan imply that regions on opposite sides of the Tibetan Plateau/Kunlun Mountain Chain were benefiting from higher and more regular rainfall during this interval.[490] With higher rates of biomass production populations of sylvatic rodents can be expected to have risen and further epizootic amplification will have occurred.

Any easing of aridity will have facilitated transportation of plague across the vast, parched and sparsely populated upland region that separated Qinghai from Issyk-Kul. Starting in the 1270s, plague would need to have travelled along the branch of the Silk Road that led to Kirgizia at a rate of over half a kilometre a week and thirty kilometres a year to have reached Issyk-Kul by 1338. Alternatively, starting in the late 1290s would have required faster speeds of one kilometre a week and fifty kilometres a year. Given the scale of the natural barriers of climate and terrain to be overcome, it is inconceivable that plague could have achieved these speeds and completed this most difficult leg of its westward

---

[485] Bos and others (2011), 509.   [486] Baillie (2006), 135–41.
[487] Note that these wetter conditions prevailed solely in those parts of Central Asia exposed to a predominantly westerly air-stream and north of the reach of the Asian monsoon. South of this critical climatic boundary drought conditions predominated from 1311 to 1351: Sun and Liu (2012), 6 of 11. For the boundary between these two zones see Chen and others (2008); Zhao and others (2013); Fang and others (2014). For the Dantean Anomaly see Brown (2001), 251–4; Campbell (2010a), 13–14, 19–20.
[488] Norris (1977), 10–11.   [489] Jordan (1996); Campbell (2011b).
[490] In contrast, drought prevailed just a few hundred kilometres to the south, due to the diminishing strength and reach of the Asian monsoon: Sun and Liu (2012).

overland journey by processes of contiguous spread alone. Instead, the most likely mechanism was transportation of infected ectoparasites via the merchandise carried by the caravans that still regularly traversed this inhospitable region. Alternatively, the camels themselves may have become infected.[491] Transportation by migratory birds and their fleas is a further possibility.[492] Probably by more means than one and in fits and starts, plague and its vectors were drawn ever further west across this vast and semi-arid terrain. It is to be expected that fleas will have attacked their preferred hosts, namely rodents, first, but by the time plague reached Issyk-Kul rodent populations must have been failing for their flea vectors were adopting humans as their hosts of last resort (Figure 3.27).

From Kirgizia plague then had to travel a further two thousand kilometres to reach the Caspian Basin and, beyond it, the lands of the Kipchak Khanate of the Golden Horde. On this leg there were no major mountain barriers or deserts to be crossed, merely a vast undulating expanse of thinly populated and semi-arid steppe grassland. To cover this distance in less than eight years its rate of spread had to accelerate to ⅔ kilometre a day and almost 250 kilometres a year, which again confirms the facilitating role of humans in the process. Whereas plague spreading contiguously between rodent communities could rarely cover as much as 0.1 kilometre a year, Benedictow reckons that spreading metastatically with human assistance 'the Black Death can be seen to spread over land by an average pace of 0.5–2.5 kilometre per day, and along main roads usually on average by 1–2 kilometre per day'.[493] Transportation rates by birds would have been even greater. In one way or another, therefore, soldiers, officials and traders travelling west by horse, ox-cart and camel caravan must have carried the plague with them, leaving infected communities of rodents and, as at Issyk-Kul, a trail of human casualties in their wake[494] It is not to be imagined that this was achieved in a single giant step, for the slowness of overland travel meant that many intermediate steps were probably needed. Nor had plague necessarily yet become a fast-spreading pandemic. Certainly, Francesco Balducci Pegolotti had no inkling of the dangers it posed when, in the early 1340s, he recorded how safe it was for merchants and traders to travel to Cathay via this route.[495] Within another five years, for a combination of political and epidemiological reasons, this route had become altogether more hazardous.

[491] Schmid and others (2015).
[492] Heier and others (2011), 2921: the Isabelline wheatear (*Oenanthe isabellina*) nests in gerbil burrows and, in order to find a suitable nesting place, flies from burrow to burrow, possibly transporting infected fleas.
[493] Benedictow (2010), 170, 173.   [494] Norris (1977), 13–15.
[495] Pegolotti (*c*.1340 and 1936), 21–3.

After the almost unfettered growth of the twelfth- and early thirteenth-century commercial revolution, the first serious setbacks to European mercantile expansion occurred between 1258 and 1291 in the Levant at the very time that enticing new commercial opportunities in the Far East were beckoning. This commercially strategic region sat astride the trans-Syrian trade routes that linked the commerce of the Mediterranean with that of the Persian Gulf, Arabian Sea, Indian Ocean and beyond and were the principal conduits by which the spices of India and ceramics and silks of the Orient were delivered to European markets.[496] The Levant also constituted an important market for European exports, especially of cheap, light coloured cloth.[497] Yet between the capture of Baghdad by the Mongols in 1258 and the fall of Acre to the Mamluks in 1291 its caravan routes were increasingly obstructed and European merchants progressively excluded from its ports and markets. Final elimination of the crusader states substituted increasingly punitive papal embargoes on trade with the Egyptian Mamluks for the lucrative trading privileges hitherto enjoyed by Genoa and Venice.[498] These were the more harmful given that the Red Sea route to Alexandria remained the sole un-constricted artery by which the maritime commerce of the Indian Ocean and Arabian Sea could reach Europe. With most rival trade routes closed (apart from those requiring lengthy trans-shipments between Hormuz and Basra on the Gulf via Tabriz in Persia to either Ayas in Cilicia on the Mediterranean or Trebizond on the Black Sea), the Kārimīs cartel of Muslim merchants who controlled the Red Sea trade were in a strong position to levy monopoly profits and the sultan of Egypt to dictate commercial terms to Christian merchants. The latter curried favour with the sultan by supplying slaves from southern Russia and Scythia to his Mamluk armies and timber, iron and other military stores.

Unsurprisingly, from the 1260s and especially the 1290s the focus of Italian commercial activity was deflected north to the Black Sea and the substitute markets it offered, the alternative access it gave via the *Pax Mongolica* to the East, and the vital slave trade with the Mamluks that it afforded.[499] Between 1291 and 1299 the Genoese and Venetians fought a bitter naval war for domination of this strategic economic region, from which Genoa emerged the victor and Marco Polo one of its captives. From the Black Sea its merchants penetrated southeast to Persia and east into the Caspian Basin, thereby unwittingly providing the critical link by which *Y. pestis* would in due course be introduced to Europe.[500]

---

[496] Abu-Lughod (1989), 185–211.   [497] Munro (1999b).   [498] Above, Section 3.01.
[499] Above, Figure 2.1 and 129.   [500] Below, Sections 4.03 and 4.04.

Meanwhile, loss of crusading outlets in the Holy Land seems to have fed an upsurge in major military conflicts within Europe, waged for an array of feudal, dynastic, territorial and religious reasons.[501] The most bitter and costly of these, between Angevins and Aragonese, England and France, France and Flanders, Scotland and England, and rival Guelph and Ghibelline supporters of the pope and the Holy Roman Emperor, proved destructive of property, disruptive of trade and excessively demanding of finance. They also displaced commerce from its long-established channels and begot brigandage on land and piracy at sea, thereby driving up freight rates and in the process contributing to the general rise in risks and transaction costs.[502]

Especially damaging was Philip IV's interference from the late 1280s in conduct of the Champagne fairs, whose commercial and juridical neutrality he ruthlessly sacrificed in order to advance his feudal and territorial ambitions respecting the semi-autonomous French fief of Flanders.[503] Philip's overt discrimination against Flemish merchants and their Italian counterparts led them to conduct much of their business elsewhere, to the permanent loss of this once pre-eminent focus of exchange between the commerce of the Mediterranean and that of the North Sea region. Higher freight rates on the new maritime route via the Strait of Gibraltar to Bruges, Southampton and London relative to those on the old trans-Alpine overland routes further reinforced the trend towards higher transaction costs.

Although a few ports, such as Bruges, profited from these developments, the aggregate volume of European long-distance trade shrank.[504] Italy's great maritime entrepôts were squeezed hard by loss of commercial opportunities in the eastern Mediterranean, the dwindling supply and higher price of Oriental trade goods, and decline of the Champagne fairs as an efficient and convenient focus for their commercial dealings with northern Europe. Although the country's merchant companies were pioneers of the new business methods of the age, numbers of them were tempted to grow too big and then, unwisely, became drawn into the supply of war finance to credit-hungry monarchs.[505] Bankruptcies inevitably ensued whenever business confidence faltered, there was a run on their reserves and/or they found themselves unable to meet their own sometimes overwhelming obligations. It did not help that profits on the bulk trade in grain which had long been one of their mainstays became seriously squeezed during the second quarter of the fourteenth century when

[501] Munro (1991), 121–4.   [502] Munro (1991); Munro (1999b).
[503] Above, 139; Figure 3.1.   [504] Munro (1991), 124–7.
[505] Above, 147–8; Hunt and Murray (1999), 116–19.

a series of weather-induced back-to-back harvest failures led several Italian urban governments to make their own bulk purchases of grain which they then processed into bread and sold at subsidized prices.[506] Urban growth in the developed centre and north of Italy consequently stagnated as the region's economy declined. Italian daily real wage rates and GDP per head were both trending decisively downwards from at least 1310.[507]

In northern Europe the effect of the rise in transaction costs was to undermine commercial viability of the manufacture for export of cheap, light, unfinished cloths upon which the prosperity of both the English and Flemish urban textile industries had in large part depended.[508] Since the Flemish industry was by far the larger of the two, and indeed the single greatest industrial employer of labour in northern Europe, this constituted a major economic setback. Diversification into manufacture of luxury woollens better able to withstand the increased costs of transport ensured survival of the Flemish industry but on a reduced scale in terms of the aggregate value of output and volume of employment. It also reinforced dependence upon imports of English fine wool, for which the Flemings faced growing competition from rival Brabantine and Italian purchasers. Problematically, deliveries of English wool were susceptible to the ravages of sheep murrain and manipulation by the English Crown in furtherance of its own political and military objectives. Industrially based urban growth therefore ceased, recurrent trade recessions aggravated political tensions and begot a series of sometimes violent urban revolts, and, as the once thriving and dynamic cloth industry stagnated and declined, it seems likely that, as in Italy, output and incomes per head trended downwards.[509]

Neither Italy (centre-north) nor Flanders was self-sufficient in either essential industrial raw materials – wool, alum and dyestuffs – or staple foodstuffs. Loss of export earnings was therefore economically compromising to them and in Italy caused agricultural prices to rise ahead of those for manufactured goods (Table 3.1), thereby dampening domestic demand for products of the secondary and tertiary sectors. Each was densely populated, with average densities in excess of forty per square kilometre and double that in the most crowded districts, and both retained large agricultural sectors within which morcellation of holdings had been taken to extremes.[510] Shrinking employment opportunities in the service and manufacturing sectors consequently entrapped excess

---

[506] Abulafia (1981); Hunt and Murray (1999), 119; Jansen (2009).
[507] Above, Section 3.01.1; Figure 3.2.
[508] Above, 155–8 and 175; Figure 3.5; Figure 3.12A.
[509] Above, Section 3.01.2.   [510] Above, 62–4.

labour on the land at densities which the slowing but nonetheless ongoing momentum of population growth drove ever higher. Malanima's estimates suggest that Italian rural population densities did not peak until the 1320s, by which time a high proportion of rural households were attempting to subsist on holdings that were marginal for subsistence. A similar problem prevailed in Flanders where growing numbers of rural households resorted to textile manufacture as a means of augmenting their incomes, a development which brought them into direct conflict with the beleaguered urban textile producers intent upon quashing this unwelcome rural competition.[511] The more the international commercial recession deepened, the worse these problems became and the greater the proportion of households exposed to serious subsistence risk whenever harvests failed, the prices of staple foodstuffs soared, or dislocations to trade depressed non-agricultural earnings. Urban textile artisans, squeezed by massively inflated food prices in combination with an abrupt contraction in demand for cloth, perished in large numbers during the Great European Famine.[512]

England's problems at this time were rather different for, except in years of extreme scarcity, it was self-sufficient in staple foodstuffs and a net exporter of vital raw materials – wool, hides, tin and lead – that remained in strong international demand. Loss of its export industry of cheap, light, unfinished cloths was a blow, especially to the towns most directly affected, but from the 1330s, sheltered by rising export duties on wool and aided by declining cloth imports, its textile industry, producing mostly for the domestic market, began to revive.[513] At the same time, although the aggregate volume of the country's overseas trade undoubtedly shrank, withdrawal by foreign merchants created commercial opportunities for those native merchants with the capacity to expand.[514] Nevertheless, these were achievements born out of adversity rather than prosperity, as declining business at the country's main international fairs and London's own faltering fortunes bear witness (Figure 3.11). For as long as the international economy remained in recession there was little prospect of the metropolitan economy reviving, let alone the country expanding its modest secondary and tertiary sectors and relieving its over-dependence upon primary production. Low daily real wage rates and GDP per head, in turn, depressed domestic demand for non-agricultural goods and services.[515]

Low labour productivity in agriculture was a particular problem due to the sub-optimal size and scattered layout of so many holdings. In the

[511] Nicholas (1968); Bavel (2010), 346.   [512] Jordan (1996), 144–8.
[513] Above, 176–7.   [514] Above, Section 3.01.3c.   [515] Above, Section 3.01.3a.

most crowded parts of the countryside there was too little work to keep the whole of the able-bodied workforce fully and efficiently employed. Proto-industry might have soaked up the surplus labour force, giving employment to women and children and thereby boosting household incomes, but was as yet but weakly developed. Tenure rather than technology and the limited scale of concentrated urban demand for foodstuffs and raw materials lay at the root of agriculture's problems. The ease with which land could be obtained and extra holdings created placed little hindrance in the path of new household formation and, thus, underwrote perpetuation of population growth.[516] The abundance of freehold land and lax seigniorial control of much customary land gave licence to active morcellation.[517] Sub-economic head rents fostered rent seeking via subdivision and subletting for the full rack rent. Operation of land and credit markets in conjunction with customary forms of inheritance, both partible and impartible, under conditions of population growth promoted morcellation rather than engrossment of plots and holdings.[518] The upshot was the multiplication of immiserated households – smallholders, cottagers, commoners and labourers – living on holdings incapable of providing more than a bare-bones level of subsistence.[519]

The burden of poverty which operation of these processes imposed upon the economy constituted an almost insurmountable obstacle to the kinds of structural change that might have generated positive economic growth. It also created a harvest-sensitive society in which each crisis precipitated a new round of debt default and distress land sales and inexorable increase in morcellation.[520] Landlessness rose and with it the influx of rural paupers to the towns. There could be no reversal of this vicious circle without profound reform of tenures and wholesale transformation of the economic and demographic context within which factor markets operated.[521] Over the course of the early fourteenth century England consequently experienced a growing polarization of wealth and purchasing power between a minority of wealthy households with land, capital and income in excess of their subsistence requirements, who were thereby able to profit from trends in relative factor prices, and a growing majority of impoverished and under-employed households who eked out a hand-to-mouth existence on inadequate and under-capitalized holdings and who attempted to sell their excess labour on a glutted labour market.[522]

---

[516] Above, Section 3.01.3d.   [517] Campbell (2005).   [518] Bekar and Reed (2013).
[519] Above, Section 3.01.3b; Figure 3.10. Appendix 3.1, Table 3.4.
[520] Above, Section 3.01.3d.   [521] Campbell (2013b).   [522] Above, Section 3.01.3b.

This bottom-heavy socio-economic structure ensured that harvest shortfalls had a selective but disproportionate economic and demographic impact, inflating food prices, reducing demand for inessentials, amplifying the activity of factor markets, inducing a widespread resort to crime, and, in the most extreme instances, depressing marriage rates and elevating mortality rates.[523] Periodic harvest shortfalls were an inescapable fact of agricultural life.[524] Yet from the late thirteenth century, as a result of a far-reaching global reorganization of atmospheric circulation associated with ending of the MCA and onset of the Wolf Solar Minimum, Europe's climate entered a period of heightened instability and extreme weather and serious harvest failures became more common.[525] Risks of substantial back-to-back shortfalls also rose.

Incessant heavy rain was the greatest hazard facing grain producers and in 1315–16 and 1329–30 such weather brought famine to first northern and then southern Europe.[526] Neither was an isolated or random event since each was an outcome of changes then taking place in North Atlantic sea-surface temperatures, the strength of the North Atlantic Oscillation, and the direction and force of the winter westerlies. They were also teleconnected to concurrent changes in climate taking place around the world.[527] Each famine episode brought the weaknesses and vulnerabilities of these struggling societies to the fore and had an impoverishing effect upon them. Neither, however, was a purely Malthusian event since both arose during, and were products of, changes in atmospheric circulation patterns on a hemispherical scale. Nor does either famine appear to have been a watershed event.

At this critical juncture in history serious famines had major short-term impacts but, except in a few specific contexts, rarely resulted in any lasting transformation of the socio-ecological status quo, other than to erode resilience and shift the socio-ecological system closer to a tipping point. In a demographically comparatively crowded and politically contested world, climate change compounded rather than caused the generally worsening economic situation and added to the, sometimes acute, downward pressure upon living standards.[528] Its impacts tended to be greatest and most enduring upon marginal groups and environments, especially those simultaneously affected by harvest failure, social dislocation and/or war, under which circumstances it occasionally initiated large-scale environmental degradation or settlement retreat.[529]

523   Above, Section 3.01.3a; Campbell (2010a); Figure 3.18.
524   Campbell and Ó Gráda (2011).   525   Above, Section 3.02.
526   Above, Figures 3.3, 3.8A, 3.8B; above, Section 3.01.3e.
527   Above, Sections 1.01.1 and 3.02.   528   Above, Figures 3.3, 3.8A, 3.8B.
529   Above, Section 3.03.1a; McNamee (1997), 72–122; Dotterweich (2008).

The adverse effects of extreme weather were also greatly amplified when combined with disease, as most conspicuously in the case of the English sheep murrains and European cattle panzootic of 1315–25.[530] The former depressed production and supply of fine English wool to European textile manufacturers at a time when market conditions were already turning against them.[531] The latter destroyed vital working capital, drastically curtailed draught-power resources, and deprived an already malnourished population of an important source of protein.[532] They greatly prolonged the weather-induced agrarian crisis, since flocks and herds took longer to rebuild than grain stocks and were integral to full reinstatement of ecologically balanced mixed-farming systems.[533] These zootics also ensured that pastoral producers were as grievously affected at this time as grain producers.[534]

In the case of sheep murrain there was a fairly straightforward connection between incessant rain, water-logged pastures, proliferation of *Fasciola hepatica* and its water-snail hosts, and ingestion by sheep and other livestock of liverfluke. Immediate post-famine introduction of the rinderpest virus to England, in contrast, was entirely coincidental and merely the latest stage in a biological process of contagious diffusion from an initial outbreak in or near Bohemia in central Europe.[535] The latter did, however, coincide with the extreme weather and may therefore have been set in motion when biologically naïve livestock came into close contact with infectious animals under conditions of extreme ecological stress.[536] From this initial source the deadly pathogen then spread through the cattle-rearing and ox-ploughing regions of Europe at a rate of one kilometre a day to reach England three years, and Ireland five years, after its reported appearance in Bohemia.[537] How much of Europe escaped this bovine plague remains to be established, but to date no references to it have been discovered from south of the Alps. It was northern Europe, therefore, which bore the brunt of this double climatic and biological disaster.

As yet plague had not reached Europe and would not do so until 1346/7. Nevertheless, among host populations of gerbils and marmots in the semi-arid interior regions of central Asia it had already been reawakened from its enzootic state. Penetration of central Asia by a moister westerly air-stream originating in the North Atlantic consequent upon weakening of the NAO seems to have been material to this development.

---

[530] Above, Section 3.03.1.   [531] Above, Figures 3.4 and 3.24.
[532] Above, Figures 3.24 and 3.26.   [533] Above, Figure 3.24.
[534] For example, Oram and Adderley (2008b).   [535] Above, Figure 3.25.
[536] Above, Section 3.03.1b.   [537] Above, Figure 3.25.

Marginal gains in precipitation initiated a trophic cascade of increased vegetation growth, enlarged sylvatic rodent populations and increased flea activity that intensified transmission of the pathogen and helped advance plague to a more active epizootic state within its primary focus, now identified as most probably the Tibetan–Qinghai Plateau of western China. In the process, as stocks of the pathogen became amplified, so autonomous biological changes brought several new lineages of Y. pestis into existence. Sudden proliferation of new polytomies on plague's phylogenetic tree is a sure sign that sometime in the late thirteenth century the pathogen had entered a more active phase. Fatefully, these ecological and biological developments were occurring in the very region traversed by the northern branch of the Silk Road, which in the late thirteenth and early fourteenth centuries was close to the zenith of its medieval commercial importance. Long-distance caravan traffic along this important artery of East–West trade appears inadvertently to have been responsible for effecting plague's steady westward colonization of regions from which it had long been absent. Very likely a mini-pluvial episode from 1310 to 1340 also helped expedite this process, with the result that by the 1330s plague seems to have reached the extensive steppe lands to the east of the Caspian Basin. Once established there it was only a matter of time before Y. pestis reached the western terminus of the Silk Road and came into contact with the crowded populations of black rats and humans that occupied the busy mercantile ports of the Black Sea. In the early 1340s, however, that ominous development lay in the future and few, if any, Europeans can have had any inkling of the massive demographic threat that this re-emergent and inexorably spreading pathogen potentially posed.

Contemporaries may have been oblivious of plague but they could hardly ignore the increasing fickleness of the weather. In northern Europe the weather-induced agrarian crisis that began in 1315 was not effectively over until 1332, by which time it was southern Europe's turn to be on the receiving end of extreme weather.[538] Almost no part of the continent therefore escaped unscathed during these difficult decades. At the same time, climate change was having a destabilizing effect upon the rice-growing civilizations of Southeast Asia and China, as the South Asian monsoon began to fluctuate in strength.[539] Environmental change, often for the worse and almost invariably destabilizing, was therefore felt right across Eurasia and greatly exacerbated the array of economic problems that were coming to the fore at much the same time. War, too, fought on many fronts and for a range of reasons, massively contributed to the

---

[538] Above, 148–50 and Section 3.01.3e.
[539] Above, Section 3.02; Brook (2010), 50–73.

difficulties of the age and from the 1330s impelled Latin Christendom's flagging commercial economy deeper into decline. The direct and indirect effects of war in combination with heightened climatic instability and ecological stress and the continued pressure of population upon resources ensured that for ordinary people the 1340s would prove to be one of the most difficult decades of the Middle Ages. Once plague finally reached Europe it also became the most deadly.

Appendix 3.1 The landed incomes of English households in 1290

The social distribution of English household incomes in 1290 can be reconstructed with some confidence, as summarized in Table 3.4. The king was, of course, the greatest magnate in the land. The Crown estate contained about one-thirtieth of all the land in the realm and yielded Edward I a landed revenue of about £13,500.[540] Partly because of its great size and wide dispersal and the peculation and corruption of those charged with its management, it yielded significantly less income than it ought and far less than the king needed to run the country even in times of peace.[541] It therefore had to be augmented with regular direct and indirect taxation, the scale and frequency of which increased at times of war (Figure 4.1). To finance his costly wars in Wales, France and Scotland Edward borrowed bridging funds from first the Ricciardi company of Lucca and then the Frescobaldi company of Florence, taxed the movable goods of the laity, received direct subsidies from the clergy, was granted the revenues of several papal taxes, and imposed customs duties on overseas trade (from 1303 taxing alien merchants on a wider range of goods than denizens).[542] From these various sources he received on average three times as much income throughout the 1280s and 1290s as that yielded him by the Crown Estate (Tables 3.4 and 3.5). War was the driving force behind these tax demands and the associated growth of government administration and record creation and keeping which they engendered. Between 1295 and 1298, when Edward was most actively asserting his territorial claims in Gascony and Scotland, he received and spent taxes totalling £345,000 (Figure 3.13).[543] Raising such massive sums over such a short period placed the incomes of many ordinary people under great strain and renders the capacity of the country to deliver them all the more impressive.

Next in status and wealth after the king were the 149 noble households, with mean annual landed incomes of £376 (Table 3.5). Apart from the

---

[540] Hoyt (1950), 85–92; Wolffe (1971), 36–7.   [541] Hoyt (1950), 156–70.
[542] Ormrod (1991); Lloyd (1982).   [543] Ormrod (2010).

Table 3.4 *A social table of England, c.1290*

Socio-economic category	Estimated no. of households	Assumed mean household size	Estimated population	Assumed arable land per household (hectares)	Total arable area (,000s hectares)	Annual income per household (£)	Estimated total income (£,000s)
Minor clergy, professionals, lawyers, merchants, tradesmen, craftsmen, builders; urban labourers	130,000	5.50	715,000			£5.50	£715
Landowners (spiritual lords, aristocracy, gentry, clergy)	21,000	8.50	178,500	50.0	1,050	£28.00	£588
Substantial tenants	12,500	7.00	87,500	20.8	260	£12.00	£150
Yardlanders	180,000	5.50	990,000	12.5	2,250	£6.00	£1,080
Smallholders	300,000	4.00	1,200,000	5.0	1,500	£3.00	£900
Cottagers & agricultural labourers	240,000	3.50	840,000	0.8	200	£1.50	£360
Rural craftsmen, non-agricultural labourers, paupers, vagrants	160,000	3.50	560,000	0.3	50	£1.75	£280
Men-at-arms, miners, fishermen & sailors	50,000	3.50	175,000			£2.50	£125
ENGLAND TOTAL	1,093,500	4.34	4,746,000		5,310	£3.84	£4,198

Notes: The poverty line (dashed line) is the minimum income required for a family to afford the respectability basket. The annual cost of a 'respectability' basket of consumables (190 kg bread; 40 kg beans/peas; 26 kg meat; 5.2 kg butter; 5.2 kg cheese; 52 eggs; 182 ltr beer; 2.6 kg soap; 5 m linen; 2.6 kg candles; 2.6 ltr lamp oil; 5.0 M BTU fuel) is estimated at 17s. 3d. per adult male and £2 16s. 1d. for a family of two adults and three children. To afford a 'bare-bones' basket of consumables (155 kg oats; 20 kg beans/peas; 5 kg meat; 3 kg butter; 1.3 kg soap; 3 m linen; 1.3 kg candles; 1.3 ltr lamp oil; 2.0 M BTU fuel) an adult male needed a minimum annual income of 7s. 3¼d. and a family of five £1 3s. 8d. Both baskets of consumables met the minimum dietary requirement of approximately 2,000 kcal. per day. Quantities are derived from Allen (2009), 36–7, and costed using average prices for 1286–95 from Allen (2001). M BTU = millions of British thermal units.
Source: adapted from Campbell (2008), 940

Table 3.5 *Estimated numbers and landed revenues of English landlords, c.1290*

Social group	Number of households		Mean annual landed income per household		Total landed income per status group		% total landed incomes
GREATER LANDLORDS:	993		£258		£256,550		47.4
CROWN		1		£13,500		£13,500	2.5
Nobility (earls, barons, noble women)		149		£376		£56,050	10.4
Greater clergy (archbishops & bishops, religious houses)		843		£222		£187,000	34.5
MINOR LANDLORDS:	19,600		£15		£284,800		52.6
Gentry (knights, lesser gentry, gentry women)		11,100		£16		£182,800	33.8
Parish clergy		8,500		£12		£102,000	18.8
ALL LANDLORDS:	20,593		£28		£541,350		100.0

Source: Campbell (2005), 12–13

greatest prelates, no other social group commanded so substantial a disposable income. Merchants and financiers certainly had the potential to make considerable fortunes but no native merchant could yet rival the wealth of the greatest aristocrats. This tiny social elite received a tenth of all landed wealth and, as a class, Dyer believes that their incomes had grown over the thirteenth century.[544] Even so, the desire to lead a lavish lifestyle, maintain a substantial retinue, and indulge in the tempting array of high-status consumption goods now available to them, including castle and church building on ever more elaborate scales, caused numbers of noble households to succumb to indebtedness. The building earl of Norfolk, Roger IV Bigod, 'spent his way to disaster' notwithstanding gross revenues of £2,500–£4,000.[545] The greatest of the greater clergy were as wealthy, none more so than the bishops of Winchester, but typically husbanded their resources more prudently. Their average incomes were lower than those of the high nobility but in aggregate were more than three times as great (Table 3.5). The wealthiest monastic houses, like the greatest prelates, commanded incomes of several hundred pounds a year. Individual monks may have espoused a life of poverty but the households to which they belonged were anything but poor, hence a monastic life was materially one of the most secure. Bequests and donations by the faithful also meant that, until arrested by the Statutes of Mortmain of 1279 and 1290, their landed estates had steadily grown by accretion.

Collectively, greater landlords received a little under and minor landlords a little over half of total landed incomes (Table 3.5). By the close of the thirteenth century minor lords found their incomes under increasing pressure. Most depended for their income upon the revenues of a single small manor or knight's fee. Profits from their demesne lands, rents (many of them fixed) paid by their tenants, fines, multure, tollage and stallage from their courts, mills and markets, and whatever additional perquisites came their way, yielded them an average of £16 a year (Table 3.5). On this they endeavoured to maintain their social position.[546] Although they ranked as the smallest fry in a landlord class which contained some very big fish, collectively they received around a third of total seigniorial revenues. A further 19 per cent was received by their ecclesiastical counterparts, the 8,500 parish clergy, from the produce of rectorial glebes and tithe receipts. Foundation and endowment of parish churches and religious houses had made the Church the single greatest landowner in the land, in receipt of over half of all seigniorial revenues (Table 3.5) and perhaps 7 per cent of national income.

[544] Dyer (1989), 35–41.   [545] Morris (2005), 148–9, 190.
[546] Dyer (1989), 38–9; Coss (1991), 264–304.

The upper echelons of the tenantry including most servile yardlanders also received incomes which placed them well above the poverty line. A well-managed and well-resourced villein yardland of 12½ hectares, typically held in return for a sub-economic rent, guaranteed an income of around £6 and was thus an attractive proposition.[547] Those farming on this scale comprised approximately a fifth of rural households but held more than two-fifths of all arable land and enjoyed household incomes that were approximately 50 per cent above average (Table 3.4). Such men were in a position to invest in their holdings, produce surpluses for sale, hire labourers and servants, and must often have sent substitutes to perform their labour services.[548] Within the countryside they were a conspicuously well-off and often influential group, playing a leading role in the management and regulation of commonfields and pastures, operation of manor courts, and supervision of demesnes. Among rural households, apart from landlords, only the dwindling number of substantial free tenants and those operating successful mills and smithies fared as well or better and regularly had surplus income at their disposal.

Half-yardlanders lived closer to the poverty line, although how close remains a matter of dispute. The implication of the estimates given in Table 3.4 is that smallholders with an average of five hectares per household were usually just about able to afford a respectability basket of consumables. This accords with Mark Page's recent optimistic verdict on the economic wellbeing of the many tenants in south Hampshire who successfully supported families on as little as three hectares and survived the shocks of famine and agrarian crisis.[549] Harry Kitsikopoulos, in contrast, concluded from a hypothetical reconstruction of the pre-Black Death budgets of tenant producers that villeins farming in a three-field township in the English midlands required at least seven and a half hectares of arable to be able to make ends meet and maintain their families in a modest degree of comfort.[550] A smallholding of three to six hectares would have been insufficient to achieve this. Nonetheless, tenants of such meagre holdings existed in very large numbers and in practice succeeded in maintaining themselves in all but the worst harvest years, which implies that Page's optimism respecting the viability of these holdings is well founded. Inevitably, poor harvests squeezed them hard, eliminating their slender surpluses, shrinking casual labouring opportunities, withering demand for by-products, inflating the prices of essential foodstuffs, destabilizing fragile credit arrangements and driving many

---

[547] Hatcher (1981), 268; Raftis (1997), 125, 131.
[548] Fox (1996), 539–60; Raftis (1997), 34–5.
[549] Page (2012), 194–5.   [550] Kitsikopoulos (2000), 237–61.

to part with land.[551] In 1290 over a quarter of a million rural house-holds were living in this vulnerable situation. Their numbers increased the proportion of rural households living on or below the poverty line to maybe two-thirds of the total. No doubt a significant proportion of urban households were similarly circumstanced since many depended for their livelihoods upon equally slender means and suffered significant reductions of income in years of high food prices when the terms of trade turned against them.

Those most deficient in land were typically those worst off and there can be no question that these semi-landless groups constituted a far larger component of English society in 1290 than in 1086. Moreover, in a striking inversion of status and income, many of them were free, for it was the households of free tenants which had multiplied most rapidly and whose holdings had succumbed to the most extreme morcellation during the intervening two centuries. In fact, the proliferation of petty free holdings by a combination of piecemeal reclamation, subdivision and subletting, aided and abetted by the unrestrained working of an active land market, is one of the most striking features of the age.[552] Customary holdings were not immune to these processes but lords were in a stronger position to regulate the operation of land markets and application of inheritance customs. The higher rents owed for villein land also meant that, if holdings were to remain viable, subdivision could not be taken to such an absolute extreme.[553] Within the area encompassed by the 1279 Hundred Rolls, 59 per cent of free holdings were smaller than six acres, compared with 36 per cent of villein holdings; and 33 per cent of free holdings were smaller than one acre, compared with 22 per cent of villein holdings.[554] As the warden and fellows of Merton College, Oxford discovered on their manor of Thorncroft in Surrey, whatever tenurial control they may have exercised over their villein holdings did not extend to those held by their free tenants, whose disintegration they were powerless to prevent.[555]

---

[551] Campbell (1984); Schofield (1997); Briggs (2008), 149–75.
[552] Campbell (2005), 45–70; Bekar and Reed (2009); Bekar and Reed (2013).
[553] Witney (2000), lxxvii–lxxx.   [554] Kanzaka (2002), 599.
[555] Evans (1996), 236–7.

During the 1340s processes which had been in train since the beginning of the Great Transition came to a head. Escalating warfare inflated transaction costs, disrupted trade and destroyed working capital, thereby sending Latin Christendom's flagging commercial economy deeper into decline (Section 4.01). Atmospheric circulation patterns shifted, as the Medieval Climate Anomaly ended for good, and growing conditions were depressed almost everywhere (Section 4.02). Once again famine stalked both northern and southern Europe. Conditions were even worse in China and eastern Asia, where onset of mega-drought on an unprecedented scale undermined the agrarian foundations upon which established socio-political relations rested and contributed to the collapse of the Yuan Dynasty. And in the midst of these difficulties, plague, which had silently been spreading across Asia, finally reached the Black Sea. There, it ignited into a fast-spreading pandemic and within the space of seven years had devastated populations throughout the greater part of Asia Minor, the Middle East, North Africa and Europe, transforming at a stroke the demographic status quo (Section 4.03). Each of this trio of crises compounded the misery inflicted by the others, so that collectively they cohered into a single complex transformative event. Its shock was immense. This was the Great Transition's decisive tipping point. The socio-ecological changes and adjustments which then ensued ensured that nowhere in the Known World would life ever be quite the same again. Relations between the Christian and Muslim trading blocs hardened, transition to the altered and less stable circulation patterns of the Little Ice Age continued, and a new plague-dominated epidemiological age dawned (Section 4.04).

4.01   Escalating warfare and deepening commercial recession

Latin Christendom was no stranger to warfare, indeed, its ruling feudal elites were predisposed to it. For the greater part of the twelfth and thirteenth centuries, however, their innate belligerence failed to thwart the progress of Europe's commercial revolution. Indeed, crusader conquests in the Holy Land and the opportunistic capture of Constantinople had been instrumental in giving European merchants access to Levantine and Black Sea markets and the lucrative overland trade routes that linked the commerce of the Mediterranean and Black Sea with that of the Persian Gulf and Arabian Sea.[1] The Peace of God movement promoted by the Church in combination with the preaching of crusade against the infidel also brought a degree of internal order to Europe, sufficient to lower transaction costs and enable regional, national and international trade to flourish. From the end of the thirteenth century, in contrast, warfare became an increasing obstacle to continued economic progress along established lines. One by one the crusader states had fallen and European merchants become progressively excluded from the Levant. In the Middle East and western Asia, including Asia Minor, Islam was resurgent, and although trade continued those Christians who engaged in it faced greater risks. And within Christendom the Church had lost its moral authority and the Peace of God movement was no more, with the result that there was little to restrain Christian monarchs from waging war against each other on a variety of dynastic, feudal and territorial pretexts and on an ever greater scale. Warfare now posed a direct threat to the prevailing market-based economic order. Especially damaging, at this watershed point in Europe's economic development, were those wars that obstructed trade and commerce, raised its costs, destabilized fragile credit structures and resulted in forfeiture of trading privileges and exclusion from lucrative overseas markets, to the detriment of market-generated Smithian growth.[2]

In the West, the Hundred Years War (1337–1453) between England and France, in which Scotland, Flanders, Italy and Spain all became variously embroiled, proved to be an especially damaging conflict, impoverishing its protagonists, ruining its Italian financial backers, displacing and depressing trade and commerce, diverting investment and destroying productive capacity. The dispute that ignited into war in 1337 had long been brewing and stemmed from the ambiguity of the king of England's status as both autonomous ruler and, as duke of Aquitaine, a vassal of the king of France.[3] Edward III had sought to evade the humiliation of feudal subordination to the French king by asserting his own strong dynastic claim to the French Crown, but this was repudiated in 1328 and insult was then added to injury when in 1337 Philip VI (r. 1328–50)

---

[1] Abu-Lughod (1989), 137–49.
[2] This thesis is expounded in detail in Munro (1991) and further elaborated in Munro (1999b) and Munro (1999c).
[3] Ormrod (1990), 7–10.

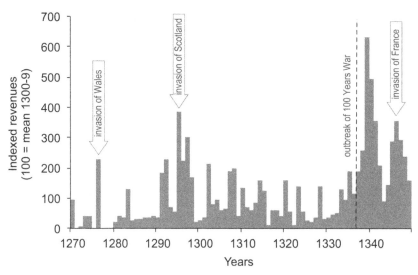

Figure 4.1 England: total deflated net receipts from direct and indirect taxation, 1270–1349
Source: Ormrod (2010)

confiscated Edward's French duchy. No doubt Philip VI thought he had the stronger hand in this dispute. France was the larger, richer and more populous of the two realms and initially the financial strain of taking on such a formidable foe proved to be punitively expensive for England. In the opening stages of a conflict that would drag on for over a hundred years it certainly looked as though Edward III had seriously overreached himself. By 1340, when he formally claimed the title of king of France, his kingdom's economic resources had been sapped by repeated taxation, heavy expenditure overseas had drained the economy of bullion (Figure 4.1), deflated the currency and produced a serious shortage of specie, and the strength of baronial opposition to his policies had plunged Edward into the gravest constitutional crisis of his long reign.[4]

To advance his cause Edward III believed that he needed powerful continental allies and he was prepared to pay dear and disrupt the lucrative wool trade to enlist the support of the Flemish and the Holy Roman Emperor. He therefore taxed the realm more heavily than ever before, more than quadrupling the country's real annual tax burden during the first five years of the war, 1337–41 (Figure 4.1).[5] Impatient for cash,

[4] Ormrod (1990), 11–15; Ormrod (1991), 182–3; Allen (2012), 263.
[5] Ormrod (2010).

Edward III negotiated substantial loans at costly rates of interest from the Florentine Societies of the Bardi and Peruzzi and some others at what proved to be considerable risk to their own finances.[6] In addition, he imposed politically coercive embargoes on the export of wool, made geographically selective use of purveyance to supply his armies both on the Scottish border and abroad, and assembled a fleet by requisitioning merchant vessels to naval use.[7]

Meanwhile, Edward's declaration of war had attracted a series of destructive hit-and-run raids by the French under Admiral Nicholas Béhuchet on the Channel Islands and the countryside, ports and shipping of England's south coast.[8] The Isle of Wight was raided three times and in June and October 1338 the towns of Portsmouth and Southampton were sacked. These damaging attacks were not halted until the English naval victory at Sluys in June 1340. This belated success was won at a high price but proved impossible to follow up, for political opposition to the king's policies was too strong, the country's tax base was too depleted, money was scarce, the crucial wool trade had been thrown into disarray, maritime commerce had been disrupted and there was little prospect of obtaining additional credit from the now financially embarrassed companies of the Bardi and Peruzzi.

To compound matters, due to exceptionally severe winter weather the wheat and rye harvest of 1339 was disastrous and because of subsequent summer drought even oats, the staple of the poor, yielded indifferently (Figure 4.6).[9] Provisions were therefore scarce and dear, making the hardship of those faced with renewed heavy tax demands all the more acute. Extant returns to the tax of a ninth of all corn, wool and lambs (equivalent to an additional tithe upon agricultural output) granted to Edward III in 1340 leave little doubt of the parlous state to which many in the countryside had been reduced.[10] At West Wratting in Cambridgeshire 'the men of the parish were said to be "worn down by many taxes"', at Kimpton in Hampshire 'the payment of fifteenths was said to have impoverished the people and it was not possible for a certain portion of the land to be sown', while at Clungunford in Shropshire twenty virgates lay waste 'because of poverty and the king's many taxes'.[11] The far from complete surviving returns to the *Nonae* imply that arable land

---

[6] Hunt (1990); Bell and others (2009a), 419, 432.

[7] Lloyd (1977), 144–92; Nicholas (1987), 3, 48–52, 150–1; Ormrod (1991), 175–81; Maddicott (1987), 329–51; Hewitt (1966), 50–63, 77–8; Saul (1979).

[8] Hewitt (1966), 1–5.   [9] Britton (1937), 139; Titow (1960), 363, 396–7.

[10] Baker (1966); Maddicott (1987), 346–8; Livingstone (2003), 321–30, 344–52.

[11] Livingstone (2003), 349; cited in Maddicott (1987), 347.

sufficient to provision a city the size of London had been withdrawn from cultivation.[12]

Edward III's political and financial fortunes revived with a change of policy, of administrative personnel and of strategy, helped by the fortuitous outbreak in 1341 of the Breton war of succession. From 1343 it became his intention 'to launch a major continental offensive involving simultaneous attacks on several different fronts', funded by a renewed spate of taxation and, since the Bardi and Peruzzi were now bankrupt, by loans advanced by consortia of English merchants.[13] Again, bad weather and a poor harvest in 1346 aggravated the exactions of the king's taxers and in spring and summer of the following year, when grain stocks were becoming scarce, attempts to export grain under royal licence to Bordeaux sparked food riots in the ports of Bristol, Boston, Lynn, Thetford and unidentified ports in Kent.[14] Nevertheless, on this occasion the king's costly military gamble paid off with a successful invasion of Normandy in July 1346, crushing defeat of the French army led in person by Philip VI at Crécy in August, and the key Channel port of Calais invested. To cap Edward's success, in October a counter attack on northern England by a Scottish army led by David II was routed at the battle of Neville's Cross and the Scots' king taken captive.[15] With his northern border secure, David II imprisoned in England and the Scots burdened with a punitive ransom demand, and, in August 1347, Calais at last in his hands, the way was open for Edward III to employ force of arms to pursue his French ambitions, doing so now at the expense of the French realm.

It was France's turn to bleed and she did so from her arteries. Normandy, one of her richest and most populous provinces, initially bore the brunt of the English invasion. Here, the burden of taxation, purveyance and military levies imposed by a monarchy on the brink of bankruptcy had been rising since the outbreak of hostilities in 1337 and placing an ever greater financial strain upon a population, three-quarters of whom were 'wretched smallholders living in the main on one or two acres of land'.[16] Guy Bois is in no doubt that outbreak of the Anglo-French war marks a turning point in the Duchy's economic fortunes 'because it tended to destroy the already precarious equilibrium of the peasant economy and to open an era of decline, with cumulative effects'.[17] French defeats then exposed the countryside to plunder by marauding English armies and bands of mercenaries, while the hefty ransom demands imposed upon the estates of captured French nobles

---

[12] Livingstone (2003), 352–61.   [13] Ormrod (1990), 17.
[14] Below, Figure 4.6; Titow (1960), 363, 399–400; Sharp (2000).
[15] Ormrod (1990), 17, 26.   [16] Bois (1984), 287.   [17] Bois (1984), 277.

further undermined the failing resource base. The upshot, on Bois's analysis, was a vicious circle, whereby 'population declined, fiscal pressure on the survivors was intensified, production declined further, and so on'.[18] War, in short, was the instrument of a massive economic and demographic implosion.

By the beginning of 1348 society in eastern Normandy was 'already foundering': tax returns were falling, taxpayers rebelling, and successive debasements had undermined commercial confidence in the monetary system.[19] Where English wage earners benefited from the war-induced deflation of these years, their French counterparts were squeezed hard by a debasement-fuelled inflation.[20] Even before the English invasion, shrinking commercial activity is implicit in the reduced tax receipts obtained in 1340–1 from the five Champagne fairs of Troyes (St Jean and St Remy), Provins (St Ayoul fair), Lagny-sur-Marne and Bar-sur-Aube, which, collectively, are the lowest on record and almost a third down on their already much reduced level of twenty years earlier (Figure 3.1). The alliance of Flanders with England had further damaged the fairs' business and, besides, by the 1340s Flemish textile output, harmed by political interruptions to wool exports from England, was itself much reduced. Compared with their levels a decade earlier, by the late 1340s receipts from the drapery tax farm at Ghent were down by 20 per cent, numbers of cloths sealed at Ypres down by 34 per cent and receipts from the drapery tax farm at Mechelen down by 60 per cent (Figure 3.5). In Flanders, as in France, war was clearly making an already difficult economic situation far worse.

Reverberations of the Anglo-French war were felt as far away as Florence, where chronicler Giovanni Villani blamed Edward III for the bankruptcy of the last of that city's great banking companies, the Bardi and Peruzzi.[21] Modern scholarship attributes the collapse of these super companies less to Edward's purported reneging on his war loans, than to the over-extended and top-heavy scale of their operations in a fast-shrinking market. What then pushed them under was a run on savings and attendant failure of liquidity precipitated by a war-induced international credit crunch.[22] Certainly, the tide of commerce was turning against them, especially once fear of food riots obliged urban governments to intervene in the once lucrative grain trade from southern Italy, thereby cutting into the profits upon which the business fortunes of these merchant companies had in part been founded.[23] Meanwhile, Florence

---

[18] Bois (1984), 287.   [19] Bois (1984), 288.   [20] Spufford (1988), 304–5.
[21] Russell (1918); Hunt and Murray (1999), 116–17.
[22] Hunt (1990); Hunt (1994); Hunt and Murray (1999), 116–19; Bell and others (2009a), 432; Bell and others (2009b).
[23] Hunt and Murray (1999), 119.

had just fought an expensive and futile war with Pisa over Lucca and the old dynastic conflict between the Angevin kingdom of Naples and Aragonese kingdom of Sicily rumbled on and placed its own strains upon Italian mercantile credit and exports of Sicilian grain.[24]

The fortunes of the greater Italian trading cities, especially Venice and Genoa, were, of course, at least as dependent upon commercial opportunities in the eastern Mediterranean, Aegean and Black Sea as upon those north of the Alps. Yet in the 1340s these, too, were contracting as the Egyptian Mamluks continued to make territorial advances in the Levant and Christian relations with the increasingly Islamicized Mongol Kipchak Khanate and Il-Khanate deteriorated. Following the fall of Acre in 1291 the Venetians and other Italians had made Cyprus their base, whence, insofar as papal embargoes allowed, they continued to trade with the sultan of Egypt at Alexandria as also with the remaining Christian kingdom of Cilicia in Lesser Armenia at Ayas (medieval Ajazzo or Lajazzo), western terminus of the circuitous but important caravan route followed by Marco Polo in 1271 that led, via Sivas, Erzingan, Erzerum and Tabriz, to Hormuz on the Persian Gulf.[25] Yet in 1347 Ayas was definitively taken by the Mamluks, giving them monopoly control of the remaining Mediterranean branches of the lucrative Indian spice trade, the bulk of which was now channelled through Alexandria.[26] Instead of the multiple competing routes by which exotic goods had once reached the Mediterranean from the Persian Gulf and Red Sea there was now effectively just one.[27] From this point Venetian appeals to the papacy to lift its embargoes on direct Christian trade with Muslim Egypt became increasingly urgent (and the levies charged on that trade by the Mamluks ever more exorbitant).[28] As the Mamluks tightened their grip on the spice trade, pepper prices in England rose. By 1343–5 prices were already 30 per cent above their level on the eve of the fall of Acre, they rose further in 1346 and by 1348 had increased by 70 per cent as the Mamluk monopoly bit hard and the Black Death further disrupted this quintessentially long-distance trade.[29] Between 1345 and 1351 pepper prices rose by no less than 150 per cent.

At the very time that the Mamluks were consolidating their monopoly of the spice trade, serious setbacks were sustained by Italian commercial interests in Persia and the northern Black Sea, terminus of the northern caravan route across the Eurasian interior and source of the

---

[24] Russell (1918); Epstein (1992), 316, 397.
[25] Lopez (1987), 352; Abulafia (1987), 458–60; Abu-Lughod (1989), 185–6.
[26] Phillips (1988), 119; Abu-Lughod (1989), 212–47.
[27] Lopez (1987), 387; Abu-Lughod (1989), 359–60.
[28] Lopez (1987), 387–8; Abu-Lughod (1989), 189, 207, 214–15.
[29] Calculated from Clark (2009).

prized Scythian slaves exported to Egypt. Following the fall of Baghdad in 1258 the Mongol Il-Khanate's capital of Tabriz in Persia, strategically located on the routes that linked Hormuz on the Persian Gulf with Ayas on the Mediterranean and Trebizond on the Black Sea, had become a mecca for Italian and especially Genoese merchants.[30] Islam had become the state religion in 1295 but Hulagu's descendants remained tolerant of other religions including Shamanism, Buddhism and Christianity. Disastrously, that changed in 1338 with the death of Khan Abī Sa'īd: Tabriz was seized by a tyrant and its community of Italian merchants either robbed or slaughtered.[31] Thereafter the Italians could not be enticed to return and retreated to their secure Black Sea base in the empire of Trebizond.

Meanwhile, relations between their compatriots in the northern Black Sea entrepôts of Kaffa and Tana and the Kipchak Khanate of the Golden Horde were also taking a turn for the worse. Kaffa, established by the Genoese in 1266, was a major slave market and supplier of agricultural products, and its consul was in overall charge of all the Genoese Black Sea colonies.[32] It plied a busy maritime trade across the Black Sea to Trebizond, Constantinople and beyond. Tana gave complementary access to the Khanate's capital at Sarai Batu and was the western terminus of the long caravan route that traversed central Asia via Issyk-Kul and Qinghai to Beijing, which as recently as c.1340 had been pronounced by Francesco Balducci Pegolotti to be 'perfectly safe, whether by day or by night'.[33]

Partly because of their slave-trading activities, relations between the Italian merchants and their Mongol hosts had never been entirely easy. In 1307/8 displeasure at the trade in Turkic slaves had led Toqtai, Khan of the Golden Horde (r. 1299–1312), to arrest the Italian residents of his capital at Sarai Batu, and compel the Genoese to abandon Kaffa.[34] His successor, Özbeg (r. 1312–40), successfully Islamicized the Horde but nevertheless treated Christians liberally and welcomed back the Genoese to Kaffa, where they proceeded to flout the 1295 papal embargo upon trade with Muslims, so that by 1316 it was again in a flourishing state with a cosmopolitan population of Italians, Armenians, Greeks, Jews, Mongols and Turks.[35] Later, he authorized rebuilding of Kaffa's

---

[30] Abulafia (1987), 460; Phillips (1988), 108–9; Abu-Lughod (1989), 165, 185; Di Cosmo (2005), 411.
[31] Lopez (1987), 387; Phillips (1988), 119; Di Cosmo (2005), 403, 418.
[32] Malowist (1987), 588; Phillips (1988), 108; Abu-Lughod (1989), 124; Di Cosmo (2005), 398–9.
[33] Cited in Abu-Lughod (1989), 168.   [34] Di Cosmo (2005), 412–13.
[35] Wheelis (2002).

warehouses and walls and ceded land at Tana on the Don to the Venetians so that they could expand their commercial enterprise.[36]

Matters went into reverse in 1343, when a brawl between Christians and Muslims in Tana led the new khan, Janibeg, to expel the Italians from the town. The refugees from Tana fled to Kaffa, to which Janibeg then promptly laid siege.[37] Therefore 1343 effectively marks final closure to Christians of the overland route from the Black Sea to Cathay and by 1345 traffic along it was further interrupted by insurrection in the Chaghataid Khanate in the heart of central Asia.[38] In the Kipchak Khanate growing 'hostility to Westerners went hand-in-hand with a fresh wave of Islamicisation' and further strengthening of diplomatic links with the Mamluks.[39] The siege of Kaffa lasted until February 1344, when it was broken by an Italian relief force, but was renewed in 1345 until a devastating outbreak of plague among the besiegers obliged Janibeg to lift it.[40] Eventually, an Italian blockade of Mongol ports forced Janibeg to negotiate, and in 1347 the Italians were allowed to re-establish their colony at Tana. Within ten years, however, Janibeg had embarked upon the conquest of Azerbeijan and capture of Tabriz. The Mongol Empire was fast fragmenting and the *Pax Mongolica* that until the 1340s had allowed caravans such safe passage across central Asia was no more.[41]

One by one the commercial links between West and East upon which the maritime fortunes of Genoa and Venice had in part been built were severed. The rise of Mamluk power, disintegration of the Mongol Empire and the spread of Islam were together erecting an impermeable political, military and religious barrier between, on the one hand, the seaborne trades of the Mediterranean and Black Sea in the west and, on the other, those of the Arabian Sea and Indian Ocean to the east. By the close of the 1340s Genoese merchants, hitherto the most enterprising in Europe, were fast losing heart and confidence and curtailing the geographical orbit of their activities.[42] Since such Asian trade as reached Europe now mostly did so via the bottleneck of Egypt, the Venetians, more dependent than the Genoese on the Indian spice trade, were left with little option but to turn a blind eye to the papacy, deal with Muslim middlemen, broker the best terms they could obtain from the Mamluk sultan, and pay dear for these now essential luxuries with cumulatively deflationary exports of gold and silver bullion.

In a further ominous development, the debilitating Byzantine civil war of 1341–7 reduced that once-mighty empire to a rump state, whose

---

[36] Grousset (1970), 404; Wheelis (2002).
[37] Wheelis (2002); Di Cosmo (2005), 413–14.   [38] Abu-Lughod (1989), 169.
[39] Grousset (1970), 405.   [40] Wheelis (2002).
[41] Yule and Cordier (1916), 143–71; Abu-Lughod (1989), 169.   [42] Kedar (1976), 1.

depleted manpower resources left it increasingly vulnerable to the rising and encircling power of the Ottoman Turks.[43] Within a year, in a repeat of the events of the Justinianic Plague of AD 542, the Black Death had further reduced the decayed metropolis's population. This double disaster enabled the Ottoman Turks to capture Gallipoli in 1352 and, having established themselves astride the Bosphorus, embark upon conquest of the Balkans. From this point it was only a matter of time before they captured Constantinople, secured exclusive control of access to the Black Sea and closed it to the Italians. Once this was achieved, between 1453 and 1475 (following a failed attempt in 1394), the commercial isolation of Europe from Asia would be almost complete.

By the 1340s, in place of the widening markets, alternative and competing trade routes, and falling transaction costs of the twelfth- and thirteenth-century commercial revolution, an era of contraction had dawned which condemned much of Europe to shrinking trade, dwindling bullion stocks, stagnating urbanization and an over-dependence upon primary production.[44] War, fought on many fronts and for an array of reasons, was in large measure directly responsible for the worsening situation.[45] In 1346 – when the English invaded France, the Scots invaded England, in Florence the Society of the Bardi was declared bankrupt, in the Crimea the troops of Khan Janibeg were besieging Kaffa, the Byzantine Empire was still locked in a self-destructive civil war, in Asia Minor Ottoman power was in the ascendant, and in the eastern Mediterranean the Mamluks were poised to capture Ayas in Lesser Armenia – Latin Christendom's economic prospects looked bleak. Currencies had been destabilized and credit exhausted, the volume of international trade was much reduced, brigandage and piracy were rampant, the Champagne fairs were a shadow of their former selves and the once great Flemish textile industry was at a decidedly low ebb.[46] In Europe's leading economies GDP per head was stagnant or depressed and daily real wage rates were at or close to their late-medieval nadir.[47]

Economically and commercially an impasse had been reached from which there was no immediate prospect of deliverance. Almost everywhere under the deteriorating political and military conditions then prevailing this economically dire state of affairs looked set to continue and quite possibly to get worse. In the summer of 1346 no European could have foreseen that release from this impasse was imminently to

---

[43] Smyrlis (2012), 145.
[44] Lopez (1987), 390: 'We are in the presence of an all-European depression. We must explain it chiefly by all-European causes.'
[45] Munro (1991).   [46] Above, Table 2.3, Figures 3.5 and 3.11.
[47] Below, Figures 5.8A, 5.09A and 5.14.

hand in the form of a sudden and massive downsizing of Old World populations. Yet it was then that plague spread from Asia into Europe and contaminated the Mongol siege lines around the Crimean port of Kaffa. Its hosts and/or vectors had only to surmount that city's defences and stow away on board the Genoese galleys moored in its harbour to be spread with devastating and transformative demographic consequences throughout Europe's extensive and close-knit commercial system. Unlike other more belligerent invaders, plague ratcheted populations down but left infrastructures, institutions and capital assets largely intact. It selectively delivered windfall gains to many of the survivors by redistributing resources, realigning relative factor prices, and reflating coin supplies. Further, it spared northern Europeans a repeat of the Great European Famine by curtailing the numbers of mouths to be fed at the very time when anomalous weather caused three consecutive outright harvest failures in 1349, 1350 and 1351.

4.02 Old World climates on the cusp of change

4.02.1 The climate anomaly of the 1340s and 1350s

Across an array of palaeoclimatic records the 1340s and early 1350s stand out as an almost uniquely disturbed and climatically unstable period when long-established atmospheric circulation patterns were on the cusp of lasting change. On the Loehle and McCullough index of global temperature anomalies, these years mark the end of almost a hundred years of cooling, whose depressing effect upon growing conditions right the way across the temperate world and in both the northern and southern hemispheres is borne out by the major growth trough registered by trees between 1343 and 1355, with a collective growth minimum at 1348–50 (Figure 4.2B).[48] Temperature reconstructions for the northern hemisphere, western China, eastern, central and northern Europe, and Greenland confirm the coldness of these years (Figure 4.2A).

Across Europe there is abundant evidence of the harshness of the weather during the 1340s and 1350s. Thus, a tree-ring derived early-summer temperature series for Slovakia reveals that May/June temperatures were well below normal in 1348–54 and again in 1361–2, while extensive sea ice is recorded around Iceland in 1348–51.[49] A marked

---

[48] Above, Figure 2.2. In the western USA Bristlecone Pine chronology, 1348–50 stand out clearly as exceptionally cold years: Salzer and Hughes (2007), 62.

[49] Above, Figure 3.22; Büntgen and others (2013); Dawson and others (2007), 432; Massé and others (2008).

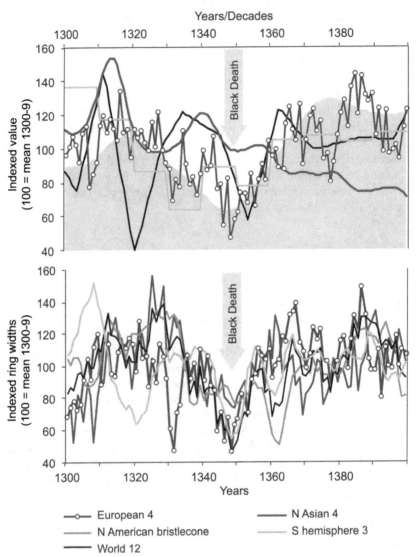

Figure 4.2 The environmental downturn of the mid-fourteenth century: (A) temperatures and (B) tree growth, 1300–1400
Sources: (A) Annual northern hemisphere temperatures, Mann and others (2008); decadal northern hemisphere temperatures, Ljungqvist (2009); annual Greenland temperatures, Kobashi and others (2010); European annual summer temperatures = mean of northern Fenno-scandia, Grudd (2010); central Europe, Büntgen and others (2011);

inflation in English salt prices in 1350–2, with prices doubling in 1351, shows that the cool and wet weather of 1349–51 depressed salt output (both home-produced and imported) by solar evaporation (Figure 4.3).[50] Further corroboration of the abnormal nature of these years and, especially, their unusual coldness is provided by an index of cold derived from the deuterium content of Greenland ice-cores. This shows that western Greenland witnessed several episodes of intense cold during the fourteenth century, most notably in 1312–14, 1323–7, 1336–8, 1349–53, 1378–82, 1389–90 and 1392–4. None, however, was more extreme than the 1349–53 event.[51] In fact, Dawson and others estimate that in 1352–3 temperatures sank to a minimum lower than those at any subsequent point in history, including the notoriously cold 1690s – the coldest decade of the Maunder Minimum.[52] The years 1355–6 also show up as intensely cold in Scotland.[53] Plainly, these 'icy' years were symptomatic

---

Figure 4.2 (*cont.*) and eastern Europe, Büntgen and others (2013); annual western China temperatures, Shi and others (2012). Eurasian Four ring-width chronology (3-year moving average) combines dendrochronologies for European oaks, Fennoscandian pines and Aegean oaks (data supplied by M. G. L. Baillie), with a chronology for Mongolian Siberian larch (Jacoby and others (no date)).
(B) European 4 = European oaks, Fenoscandian pines and Polar Urals pines (data supplied by M. G. L. Baillie), plus Alpine conifers (Büntgen and others (2011)). North Asian 4 = Tien Shan junipers (data supplied by Jan Esper), Qinghai junipers (Yang and others (2014)), Mongolian Siberian larch (Jacoby and others (no date)), plus Siberian Siberian larch (data supplied by M. G. L. Baillie). North American bristlecone pine (data supplied by M. G. L. Baillie). Southern hemisphere 3 = Chilean and Argentinian *Fitzroya*, New Zealand cedars and Tasmanian Huon pine (data supplied by M. G. L. Baillie). All chronologies are indexed on 1300–99 and standardized to have the same coefficient of variation.

---

[50] The single greatest inflation in salt prices on record was in 1316, at the height of the Great European Famine and following a year of incessant rain: Campbell (2010c), 20–1. One reason the price inflation was less pronounced in 1350–2 than in 1315–17 is because England had swung from being a net exporter to a net importer of salt, with substantial supplies sent from France's Bourgneuf Bay, where sea salt was cheaply produced by a process of solar evaporation: Bridbury (1955), 29–30, 46–7, 50, 95, 110–11, 151–2. That the high prices of 1350–2 had at least as much to do with the weather as with the sudden plague-induced scarcity of workers is borne out by the fact that in 1350–1 excessive rain ruined harvests at Chartham, Great Chart and Ickham in Kent: Campbell (2010c), 47n.
[51] Above, Figure 3.22.   [52] Dawson and others (2007), 430.
[53] Baker and others (2002), 1342.

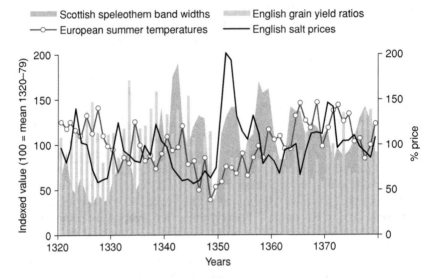

Figure 4.3 Evidence of harsh weather in northern Europe and England in the 1340s and 1350s

Speleothem band widths (the lower the value the wetter the weather), European summer temperatures and English grain yields are indexed on their respective means for 1320–79; salt prices are expressed as a percentage of their mean over the previous 25 years.

Sources: Scottish speleothem band widths, Proctor and others (2002b); northern Europe summer temperatures, combined index derived from Grudd (2010), Büntgen and others (2011), Büntgen and others (2013); English grain yields per seed gross of tithes and net of seed, Campbell (2007); salt prices, calculated from Clark (2009)

of the same climate anomaly responsible for the pronounced downturn in global tree growth that had set in from 1342/3.

As temperatures cooled, atmospheric circulation patterns shifted and extreme weather events became more common. This is manifest in the greatly increased inter-annual variation of reconstructed northern hemisphere temperatures and North Atlantic sea-surface temperatures (Figure 4.4). Over the 1,400 years spanned by these two reconstructed temperature series the level of variance (calculated over 51-year periods) varied by a factor of four or five. Episodes of heightened instability show up in the 950s, 1090s, 1350s, 1440s and 1670s, of which the most pronounced, in terms of both hemispherical and sea-surface temperatures, was that of the 1350s.

Environmental instability was relatively low during the final phase of the MCA in the mid-thirteenth century, then rose to much higher levels

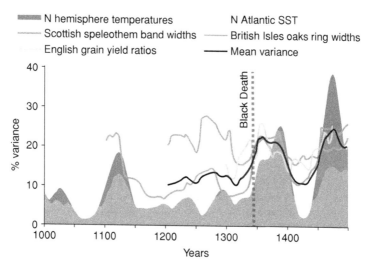

Figure 4.4 Percentage variance as an indicator of the level of environmental instability, 1000 to 1500

Note: variance is calculated for 51-year (grain yields 25-year) moving periods and end plotted, then 5-year smoothed. The variance of grain yields is for a combined index of wheat, barley and oats yields gross of tithes and net of seed.

Sources: northern hemisphere temperatures and North Atlantic sea-surface temperatures (SST), Mann and others (2008); Scottish speleothem band widths, Proctor and others (2002b); British Isles oaks ring widths (25-series master chronology), data supplied by M. G. L. Baillie; English grain yields per seed, Campbell (2007)

in the early years of the fourteenth century as the MCA weakened, and finally increased to peak levels in the mid-fourteenth century as transition to the circulation patterns of the LIA gathered momentum (Figure 4.4). Note that it was at that strategic tipping point that zoonotic plague broke out in the Kipchak Khanate of western Asia. As annual weather patterns within the northern hemisphere swung between ever wider extremes, the variance of the band widths of a Scottish speleothem, the ring widths of British Isles oaks and the yield ratios of English grain crops all increased sharply, so that by the 1350s the variance of oak ring widths had risen by 50 per cent and the variance of both speleothem band widths and grain yields had doubled, with the greatest gains occurring during the very years when plague was spreading across western Eurasia (Figure 4.4).[54]

---

[54] Oaks grew best when cold winters were followed by mild, wet, spring and summer weather; marked annual variations in winter temperature and summer rainfall thus heightened the annual variability of oak growth.

This congruence is all the more impressive given that each time series is independently generated from intrinsically different data sources: a stalagmite, oak trees and manorial accounts.

Contemporaries, of course, lacked the meteorological information and knowledge required to make sense of the climatic changes that were afoot. Even so, by the late 1340s they were certainly conscious that the weather was behaving in strange and unaccustomed ways and, once plague broke out, their belief in the miasma theory of disease meant that they drew particular attention to it. Thus the Paris Medical Faculty reported in October 1348:

For some time the seasons have not succeeded each other in the proper way. Last winter [1347/8] was not as cold as it should have been, with a great deal of rain; the spring windy and latterly wet. Summer was late, not as hot as it should have been, and extremely wet – the weather very changeable from day to day, and hour to hour; the air often troubled, and then still again, looking as if it was going to rain but then not doing so. Autumn too was very rainy and misty.[55]

One of the most precisely dated and telling indications of the profound changes then afoot is provided by analysis of the annual record of the minimum and maximum discharge of the River Nile taken at the nilometer on Rhoda Island opposite Old Cairo.[56] In a statistically sophisticated analysis of these data, Jianmin Jiang and others (2002) identified alternating episodes of 'dry' (935–1095, 1195–1245, 1282–1340) and 'normal' (1096–1194, 1246–81) discharge until 1341, when an abrupt change to 'wet' conditions occurred which endured, with some modification between 1395 and 1427, until the end of the record in 1469 (Figure 4.5).[57] These successive changes from one discharge phase to another

---

[55] Horrox (1994), 161.
[56] The term nilometer was coined by the Greeks to describe the stepped gauges constructed by the Egyptians to enable the Nile's rise and fall to be observed and recorded with precision. The extant Rhoda Island nilometer at Old Cairo constructed by the Arabs follows in this tradition. The interior c.1800 is depicted in an original watercolour by Luigi Mayer in the collection of the Victoria and Albert Museum, London, and reproduced in his (1804) *Views in Egypt*, London. By tradition, respective readings of the Nile's minimum and maximum discharge were always taken on 20 June, Julian calendar (i.e. 3 July, Gregorian calendar), and in late September at the point when the Blue Nile was in spate and the Nile flood reached its highest level. They capture, respectively, precipitation over equatorial Africa, source of the White Nile, and that of the Ethiopian monsoon, source of the Blue Nile and Atbara. Making and keeping these measurements was the responsibility of the hereditary guardians of the nilometer, first built in AD 715 for that purpose, and for over eight hundred years between 641 and 1469 (the pre-715 observations are from an earlier nilometer) they are reported in the chronicle of Ibn Taghrī Birdī, itself written between 1441 and 1469. These statistics were published by Prince Omar Toussoun (1922), *Mémoires présentés à l'Institut d'Égypte*, IV, Cairo, 135–45, and became, in turn, the subject of the definitive study of the Cairo nilometer by Popper (1951).
[57] Jiang and others (2002).

were typically abrupt, none more so than that of 1341–2.[58] The higher discharge levels that prevailed from this date imply heavier rainfall over equatorial Africa in combination with a greatly strengthened Ethiopian (East African) monsoon. From this time, also, discharge levels became more variable, with an increased incidence of both very high and very low floods.[59]

This unique record of the annual discharge of one of the world's longest rivers thus pinpoints a significant shift in atmospheric circulation patterns at the very time that military conflicts were multiplying and immediately prior to the recorded outbreak of the Black Death in the Kipchak Khanate of the Golden Horde in 1345/6 (Section 4.02.2). As is characteristic of environmental tipping points on this scale, it was accompanied by a marked increase in variability and uncertainty.[60]

Intriguingly, 1341/2 also emerges from other environmental records as a year of weather extremes. In central Asia the mini pluvial of 1310–40 came to an abrupt end and in east Asia the monsoon failed (Figure 4.5).[61] In China Timothy Brook has identified 1342–5, which he names the Zhizheng Slough, as a time of particularly acute environmental difficulty, when recurrent massive drought, locust attacks and floods begot devastating famines and epidemics.[62] In northern Europe storm surges brought flooding to the low-lying coasts around the southern North Sea,[63] while in Germany in 1342 a rare Genoan Low delivered torrential rainfall on an altogether unprecedented scale to the catchment area of the River Main and other central European rivers, resulting in the St Magdalene's Day flood of late July 1342 when the Main at Würzburg rose higher than ever before or since.[64] The same year in western Scotland was the driest in over 250 years (Figure 4.3).[65] And in the North Atlantic the alternation of pronounced cooling and warming events (the former associated with winter storms, the latter with heavy summer rainfall) which had attained its fullest development between 1315 and 1342, began to subside.[66]

---

[58] Fraedrich and others (1997).   [59] Hassan (2007); Hassan (2011).
[60] Above, Section 3.03.2c. Scheffer (2009), 286: 'Variance in fluctuations may often increase as a critical transition is approached'.
[61] Above, Figure 3.30.   [62] Brook (2010), 72.
[63] Britton (1937), 139–41; Bailey (1991), 189–94.
[64] Tetzlaff and others (2002); Böhm and Wetzel (2006). An extant inscription in the historical museum at Würzburg describes the flood thus: 'A.D. 1342, on the twelfth day before the calends of August on the Sunday before Jacobi, the River Main rose as high as never before. The water level reached the steps of the cathedral of Würzburg and flowed around the first stone statues. The bridge with the tower, the walls and many stone houses in Würzburg collapsed. In the same year there were similar floods all over Germany and in other regions. And this house was built by master Michael of Würzburg.' Hoffmann (2014), 325–6.
[65] Proctor and others (2002a); Proctor and others (2002b).
[66] Above, Figure 3.19B; Dawson and others (2007).

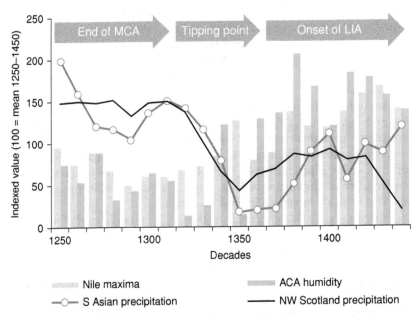

Figure 4.5 The 1340s as a tipping point in the transition from the Medieval Climate Anomaly (MCA) to the Little Ice Age (LIA), 1250–1450

Sources: Nile maxima, Popper (1951), 221–3; South Asian precipitation, estimated from Berkelhammer and others (2010b), Zhang and others (2008); Arid Central Asia (ACA) humidity index, Chen and others (2010); northwest Scotland precipitation, Proctor and others (2002b)

These coincidental weather events are consistent with the observation of Jiang and others that 'climate episodes in Nile River floods are linked to climate variability in disparate locations via global teleconnection processes'.[67]

Evidently, as rainfall over Ethiopia rose, so it declined over India and especially south China (Figure 4.5). By the 1340s the regular heavy monsoon rains that had prevailed with rare interruption for the better part of two hundred years from 1082 to 1268 had ended for good, with disastrous consequences for the paddy-rice dependent civilizations of south China and Southeast Asia.[68] These strong monsoon rains had been the product of a positive El Niño Southern Oscillation (ENSO) and La Niña

---

[67] Jiang and others (2002), 112.
[68] Lieberman (2009), 554–9; Lieberman and Buckley (2012), 1073–5; Tana (2014), 332–5.

dominated Pacific Ocean, which ensured that sea-surface temperatures and humidity levels were both significantly higher in the western (Asian) than eastern (American) Pacific.[69] As, from the 1270s and especially the 1330s, the ENSO weakened, so too did the South Asian monsoon, and by the 1340s the transition to a profoundly different monsoon regime was well advanced. The ENSO was also closely correlated with the North Atlantic Oscillation (NAO), so that when the ENSO became negative and precipitation over South Asia failed, the NAO also weakened and the winter westerlies shifted south, admitting colder, drier polar air to northern Europe (Figure 4.3).[70] According to the Cnoc nan Uamh speleothem record, the winters of 1340–4 were the driest and coldest experienced since the eleventh-century Oort Solar Minimum and those of 1357–9 were even more extreme (Figures 4.4 and 4.5).

Dendrochronology sheds further high-definition light on these developments. In the early 1340s the conspicuous inversion that had prevailed since the 1310s between tree growth in the Old World and that in Asia and the New World abruptly ended, at which time world tree growth was close to average.[71] Then, almost everywhere, commencing in 1342/3, growth across the temperate world declined: in the northern hemisphere the growth minimum occurred in 1346 (the year when plague broke out in the Crimea) and in the southern hemisphere in 1348 (the year that the fast-spreading pandemic reached Europe's Atlantic and North Sea coasts) (Figure 4.2B).[72] In Qinghai (junipers) the minimum value occurs in 1344, in western Europe (oaks), the Polar Urals (pines) and northern Scandinavia (pines) in 1345–6, in Mongolia (Siberian larch) and the Tien Shan (junipers) in 1348, and in California (bristlecone pines) in 1349. Corresponding dates in the southern hemisphere are 1347 in Tasmania (Huon pine), 1348 in Chile and Argentina (*Fitzroya*) and 1350 in New Zealand (cedar). For reduced growth on such a scale to have been replicated by so many dendrochronologies from such diverse locations and environments implies exceptionally strong negative environmental forcing on a global scale. Unsurprisingly, correlations between tree growth in Asia, the Old World and the New World are consistently positive across these years and average over +0.5 for the period 1340–68. This major growth anomaly, one of the greatest and most prolonged of the second millennium, coincides almost exactly with the point when in western Asia *Y. pestis* finally spilled over from sylvatic to commensal rodent populations and then began to spread far and wide with devastating consequences for human populations (Figure 4.2). The connection

[69] Above, Section 2.02.1.   [70] Trouet and others (2009a); Trouet and others (2009b).
[71] Above, Figure 3.19C.   [72] Baillie (2000), 62–5; Baillie (2006), 33–8.

between these environmental and biological developments is provided by the climatically influenced ecological conditions that shaped pathogen–host–vector inter-relationships.

4.02.2   Interactions between climate and plague

It is unlikely to be a coincidence that the first recorded major human plague outbreak occurred within four years of the 1341/2 climate downturn. Its victims were the population occupying the lands of the Kipchak Khanate between the Caspian Basin and the Black Sea. The trigger is likely to have been ecological stress arising from a sudden change in the weather, leading to a crossover of infection, either directly from sylvatic rodents to humans or indirectly to commensal rodents and then humans (Figure 3.27). Any failure of precipitation and abrupt reduction in vegetation growth in these water-limited grasslands will have undermined the viability of gerbil colonies and displaced plague-infected animals in ways that facilitated human contact with their flea vectors.[73] Further, as these sylvatic host populations collapsed, the heavy and hungry flea burdens they supported will have been driven to seek substitute hosts. This may have been humans, thus giving rise to increased cases of zoonotic plague, but is more likely to have been commensal rodents (i.e. rats), since these were the preferred alternative hosts of fleas. If so, this will have caused rapid amplification of plague and its progression from an epizootic state to a fast-spreading and deadly panzootic of domestic rodents. From this point humans will have been increasingly at risk from full-blown zoonotic plague, especially once mass die-offs of commensal rodents occurred and their starving fleas were again driven to seek alternative hosts. It was at this stage in the plague cycle that the Second Pandemic ignited (Figure 3.27).

The scene was now set for a repeat of the events which had been enacted almost exactly 800 years earlier at the start of the First Pandemic, when, following a comparably sharp climatic perturbation, *Y. pestis* had similarly spilled over from sylvatic to commensal rodents and, thus, humans and then spread to Constantinople and from there to the whole of the Roman Empire and beyond (Appendix 4.1). In the case of the Second Pandemic, plague contaminated the Black Sea port of Kaffa in the Crimea in 1346, Constantinople in May the following year and then Messina in Sicily that autumn. Thereafter, it was only a matter of time before the greater part of the Old World became infected. Both pandemics sprang from climatically driven macro episodes of complex

---

[73] McMichael (2010), 2 of 3.

ecological change. Each hinged upon biological developments occurring independently within the evolving inter-relationship between *Y. pestis*, its hosts and vectors. The result was that a disease which had been slowly growing in virulence among ground-burrowing wild rodents suddenly became a major killer of humans and invaded countries from which it had long been absent and whose climates and ecologies were very different from those of its reservoir regions deep in the Eurasian continental interior.

Humans may have become the most conspicuous victims of this unfolding scenario but its principal protagonists were the flea vectors that successively migrated en masse from sylvatic rodents to commensal rodents and then humans. Probably it was human transportation of fleas from the core reservoir region of *Y. pestis* in the northeast Tibetan–Qinghai Plateau that had been instrumental in making the Second Pandemic possible. Fleas thrived on humid and warm weather, which is why plague mortality typically peaked in the summer (Figure 4.7). For the same reason, the unseasonably humid and wet weather described by the Paris Medical Faculty may explain why in southern Europe plague advanced in the wake of the washed-out harvests of 1346–7 and then in northern Europe dismal weather, harvest failure and plague proceeded together.

Fleas may have thrived on the damp summer weather but grain crops did not. Complaints recorded in English manorial accounts leave no doubt of the damage inflicted upon agricultural operations during 1348/9 by the inclement weather.[74] Already there had been dismal harvests in 1339 and 1346 but these were overshadowed by the run of disastrous harvests that began in 1349 (Figures 4.3 and 4.6). Over the nine years 1349–57 mean net grain yields per seed were 27 per cent below their long-term average; during the four consecutive years 1349–52 they were 40 per cent below that average; and in the two worst years of all, 1349 and 1350, they were 52 per cent below average.[75] Over the entire span of years for which continuous yield data are available – 1270 to 1455 – these are the most deficient harvests on record.[76] Historians have tended to attribute them to the mass mortality of managers and workers but it

---

[74] England, Chester, 1348: 'there was inordinately heavy rain between Midsummer and Christmas, and scarcely a day went by without rain at some time in the day or night': Horrox (1994), 62, also 54, 66, 74. Autumn 1347 was wet, as were winter and autumn 1348, and the whole of 1349, and waterlogged soils were reported in winter and summer 1350: Titow (1960), 401–3; Stern (2000), 100, 164–6.

[75] Farmer (1977), 557, reports mean yields of wheat, barley and oats respectively 33.5 per cent, 28.2 per cent and 46.2 per cent below average in the two harvest years 1349–50. A reduction of 1°C in summer temperature reduced wheat yields by 5 per cent.

[76] Campbell (2007); Campbell (2009b), 25–9.

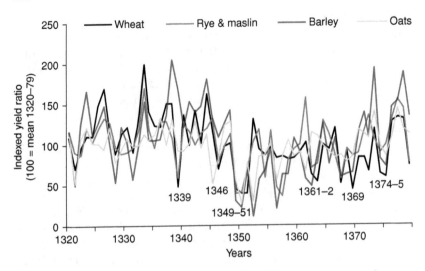

Figure 4.6 English grain harvests, 1320–79
Source and note: Campbell (2007). Yield ratios are gross of tithes and net of seed.

is clear that the inclement weather was arguably far more to blame.[77] In fact, without the huge reduction in population precipitated by the plague, England along with much of the rest of northern Europe would undoubtedly have been in the grip of another great famine.[78] Scarcity of labour and discontinuities of management simply made bad harvests worse.[79]

[77] Stone (2005), 101–4. Poor yields on the Westminster demesne of Kinsbourne, Hertfordshire, in 1349–53 were the product of a combination of weather and labour-supply problems: Stern (2000), 164–6, 178–9. Benedictow (2004), 351, nevertheless emphasizes the latter: 'Dearth and famine were a usual consequence of the Black Death (and later plague epidemics), because normal work in agriculture and urban industries tended to grind to a halt under the impact of the epidemic onslaught, with severe consequences for production and income'. This interpretation is supported by much contemporary comment of labour scarcity and crops left un-harvested in the fields: Horrox (1994), 64, 66, 70, 72–3, 78. For a case analysis of the massive production shock experienced during these years within a single distinctive region, see Stone (2011).

[78] Campbell (2009b), 23–6; Campbell (2010a), 144–7; Campbell and Ó Gráda (2011), 871–3.

[79] On the Kent estate of Canterbury Cathedral Priory in 1349 the reeves at Agney and Ruckinge complained, respectively, that peas and vetches and winter barley were left un-harvested because of the lack of labourers; presumably for much the same reason, livestock were fed un-harvested barley at Chartham and un-threshed wheat at Mersham; the following year there were still insufficient reapers to harvest all the vetches at Mersham: Campbell (2010b), 47n.

Failed harvests, by increasing poverty, malnutrition and the congregation of vagrants, will, of course, have created ideal conditions for vector transmission by rodent and/or human ectoparasites. Large-scale movements of troops, munitions and provisions in conjunction with the ongoing wars between England and France and between Scotland and England will have further aided the pathogen's dissemination. Plague, inclement weather, harvest failure and war were a toxic combination, all the more so if epidemic typhus, which thrived on these conditions, was an ingredient in the equation.[80]

Yet there is a paradox in this unfolding scenario, insofar as a disease normally associated with continental regions characterized by semi-arid climates struck northwestern Europe with devastating force and penetrated as far north as latitude 63° when the weather over much of the region was exceptionally cool. Such weather conditions are more characteristic of typhus outbreaks, whereas early-phase transmission by fleas typically requires a minimum temperature of 10°C and transmission by blocked fleas (the method identified by Alexandre Yersin and emphasized by Benedictow) was most effective at temperatures in the range 16–22°C.[81] Unless there was a double pandemic of typhus and plague, other things being equal, these climatic requirements ought to have constrained flea-borne transmission of the bacillus in both time and space and thereby inhibited the pandemic. Furthermore, subsequent major European plague outbreaks were similarly associated with adverse weather and depressed growing conditions.[82] Cool temperatures evidently did little or nothing to inhibit the progress of plague. Why this was clearly hinged upon the precise vectors involved in plague's transmission and the ecological parameters that determined and shaped their activity. It certainly implies that as plague spread north into cooler latitudes, early-phase transmission must have come increasingly to the fore.[83]

4.03   Eruption of the Black Death in Europe

4.03.1   A killer unmasked: the identity of the Black Death pathogen

In 1984 Graham Twigg initiated a debate about the biological identity of the Black Death which took until 2010 to be resolved to general

---

[80] Bechah and others (2008), 417, 418: 'R. prowazekii is responsible for epidemic typhus, a disease of cold months when heavy clothing and poor sanitary conditions are conducive to lice proliferation'. Historically, it has been 'responsible for massive mortality in the wake of wars, famines, and migrations'.

[81] Eisen and others (2006); Eisen and others (2015); Benedictow (2010), 396–8.

[82] Below, Figure 5.5.   [83] Eisen and others (2015).

satisfaction.[84] Opinion became divided between those convinced that the vector-borne bacterial infection *Yersinia pestis* was responsible for this pandemic and those who argued that, notwithstanding contemporary descriptions of many of bubonic plague's classic physical symptoms, the disease was too contagious and fast-moving, with too long an incubation period (as witnessed by its ability to survive long sea journeys), and too mortal in its aggregate demographic impact, for the conventional bubonic-plague diagnosis to hold.[85] Instead, it was something else: anthrax (Twigg, 1984); a viral haemorrhagic fever (Scott and Duncan, 2001); a deadly but now extinct viral disease (Cohn, 2002a); or conceivably even the biological fallout from an extra-terrestrial impact on 25 January 1348 (Baillie, 2006).[86] Many were deceived by the closer resemblance of the Black Death's speed and pattern of diffusion to those of a viral infection spread from person to person, than those of a vector-borne zoonotic.[87]

In their 2007 review of the debate, John Theilmann and Frances Cate conceded that the doubts and objections expressed by such prominent plague sceptics as Twigg, Scott and Duncan, and Samuel Cohn Jr are not without legitimacy and acknowledged that these 'plague critics' have 'made a convincing case that the great pestilence exhibited characteristics different from those of the third plague epidemic' which began in the Yunnan Province of China in 1855 and subsequently spread to all inhabited continents.[88] While themselves subscribing to the bubonic plague diagnosis, Theilmann and Cate hypothesized that this discrepancy between the Second and Third Pandemics may be because plague acted in conjunction with other dangerous and infectious diseases, such as typhus and influenza, or was a particularly virulent strain of *Y. pestis*.[89] Even so, they doubted whether conclusive laboratory evidence would ever be forthcoming that would permit clinical identification of the

---

[84] For a critical response to this debate see Benedictow (2010). See also the response of Morris (1971) to Shrewsbury (1970).

[85] Nutton (2008a); Scott and Duncan (2001), 356–62; Cohn (2008), 77–88.

[86] The 25 January 1348 event is generally considered to have been an earthquake centred on northern Italy: Hoffmann (2014), 306–7. Contemporaries attributed the Black Death to noxious air thereby released from the bowels of the earth: Horrox (1994), 158–63.

[87] For example Wood and others (2003); Christakos and others (2005); Welford and Bossak (2010a).

[88] Theilmann and Cate (2007), 390. The views of Twigg, Scott and Duncan, Cohn, and several other 'plague deniers' are systematically refuted in Benedictow (2010).

[89] Shrewsbury (1971), 197, 124–5, similarly proposed that plague was accompanied by typhus spread by human ectoparasites; Theilmann and Cate (2007), 392–3. In contrast, Benedictow (2010) is adamant that there were few significant differences between the Second and Third Pandemics.

Black Death pathogen. In this they, in their turn, have been proven wrong.

It was Michel Drancourt and Didier Raoult's Marseille plague team who published the first forensic evidence that identified the etiological agent responsible for plague. In a key paper published in 2000 they demonstrated that *Yersinia* (chromosomal) ancient deoxyribonucleic acid (aDNA) could be clinically identified from the dental pulp of teeth extracted from the skeletons of plague victims.[90] To be precise, the Marseille team claimed they had discovered *Yersinia* aDNA in the teeth of one child and two adults excavated from a purportedly fourteenth-century cemetery at Montpellier in France.[91] Their finding proved controversial. In the first place, this did not establish beyond doubt that the *Yersinia* organism was indeed *Y. pestis*. Secondly, the existence of bubonic plague in Mediterranean France does not necessarily mean that *Y. pestis* was the cause of the pan-continental pandemic, given that several earlier and later plague outbreaks failed to spread beyond the Mediterranean.[92] Thirdly, since laboratory analysis of DNA is highly susceptible to contamination, the most fervent plague critics maintained that these results were deficient in scientific rigour and could not be trusted until independently corroborated. Indeed, their scepticism appeared justified when a corresponding study undertaken by M. T. Gilbert and others (2004) drew a blank and concluded 'no *Y. pestis* DNA could be amplified from DNA extracted from 108 teeth belonging to 61 individuals, despite the amplification of numerous other bacterial DNA sequences'.[93]

It took until 2010 before the contested results of the Marseille team were corroborated and extended by the conclusions of a twelve-strong international and interdisciplinary team. Their breakthrough results came from successful aDNA analysis of the dental pulp of seventy-six human skeletons excavated from five suspected plague-burial sites in Italy, France, Germany, the Netherlands and England, all with radiocarbon dates between the fourteenth and seventeenth centuries.[94] From the fourteenth-century burials, dental pulp from one skeleton from Saint-Laurent-de-la-Cabrerisse (France), two from Hereford (England) and seven from Bergen-op-Zoom (Netherlands) yielded unambiguous evidence of infection with what was now definitively identified as *Y. pestis*. Additionally, a separate rapid diagnostic test found traces of the *Y. pestis*

---

[90] Raoult and others (2000).
[91] Raoult and others (2000). Notwithstanding the scepticism of some, Noymer (2007), 620, acknowledged the significance of this aDNA result.
[92] Stothers (1999); Hays (2005), 134–42; Alfani (2013).
[93] Gilbert and others (2004), 341; Duncan and Scott (2005).
[94] Haensch and others (2010).

specific F1 antigen on seven skeletons from Saint-Laurent-de-la-Cabrerisse, four from Hereford, and three from Bergen-op-Zoom, plus four from Augsburg (Germany) and six from Parma (Italy). On the strength of these more detailed findings, obtained using scrupulous scientific methods, Stephanie Haensch and her colleagues concluded:

> two independent methods demonstrate that humans buried in mass graves that were historically and contextually associated with the Black Death and its resurgences, were consistently infected by Y. pestis in southern, central and northern Europe. Thus, the second pandemic was probably caused in large part by Y. pestis . . .[95]

Equivalent results have since been published respecting Black Death burials at East Smithfield in London and plague burials at Venice.[96] Crucially, these aDNA results have been obtained in separate laboratories using the most rigorous methods by independent teams of scientists. Bioarchaeological work is now focused upon identifying exactly which strains of the bacterium were involved and their respective genetic genealogies. These findings have certainly convinced the geneticists that one or more strains of Y. pestis, acting alone or in conjunction with other pathogens, were responsible for the Black Death. Geneticists have also been quick to establish how these Black Death genomes fit into the reconstructed phylogenetic tree of Y. pestis and what this might reveal about the chronology and geography of the Second Pandemic's origins and spread.[97] In the face of this forensic evidence, alternative circumstantially based diagnoses of the pandemic have been abandoned.[98]

Working from extant isolated and cultured strains of Y. pestis, scientists have also decoded the Y. pestis genome.[99] The bacterium evolves clonally and is notable for its limited genetic diversity, with little to suggest that any of its variant genotypes were or are intrinsically more virulent and dangerous than the others.[100] When mutations occur, mostly due to neutral processes such as genetic drift, distinct genomic strains result, each defined by its single-nucleotide polymorphisms (SNPs) and deriving from a common ancestor.[101] From this information the genealogy of Y. pestis has been reconstructed, with no strain older than its first mutant ancestor.[102] Genomes extracted from datable plague burials are used to

---

[95] Haensch and others (2010), 5 of 14.
[96] Bos and others (2011); Schuenemann and others (2011); Tran and others (2011).
[97] Achtman and others (2004); Morelli and others (2010); Cui and others (2013).
[98] The key paper spelling out the purport of these scientific discoveries to historians is Little (2011).
[99] Achtman and others (2004); Morelli and others (2010).
[100] Bos and others (2011); Cui and others (2013).
[101] Cui and others (2013).   [102] Above, Figure 3.28.

determine the first appearance of key branches. The result is known as a phylogenetic tree, whose successive branches (or polytomies) represent the different lineages of the bacterium which have evolved since the disease became genetically differentiated from its parental species, *Yersinia pseudotuberculosis*, at some time within the last twenty thousand years.[103] Most of these lineages are capable of causing human plague.[104]

Reconstruction of the *Y. pestis* genome is now allowing the bacterium's spread through space and time to be deduced independently of historical documentation of plague outbreaks. In a key sequel study, Cui and others (2013) identify a 'big bang' sometime during the thirteenth century, when several new lineages emerged within a short time period, including the Black Death sequences defined by aDNA studies for the plague fatalities at Saint-Laurent-de-la-Cabrerisse, Hereford and Bergen-op-Zoom.[105] A clear consensus has now emerged among geneticists and biologists that the geographical distribution of these lineages implies that *Y. pestis* first evolved in China whence it spread on multiple occasions to other areas in Eurasia and Africa and, eventually, in the Third Pandemic, throughout the world.[106] The outcome of this process is the country-specific genetic diversity that exists today, whereby plague deaths in Kyrgyzstan and Madagascar arise from genealogically and chronologically different strains of the same pathogen.[107]

With the decoded *Y. pestis* genome sequence for reference, Haensch and others point out that the strain responsible for the Black Death pre-dated evolution of the three main modern plague lineages, *orientalis*, *medievalis* and *antiqua*.[108] In other words, the disease which between 1347 and 1353 sent millions in west Asia, Europe and North Africa to premature graves was biologically non-identical with the plague studied and diagnosed by bacteriologist Alexandre Yersin in Hong Kong in 1894–7, whose spread throughout India between 1896 and 1907 was the subject of the Indian Plague Commission's detailed reports, and which

---

[103] Above, Figure 3.28; Morelli and others (2010). Suntsov (2014) has proposed that the transition to *Y. pestis* from the initial pseudotuberculosis microbe *Y. pseudotuberculosis* occurred in southern Siberia and Central Asia via the 'Mongolian marmot *Marmota sibirica*–flea *Oropsylla silatiewi*' parasitic system.
[104] Cui and others (2013), 579.   [105] Above, Figure 3.28; Cui and others (2013), 580.
[106] Achtman and others (2004), 17842; Morelli and others (2010), 1140; Bos and others (2011), 509.
[107] Morelli and others (2010). On Tuesday 27 August 2013 (http://www.bbc.co.uk/news/world-asia-23843656) and 11 December 2013 (http://www.bbc.co.uk/news/world-africa-25342122) BBC World News reported plague deaths in Kyrgyzstan and Madagascar. In Kyrgyzstan plague was contracted from an infected marmot, as was the fatality reported from Yumen City, Gansu Province, western China (to the northwest of Qinghai): http://www.bbc.com/news/world-asia-china-28437338.
[108] Haensch and others (2010), pp. 1–2 of 14.

many historians have taken as the model for the plagues which ravaged Europe from the fourteenth to the eighteenth centuries.[109] This also lays to rest the oft-repeated thesis advanced by R. Devignat in the 1950s that *Y. pestis medievalis* was the strain of plague responsible for the so-called 'second pandemic' of the Black Death (as *Y. pestis antiqua* was for the great pandemics of ancient times and *Y. pestis orientalis* for those of modern times).[110] As it is now understood, the *Y. pestis* genome had a more ancient pedigree, which preceded development of the *antiqua*, *medievalis* and *orientalis* branches and evolved geographically from east to west.[111]

The capacity for *Y. pestis* to mutate during epidemics is also borne out by the intriguing discovery of Haensch and others that the genotype commonly responsible for the French and English deaths was one evolutionary stage less advanced than the strain which caused the deaths at Bergen-op-Zoom, from which they deduce that 'distinct bacterial populations spread throughout Europe in the fourteenth century'.[112] Because the Bergen-op-Zoom strain differed from all known modern *Y. pestis* populations from Eurasia they believe it to be extinct but they do not rule out the possibility that the Saint-Laurent-de-la-Cabrerisse/Hereford genotype may still exist.[113] As more aDNA evidence accumulates it is also to be expected that further European variants of the genome will come to light, especially if at some stage plague became enzootic within Europe instead of being reintroduced each time from plague reservoirs in Asia, as Schmid and others have recently proposed.[114] A key lesson from the study by Cui and others (2013) is that the larger and geographically more extensive the aDNA sample base, the greater the light that will be shed into past patterns of plague spread and their provenance. In the case of the Black Death, current absence of such information for those regions around the Black Sea and Aegean into which it is known the human disease first spread in 1346–7 is a conspicuous lacuna.

---

[109] For example Ziegler (1969); Shrewsbury (1971); Hatcher (1977); Bolton (1980); Benedictow (2010). For a revised view see Theilmann and Cate (2007), 390–1. Nutton (2008b), 16: 'If *Yersinia pestis* was the biological agent of the Black Death . . . its behaviour then, and for centuries afterwards, differed at times considerably from what has been observed over the last century and more. The symptoms of plague are recognizably the same, but its epidemiology and demographics are clearly distinct'. Also, Royer (2014).

[110] Devignat (1951), 260–1: 'Variety III (from south-east Russia) which ferments glycerin and does not produce nitrous acid . . . seems to have spread in the 14th century from the Caspian Sea throughout the whole of Europe, where it caused the "Black Death" and, through the black rat, established itself endemically during four centuries'.

[111] Above, Figure 3.28.   [112] Haensch and others (2010), 7 of 14.

[113] Haensch and others (2010), 8 of 14.   [114] Schmid and others (2015).

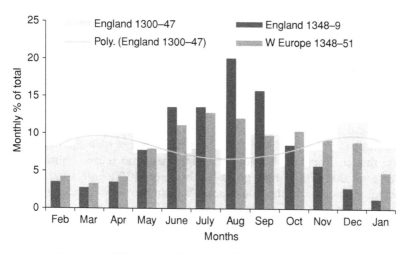

Figure 4.7 The seasonal impact of the Black Death in England and western Europe
Note: England = monthly % of total deaths of tenants-in-chief of the Crown; W. Europe = mean monthly % of estimated total territorial advance by plague.
Sources: calculated from Christakos and others (2007), 715; Campbell and Bartley (2006), 15

4.03.2   The temporal profile of the epidemic

Plague's temporal advance assumed a wave-like seasonal pattern (Figure 4.7). The estimates of George Christakos and others (2007) may be flawed (they were obtained using a Reed–Frost epidemiological model which assumes that plague was a viral infection) but the evidence upon which they are based can be trusted. Their extrapolations indicate that the Black Death was least active in the winter months and in each of the three consecutive plague years 1348–9, 1349–50 and 1350–1 its lowest rate of spread appears to have occurred between January and April (Figure 4.7). From May, with the advent of warmer spring weather, it grew more virulent and each year seemingly began to spread with greater speed. Rates of territorial expansion tended to peak in July, when temperatures were warmest and fleas would have been most active, but then gradually abated. The exception was 1348, when, as plague consolidated its grip upon Italy, southern France and Iberia, the epidemic revived in the autumn and peaked at an even greater rate of expansion in November (Figures 4.7 and 4.10). This double peak in summer and autumn was never repeated. Subsequently, as the epidemic spread north into cooler climatic and more sparsely populated zones, the seasonal contrast between winter quiescence and summer activity became more pronounced and the momentum of its territorial expansion diminished until, in 1353, it halted altogether.[115]

The clear seasonality of plague's spread, with summers significantly more dangerous than winters, implicates the influence of temperature and humidity upon both the activity of the fleas that transmitted the infection and the mobility of the humans who, on their persons, clothes and goods, transported the fleas.[116] For obvious reasons, shipping and traffic volumes were greater in the summer than the winter.[117] Note that in England this seasonal pattern of mortality is almost the inverse of that which had prevailed between 1300 and 1347, when December had been the most and August the least deadly months (Figure 4.10).

Plague deaths within individual communities displayed a similar temporal profile. In the zoonotic form of plague there was always a lag between when the first commensal rodents became infected and the first human plague deaths occurred. This is because, where transmission by blocked fleas predominated, it took an infected flea vector 10–14 days to ignite a plague panzootic in a hitherto uninfected rat population, a further 3 days for fleas to then transmit the infection to the first humans, 3–5 days for infected humans to incubate the disease and then 1–3 days for it to run its course. From first infection of rats to death of the first human plague victims could thus take 19–27 days.[118] Early-phase transition, in contrast, could achieve the same result in half the time.[119] Benedictow believes that it is the lags intrinsic to blocked-flea transmission that explain why, in the well-documented late sixteenth-century case of Penrith in Westmorland, 22 days elapsed between the first plague death on 22 September 1597 and the second on 14 October.[120] Thereafter at Penrith onset of winter, with its lower temperatures and reduced flea activity, slowed progress of the epidemic and in January 1598 it appeared to have subsided altogether (Figure 4.8). In March, however, as warmer temperatures rekindled flea activity, plague deaths started to mount and in June, July, August and September, the warmest months of the year, they surged to a peak.

This pattern of an initial sporadic trickle of deaths and then a sudden surge of mortality followed by an equally abrupt decline appears to have

---

[115] Benedictow (2010), 398.
[116] Gage and Kosoy (2005), 506–9, 515–16; Bossak and Welford (2009); Benedictow (2010), 396–8.
[117] Twigg (1984), 51–2; Bossak and Welford (2009).
[118] Benedictow (2010), 6.   [119] Eisen and others (2015).
[120] Benedictow (2010), 639–53 (in response to Scott and Duncan (2001)).

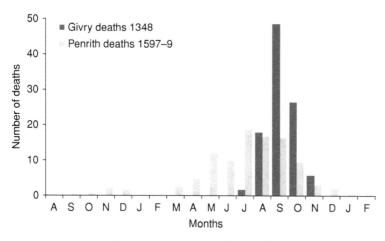

Figure 4.8 The contrasting mortality profiles of the plague outbreaks at Givry, Burgundy, 1348, and at Penrith, Cumbria, 1597–9
Note: total deaths amounted to an estimated 31 per cent of Givry's pre-plague population and 45 per cent that of Penrith.
Sources: Givry – Christakos and others (2005), 127 (derived from Gras (1939)); Penrith – Scott and Duncan (2001), 120

been typical and reflects the parallel mortality profiles of rats and fleas.[121] At Penrith, as elsewhere, the town's non-immune population of rats will have been the first to succumb to the importation of infection and the first human fatalities will have been the incidental result of that epizootic. It was only after the rat population had collapsed that the human outbreak really got under way, as starving fleas began en masse to adopt humans as substitute hosts. Warm and humid summer weather greatly amplified flea activity and at Penrith brought the mortality crisis to its peak in late summer, by which time the town's rat population must have been close to extinction. Once this happened it was only a matter of another four to five months before flea numbers, in turn, also collapsed, since humans are incapable of acting as permanent maintenance hosts of rodent fleas. At Penrith the return of colder weather reinforced this trend and by December, following mass die-offs of first rats and then starved fleas, the plague had largely burnt itself out: the last flea capable of transmitting plague had probably perished a fortnight before the final plague burial on 6 January 1599. The latter occurred 15½ months after the first plague

---

[121] For a corresponding analysis of the 1613–14 plague outbreak at Freiberg in Saxony see Monecke and others (2009). I am grateful to Ann Carmichael for alerting me to this reference.

burial and almost 6 months after the peak of the crisis. Plague must have cleared the town of rats and their fleas but it had also killed 485 (36 per cent) out of a pre-plague urban population of at least 1,350.[122]

According to Monecke and others, human plague outbreaks typically began slowly, then rapidly escalated before subsiding and then dying out because of the preceding and parallel mortalities of non-immune rats and their fleas. They claim that outbreaks were far more muted when plague-resistant rats were present because rats were strongly preferred as hosts by fleas. Humans were the starved rodent fleas' hosts of last resort.[123]

Plague's summer mortality peak, as manifest at Penrith, is one of the most defining features of this vector-transmitted disease and is consistent with the effect of temperatures and humidity upon flea reproduction and activity.[124] The same seasonal peak shows up at comparably sized Givry in Burgundy in 1348. Here, on the evidence of a uniquely preserved parish register, the disease advanced three times faster than at Penrith, running its course in maybe just four months, with the upsurge of plague deaths commencing in mid-July (the earliest deaths may have gone unnoticed), the peak in deaths following six weeks later, and the last of over six hundred deaths occurring on 19 November.[125] The difference of duration between the mortality profiles of the outbreaks in these two small towns is striking and implies that at Givry ecological conditions were especially favourable to the disease's rapid progression through both rodent and human populations, with early-phase transmission probably playing a more prominent role (Figure 4.8). Alternatively, as the Marseille plague team have speculated, human ectoparasites may have been responsible for plague's rapid and correspondingly human-to-human advance at Givry and rodent ectoparasites for its more drawn-out diffusion and long periods of seeming inactivity at Penrith.[126]

The rapidity with which the Black Death progressed at Givry appears to have been typical of this first and most deadly strike of the Second Pandemic. At Bordeaux in late summer 1348 the former English royal chancellor, Robert Bourchier, and his charge, bride-to-be Princess Joan de la Tour, expired respectively within 10–15 days and 30 days of their arrival in the plague-infested city.[127] The next year, in the English diocese of Coventry and Lichfield, the chronology of clerical deaths recorded in the bishop's register indicates that plague swept through local areas in a matter of just 4–6 months.[128] Elsewhere the swiftness with which

---

[122] Scott and others (1996); Scott and Duncan (2001), 115–48.
[123] Monecke and others (2009).   [124] Benedictow (2010), 396–8.
[125] Figure 4.8; Benedictow (2010), 108.   [126] Drancourt and others (2006).
[127] Christakos and others (2005), 226–7, 281.   [128] Wood and others (2003).

the healthy sickened and died attracted much comment. As Giovanni Boccaccio graphically observed of Florence in 1348, 'whenever those suffering from [this pestilence] mixed with people who were still unaffected, it would rush upon these with the speed of a fire racing through dry or oily substances'.[129] Although difficult to reconcile with blocked-flea transmission, this is consistent with early-phase transition, whereby fleas can transmit *Y. pestis* from host to victim in a matter of hours and typically less than four days, provided that levels of bacteremia in the former are sufficiently high.[130] In modern plague outbreaks humans then experience a short incubation period of just 1–8 days between infection and first manifestation of symptoms (high fever, chills, aching muscles, extreme weakness, swollen and tender lymph nodes, diarrhoea, nausea and vomiting). The incubation period for the rarer and less transmissible pneumonic form of the disease is shorter, just 1–3 days.[131] The puzzle is that in the fourteenth century those who sickened so quickly would have had limited opportunity to complete long overland journeys and arduous sea voyages before incapacitating sickness and death intervened. Further, if rodent populations had to collapse before human deaths mounted, the speed with which rat colonies became infected and overwhelmed must have been equally rapid.

Exactly how the disease succeeded in infecting an entire continent within barely six years remains one of the most puzzling features of the Black Death. Certainly, striking as it did out of the blue, there were no quarantine or other preventive measures in place that might have impeded it. In later outbreaks the quarantine measures developed and enforced by Italian towns and cities from the end of the fourteenth century presumed that individuals had to be isolated and kept under observation for several weeks before they could be considered to be plague free and no risk to others.[132] In July 1377 the Dalmatian Republic of Ragusa promulgated the first quarantine legislation in the world when it imposed a 30-day period of isolation upon visitors, travellers, traders, merchandise and ships coming to Dubrovnik from plague-infested areas, and followed this in 1390 with establishment of a permanent Health Office.[133] Venice followed Ragusa's example and lengthened the period of quarantine to 40 days (*quarantena* = forty-day period). Here, those arriving from overseas when quarantine regulations were actively enforced were kept in isolation on the small island of Santa Maria di Nazareth (now Lazzaretto

---

[129] Horrox (1994), 27–8.   [130] Eisen and others (2015).
[131] Kool (2005).   [132] Cliff and others (2009); Henderson (2010), 373–4.
[133] Frati (2000); Blažina Tomić and Blažina (2015), 106–12.

Vecchio) in the southern part of the Venetian lagoon. Those who survived this period (well in excess of the time required for both rats and humans to become infected and die) were deemed infection free. Over the course of the fifteenth century many other Italian cities adopted similar measures, founded permanent health offices and enacted legislation aimed at raising standards of sanitation and hygiene, which may be why the spread of plague slowed and outbreaks became more circumscribed in their territorial extent.[134] The mortality and geographical scale of the initial devastating strike in 1347–53 would never, in fact, be replicated.

4.03.3   The spread of plague in Europe

Plague finally spread from Asia into Europe around or before the second half of 1346, when several chroniclers report that it reached the Crimean coast of the Black Sea (Figure 4.9).[135] Here it immediately displayed its full destructive potential by cutting a swathe through Khan Janibeg's Mongol army, then encamped outside the busy Genoese port of Kaffa.[136] At Kaffa, if not before, plague very likely came into contact with colonies of black rats, including the ship rats that were the inevitable stowaways on every Genoese galley and merchantman. Flea vectors then transported *Y. pestis* from one highly susceptible rat colony to another, from ship to ship and from port to port. Once in direct contact with European traders and their commerce plague's rapid dissemination through the dense maritime networks, ports and settled coastlands of the Black Sea and Mediterranean was therefore assured. Travelling now on far busier routes by both water and land, its rate of spread rose to up to six kilometres a day and two thousand kilometres a year.[137] Over the next six years it penetrated wherever people lived, interacted and traded so that, with very few exceptions, the only regions 'of western Europe that were not affected by [the] Black Death were uninhabited areas' (Figure 4.10).[138]

Gabriel de Mussis is the source of the oft-repeated story that at Kaffa plague was transferred from the besiegers to the besieged when the Mongols catapulted corpses into the city.[139] Presumably it was the live and still infectious insect vectors present on the bodies and in the clothing

---

[134] Cliff and others (2009); Blažina Tomić and Blažina (2015), 134–7.
[135] Above, Section 3.03.2c.   [136] Norris (1977), 11; McNeill (1977), 146–7.
[137] Christakos and others (2007). These estimates are compromised by reliance upon a Reed–Frost model that assumes a viral rather than vector-dependent mechanism of spread.
[138] Christakos and others (2007), 706, 711.   [139] Wheelis (2002).

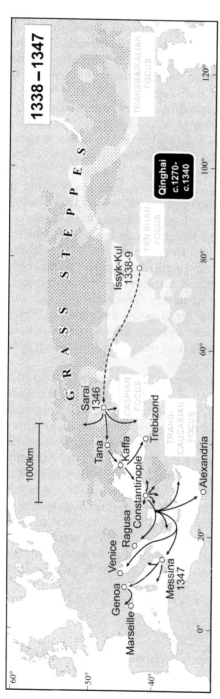

Figure 4.8 The spread of plague from Asia to Europe, 1338–47

Sources: Norris (1977), 12, 20; Benedictow (2004), map 1; Christakos and others (2005), 241–59

of their recently deceased victims that transmitted *Y. pestis* to those within the city's walls and the rats with which they cohabited. The Genoese merchants and mariners who in spring 1347 then took ship and fled the city, its siege and pestilence carried these infected ectoparasites, and no doubt numbers of their rodent hosts, across the Black Sea with them. By May 1347 the contamination had been introduced to Pera and Constantinople. Then, over the summer, it was spread to the ports of the Aegean and by early autumn had reached both Alexandria in Egypt and Messina in Sicily. Infection of Italy and Croatia followed and eventually, by November 1347, plague reached Marseille (Figure 4.9).[140]

This process probably entailed many ships and crews rather than a few and was spread over a period of about half a year, which is the time it took for plague to reach southern Europe from the Crimea (the comparable overland journey of 3,300 kilometres from Issyk-Kul to the Crimea is likely to have taken from eight to twelve years).[141] It is both overdramatic and unrealistic, given the length of the voyage, number of intermediate ports en route and scale of maritime activity in this region, to suppose that a single shipload of fleeing Genoese was responsible for transferring plague to Italy or that the Genoese alone were its carriers.[142] Nonetheless, contemporaries were virtually unanimous in denouncing the Genoese as the human vectors who transmitted the deadly infection wherever they went.[143]

Once plague reached Sicily at the maritime crossroads of the Mediterranean, so dense and extensive were that island's commercial connections that the infection was quickly disseminated to the four corners of the Mediterranean.[144] This ensured that populations throughout almost the entire Mediterranean maritime trading area then became contaminated over the course of 1348 (Figure 4.9). In Tuscany, Provence and Catalonia it struck communities still reeling from the effects of the extreme weather and near famine of 1346–7.[145] From the coastal towns the pandemic spread inland to their hinterlands and beyond, following the main arteries of trade and travel and advancing from east to west and south to north across Europe along a series of fronts.[146] It thus reached Bordeaux on the French Atlantic coast and Rouen and Paris in northern France by summer 1348, and Weymouth (alias Melcombe Regis) and Bristol in

[140] Benedictow (2004), 61; Christakos and others (2005), 213–18, 243, 244–51, 256–9; Benedictow (2010), 585–7.
[141] Schmid and others (2015).
[142] Twigg (1984), 49–53; Scott and Duncan (2001), 370–1.
[143] Horrox (1994), 18–20, 35–6, 41–2, 45–6.
[144] Benedictow (2004), 60–104; Christakos and others (2005), 243–59.
[145] Figure 3.22.
[146] Christakos and others (2005), 208–9; Christakos and others (2007), 714.

southwestern England and Drogheda and Dublin in eastern Ireland at about the same time (Figure 4.10).

The next year, 1349, it spread to southern Spain and Portugal, virtually the whole of England, Wales and Ireland, plus the rest of France, the Southern Low Countries, the Rhineland and Danube valley, Norway (penetrating as far north as Trondheim, just 200 miles short of the Arctic Circle), and the southern Baltic port of Danzig and its grain-growing hinterland (Figure 4.10).[147] In these northerly regions plague's advance coincided with onset of cool wet weather and a run of serious harvest failures, whose consequent misery it greatly compounded (Figures 4.3 and 4.6). In 1350, as the cold and wet weather continued, it moved further north and east and infected Scotland, the Northern Low Countries, Germany, Denmark, southern Sweden, northern Poland, Bohemia and Slovakia.[148] Thence, it penetrated the Baltic countries of eastern Poland, Lithuania and Latvia in 1351, and, having come almost full circle and left few parts of Europe unscathed, finally burnt itself out in eastern and central Russia in 1352–3.[149]

Although plague later came to be regarded as a largely urban phenomenon, in this first and most deadly outbreak Christakos and others found no correlation between settlement size and mortality and no essential difference between the susceptibilities of rural and urban dwellers.[150] The countryside was therefore no safe haven; attempts to flee the contagion proved in vain and merely added impetus to plague's seemingly relentless spread. Once a settlement had become infected, as at Givry in or before July 1348 (Figure 4.8), the disease typically progressed rapidly to a climax and then, as quickly, abated.[151] Such conspicuously high rates of infection meant that substantially larger populations of rodent susceptibles were necessary to sustain epidemics for longer, so that the greater the physical scale of a settlement the longer the duration of an epidemic. Only in European cities with more than 60,000 inhabitants did it take more than 12 months for plague to run its course.[152] In London, with around 80,000 inhabitants, the plague lasted for at least 15 months, in Paris (probably twice the size of London) for 16 months, and in Venice (population 110,000–120,000) for

---

[147] Hinde (2003), 43, maps the Black Death's spread across England in 1348–9. On Norway see Hufthammer and Walløe (2013).
[148] The Swedish evidence is reviewed by Myrdal (2006); for Slovakia see Büntgen and others (2013).
[149] Benedictow (2004), 209–15, 218–21; Christakos and others (2005), 260.
[150] Christakos and others (2005), 144–51, 223–5.
[151] Gras (1939), 305–6; Christakos and others (2005), 126–7; Benedictow (2010), 108.
[152] Olea and Christakos (2005); Christakos and others (2005), 224–5.

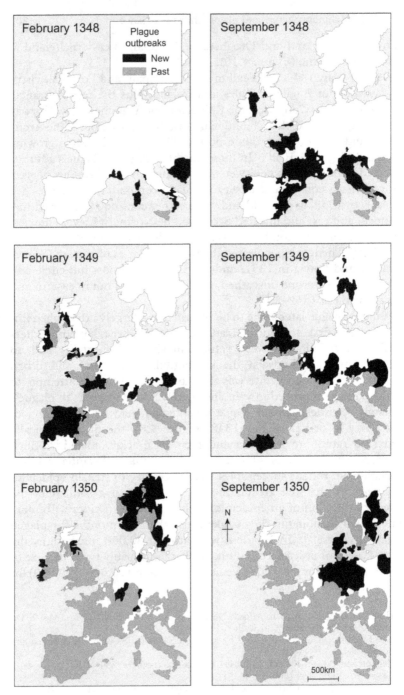

Figure 4.10 The spread of plague in western Europe, February 1348 to September 1350
Source: redrawn from Christakos and others (2007), 709–10

18 months.[153] The sheer size of these great urban populations ensured that exposure of rodents and humans to the pathogen was a more protracted process than in small towns like Givry with a few thousand inhabitants or substantial villages like Walsham in Suffolk with just a few hundred.[154] In the latter, maximum exposure was achieved within a space of weeks rather than months. The speed of the plague's passage therefore magnified its shock. In its wake it left traumatized and wasted populations.

Historical reconstructions from surviving written records of plague's pattern of spatial diffusion imply the facilitating role of human agency. Unless an artefact of the evidence and its analysis, the Black Death appears to have followed established trade routes, moving in a chain reaction from town to town, hierarchically between centres of descending rank, and outwards from ports and cities to their rural hinterlands (Figure 4.10). Had it been an airborne infection, as contemporaries believed it to have been given the prevailing miasma theory of disease, carried by the wind from place to place, its pattern of dissemination would have been entirely different, with simultaneous outbreaks at widely scattered and seemingly unrelated locations, exhibiting in their broad distribution the influence of prevailing winds.[155] In fact, the pattern of spread more closely resembles that of a viral infection transmitted directly from person to person than that of a vector-borne zoonotic whose spread was contingent upon a corresponding panzootic of its rodent hosts.[156] This is one reason why a number of historians and some scientists doubted that the Black Death could have been *Y. pestis*, a diagnosis now, however, confirmed by analysis of aDNA.[157] A switch of vector from rodent to human ectoparasites would go some way towards explaining the discrepancy.[158]

---

[153] Christakos and others (2005), 249, 259, 278.

[154] Walsham had a pre-plague population of about 1,500. The first plague deaths probably occurred in late March and the last in mid-July 1349. The traumatic events of these months are imaginatively reconstructed in Hatcher (2008). See also Ziegler's reconstruction of the impact of the Black Death upon the fictional village of 'Blakwater': Ziegler (1969), 202–23.

[155] Bossak and Welford (2010). For contemporary miasmatic diagnoses of the Black Death see Horrox (1994), 158–86. Potato blight, a vampire fungus, brought to Ireland from Belgium in September 1845 by an unusual easterly air-stream, is a good example of an airborne infection.

[156] Scott and Duncan (2005); Cohn (2008), 79–81; Welford and Bossak (2010a).

[157] Scott and Duncan (2001), 356–62, list the problems posed by conventional diagnoses of the Black Death as *Y. pestis*; also, Cohn (2008), 77–88. Scientists Sharon DeWitte and James W. Wood both doubted that plague could have been *Y. pestis* until convincing aDNA evidence was forthcoming: Schuenemann and others (2011), E751.

[158] Above, Sections 3.03.2a and 3.03.2b and Figure 3.27.

Contemporary accounts leave no doubt of the devastation wrought by the Black Death. To eyewitness Gabriel de Mussis, its mass mortality represented divine retribution for the manifold sins of society. He describes death and bitterness everywhere, cities and towns left partially depopulated, and the mass funerals and communal grave pits resorted to in order to dispose of the multitudes of dead.[159] Giovanni Boccaccio estimated that in Florence alone this 'lethal catastrophe' may have killed 'over 100,000'.[160] In Avignon, one observer believed that at least half the population perished, mainly because 'when one member of a family dies, almost all the rest follow'.[161] Writing at the monastery of St Giles of Tournai in Flanders, Abbot Gilles li Muisis reported that 'in 1347 the mortality grew strong in Rome, the Romagna, Sicily, Tuscany, Italy, Gascony, Spain and various other countries, at last entering France in 1348'.[162] On his reckoning 'the mortality was so great that in many places a third of the population died, elsewhere a quarter or a half, and in several areas only one or two people out of ten survived'.[163]

In northern Europe's largest city of Paris, the Great Chronicle of Saint-Denis enumerates a daily death rate of 800, so that in the space of eighteen months 66,000 died in Paris and Saint-Denis.[164] In London, clerk Robert of Avesbury noted that over the ten weeks prior to Easter 1349 'more than 200 corpses were buried almost every day in the new burial ground made next to Smithfield, and this was in addition to the bodies buried in other churchyards in the city', which implies 15–20,000 deaths in the space of less than two months, and those by no means the most deadly of the fifteen months that the contagion raged in the capital.[165] Meanwhile, the chronicle of the Austrian monastery of Neuberg claimed that Vienna and all its territories lost almost two-thirds of their population.[166] To Scottish clerk, John of Fordun of Aberdeen, 'so great a plague has never been heard of from the beginning of the world to the present day, or been recorded in books; for this plague vented its spite so thoroughly that fully a third of the human race was killed'.[167]

Collectively these and other commentators emphasize the deadliness of plague, the swiftness with which the disease ran its course once the first symptoms had appeared, its lack of discrimination with respect to age, gender and class, the speed and ease with which it spread, the futility

---

[159] Horrox (1994), 14–26.   [160] Horrox (1994), 33–4.   [161] Horrox (1994), 43.

[162] Horrox (1994), 46.   [163] Horrox (1994), 49.   [164] Horrox (1994), 58.

[165] Horrox (1994), 65; Christakos and others (2005), 249.   [166] Horrox (1994), 61.

[167] Horrox (1994), 84. For the impact eight hundred years earlier of the First Pandemic of plague see Little (2007).

of flight, and the role of fugitives, mariners and travellers in spreading it. They also convey a powerful impression of the massive scale of its death toll in cities, towns and countryside right across Europe, to as far west as Ireland and north as Scotland and Norway. Constantinople was the first European city to suffer, in spring 1347, and Pskov in Russia one of the last, in spring 1352.[168] If chroniclers' estimates that around a third of the population died of plague are at all reliable, then at least 25 million Europeans are likely to have succumbed to the disease over these six years and maybe far more.[169] Both proportionately and absolutely it therefore probably ranks as the single greatest public health crisis in recorded European history. Nor was it a transitory shock, for plague remained a recurrent feature of European life for the next three hundred years, although the mortality rate of the first wave of plague was never repeated and the disease gradually changed in epidemiological character as maybe, too, did the population's genetic capacity to withstand it.[170]

Staggering as was the death toll during the Black Death, it is worth stressing that over half the population managed to survive this first strike by this most lethal of diseases. Probably a fifth of those stricken recovered and significant numbers were lucky enough to escape exposure to the pathogen and its vectors.[171] Varying residential levels of rodent and flea infestation meant that plague was more effective at spreading *within* than *between* households. Medics and clerics, in the frontline of ministering to the sick in their homes and the dying on their deathbeds, were especially exposed to infected flea vectors and therefore at risk of themselves contracting plague.[172] In contrast, as one commentator remarked, 'amazingly during this plague no king, prince, or ruler of a city died'.[173] In England, Edward III and his immediate family, with the exception of his daughter Princess Joan de la Tour (who died in Bordeaux en route to her wedding to Prince Pedro of Castile), all escaped unscathed.[174] Others spared included England's first great vernacular prose writers, William Langland (born c.1330) and Geoffrey Chaucer (born c.1343).

Although numbers of senior government officials perished (the lord chancellor, three senior clerks of chancery, the royal chamberlain, the king's chamberlain, two king's attorneys, the auditor of the chamber,

---

[168] Benedictow (2004), 61, 69–70, 212–13.
[169] See Table 2.1, for estimates of Europe's pre-Black Death population.
[170] Laayouni and others (2014); Crespo (2014).
[171] '80 per cent of those who contract the disease die from it': Benedictow (2010), 9.
[172] Modern case studies of plague in Africa are shedding some light on the factors that determine exposure to plague at the level of individual households: MacMillan and others (2011); Vogler and others (2011).
[173] Horrox (1994), 35.   [174] Horrox (1994), 250.

the keeper of the wardrobe, and four sheriffs), apart from some temporary suspension of business, the wheels of administration continued to turn.[175] On the hard-hit Winchester estate, Elizabeth Levett famously demonstrated that enough of the rural population outlived the Black Death to fill the vacant tenancies and maintain cultivation of the bishop's demesnes.[176] The same applied on the vast majority of other English estates and manors. It required repeated visitations of the disease, in combination with other factors, before villages were emptied of all their inhabitants and landlords gave up direct management of their demesnes.

Plague may little have respected person, rank or office, but it did not kill indiscriminately. Today, plague is above all a disease of poor people in poor countries and the same applied in the fourteenth century.[177] The more detailed historical evidence available for England indicates that the rich experienced lower mortality than the poor, probably because ecologically they were less directly and regularly exposed to the disease's insect vectors.[178] Thus, it was the poor who lived in the most overcrowded and least sanitary conditions and in closest proximity to plague's vermin hosts and vectors. It is to be expected that their persons, bedding and clothing were particularly heavily infested with ectoparasites. Analysis of skeletal remains from Black Death burials also indicates that the malnourished, physically frail and ageing were disproportionately represented among the dead.[179] Consequently it is no surprise that the death rate of 27 per cent estimated for English male tenants-in-chief of the Crown was among the lowest of any social group.[180] Only bishops, with a death rate of 18 per cent, appear to have escaped more lightly, although high-profile episcopal casualties included two successive archbishops of Canterbury, John de Ufford and Thomas Bradwardine (upon his return from the perilous journey to Avignon).[181] Abbots, in contrast, fared far worse, probably because they lived and worked in close-knit cloistered communities. Their death rate of 42 per cent was much the same as the 44 per cent death rate of monks in twelve of the most important monasteries.[182] At the major

---

[175] Ormrod (1996), 178.   [176] Levett (1916); Robo (1929).

[177] Today 1,000–2,000 cases of plague a year are reported to the World Health Organisation, the bulk of them from sub-Saharan Africa, where poverty remains an acute problem. Madagascar is one of the worst-affected countries: for a detailed case study see Vogler and others (2011).

[178] Monecke and others (2009), 590–1, attribute lower plague mortality in 1613–14 among the richer households of Freiberg in Saxony to better housing conditions and related ecological factors.

[179] DeWitte and Wood (2008).   [180] Russell (1948), 216; Ziegler (1969), 227–30.

[181] Hatcher (1977), 22; Horrox (1994), 71–2, 74, 78.

[182] Russell (1948), 223–5; Ziegler (1969), 228.

Benedictine abbey of St Albans plague thus claimed the lives of the abbot, prior and sub-prior and numbers of monks.[183] High-quality stone-built accommodation, good sanitation and regular and healthy diets evidently counted for naught once the infection's vectors had penetrated shared dormitories, refectories and presbyteries.[184]

Monastic chroniclers such as John Clynn and Henry Knighton naturally stressed the heavy losses sustained by the conventual Orders, thereby conveying the misleading impression that the regular clergy were disproportionately hard hit.[185] Although Russell concedes that in England monastic mortality was 'occasionally very high', overall he reckons that 'the mortality of the monks at large . . . does not seem to have been much more than a fourth on the average'.[186] Instead, it would appear that the secular clergy sustained the heavier losses, since, by entering the homes of the sick and dying to administer Extreme Unction, they were at the forefront of exposure to this vector-transmitted infection.[187] On the evidence of the numbers of parish priests who died and had to be replaced during the epidemic, death rates have been estimated for the beneficed clergy of ten English dioceses ranging from 39 per cent for York to 49 per cent for Exeter, Winchester and Norwich and with an overall mean of 45 per cent.[188] There is good reason to suppose that these mirrored the death rates among the communities they served.

On the four Essex manors of High Easter, Great Waltham, Margaret Roding and Chatham Hall, adult males enrolled in tithings fell by 30–40 per cent as a consequence of the epidemic.[189] On the large Worcestershire manor of Halesowen the death rate of adult male tenants was at least 40 per cent and on the small but crowded Norfolk manor of Hakeford Hall in Coltishall it probably exceeded 55 per cent.[190] Among landless men on the estates of Glastonbury Abbey plague mortality averaged 57 per cent, and J. Z. Titow has estimated that it reached 65 per cent among tenants on the bishop of Winchester's Hampshire manor of Bishops Waltham.[191] Such figures imply that a national death toll of one-third is an

---

[183] Horrox (1994), 252–3; Russell (1948), 223; Harper-Bill (1996), 97.
[184] Harvey (1993), 129–34.
[185] This bias comes across strongly in Henry Knighton's celebrated account, written in the 1390s, of the devastation wrought by plague in and around the papal city of Avignon between January and July 1348 (Knighton was an Augustinian Canon of Leicester): Horrox (1994), 75–80.
[186] Russell (1948), 225–6.
[187] Shrewsbury (1971), 54–119; Harper-Bill (1996), 84–90.
[188] Russell (1948), 221–3.
[189] Poos (1985). I am grateful to Larry Poos for making his raw data available.
[190] Razi (1980), 106–7; Campbell (1984), 96.
[191] Ecclestone (1999), 26; Titow (1969), 69–70.

underestimate. Instead, a death rate of at least 40 per cent is more likely, and the 45 per cent mortality of parish priests may yet prove to be representative of the average scale of losses among their parishioners.[192]

Since England had a pre-plague population of approximately 4.8 million, a mortality rate of 45 per cent would have produced over 2 million excess deaths within the narrow space of twenty months between August 1348 and March 1350.[193] Of these, probably 1 million would have occurred during the three most deadly months of June, July and August 1349 (Figure 4.7), creating enormous logistical problems in administering the expected Christian last rites and then disposing of so many corpses.[194] Recourse eventually was made to mass graves, such as the plague pits recently unearthed at the Royal Mint and East Smithfield sites in London.[195] If the same 40–45 per cent mortality rate were repeated at a European-wide scale it would have produced a colossal 30–36 million excess deaths.[196] Everywhere this unprecedented demographic haemorrhage occurred within a similarly concentrated span of a few months and, significantly, in terms of the epidemiology of the pandemic, in each affected community once the epidemic had spent its force it moved on, neither lingering nor, at least for the time being, recurring.[197]

Agricultural labourers who survived the plague found that their labour was now worth a great deal more, since the work of producing food and organic raw materials continued but there were far fewer workers to undertake it. The immediate 50 per cent hike in the daily real wage rates of English farm workers bears grim testimony to the massive reduction in their numbers relative to the amount of land in agricultural use. It was this wage inflation that the Ordinance of Labourers of 1349 and, then, the Statute of Labourers of 1351 were intended to restrain. Building labourers, in contrast, did not benefit so immediately, for plague brought a temporary or sometimes permanent halt to many construction projects. The slump in construction activity was Europe-wide. In the Tuscan city of Siena the half-completed scheme to add a vast new nave to the cathedral of Santa Maria Assunta was the most conspicuous casualty; today, the unfinished structure stands as Europe's most tangible

---

[192] Broadberry and others (2015), 14–15, estimate an overall population reduction of at least 45 per cent as a result of the first plague outbreak.

[193] For the size of England's pre-plague population see Broadberry and others (2015), 10–22.

[194] For examples see Horrox (1994), 266–74.

[195] Antoine (2008), 101–3; Grainger and others (2008).

[196] For Europe's pre-plague population see Table 2.1 and 60 (n. 70).

[197] Christakos and others (2005), 113; Christakos and others (2007), 717.

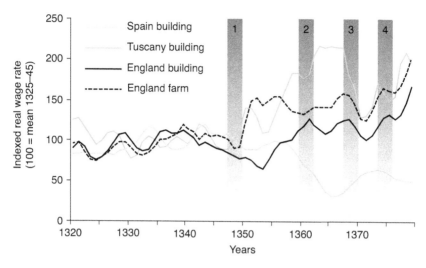

Male labourers' daily real wage rates before and after the Black Death: Spain, Tuscany and England
Numbers = major plague outbreaks (1 = 1348–9; 2 = 1360–2; 3 = 1369; 4 = 1374–5)
Sources: Spain, data supplied by Leandro Prados de la Escosura; Tuscany, Malanima (2012); England, building labourers, Munro (no date); England, farm labourers, Clark (2007b)

monument to the human devastation wrought by the Black Death.[198] In Florence, Giotto's new polychrome campanile fared better; construction was suspended with just two of its projected five stories completed but then resumed after ten years.

Almost everywhere, it took at least half-a-dozen years before demand for building workers began to recover and their daily real wage rates started to improve (Figure 4.11).[199] In this respect, Florentine survivors of the Black Death working in the building trades fared better than their English counterparts, insofar as their daily real wage rates improved sooner. Tuscany was, of course, a richer and more urbanized economy than England, with a larger construction sector, so it is perhaps to be expected that post-plague demand for building labourers should have proved to be more buoyant than in England. It was an altogether different matter in Spain, where the Black Death clearly initiated a major slump in

[198] http://en.wikipedia.org/wiki/Siena_Cathedral. Monuments to later plague epidemics include the Venetian votive churches of Il Redentore and the Bassilica de Santa Maria della Salute, built to mark deliverance from the plague epidemics of 1575/6 and 1630/1.
[199] Munro (2009).

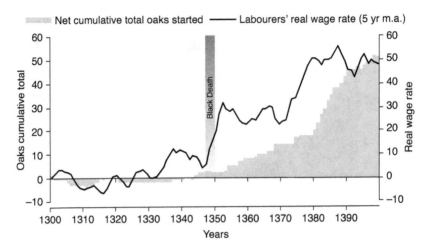

Figure 4.12 Regeneration rates of Irish oaks and English male labourers' daily real wage rates, 1300–1400
Negative numbers of oaks = depletion; positive numbers of oaks = regeneration
Sources: data on Irish oaks start and end dates supplied by M. G. L. Baillie; combined index of English building and farm labourers' daily real wage rates calculated from Munro (no date) and Clark (2007b)

the construction industry so that by the mid-1360s building workers were 50 per cent worse off than they had been before the plague. Irrespective of the precise price response, it is clear that in all three of these economies the Black Death marks a major watershed in the rates at which labour was remunerated (Figure 4.11).

The sudden scaling down of building activity meant that fewer trees were being felled. At the same time, with 30–45 per cent fewer people to feed, the withdrawal of land from cultivation allowed extensive woodland regeneration. This twin boost to tree growth stands out as a clear discontinuity in the European dendrochronological record. In Ireland comparison of the start and end dates of datable oak timbers implies a progressive depletion of woodland down to the 1340s, with many of the trees then being felled exhibiting the narrow rings characteristic of long-lived oaks (Figure 4.12). Then, from the plague decade onward, the number of start dates relative to end dates rises dramatically as the abrupt reduction in population pressure allowed widespread regeneration of woodland. These new young trees display the wide rings typical of their early stage of growth and this mid-fourteenth-century shift from predominantly narrow to wide ring widths is apparent in other European dendrochronologies. In Ireland an acceleration in the rate of regeneration from the 1380s echoes the upturn in English daily real wage rates at the same time as, in the wake of successive plague outbreaks, land use in Ireland and labour markets in England adjusted to significantly lowered population levels (Figure 4.12).

The German oak dendrochronology similarly reveals a conspicuous cessation of new building activity from 1347. Further, when construction recovered at the end of the fifteenth century many of the timbers then felled had begun growing in the immediate aftermath of the Black Death.[200] In Slovakia, too, felling rates declined from the end of the thirteenth century and then slumped in the second quarter of the fourteenth century centring on the Black Death. Thereafter, until c.1500, felling rates remained well below the level of the early fourteenth century and when eventually they rose, in the late fifteenth and the sixteenth centuries, most of the trees being cut were found to have commenced growing within a decade of the plague.[201] Greek dendrochronology reveals a very similar story.[202] Almost everywhere, in fact, the Black Death marks the point where the tide turned and a sustained phase of woodland depletion gave way to one of widespread regeneration.[203] Only a major demographic event with enduring consequences could have brought about such a profound landscape transformation.[204]

4.04   The Black Death's lasting epidemiological legacy

4.04.1   The second plague of 1360–3

After a lull of almost a decade, Biraben's survey of European chronicles shows that, with the conspicuous exception of Iberia, plague returned in a second major European onslaught between 1360 and 1363 (Figure 4.13). In Italy and France there are multiple references to plague in 1360 and 1361, whereas in the British Isles the peak comes in 1361 and 1362. Similarly, Cohn's count of testamentary bequests and wills identifies crisis-related peaks at Besançon (France) and Tournai (Flanders) in 1360, at London (England) in 1361, but, curiously, not until 1363 in six Tuscan and Umbrian cities (Figure 4.13). Milan, however, which appears to have been spared the Black Death, became infected in spring 1361.[205] Ragusa was struck the same year, provoking a ten-fold increase in the number of wills.[206] Although European losses were substantially

---

[200] Baillie (2006), 21–3.   [201] Büntgen and others (2013), 1776.
[202] Baillie (2006), 22–3.   [203] Kaplan and others (2009), 3023.
[204] Lagerås (2006), 77–92, provides an analysis of post-Black Death vegetation change in southern Sweden based upon pollen analysis.
[205] Carmichael (2014).   [206] Blažina Tomić and Blažina (2015), 51.

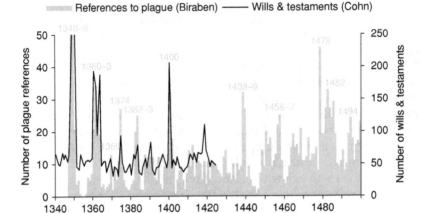

Figure 4.13 Numbers of last testaments and wills in nine cities, 1340–1424, and numbers of contemporary references to plague in Italy, Iberia, France, the Low Countries and British Isles, 1345–1499.

Numbers of last testaments and wills are for six Tuscan and Umbrian cities (Italy), Besançon (France), Tournai (Flanders) and London (England). The off-the-scale values for 1348 and 1349 are, respectively, 134 and 60 (references to plague) and 262 and 538 (testaments and wills). *Sources*: Cohn (2002a), 193, 197, 198, 199; Biraben (1975), 363–74 (I am grateful to Cormac Ó Gráda for sharing these data)

less than those during the Black Death, they were on a sufficient scale to indicate that death rates must have been at least one-third those of 1347–53.[207] Moreover, although adults plainly died in large numbers, contemporaries commented that this pandemic was especially fatal for children. This, however, probably reflects an age distribution in which those born during the fertility boom of the preceding plague-free decade, and all still aged ten or less, constituted a particularly prominent and vulnerable cohort.[208] Because they represented the next generation, their

---

[207] Nightingale (2005), 46–7, estimates the mortality rate of adult male creditors at 34 per cent in 1349 and 14 per cent in 1362, declining to 10.5 per cent in 1363: the equivalent mortality rate in 1369 was 10 per cent.

[208] Russell (1948), 217, 222, 229, gives death rates of 23 per cent for lay tenants-in-chief of the Crown and 9.4–19.3 per cent for the beneficed clergy; he also quotes contemporaries who described the 'second plague' of 1361 as a *mortalité des enfants*. Cohn (2002a), 212–19, likewise documents a growing bias of plague mortality towards the young. For the pestilence in England see Horrox (1994), 85–8. Benedictow (2010), 218–35, believes that the death of so many children had more to do with the youthful age structure of the population than any acquisition of immunity by those who had survived the Black Death.

deaths sapped the population's ability to reproduce itself.[209] Overall, when deaths of all age groups are taken into account, this probably ranks as the second greatest mortality crisis of the later Middle Ages, worse even than the Great Famine of 1315–22.[210] Nevertheless, it is one of the least studied and understood.[211]

Shrewsbury, who was in no doubt that the 1348–9 epidemic in Britain was bubonic plague (compounded, perhaps, by typhus), was less convinced that the 1361–2 epidemic (to which he devotes considerable attention) was the same disease.[212] In his view, 'contemporary references to this pestilence provide no justification for its identification as an outbreak of bubonic plague'.[213] Instead, he suggests that several distinct diseases may have been active, including smallpox, influenza and maybe diphtheria. A widespread presumption nonetheless prevails that this was a return visitation by the same disease that had killed with such ferocity a dozen years earlier.[214] What is lacking is clinching aDNA evidence from burials directly attributable to this event that would establish whether *Y. pestis* was the pathogen wholly or partially responsible for the heavy mortality and, if so, whether the strain of the genome was identical with, or a mutation of, those responsible for the Black Death itself.[215] If, as seems most likely, it was plague, whence it came is a puzzle. Maybe, it emerged from a reservoir of enzootic infection temporarily established among commensal or more probably sylvatic rodents somewhere in Europe during the Black Death?[216] Alternatively, and more likely, it may have been reintroduced from western or central Asia to a Europe temporarily free of *Y. pestis*.[217] This would be consistent with the claim of an anonymous chronicler that the plague that devastated Ragusa had originated in Alexandria, pivot of the Indian spice trade.[218] Until its origins and routes of dissemination have been tracked, greater certainty is not possible.

In the case of England, it looks as though the pestilence may have broken out first in London, the city with the most extensive overseas

---

[209] Razi (1980), 134–5, 150–1: at Halesowen 'the population of the parish was overwhelmed at the end of the fourteenth century by the middle-aged and elderly and was doomed to a long period of stagnation and decline' (p. 151).

[210] Cohn (2002a), 191–203; Hatcher (1977), 26–30, 71.

[211] Specific case studies include Glénisson (1971); Mullan (2007/8).

[212] Shrewsbury (1971), 127–33.   [213] Shrewsbury (1971), 131.

[214] Hatcher (1977), 21–6; Bolton (1980), 59–63; Horrox (1994), 11–14; Aberth (2001), 128–9; Cohn (2002a), 188–209; Nightingale (2005), 47–8; Benedictow (2010), 222–4.

[215] Haensch and others (2010) offer no results specifically dated to the 1360–3 pandemic. Tran and others (2011) identify evidence of *Y. pestis* in two fourteenth-century Venetian skeletons, neither of which is dated more precisely.

[216] Carmichael (2014).   [217] Schmid and others (2015).

[218] Blažina Tomić and Blažina (2015), 51, 278.

connections and at the nerve-centre of the nation's commerce. Here, once again, several senior government officials died.[219] Over the course of 1361 and into 1362 plague then spread to most other parts of the country, where its victims included senior prelates, a number of sheriffs and escheators, 24 per cent of the nobility and 23 per cent of tenants-in-chief of the Crown.[220] Excess deaths among parish clergy in the diocese of Winchester started to mount from late March 1361, rose steeply to a peak in the summer of that year, continued at a reduced rate during the ensuing autumn and winter and did not finally cease until late summer 1362. Over this period John Mullan estimates that the epidemic may have claimed the lives of 30 per cent of the diocese's parish priests.[221] In contrast, among beneficed clergy in the diocese of York the equivalent death rate was 9–19 per cent, which compares with estimated death rates of 13 and 14 per cent among tenants at Bishops Waltham (Hampshire) and Halesowen (Worcestershire) and 10–14 per cent among adult male Statute Merchant creditors.[222]

At Oakington in Cambridgeshire, the epidemic disrupted normal levels of lending between tenants, while on the extensive southern English estate of the bishops of Winchester a peak in *post mortem* land transfers identifies 1361–2 as a year of serious crisis, the worst of the second half of the fourteenth century.[223] Although a few manors (East Knoyle, Cheriton, Twyford, Warfield, Hambledon, and Waltham St Lawrence) were as badly affected as in 1348–9, at an aggregate estate level mortality was both substantially lower and demographically more selective.[224] Nationally, whatever demographic gains had been made since 1350 were wiped out and, if the Worcestershire manor of Halesowen is representative, age and sex structures were changed in ways that made further recovery more difficult.[225] In its wake, the nominal daily wage rates of adult male agricultural labourers, which had been drifting downwards, made a cumulative 12 per cent gain (Figure 4.14).

4.04.2   Later plague outbreaks

Plague returned to much of Europe in 1369, 1374–5 and 1382–3 (Figures 4.13 and 4.14). The pope's personal doctor, Raymundus Chalmelli de Vinario, believed these to be successive strikes by the same

[219] Horrox (1994), 85–7; Mullan (2007/8), 3–4; Ormrod (1996), 178.
[220] Russell (1948), 217, 224; McFarlane (1973), 168–71; Ormrod (1996), 180.
[221] Mullan (2007/8), 14–16.
[222] Russell (1948), 222; Titow (1969) 70; Razi (1980), 126–7; Nightingale (2005), 47.
[223] Briggs (2009), 198–9; Mullan (2007/8), 17.   [224] Mullan (2007/8), 17–22, 27.
[225] Razi (1980), 134–5, 150–1.

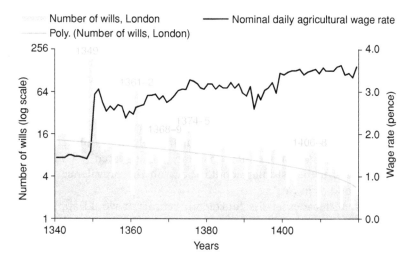

Figure 4.14 Nominal daily wage rates of male agricultural labourers and numbers of wills proved in the London Court of Hustings, 1340–1419
Note: the trendline of numbers of wills is a second-order polynomial, calculated with the values for 1348 and 1349 omitted.
Sources: Clark (2009); Clark (2007b); Cohn (2002a), 197

disease and the aDNA evidence from Saint-Laurent-de-la-Cabrerisse in southern France may possibly incriminate the Black Death strain of *Y. pestis* in the 1374–5 pandemic.[226] Intriguingly, according to historical evidence assembled by both Cohn and Nightingale, morbidity and mortality declined with each successive strike, a development which Cohn attributes to the acquisition by survivors of immunity (Figures 4.13 and 4.14).[227] This claim is not uncontroversial, for it has been doubted whether exposure to plague could confer more than temporary immunity upon survivors.[228] This is one of a number of aspects of the pandemics that await closer investigation, together with the possibility that, for whatever reason, a minority of the population may have possessed natural immunity to the plague bacillus, enabling them to survive unscathed.[229]

One possible effect of repeated and selective plague outbreaks may have been to enhance the proportion of the population possessing such a genetic predisposition to immunity. The hypothesis 'that plague had

---

[226] Cited in Cohn (2002a), 85; Haensch and others (2010).
[227] Cohn (2008), 85–7; Nightingale (2005), 48.
[228] Walløe (2008), 67–8; Benedictow (2010), 212–17.   [229] Walløe (2008), 68.

major evolutionary effects on the immune system of European populations' is consequently now on the research agenda of biologists.[230] Alternatively, the death tolls from successive plague strikes may have fallen because populations were becoming more adept at evading infection. Improved housing standards are likely to have rendered domestic ecological conditions less favourable to rats and thereby lowered human exposure to plague's flea vectors. A further possibility considered by Monecke and others is that 'the catastrophic epidemics of the fourteenth century would have been replaced by comparatively small outbreaks once a naturally immunised subpopulation of rats had appeared'.[231] They recommend that 'further studies should focus on the prevalence of anti-*Yersinia* antibodies in rats'.

By the final decades of the fourteenth century it would appear that the intervals between pan-continental plague pandemics were lengthening. From Biraben's survey of contemporary chronicles it is clear that there were still many recorded plague outbreaks (Figure 4.13), but geographically the extent of each was more circumscribed. It looks very much as though plague was now maintaining itself by circulating between towns and villages within Europe and was only occasionally reinforced by reintroductions of the disease from central Asia, as, for instance, in 1408/9.[232] When outbreaks of human plague occurred they now did so as zoonotics accompanying mostly localized epizootics and panzootics.[233] It cannot yet be ruled out that plague may have gone to ground among rodent communities in Europe's greatest port towns and cities, as, by the late sixteenth century, seems to have become the case of London.[234] Alternatively, given that plague's natural reservoirs are almost invariably rural and remote, it is reasonable to hypothesize that plague may have became enzootic among European counterparts of Asian gerbils and marmots and North American prairie dogs. Intriguingly, Ann G. Carmichael has shown that in the case of sixteenth-century Milan, plague typically spread from the countryside to the city, and not vice versa. Further, she has linked the persistence of plague in Europe to possible establishment of semi-permanent reservoirs of *Y. pestis* among ground-burrowing Alpine marmots.[235] This is also a valuable reminder that plague in

[230] Laayouni and others (2014).   [231] Monecke and others (2009), 591.

[232] Schmid and others (2015).

[233] Nightingale (2005), 48: by the end of the fourteenth century 'plague was already assuming the characteristic it had in the sixteenth century of spreading slowly along the lines of communication from town to town, and region to region, with different rates of mortality in each'.

[234] Cummins and others (2013).

[235] Carmichael (2014). Schmid and others (2015) are sceptical that reservoirs of plague ever became established in Europe.

fifteenth- and sixteenth-century Europe was less exclusively urban than it has often been represented. During these most chilly of centuries, it is also likely that plague increasingly operated in conjunction with other infections in what, epidemiologically, was clearly a remarkably unhealthy age.[236]

4.05 The Black Death: an enigma resolved?

The Black Death stands out in popular memory as a frightening demonstration of the prodigies of destruction that can result when a lethal disease is introduced to a biologically naïve and medically unprotected human population. It struck at a time of population pressure, relative resource scarcity, low living standards, economic difficulty, and burgeoning warfare on many fronts. Smithian growth may effectively have ceased and to some degree gone into reverse but the commercial infrastructure necessary for the pathogen's rapid and wide geographical diffusion remained intact and fully operational. The demographic catastrophe nonetheless owed more to ecological than to economic circumstances. The economic situation that it relieved may have been intrinsically Malthusian but in origin and character the Black Death was a crisis not of subsistence but of health.

The weight of available historical evidence leaves little doubt that in the Old World the Black Death constituted the single greatest public health crisis of the second millennium, with the second plague of 1360–3 a close runner-up. In fact, it was the latter and its successor plague outbreaks that were responsible for aborting the incipient post 1347–53 Malthusian recovery and for transforming age structures in ways that made full inter-generational replacement impossible. Notwithstanding Shrewsbury's efforts to play down the scale of plague mortality, there is now a clear consensus that at least a third of Europeans perished in the first wave of plague between 1347 and 1353 and in the worst-hit cities, regions and countries this proportion very likely exceeded 40 per cent.[237] By the end of the fourteenth century successive waves of plague had resulted in a net halving of Europe's population. Nor did the population begin to recover until the final quarter of the fifteenth century, intriguingly doing so a full two centuries before plague itself finally disappeared.

Such a momentous and terrible historical event has naturally generated great interest, debate and research. Meanwhile, current concern about

---

[236] Hatcher (2003), 95–9; Hatcher and others (2006); Nightingale (2005).
[237] Shrewsbury (1971).

the rising death toll from *Y. pestis* in some of the poorest countries of the world, especially in sub-Saharan Africa, has sparked fears that plague is re-emerging as an infectious disease and may prove increasingly difficult to contain if the antibiotics used to combat it lose their effectiveness.[238] The possible effects of global climate change upon the pathogen, its hosts and vectors are an added source of anxiety.[239] Curiosity about plague's three historical pandemics coupled with worries about the dangers still posed by the disease have consequently stimulated much fresh scientific research into the biology of the pathogen, the entomology of its vectors, zoology of its mammalian hosts, ecology of its reservoirs and the respective effects of climatic conditions upon each. New knowledge about plague in both the present and the past has consequently grown fast and is extending and qualifying an older body of medical and biological knowledge obtained from close observation and analysis of the Third Pandemic.[240] These scientific advances have shed fresh light on the Second Pandemic, enabled some old issues to be laid to rest and opened up several new historical lines of enquiry especially respecting the history of the plague in Asia.

By far the most important scientific result to date has been demonstration that individuals interred in fourteenth-century plague cemeteries in Italy, France, England and the Netherlands were infected with *Y. pestis*. Whereas the first aDNA results to demonstrate this were received with scepticism, those now available have been obtained by different laboratories and teams of researchers in accordance with the most rigorous scientific procedures. This effectively resolves the at times heated debate about the causative agent of the Black Death. It does not mean that *Y. pestis* was responsible for *all* deaths during the Black Death but it establishes beyond reasonable doubt that plague was present and a cause of death at all sites where aDNA analysis has so far been undertaken. The task now is to amplify these results, since they are representative neither of Europe as a whole nor of all waves of plague. Evidence is so far lacking from those regions and places where plague first struck in 1346–7, notably the Crimea, Constantinople, the Aegean and Sicily (plus, of course, Asia Minor, Egypt and the Middle East). The want of aDNA results for the Second Plague of 1360–3 is also a conspicuous lacuna. Without them this sequel mortality crisis cannot be confirmed as plague, nor can it be established whether, if plague, it was the

---

[238] Galimand and others (1997); Gratz (1999); Anker and Schaaf (2000). For reaction to a plague death on 16 July 2014 in one of the disease's core reservoir regions in northwest China see http://www.bbc.com/news/world-asia-china-28437338.

[239] Patz and others (2005); Semenza and Menne (2009).

[240] Eisen and others (2015).

same strain as that which had killed on an even greater scale in 1347–53. Only with fuller genetic information will it be possible to resolve whether within Europe each wave of plague represented a fresh invasion and, if so, whence it came, or whether by the fifteenth century plague persisted largely by circulating between ports, cities, towns and villages.[241]

Decoding the *Y. pestis* genome has been fundamental to identifying these historical strains of plague and locating them on the *Y. pestis* phylogenetic tree (Figure 3.28). Since plague's various lineages evolved sequentially and most variant strains emerged in geographically specific contexts, the plague genome embodies its own evolutionary history and pattern of spread. The position in the genome of historically specific strains of *Y. pestis* retrieved from the aDNA of burials securely dated from historical and/or archaeological evidence (including radiocarbon) has enabled absolute dates to be attributed to the emergence of specific strains and development of key polytomies. Fresh lineages or polytomies emerged unevenly and were particularly prone to occur during major plague epizootics and panzootics, as was the case immediately prior to the Black Death, whose outbreak in the West was preceded by development of several new polytomies (Figure 3.28). Further amplification and refinement of the *Y. pestis* phylogenetic tree has resulted from gathering and analysis of additional genome data for China and it is to be expected that more work along these lines will contribute additional detail. Careful sifting of aDNA from European plague burials, for instance, should reveal whether a distinctively European sub-branch of *Y. pestis* developed between the arrival of plague in the mid-fourteenth century and its disappearance in the second half of the seventeenth century (as ought to have occurred if independent reservoirs of enzootic plague did, indeed, become established in Europe). Fuller information for central, western and South Asia would also help clarify the land and sea routes by which plague spread west across Eurasia. At present these remain a matter of conjecture.

From phylogenetic analysis of *Y. pestis* it is now clear that the disease's genetic diversity is relatively low and that most strains of plague (the exception is 0.PE4C) are capable of infecting and killing humans. There has been speculation that the uniquely heavy death toll of the Black Death, unmatched at national and continental levels in any subsequent plague outbreaks, was the result of an exceptionally lethal strain of the bacterium. However, this is not borne out by the genetic evidence, according to which the Black Death strains of *Y. pestis* were no more or

[241] Schmid and others (2015).

less dangerous than others.[242] Nor were they lineally related to the now extinct strain identified in two sixth-century burials from the cemetery at Aschheim in Bavaria. In the case of the First Pandemic, 'genotyping results confirm that the *Y. pestis* strain from the Aschheim victim is more basal on the global phylogeny than the *Y. pestis* populations that caused the Black Death and the Third Pandemic'.[243] The First and Second Pandemics therefore arose from independent crossovers of the pathogen from animals to humans and the long period of quiescence which separated the end of the First from the start of the Second Pandemic coincided almost exactly with the MCA.

Contrary to those historians who have argued for an African origin of the First Pandemic and western Asian origin for the Second Pandemic, the phylogenetic evidence strongly implies that both pandemics were caused by *Y. pestis* strains that originated in Asia and, most probably, in western China. The semi-arid northeast Tibetan–Qinghai Plateau emerges as the probable core region from which emerged the strains of *Y. pestis* responsible for the Black Death. Whereas little unambiguous evidence has so far been identified in Chinese records to suggest that the Black Death ever occurred there, Cui and others (2013) believe that the genetic evidence points to 'historically undocumented epidemics in China'. There is now a clear need to reassess the historical evidence in the light of these important inferences advanced by the biologists.[244] Likewise, more detailed genetic mapping is needed to establish the route(s) by which *Y. pestis* either surmounted or circumvented the formidable ecological barrier presented by the Kunlun Mountain Chain and travelled west from the Tibetan–Qinghai Plateau to the Caspian Basin.

The biological evidence confirms that the Black Death was not anthrax, a haemorrhagic fever, a deadly but now extinct virus, or biological fallout from a comet. It was a bacterial infection of small mammals, mostly transmitted by insect vectors, which had spilled over and, as a zoonotic, infected humans. Today, plague can be effectively treated with antibiotics but in the Middle Ages there was no known remedy and it had a case-fatality rate of around 80 per cent. Nor were the connections between rodents, fleas and human plague explicitly recognized and understood. The breakthrough identifications of the black rat (*Rattus rattus*) as the principal amplifying host of *Y. pestis*, of the flea, *X. cheopis*, as its principal vector, and of blood meals taken by infected fleas (their stomachs

---

[242] Bos and others (2011), 509: 'few changes in known virulence-associated genes have accrued in the organism's 660 years of evolution as a human pathogen'. Cui and others (2013), 579.

[243] Harbeck and others (2013), 2.   [244] Hymes (2014).

blocked with the plague bacillus) as the principal mechanism of transmission, were not made until the early twentieth century, following outbreak of the Third Pandemic. *Y. pestis* transmitted in this way gave rise to bubonic plague with its distinctive swelling and discolouration of the lymph glands, which has almost always been the most common form of plague, responsible for the greatest numbers of plague deaths. Other routes of transmission and types of plague exist but have rarely accounted for more than a minority of fatalities. Pneumonic plague is more lethal and runs its course more swiftly but partly for these reasons was incapable of sustaining the great pandemics.

Transmission by blocked fleas, as expounded by Alexandre Yersin, has become the predominant paradigm and with it the belief that black rats were and remain the primary hosts of *Y. pestis*.[245] In fact, neither provides a complete explanation. It has long been recognized, but often overlooked, that early-phase transmission is an equally influential mechanism of spread.[246] Moreover, plague is highly adaptable and a variety of different ground-burrowing rodents and small mammals can act as its hosts. In Asia it is sylvatic populations of gerbils, marmots, tarbagans and susliks that have served as plague's primary hosts and among which it has existed in an enzootic state for centuries and probably millennia.[247] These sylvatic populations have been able to co-exist with plague, sustaining it without being exterminated by it, although the precise mechanisms by which this has been achieved are imperfectly understood.[248] Among them the disease might flare up and become an epizootic but did not necessarily proceed further than that before subsiding once again.[249] Hunters, trappers and herdsmen who came into contact with these mammals or their insect vectors might be unfortunate enough to contract the infection but in most cases the disease stopped with them.

Biologically naïve commensal rats, in contrast, were significantly less tolerant of plague and initially suffered far higher mortality when exposed. Once they became infected, epizootic plague rapidly escalated and became a panzootic.[250] Fundamental to the great pandemics of the past has therefore been the crossover of infection from sylvatic rodents to commensal rodents, with their lower resistance to the infection and far greater physical proximity to vulnerable human populations. Any analysis of the eruption of these pandemics consequently needs to account for the timing and location of this crucial spillover event. Obviously, once rats became amplifying hosts of the infection human exposure to it was

[245] Royer (2014).   [246] Eisen and others (2015).   [247] Above, Figure 3.27, Stage 1.
[248] Davis and others (2004); Eisen and Gage (2009).
[249] Above, Figure 3.27, Stage 2.   [250] Above, Figure 3.27, Stage 3.

greatly increased and there was a real risk that a panzootic of rats would ignite a concurrent zoonotic of humans.[251] Transportation of infected rats on ships and in cargoes of grain and other commodities also enabled the disease to spread further and faster than was possible solely by processes of contiguous spread among sylvatic rodent populations. This was how plague achieved its respective metastatic leaps from Alexandria to Constantinople in AD 542 and from Kaffa to Constantinople in 1347 and, thence, throughout that imperial city's far-flung maritime dominions. In the process, rats and other rodent species had to adapt and become capable of co-existing with *Y. pestis* without being wiped out. Otherwise colonies of rodents could not have functioned as the enzootic reservoirs of plague that they evidently became for periods at a time. During the worldwide Third Pandemic it was from rats that plague returned to the wild, spreading to various species of sylvatic mammal, such as the prairie dogs and ground squirrels of the southwestern United States, among which plague is now enzootic. It cannot yet be discounted that something like this may have happened in late-medieval Europe.[252]

Numbers of different species of fleas are parasitic upon these sylvatic and commensal host animals. In the plague foci of central and western Asia at least sixteen are capable of transmitting *Y. pestis* but not all with equal efficiency and rarely as effectively as *X. cheopis*.[253] In order to transmit *Y. pestis* in sufficient quantities to cause infection, the hosts from which the fleas take their blood meals need to be experiencing high levels of bacteremia, and the fleas must live long enough for the bacteria to multiply in the numbers required for concentrated transmission.[254] Blocked fleas can achieve this but so, too, can early-phase transmission by unblocked fleas.[255] The scale of the flea burden and rhythm of the flea lifecycle are also fundamental to the ability of fleas to play a key role in maintenance of enzootic transmission cycles and act as bridging vectors between rodent species and between rodents and humans. Fleas are therefore critical to the dynamic of the plague cycle, as well as to the lengths of incubation periods between introduction of infected fleas to a rodent community, eruption of a panzootic among that community, wholesale collapse of rodent numbers, spillover transfer of the infection to humans, collapse of flea populations and end of the outbreak. Fleas of whatever type are strongly influenced by temperature and humidity, which is partly why plague pandemics display such a markedly seasonal profile, increasing in the spring, peaking in high summer and declining

---

[251] Above, Figure 3.27, Stage 4.   [252] Carmichael (2014).
[253] Eisen and Gage (2012), 70–1.   [254] Eisen and Gage (2012), 69.
[255] Eisen and others (2006); Eisen and others (2015).

in the autumn. Fleas also lend themselves to metastatic spread of plague, on the persons and in the clothes and merchandise of humans, as well as perhaps by birds, and are capable of surviving journeys of considerable duration without losing the ability to transmit infection.

Research into plague's vectors is ongoing and Eisen and Gage (2012) believe that 'it is quite likely that the list of plague vectors is considerably longer than what has been described to date, and when early-phase time points are considered, transmission efficiency for some flea species may be higher than initially realized'.[256] Interest particularly attaches to the effectiveness of the human flea (*Pulex irritans*) as a plague vector since its involvement might account for the person-to-person pattern of infection during the initial waves of the Second Pandemic. Evidence in support of *Pulex irritans* as a plague vector is both limited and controversial but this has not prevented significant claims being made of it and the matter is now under active investigation, as is the possibility that the human louse may have been capable of transmitting the bacillus.[257] If a convincing case can be made for human ectoparasites as vectors of plague it would help explain some of the features of the Black Death which misled several historians and some scientists into believing it could not have been *Y. pestis* at all.[258] Certainly, the Marseille plague team have speculated that vector transmission from human to human constituted a fifth stage of the plague cycle, when the disease finally broke loose from an accompanying panzootic and became a full-blown pandemic.[259] As yet, however, this hypothesis remains unverified (and, historically, may prove unverifiable).

The unstoppable momentum of infection acquired by the Black Death was the end product of successive changes of hosts and vectors under conditions of considerable ecological stress. Cui and others (2013) have proposed that the whole process was set in train sometime around or after *c*.1270, coinciding with the end of the MCA and onset of the Wolf Solar Minimum. Possibly the brief but sharp climatic downturn of the mid-1290s was the decisive trigger event. The impact of climate change upon ecological conditions in plague's parched core-reservoir region of the northeast Tibetan–Qinghai Plateau to the east of the 3,000-kilometre wide Kunlun Mountain Chain appears to have been the catalyst that advanced plague from an enzootic to an epizootic state and galvanized its wider geographical dispersal. Seemingly, the minor pluvial episode that prevailed from the 1310s until 1340 lent momentum to the process

---

[256] Eisen and Gage (2012), 72.
[257] Houhamdi and others (2006); Walløe (2008); Piarroux and others (2013); Leulmi and others (2014); Ratovonjato and others (2014); Eisen and others (2015).
[258] Cohn (2002b).   [259] Above, Figure 3.27.

and temporary termination of these conditions in the early 1340s, at a tipping point in global circulation patterns, may have been the shock that caused mass migration of flea vectors from sylvatic to commensal rodents, with the heightened risks this then posed to human populations. Certainly, by 1343 the strains of *Y. pestis* that would become the mother of all future plagues had come into being.[260] By 1346 plague's arrival at Kaffa on the Crimean shore of the Black Sea provided the springboard for its subsequent penetration of the rest of Europe. Here, in 1347, its flea vectors and rodent hosts boarded Genoese galleys, to be spread far and wide via the busy sea-lanes that, even in the midst of commercial recession, linked the medieval commercial world and extended to the furthest reaches of Christendom. From this point, human agency became more material than ever to the Black Death's deadly progress.

Plague struck southern Europe in late 1347 and early 1348 in the wake of abnormally wet weather and serious harvest failures. As Florentine chronicler Giovanni Villani lamented, 'not in a hundred years had there been such a bad harvest of grain and fodder and wine and oil and everything else in this country as there was in this year [1347]...all because of too much rain'.[261] It reached northern Europe in midsummer 1348 just before persistently inclement weather ruined a run of harvests there. These exceptional weather conditions were a manifestation of the heightened climatic instability prevailing at that time right across Eurasia and beyond. In Europe they did not cause plague, except that the humid weather will undoubtedly have stimulated flea reproduction and activity and thereby aided plague's advance, but they greatly exacerbated the misery and social and economic dislocation arising from the biological disaster. They also raise the possibility that plague acted not alone but in combination with epidemic typhus.

Normally a hot-weather disease which thrived on temperatures of around 20°C, progress of *Y. pestis* appears to have been unimpeded by summer temperatures that must have been substantially below this optimum across most of northern Europe throughout the plague years. Quite why this was, along with the precise configuration of the strange weather patterns prevailing at that time, has yet to be teased out. Nor did continuing poor weather throughout the 1350s, 1360s and early 1370s inhibit plague's repeated return; on the contrary, it seems to have encouraged plague. This meant that an entire generation experienced little respite from poor weather, inferior harvests and recurrent bouts of heavy disease mortality with the result that the initial post-Black Death

[260] Bos and others (2011), 509.   [261] Jansen (2009), 22–3.

demographic bounce back did not endure. Instead, naturally heavier infant and child mortality ensured that inter-generational adult replacement rates remained negative, locking populations across Europe into a self-perpetuating downward trajectory. A socio-ecological threshold had been crossed.

Meanwhile, it is entirely possible that the sheer scale of these repeated demographic losses shifted the genetic composition of the survivor population in favour of those with a degree of resistance to *Y. pestis*, so that plague gradually became a disease that eroded rather than devastated populations and one from which Europe's population could eventually recover.[262] If rats, too, were acquiring a degree of resistance, this would also have damped down the human death toll during plague outbreaks and curbed the pathogen's ability to spread.[263] It also became a disease which increasingly acted in concert with other infections, with the breakdowns of nutrition, hygiene and health that accompanied serious harvest failure, and with active warfare. The great tsunamis of infection ceased and a new pattern of European plague epidemics became established, comprising many small ripples and the occasional greater wave, until the disease's final retreat from the continent during the second half of the seventeenth century.[264]

The Black Death constituted a massive and enduring biological shock, the outcome of a unique conjunction of climatic, ecological, biological and human circumstances.[265] Collectively, these transformed a long-dormant enzootic infection of sylvatic rodents, largely confined to Arid Central Asia, into a fast-spreading 'global' pandemic of humans. Analysis of *Y. pestis* aDNA retrieved from Black Death burials suggests that there was little special or unusual about the strains of the bacterium that were being transmitted. Instead, the Second Pandemic owed its many distinctive features to the precise micro and macro ecological conditions prevailing when it arose and the particularly acute environmental, political and military instability and stress then prevailing. In conjunction with ongoing climate change, it initiated a dynamic new biological and demographic era from which there could be no return to the socio-ecological status quo ante. In Europe, although the close association between climate downturns, bad harvests and major plague outbreaks continued, resource scarcity and population pressure ceased to be problems.[266] Epidemiologically, genetically, demographically, economically and in many other ways the Black Death cast a very long shadow. Breakthrough research by biologists is transforming understanding of

[262] Laayouni and others (2014).   [263] Monecke and others (2009), 591.
[264] Alfani (2013).   [265] Above, Figure 1.2.   [266] Below, Figure 5.5.

the disease itself, as that by palaeoclimatologists is of the environmental context within which it arose, and in both cases this is demonstrating that as an event it can only be properly understood within a pan-Eurasian and, to some degree, global context.

4.06   Three in one: the perfect storm

4.06   Three in one: the perfect storm

By the 1340s irreversible changes in the military and political balances of power across Eurasia meant that the prospect of any return to the economic heyday of the commercial revolution had gone for good. In Latin Christendom an era of contraction had dawned characterized by heightened warfare, riskier trade, rising transaction costs, the loss of lucrative overseas markets and commercial privileges, reduced output of many commodities and declining purchasing power. Ricardian growth had effectively stalled and proliferating poverty was stifling any prospects of restarting it. At the same time, the cumulative effects of decades of diminished solar irradiance during the Wolf Solar Minimum were taking their toll: global and northern hemisphere temperatures were depressed and a profound readjustment of atmospheric circulation patterns was under way. As climates entered a less stable phase, environmental instability increased right across Eurasia and the incidence of extreme weather events rose. The counterparts of the sea and river floods and washed out harvests in Europe were the monsoon failures and mega-droughts of China and South Asia and sudden heightening of the annual Nile flood. Experience of these extreme events varied widely but, in one form or another, they spared no part of Eurasia.

It was into this fast-deteriorating political, economic and environmental situation, and out of this very specific ecological context, that plague erupted with explosive force in the early 1340s. The lands of the Kipchak Khanate between the Caspian Basin and the Black Sea and astride the arterial caravan routes that traversed the *Pax Mongolica* appear to have been struck first, whence, in 1345/6, the contagion crossed the River Don and entered Europe. The next year, 1347, aided and abetted by the far-flung maritime connections of the Genoese, it took ship, spread across the Black Sea and penetrated Europe's commercial arteries. Everywhere it sent populations tumbling and initiated a long era of demographic decline and shrinking economic output. Plague changed public health for the worse, altered age structures and depressed reproduction rates. Exposure to the disease changed human behaviour, mentalities and beliefs and conceivably acted as a genetic filter on the survivors. The distinctive institutional responses it elicited shaped labour markets and influenced decisions about household formation for centuries to come.

With far fewer mouths to be fed, cultivation contracted, pasture farming expanded and woodland regenerated.

Although an intrinsically biological event, plague emerged from a specific climatic and ecological context at a tipping point in global atmospheric circulation patterns. Normally a vector-borne bacterial disease of wild rodents, it owed the extent of its geographical diffusion and scale of its human impact to the population densities that had built up, the dense networks of commerce and communications that had developed, and the inter-linked international orbits of exchange that had been created during the preceding plague-free era of growth and efflorescence. Plague therefore acted not in isolation but in combination with an array of mutually reinforcing environmental and human processes, each animated by an internal dynamic of its own.[267] The effect of the latter, over the course of the first half of the fourteenth century, had been to amplify biological developments in a remote, environmentally marginal and thinly peopled region in the heart of Asia and transpose the result over a distance of several thousand kilometres to far more developed European regions supporting large and vulnerable populations. The perfect storm this generated possessed truly transformative force. Europe's already floundering socio-ecological regime was terminally undermined and a long downturn initiated upon whose course war, climate change and disease continued to exercise a powerful influence.

Appendix 4.1 Outbreak of the Justinianic Plague and the weather

The First Pandemic is first recorded in Egypt in AD 541. Although Peter Sarris believes that its ultimate origin may have been somewhere in Africa, the new genomic evidence points to central Asia as the likelier source.[268] By spring AD 542 it had been shipped across the Mediterranean in grain cargoes destined for the imperial capital and teeming metropolis of Constantinople, whence, over the next two years, it was disseminated east to the Levant, south to North Africa, west to Italy, Spain and Gaul, and eventually north to Britain and Ireland.[269] Populations were devastated wherever it went, with far-reaching demographic, social, economic and political consequences that have long been debated.[270] Not until the 760s did this first great pandemic finally burn itself out, disappearing so completely that the strains of *Y. pestis* that caused it have 'no known contemporary representatives' and, consequently, are 'either extinct or

---

[267] Above, Section 1.03 and Figure 1.2.   [268] Wagner and others (2014).
[269] Sarris (2002), 169–70.   [270] Little (2007).

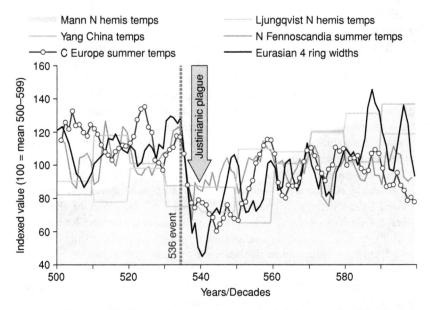

Figure 4.15 The environmental context of the outbreak of the Justinianic Plague in AD 541/2
Sources: annual northern hemisphere temperatures, Mann and others (2008); decadal northern hemisphere temperatures, Ljungqvist (2009); northern Fennoscandian summer temperatures (3-year moving average), Grudd (2010); central Europe summer temperatures (3-year moving average), Büntgen and others (2011); decadal Chinese temperatures, Yang and others (2002); Eurasian Four ring-width chronology (3-year moving average) combines dendrochronologies for European oaks, Fennoscandian pines and Aegean oaks (data supplied by M. G. L. Baillie) with a chronology for Mongolian Siberian pines (Jacoby and others (no date))

unsampled in wild rodent reservoirs'.[271] In fact, plague had retreated to the continental interior of Asia where, for the next five hundred years, it persisted as an enzootic infection among reservoir populations of sylvatic rodents.

David Wagner and the team of twenty-six scientists who reconstructed the Justinianic Plague's genome speculate that its emergence, in terms of the pathogen's vital spillover from rodents to humans, can be linked to climatic instability and its disappearance to the onset of the more settled conditions of the MCA.[272] Baillie has reconstructed the environmental

---

[271] Wagner and others (2014), 322.   [272] Wagner and others (2014), 325.

context of the First Pandemic in some detail.[273] It had been preceded in AD 536 by a well-attested dust-veil event probably caused by a major volcanic eruption, extra-terrestrial impact or cometary outburst. The environmental fall-out from this event resulted in depressed tree growth across Eurasia, so that AD 536 stands out as a pronounced narrow-ring event in most dendrochronologies (Figure 4.15). The following year, however, tree-growth in many regions was back to normal and it was not until AD 539 that the real environmental downturn began, marked by a depression in tree growth of seven years' duration with minimum values in the plague years AD 540–2, when mean ring widths in some chronologies were significantly narrower than in AD 536.[274] Reduced temperatures were clearly to blame and temperature reconstructions for the northern hemisphere, China, central Europe and northern Scandinavia all register a sharp downturn during these years (Figure 4.15). In the European oak chronology these years stand out as one of the most pronounced and prolonged narrow-ring episodes of the last two millennia and the same years show up similarly in several other chronologies from around the northern hemisphere. In short, outbreak of the Justinianic Plague occurred within the context of a pronounced climatic perturbation, with the link between climate and disease provided by the effects of acute ecosystem stress upon pathogen–host–vector relationships in reservoir regions where plague existed as an enzootic.

[273] Baillie (1994); Baillie (2008).   [274] Baillie (2001).

5 Recession

The inhibiting environment and Latin Christendom's
late-medieval demographic and economic contraction

5.01 From a tipping point to a turning point

In the 1340s the perfect storm generated by war, climate change and plague sealed the shift in socio-ecological regime that attained its fullest expression in the middle decades of the fifteenth century.[1] The greatly increased epidemiological burden that was the Black Death's enduring legacy ensured that demographic replacement rates remained negative for the next 100–150 years (Section 5.03.2). Shrinking populations then curbed both the production and consumption of goods and services and set in train far-reaching adjustments to the infrastructure of commercial exchange, to land use and settlement, and to the intensity of resource exploitation (Section 5.04). The environmental implications of these developments were profound. So, too, were those that emanated from continued advance of LIA circulation patterns (Section 5.02.1). With the exception of one brief interlude, during the final quarter of the fourteenth century, societies across Europe had to cope with environmental conditions which were altogether more challenging than those that had prevailed during Latin Christendom's great twelfth- and thirteenth-century efflorescence.[2] These environmental constraints further inhibited demographic and economic reproduction already squeezed hard by commercial recession, bullion scarcity and market contraction.

The first sustained cold episode of the LIA spanned the middle decades of the fifteenth century, during the Spörer Solar Minimum, when global and northern hemisphere temperatures sank to their lowest levels in a thousand years and extreme weather events became increasingly common (Section 5.02.2).[3] Recurrent episodes of weather-induced ecological stress across Eurasia depressed harvests of grain, wool and grapes and drove the flare-ups of plague and other diseases which kept European society demographically in thrall to periodic surges in mortality

---

[1] A *regime shift* may be defined as 'a sudden jump from one dynamic regime to another': Scheffer (2009), 104.

[2] Above, Section 2.02.   [3] Below, Figures 5.1 and 5.2.

(Sections 5.03.1 and 5.03.2).[4] For agricultural producers the deterioration in growing conditions was at its most pronounced between 1453 and 1476.[5] This was when supply-side constraints were tightest and, unsurprisingly, when European populations and the total volume of economic activity were at their lowest ebbs (Sections 5.03.2 and 5.04).

The situation would have been worse had not these difficulties been offset in part by significant improvements in the balance between populations and available resources, which allowed the withdrawal of settlement from environmentally and politically marginal locations, reversed the ruinous trend towards ever-smaller production units, enabled a better ecological balance to be established between the arable and pastoral sectors and shifted factor prices in favour of labour (Section 5.04.2). The climate may have been deteriorating but, with far fewer mouths to be fed, food security and standards of nutrition improved and, for a time, the real incomes of many households rose and income distributions became more egalitarian. It helped that the sudden shrinkage of population reflated money supplies per head and postponed the worst effects of falling European silver output until the fifteenth century. The second half of the fourteenth century, consequently, was characterized by a brief economic boom (Section 5.05). While populations continued to erode there was, however, scant prospect of this fructifying into a self-sustaining process of growth since without expanding market demand there was limited scope for achieving significant productivity gains through a greater division of labour. The want of any real economic vitality is reflected in urbanization ratios which, in all but a few exceptional regions, remained stubbornly at or slightly below their pre-Black Death levels (Section 5.04.3). With only half its pre-plague population, Europe, in fact, was left with excess urban capacity, with the result that most towns were caught up in a competitive survival of the fittest, which left many diminished in population, narrowed in function and downgraded in status. The prosperity that sprang from the improved balance between population and resources was therefore decidedly limited in duration and qualified in the benefits that it bestowed.

Latin Christendom's internal divisions remained as pronounced as ever. While state power remained weak and fragmented it was difficult to achieve greater market coordination and lower transaction costs.[6] Nor did the Latin Church any longer command the over-arching authority and respect it had possessed at the height of the twelfth-century reform movement.[7] On the contrary, long-running disputes between the pope

[4] Below, Figure 5.5.   [5] Below, Figure 5.13.
[6] Epstein (2000a), 38–72.   [7] Above, Section 2.04.1.

and the Holy Roman Emperor, the Western Schism between 1378 and 1417, and influential criticisms levelled at the Church by reformers John Wycliffe and Jan Hus were seriously detrimental to the the Latin Church's standing. Indeed, religious conflicts and heretical movements were one source of the endemic warfare that continued to consume resources and disrupt trade and commerce across Europe. Bandits on land and pirates and slave raiders at sea all flourished for want of strong public authority and imposed burdensome costs of self-defence and protection upon those who engaged in long-distance trade.

As if these internal difficulties were not bad enough, the orbit of Mediterranean commerce was significantly curtailed by the Mamluks' consolidation of their power base in North Africa and the Middle East and by Ottoman conquests in Asia Minor and the Balkans, culminating in the fall of Constantinople in 1453 and of Trebizond in 1461 (Section 5.06). Byzantine defeat effectively ousted the Genoese from the Black Sea and left the Venetian–Alexandrian axis as almost the sole remaining conduit by which Indian spices and Oriental silks and ceramics reached European markets. These continued to be paid for in the main by the export of precious metals, whose value, when combined with losses from wear-and-tear on the coinage, now exceeded that of the output from those European silver mines still in production. In the most cash-strapped economies processes of de-monetization were set in train, as, for want of hard money, established multilateral patterns of exchange became difficult to sustain. In effect, bullion famine, at its worst from c.1395 to c.1415 and 1457–64, locked Europe into a state of commercial recession from which only the most enterprising or commercially aggressive economies, notably the Portuguese and Northern Low Countries, were able to escape.

Socio-ecological conditions were at their most straitened in the middle decades of the fifteenth century. That was when growing conditions were at their most depressed, serious back-to-back harvest shortfalls returned large parts of Europe to the brink of famine, plague and other as yet poorly diagnosed diseases were resurgent, the effects of generations of population decline were at their most pronounced, mints were going out of production everywhere, markets were slack and long-distance trade faced increasing obstacles (Section 5.04.4). Thereafter, many of these constraints gradually eased. Solar irradiance strengthened, temperatures edged upwards, mortality subsided, populations began fitfully to recover, the tempo of the Portuguese, Brabantine and Dutch economies quickened, and renewed efforts were made to explore the Atlantic and to profit from its islands, fishing grounds and alternative sea routes. Blocked from getting to India and the Orient by heading east, the most promising option available to the West was to investigate whether Africa could be circumnavigated (Section 5.06). Advances in ship design and navigation, coupled with the accumulated experience of coping with the Atlantic's challenging sailing conditions (begun when the Genoese opened their sea route to Bruges in 1277), now made this a realistic prospect.

The final quarter of the fifteenth century therefore marks the turning point, when the Great Transition finally came to an end and a resurgent western Europe embarked upon a new sustained phase of expansion and growth in a world enlarged, reorientated and commercially reinvigorated by the European voyages of discovery. One socio-ecological dynamic had spent its force and another was gathering momentum. Over the centuries that had elapsed since Latin Christendom's twelfth-century efflorescence, knowledge had accumulated, technology had advanced, an array of useful macro and micro institutions had been put in place, and in modest but significant ways numbers of European economies had become richer.[8] The leading protagonists in this new socio-ecological age therefore began their recovery from a higher base. Portugal, the Northern Low Countries and England had all narrowed the economic lead long held by Italy, which, as the sixteenth century opened, Brabant and Holland were poised to overtake. The focus of European dynamism was in the process of shifting from Italy and the Mediterranean to the thrusting economies on the shores of the Atlantic and North Sea, further removed from the looming threat of the Ottomans and better suited and placed to exploit the new opportunities of the age. The autonomous economies of Brabant and Holland in the Northern Low Countries seized the initiative and led the reintegration of Eurasian commerce, in which, in contrast to the situation in the eleventh and twelfth centuries, European states and merchants now played a more dominant role.

5.02   Advance of the Little Ice Age (LIA)

5.02.1   The reconfiguration of atmospheric circulation patterns

Between the 1270s and 1340s the Medieval Climate Anomaly came to an end. Thereafter, as global temperatures cooled, the ENSO, the Asian monsoon and the NAO all weakened, and long-established patterns of atmospheric circulation were profoundly reconfigured. This new climate era has become known as the Little Ice Age because in polar and alpine regions heavy snow accumulation during bouts of intense winter cold fed the expansion of sea ice and advance of glaciers.[9] Sustained reductions

---

[8] Below, Figure 5.14B.   [9] Grove (1988); Grove (2004).

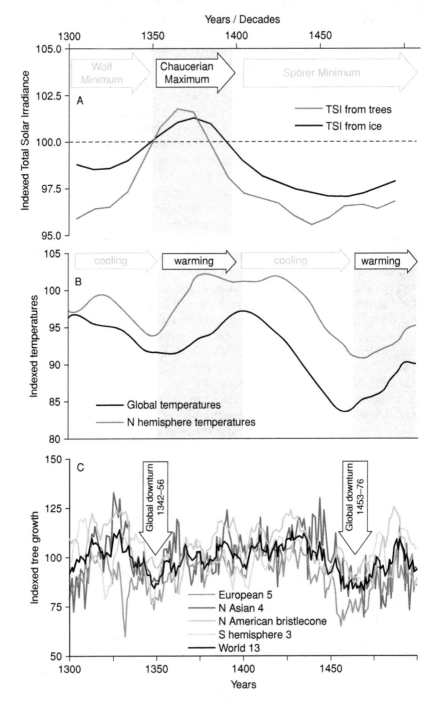

Figure 5.1 (A) Total Solar Irradiance, (B) global and northern hemisphere temperatures and (C) world tree growth, 1300–1500
Sources and notes: (A) Delaygue and Bard (2010b); Vieira and others (2011). (B) Loehle and McCulloch (2008); Mann and others (2008).

in solar irradiance helped set these developments in train, first during the Wolf Solar Minimum of *c*.1282 to *c*.1342 and then during the extended Spörer Solar Minimum of *c*.1416 to *c*.1534 (Figures 5.1A and 5.1B). A brief Solar Maximum, at its most pronounced in the 1370s and 1380s (at the very time that Chaucer's fictional band of pilgrims set out for Canterbury), occupied the fifty-year interval between these two minima and temporarily restored irradiance to the elevated levels of the MCA. Within a further sixty to seventy years, however, prevailing levels of solar irradiance and concurrent global temperatures had sunk lower than at any time in the previous 1,500 years.[10] As a result, corresponding patterns of air pressure, wind direction and force, precipitation and temperature at this initial nadir of LIA cold in the 1450s were profoundly different from those that had characterized the final resurgent phase of the MCA during the 1250s.[11]

Whereas the MCA had sustained relatively settled patterns of atmospheric circulation, one of the most striking features of LIA climates was their instability, with marked annual variations in temperature and precipitation. Societies, as a result, had to cope with far greater environmental uncertainty at a time when they were also contending with heightened biological risks from plague and other diseases. Synergies plainly existed between climate and disease which help to account for the recurrent bouts of high morbidity and mortality which sapped post-Black Death populations of their capacity for recovery until this long episode of climatic adversity was past its worst. Eventually, from the 1460s and 1470s, output of solar irradiance began slowly to increase once again (Figure 5.1A). It increased further from the 1530s, but so great had been the damping of solar activity during the Spörer Minimum that it

---

Figure 5.1 (*cont.*) (C) European 5 = European oaks, Fennoscandian pines and Polar Urals pines, Aegean junipers and oaks (data supplied by M. G. L. Baillie), plus Alpine conifers (Büntgen and others 2011). North Asian 4 = Tien Shan junipers (data supplied by Jan Esper), Qinghai junipers (Yang and others (2014)), Mongolian Siberian larch (Jacoby and others (no date)), plus Siberian Siberian larch (data supplied by M. G. L. Baillie). North American bristlecone pine (data supplied by M. G. L. Baillie). Southern hemisphere 3 = Chilean and Argentinian *Fitzroya*, New Zealand cedars and Tasmanian Huon pine (data supplied by M. G. L. Baillie). All chronologies are indexed on 1250–9 and the dendrochronologies are standardized to have the same coefficient of variation.

[10] Figures 2.2 and 2.9.   [11] Above, Section 2.02.

was not until the opening decades of the seventeenth century that irradiance was back to the peak levels of the 1370s and 1380s. Intriguingly, demographic recovery followed the upturn in irradiance levels.

Because the oceans act as stores and sinks of heat, trends in global and northern hemisphere temperatures tended to follow the varying output of solar irradiance but with a lag, often of several decades (Figure 5.1B). Thus, global cooling was at its most intense in the 1340s and 1350s, some time after output of solar irradiance had begun to revive. At this time northern hemisphere temperatures plunged to their lowest level in over a thousand years.[12] Together, diminished irradiance and reduced temperatures depressed tree growth almost everywhere, with composite dendrochronologies for northern Asia, Europe and the New World all well below trend from 1342 to 1356 and a minimum mean value at 1348 (Figure 5.1C). Coincidentally, there is evidence of severe cold in Greenland, which seems to have triggered a re-expansion of sea ice around Iceland.[13] Meanwhile, the Asian monsoon, which had been weakening since the 1280s, continued to diminish in strength and in the 1350s failed for several years in succession, with calamitous consequences for all those regions reliant upon the monsoon for the bulk of their precipitation.[14] Not in five centuries had there been drought of such severity and persistence. In Europe, in contrast, it was sunshine and warmth that were in short supply.

Across Europe, summer temperatures reconstructed from dendrochronology sank to a historic low during the years 1348–53, with 1349 the coldest summer of all (Figure 5.2B). In England inclement weather exacerbated by heavy plague-induced mortalities of agricultural workers and managers ensured that the grain harvests of 1349–51 were outright failures and the only major double back-to-back shortfall on medieval record.[15] Nor did grain yields soon recover, for weather conditions remained persistently unfavourable, with plague and heavy mortalities of workers and managers recurrent, for the next twenty-five years.[16] By the 1360s solar irradiance may have been strongly resurgent and global and northern hemisphere temperatures both rising

---

[12] Figure 2.2.   [13] Figure 3.22; Dawson and others (2007).
[14] Figure 2.8C. Brook (2010), 59, 68; Lieberman and Buckley (2012), 1052, 1057–8, 1073–4, 1078; Tana (2014), 333–5. 'Proxy reconstructions of precipitation from central India, north-central China, and southern Vietnam reveal a series of monsoon droughts during the mid-14th–15th centuries that each lasted for several years to decades. These monsoon *megadroughts* have no analog during the instrumental period': Sinha and others (2011), 47.
[15] Campbell (2011a), 144–7; Campbell and Ó Gráda (2011), 869.
[16] Campbell (2011a), 147–9; Hatcher (1977), 21–6; Baillie (2006), 36–7.

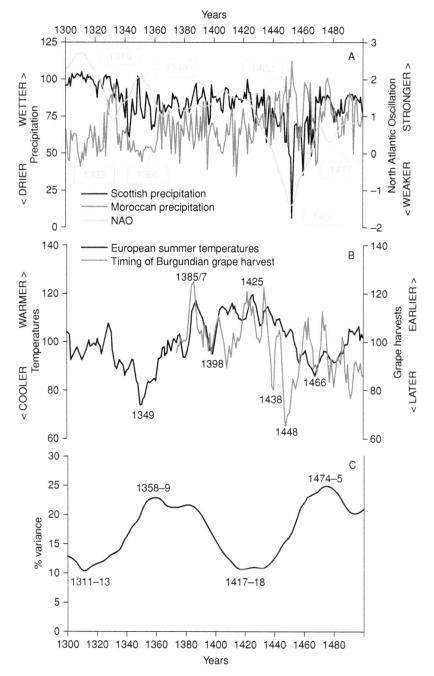

Figure 5.2 (A) The North Atlantic Oscillation, (B) European summer temperatures and (C) an index of environmental instability in Britain, 1300–1500

(Figures 5.1A and 5.1B), but in Europe arctic winters still occurred, most notably in 1363–4, and in the Swiss Alps glaciers maintained their advance.[17] In fact, it was in the 1370s that Icelandic sea ice attained its maximum fourteenth-century extent, accompanied by a succession of high-amplitude cooling events in North Atlantic sea-surface temperatures.[18] These harsh and unsettled weather conditions proved agriculturally challenging for societies across this broad region, still adjusting to the economic impact of heavy plague mortality.[19]

It took twenty to thirty years for the rising output of solar irradiance to make itself felt. Eventually, from 1366, the NAO became less volatile and stabilized at a moderately positive level, well below that of the 1250s but nonetheless gradually gaining in strength until 1405 (Figure 5.2A). In 1366 world tree growth had briefly turned positive in all thirteen master chronologies, as it would do again in the ten northern hemisphere chronologies in 1384 and 1387 (Figure 5.1C). The 1385 Burgundian grape harvest stands out as the earliest on medieval record and two years later European summer temperatures, which had been rising more-or-less continuously since 1350, attained their fourteenth-century peak (Figure 5.2B).[20] Meanwhile, severe winters virtually ceased, high-amplitude cooling events in the North Atlantic died out, Icelandic sea ice shrank and Alpine glaciers contracted.[21]

As climatic conditions ameliorated, year-on-year temperature variations in Greenland, northern Sweden, central Europe and the northern hemisphere diminished, as did the statistical variance of North Atlantic sea-surface temperatures, British Isles oak ring widths, English grain

---

Figure 5.2 (cont.) Sources and notes: (A) Proctor and others (2002b); Esper and others (2009); Trouet and others (2009b): Scottish and Moroccan precipitation are indexed on 1250–9. (B) European annual summer temperatures = mean of northern Fennoscandia, Grudd (2010); Netherlands, Engelen and others (2001); central Europe, Büntgen and others (2011); and eastern Europe, Büntgen and others (2013); all series are indexed on 1300–1499 and standardized to have the same coefficient of variation: Burgundian grape harvest dates, Chuine and others (2005). (C) mean variance of northern hemisphere temperatures (Mann and others (2008)), British Isles oak ring widths (data supplied by M. G. L. Baillie), Scottish speleothem band widths (Proctor and others (2002b)) and English grain yield ratios (Campbell (2007)).

---

[17] Pfister and others (1996); Grove (2004), 153–9.   [18] Figures 3.19A and 3.22.
[19] Campbell (2011a).   [20] Chuine and others (2005).
[21] Figures 3.19B and 3.22; Grove (2004), 153–9.

yields and Scottish speleothem band widths (Figure 5.2C).[22] The greatly heightened environmental instability of the mid-fourteenth century had abated and, while this brief interlude of strong solar irradiance lasted, circulation patterns became more settled in northern Europe and favourable growing conditions prevailed once again. In southern England, harvests obtained during the final quarter of the fourteenth century are among the best and most reliable on medieval record and transformed a situation of grain scarcity and high prices into one of grain glut and low prices, to the benefit of wage earners but at the expense of agricultural producers.[23] Warmer temperatures and increased solar output together stimulated plant growth almost everywhere (Figures 5.1A and 5.1B), so that in a remarkable inversion of the situation before 1346, for a period of almost twenty-five years English grain yields and British Isles oak ring widths were positively correlated. This testifies to the powerful environmental forcing effect of the climatic changes then afoot, which sprang in large measure from improved output of solar irradiance. Here, it might seem, were the environmental preconditions for a repeat of what had happened following the Oort Solar Minimum of c.1010–c.1050, namely a full reinstatement of the atmospheric circulation patterns of the MCA. That this failed to materialize implies that the transition to an altered climatic regime had already passed the point of no return.

The incomplete reinstatement of pre-Wolf circulation patterns is especially apparent in China, Southeast Asia, India and Ethiopia. In China average temperatures certainly bounced back as solar irradiance increased and for much of the last quarter of the fourteenth century matched those of the 1250s (Figure 5.3B). There was, however, no commensurate recovery of the monsoon. Precipitation levels certainly rose, so that from the 1370s drought eased as a problem, but remained well below those that had prevailed during the MCA when the ENSO had been at fullest strength (Figure 5.3B).[24] Even in Southeast Asia, where, on the evidence of the ring widths of *Fokienia hodginsii*, recovery of precipitation levels went furthest, it was only in exceptional years that the monsoon regained its earlier strength, as most notably in 1396–8 (Figure 5.3B).[25] In China the same decade delivered the heaviest monsoon rainfall since the 1320s and on the American side of the Pacific the partially restored strength of the ENSO suddenly faltered and returned much of the west coast of the Americas to a state of drought (Figure 5.3A), although not on the scale of the mega-droughts of the thirteenth century. Nevertheless, as output of solar irradiance began to wane once again, so too did the

---

[22] Figure 3.20.   [23] Campbell (2011a), 149–51.
[24] Sinha and others (2011).   [25] Buckley and others (2010).

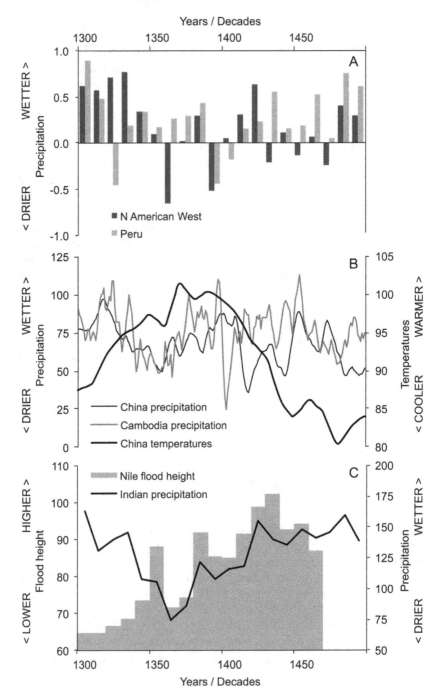

Figure 5.3 (A) Precipitation in the American Pacific West, (B) temperatures in China and precipitation in China and Cambodia and (C) precipitation in India and Pakistan and the flood discharge of the River Nile, 1300–1500

strength of the ENSO and, with it, both the grip of drought upon the Pacific West of the Americas and the volume of rainfall over Asia (Figures 5.3A, 5.3B and 5.3C).

The history of the Indian monsoon followed a somewhat different course. Over India and Pakistan the worst monsoon failures were delayed until the 1360s and early 1370s (Figure 5.3C). Thereafter, for the remainder of the fourteenth century, precipitation levels fell well below those of the mid-thirteenth century. They were also less reliable, so that when the monsoon failed in the 1390s serious famine resulted once again.[26] The altered character of the monsoon is also evident in a change in the relationship between precipitation levels over the Indian sub-continent and those over northeast Africa as measured by the scale of the annual Nile flood at Cairo (Figure 5.3C). Until the 1340s a weak Ethiopian monsoon had been the counterpart of a strong Indian monsoon. Subsequently, however, rainfall over both regions tended to move in step, rising in the 1380s, rising further in the 1410s and peaking in the 1430s, when, in India, it briefly returned to the level of the 1250s. To the east, in Cambodia and China, the opening decade of the new century had brought monsoon failures more complete than any experienced during the fourteenth century (Figure 5.3B). Flood events initiated by sporadic mega-strength monsoons further compounded the deteriorating environmental situation, as atmospheric circulation patterns destabilized once again and conditions swung between climatic extremes, wreaking havoc with drainage and irrigation systems.[27] In India, Pakistan and Ethiopia this phenomenon of mega-wet monsoons did not emerge until the 1420s and 1430s (Figure 5.3C), by which time atmospheric circulation over northern Europe was also changing once again, possibly more radically than ever before.

Figure 5.3 (cont.) Sources and notes: (A) adapted from Cook and others (2004c); Rein, Lückge and Sirocko (2004). (B) Temperatures, Yang and others (2002); precipitation, adapted from Zhang and others (2008), Wang and others (2006): all indexed on 1250–9. (C) Precipitation, adapted from Rad and others (1999), Berkelhammer and others (2010b); Nile flood from Popper (1951), 221–3, both indexed on 1250–9.

[26] Sinha and others (2007).

[27] In Cambodia 'several abrupt reversals from drought to very intense monsoons occurred during this period of generally weak monsoon strengths, such that 6 of the 20 wettest years occurred during the latest fourteenth and earliest fifteenth centuries': Buckley and others (2010).

Compared with the dramatic climatic developments taking place in many parts of Monsoon Asia, the first quarter of the fifteenth century in northern Europe was climatically less eventful, apart from a well-documented increase in North Atlantic storminess between c.1400 and 1420.[28] Generally mild conditions prevailed over the North Atlantic and temperatures over Greenland actually seem to have improved.[29] After 1400 there was a modest expansion of sea ice off Iceland but its area remained a fraction of that prevailing in the 1330s and 1370s, when temperatures over the North Atlantic had sunk to their coldest.[30] Dutch tithe receipts point to a massive 75 per cent contraction in grain output from the 1390s to 1420s, as rising water tables forced a switch from arable to pasture, but in England the reduction in actual yields across this period was only 15 per cent.[31] Although there were few bumper harvests, and none as bountiful as those of the 1380s, there were no outright disasters; the worst were those of 1401, 1408 (the poorest of four indifferent harvests) and 1422.[32] In 1422 the NAO remained moderately positive, environmental instability was relatively low, and across northern Europe the summer of 1425 was the warmest of the fourteenth and fifteenth centuries (Figure 5.2B). Overall, there is little to indicate that an environmental threshold was about to be crossed as onset of the Spörer Solar Minimum began to bite and global, northern hemisphere and Chinese temperatures all became significantly cooler (Figures 5.1A, 5.1B and 5.3B).

5.02.2   Climatic conditions during the Spörer Solar Minimum

In Asia the second quarter of the fifteenth century brought renewed monsoon failures: drought returned to Cambodia in 1424, India in the mid-1430s, central and southern China in c.1439–45 and Pakistan in the mid-1440s (Figures 5.3B and 5.3C). Then, from the 1440s, excessive monsoon rains in India, Cambodia and China became the greater problem.[33] Notably wet years included 1453–4 in Cambodia and 1450–6 in southern China. Their counterpart in the American Pacific West was a return to aridity (Figure 5.3A). Around this time, atmospheric loading arising from the c.1458 explosive mega-eruption of Kuwae in the South Pacific may have reinforced the global cooling which had been taking

---

[28] Dawson and others (2007).   [29] Figures 3.19A, 3.19B and 3.22.
[30] Figure 3.22.   [31] Campbell (2011a), 152–3.
[32] Campbell (2007). 1401 was also a major plague year: below, Figure 5.5.
[33] Sinha and others (2007); Berkelhammer and others (2010a); Buckley and others (2010); Zhang and others (2008).

place since at least the 1420s.[34] The 1450s were consequently the coldest decade of the fifteenth century and the coldest of the Middle Ages, significantly colder than the 1350s and almost as cold as the coldest decades of the LIA in the 1590s and 1690s.[35] During these years of significant climatic disturbance in Asia and America, from the 1440s to the 1470s, world tree growth registered a further sustained decline (Figure 5.1C). The downturn was synchronous across both the Old and the New Worlds and took the form of a double dip: the first began in 1446 and was at its most pronounced in 1448–50 (when the Burgundian grape harvest was seriously delayed (Figure 5.2B)); the second is associated with the eruption of Kuwae in c.1458, lasted until the early 1470s and was especially marked from 1459 to 1468.[36] Although European trees registered the greatest growth reduction, this was a global phenomenon and first and foremost undoubtedly resulted from the depressing effect upon growing conditions in both hemispheres of the Spörer Solar Minimum (Figures 5.1A and 5.1C).

In northern Europe it was during the second quarter of the fifteenth century that the transition was completed to a LIA climate characterized by a weak or negative NAO, with cold and relatively dry winters dominated by polar high pressure (Figure 5.2A). Analysis of Greenland ice-cores has revealed that as the fifteenth century opened, atmospheric pressure was falling over Iceland and building over eastern Siberia until, by the 1420s, the widening pressure gradient had initiated a profound shift in northern hemisphere circulation.[37] From this time winter conditions over northwestern Europe became colder and more unsettled and summers, with some notable exceptions, cooler (Figure 5.2B). L. D. Meeker and P. A. Mayewski consider this to have constituted 'the most rapid onset of any such event recorded in the North Atlantic region over the last 10,000 years'.[38] A synchronous change shows up in the Scottish speleothem record, which documents a massive dislocation to established rainfall levels and patterns from c.1420 to c.1470, with a minimum value in 1452 (Figure 5.2A). Circa 1450, 1460 and 1475 also stand out as years of exceptional coldness.[39] From 1423 to 1492 bitterly cold winters

---

[34] Figure 2.9; Buckley and others (2010); Gao and others (2009a). Eruption of Kuwae has hitherto been dated to 1452/3 but Bauch (2016) argues that a later date is more consistent with recorded atmospheric phenomena. Sulphate deposits in the Greenland ice-cores indicate that Kuwae erupted in c.1458 and was preceded by a lesser tropical eruption in c.1453 and followed by a high latitude northern hemisphere eruption in c.1462: Frank Ludlow, personal communication.

[35] Figure 1.1A.   [36] Bauch (2016); Frank Ludlow, personal communication.

[37] Meeker and Mayewski (2001).   [38] Meeker and Mayewski (2001), 263.

[39] Baker and others (2002), 1342.

are also documented with much increased frequency in the Netherlands: those of 1432, 1435, 1437 and 1443 stand out as notably harsh.[40]

In Greenland the unprecedented cold, in combination with growing competition for hunting grounds from the Inuit and lengthening intervals between visits from European traders, seems to have precipitated evacuation of the last of the Norse inhabitants.[41] Advent of these colder conditions lowered the altitudinal limits of cultivation, shortened growing seasons and placed a greater premium upon winter housing of livestock and production of fodder crops across Europe. Harsh winters, late springs and cool summers also presented a major challenge to grain producers and wine growers. In England the 1428 harvest was the worst since 1356 and yields were poor again in 1432. In 1436 the Burgundian grape harvest was seriously delayed and the next year wine imports to England were substantially reduced as the bad weather disrupted trade and travel.[42] Then in 1437 and 1438 grain harvests failed for two consecutive years, precipitating the single greatest English subsistence crisis and grain-price inflation of the fifteenth century.[43] On the Winchester estate sheep farming was adversely affected by the harsh winter conditions: expenditure on supplementary feeding increased, mortality rates soared, reproduction rates were depressed, and fleece weights are among the lowest on record.[44] Nationally, wool exports slumped in 1437–9.[45] The concurrent sharp inflation in salt prices, much of it imported French Bay salt produced by solar evaporation, implies that conditions were probably wet as well as cold.[46]

Unfavourable weather returned in 1441 and 1442, causing harvests to fail again, although this time more selectively. In Burgundy, delays to the *pinot noire* grape harvest became ever longer from 1442 to 1448. The international dimensions of this pronounced downturn in agricultural output are reflected in an aggregate decline of 13 per cent in GDP per head in Italy, Holland and England between 1435 and 1442.[47] No doubt these adverse conditions underscored contemporaneous fashion shifts to fuller, darker, heavy woollen and fur-lined clothes, and to snug private solars with their own fireplaces.[48] The harsh weather also encouraged construction of barns, stables, byres, cotes and sties to protect

[40] Engelen and others (2001).   [41] Dugmore and others (2007), 19–22.
[42] Chuine and others (2005); James (1971), 58.   [43] Campbell (2011a).
[44] Stephenson (1988), 383–4.   [45] Carus-Wilson and Coleman (1963), 59–61.
[46] Campbell (2011a), 153–4.
[47] Calculated from Malanima (2011), 207; Zanden and Leeuwen (2012); Broadberry and others (2015), 232.
[48] Piponnier and Mane (1997); Munro (2007); Pedersen and Nosch (2009); Veale (1966); Dresbeck (1971).

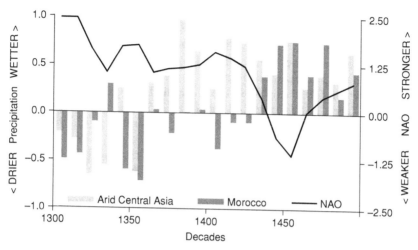

Figure 5.4 The North Atlantic Oscillation (NAO) and precipitation indexes for Morocco and Arid Central Asia, 1300s to 1490s
Sources: Chen and others (2010); Esper and others (2009); Trouet and others (2009b)

vulnerable crops and livestock.[49] Freezing Dutch winters, inferior English grain yields and late Burgundian grape harvests recurred sporadically for the remainder of the century. From the 1450s temperatures fell over Greenland and sea ice re-expanded around Iceland, with notable peaks in the 1470s, 1480s and 1490s.[50]

More southerly climes were also caught up in these changes. During the opening decades of the fourteenth century, when the NAO had been strong, the northerly course taken by the Atlantic winter westerlies had deprived southern Europe, North Africa and most regions to their east of precipitation and maintained central Asia in a state of aridity. But when the NAO weakened, temporarily in the 1320s and 1330s and then more permanently from the 1360s, these rain-bearing winds veered south and brought increased precipitation to these hitherto rain-deficient regions. Precipitation indexes for Morocco and Arid Central Asia highlight the climatic transition that set in across this broad region as the NAO at first weakened and then became strongly negative (Figure 5.4). Initially, from the 1360s, drought eased in Morocco as humidity rose in central Asia, boosting growth of juniper trees in the Tien Shan mountains and

[49] Dyer (1995); Brady (1997); Gerrard and Petley (2013).
[50] Figure 3.22; Trouet and others (2009a and b); Kobashi and others (2010); Massé and others (2008).

northeastern Tibetan Plateau and Siberian larch trees in Mongolia and Siberia (Figure 5.1C).[51] Then, from the 1430s as the westerlies shifted further to the south, humidity diminished somewhat in central Asia but rose in Morocco. The 1440s and 1450s brought significantly increased precipitation to North Africa, at the expense of northwest Europe, as the pressure difference between the Icelandic Low and Azores High narrowed to levels not experienced since the 1050s during the Oort Solar Minimum. For the remainder of the fifteenth century it was this altered pressure regime that prevailed.

By the 1450s, impelled by significant reductions in solar irradiance, as mediated by complex ocean–atmosphere feedback mechanisms, the transition from the atmospheric circulation patterns of the MCA to those of the LIA was complete. Temperatures both globally and hemispherically had cooled significantly. Across northern Europe summer warmth was diminished and winter incursions of polar high pressure were increasingly common, displacing the winter track of Atlantic cyclones southwards across the Mediterranean and North Africa. Everywhere, agricultural producers were obliged to adapt to greatly altered growing conditions and there was much withdrawal from land that was marginal for cultivation. Producers in upland areas experienced a significant lowering in the altitudinal limits to cultivation, while flooding and rising water tables became significant problems in the estuarine marshlands that bordered the North Sea. High labour costs in combination with low food prices encouraged conversion of heavy and ill-drained land from arable to pasture, giving rise to the phenomenon of shrunken and deserted villages, while the poorest soils were allowed to revert to woodland.[52]

Longer, harder winters placed a premium upon storing crops and housing livestock and northern Europeans found they had greater need of fuel, food and clothing than at any time in the previous thousand years. Cooling ocean waters also caused some fish stock to migrate to new grounds: for cod the critical threshold was a sea-surface temperature of at least 2°C.[53] The Norse had long withdrawn from Greenland but the parent colony of Iceland was now encountering increasing environmental difficulties. These changes were the more profound because they were matched by concurrent climatic transformations across the northern hemisphere, to the benefit of some geographical regions but disadvantage of others. In China and much of South Asia the unreliability of the monsoon played havoc with irrigation-based farming systems as it swung between drought and flood. Intensive cultivation of wet rice

[51] Sun and Liu (2012), 6 and 9 of 11.   [52] Broadberry and others (2015), 57–64.
[53] Grove (2004), 607.

proved far less adaptable to the altered environmental conditions than the more diversified and land-extensive mixed-farming systems of northern Europe with their alternative crops and animals and shifting frontier between grain and grass.[54]

5.03   A golden age of bacteria?

5.03.1   Climate and disease

This prolonged and fitful episode of climate change, with its lulls, reversals and sudden progressions, compounded the challenge presented to European society by the eruption and spread of plague and other diseases from the mid-fourteenth century. Crucially, it was the ecological stress engendered by onset of the Wolf Solar Minimum (1282–1342) that appears to have triggered plague's reactivation from an enzootic to an epizootic state in its reservoir regions within the semi-arid interior of Asia.[55] It was at the climax of this climatic anomaly, when weather conditions were most unstable and summer temperatures and tree growth most depressed, that plague spread westwards across Eurasia. While the Black Death raged, cool and persistently wet weather brought harvest failure to much of Europe.[56] Climate change having generated the ecological stress that relaunched plague, plague in its turn magnified and transformed the impact of this ongoing climatic transition upon human societies across the Old World, and especially in Europe. Both separately and in combination, climate and disease brought about a significant deterioration in public health, notwithstanding countervailing post-Black Death improvements in living standards.[57]

Figure 5.5 explores the relationship between downturns in growing conditions, as measured by a European Five master dendrochronology and the quality of English grain harvests, and those major plague outbreaks recorded in at least ten chronicles from France, the Low Countries, Britain and Ireland, as enumerated by Biraben. As will be observed, beginning with the Black Death, plague outbreaks were more likely than not to occur during or immediately following years of depressed tree growth and inferior harvests. Between 1346 and 1475, this was true of the plagues of 1348–50, 1360–2, 1369, 1374, 1399–1401, 1438–9, 1450–2, 1454–7 and 1463–75. Indeed, the first and last of these plagues coincided with the periods when negative forcing of European and world

---

[54] Buckley and others (2010); Brook (2010), 72, 77, 97; Lieberman and Buckley (2012), 1073–5.
[55] Above, Sections 3.03.2.   [56] Above, Figures 4.3 and 4.6.
[57] Above, Section 4.04.

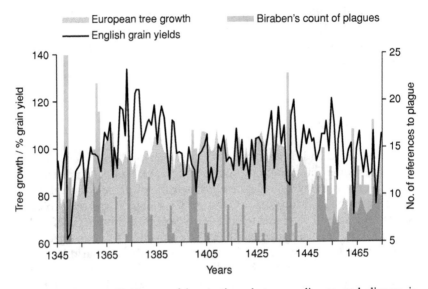

Figure 5.5 Evidence of interactions between climate and disease in northern Europe, 1345–1475

Sources and notes: European Five master dendrochronology from Figure 5.1C, indexed on 1250–9; English gross grain yields per seed (wheat, barley and oats) calculated from Campbell (2007) as % of average of previous 25 years; total references to plague from French, Low Countries and British and Irish sources (minimum of five) from Biraben (1975), 363–74

tree growth was exceptionally strong at the respective climaxes of the Wolf and Spörer Solar Minima (Figure 5.1C).

Of course, poor weather and inferior harvests did not guarantee that plague would break out but few widely reported plagues were associated with the opposite conditions. Those of 1382–3 (mostly confined to France and Italy) and 1412 (little reported outside France) are the sole exceptions (Figure 5.5). They contrast with the self-evidently weather-related plagues of 1399–1401, 1438–9, 1457 and 1464–5. Where these recurrent European plague outbreaks originated is a moot point. Although Schmid and others (2015) have argued that *Y. pestis* failed to establish a natural wildlife reservoir within Europe, they concede that plague could have persisted as a background disease 'circulating between cities and villages' and 'revisiting them as their population of susceptible individuals recovered from earlier outbreaks', presumably when enabling economic and ecological conditions were ripe. Further, they acknowledge that black rats may have 'played an important role as an urban reservoir of plague in those harbour cities with a substantial black rat population'.[58]

Part of the explanation for the observable association within Europe between an upturn in reported plague outbreaks and depressed growing conditions and poor harvests (Figure 5.5) plainly lies in the fact that pathogen–host–vector interactions were sensitive to variations in temperature and humidity. Fleas, in particular, multiplied under humid conditions. Moreover, plague then as now was a disease of poverty, breaking out and flaring up whenever ecological and economic stress brought humans into closer contact with plague's rodent hosts and flea vectors. At such times it probably acted in combination with other infections that thrived on the malnutrition, over-crowding and poor hygiene engendered by harvest failure, notably murine typhus and possibly epidemic typhus. Disease, consequently, endowed these years of adverse weather and scarcity with a demographic significance out of all proportion to their economic impact. Herein possibly lies the greatest and most insidious influence of contemporary climate changes upon society. These complex interactions between climate, disease and society were a key feature of the Great Transition.

5.03.2   The downward demographic trend

Had the Black Death been a one-off event it is unlikely that its immediate socio-ecological impact would have endured for more than a generation or two. Instead, populations would most likely have bounced back in much the way that Malthus envisaged populations should, as survivors of this greatest of mortality crises responded to the dramatically improved economic opportunities bestowed upon them. Labour was now relatively scarcer, dearer and, despite the punitive new labour legislation, better remunerated (Figures 4.11 and 4.14), in contrast to capital and land, which were now more available and cheaper.[59] Immediate demographic recovery was further encouraged by the temporary disappearance of plague, which in this first outbreak came, killed and vanished.[60] Biraben's trawl for references to plague in European chronicles drew a virtual blank for the years 1353–6 (Figure 4.13). With the peril apparently past, the traumatized survivors of this first and most deadly outbreak of plague set about rebuilding their families.

---

[58]   Schmid and others (2015), 3–4 of 6; Cummins and others (2013).
[59]   Clark (1988), 271–5; Clark (2010).
[60]   Christakos and others (2007), 713–14, 716–17.

Unsurprisingly, the sudden availability of so many dead men's shoes prompted a bonanza of marriages.[61] At Givry in Burgundy, where 11–29 marriages a year had been celebrated between 1336 and 1341, no weddings were recorded during the plague year of 1348 but 86 took place the next year and 33 in 1350.[62] On the estates of both the bishop of Winchester in southern England and the prior of Halesowen in the west midlands, payments for licence to marry doubled in the immediate wake of the plague, notwithstanding that their base populations were substantially reduced.[63] In the Lincolnshire fens on five manors belonging to Spalding Priory there were three times as many merchet payments in 1350 as there had been during an average year before the plague.[64] With 40–50 per cent fewer people but two to three times as many marriages, nuptiality rates, at least in the short term, soared and, although it cannot be documented, it is to be expected that an upsurge in births soon followed.

This happy demographic situation did not last, for within twelve years the first of a succession of sequel plague outbreaks swept across Europe, with many of the fresh cohort of children born immediately after the Black Death prominent among its victims. Each disease outbreak triggered a surge in mortality, which ratcheted populations down in size and, by elevating infant and child mortality rates, sapped populations of the capacity to reproduce themselves. Male replacement rates, consequently, sank below those necessary to ensure full generational replacement.[65] This downward slide of populations continued almost everywhere for at least four consecutive generations and was not halted until the second half of the fifteenth century, when a fitful recovery began. There has been considerable speculation that women may have been responding to the new wage-earning opportunities and marrying later, thereby lowering fertility, although there is little substantive evidence to support this.[66] Rural to urban migration is also likely to have redistributed population from low- to high-mortality locations and altered gender ratios and age structures in the donor and recipient populations. In the case of the English manors of High Easter, Great Waltham, Margaret Roding and Chatham Hall in Essex it was from the 1370s that the prospects

---

[61] Benedictow (2010), 268–71.   [62] Benedictow (2010), 271.

[63] Winchester marriage licences derived by Cormac Ó Gráda from Page (2001); Halesowen marriage licences from Razi (1980), 48, 133.

[64] Jones (1996), 466.

[65] Russell (1948), 216–18; Cohn (2002a), 192–203; Thrupp (1962), 191–206; Thrupp (1965); Hollingsworth (1969), 378–9.

[66] Goldberg (1992); Bailey (1996); Hatcher (2003), 92–5; Humphries and Weisdorf (2015). For an analogous post-plague reduction in nuptiality and fertility in seventeenth-century Colyton see Wrigley (1966).

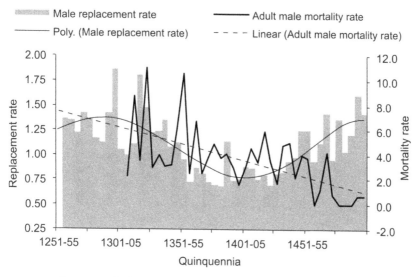

Figure 5.6 Quinquennial adult male replacement rates and mortality rates of English tenants-in-chief and creditors, 1256–1500
Sources: Hollingsworth (1969), 378–9; Nightingale (2005), 53

of demographic recovery were finally extinguished as numbers of adult males began a century-long decline.[67] Tenant numbers dwindled almost everywhere and as the labour supply shrank so nominal daily wage rates rose again, until by 1375 they were more than double their immediate pre-Black Death level.[68]

Post-Black Death populations may have been increasingly well fed, clothed and housed but this was insufficient to ward off the negative effects upon health of longer and harder winters, cooler summers and an increased epidemiological burden.[69] In the new disease-dominated demographic environment the experience of English male tenants-in-chief of the Crown demonstrates that even this most advantaged socio-economic group had lost the capacity to maintain inter-generational replacement (Figure 5.6). Male replacement rates for this social elite remained negative for four successive generations following the Black Death and then for a further generation swung between positive and negative. Not until the final quarter of the fifteenth century were numbers of sons once again consistently in excess of numbers of fathers. At around the same time, the mortality rate of Statute Merchant creditors also

---

[67] Poos (1985).   [68] Above, Figure 4.14.
[69] Grove (1988); Campbell (2011a), 122–3, 152–6.

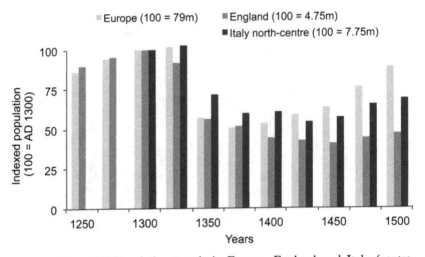

Figure 5.7 Population trends in Europe, England and Italy (centre-north), 1250–1500
Sources: Europe, McEvedy and Jones (1978), 19; England, Broadberry and others (2015), 20, 227–33; Italy (centre-north), Malanima (no date)

abated (Figure 5.6).[70] Over this century-long period of negative replacement rates, independently reconstructed population trends for England, Tuscany and Europe as a whole chart a broadly similar downward course (Figure 5.7).

When population growth belatedly resumed in England it was the superior health and dynamism of rural populations in the economically expanding northwest, the west midlands and the southwest that kickstarted and led the process.[71] From a slow and fitful start, recovery then accelerated until by the second quarter of the sixteenth century the population was increasing vigorously once more and plague, while still recurrent, had lost its capacity to stall the process. When, in the late seventeenth and early eighteenth centuries, plague finally died out and disappeared, it did so largely of its own volition, retreating successively from Ireland, Britain, northwestern and southern Europe but lingering longer in the Russian and Ottoman Empires.[72] Eventually, *Y. pestis* became mostly confined once again to the ancient enzootic reservoir areas in the interiors of western and central Asia whence it had emerged

---

[70]   Further evidence that mortality was easing from the mid-fifteenth century is provided by Thrupp (1965), 114; Gottfried (1978), 204–13.
[71]   Broadberry and others (2015), 22–7.   [72]   Alfani (2013).

with such deadly consequences during the decades around *c.*1300 and would reappear intermittently during the next several centuries, whenever ecological conditions triggered a renewed escalation from epizootic to panzootic plague.[73]

5.04   Economic and commercial contraction

5.04.1   Shrinking national incomes and changes in relative factor and commodity prices

Irrespective of whether economic output had been rising (Spain), fluctuating (England) or falling (Italy) before the Black Death, the simultaneous shock that plague then inflicted upon the supply of labour and demand for goods and services set in train an immediate and enduring contraction in economic activity. Between the 1340s and 1370s, real GDP in current prices shrank by 26 per cent in Spain, 35 per cent in England and 35–40 per cent in Italy and as late as 1500 in all three of these countries remained 15–35 per cent below its immediate pre-plague levels (Figure 5.8A). The Black Death itself slashed GDP by a fifth in Italy and by a third in England; mortality from sequel plague outbreaks then reduced GDP further until minimum levels were reached in the plague year 1374/5. In Italy GDP would never again sink as low but in England the nadir did not come until 1441, at the climax of a severe short-term recession which affected both Italy and Holland as adverse weather depressed the outputs of grain, wool and wine (Figure 5.8A).[74] Annual growth rates of GDP highlight the economic nosedive that dominated the third quarter of the fourteenth century and the modest recovery which then followed during the climatically benign final quarter of that century, when plague also, for a time, became less punitive in its effects (Figures 5.2, 5.5 and 5.8B). Here were the seeds of a post-crisis Malthusian economic recovery but they failed to germinate and in the opening decade of the fifteenth century, when poor harvests and plague returned (Figure 5.5) and bullion was in extremely scarce supply (Figure 5.11), growth rates turned negative once again.[75] Thereafter, until the final quarter of the fifteenth century, growth rates of GDP fluctuated between positive and negative as national income rose and fell but displayed no sustained tendency to grow. A new post-plague economic equilibrium had become

---

[73] Above, Figure 3.27; Schmid and others (2015).
[74] Hatcher (1996); Nightingale (1997).
[75] On the scarcity of bullion see Day (1987), 1–54; Spufford (1988), 339–62; Bolton (2012), 232–6.

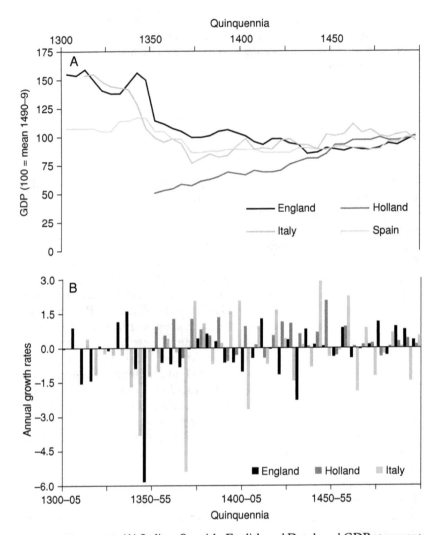

Figure 5.8 (A) Italian, Spanish, English and Dutch real GDP at current prices (100 = 1500), 1300–1500. (B) Inter-quinquennial annual growth rates of Italian, English and Dutch GDP, 1300–1500

Sources and notes: Italy – Malanima (2011), 205–9; Spain – data supplied by Leandro Prados de la Escosura; England – Broadberry and others (2015), 227–33; Holland – data supplied by Bas van Leeuwen. Italian, English and Dutch GDP trends are 3-year double smoothed; Spanish GDP trends are decadal means

established from which the small Dutch economy alone showed signs of escaping (Figures 5.8A and B).[76]

Major adjustments to the relative values of land, labour and capital accompanied this scaling-down of economic activity, as labour became scarcer and, per head, land and capital more abundant. Attention has already been drawn to the surge in nominal wage rates that followed the Black Death in England, notwithstanding the best efforts of the justices of labourers to restrain them, as male workers capitalized upon their improved bargaining power and played off one employer against another.[77] From the late 1370s, falling food prices kept daily real wage rates rising, so that by the 1440s the daily wages paid to building labourers and farm labourers purchased two-and-a-half times what they had bought in the 1340s (Figure 5.10A). Wage rates then fluctuated around this historically elevated level until almost the end of the fifteenth century, when they slowly started drifting down again (Figure 5.9A).[78] Throughout this long period wage-bargaining power advantaged labourers over employers, especially during the peak seasons of agricultural labour demand and above all in late summer when hands were desperately needed to bring in the harvest. Daily wages paid to casual workers at such times were far above those earned by farm labourers hired on annual contracts according to the statute, a point recently highlighted by the clear differential identified by Jane Humphries and Jacob Weisdorf between the wages paid to women in fixed and in casual employment.[79]

Since the unskilled workforce had shrunk more than the skilled, building labourers, for example, were now paid at two-thirds rather than half the rate of a master craftsman.[80] Building labourers in Florence made similar wage gains and, in fact, by the 1420s had increased their daily real wage rates by marginally more than their counterparts in London and Oxford.[81] Indeed, the middle decades of the fifteenth century were good for urban building labourers right across Europe and it would be at least another four centuries before most were again paid at such generous rates (Figure 5.9A).[82] These high wage rates were sustained in an era of relative under-population by the increased return to labour as a factor of production, reinforced by the reduced number of days that labourers needed to work in order to meet their subsistence needs and those of their

---

[76] Bavel and Zanden (2004). The Duchy of Brabant and Portugal may also have been exceptions.
[77] Figure 4.14; above, Section 4.04; Farmer (1988), 483–90; Cohn (2007). Female workers were less successful: Humphries and Weisdorf (2015).
[78] Clark (2007b); Munro (no date).
[79] Hatcher (2011); Humphries and Weisdorf (2015).
[80] Allen (2001); Munro (no date).
[81] Federico and Malanima (2004), 459–60.   [82] Allen (2001).

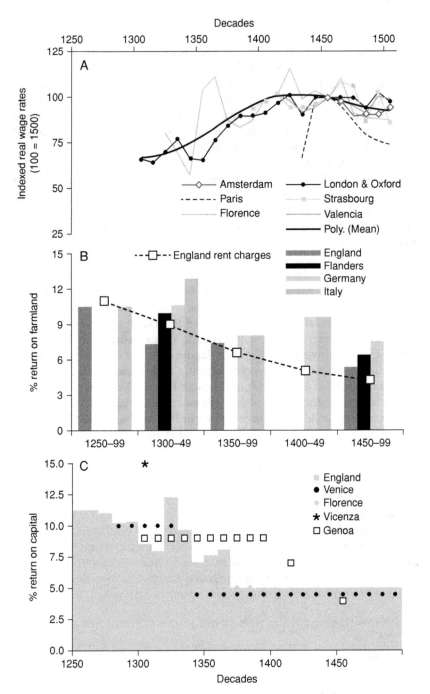

Figure 5.9 (A) Urban building labourers' daily real wage rates in a selection of European cities, 1300s to 1490s. (B) Rent charges in England and the return on farmland in England, Flanders, Germany and Italy, 1250–99 to 1450–99. (C) Return on capital in England and nominal interest rates on public debt paid by Italian urban republics, 1250s to 1490s

Sources and notes: (A) Allen (2001); (B) Clark (2005), 34–5; (C) Clark (2010); Epstein (2000a), 20

households.[83] The shrinkage in the labour supply was therefore greater than the shrinkage in the number of able-bodied workers.[84]

Meanwhile, land, whose relative supply increased, declined in value. Tracking that decline has barely begun and is anything but straightforward given the nature of the available historical sources.[85] Clark has nevertheless assembled such data as are currently available on the rate of return to farmland in England, Flanders, Germany and Italy, which collectively point to a reduction of around one-third from 7.3–12.9 per cent in the first half of the fourteenth century to 5.4–7.6 per cent during the second half of the fifteenth century (Figure 5.9B).[86] In Germany and especially Italy there appears to have been a particularly marked drop in the return on farmland following the Black Death. This is less evident in England, although Mark Bailey has identified an average decline of 35 per cent in the value of customary land on six manors in the east midlands and East Anglia between the 1340s and the 1360s.[87] Studies of the freehold and customary land markets have similarly demonstrated that land was suddenly in greatly increased supply.[88] Where before the Black Death transactions of individual plots had tended to dominate the market, a century later transactions were increasingly of multiple plots and often of entire holdings.[89] Since land markets were closely tied to credit markets, this change in the character of land markets reflected a fall in the price of capital.

The pioneering work on interest rates has, again, been undertaken by Clark, who has charted a significant decline in the rate of return on capital in England, with an approximate halving of interest rates over the course of the fourteenth century (Figure 5.9C).[90] The reduced interest rates established by the 1370s then prevailed for the remainder of the Middle Ages. This trend is paralleled by a fall in the nominal rates of interest paid on long-term public debt by the Italian city republics of Florence, Genoa, Venice and Vicenza, as documented by Epstein (Figure 5.9C).[91] Whereas at the opening of the fourteenth century the two great republics of Genoa and Venice were paying respective interest rates of 6–12 and

---

[83] Broadberry and others (2015), 260–5, 414–15.
[84] For the influence of changes in labour supply per head upon daily real wage rates see Angeles (2008).
[85] For a demonstration of what can be achieved see Bailey (2014), 303.
[86] Clark (2005); also Clark (1988) and Clark (2010).
[87] Bailey (2014), 303: the declines ranged from a reduction of 15 per cent in leasehold rents at Cuxham in Oxfordshire to a fall of 53 per cent in entry fines levied on customary arable land at Dunningworth in Suffolk.
[88] Howell (1983), 47–8; Campbell (1984); Yates (2013), 586–92.
[89] Campbell (1980), 188–91; Campbell (1981), 26–9; Yates (2003).
[90] Clark (1988); Clarke (2005).
[91] Epstein (2000a), 20. For the calculation of interest rates from medieval sources see Bell and others (2009a).

8–12 per cent, by the mid-fifteenth century these rates had reduced to 4–5 per cent.[92] Florentine interest rates were a third lower again and, backed by a sophisticated banking sector, sank to less than 3 per cent in the final years of the fifteenth century.[93] These reductions in the cost of capital began before the Black Death and continued in its aftermath until a new lower equilibrium was established from early in the fifteenth century. What caused this decline in interest rates remains obscure but it had the obvious effect of making capital investment much cheaper.[94] Investment in labour-saving technology – spinning wheels, horizontal looms, fulling and gig mills, mechanized forges, blast furnaces, printing presses and three-masted ships – offered real pay-offs in an age when labour was becoming dearer.[95] Harsher winter weather also required increased investment in storage facilities and better housing for humans and valuable livestock.

These changes in relative factor prices, in turn, drove changes in relative commodity prices, with labour-intensive products becoming relatively dearer and land-intensive and capital-intensive products cheaper. In a largely pre-mechanized age of human-operated hand tools, that meant that industrial prices tended to rise relative to agricultural prices. As will be seen from Figure 5.10A, English relative prices were already favouring manufactured goods before the Black Death, when the country's wool-textile industry began its recovery, and they swung even more strongly in favour of industrial production from the 1350s, as the population shrank and daily real wage rates rose. Unsurprisingly, the disparity between industrial and agricultural prices was greatest in the 1440s, when population levels were lowest and daily real wage rates highest (Figure 5.10A). This shift in the terms of trade between these two sectors had two countervailing effects. On the one hand, it encouraged increased consumption of foodstuffs, especially those that were the most land-intensive to produce, notably brewing grains and all livestock products.[96] On the other, high product prices promoted an expansion of industrial output and the occupational migration of labour from agriculture to manufacturing. Already by 1381 15 per cent of the male, 28 per cent of the female and 19 per cent of the total English labour force were employed in industry.[97]

---

[92] Epstein (2000a), 20.   [93] Epstein (2000a), 19–20.

[94] Clark (2005), 1: 'The magnitude of this decline [in interest rates] is little appreciated, its cause is a mystery, and its connection to the shift to an economic system with persistent efficiency advance is unknown'.

[95] Mokyr (1992), 34–5, 51–4.

[96] Campbell (1997b); Broadberry and others (2015), 288–91.

[97] Broadberry and others (2013), 17.

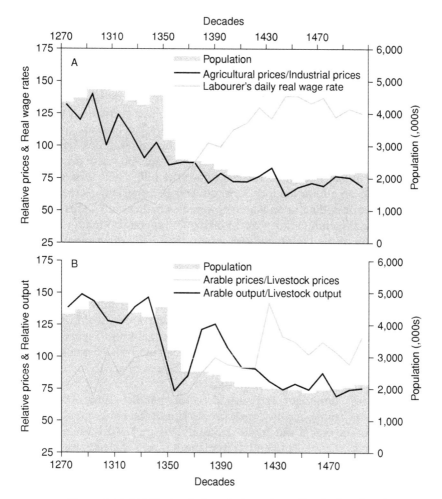

Figure 5.10 (A) England: the relative prices of agricultural and manufactured goods, indexed male labourers' daily real wage rates, and total
population, 1270s to 1490s. (B) England: the ratios of arable prices
to livestock prices and of arable output to livestock output, and total
population, 1270s to 1490s

Sources and notes: Relative prices and outputs as described, and population totals as given, in Broadberry and others (2015), 189–94, 227–33,
and supplied by Bas van Leeuwen; wage rates (building and farm labourers' combined) from Clark (2007b) and Munro (no date) using the
basket of consumables from Munro (no date). Relative prices, outputs
and wage rates are indexed on their respective means for 1300s–1490s.

In an era of high wage costs, industrial locations with relatively cheap labour enjoyed a real comparative advantage. Hence manufacturing tended to forsake expensive and often well-organized urban labour markets and latch onto cheaper rural labour working part time and unrestricted by guild controls. Areas of pastoral husbandry, mixed farming and woodland proved particularly receptive to this development since part-time employment in manufacturing combined particularly well with animal husbandry and wood-pasture economies.[98] These areas also furnished an array of useful raw materials, notably tallow, hides, bark, charcoal and, not unusually, minerals. Access to water-power to drive fulling mills, gig mills, forges and furnaces gave the hillier and least arable of these areas an additional locational advantage, especially as the priority claim of corn milling upon water-power sites had eased.[99] This explains why in the fifteenth century clothmaking and metalworking took root in many parts of the countryside as long-established urban manufactures languished and declined.[100] The rise of textile production in the West Riding and its demise in York is one of the best-known exemplars of this trend.[101] The post-Black Death rise of an English rural wool-textile industry is reflected in the progressive shrinkage of exports of raw wool from an annual average of 31,500 sacks in the 1350s to 17,700 sacks by the 1390s and then just 7,400 sacks by the 1450s (Figure 5.12B), although by then wool output and thus exports were also being squeezed by declining fleece weights arising from changes in sheep management and deteriorating weather conditions.[102]

Within the dominant agricultural sector, parallel shifts occurred in the prices of arable and livestock products and the consequent balance struck between arable and livestock output (Figure 5.10B). Following the Black Death, cheaper land and dearer labour increasingly swung prices in favour of pastoral land uses and animal husbandry, with its significantly smaller labour requirements than arable production. Poor harvests in the 1350s and 1360s worked against this trend but bumper harvests in the 1380s and 1390s reinforced it.[103] Relative prices tipped most decisively towards livestock products in the 1420s and thereafter remained consistently favourable for the rest of the fifteenth century (Figure 5.10B). Throughout this long period slack demand, low prices and high wage costs depressed arable production. At the opening of the fourteenth century it had been otherwise. With the population at a maximum and

[98] Thirsk (1961); Thirsk (1973); Birrell (1969).
[99] Baker (1973), 222, 225, 229–30.   [100] Baker (1973), 222–5, 228–9.
[101] Kermode (1998), 274–5, 316–18.   [102] Stephenson (1988), 377–80.
[103] Campbell (2011a), 142–51.

demand for crops at an all-time high, arable output had exceeded livestock output by a significant margin (Figure 5.10B).[104] That situation
changed dramatically in the 1340s with the Black Death and the run of
dismal harvests that accompanied and followed it.[105] During the ensuing
Chaucerian Solar Maximum (Figure 5.1) bumper harvests briefly tipped
the balance back towards the arable sector (Figure 5.5), until from the
end of the fourteenth century relative prices and production costs finally
advantaged livestock over crop production (Figure 5.10B). This production shift, with its implications for land use, agricultural labour productivity and the composition of diets, was a further dimension of the Great
Transition.

5.04.2   Land-use substitution and the reconfiguration of rural populations

Under the economic and environmental conditions prevailing during
the fifteenth century it made sense to withdraw marginal land from
agricultural use and convert the heaviest and most intractable soils to
permanent pasture. As the Spörer Solar Minimum advanced, the shift
towards cooler summers and colder winters made grass a better bet for
many farmers than grain and, in upland areas, lowered the altitudinal
limits of cultivation.[106] Woodland typically became the default land-use
wherever land lapsed from agricultural use and attention has already
been drawn to its post-plague expansion.[107] Where cultivation continued, most agricultural settlements shrank in size and the least successful
often withered to a single farm, especially when landlords discovered the
superior profits that could be obtained by evicting any remaining tenants and replacing them with sheep.[108] Creation of large pastoral enterprises formed part of the general reconfiguration of farming systems
taking place at this time, as land-intensive farming systems gained, and
labour-intensive farming systems waned, in importance.[109] Incentives to
specialize, invest and innovate weakened as urban populations shrank
and their provisioning hinterlands contracted, so that low economic rent
locked most farming regions into low-yielding, land-intensive systems of
production.[110]

---

[104] Power and Campbell (1992); Campbell (2000), 94–101, 411–30.
[105] Campbell (2011a), 142–9; Figures 4.6 and 5.5.
[106] Above, Section 5.3; Parry (1978); Malanima (2012), 98–9.
[107] Figure 4.12; above, Section 4.03.4; Baillie (2006), 21–3; Büntgen and others (2013),
       1776.
[108] Baker (1973), 207–17; Broadberry and others (2015), 57–61.
[109] Campbell (2000), 430–6; Campbell and others (1996), 173–9.
[110] Campbell and others (1996), 177–9.

Meanwhile, far-reaching structural changes to farms and fields took place, as under the prevailing conditions of population decline, the cumulative effects of *post mortem* and *inter vivos* land transfers were now the amalgamation of land parcels and engrossing of holdings.[111] These, in turn, led to much piecemeal enclosure of former open-field land.[112] As lords relaxed tight tenurial control of the land, some tenant dynasties added yardland to yardland and successfully built up yeoman-sized holdings.[113] Meanwhile, serfdom faded away, villein tenures metamorphosed into copyhold tenures free of the taint of servility, former demesne lands were converted to fixed-term leaseholds, and subletting for profit rents ceased to be viable.[114] At the same time, the subsistence imperative to engage in market exchange abated and production for household consumption became an increasingly viable option for many. Dwindling money stocks also obliged rural producers to resort to non-monetary forms of exchange and acted as a restraint upon fuller commercialization of agriculture.[115]

In England these developments collectively gave rise to a profound redistribution of rural populations as difficult and marginal environments were abandoned, tenants were displaced and dispossessed by the expansion of pasture farming, tenant engrossment of land reduced the availability of holdings, manors offering tenures on generous terms attracted tenants, and industrializing localities, often of wood-pasture and weak lordship, prospered and grew.[116] England's reconfigured population geography reflected the cumulative adjustments made as rural society adapted to the new economic and environmental status quo with its greatly reduced scale of economic activity and transformed relative factor and commodity prices. Rural societies across Europe faced similar challenges although the precise character of their responses was shaped by the character of prevailing property rights and the tenurial balance of power between lords and tenants.[117]

5.04.3   Urban stagnation and commercial depression

The 25–40 per cent contraction in economic output initiated by the Black Death (Figure 5.8A) also left the urban and commercial sectors with

---

[111] Campbell (1980) 188–91; Campbell (1981), 5–15, 26–9; Whittle (2000), 108–10.
[112] Baker (1973), 211–15.   [113] Whittle (2000), 167–77.
[114] Bailey (2014). These developments are reviewed in greater detail in Campbell (2002a).
[115] Britnell (1993a), 179–85.
[116] Darby and others (1979); Broadberry and others (2015), 22–7.
[117] These power relationships and their consequences are extensively discussed in Aston and Philpin (1985).

excess capacity. Many of the markets, fairs and boroughs that had been so optimistically founded during the commercial revolution of the twelfth and thirteenth centuries suffered a loss of critical mass and downgrading of functions.[118] As the economic contraction became entrenched and manufacturing forsook the larger cities for lower-cost locations in small towns and villages, so the economic base of many towns narrowed and their problems multiplied.[119] Townsmen also appear to have experienced greater exposure to potentially deadly infections than their rural cousins; consequently it was only by in-migration that many towns succeeded in replacing their populations.[120] With rare exceptions, the majority of towns were substantially smaller in 1450 than they had been in 1300 and, in aggregate, European towns probably contained 3 million fewer townsmen.[121] Even with higher consumption per head, almost all could be provisioned from narrower hinterlands.

That towns managed to maintain their estimated 10–11 per cent share of Europe's population was therefore a considerable achievement.[122] Apart from the successful maritime economies of the Northern Low Countries and Portugal, and with the possible exception of south Germany where mining of non-ferrous metals and realigned trans-Alpine trade routes were sources of prosperity, urbanization had effectively ceased as a process.[123] Deprived of the powerful Smithian dynamic that had spurred urbanization during the heady days of the commercial revolution in the twelfth and early thirteenth centuries, there was little to propel large-scale urban growth. Instead, as demand subsided and markets shrank, towns competed with each other in an urban survival of the fittest. Those able to secure a new commercial niche – Milan, Antwerp, Geneva, Nuremberg and Lisbon – fared well and grew, but 'success' for most meant the avoidance of decline. London out-performed most other leading English towns and just about held its own, but only did so by claiming a greater share of the nation's trade and commerce (Figure 5.12B), to the disadvantage of once prosperous regional capitals such as York.[124] Nonetheless, the real rental values of properties in the capital's central

[118] Britnell (1993a), 156–61, 169–71; Masschaele (1994); Bailey (2007), 265–8.
[119] Hatcher (1996), 266–70; Kermode (1998), 261–75; Nightingale (2010); Phythian-Adams (2002).
[120] Kermode (1998), 73–4; Kermode (2000), 458–9; Kowaleski (2014), 583–97.
[121] Urbanization ratio from Bairoch and others (1988), 259, applied to European population estimates from McEvedy and Jones (1978), 19.
[122] Bairoch and others (1988), 259.
[123] For the situation in hitherto dynamic Italy see Epstein (2000a), 91–6; Malanima (2005). On south Germany see Scott (2002), 58–65, 113–37.
[124] Nightingale (1996), 100–6; Nightingale (2010); Keene (2000a), 60–9, 79; Kermode (1998), 263–5, 274–5, 318–19.

business district of Cheapside were marginally lower at the close of the fifteenth century than they had been at that century's opening.[125] The most successful late-medieval English towns were invariably small and owed their vitality to the expansion of manufacturing within them and their hinterlands.[126] Until European commercial growth could be rekindled, however, England's urban sector as a whole, like that of most other European countries, trod water.[127]

For the greater part of the fifteenth century European commerce was held in check by four mutually reinforcing problems. First, domestic demand was effectively flat. Per head, people may have been better off but while populations continued to dwindle, as they did until at least the third quarter of the fifteenth century, aggregate demand was not expanding (Figure 5.7). Until almost the end of the fifteenth century the GDPs of Italy, Spain and England remained trendless (Figure 5.8A). Higher daily real wage rates certainly enabled labourers to indulge their preferences and trade up to a more lavish basket of consumption goods but once these needs were satisfied labourers seem to have opted for less work and more leisure rather than greater industriousness and more goods.[128] Their enhanced demand per head was more dispersed than concentrated and benefited rural producers of food, drink, fuel, building materials, textiles and leather, metal wares and pottery far more than urban suppliers of services and manufactured goods, which is why their improved living standards did not ignite a minor growth-generating consumer revolution. Second, warfare, piracy and, within the Mediterranean, slave raiding had all become endemic, thereby ensuring that international trade remained in thrall to high transaction costs.[129] To counter these multiple threats, Venetian and Genoese maritime trade relied upon convoys of heavily armed galleys while in northern waters the Hanseatic consortium gave protection to its members. Third, east–west routes across Arabia had narrowed to a single artery over which the Egyptian Mamluks enjoyed monopoly control. An unholy alliance between Christian Venice and Muslim Egypt kept this route open and European elites supplied with the Indian spices and Oriental silks and ceramics they craved, but at an almost ruinous cost to the Europeans in terms of the tolls charged, the bias of the trade in favour of the Muslim middlemen, and the size of Europe's recurrent trade deficit.[130] Fourth, from the closing years of the

---

[125] Keene (1985), 20.   [126] Britnell (1993a), 170–1; Yates (2007), 67–124.
[127] Rigby (2010).   [128] Broadberry and others (2015), 257–65.
[129] Munro (1991), 120–30; Davis (2003), 23–48, 139–74, cited in Brooke (2014), 422. Epstein (2000a), 38–72, offers a more optimistic assessment of demand, transaction costs and trade during the century following the Black Death.
[130] Day (1987), 3–10.

fourteenth century all European exchange was handicapped by a chronic shortage of bullion.[131]

From its inception, trade with the Levant had been conducted at a hefty deficit to Europe, largely made good by substantial bullion payments of gold and especially silver.[132] During the European silver-mining boom of the twelfth and thirteenth centuries this had not posed a serious financial problem, as silver stocks were expanding, but this changed from the second quarter of the fourteenth century as mines became exhausted and European silver output first dwindled and then virtually ceased.[133] Thereafter, wear and tear on the coinage and the expenditure by countless pilgrims to the Holy Land exacerbated the effects of this recurrent trade deficit and progressively depleted the stocks of silver available for re-minting, forcing closure of a growing number of European mints. Bullion famine was the inevitable result. Want of silver kept Europe's highly commercialized and monetized economy desperately short of the hard cash upon which market transactions still in large measure depended (Figures 5.11A and 5.11B). Problems were particularly acute between c.1390 and c.1410 and, again, between c.1435 and c.1470 and 'reached crisis proportions during the seven worst years of the bullion-famine, from 1457 to 1464'.[134] Turkish capture of the declining Croatian mines between 1455 and 1460 made a bad situation worse.[135] Commerce was squeezed hard.[136] Scarcity proved the mother of invention and various fiscal, financial and accounting expedients were adopted to alleviate the situation and keep the wheels of commerce turning, although, unavoidably, they revolved more slowly and with greater friction.[137] Within the most cash-strapped economies this is evident in the resort to payments in labour and in kind and to trade by barter, to the detriment of multilateral exchange.[138]

Energetic prospecting revealed no rich new sources of ore and, in desperation, old mines were reopened. In the final years of the fifteenth century, however, this trickle of new silver was quickly absorbed by a concurrent increase in population, so that mint output per head remained

---

[131] Spufford (1988), 339–62. For monetarist interpretations of the late-medieval English economy see Nightingale (1990); Bolton (2012), 263–7.

[132] Day (1987), 3–10.

[133] Above, Section 2.05.2c; Spufford (1988), 348, 352, 380; Day (1987), 33–5.

[134] Spufford (1988), 361.   [135] Spufford (1988), 359–60.

[136] Hatcher (1996); Nightingale (1997).

[137] Day (1987), 24, 27–8, 44–5; Spufford (1988), 358; Nightingale (2004a); Bolton (2012), 280–95.

[138] Spufford (1988), 348; Day (1987), 82–9. Rural Ireland, for example, lapsed into coinlessness: Cosgrove (1993), 425–6, 822–5.

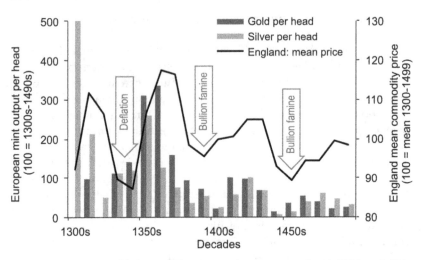

Figure 5.11 Estimated European mint output per head, 1300s to 1490s, and English mean price level (11-year moving average), 1300–1499
Sources and notes: (A) mint estimates from Spufford (1988), 419; population estimates (interpolated to decadal level) from McEvedy and Jones (1978), 19. (B) Composite price indices as described in Broadberry and others (2015), 189–94, and supplied by Bas van Leeuwen.

virtually static (Figure 5.11).[139] Under such impecunious conditions it is hardly surprising that trade and commerce at all levels – from petty exchanges paid for in coin to the high-value overseas trade upon which depended the prosperity of the greatest towns and cities – languished. While these conditions lasted, want of adequate stocks of bullion doomed European commerce to self-perpetuating stagnation. The economies that fared best, like the Northern Low Countries, were those able to capture a larger share of intra-European trade and maintain a positive trade balance. Portugal, too, bucked the trend by tapping, from the 1440s, into external supplies of African gold bullion.

Few of these problems materialized during the plague-dominated era from 1347 to 1375, since each wave of deaths effectively raised money supply per head among the survivors. Plague, in effect, served as a surrogate silver mining boom. Post-Black Death mint output per head of silver coins peaked in the 1350s and that of gold coins in the 1360s, after which output of both quickly subsided (Figure 5.11). The Black Death also triggered a sharp price inflation, which, reinforced by poor harvests, in England caused prices to rise to a peak *c*.1370 (Figure 5.11). Thus

---

[139] Spufford (1988), 358–9, 363–4; Bolton (2012), 244.

encouraged, trade bounced back. English wool exports peaked in the late 1350s and remained high until well into the 1370s, by which time cloth exports were at last rising strongly (Figure 5.12B). These were prosperous times in England's northern towns of Beverley, Hull and York.[140] Similarly, in the western Mediterranean, Marseille's port traffic in c.1360 remained at pre-Black Death levels and that of Genoa peaked in the early 1370s (Figure 5.12A). Only at Pera, across the Golden Horn from Constantinople, was there a post-plague slump and not a boom (Figure 5.12A), which proved to be an augury of what was to follow once the bountiful bullion bestowed by the Black Death had been spent. By the late 1380s the downturn was clearly apparent in England and at Marseille (Figure 5.12A), while Genoese trade with Catalonia, France, Flanders and England was falling fast. Commercial contraction had become contagious and, as traded volumes withered and the geographical orbits of European foreign trade narrowed, erstwhile major entrepôts, like Marseille, became reduced to the status of modest regional markets.[141] All branches of Europe's trade were at their lowest ebb during the first of the fifteenth-century bullion famines, c.1410, and had scarcely improved by c.1440, when the second bullion famine began to bite (Figures 5.11 and 5.12A).

These difficulties were rarely of recent origin. Problems of narrowing access to the trade of the Orient began in the 1260s and transaction costs in international trade were rising strongly from at least the 1290s. Even the scarcity of money, which surfaced as a constraint in the post-plague era, had its roots in Europe's long-established trade imbalance with Asia and the pre-Black Death decline of European silver output as deposits became exhausted. From 1347 to 1352, however, the adverse effects of dearer and more difficult long-distance trade, dwindling bullion stocks and an ever greater trade deficit were lent added force by the contraction of economic output and market demand consequent upon the collapse and long-postponed recovery of Europe's population. Collectively, these constraints thwarted the incipient economic recovery that followed the plague and, even though institutions and property rights remained favourable, made it difficult to launch any sustained and widespread growth of GDP. They constituted the economic component of the new socio-ecological dynamic that emerged following the momentous developments of the mid-fourteenth century. Moreover, in a conjuncture as striking as that of the mid-fourteenth-century tipping point itself, their grip was tightest during the very decades of the mid-fifteenth century when the Spörer Solar Minimum was most pronounced (Figure 5.1A),

[140] Kermode (1998), 261–3, 268–9, 274.   [141] Day (1987), 208.

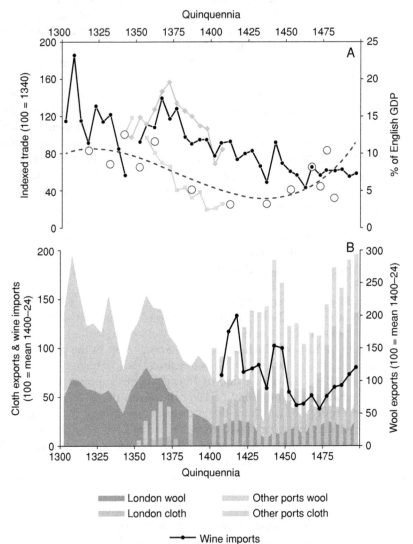

Figure 5.12 (A) The port trade of Genoa and Marseille and the overseas trade of England, 1300–1499. (B) English exports of wool and cloth via London and other ports, 1300–1499

Sources and notes: (A) Day (1987), 204 and 207, with interpolation of values for missing years; English estimates are very approximate and are made and supplied by Bas van Leeuwen. (B) Mitchell (1988), 358–9; James (1971), 57–8.

atmospheric fallout from the *c.*1458 mega-eruption of Kuwae was making itself felt, environmental instability was greatly heightened (Figure 5.2C), and outbreaks of plague and other diseases were most widely reported (Figure 5.5).[142]

5.04.4   The negative environmental and economic conjuncture
          of the mid-fifteenth century

As Figures 5.13A and 5.13B highlight, the economic difficulties generated by bullion scarcity, price deflation and a sharp contraction in overseas trade were greatly compounded by the entirely coincidental deteriorations in growing conditions and summer temperatures and dislocation of normal weather patterns arising from the dramatic weakening of the NAO. As ecological stresses mounted, sustained outbreaks of disease levied a heavy toll on European populations. Warfare, too, assumed a dangerous new aspect. In 1453 Constantinople finally fell to the Ottomans, who thereby gained control of the Bosphorus and the commerce of the Black Sea and the opportunity to advance against the Venetians in the Balkans and Aegean. By the final quarter of the fifteenth century virtually the entire eastern half of the Mediterranean was under Muslim control and Christian merchants were effectively excluded from all direct contact with the commerce of the Indian Ocean. That same year France finally brought its long-running war with England to a victorious close. Thwarted in France, England's high aristocracy chose this moment to engage in the murderous dynastic conflict which has become known as the Wars of the Roses and fought their bloodiest battle at Towton in Yorkshire in atrocious wintry weather on Palm Sunday 1461.

Economically, politically, climatically and epidemiologically, the 1430s to 1470s were an extremely testing time when the brakes were firmly on and European societies were in retreat on many fronts. A situation more different from that prevailing in 1271 when the three mercantile Polos had set out on their Chinese adventure would be hard to imagine. To resolve this impasse, environmental and biological constraints had to ease, population growth had to replace stagnation and decline, the Muslim stranglehold upon European trade with the East had to be circumvented or broken, and stocks of bullion had to be replenished, especially the silver used in everyday monetary exchange. The sixteenth century brought progress on all fronts and initiated a fresh wave of institutional and technological innovation but this was presaged during the closing

---

[142] Figure 2.9; Gao and others (2009a); Bauch (2016); Frank Ludlow, personal communication.

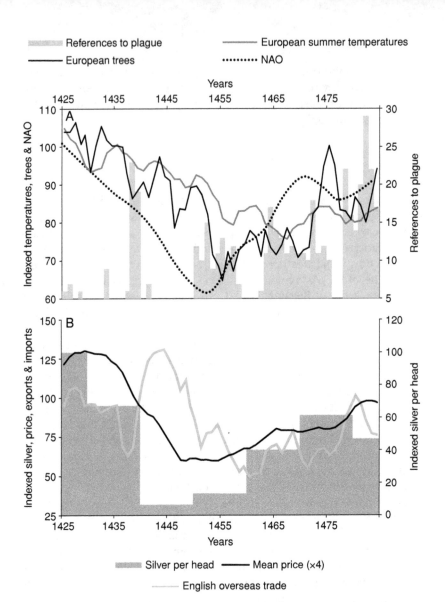

Figure 5.13 (A) The environmental and (B) the economic conjuncture of the 1430s to 1470s

Sources and notes: (A) Figures 5.1A and C, 5.2A and B, and 5.05, with the NAO, summer temperatures, and tree growth re-indexed on the 1420s. (B) silver per head from Figure 5.11 combined agricultural and industrial prices (five-year moving average, indexed on 1420s and amplified ×4) as described by Broadberry and others (2015), 189–94, and supplied by Bas van Leeuwen; English overseas trade (3-year moving average, indexed on 1420s), wool and cloth exports from Figure 5.12B combined with imports of non-sweet wine from James (1971), 58.

decades of the fifteenth century by a gradual upturn in solar irradiance, absence of further volcanic forcing and concomitant easing of climatic conditions, growing demographic resilience to plague outbreaks, and increasingly successful exploration of the Atlantic by the Portuguese and other mariners. These stirrings indicate that a fresh episode of expansion was about to begin under the greatly altered socio-ecological conditions that the Great Transition had brought into being.

5.05   Prosperity amidst adversity?

For all the negative forces ranged against demographic and economic re-expansion and growth, and the clear evidence that morbidity in the new disease environment had increased and life expectancies shortened, there are good reasons to suppose that at least materially many Europeans were better off after the Black Death. With far fewer people to feed, clothe and house there were plainly more landed resources per head and hence the real prospect of more abundant and varied diets and improved standards of clothing and housing. Involuntary landlessness and under- and unemployment had been eliminated almost at a stroke and, with empty houses going begging and rents falling, over-crowding ceased to be the inevitable condition of both the rural and urban poor. Poverty and vagrancy did not disappear, but they became the unavoidable lot of a significantly reduced proportion of households, with the result that Christian charity went further. In England, for instance, households living below the poverty line and unable to afford a respectability basket of consumption goods shrank from over 40 per cent of the total in 1290 to fewer than 20 per cent by 1381, when they likely contained no more than one in seven of all individuals.[143]

Poverty became more manageable as a problem as its scale diminished, so societies were better able to create institutions and adopt measures that would relieve it.[144] Those on low incomes benefited from the fact that it was now labour and not work that was in short supply, that labour was of enhanced value and therefore, notwithstanding the efforts of ruling elites to impose wage restraints, better remunerated, and at least in England the potential existed to augment household incomes by engaging in industrial by-employment. Given that by the mid-fifteenth century, in cities across Europe, urban building labourers were paid at daily rates that would not be bettered until the very end of the nineteenth century, it is tempting to regard the century or so that followed the Black Death as the golden age of waged labour, when ordinary working people were better

---

[143] Broadberry and others (2015), 314–21, 421.   [144] McIntosh (2012), 37–112.

off than they had been or would be for centuries and could look forward to steadily rising incomes. As Allen has argued, dearer labour may also have established a momentum of investment in labour-saving technology and human-capital formation that centuries later in the high wage economies of the southern North Sea region bore fruit in the industrial revolution.[145]

Certainly, the available daily real wage rate data provide compelling evidence that daily rates of remuneration, if not necessarily annual earnings, dramatically improved following the Black Death. In England these peak late-medieval wage rates have long been known from the pioneering work of Phelps Brown and Hopkins but it is only relatively recently that similar trends have been identified in Italy, Spain, Holland and in numbers of cities across Europe (Figure 5.14A).[146] Inevitably, there has been a tendency to equate daily real wage rates with living standards, notwithstanding that they measure rates of payment not levels of earnings and take no account of the numbers of days for which labourers actually obtained paid employment. In fact, when the drudgery involved in labouring was high, as in much building work, higher wage rates gave workers a clear incentive to labour for fewer days and enjoy more leisure.[147] Likewise, the daily wage rates paid to a single occupational cohort of male workers employed on tasks least subject to technological change provide an imperfect proxy for estimations of GDP per head, and thus economic growth, because they fail to encompass changes taking place elsewhere in the economy and are likely to reflect variations in the total numbers of days worked and the price of labour relative to other essential factor inputs as much as changes in output per head.[148] The one thing that daily real wage rates do unequivocally reveal is whether workers were getting better paid or not.

Trends in daily real wage rates in England, Spain and Italy from the start of the fourteenth century are plotted in Figure 5.14A, together with the earliest available wage series for Holland, that for building labourers in Amsterdam from the 1420s. Note that the Black Death was followed by an almost immediate rise in daily real wage rates in both Italy and England, with demand for construction workers recovering more strongly in more urbanized Italy than rural England. Demand then fell back in Italy following the plagues of the mid-1370s before recovering from this reduced base, whereas in England it continued to strengthen. By the

---

[145] Allen (2001); Allen (2009).
[146] Phelps Brown and Hopkins (1956), who built on earlier work by Rogers (1866–1902) and Beveridge (1939).
[147] Blanchard (1994), 19–22; Allen and Weisdorf (2011).
[148] Broadberry and others (2015), 247–78.

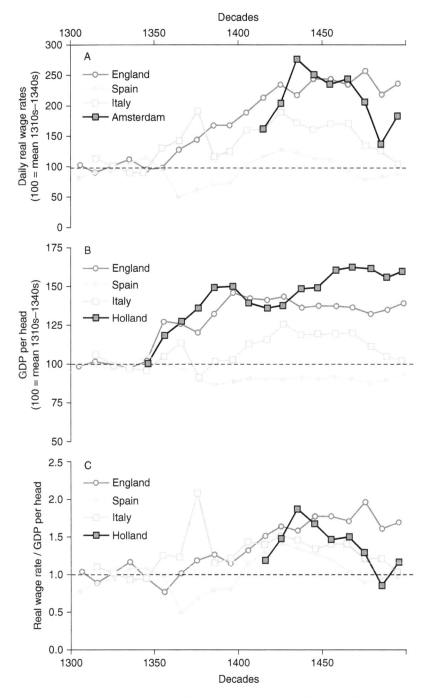

Figure 5.11 (A) Indexed daily real wage rates of male building labourers, England, Spain, Italy and Amsterdam, 1300s to 1490s. (B) Indexed
GDP per head, England, Spain, Italy and Holland, 1300s to 1490s.

1430s, when daily real wage rates were close to their respective post-Black Death peaks in both economies, building labourers were being paid at more than double the rate for the same job as in the early fourteenth century. English workers appear to have made the greater gains and by the mid-fifteenth century Amsterdam building workers were also being paid at close to English rates. Gains made by English farm labourers were of an equivalent order of magnitude.[149] Skilled craftsmen were also getting paid more but the gap between their wage rates and those of unskilled workers in the same occupations had narrowed as the skill premium diminished.[150] Provided that they worked for sufficient days, at these improved wage rates both categories of workers should have been able to afford a substantially improved standard of living. Nevertheless, there were important exceptions, as the case of building labourers in Spain illustrates.

Spanish demand for construction workers evidently collapsed following the first plague and the daily rates at which building labourers were paid remained depressed for the rest of the fourteenth century (Figure 5.14A). It took until the beginning of the fifteenth century for Spanish daily real wage rates to recover to their pre-Black Death level and they then rose to a modest peak in the 1420s, barely 12.5 per cent above the rates paid in the early 1340s, when Spain's under-populated frontier economy had been in a state of economic catch-up.[151] This evidence cautions against assuming that the post-Black Death gains in daily real wage rates won by male workers in Europe's larger towns and cities, urbanized Italy, and still populous but largely rural England, were necessarily shared by workers everywhere.[152] It also confirms that any gains made had been largely secured by the 1420s (Figure 5.14A). Thereafter, Spanish and Italian daily real wage rates drifted gently down again

---

← ————————————————————————————

Figure 5.14 (cont.) (C) Daily real wage rates divided by GDP per head, England, Spain, Italy and Holland (all series are indexed on 1310s–1340s), 1300s to 1490s
Sources and notes: England, Munro (no date); Broadberry and others (2015), 227–33. Spain, data supplied by Leandro Prados de la Escosura. Italy, Malanima (2008), 31–5; Malanima (2011), 205–9. Holland, data supplied by Bas van Leeuwen.

---

[149] Campbell (2013c), 172–4.   [150] Allen (2001).
[151] Álvarez-Nogal and Prados de la Escosura (2013), 2–3. For the favourable daily real wage rates paid in pre-Black Death Portugal see Henriques (2015), 160–1.
[152] For the substantially smaller post-Black Death gains made by English women workers see Humphries and Weisdorf (2015).

whereas English and Amsterdam wage rates edged upwards for a further couple of decades to the peak levels reached by the 1440s. English wage rates then fluctuated at this high level for the rest of the century, in contrast to Spanish, Italian and Amsterdam wage rates, which were all trending down from the 1470s. In all four of these economies a clear contrast is to be observed between the relatively buoyant employment situation before c.1420 and the far slacker conditions which then prevailed for the rest of the fifteenth century and especially during the third quarter of the century, when bullion was scarcest, trade most depressed and market demand most reduced (Figures 5.13 and 5.14A).

Reconstructions of GDP per head (Figure 5.14B and Table 5.1) further qualify and refine this picture. First, in Italy, England and, probably, Holland, real post-Black Death gains in GDP per head were only half as great as the concurrent improvements in daily real wage rates. Second, the strong surge of economic growth that came in the wake of the Black Death lasted barely a generation in England and Holland, while in Italy, following a false start in the 1350s and 1360s, it had largely spent its force by the 1420s. Thus, economic growth ceased some time before daily real wage rates stopped rising (Figures 5.14A and B). Third, in Spain GDP per head actually declined following the plague and remained below its pre-Black Death level until the end of the Middle Ages. Álvarez-Nogal and Prados de la Escosura believe that this was because population levels sank below the threshold necessary to sustain established commercial relationships and associated levels of productivity, with the result that living standards sagged.[153] Fourth, common to all four countries was the state of stasis that prevailed once initial adjustment to the transformed post-Black Death economic situation had been accomplished and the effects of shrunken demand, shrinking commerce and trade and scarce bullion had asserted themselves. Europe undoubtedly possessed the institutional and technological preconditions for growth but the essential motor of growth was lacking. In effect, the Black Death had resolved one intractable problem – rural and urban congestion – only to create another, that of inadequate demand, which was then exacerbated by the continued leaching of bullion to the East, progressive loss of overseas markets, and seemingly permanent inflation of transaction costs.

These estimates of GDP per head thus reveal three different trajectories of development following the Black Death: decline in the case of sparsely populated and post-reconquest Spain, recovery to earlier levels

---

[153] Day (1987), 207–8, characterizes 'the entire period from 1380 until 1490' in Catalonia 'as one of economic decline'.

Table 5.1 *GDP per head and urbanization ratios for selected European (and east Asian) countries and benchmark dates, 1300–1500*

	1300	1340	1400	1450	1500
(A) GDP per head (1990 Int$)					
S. Low Countries					c.$1,600
Holland		$876	$1,245	$1,432	$1,483
Italy	$1,482	$1,376	$1,601	$1,668	$1,403
Germany					$1,385
France			$1,300		$1,244
Portugal				c.$1,125	
England	$755	$777	$1,090	$1,055	$1,114
Spain	$957	$1,030	$885	$889	$889
China			$960	$983	$1,127
Japan				$554	
(B) Urbanization ratio (%)					
Belgium	22.4			33.5	
Netherlands	13.8		21.7	25.6	29.5
Italy	21.4	*17.7	17.6	17.0	21.0
Portugal	9.5			14.7	
Germany	7.9		11.1		8.2
France	8.0		10.8		8.8
UK	4.4		5.7		4.6
Spain	8.8		7.8		c.8.0

Note: The urbanization ratios in Part B are calculated for the modern countries/territories specified.
Sources: (A) Southern Low Countries, Buyst (2011); Portugal, Palma and Reis (2014); all other countries, Broadberry and others (2015), 375: figures are 10-year averages, starting in the stated year (1310 in the case of Italy). (B) Urbanization ratio, Italy (* = 1350): Malanima (2005), 108; Spain: Álvarez-Nogal and Prados de la Escosura (2013), 14; Belgium, Netherlands, Portugal, Germany, France and UK: Bairoch and others (1988), 259.

of prosperity in the case of Mediterranean Italy, and progress to higher levels of productivity with respect to the southern North Sea economies of England and Holland. Spain's GDP per head had slipped down from over $1,000 (1990 Int$) on the eve of the Black Death to just under $900 during the whole of the fifteenth century (Table 5.1). England and Holland had both overtaken Spain and after fifty years of vigorous growth boasted substantially improved GDPs per head of £1,090 and $1,245. Both, however, remained substantially behind Italy (centre-north), even though it had been experiencing serious economic difficulties before the

Black Death. Italy did eventually regain its former prosperity and until almost the end of the fifteenth century could claim to be the richest country in Europe, with an average GDP per head of over $1,600, which rose to an impressive $2,000 in the 1420s, late 1440s and early 1460s.[154] By 1500, however, Italy's economic fortunes were once again waning and its GDP per head and urbanization ratio had begun their respective long declines. Already the Northern Low Countries was demonstrating its superior dynamism and Holland in particular was firmly launched on the growth path that would make it the richest country in the world by the end of the sixteenth century.[155]

In the eleventh century, on the eve of its commercial revolution, no country in Europe had been as developed as Song China and all were poorer. Even after the devastation of the Mongol invasion and conquest the most developed parts of Yuan China may still have had the edge over their European counterparts. Yet, by the end of the Great Transition, England, the Low Countries, France, Germany and Italy were collectively on a par with Ming China and GDP per head in Europe's richest and most urbanized regions – the Northern and Southern Low Countries and the centre and north of Italy – matched that of the most developed region of the Far East, notably the Yangzi Province of China.[156] Moreover, the richest parts of Europe were three times richer than contemporary Japan.[157] Where the leading European economies had stagnated those of the Far East had slipped backwards, so that by the close of the fifteenth century any 'great divergence' that may once have existed between the economies of eastern China and western Europe had effectively disappeared (Table 5.1).[158]

Note that the daily real wage rate data imply that gains in living standards following the Black Death were greater and more sustained than concomitant improvements in GDP per head (Figures 5.14A and B). Figure 5.14C plots the ratio obtained by dividing the indexed trend of daily real wage rates by that of GDP per head. Values above (below) unity imply that daily real wage rates were high (low) relative to GDP per head. Within a generation of the Black Death in all four countries, this ratio began to move steadily in favour of daily real wage rates and peaked at ratios of 1.4 (Spain) to 1.9 (Holland) in the 1420s and 1430s, before, with the conspicuous exception of England, drifting back towards unity

---

[154] Malanima (2011), 205–9.
[155] Malanima (2011); Zanden and Leeuwen (2012); Campbell (2013c), 191.
[156] It is reasonable to suppose that GDP per head in Yangzi Province was at most 50 per cent above the Chinese average of $1,127, i.e. approximately $1,700: Broadberry and others (2015), 386.
[157] Broadberry and others (2015), 375, 384–7.   [158] Pomeranz (2000).

by 1500. These divergences reflect changes in the return to labour as a factor of production, the supply per worker of labour to the market, and the relative prices of staple consumption goods.[159]

That relative factor values shifted in favour of labour and raised its market price following the Black Death has already been demonstrated (Figure 5.9). Higher rates of pay, in turn, meant that manual workers needed to work for fewer days in order to satisfy their subsistence needs. The more that workers withdrew labour from the market the more this exerted upward pressure upon wage rates, so that trends in daily real wage rates and GDP per head increasingly diverged. In effect, once they had secured whatever subsistence standard satisfied them, workers were opting to consume more leisure rather than goods (although many may have had little choice given the slack demand for labour). This was a further reason why aggregate market demand stubbornly refused to expand for the better part of a hundred years.

These inferred reductions in the annual numbers of days worked by English, Italian, Dutch and even Spanish labourers chime with Allen and Weisdorf's analysis of the number of days per year that English urban and rural labourers needed to work in order to provide their households with a respectability basket of consumables (Figure 5.15A).[160] By the mid-fifteenth century, when daily real wage rates were at their peak, Allen and Weisdorf reckon that labouring for just three days a week was sufficient to provide workers with a satisfactory standard of living.[161] As they point out, this gave manual labourers the option of enjoying more leisure or working more industriously in order to acquire more consumables.[162] Further, they suggest that agricultural workers were more likely to opt for leisure and urban and industrial workers for industriousness. On this reasoning, it is therefore unsurprising that in predominantly agrarian England there appears to have been no corresponding rise in the urbanization ratio.[163] Contrary to Wrigley's dictum that higher real incomes

[159] Angeles (2008); Broadberry and others (2015), 260–5.

[160] The respectability basket of consumables is defined in Appendix 3.1, Table 3.4.

[161] Blanchard (1994), 17, reckoned that tenant families spent 125–135 days a year on farm work 'leaving them 130–140 days of "dead time" . . . free from the agricultural round'.

[162] Allen and Weisdorf (2011). Leisure time comprised approximately 100 holy days ordained by the Church and up to 140 days available for popular recreations: Blanchard (1994), 19–23. For the array of leisure pursuits cheaply or freely available to ordinary people see Reeves (1995).

[163] Rigby (2010), 411: 'the share of England's population living in its provincial towns in 1524 was, at most, no higher than that in 1377 and may even have been slightly lower'. Including an estimate for London taxpayers suggests to Rigby (personal communication) that England's urbanization ratio was the same in 1524 as it had been in 1377.

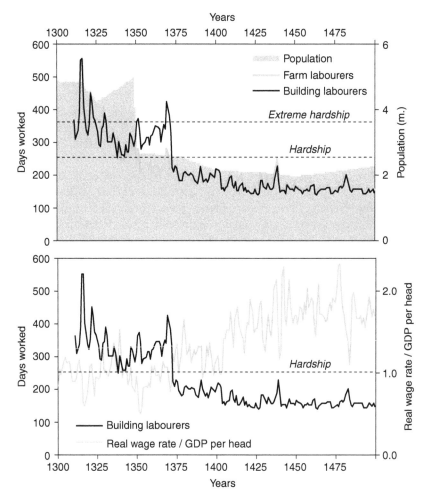

Figure 5.15 (A) The number of days that English labourers needed to work in order to satisfy their subsistence needs, compared with (B) the ratio of GDP per head to the daily real wage rates of male building labourers, 1300–1499
Sources: data on days worked supplied by Jacob Weisdorf (Allen and Weisdorf, 2011); building labourers' real wage rates from Munro (no date); GDP per head from Broadberry and others (2015), 227–33

typically generated higher urbanization ratios, during this period rising daily real wage rates did not necessarily translate into a rising proportion of urban dwellers, and to judge from the national estimates of urbanization summarized in Table 5.1B, this seems to have been repeated to varying degrees right across Europe.[164] Differences did nevertheless exist in the magnitude of the divergence between daily real wage rates and GDP per head, which was greatest in England and greater in Italy than Spain (Figure 5.14C). Probably this was because the potential for wage inflation in formerly labour-surfeited England exceeded that in already labour-scarce Spain.

Comparison of the Allen and Weisdorf index of days worked (Figure 5.15A) with the ratio of GDP per head to daily real wage rates (Figure 5.14C) reveals a clear inverse relationship (Figure 5.15B). The fewer days labourers needed to work to satisfy their preferred consumption needs, the higher daily real wage rates rose relative to GDP per head. The vital crossover between the two graphs occurred in the 1370s, as the after-effects of four major plague epidemics made themselves felt, the bargaining power of labour strengthened, price deflation began to lower the costs of subsistence and daily real wage rates rose above hardship levels. From c.1400, as plague returned and scarce bullion further deflated prices, the gap between these two measures widened decisively. Conspicuously, it was during the commercially depressed and bullion-scarce middle decades of the fifteenth century, when labourers could earn enough from just three days' work to purchase a respectability basket of consumption goods, that daily real wage rates were most inflated relative to GDP per head. This was prosperity achieved by the opposite of modern economic growth, since it sprang from a combination of labour scarcity and price deflation.

In England, it was rural producers and craftsmen rather than urban artisans and traders who most benefited from rising consumption per head of the basic subsistence goods of food, clothing, housing and religion. This shows up in changes in the agricultural product mix, as producers responded to the stronger demands for bread grains (wheat and rye) than for pottage grains (oats), for brewing grains (barley) than for food grains, and for dairy produce and meat than for food grains (Table 5.2). Increasingly, consumers wanted refined wheaten bread, not coarser and cheaper rye and multi-grain bread; ale brewed from the best barley malt, not oats malt; and beef rather than bacon. Their consumption of kilocalories went up and the forms in which those kilocalories were consumed became more highly processed, as witnessed by lower food-extraction rates.

---

[164] Wrigley (1985), 683; Bairoch and others (1988), 259: Germany, Belgium, Spain, France, Italy, Switzerland, Austria, Hungary and the Czech lands, the Balkans and European Russia all had lower urbanization ratios in 1500 than in 1400, while Romania's remained unchanged.

Table 5.2 *Output per head of crops and livestock products in English agriculture and estimated daily kilocalorie consumption of the same for benchmark years, 1300–1450*

	Estimated output per head (100 = AD 1300)						
Year	Wheat bus.	Rye etc. bus.	Barley bus.	Oats bus.	Pulses bus.	Milk gallons	Meat lbs
1300	100	100	100	96	100	100	100
1350	105	83	134	82	121	173	175
1400	113	78	192	83	157	190	170
1450	92	118	162	107	143	206	206

	Estimated daily kilocalories per head				
	Crops	Extraction rate (%)	Livestock products	Other	Total
1300	1,625	54	131	300	2,056
1400	1,896	49	211	200	2,307
1450	1,712	48	264	200	2,176

Source: Broadberry and others (2015), 98, 112, 227–33, 289

During the fifteenth century, country people ate, drank and made merry more heartily than ever before, thereby creating work for millers, bakers, maltsters and brewers. In an age when sudden death was omnipresent, most took their religion seriously and invested heavily in church building and private devotion. As the climate cooled, they dressed more warmly and rebuilt their houses and farm buildings. A minority worked industriously, amassed land, property and material possessions and hired domestic and farm servants. Nevertheless, because their demand was dispersed rather than concentrated it offered few of the Smithian gains from specialization generated by large and expanding urban centres, with their highly differentiating influence upon land use and economic rent.[165] Instead, it was the relocation of cloth making and metalworking to low-cost rural locations that contained the seeds of future economic growth and which during this period began to make the English economy less exclusively dependent upon primary production.[166]

[165] For the contrasting influences of London and Cambridge see Campbell and others (1993); Lee (2003).
[166] Broadberry and others (2013).

More urbanized Italy remained significantly richer than England and the first half of the fifteenth century, when Italian daily real wage rates and GDP per head both peaked, was ostensibly an economic as well as artistic golden age (Figures 5.14A and B).[167] Italy, however, owed this prosperity, not to growth, but to the differential contraction of population at a time of shrinking national income. As a result, the country was becoming less, not more, urbanized (Table 5.1B). In the absence of natural increase, the gains per head thereby obtained were sufficient to offset the losses incurred from the contraction of Italian overseas trade and commerce. Genoese trade with the Black Sea, Catalonia and northern Europe was in advanced decline, Venice was in virtually sole control of the lucrative but heavily taxed Indian spice trade, merchants were more risk averse than formerly, so that local orbits of exchange were now the mainstay of most mercantile activity, and, with smaller populations to supply, markets were less integrated.[168] Without reinvigorated commercial expansion to underpin it, the renewal of Italian population growth during the final decades of the fifteenth century consequently exerted negative pressure upon both daily real wage rates and GDP per head, while the country's urbanization ratio continued its inexorable decline.[169] In Italy's case the post-plague windfall economic gains lacked durability and withered once the exceptional demographic circumstances responsible for them had passed.

The Northern Low Countries fared better and by 1500 had probably overtaken Italy and become Europe's richest and most urbanized region (Table 5.1). By then financial and commercial leadership had passed from Bruges, whose harbour was silting, to Antwerp in the Duchy of Brabant, whose vibrant economy had long bucked the European trend.[170] Progress was also evident in neighbouring Holland.[171] Initially, following the Black Death, trends in Dutch GDP per head resembled those in England, with the difference that Holland was marginally the richer. In an age of contraction, the province's small size was an advantage: with a population of around 0.2 million (compared with England's 2.5 million in 1377), its national income was roughly one-tenth that of England. It possessed an excellent network of navigable waterways and canals, was blessed with abundant supplies of peat for fuel and clay for brick and tile manufacture, and was strategically well placed to profit from the

167 Brunelleschi, Donatello and Masaccio were all active in the 1420s and Piero della Francesca was in the early stages of his artistic apprenticeship.
168 Day (1987), 204–6; Kedar (1976); Bateman (2011), 464.
169 Malanima (2011); Campbell (2013c), 186.
170 Day (1987), 211–12; Bolton and Bruscoli (2008); Limberger (2008), 1–3, 215–19.
171 Bavel and Zanden (2004).

established maritime commerce of the North Sea and Baltic and the new opportunities for fishing and trade opening in the North Atlantic. Set against this, shrinking peat and rising water tables in the late fourteenth and early fifteenth centuries were a major environmental setback, displacing population from the land, obliging farmers to switch from arable to pastoral production, deflecting investment into fishing and shipping, and breeding a dependence upon imported grain supplies.[172] Confronted by these environmental challenges, Dutch GDP per head sagged between 1390 and 1430, by which date it was more-or-less on a par with that of England (Figure 5.14B).

Then, from the 1430s, when growth had ceased almost everywhere else, the Dutch economy appears to have entered a new growth phase and started to forge ahead of its neighbours (Figure 5.14B). From this time shipping, fishing, dairying, brewing, textile manufacture, brick and tile making and peat digging all grew in economic significance. By aggressively competing with the Hanse and expanding their activities into the Baltic, Dutch merchants successfully claimed an enlarged share of northern Europe's maritime commerce. Sustained by favourable marketing institutions, well-defined property rights, migration from the countryside and immigration from elsewhere around the North Sea, Holland's towns prospered, so much so that by 1500 the urbanization ratio had reached almost 30 per cent (Table 5.1B). Concurrently, GDP per head had recovered and risen to $1,480. Given that the population was also steadily rising, urbanization increasing, commerce expanding, the structure of the economy changing and technology advancing, this was real expansion-based growth and, with equally dynamic neighbouring Brabant, was rare in Europe at the time. It laid the foundation for rapid take-off of the Dutch economy in the following century.[173]

The only other country in which urbanization was actively increasing was Portugal (Table 5.1). Newly independent from, and richer than, Castile, from 1415, with backing from the more experienced Genoese, it was at the forefront of contemporary maritime exploration, south down the coast of Africa and southwest out into the Atlantic.[174] By the 1440s it had circumvented the Saharan caravan routes and was importing gold and ivory directly from West Africa, and from the 1450s its newly established Madeiran plantations were actively supplying markets across Europe, headed by Antwerp, with sugar.[175] Buoyed up by these successes, during the 1480s state-backed Portuguese mariners made a

---

[172] Bavel and Zanden (2004).   [173] Zanden and Leeuwen (2012).
[174] Phillips (1988), 239–41; Fernández-Armesto (1987), 198–200, 217.
[175] Spufford (1988), 369; Butel (1999), 36–9.

further determined effort to break Venice and Egypt's monopoly control of the Indian spice trade by discovering how to sail directly round Africa and into the Indian Ocean. In contrast to the older Mediterranean-focused economies of Italy and Spain, Portugal's orbits of trade, like those of Holland, were expanding, with the result that it was certainly more prosperous and probably richer at the end of the fifteenth century than it had been at the beginning.[176]

5.06   The end of the Great Transition: from an eastward to a westward enterprise

During the long era of efflorescence that preceded the Great Transition, Christianity, as expressed by pilgrimage and crusades, predisposed the West to look east, while commercial desire to acquire the spices, silks and ceramics of the Orient powerfully reinforced this inclination. Italian merchants led the way in developing this long-distance trade in luxury commodities, which they partially balanced by supplying the Levant with cheap, light, coloured, northern European cloths, and whatever else could be shipped and sold at a profit, including materials needed by the Mamluks for military purposes. The deficit they made good with exports of precious metals in the form of ingots, coins and plate.[177] For as long as Europe's silver-mining boom lasted, this long-distance trade in luxury commodities was a source of growth. European orbits of commerce widened and deepened as complex multilateral patterns of trade evolved to supply raw materials to textile manufacturers and finishers, sustain the mining, smelting and minting of silver, and distribute imported luxury goods to the feudal and mercantile elites who most craved them. Western Europe's great national and international fairs thrived on this commerce, which also fed growth of the greater port cities and manufacturing centres and elevated economic output to new levels.[178]

Parallel developments also took place in the Asian source regions of silk, ceramic and spice production.[179] In common with Europe, they benefited from a relatively stable climatic regime consequent upon high levels of solar irradiance and, it would appear, an equally benign epidemiological environment.[180] As Abu-Lughod has demonstrated, by the mid-thirteenth century an inter-linked Eurasian system of trade had evolved which connected producers in the Far East to consumers in the

---

[176] Fernández-Armesto (1987), 217.   [177] Day (1987), 58–63; Munro (1991), 110–21.
[178] Above, Sections 2.04.3 and 2.05.3.
[179] Lieberman (2009), 548–58; Lieberman and Buckley (2012), 1056–68; Tana (2014), 328–30.
[180] Lieberman (2009), 552–6; above, Sections 2.02 and 4.03.

Latin West.[181] Luxury merchandise flowed in one direction and silver, and to a lesser extent gold, in the other, all handled by a legion of agents, dealers, shippers, caravaners and carriers. While these trans-continental trade flows remained unobstructed and the output of Europe's silver mines exceeded the combined losses from wear and tear, the expenditure of pilgrims and exports of bullion, the prosperity of those who participated in this trade was assured.[182] Unfortunately, from the 1260s this progressively ceased to be the case.

During the opening phase of the Great Transition, when prevailing atmospheric circulation patterns began to destabilize and rinderpest probably spread from western Asia to Europe, these established trade connections ruptured and foundered and European attempts to maintain its once profitable eastward enterprise became increasingly problematic, conditional and costly.[183] Between the 1250s and 1340s the military, political and religious map of the Middle East was redrawn and in the process, one by one, the caravan routes that linked the Persian Gulf with the Mediterranean and Black Sea, together with those that crossed the interior of Eurasia, were effectively closed.[184] Eventually, this left trans-Eurasian commerce dependent on the trickle of overland trade that still reached Trebizond on the Black Sea via Tabriz in Persia and the far greater maritime flow that reached Alexandria on the Mediterranean via Cairo, the Red Sea and the Indian Ocean.[185] Where once there had been competition between multiple alternative routes there was now in effect an Egyptian monopoly. The sultan of Egypt was therefore able to insist that the Italian maritime republics pay dearly for the privilege of doing business with him. Indian spices still reached European markets but at a greatly increased cost and in the teeth of papal disapproval.

To compound the problem, final defeat of the crusader states, following the fall of Acre in 1291, had deprived European textile manufacturers of their lucrative Levantine market and thereby greatly exacerbated the one-sidedness of the spice trade.[186] Payment for that trade, now mostly handled by Venice, placed an ever greater strain upon fast-dwindling European stocks of precious metals. Until the 1320s output of European silver had been equal to the demands made of it within and beyond Europe. Thereafter, as existing ore deposits became worked out and prospecting revealed no rich new sources, supplies dried up and it was only a matter of time before the recurrent trade deficit with the East drained Europe dry of the bullion upon which its monetized and

[181] Abu-Lughod (1989), 352–6; above, Figure 2.1.   [182] Day (1987), 4–10, 60–2, 213.
[183] Above, Sections 3.01.1 and 3.03.1.   [184] Above, Section 3.01.
[185] Abu-Lughod (1989), 360.   [186] Munro (1991), 121–4.

commercialized economy depended.[187] By the mid-fourteenth century, therefore, the Indian spice trade was fast becoming a luxury that Europe could ill afford.

It was at this point that the Black Death struck and further undermined the already deteriorating socio-ecological status quo. Its sudden advent marks the brief and dramatic second phase of the Great Transition. Economically, by temporarily reflating coinage supplies per head (Figure 5.11), the massive haemorrhage of population postponed the impending financial and commercial crisis by a generation and delivered a transitory prosperity to Europe's more populous and commercialized regions and countries. Nevertheless, it was only a matter of time before the problems generated by loss of overseas markets, shrinking silver output and the persistent trade deficit with Asia reasserted themselves. In the aftermath of the demographic disaster no new engine of growth or source of bullion emerged that might have saved the situation and got the European economy out of this fundamental predicament, with the result that by the end of the fourteenth century the brief post-plague surge of economic growth had largely fizzled out (Figure 5.14B). True, many European wage earners were left better off (Figure 5.14A), but until markets expanded and demand grew there was little prospect that Smithian growth could be reignited and further gains in output per head achieved.

The obstacles to economic recovery were four-fold. First, a series of military, political and religious reversals had extinguished the great eastward enterprise that had underpinned the commercial revolution of the twelfth and thirteenth centuries.[188] Second, from the 1390s and especially the 1420s, worsening climatic conditions and renewed disease outbreaks frustrated any immediate prospect of demographic recovery (Figures 5.1, 5.2 and 5.5).[189] Third, constant net monetary losses tipped Europe into a state of recurrent bullion famine, forcing the closure of mints and starving day-to-day commercial exchange of ready specie.[190] Fourth, for cognate reasons of climate change, ecological imbalance, dynastic failure and demographic decline, economic output and long established orbits of commerce were also failing in China and Southeast Asia.[191]

---

[187] Above, Section 2.05.2c; Day (1987), 58–60.
[188] Above, Sections 3.01 and 4.01.   [189] Above, Section 4.04.
[190] Day (1987), 11–48, 58–60; Spufford (1988), 339–62; Bolton (2012), 270–2.
[191] Abu-Lughod (1989), 361: 'of crucial importance is the fact that the "Fall of the East" preceded the "Rise of the West"'. Lieberman (2009), 556–8, 724–33, 793–7; Brook (2010), 50–73; Lieberman and Buckley (2012), 1068–78.

For individual European economies, success under these straitened circumstances hinged upon maintaining a positive trade balance, making the most of domestic markets, developing institutions that minimized coordination failures and kept transaction costs down, rationalizing land use, shifting manufacturing to locations with lower production costs, adopting labour-saving technologies, seeking European substitutes for Asian raw materials and luxury goods, devising effective financial methods of coping with the scarcity of hard money, and profiting at the expense of others by capturing an enlarged share of the reduced volume of commerce.[192] Exploration offered a further potential escape from this economic impasse. Its risks and costs were great but stood to be repaid many times over if new sources of bullion could be found, fresh markets for European exports secured, and ways discovered of reaching the East that avoided running the gauntlet of the Muslim middleman. All were tough options hence it is hardly surprising that sustained economic progress proved the exception rather than the rule.

During the third and final phase of the Great Transition, played out under the adverse climatic and associated epidemiological conditions that accompanied the Spörer Minimum, obstacles to any renewal of the old eastward enterprise became insurmountable. Enfeebled Europe, depleted of population and preoccupied with its own internal divisions and conflicts, proved incapable of preventing the consolidation of Ottoman power in Asia Minor and its extension across the Bosphorus into the Balkans, culminating in the final defeat of the rump of the Byzantine Empire and the fall of Constantinople in 1453. Once this happened the Ottoman and Mamluk power blocs between them secured effective control of all the overland and maritime routes that in the heyday of the commercial revolution had given Europeans direct access to the commerce of the East.[193] Christian merchants wishing to conduct trade with the Muslim-controlled ports of the Aegean and eastern Mediterranean were left with little option but to seek concessions from the Turkish and Egyptian sultans on the best terms negotiable. Ottoman control of the Bosphorus effectively removed the Black Sea from the orbit of Italian commerce, placed the Genose and Venetian colonies of Mytilene, Chios, Crete and Cyprus under threat and set the seal on Italian commercial stagnation. To compound matters, the principal Serbian and Bosnian silver mines fell into Ottoman hands between 1455 and 1460, depriving Venice of two of its most important residual silver suppliers.[194] In the aftermath of these Turkish victories, bullion famine again handicapped

---

[192] Epstein (2000a), 52–72.   [193] Figure 2.1.
[194] Spufford (1988), 342, 349–52, 359–60.

European commerce and trade and business activity at all levels slumped (Figure 5.13).[195] It was in fact a mercy that populations were not yet recovering, for that would have placed the shrinking supply of coinage under even greater strain.

Throughout these difficult times Venice preserved its prosperity by maintaining the monopoly stake it had established with Egypt in the Indian spice trade. Accordingly, it became the chief conduit by which bullion was siphoned out of the European economy.[196] Determined prospecting yielded no significant new sources of ore and Europe yet lacked the export commodities and overseas markets that might have mitigated its heavy losses on the spice trade. To add to these difficulties, low temperatures, poor weather and zoonotics of livestock collectively depressed agricultural output by delaying grape harvests, reducing yields of grain and wool, and devastating flocks and herds.[197] They also dislocated trade flows and added to the risks of travel. Faced with these difficulties English overseas trade sank to its lowest ebb (Figure 5.12A). As the NAO weakened dramatically, deep winter cold penetrated northern Europe and the track of the Atlantic westerlies shifted south, delivering heavier rainfall to southern Europe and North Africa (Figures 5.2 and 5.4). Under these abnormal climatic conditions Portuguese mariners sailing with Genoese assistance began venturing ever further south down the West African coast in their quest for the gold-rich lands of the fabled Mali Empire. By the 1440s they had reached modern Mauritania, Senegal, Gambia and Guinea and in 1443, in direct competition with Italy, sent the first maritime consignment of African gold and ivory back to Lisbon.[198]

Blocked from pursuing an eastward enterprise, Europe's maritime nations latched onto the possibilities that might lie in other directions. Significantly, the first recorded attempt to reach India by sailing round Africa was made by the Genoese Vivaldi brothers in 1291, the year that Acre fell.[199] They exited the Mediterranean and sailed south into the Atlantic in two well-provisioned galleys, never to return. The Genoese had been undertaking regular long-distance voyages to Bruges since 1277 and thereby acquired first-hand experience of the Atlantic's challenging sailing conditions. They went on to pioneer the fully rigged, three-masted, high-sided, armed carracks that were more economical to crew, easier to defend and capable of carrying larger cargoes over longer

---

[195] Spufford (1988), 357–62.   [196] Day (1987), 8–9; Spufford (1988), 350–3.
[197] Stephenson (1988); Chuine and others (2005); Campbell (2011a), 152–6.
[198] Fernández-Armesto (1987), 140–8, 192–4; Spufford (1988), 369.
[199] Fernández-Armesto (1987), 152; Phillips (1988), 102, 252; Abu-Lughod (1989), 121–2, 188–9.

distances than heavily manned galleys. The addition of topsails and fore-masts increased their range and the incorporation of lateen sails enabled them to sail closer to the wind. These were the vessels that Bartolomeu Dias, Vasco da Gama, Cristoforo Colombo and Amerigo Vespucci would use in their epic voyages.[200] As ship design improved and navigational experience accumulated, mariners and fishermen from around Europe's Atlantic shores became more confident at dealing with that ocean's tricky winds, tides and currents and ventured ever further out to sea.

Iceland and occasionally Greenland had been destinations for mer-chants and fishermen from around the North Sea for centuries; then, from the late fourteenth century, the Atlantic fisheries grew in impor-tance at the expense of those of the North Sea, attracting Basque, Breton and English west-country fishermen and Dutch whalers.[201] Knowledge accumulated about the Atlantic's stock of available marine resources and from the mid-fifteenth century it was only a matter of time before the rich fishing grounds of the Grand Banks were stumbled upon. Mean-while, interest grew in the scattering of remote Atlantic islands, both known and rumoured, and speculation grew about where this seem-ingly limitless ocean might lead. Efforts at exploration, however, were mostly directed to the south, where, from the late fourteenth century, the 'Fortunate Islands' became the object of Iberian interest.[202] By 1415 the Canary Islands, as they now became known, had been explored and annexed by Spain and in 1420 Portugal claimed deserted Madeira and shortly afterwards went on to rediscover and annex the Azores.[203]

By this time informed Europeans realized that if they wanted to recon-nect with the Orient and find a cheaper way of obtaining Indian spices and other exotic and luxury wares than via the Venetian–Egyptian monopoly, they had to do so by heading in the opposite direction from that taken two hundred years earlier by Marco Polo. The most promising options seemed to lie in sailing either south around Africa or west around the globe. The key protagonists in this venture were the Genoese in collab-oration with the Portuguese, although it was eventually under Span-ish colours that Genoese Cristoforo Colombo sailed and it was the English who backed Venetian Giovanni Caboto (alias John Cabot). When the justly celebrated breakthrough discoveries finally came they did so quickly. Between 1488 and 1499 Bartolomeu Dias rounded the Cape of Good Hope, Vasco da Gama reached India by sea, and Cristoforo Colombo, Giovanni Caboto and Amerigo Vespucci made landfalls on

---

[200] Unger (1980), 201–50; Phillips (1988), 230.
[201] Childs (1995); Butel (1999), 57–8; Kowaleski (2000), 27–8.
[202] Fernández-Armesto (1987), 171–92. [203] Phillips (1988), 229–30.

the West Indies, North America and Brazil. Their epic voyages sprang from complex impulses whose origin lay in the commercial and economic setbacks and reversals of the Great Transition of the fourteenth and fifteenth centuries. In these developments, the reorientation of Genoese enterprise from the eastern to the western Mediterranean and beyond proved to be of decisive importance.[204]

In the 1490s Europeans finally regained the direct access to the commerce of the East which they had lost in the 1340s. They also gained access to the undreamt-of mineral wealth of the, to them, hitherto unknown Americas. Within the space of fifty years Europe's commercial isolation had been ended and state of bullion scarcity reversed. At about the same time, for reasons that remain to be convincingly explained, epidemiological constraints upon European demographic recovery were finally relaxed so that from c.1500, notwithstanding continued outbreaks of plague and other diseases, populations were at last growing again almost everywhere. It must also have helped that the coldest phase of the Spörer Solar Minimum was over, with output of solar irradiance once again increasing.[205] The Great Transition was over and a new growth-generating socio-ecological regime had at last been established. With gathering momentum, a fresh phase of cultural, commercial and economic efflorescence had opened.

Within Europe, however, a striking reversal of fortunes had occurred, insofar as this next phase of European expansion was led not by long-commercialized Italy, which had lost its earlier comparative advantage, or even by newly colonial Portugal and recently reunited and imperial Spain, but by the entrepreneurial and mercantile Northern Low Countries. Already on an upward trajectory and with well-developed shipping and financial sectors when Portugal and Spain's breakthrough overseas discoveries were made, Brabant and Holland were quick to seize the commercial initiative and take advantage of these new opportunities[206] Antwerp was the runaway urban success story of the age and the Dutch towns soon followed. During the sixteenth century Holland became the fastest-growing economy in Europe and by the close of that century almost certainly the richest region in the world, ahead of both Italy (centre-north) and, probably, the Yangzi Province of China (Table 5.1).[207] It also outstripped its close neighbour England, whose big growth opportunity would not come for another two centuries.[208]

---

[204] Fernández-Armesto (1987), 96–120, 206–7, 219–20; Abu-Lughod (1989), 362–3; Butel (1999), 34–6.
[205] Figure 2.9.   [206] Bavel and Zanden (2004); Zanden and Leeuwen (2012).
[207] Campbell (2013c), 179–80, 189–92; Broadberry and others (2015), 374–87.
[208] Broadberry and others (2015), 208–12, 395–7.

Over the course of the fourteenth and fifteenth centuries England had nevertheless laid the institutional, agrarian and industrial foundations of its future prosperity. The Black Death had worked to its economic advantage by relieving the country of the oppressive burden of poverty and opening the way to structural economic change. Slowly, and with the protection of selective customs duties, England began to take advantage of its latent comparative advantages in mixed farming, textile manufacture, and mining and metalworking, and English merchants started to play a greater role in the nation's commerce.[209] When vigorous population growth resumed in the sixteenth century England thereby held onto its post-plague windfall gains in productivity, albeit at the price of most households having to work more industriously. Crucially, unlike most other European economies and in direct contrast to the situation in the thirteenth century, expansion of industrial and service sector employment absorbed most population growth with the result that GDP per head held steady and labour productivity in agriculture rose. England, too, had successfully made the Great Transition to a more dynamic demographic and economic trajectory.

For western Europe as a whole the net effect of the Great Transition was a profound reconfiguration of commercial activity, redefinition of comparative advantages and selective renewal of demographic and economic vitality. Yet the far-reaching changes and reversals of fortune that occurred between Marco Polo's journey to China and Vasco da Gama's voyage two centuries later to India are inexplicable without reference to the physical, ecological and biological stresses generated by global climate reorganization. The fate of late-medieval European populations, in fact, was intimately bound up with environmental developments taking place more than six thousand kilometres to the east in the semi-arid and sparsely populated interior of central Asia, for without the ecologically triggered eruption of the Black Death the trajectory of socio-ecological trends would undoubtedly have followed a different course. Microbial-scale developments in this case had macro-scale consequences.

The Great Transition began with the quasi-autonomous changes in climatic, ecological, biological, political, commercial and economic processes set in motion in the 1260s and 1270s, as the MCA came to an end and the Wolf Solar Minimum commenced. A regime-changing tipping point was then reached in the 1340s, when a perfect storm of environmental and societal events precipitated the implosion of established levels of population and economic activity. Incipient post-crisis Malthusian recovery was aborted by a sequence of repeat plague outbreaks,

---

[209] Broadberry and others (2013).

the first in 1360–3. By the 1390s the point of no return had been passed, as populations and economic output became locked onto a downward path and the post-Black Death bonanza of economic growth petered out. Onset of the Spörer Solar Minimum reinforced these negative trends, which finally bottomed out in the third quarter of the fifteenth century. By then, temperatures were much reduced, the atmospheric circulation patterns of the LIA were firmly in the ascendant, plague and an array of undiagnosed diseases were resurgent, human populations were at their lowest ebb, bullion supplies were drying up, economic growth had effectively stalled and western Europe was experiencing increasing commercial isolation. This was the baseline from which, in the closing years of the fifteenth century, the next phase of expansion and efflorescence would be launched, when Europe's most enterprising maritime nations and regions first redefined and then proceeded to dominate the world. This was when Europe achieved the commercial hegemony that it had so conspicuously lacked in the thirteenth century.[210] In this vital respect, the Great Transition was the precursor to the Great Divergence.

[210] Abu-Lughod (1989).

Epilogue
Theory, contingency, conjuncture
and the Great Transition

Neoclassical economics, Marxist theory and the New Institutional Economics have all been employed to obtain valuable insights into aspects of the Great Transition.[1] Each approach has had powerful advocates and the conflict between rival theoretical camps has sometimes been intense.[2] None, however, has succeeded in providing a historically convincing account of the entirety of this chronologically extended and geographically extensive socio-ecological transformation. In particular, the pan-continental pivotal environmental disasters of famine, murrain and plague defy classification as Malthusian positive checks plain and simple and stubbornly refuse to fit comfortably within explanations that give causal primacy to mostly territorially specific human processes and relationships.[3] The scale of the Great Transition requires analyses that transcend national historiographies. Nor is going to the opposite extreme, and treating the environmental agencies of climate and disease as paramount, any less unsatisfactory. To claim, as do David Zhang and others, that 'climate change was the ultimate cause, and climate-driven economic downturn was the direct cause, of large-scale human crises in preindustrial Europe and the northern hemisphere', patently fails to do justice to the complexity of human actions and reactions, let alone the autonomy of biological agents.[4] In the case of the large-scale human crisis of the 1340s, climate's impact upon society was mediated through the intervening influence of ecology, disease, microbes and many aspects of human behaviour (Figure 6.1). As should be apparent from Sections 3 and 4 of this book, unravelling these interactions with due regard to the available scientific and historical evidence is far from straightforward. Sweeping claims which assert the primacy of one agency or set of relationships over all others will never wash with historians, who are acutely aware that the devil is always in the detail.

---

[1] For a comprehensive review see Hatcher and Bailey (2001).
[2] For example, Aston and Philpin (1985).   [3] Hoffmann (2014), 342–51.
[4] Zhang and others (2011), 17296.

The mistake, of course, is to create a binary divide between human and environmental agencies and treat the former as the concern of historians and the latter as 'but a backdrop to human affairs, having no or insignificant actual effects on them'.[5] That includes labelling human actions as 'endogenous', and therefore to be understood and explained, and environmental variables as 'exogenous', and consequently less worthy of examination or to be relegated to the status of 'acts of providence'.[6] To do justice to a complex past and the dynamism of the natural world in which people lived, worked and reproduced it is necessary to understand how climate and society, ecology and biology, microbes and humans, acting separately and in combination with each other, shaped the course of history (Figure 6.1).[7] Such a holistic approach necessarily creates a multi-layered narrative which breaches conventional historical boundaries of time and place.[8] The Great Transition spared no part of the Old World and underpinned parallel changes in the New World. As it unfolded, interactions and feedbacks, both environmental and human, occurred at a range of nested temporal and spatial scales – from the short-term to the long-term and the micro to the macro – as change cascaded through the prevailing socio-ecological system (which itself existed in a state of dynamic equilibrium) in complex ways. Such a cascading process of contingent chaotic development defies any simple law of 'cause and effect' and is a reminder that each stage of each component in the transition was unique, with outcomes that were rarely predetermined and always prone to unpredictability.[9]

Mega events, such as the VEI 7 eruption of Samalas volcano in 1257/8, which is believed to have been the single greatest explosive eruption of the Holocene, did not necessarily have proportionately substantial and enduring environmental and human impacts.[10] Conversely, plague's successive transformation and crossover from a dormant enzootic state, confined to reservoirs of infection in the semi-arid interior of central Asia, to a devastating human pandemic which spread throughout the greater part of the Old World, classically illustrates the capacity of ostensibly small developments, such as a change of plague hosts from sylvatic to commensal rodents or of plague vectors from *X. cheopis* to *P. irritans*, to have

---

[5] Hoffmann (2014), 6.

[6] Harvey (1991), 2–3, who nevertheless argues that 'to determine the importance of the exogenous factors in relation to others is the most important task facing the historian'.

[7] Hoffmann (2014), 7–11.

[8] Examples include Abu-Lughod (1989); Lieberman (2009).

[9] Hatcher and Bailey (2001), 213–16. I am grateful to Terry Pinkard for the term 'contingent chaotic development'.

[10] Oppenheimer (2003); Lavigne and others (2013); Campbell (2013a).

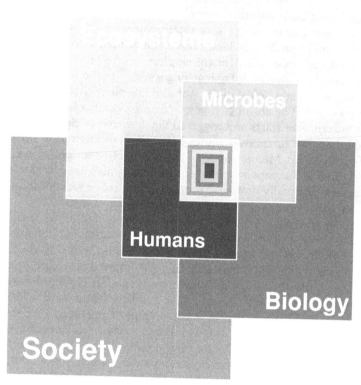

Figure 6.1 The six core components of a dynamic socio-ecological system
Source: based on National Academy of Sciences (2008), Figure SA-4, 14

far-reaching historical consequences.[11] Likewise, creation of the Mongol Empire might never have occurred had not mega-drought impelled the Mongols to raid and then invade the Western Xia between 1205 and 1209, sudden onset of pluvial conditions from 1210 then fortuitously ensured that the Mongol cavalry was kept amply supplied with fresh mounts and fodder, and, crucially, a leader with the political and military genius of Chinggis Khan emerged capable of welding the feuding Mongol tribes into an invincible army.[12] The Mongol Empire, in turn,

---

[11] Section 4, above.   [12] Hessl and others (2013).

opened up the Eurasian interior to increased latitudinal movement, making possible the eastward journey of Westerners such as Marco Polo and the westward spread of diseases, notably rinderpest and plague. McNeill may have been mistaken in his belief that the Black Death originated in eastern China but he was surely correct in his observation that 'the intensification of over-land caravan movement across Asia that reached its climax under the Mongol empires... affected both macro- and micro-parasitic patterns in far-reaching ways'.[13] In the Middle East, it was of course Mongol defeat of the Abbasid Caliphate that caused the first domino to fall. The ensuing Mongol–Mamluk conflict hastened the demise of the crusader states and triggered the diversion or closure of the long-established Syrian caravan routes by which trade flowed between the Persian Gulf and Mediterranean. This brought to an end the era of relatively free and competitive movement across this vital corridor of commerce and eventually bestowed monopoly control of residual East–West commerce upon the ultimately victorious sultan of Egypt.

In politically fragmented Europe peace was fragile and all too easily broken. Had descent of the Scottish and French royal houses remained uninterrupted in the male line following the deaths, respectively, of Alexander III in 1286 and Charles IV in 1328, there might have been no destructive Scottish War of Independence or ruinous Hundred Years War. Moreover, the timing of both great conflicts could hardly have been worse. Post-Bannockburn Scottish raiding of northern England between 1314 and 1322 and Edward Bruce's wholesale invasion of Ireland in 1315 had particularly enduring negative effects because military pillaging and destruction coincided with the worst years of the Great European Famine. Together, troop movements and cattle raiding also helped fan the independent spread of cattle plague with devastating consequences for societies geared towards pastoral production.[14] The commercial, economic and political repercussions of the far greater and costlier Anglo-French conflict were felt even more widely and extended beyond the principal combatants to include Italian merchant bankers, Flemish textile manufacturers and, again, the Scots. What mattered here was not just the contingent causes of these specific events but the conjuncture at one and the same time of an array of political, military, financial, economic, demographic, environmental and epidemiological developments. During the Great European Famine of 1316–22 the near-perfect storm these collectively generated came close to

---

[13] McNeill (1977), 162 (a view echoed by Hymes (2014)).
[14] Campbell (2010a), 7–13; Slavin (2012); Slavin (2014).

overwhelming the prevailing socio-ecological regime's precarious balance and certainly advanced it closer to what ecologists term a bifurcation or tipping point.[15]

For Europe the long phase of efflorescence that preceded the Great Transition had been characterized by a broadly benign conjuncture between onset of the Medieval Solar Maximum, prevalence of fairly stable and favourable climatic conditions, a relatively low epidemiological burden, buoyant agricultural output, adoption of an array of macro and micro institutional innovations which defined property rights, lowered transaction costs and promoted commercial exchange, the success of the crusades, a prolonged silver mining boom and much else. The positive synergies thereby engendered sustained demographic and economic expansion for the better part of two centuries.[16] Then, in the fourteenth century, it was the unlucky conjuncture of the Wolf Solar Minimum, climate change and associated worsening weather, destabilizing ecosystems, eruption of major panzootics, escalating warfare, rising transaction costs, deepening commercial recession and falling silver output that first halted economic growth and then triggered the implosion of populations and economic activity.[17] This combination of adverse circumstances was at its worst in the 1340s and provided the context within which the Black Death erupted and spread.

This was the perfect storm that initiated irreversible regime change. What made the effects of the Black Death so profound was that it struck when socio-ecological conditions were already on the cusp of a tipping point.[18] Developments in the aftermath of the Black Death were then shaped by the conjuncture of an increased epidemiological burden, onset from the 1390s of the prolonged Spörer Solar Minimum, ongoing global climate reorganization, the rising political and military power of the Mamluks and Ottomans, deepening commercial recession, the joint Venetian and Egyptian monopoly of the Indian spice trade, drying up of European silver output and consequent bullion famine.[19] These constraints were at their most extreme in the 1450s and 1460s. It was then that output of solar irradiance sank to a minimum, global and northern hemisphere temperatures were the coldest for over a thousand years, the NAO was at its weakest and plague outbreaks were widely reported across Europe. Further, between 1453 and 1461 Constantinople, the Serbian and Bosnian silver mines and Trebizond all fell to the

[15] Above, Sections 3.01.3 and 4.01; Scheffer (2009), 18–22.
[16] Above, Section 2.   [17] Above, Sections 3 and 4.
[18] Scheffer (2009), 282–95.   [19] Above, Section 4.

Ottomans, acute bullion famine set in from 1457 to 1464, Kuwae in the South Pacific erupted in $c.$1458 with mega-explosive force, and international trade slumped.[20] It was the easing of some, but by no means all, of these constraints and initiation of a new phase of expansion during the last quarter of the fifteenth century, with some relaxation of the grip of disease upon demographic replacement and fuller exploration of the commercial opportunities provided by the Atlantic, that brought the Great Transition to an end.

It is part of the Great Transition's enduring fascination that it exemplifies no iron law of economics or ecology. Across the Old World it nevertheless brought about a profound and synchronous change in the trajectories of socio-economic development, advantaging some societies and disadvantaging others. By its close the economic dynamism of Europe's Mediterranean economies was waning and that of its Atlantic-edge economies was waxing.[21] Italy was at the brink of its long decline, Portugal and Spain were on the threshold of the colonial and imperial opportunities that their breakthrough overseas discoveries would deliver, England was steadily developing its comparative advantage in industry and manufacturing, and Holland was poised to enter its seaborne golden age.[22] The most developed of these European economies were now more-or-less abreast of their Far Eastern counterparts.[23] This was partly because Europe's mixed-farming methods of husbandry had proved more adaptable to climate change and yielded intrinsically higher levels of labour productivity than the rice-growing economies of Monsoon Asia. Plague, too, which originated in central Asia but then spread west and possibly had its most devastating effect upon Europe, had helped restore a healthier balance between population and resources within Europe's commercial core regions. Already distinguished by extensive use of non-human muscle power and mechanical energy, western Europe became a region of relatively scarce and dear labour in which it paid to develop and adopt labour-saving technology.[24]

When Europe's commercial revolution began, at the start of the Medieval Solar Maximum, Song China was technologically and economically far ahead of Latin Christendom. When the Great Transition ended, as the Spörer Solar Minimum passed its nadir, the more advanced parts of Christendom had caught up and in terms of technology and trade the West was about to switch from borrower to lender and laggard to leader.

---

[20] Above, Figure 2.1.   [21] Broadberry and others (2015), 374–83.
[22] Campbell (2013c); above, Section 5.03.1.
[23] Above, Table 5.1.   [24] Allen (2009).

It was, in fact, from this 'Great Transition' that the 'Great Divergence' between the increasingly capital-intensive and dynamic economies of the southern North Sea Region and the labour-intensive and undynamic economies of Southeast Asia and especially eastern China would in due course flow.

References

AHR   *Agricultural History Review*
BHM   *Bulletin of the History of Medicine*
C&C   *Continuity and Change*
EcHR   *Economic History Review*
EEH   *Explorations in Economic History*
EID   *Emerging Infectious Diseases*
EREH   *European Review of Economic History*
GRL   *Geophysical Research Letters*
IGBP   *IGBP PAGES/World Data Center for Paleoclimatology Data
         Contribution Series, NOAA/NCDC Paleoclimatology Program, Boulder
         CO, USA*
JEH   *Journal of Economic History*
JHG   *Journal of Historical Geography*
JIH   *Journal of Interdisciplinary History*
P&P   *Past and Present*
PNAS   *Proceedings of the National Academy of Sciences of the United States of
         America*
QSR   *Quaternary Science Reviews*

Abel, Wilhelm (1935 and 1980), *Agrarkrisen und agrarkonjunktur in Mitteleuropa
    vom 13. bis zum 19. jahrhundert (Agricultural fluctuations in Europe from the
    thirteenth to the twentieth centuries,* trans. O. Ordish, London), Berlin.
Aberth, John (2001), *From the brink of the apocalypse: confronting famine, war,
    plague, and death in the later Middle Ages,* New York and London.
Aberth, John (2005), *The Black Death: the great mortality of 1348–1350. A brief
    history with documents,* Boston and New York.
Abu-Lughod, Janet L. (1989), *Before European hegemony: the world system A.D.
    1250–1350,* Oxford.
Abulafia, David (1981), 'Southern Italy and the Florentine economy, 1265–
    1370', *EcHR* 34 (3), 377–88.
Abulafia, David (1987), 'Asia, Africa and the trade of medieval Europe', 402–73
    in M. M. Postan and Edward Miller, eds., *The Cambridge economic history of
    Europe, II, Trade and industry in the Middle Ages,* 2nd edn, Cambridge.
Abulafia, David (2005), *The two Italies: economic relations between the Norman
    kingdom of Sicily and the northern communities,* Cambridge.

Achtman, Mark (2012), 'Insights from genomic comparisons of genetically monomorphic bacterial pathogens', *Philosophical Trans. Royal Soc. B: Biological Sciences* 367 (1590), 860–7.

Achtman, Mark; Morelli, Giovanna; Zhu, Peixuan; Wirth, Thierry; Diehl, Ines; Kusecek, Barica; Vogler, Amy J.; Wagner, David M.; Allender, Christopher J.; Easterday, W. Ryan; Chenal-Francisque, Viviane; Worsham, Patricia; Thomson, Nicholas R.; Parkhill, Julian; Lindler, Luther E.; Carniel, Elisabeth; Keim, Paul (2004), 'Microevolution and history of the plague bacillus, *Yersinia pestis*', *PNAS* 101 (51), 17837–42.

Alfani, Guido (2013), 'Plague in seventeenth century Europe and the decline of Italy: an epidemiological hypothesis', *EREH* 17 (4), 408–30.

Alfani, Guido; Mocarelli, Luca; Strangio, Donatella (2015), 'Italian famines: an overview (ca. 1250–1810)', Dondena Working Paper, Milan.

Allen, Martin (2012), *Mints and money in medieval England*, Cambridge.

Allen, Robert C. (2001), 'The great divergence in European wages and prices from the Middle Ages to the First World War', *EEH* 38, 411–47 (wages of labourers and craftsmen together with consumer price indices are available on the Global Prices and Incomes Database website at University of California, Davis: http://gpih.ucdavis.edu/Datafilelist.htm).

Allen, Robert C. (2009), *The British industrial revolution in global perspective*, Cambridge.

Allen, Robert C.; Weisdorf, Jacob L. (2011), 'Was there an "industrious revolution" before the industrial revolution? An empirical exercise for England, *c.*1300–1830', *EcHR* 64 (3), 715–29.

Allmand, Christopher (1988), *The Hundred Years War: England and France at war c.1300–c.1450*, Cambridge.

Álvarez-Nogal, C.; Prados de la Escosura, L. (2013), 'The rise and fall of Spain (1270–1850)', *EcHR*, 66 (1), 1–37.

Angeles, Luis (2008), 'GDP per capita or real wages? Making sense of conflicting views on pre-industrial Europe', *EEH* 45 (2), 147–63.

Anker, M; Schaaf, D. (2000), 'Plague', 25–37 in Department of Communicable Disease Surveillance and Response, World Health Organization, *Report on global surveillance of epidemic-prone infectious diseases*, Geneva. www.who.int/csr/resources/publications/surveillance/en/plague.pdf

Antoine, Daniel (2008), 'The archaeology of "plague"', *Medical History*, Supplement 27, 101–14.

Ari, Tamara Ben; Neerinckx, Simon; Gage, Kenneth L.; Kreppel, Katharina; Laudisoit, Anne; Leirs, Herwig; Stenseth, Nils Chr. (2011), 'Plague and climate: scales matter', *PLoS Pathogens* 7 (9), e1002160.

Ashtor, Eliyahu (1976), *A social and economic history of the Near East in the Middle Ages*, London.

Ashtor, Eliyahu (1983), *Levant trade in the later Middle Ages*, Princeton.

Astill, Grenville (1988), 'Fields', 62–85 in Grenville Astill and Annie Grant, eds., *The countryside of medieval England*, Oxford.

Astill, Grenville; Grant, Annie (1988), 'The medieval countryside: efficiency, progress and change', 213–34 in Grenville Astill and Annie Grant, eds., *The countryside of medieval England*, Oxford.

Aston, T. H.; Philpin, C. H. E., eds. (1985), *The Brenner debate: agrarian class structure and economic development in pre-industrial Europe*, Cambridge.

Atkin, M. A. (1994), 'Land use and management in the upland demesne of the de Lacy estate of Blackburnshire c 1300', *AHR* 42 (1), 1–19.

Ayyadurai, Saravanan; Houhamdi, Linda; Lepidi, Hubert; Nappez, Claude; Raoult, Didier; Drancourt, Michel (2008), 'Long-term persistence of virulent *Yersinia pestis* in soil', *Microbiology* 154, 2865–71.

Ayyadurai, Saravanan; Sebbane, Florent; Raoult, Didier; Drancourt, Michel (2010), 'Body lice, *Yersinia pestis orientalis*, and Black Death', *EID* 16 (8), 92–3.

Bailey, Mark (1991), '*Per impetum maris*: natural disaster and economic decline in eastern England, 1275–1350', 184–208 in Bruce M. S. Campbell, ed., *Before the Black Death: studies in the 'crisis' of the early fourteenth century*, Manchester.

Bailey, Mark (1996), 'Demographic decline in late medieval England: some thoughts on recent research', *EcHR* 49 (1), 1–19.

Bailey, Mark (2007), *Medieval Suffolk: an economic and social history 1200–1500*, Woodbridge.

Bailey, Mark (2014), *The decline of serfdom in late medieval England: from bondage to freedom*, Woodbridge.

Baillie, M. G. L. (1994), 'Dendrochronology raises questions about the nature of the AD 536 dust-veil event', *The Holocene* 4 (2), 212–21.

Baillie, M. G. L. (2000), 'Putting abrupt environmental change back into human history', 46–75 in K. Flint and H. Morphy, eds., *Culture, landscape, and the environment: the Linacre lectures 1997–8*, Oxford.

Baillie, M. G. L. (2001), 'The AD 540 event', *Current Archaeology* 15 (6), No. 174, 266–9.

Baillie, M. G. L. (2006), *New light on the Black Death: the cosmic connection*, Stroud.

Baillie, M. G. L. (2008), 'Proposed re-dating of the European ice core chronology by seven years prior to the 7th century AD', *GRL* 35, L15813.

Bairoch, Paul; Batou, Jean; Chèvre, Pierre (1988), *The population of European cities from 800 to 1850: data bank and short summary of results*, Geneva.

Baker, Alan R. H. (1964), 'Open fields and partible inheritance on a Kent manor', *EcHR* 17 (1), 1–23.

Baker, Alan R. H. (1966), 'Evidence in the *Nonarum inquisitiones* of contracting arable lands in England during the early fourteenth century', *EcHR* 19 (3), 518–32.

Baker, Alan R. H. (1973), 'Changes in the later Middle Ages', 186–247 in H. C. Darby, ed., *A new historical geography of England*, Cambridge.

Baker, Andy; Proctor, Christopher J.; Barnes, William L. (2002), 'Stalagmite lamina doublets: a 1000 year proxy record of severe winters in northwest Scotland', *International Journal of Climatology* 22, 1339–45.

Bard, Edouard; Frank, Martin (2006), 'Climate change and solar variability: what's new under the sun?', *Earth & Planetary Science Letters* 248, 1–14.

Bard, Edouard; Raisbeck, Grant; Yiou, Françoise; Jouzel, Jean (2000), 'Solar irradiance during the last 1200 years based on cosmogenic nuclides', *Tellus* 52B, 985–92.

Barg, M. A. (1991), 'The social structure of manorial freeholders: an analysis of the Hundred Rolls of 1279', *AHR* 39, 108–15.

Barnes, Guy D. (1984), *Kirkstall Abbey, 1147–1539: an historical study*, Publications of Thoresby Society 57 (128), Leeds.

Bartlett, Kenneth R. (1992), *The civilization of the Italian Renaissance*, Toronto.

Bateman, Victoria N. (2011), 'The evolution of markets in early modern Europe, 1350–1800: a study of wheat prices', *EcHR* 64 (2), 447–71.

Bauch, Martin (2016), 'The day the sun turned blue. A volcanic eruption in the early 1460s and its possible climatic impact – a natural disaster perceived globally in the late Middle Ages?', in Gerrit J. Schenk, ed., *Historical disaster experiences: a comparative and transcultural survey between Asia and Europe*, Heidelberg.

Bavel, Bas van (2010), *Manors and markets: economy and society in the Low Countries, 500–1600*, Oxford.

Bavel, Bas van; De Moor, Tine; Zanden, Jan Luiten van (2009), 'Introduction: factor markets in global economic history', *C&C* 24, 9–21.

Bavel, Bas van; Zanden, Jan Luiten van (2004), 'The jump-start of the Holland economy during the late-medieval crisis, c.1350–c.1500', *EcHR* 57 (3), 503–32.

Beasley, P. (1965), 'Human fleas (*Pulex irritans*) incriminated as vectors of plague in Bolivia', *United States Navy Medical News Letter* 46, 5–6.

Bechah, Yassina; Capo, Christian; Mege, Jean-Louis; Raoult, Didier (2008), 'Epidemic typhus', *Lancet Infectious Diseases* 8 (7), 417–26.

Bekar, Cliff T.; Reed, Clyde G. (2009), 'Risk, asset markets and inequality: evidence from medieval England', *University of Oxford, Discussion Papers in Economic and Social History* 79, Oxford.

Bekar, Cliff T.; Reed, Clyde G. (2013), 'Land markets and inequality: evidence from medieval England', *EREH* 17 (3), 294–317.

Bell, Adrian R; Brooks, Christopher; Dryburgh, Paul (2007), *The English wool market, c.1230–1327*, Cambridge.

Bell, Adrian R; Brooks, Christopher; Moore, Tony K. (2009a), 'Interest in medieval accounts: examples from England, 1272–1340', *History* 94 (316), 411–33.

Bell, Adrian R; Brooks Christopher; Moore, Tony K. (2009b), *Accounts of the English Crown with Italian merchant societies, 1272–1345*, List & Index Society 331, Kew.

Bell, Adrian R; Brooks Christopher; Moore, Tony K. (2011), 'Credit finance in the Middle Ages: Edward I and the Ricciardi of Lucca', 101–16 in Janet Burton, Frédérique Lachaud and Phillipp Schofield, eds., *Thirteenth-century England XIII*, Woodbridge.

Benedictow, Ole J. (2004), *The Black Death 1346–1353: a complete history*, Woodbridge.

Benedictow, Ole J. (2010), *What disease was plague? On the controversy over the microbiological identity of plague epidemics of the past*, Leiden.

Berkelhammer, Max; Sinha, Ashish; Mudelsee, Manfred; Cheng, Hai; Edwards, R. Lawrence; Cannariato, Kevin (2010a), 'Persistent multidecadal power of the Indian summer monsoon', *Earth & Planetary Science Letters* 290 (1–2), 166–72.

Data: Berkelhammer, Max; Sinha, Ashish; Mudelsee, Manfred; Cheng, Hai; Edwards, R. Lawrence; Cannariato, Kevin (2010b), 'Dandak Cave, India Speleothem Oxygen Isotope Data', IGBP # 2010-011.

Berman, Harold J. (1983), *Law and revolution: the formation of the Western Legal Tradition*, Cambridge, Mass.

Beveridge, William Henry (1939), *Prices and wages in England from the twelfth to the nineteenth century*, London.

Biddick, Kathleen (1989), *The other economy: pastoral husbandry on a medieval estate*, Berkeley and Los Angeles.

Biraben, Jean-Noël (1975), *Les hommes et la peste en France et dans les pays européens et méditerranéens, 1, La peste dans l'histoire*, Paris and The Hague.

Biraben, Jean-Noël (1979), 'Essai sur l'évolution du nombre des hommes', *Population* 34 (1), 13–25.

Birrell, Jean (1969), 'Peasant craftsmen in the medieval forest', *AHR* 17 (2), 91–107.

Blair, John, ed. (1988), *Minsters and parish churches: the local church in transition 950–1200*, Oxford University Committee for Archaeology, Monograph 17.

Blanc, G.; Baltazard, M. (1942), 'Rôle des ectoparasites humains dans la transmission de la peste', *Bulletin de l'Académie de Médecine* 126, 446–8.

Blanchard, Ian (1994), 'Introduction', 9–38 in Ian Blanchard, ed., *Labour and leisure in historical perspective, thirteenth to twentieth centuries: papers presented at Session B-3a of the eleventh International Economic History Congress, Milan 12th–17th September 1994*, Stuttgart.

Blanchard, Ian (1996), 'Lothian and beyond: the economy of the "English Empire" of David I', 23–45 in Richard H. Britnell and John Hatcher, eds., *Progress and problems in medieval England: essays in honour of Edward Miller*, Cambridge.

Blažina Tomić, Zlata; Blažina, Vesna (2015), *Expelling the plague: the health office and the implementation of quarantine in Dubrovnik, 1377–1533*, Montreal and Kingston.

Böhm, O.; Wetzel, K.-F. (2006), 'Flood history of the Danube tributaries Lech and Isar in the Alpine foreland of Germany', *Hydrological Sciences (Journal des sciences hydrologiques)* 51 (5), Special issue: *Historical hydrology*, 784–98.

Bois, Guy (1984), *The crisis of feudalism: economy and society in eastern Normandy c.1300–1550*, Cambridge.

Bolton, J. L. (1980), *The medieval English economy 1150–1500*, London.

Bolton, J. L. (2012), *Money in the medieval English economy: 973–1489*, Manchester.

Bolton, J. L.; Bruscoli, Francesco Guidi (2008), 'When did Antwerp replace Bruges as the commercial and financial centre of north-western Europe? The evidence of the Borromei ledger for 1438', *EcHR* 61 (2), 360–79.

Bos, Kirsten I.; Schuenemann, Verena J.; Golding, G. Brian; Burbano, Hernán A.; Waglechner, Nicholas; Coombes, Brian K.; McPhee, Joseph B.; DeWitte, Sharon B.; Meyer, Matthias; Schmedes, Sarah; Wood, James; Earn, David J. D.; Herring, D. Ann; Bauer, Peter; Poinar, Hendrik N.; Krause, Johannes

(2011), 'A draft genome of *Yersinia pestis* from victims of the Black Death', *Nature* 478 (7370), 506–10.

Boserup, Ester (1965), *The conditions of agricultural growth: the economics of agrarian change under population pressure*, London.

Bossak, Brian H.; Welford, Mark R. (2009), 'Did medieval trade activity and a viral etiology control the spatial extent and seasonal distribution of Black Death mortality?', *Medical Hypotheses* 72, 749–52.

Bossak, Brian H.; Welford, Mark R. (2010), 'Spatio-temporal attributes of pandemic and epidemic diseases', *Geography Compass* 4 (8), 1084–96.

Boussemaere, P. (2000), 'De Ieperse lakenproductie in de veertiende eeuw opnieuw berekend aan de hand van de lakenloodjes', *Jaarboek voor Middeleeuwse Geschiedenis* 2, 131–61.

Bradley, Raymond S.; Hughes, Malcolm K.; Diaz, Henry F. (2003), 'Climate in medieval time', *Science* 302, 404–5.

Brady, Niall (1997), 'The gothic barn of England: icon of prestige and authority', 76–105 in E. Smith and M. Wolfe, eds., *Technology and resource use in medieval Europe: cathedrals, mills and mines*, Aldershot.

Brenner, Robert (1976), 'Agrarian class structure and economic development in pre-industrial Europe', *P&P* 70, 30–75. Reprinted as 10–63 in T. H. Aston and C. H. E. Philpin, eds. (1985), *The Brenner debate: agrarian class structure and economic development in pre-industrial Europe*, Cambridge.

Brenner, Robert (1982), 'The agrarian roots of European capitalism', *P&P* 97, 16–113. Reprinted as 213–327 in T. H. Aston and C. H. E. Philpin, eds. (1985), *The Brenner debate: agrarian class structure and economic development in pre-industrial Europe*, Cambridge

Bridbury, A. R. (1955), *England and the salt trade in the later Middle Ages*, Oxford.

Briggs, Chris (2003), 'Credit and the peasant household economy in England before the Black Death: evidence from a Cambridgeshire manor', 231–48 in Cordelia Beattie, Anna Maslakovic and Sarah Rees Jones, eds., *The medieval household in Christian Europe, c.850–c.1550: managing power, wealth, and the body*, Turnhout.

Briggs, Chris (2004), 'Empowered or marginalized? Rural women and credit in later thirteenth- and fourteenth-century England', *C&C* 19 (1), 13–43.

Briggs, Chris (2009), *Credit and village society in fourteenth century England*, Oxford.

Britnell, Richard H. (1981), 'The proliferation of markets in England, 1200–1349', *EcHR* 34 (2), 209–21.

Britnell, Richard H. (1993a), *The commercialisation of English society, 1000–1500*, Cambridge.

Britnell, Richard H. (1993b), 'Commerce and capitalism in late medieval England: problems of description and theory', *Journal of Historical Sociology* 6 (4), 359–76.

Britnell, Richard H. (1995), 'Commercialisation and economic development in England, 1000–1300', 7–26 in Richard H. Britnell and Bruce M. S. Campbell, eds., *A commercialising economy: England 1086 to c.1300*, Manchester.

Britnell, Richard H. (1996), 'Boroughs, markets and trade in northern England, 1000–1216', 46–67 in Richard H. Britnell and John Hatcher, eds.,

Progress and problems in medieval England: essays in honour of Edward Miller, Cambridge.

Britnell, Richard H. (2000), 'The economy of British towns 600–1300', 105–26 in D. M. Palliser, ed., *The Cambridge urban history of Britain, I, 600–1540,* Cambridge.

Britnell, Richard H. (2001), 'Specialization of work in England, 1100–1300', *EcHR* 54 (1), 1–16.

Britnell, Richard H. ed. (2003), *The Winchester Pipe Rolls: studies in medieval English economy and society,* Woodbridge.

Britnell, Richard H.; Campbell, Bruce M. S. (1995), 'Introduction', 1–6 in Richard H. Britnell and Bruce M. S. Campbell, eds., *A commercialising economy: England 1086 to c.1300,* Manchester.

Britton, C. E. (1937), *A meteorological chronology to A.D. 1450,* London, Meteorological Office Geophysical Memoirs 70.

Britton, Edward (1977), *The community of the vill: a study in the history of the family and village life in fourteenth-century England,* Toronto.

Broad, John (1983), 'Cattle plague in eighteenth-century England', *AHR* 31 (2), 104–15.

Broadberry, Stephen N.; Campbell, Bruce M. S. (2009), 'GDP per capita in Europe, 1300–1850', unpublished paper presented at Session E4, *Reconstructing the national income of Europe before 1850: estimates and implications for long run growth and development,* XVth International Economic History Congress, Utrecht.

Broadberry, Stephen N.; Campbell, Bruce. M. S.; Leeuwen, Bas van (2013), 'When did Britain industrialise? The sectoral distribution of the labour force and labour productivity in Britain, 1381–1851', *EEH* 50 (1), 16–27.

Broadberry, Stephen N.; Campbell, Bruce M. S.; Klein, Alex; Leeuwen, Bas van; Overton, Mark (2015), *British economic growth 1270–1870,* Cambridge.

Brook, Timothy (2010), *The troubled empire: China in the Yuan and Ming Dynasties,* Cambridge, Mass.

Brooke, John L. (2014), *Climate change and the course of global history: a rough journey,* Cambridge.

Brovkin, Victor; Lorenz, Stephan J.; Jungclaus, Johann; Raddatz, Thomas; Timmreck, Claudia; Reick, Christian H.; Segschneider, Joachim; Six, Katharina (2010), 'Sensitivity of a coupled climate–carbon cycle model to large volcanic eruptions during the last millennium', *Tellus* 62B, 674–81.

Brown, Neville (2001), *History and climate change: a Eurocentric perspective,* London and New York.

Bryer, R. A. (1993), 'Double-entry bookkeeping and the birth of capitalism: accounting for the commercial revolution in medieval northern Italy', *Critical Perspectives on Accounting* 4 (2), 113–40.

Buckley, Brendan M.; Anchukaitis, Kevin J.; Penny, Daniel; Fletcher, Roland; Cook, Edward R.; Sanod, Masaki; Nam, Le Canh; Wichienkeeo, Aroonrut; Minh, Ton That; Hongg, Truong Mai (2010), 'Climate as a contributing factor in the demise of Angkor, Cambodia', *PNAS early edn,* 5pp.

Buell, Paul D. (2012), 'Qubilai and the rats', *Sudhoffs Archiv* 96 (2), 127–44.

Büntgen, Ulf; Tegel, W.; Nicolussi, K.; McCormick, M.; Frank, D.; Trouet, V.; Kaplan, J. O.; Herzig, F.; Heussner, K.-U.; Wanner, H.; Luterbacher, J.; Esper, J. (2011), 'Central Europe 2500 year tree ring summer climate reconstructions', IGBP # 2011-026.

Büntgen, Ulf; Kyncl, Tomás; Ginzler, Christian; Jacks, David S.; Esper, Jan; Tegel, Willy; Heussner, Karl-Uwe; Kyncl, Josef (2013), 'Filling the Eastern European gap in millennium-long temperature reconstructions', *PNAS* 110 (5), 1773–8.

Burton, Janet (1994), *Monastic and religious Orders in Britain, 1000–1300* (Cambridge.

Butel, Paul (1999), *The Atlantic*, trans. Iain Hamilton Grant, London and New York.

Buyst, Erik (2011), 'Towards estimates of long term growth in the southern Low Countries, c.1500–1846', unpublished paper presented at Hi-Pod Workshop *Quantifying long run economic development*, University of Warwick in Venice, Palazzo Pesaro Papafava, March 2011.

Campbell, Bruce M. S. (1975), 'Field systems in eastern Norfolk during the Middle Ages: a study with particular reference to the demographic and agrarian changes of the fourteenth century', unpublished PhD thesis, University of Cambridge.

Campbell, Bruce M. S. (1980), 'Population change and the genesis of commonfields on a Norfolk manor', *EcHR* 33 (2), 174–92.

Campbell, Bruce M. S. (1981), 'The extent and layout of commonfields in eastern Norfolk', *Norfolk Archaeology* 38, 5–32.

Campbell, Bruce M. S. (1983), 'Agricultural progress in medieval England: some evidence from eastern Norfolk', *EcHR* 36 (1), 26–46. Reprinted in Bruce M. S. Campbell (2007), *The medieval antecedents of English agricultural progress*, Aldershot.

Campbell, Bruce M. S. (1984), 'Population pressure, inheritance, and the land market in a fourteenth-century peasant community', 87–134 in Richard M. Smith, ed., *Land, kinship and lifecycle*, Cambridge. Reprinted in Bruce M. S. Campbell (2009), *Land and people in late medieval England*, Aldershot.

Campbell, Bruce M. S. (1986), 'The complexity of manorial structure in medieval Norfolk: a case study', *Norfolk Archaeology* 39, 225–61. Reprinted in Bruce M. S. Campbell (2009), *Land and people in late medieval England*, Aldershot.

Campbell, Bruce M. S. (1991), 'Land, labour, livestock, and productivity trends in English seignorial agriculture, 1208–1450', 144–82 in Bruce M. S. Campbell and Mark Overton, eds., *Land, labour and livestock: historical studies in European agricultural productivity*, Manchester. Reprinted in Bruce M. S. Campbell (2007), *The medieval antecedents of English agricultural progress*, Aldershot.

Campbell, Bruce M. S. (1992), 'Commercial dairy production on medieval English demesnes: the case of Norfolk', *Anthropozoologica* 16, 107–18. Reprinted in Bruce M. S. Campbell (2007), *The medieval antecedents of English agricultural progress*, Aldershot.

Campbell, Bruce M. S. (1995a), 'Measuring the commercialisation of seigneurial agriculture circa 1300', 132–93 in Richard H. Britnell and Bruce M. S.

Campbell, eds., *A commercialising economy: England 1086–1300*, Manchester. Reprinted in Bruce M. S. Campbell (2007), *The medieval antecedents of English agricultural progress*, Aldershot.

Campbell, Bruce M. S. (1995b), 'Ecology versus economics in late thirteenth- and early fourteenth-century English agriculture', 76–108 in Del Sweeney, ed., *Agriculture in the Middle Ages: technology, practice, and representation*, Philadelphia.

Campbell, Bruce M. S. (1996), 'The livestock of Chaucer's reeve: fact or fiction?', 271–305 in Edwin B. Dewindt, ed., *The salt of common life: individuality and choice in the medieval town, countryside and church. Essays presented to J. Ambrose Raftis on the occasion of his 70th birthday*, Kalamazoo. Reprinted in Bruce M. S. Campbell (2008), *Field systems and farming systems in late medieval England*, Aldershot.

Campbell, Bruce M. S. (1997a), 'Economic rent and the intensification of English agriculture, 1086–1350', 225–50 in Grenville Astill and John Langdon, eds., *Medieval farming and technology: the impact of agricultural change in Northwest Europe*, Leiden. Reprinted in Bruce M. S. Campbell (2008), *Field systems and farming systems in late medieval England*, Aldershot.

Campbell, Bruce M. S. (1997b), 'Matching supply to demand: crop production and disposal by English demesnes in the century of the Black Death', *JEH* 57 (4), 827–58. Reprinted in Bruce M. S. Campbell (2007), *The medieval antecedents of English agricultural progress*, Aldershot.

Campbell, Bruce M. S. (2000), *English seigniorial agriculture 1250–1450*, Cambridge.

Campbell, Bruce M. S. (2002a), 'England: land and people', 2–25 in Stephen H. Rigby, ed., *A companion to Britain in the later Middle Ages*, Oxford. Reprinted in Bruce M. S. Campbell (2009), *Land and people in late medieval England*, Aldershot.

Campbell, Bruce M. S. (2002b), 'The sources of tradable surpluses: English agricultural exports 1250–1349', 1–30 in Lars Berggren, Nils Hybel and Annette Landen, eds., *Cogs, cargoes and commerce: maritime bulk trade in northern Europe, 1150–1400*, Toronto.

Campbell, Bruce M. S. (2003a), 'A unique estate and a unique source: the Winchester Pipe Rolls in perspective', 21–43 in Richard H. Britnell, ed., *The Winchester Pipe Rolls and medieval English society*, Woodbridge. Reprinted in Bruce M. S. Campbell (2009), *Land and people in late medieval England*, Aldershot.

Campbell, Bruce M. S. (2003b), 'The uses and exploitation of human power from the 13th to the 18th century', 183–211 in Simonetta Cavaciocchi, ed., *Economia e energia secc. XIII–XVIII, Istituto Internazionale di Storia Economica 'F. Datini'*, Prato.

Campbell, Bruce M. S. (2005), 'The agrarian problem in the early fourteenth century', *P&P* 188, 3–70. Reprinted in Bruce M. S. Campbell (2009), *Land and people in late medieval England*, Aldershot.

Campbell, Bruce M. S. (2007), *Three centuries of English crop yields, 1211–1491*, www.cropyields.ac.uk

Campbell, Bruce M. S. (2008), 'Benchmarking medieval economic development: England, Wales, Scotland, and Ireland *circa* 1290', *EcHR* 61 (4), 896–945.

Campbell, Bruce M. S. (2009a), 'Factor markets in England before the Black Death', *C&C* 24 (1), 79–106.

Campbell, Bruce M. S. (2009b), 'Four famines and a pestilence: harvest, price, and wage variations in England, 13th to 19th centuries', 23–56 in Britt Liljewall, Iréne A. Flygare, Ulrich Lange, Lars Ljunggren and Johan Söderberg, eds., *Agrarhistoria på många sätt; 28 studier om manniskan och jorden. Festskrift till Janken Myrdal på hans 60-årsdag (Agrarian history many ways: 28 studies on humans and the land, Festschrift to Janken Myrdal 2009)*, Stockholm.

Campbell, Bruce M. S. (2010a), 'Nature as historical protagonist: environment and society in pre-industrial England' (the 2008 Tawney Memorial Lecture), *EcHR* 63 (2), 281–314.

Campbell, Bruce M. S. (2010b), 'Agriculture in Kent in the high Middle Ages', 25–53 in Sheila Sweetinburgh, ed., *Later medieval Kent 1220–1540*, Woodbridge.

Campbell, Bruce M. S. (2010c), 'Physical shocks, biological hazards, and human impacts: the crisis of the fourteenth century revisited', 13–32 in Simonetta Cavaciocchi, ed., *Le interazioni fra economia e ambiente biologico nell'Europe preindustriale secc. XIII–XVIII, Istituto Internazionale di Storia Economica 'F. Datini'*, Prato.

Campbell, Bruce M. S. (2011a), 'Grain yields on English demesnes after the Black Death', 121–74 in Mark Bailey and Stephen H. Rigby, eds., *England in the age of the Black Death: essays in honour of John Hatcher*, Turnhout.

Campbell, Bruce M. S. (2011b), 'Panzootics, pandemics and climatic anomalies in the fourteenth century', 177–215 in Bernd Herrmann, ed., *Beiträge zum Göttinger Umwelthistorischen Kolloquium 2010–2011*, Göttingen.

Campbell, Bruce M. S. (2013a), 'Matthew Paris and the volcano: the English "famine" of 1258 revisited', unpublished paper presented at the workshop, *Mortality crises between the plagues, c.800–c.1300 CE*, University of Stirling, November.

Campbell, Bruce M. S. (2013b), 'Land markets and the morcellation of holdings in pre-plague England and pre-famine Ireland', 197–218 in Gerard Beaur, Phillipp R. Schofield, Jean-Michel Chevet and Maria-Teresa Pérez-Picazo, eds., *Property rights, land markets and economic growth in the European countryside (13th–20th centuries)*, Turnhout.

Campbell, Bruce M. S. (2013c), 'National incomes and economic growth in pre-industrial Europe: insights from recent research', *Quaestiones Medii Aevi Novae* 18, 167–96.

Campbell, Bruce M. S.; Barry, Lorraine (2014), 'The population geography of Great Britain c.1290: a reconstruction', 43–78 in Christopher Briggs, Peter Kitson and Stephen Thompson, eds., *Population, economy and welfare, c.1200–2000: papers in honour of Richard M. Smith*, Woodbridge.

Campbell, Bruce M. S.; Bartley, Ken (2006), *England on the eve of the Black Death: an atlas of lay lordship, land, and wealth, 1300–49*, Manchester.

Campbell, Bruce M. S.; Bartley, Ken C.; Power, John P. (1996), 'The demesne-farming systems of post Black Death England: a classification', *AHR* 44 (2), 131–79. Reprinted in Bruce M. S. Campbell (2008), *Field systems and farming systems in late medieval England*, Aldershot.

Campbell, Bruce M. S.; Galloway, James A.; Keene, Derek J.; Murphy, Margaret (1993), *A medieval capital and its grain supply: agrarian production and its distribution in the London region c.1300*, Historical Geography Research Series, 30.

Campbell, Bruce M. S.; Ó Gráda, Cormac (2011), 'Harvest shortfalls, grain prices, and famines in pre-industrial England', *JEH* 71 (4), 859–86.

Campbell, Bruce M. S.; Overton, Mark (1993), 'A new perspective on medieval and early modern agriculture: six centuries of Norfolk farming c.1250–c.1850', *P&P* 141, 38–105. Reprinted in Bruce M. S. Campbell (2007), *The medieval antecedents of English agricultural progress*, Aldershot.

Carmichael, Ann G. (2014), 'Plague persistence in western Europe: a hypothesis', 157–92 in Monica Green, ed., *Pandemic disease in the medieval world: rethinking the Black Death*, The Medieval Globe 1, special issue, www .arc-humanities.org/the-medieval-globe.html.

Carus-Wilson, E. M.; Coleman, Olive (1963), *England's export trade: 1275–1547*, Oxford.

Centre for Metropolitan History (2000), 'Metropolitan market networks c.1300–1600', 5–9 in Centre for Metropolitan History, *Annual Report 1999–2000*, London.

Chen, Fa-Hu; Chen, Jian-Hui; Holmes, Jonathan; Boomer, Ian; Austin, Patrick; Gates, John B.; Wang, Ning-Lian; Brooks, Stephen J.; Zhang, Jia-Wu (2010), 'Moisture changes over the last millennium in Arid Central Asia: a review, synthesis and comparison with monsoon region', *QSR* 29 (7), 1055–68.
Data: Chen, Fa-Hu; Chen, Jian-Hui; Holmes, Jonathan; Boomer, Ian; Austin, Patrick; Gates, John B.; Wang, Ning-Lian; Brooks, Stephen J.; Zhang, Jia-Wu (2012), 'Arid Central Asia 1000 year synthesized moisture reconstruction', IGBP # 2012–023.

Chen, Fa-Hu; Yu, Zicheng; Yang, Meilin; Ito, Emi; Wang, Sumin; Madsen, David B.; Huang, Xiaozhong; Zhao, Yan; Sato, Tomonori; Birks, H. John B.; Boomer, Ian; Chen, Jianhui; An, Chengbang; Wünnemann, Bernd (2008), 'Holocene moisture evolution in arid central Asia and its out-of-phase relationship with Asian monsoon history', *QSR* 27 (3), 351–64.

Cheney, C. R. (1981), 'Levies on the English clergy for the poor and for the king, 1203', *English Historical Review* 96 (380), 577–82.

Chibnall, Marjorie (1986), *Anglo-Norman England 1066–1166*, Oxford.

Childs, Wendy R. (1981), 'England's iron trade in the fifteenth century', *EcHR* 34 (1), 25–47.

Childs, Wendy R. (1995), 'England's Icelandic trade in the fifteenth century: the role of the port of Hull', *Northern Seas: Yearbook 1995*, 11–31.

Childs, Wendy R. (1996), 'The English export trade in cloth in the fourteenth century', 121–47 in Richard Britnell and John Hatcher, eds., *Progress and problems in medieval England: essays in honour of Edward Miller*, Cambridge.

Chorley, Patrick (1988), 'English cloth exports during the thirteenth and early fourteenth centuries: the continental evidence', *Historical Research* 61 (144), 1–10.

Christakos, George; Olea, Ricardo A.; Serre, Marc L.; Yu, Hwa-Lung; Wang, Lin-Lin (2005), *Interdisciplinary public health reasoning and epidemic modelling: the case of the Black Death*, Berlin, Heidelberg, New York.

Christakos, George; Olea, Ricardo A.; Yu, Hwa-Lung (2007), 'Recent results on the spatiotemporal modelling and comparative analysis of Black Death and bubonic plague epidemics', *Public Health* 121, 700–20.

Chuine, I.; Yiou, P.; Viovy, N.; Seguin, B.; Daux, V.; Le Roy Ladurie, E. (2005), 'Burgundy grape harvest dates and spring–summer temperature reconstruction', IGBP # 2005-007.

Clanchy, Michael T. (1979), *From memory to written record: England 1066–1307*, London.

Clark, Elaine (1981), 'Debt litigation in a late medieval English vill', 247–79 in J. Ambrose Raftis, ed., *Pathways to medieval peasants*, Toronto.

Clark, Elaine (1994), 'Social welfare and mutual aid in the medieval countryside', *Journal of British Studies* 33 (4), 381–406.

Clark, Gregory (1988), 'The cost of capital and medieval agricultural technique', *EEH* 25 (3), 265–94.

Clark, Gregory (2005), 'The interest rate in the very long run: institutions, preferences and modern growth', http://dev3.cepr.org/meets/wkcn/1/1626/papers/clark.pdf

Clark, Gregory (2007a), *A farewell to alms: a brief economic history of the world*, Princeton.

Clark, Gregory (2007b), 'The long march of history: farm wages, population, and economic growth, England 1209–1869', *EcHR* 60 (1), 97–135.

Clark, Gregory (2009), 'English prices and wages 1209–1914', Global Price and Income History Group, www.iisg.nl/hpw/data.php#united.

Clark, Gregory (2010), 'The macroeconomic aggregates for England, 1209–2008', *Research in Economic History* 27, 51–140.

Claughton, Peter (2003), 'Production and economic impact: Northern Pennine (English) silver in the 12th century', 146–9 in *Proceedings of the 6th International Mining History Congress*, Akabira City, Hokkaido, Japan.

Cliff, Andrew D.; Smallman-Raynor, Matthew R.; Stevens, Peta M. (2009), 'Controlling the geographical spread of infectious disease: plague in Italy, 1347–1851', *Acta Medico-Historica Adriatica* 7 (1), 197–236.

Cobb, Kim M.; Charles, Christopher D.; Cheng, Hai; Edwards, Lawrence R. (2003), 'El Niño/Southern Oscillation and tropical Pacific climate during the last millennium', *Nature* 424, 271–6.

Cohn Jr, Samuel K. (2002a), *The Black Death transformed: disease and culture in early Renaissance Europe*, London.

Cohn Jr, Samuel K. (2002b), 'The Black Death and the end of a paradigm', *American Historical Review* 107, 703–38.

Cohn Jr, Samuel K. (2007), 'After the Black Death: labour legislation and attitudes towards labour in late-medieval Western Europe', *EcHR* 60 (3), 457–85.

Cohn Jr, Samuel K. (2008), 'Epidemiology of the Black Death and successive waves of plague', *Medical History*, Supplement 27, 74–100.

Connell, Brian; Jones, Amy Gray; Redfern, Rebecca; Walker, Don (2012), *A bioarchaeological study of medieval burials on the site of St Mary Spital: excavations at Spitalfields Market, London E1, 1991–2007* (London).

Cook, Edward R.; Anchukaitis, Kevin J.; Buckley, Brendan M.; D'Arrigo, Rosanne D.; Jacoby, Gordon C.; Wright, William E. (2010), 'Asian monsoon failure and megadrought during the last millennium', *Science* 328, 486–9.

Cook, Edward R.; Esper, Jan; D'Arrigo, Rosanne (2004a), 'Extra-tropical northern hemisphere land temperature variability over the past 1000 years', *QSR* 23, 2063–74.

Cook, Edward R.; Woodhouse, Connie A.; Eakin, Mark; Meko, David M.; Stahle, David W. (2004b), 'Long-term aridity changes in the western United States', *Science* 306, 1015–18.
    Data: Cook, Edward R.; Woodhouse, Connie A.; Eakin, Mark; Meko, David M.; Stahle, David W. (2004c), 'North American summer PDSI reconstructions', IGBP # 2004-045.

Cosgrove, Art, ed. (1993), *A new history of Ireland, II, Medieval Ireland, 1169–1534*, Oxford.

Coss, Peter R. (1991), *Lordship, knighthood and locality: a study in English society c.1180–c.1280*, Cambridge.

Crespo, Fabian (2014), 'Heterogeneous immunological landscapes and medieval plague: an invitation to a new dialogue between historians and immunologists', in Monica Green, ed., *Pandemic disease in the medieval world: rethinking the Black Death, The Medieval Globe* 1, special issue, www.arc-humanities .org/the-medieval-globe.html.

Crowley, Thomas J. (2000), 'Causes of climate change over the past 1000 years', *Science* 289 (5477), 270–7.

Cui, Yujun; Yu, Chang; Yan, Yanfeng; Li, Dongfang; Li, Yanjun; Jombart, Thibaut; Weinert, Lucy A.; Wang, Zuyun; Guo, Zhaobiao; Xu, Lizhi; Zhang, Yujiang; Zheng, Hancheng; Xiao Xiao, Nan Qin; Wu, Mingshou; Wang, Xiaoyi; Zhou, Dongsheng; Qi, Zhizhen; Du, Zongmin; Wu, Honglong; Yang, Xianwei; Cao, Hongzhi; Wang, Hu; Wang, Jing; Yao, Shusen; Rakin, Alexander; Li, Yingrui; Falush, Daniel; Balloux, François; Achtman, Mark; Songa, Yajun; Wang, Jun; Yanga, Ruifu (2013), 'Historical variations in mutation rate in an epidemic pathogen, *Yersinia pestis*', *PNAS* 110 (2), 577–82.

Cummins, Neil; Kelly, Morgan; Ó Gráda, Cormac (2013), 'Living standards and plague in London', *Social Science Research Network*, working paper, http://papers.ssrn.com/sol3/papers.cfm?abstract_id=2289094.

Darby, Henry Clifford (1940), *The medieval Fenland*, Cambridge.

Darby, Henry Clifford (1977), *Domesday England*, Cambridge.

Darby, Henry Clifford; Glasscock, Robin E.; Sheail, John; Versey, G. Roy (1979), 'The changing geographical distribution of wealth in England: 1086–1334–1525', *JHG* 5 (3), 247–62.

Davies, M.; Kissock, J. (2004), 'The Feet of Fines, the land market and the English agricultural crisis of 1315 to 1322', *JHG* 30, 215–30.

Davies, R. R. (1990), *Domination and conquest: the experience of Ireland, Scotland and Wales 1100–1300*, Cambridge.

Davis, David E. (1986), 'The scarcity of rats and the Black Death: an ecological history', *JIH* 16 (3), 455–70.

Davis, James (2011), *Medieval market morality: life, law and ethics in the English marketplace, 1200–1500*, Cambridge.

Davis, Robert C. (2003), *Christian slaves, Muslim masters: white slavery in the Mediterranean, the Barbary Coast, and Italy, 1500–1800*, New York.

Davis, Stephen; Begon, Mike; De Bruyn, Luc; Ageyev, Vladimir S.; Klassovskiy, Nikolay L.; Pole, Sergey B.; Viljugrein, Hildegunn; Stenseth, Nils Chr.; Leirs, Herwig (2004), 'Predictive thresholds for plague in Kazakhstan', *Science* 304 (5671), 736–8.

Dawson, A. G.; Hickey, K.; Mayewski, P. A.; Nesje, A. (2007), 'Greenland (GISP2) ice core and historical indicators of complex North Atlantic climate changes during the fourteenth century', *The Holocene* 17 (4), 427–34.

Day, John (1987), *The medieval market economy*, Oxford.

De Moor, Tine (2008), 'The silent revolution: a new perspective on the emergence of commons, guilds, and other forms of corporate collective action in Western Europe', *International Review Social History* 53, Supplement S16, 179–212.

Dean, James M., ed. (1996), 'The Simonie [Symonye and covetise, or On the evil times of Edward II]' in *Medieval English political writings*, Kalamazoo.

Delaygue, G.; Bard, E. (2010a), 'An Antarctic view of Beryllium-10 and solar activity for the past millennium', *Climate Dynamics early edn*, 18pp.
Data: Delaygue, G.; Bard, E. (2010b), 'Antarctic last millennium 10Be stack and solar irradiance reconstruction', IGBP # 2010-035.

Devignat, R. (1951), 'Variétés de l'espèce Pasteurella pestis: nouvelle hypothèse', *Bulletin World Health Organisation* 4 (2), 247–63.

DeWindt, Edwin B. (1972), *Land and people in Holywell-cum-Needingworth: structures of tenure and patterns of social organization in an east midlands village 1252–1457*, Toronto.

DeWitte, Sharon N. (2010), 'Sex differentials in frailty in medieval England', *American Journal of Physical Anthropology* 143, 285–97.

DeWitte, Sharon N.; Slavin, Philip (2013), 'Between famine and death: England on the eve of the Black Death – evidence from paleoepidemiology and manorial accounts', *JIH* 44 (1), 37–60.

DeWitte, Sharon N.; Wood, James W. (2008), 'Selectivity of Black Death mortality with respect to preexisting health', *PNAS* 105 (5), 1436–41.

Di Cosmo, Nicola (2005), 'Mongols and merchants on the Black Sea frontier in the thirteenth and fourteenth centuries: convergences and conflicts', 391–424 in Reuven Amitai and Michal Biran, eds., *Mongols, Turks, and others: Eurasian nomads and the sedentary world*, Leiden and Boston.

Diamond, Jared (1999), *Guns, germs and steel: the fates of human societies*, New York and London.

Dodds, Ben (2007), *Peasants and production in the medieval north-east: evidence from tithes, 1270–1536*, Woodbridge.

Dodgshon, R. A. (1987), *The European past: social evolution and spatial order*, Basingstoke.

Dols, Michael W. (1977), *The Black Death in the Middle East*, Princeton.

Dols, Michael W. (1978), 'Geographical origin of the Black Death: comment', *BHM* 52 (1), 112–23.

Domar, Evsey D. (1970), 'The causes of slavery or serfdom: a hypothesis', *JEH* 30 (1), 18–32.

Donkin, R. A. (1973), 'Changes in the early Middle Ages', 75–135 in H. C. Darby, ed., *A new historical geography of England*, Cambridge.

Donkin, R. A. (1978), *The Cistercians: studies in the geography of medieval England and Wales*, Toronto.

Dotterweich, Markus (2008), The history of soil erosion and fluvial deposits in small catchments of central Europe: deciphering the long-term interaction between humans and the environment – a review', *Geomorphology* 101, 192–208.

Dotterweich, Markus; Schmitt, Anne; Schmidtchen, Gabriele; Bork, Hans-Rudolf (2003), 'Quantifying historical gully erosion in northern Bavaria', *Catena* 50 (2–4), 135–50.

Drancourt, Michel; Houhamdi, Linda; Raoult, Didier (2006), '*Yersinia pestis* as a telluric ectoparasite-borne organism', *Lancet Infectious Diseases* 6 (4), 234–41.

Dresbeck, LeRoy (1971), 'The chimney and social change in medieval England', *Albion: A Quarterly Journal Concerned with British Studies* 3 (1), 21–32.

Duby, Georges (1974), *The early growth of the European economy: warriors and peasants from the seventh to the twelfth century*, trans. Howard B. Clarke, London.

Duby, Georges (1976), *Le temps des cathédrales: l'art et la société (980–1420)*, Paris.

Dugmore, Andrew J.; Keller, Christian; McGovern, Thomas H. (2007), 'Norse Greenland settlement: reflections on climate change, trade, and the contrasting fates of human settlements in the North Atlantic islands', *Arctic Anthropology* 44 (1), 12–36.

Duncan, Christopher J.; Scott, Susan (2005), 'What caused the Black Death?', *Postgraduate Medical Journal* 81, 315–20.

Dunsford, H. M.; Harris, S. J. (2003), 'Colonization of the wasteland in County Durham, 1100–1400', *EcHR* 56 (1), 34–56.

Dyer, Christopher (1989), *Standards of living in the later Middle Ages: social change in England c.1200–1520*, Cambridge.

Dyer, Christopher (1992), 'The hidden trade of the Middle Ages: evidence from the west midlands of England', *JHG* 18 (2), 141–57.

Dyer, Christopher (1995), 'Sheepcotes: evidence for medieval sheepfarming', *Medieval Archaeology* 39, 136–64.

Dyer, Christopher (2011), 'Luxury goods in medieval England', 217–38 in Ben Dodds and Christian D. Liddy, eds., *Commercial activity, markets and entrepreneurs in the Middle Ages: essays in honour of Richard Britnell*, Woodbridge.

Ecclestone, Martin (1999), 'Mortality of rural landless men before the Black Death: the Glastonbury head-tax lists', *Local Population Studies* 63, 6–29.

Edwards, Jeremy; Ogilvie, Sheilagh (2012), 'What lessons for economic development can we draw from the Champagne fairs?', *EEH* 49 (2), 131–48.

Eisen, Rebecca J.; Dennis, David T.; Gage, Kenneth L. (2015), 'The role of early-phase transmission in the spread of *Yersinia pestis*', *Journal of Medical Entomology advance access*, 10pp.

Eisen, Rebecca J.; Gage, Kenneth L. (2009), 'Adaptive strategies of *Yersinia pestis* to persist during inter-epizootic and epizootic periods', *Veterinary Research* 40 (1), 14pp.

Eisen, Rebecca J.; Gage, Kenneth L. (2012), 'Transmission of flea-borne zoonotic agents', *Annual Review Entomology* 57, 61–82.

Eisen, Rebecca J.; Bearden, Scott W.; Wilder, Aryn P.; Montenieri, John A.; Antolin, Michael F.; Gage, Kenneth L. (2006), 'Early-phase transmission of *Yersinia pestis* by unblocked fleas as a mechanism explaining rapidly spreading plague epizootics', *PNAS* 103 (42), 15380–5.

Eisen, Rebecca J.; Petersen, Jeannine M.; Higgins, Charles L.; Wong, David; Levy, Craig E.; Mead, Paul S.; Schriefer, Martin E.; Griffith, Kevin S.; Gage, Kenneth L.; Beard, C. Ben (2008), 'Persistence of *Yersinia pestis* in soil under natural conditions', *EID* 14 (6), 941–3.

Ell, Stephen R. (1980), 'Interhuman transmission of medieval plague', *Bulletin History Medicine* 54 (4), 497–510.

Emile-Geay, Julian; Seager, Richard; Cane, Mark A.; Cook, Edward R.; Haug, Gerald H. (2008), 'Volcanoes and ENSO over the past millennium', *Journal of Climate* 21 (13), 3134–48.

Engelen, A. F. V. van; Buisman, J.; IJnsen, F. (2001), 'A millennium of weather, winds and water in the Low Countries', 101–24 in P. D. Jones, A. E. J. Ogilvie, T. D. Davies and K. R. Briffa, eds., *History and climate: memories of the future?*, New York. Data: www.knmi.nl/klimatologie/daggegevens/antieke_wrn/nederland_wi_zo.zip.

Enscore, Russell E.; Biggerstaff, Brad J.; Brown, Ted L.; Fulgham, Ralph E.; Reynolds, Pamela J.; Engelthaler, David M.; Levy, Craig E.; Parmenter, Robert R.; Montenieri, John A.; Cheek, James E.; Grinnell, Richie K.; Ettestad, Paul J.; Gage, Kenneth L. (2002), 'Modeling relationships between climate and the frequency of human plague cases in the southwestern United States, 1960–1997', *American Journal of Tropical Medicine & Hygiene* 66 (2), 186–96.

Epstein, Stephan R. (1992), *An island for itself: economic development and social change in late medieval Sicily*, Cambridge.

Epstein, Stephan R. (2000a), *Freedom and growth: the rise of states and markets in Europe, 1300–1750*, London and New York.

Epstein, Stephan R. (2000b), 'The rise and fall of Italian city-states', London, LSE Research online: http://eprints.lse.ac.uk/archive/00000663. Reprinted from 277–94 in M. H. Hansen, ed. (2000), *A comparative study of thirty city-state cultures: an investigation*, Copenhagen.

Esper, J.; Frank, D. C.; Büntgen, U.; Verstege, A.; Luterbacher, J.; Xoplaki, E. (2007), 'Long-term drought severity variations in Morocco', *GRL* 34, L17702, 5pp.

Data: Esper, J.; Frank, D. C.; Büntgen, U.; Verstege, A.; Luterbacher, J.; Xoplaki, E. (2009), 'Morocco millennial Palmer Drought Severity Index reconstruction', IGBP # 2009-032.

Evans, Nesta (1985), *The East Anglian linen industry: rural industry and local economy, 1500–1850*, Aldershot.

Evans, Ralph (1996), 'Merton College's control of its tenants at Thorncroft 1270–1349', 199–259 in Zvi Razi and Richard M. Smith, eds., *Medieval society and the manor court*, Oxford.

Fang, Keyan; Chen, Fahu; Sen, Asok K.; Davi, Nicole; Huang, Wei; Li, Jinbao; Seppa, Heikki (2014), 'Hydroclimate variations in central and monsoonal Asia over the past 700 years', *PLoS One* 9 (8), e102751.

Farmer, David L. (1956), 'Some price fluctuations in Angevin England', *EcHR* 9 (1), 34–43.

Farmer, David L. (1977), 'Grain yields on the Winchester manors in the later Middle Ages', *EcHR* 30 (4), 555–66.

Farmer, David L. (1988), 'Prices and wages', 715–817 in H. E. Hallam, ed., *The agrarian history of England and Wales, II, 1042–1350*, Cambridge.

Farmer, David L. (1991a), 'Marketing the produce of the countryside, 1200–1500', 324–430 in Edward Miller, ed., *The agrarian history of England and Wales, III, 1348–1500*, Cambridge.

Farmer, David L. (1991b), 'Prices and wages, 1350–1500', 431–525 in Edward Miller, ed., *The agrarian history of England and Wales, III, 1348–1500*, Cambridge.

Farmer, David L. (1992), 'Millstones for medieval manors', *AHR* 40 (2), 97–111.

Farmer, David L. (1996), 'The *famuli* in the later Middle Ages', 207–36 in Richard H. Britnell and John Hatcher, eds., *Progress and problems in medieval England: essays in honour of Edward Miller*, Cambridge.

Federico, Giovanni; Malanima, Paolo (2004), 'Progress, decline, growth: product and productivity in Italian agriculture, 1000–2000', *EcHR* 57 (3), 437–64.

Fernández-Armesto, Felipe (1987), *Before Columbus: exploration and colonisation from the Mediterranean to the Atlantic, 1229–1492*, Basingstoke.

Findlay, Ronald; O'Rourke, Kevin H. (2007), *Power and plenty: trade, war, and the world economy in the second millennium*, Princeton.

Fox, Harold S. A. (1986), 'The alleged transformation from two-field to three-field systems in medieval England', *EcHR* 39 (4), 526–48.

Fox, Harold S. A. (1996), 'Exploitation of the landless by lords and tenants in early medieval England', 518–68 in Zvi Razi and Richard M. Smith, eds., *Medieval society and the manor court*, Oxford.

Fraedrich, K.; Jiang, J.; Gerstengarbe, F.-W.; Werner, P. (1997), 'Multi-scale detection of abrupt climate changes: application to River Nile flood levels', *International Journal of Climatology* 17, 1301–15.

Frati, P. (2000), 'Quarantine, trade and health policies in Ragusa-Dubrovnik until the age of George Armmenius-Baglivi', *Medicina nei secoli* 12 (1), 103–27.

Fryde, E. B. (1988), *William de la Pole, merchant and king's banker*, London.

Furió, Antoni (2011), 'Disettes et famines en temps de croissance. Une révision de la "crise de 1300": le royaume de Valence dans la première moitié du XIVe siècle', 343–416 in Monique Bourin, John Drendel and François Menant, eds., *Les disettes dans la conjoncture de 1300 en Méditerranée occidentale*, Rome.

Furió, Antoni (2013), 'La primera gran depresión Europea (siglos XIV–XV)', 17–58 in Enrique Llopis and Jordi Maluquer de Motes, eds., *España en crisis: las grandes depresiones económicas, 1348–2012*, Barcelona.

Gage, Kenneth L.; Kosoy, Michael Y. (2005), 'Natural history of plague: perspectives from more than a century of research', *Annual Review Entomology* 50, 505–28.

Galimand, Marc; Guiyoule, Annie; Gerbaud, Guy; Rasoamanana, Bruno; Chanteau, Suzanne; Carniel, Elisabeth; Courvalin, Patrice (1997), 'Multidrug resistance in *Yersinia pestis* mediated by a transferable plasmid', *New England Journal of Medicine* 337 (10), 677–81.

Galloway, James A.; Keene, Derek J.; Murphy, Margaret (1996), 'Fuelling the city: production and distribution of firewood and fuel in London's region, 1290–1400', *EcHR* 49 (3), 447–72.

Gao, Chaochao; Robock, Alan; Ammann, Caspar (2008), 'Volcanic forcing of climate over the past 1500 years: an improved ice core-based index for climate models', *Journal of Geophysical Research* 113, D09103, 15pp.

Gao, Chaochao; Robock, Alan; Ammann, Caspar (2009a), 'Correction to "Volcanic forcing of climate over the past 1500 years: an improved ice core-based index for climate models"', *Journal of Geophysical Research* 114, D09103, 1p. *Data*: Gao, Chaochao; Robock, Alan; Ammann, Caspar (2009b), '1500 Year ice core-based stratospheric volcanic sulfate data', IGBP # 2009-098.

Ge, Quansheng; Zheng, Jingyun; Fang, Xiuqi; Man, Zhimin; Zhang, Xueqin; Zhang, Piyuan; Wang, Wei-Chyung (2003), 'Winter half-year temperature reconstruction for the middle and lower reaches of the Yellow River and Yangtze River, China, during the past 2000 years', *The Holocene* 13 (6), 933–40.

Gerrard, Christopher M.; Petley, David N. (2013), 'A risk society? Environmental hazards, risk and resilience in the later Middle Ages in Europe', *Natural Hazards* 69 (1), 1051–79.

Gilbert, M.; Thomas, P.; Cuccui, Jon; White, William; Lynnerup, Niels; Titball, Richard W.; Cooper, Alan; Prentice, Michael B. (2004), 'Absence of *Yersinia pestis*-specific DNA in human teeth from five European excavations of putative plague victims', *Microbiology* 150 (2), 341–54.

Glaser, R.; Riemann, D. (2009), 'A thousand-year record of temperature variations for Germany and Central Europe based on documentary data', *Journal of Quaternary Science* 24, 437–49. *Data*: Glaser, R.; Riemann, D. (2010), 'Central Europe 1000 year documentary temperature reconstruction', IGBP # 2010-040.

Glasscock, Robin E., ed. (1975), *The lay subsidy of 1334*, London.

Glénisson, Jean (1971), 'La seconde peste; l'épidémie de 1360–1362 en France et en Europe', *Annuaire-Bulletin de la Société de l'histoire de France 1968*, 27–38.

Goldberg, P. J. P. (1992), '"For better, for worse": marriage and economic opportunity for women in town and country', 108–25 in P. J. P. Goldberg, ed., *Woman is a worthy wight: women in English society c.1200–1500*, Stroud.

Golding, Brian (2001), 'The Church and Christian life', 135–66 in Barbara Harvey, ed., *The twelfth and thirteenth centuries*, Oxford.

Golding, William (1964), *The spire*, London.

Goldstone, Jack A. (2002), 'Efflorescences and economic growth in world history: rethinking the "rise of the West" and the industrial revolution', *Journal of World History* 13 (2), 323–89.

Goody, Jack (1983), *The development of the family and marriage in Europe*, Cambridge.

Gottfried, Robert S. (1978), *Epidemic disease in fifteenth century England: the medical response and the demographic consequences*, Leicester.

Graham, Brian J. (1979), 'The evolution of urbanization in medieval Ireland', *JHG* 5, 111–25.

Graham, N. E.; Ammann, C. M.; Fleitmann, D.; Cobb, K. M.; Luterbacher, J. (2010), 'Support for global climate reorganization during the "Medieval Climate Anomaly"', *Climate Dynamics, online first*, 29pp.

Grainger, Ian; Hawkins, Duncan; Cowal, Lynne; Mikulski, Richard (2008), *The Black Death cemetery, East Smithfield, London*, London.

Grantham, George (1999), 'Contra Ricardo: on the macroeconomics of pre-industrial economies', *EREH* 3 (2), 199–232.

Gras, P. (1939), 'Le registre paroissial de Givry (1334–1357) et la Peste Noire en Bourgogne', *Bibliothèque de l'Ecole des Chartes* 100, 295–308.

Gratz, Norman G. (1999), 'Emerging and resurging vector-borne diseases', *Annual Review Entomology* 44, 51–75.

Green, Monica, ed. (2014), *Pandemic disease in the medieval world: rethinking the Black Death, The Medieval Globe* 1, special issue, www.arc-humanities.org/the-medieval-globe.html.

Greif, Avner (2006), *Institutions and the path to the modern economy: lessons from medieval trade*, New York.

Grousset, René (1970), *The empire of the steppes: a history of Central Asia*, trans. Naomi Walford, New Brunswick.

Grove, Jean M. (1988), *The Little Ice Age*, London.

Grove, Jean M. (2004), *Little Ice Ages: ancient and modern*, 2 vols., 2nd edn, London.

Grove, Richard H. (1998), 'Global impact of the 1789–93 El Niño', *Nature* 393, 318–19.

Grove, Richard H.; Chappell, John, eds. (2000), *El Niño – history and crisis: studies from the Asia-Pacific region*, Cambridge.

Grudd, H. (2008), 'Torneträsk tree-ring width and density AD 500–2004: a test of climatic sensitivity and a new 1500-year reconstruction of north Fennoscandian summers', *Climate Dynamics* 31, 843–57.
Data: Grudd, H. (2010), 'Torneträsk tree ring MXD temperature reconstruction AD 500–2004', IGBP # 2010-027.

Gunten, L. von; Grosjean, M.; Rein, B.; Urrutia, R.; Appleby, P. (2009a), 'A quantitative high-resolution summer temperature reconstruction based on sedimentary pigments from Laguna Aculeo, central Chile, back to AD 850', *The Holocene* 19 (6), 873–81.

Data: Gunten, L. von; Grosjean, M.; Rein, B.; Urrutia, R.; Appleby, P. (2009b), 'Laguna Aculeo, Chile austral summer temperature reconstruction', IGBP # 2009-088.

Haensch, Stephanie; Bianucci, Raffaella; Signoli, Michel; Rajerison, Minoarisoa; Schultz, Michael; Kacki, Sacha; Vermunt, Marco; Weston, Darlene A.; Hurst, Derek; Achtman, Mark; Carniel, Elisabeth; Bramanti, Barbara (2010), 'Distinct clones of *Yersinia pestis* caused the Black Death', *PLoS Pathogens* 6 (10), e1001134.

Hall, David (1982), *Medieval fields*, Aylesbury.

Hallam, H. E. (1965), *Settlement and society: a study of the early agrarian history of south Lincolnshire*, Cambridge.

Hallam, H. E. (1988), 'Population movements in England, 1086–1350', 508–93 in H. E. Hallam, ed., *The agrarian history of England and Wales, II, 1042–1350*, Cambridge.

Hanawalt, Barbara A. (1976), *Crime in East Anglia in the fourteenth century: Norfolk gaol delivery rolls, 1307–1316*, Norfolk Record Society 44, Norwich.

Hanawalt, Barbara A. (1979), *Crime and conflict in English communities, 1300–1348*, Cambridge, Mass.

Harbeck, Michaela; Seifert, Lisa; Hänsch, Stephanie; Wagner, David M.; Birdsell, Dawn; Parise, Katy L.; Wiechmann, Ingrid; Grupe, Gisela; Thomas, Astrid; Keim, P.; Zöller, Lothar; Bramanti, Barbara; Riehm, Julia M.; Scholz, Holger C. (2013), '*Yersinia pestis* DNA from skeletal remains from the 6th century AD reveals insights into Justinianic Plague', *PLoS Pathogens* 9 (5), e1003349.

Harding, A. (1973), *The law courts of medieval England*, London.

Harper-Bill, Christopher (1996), 'The English Church and English religion after the Black Death', 79–124 in W. Mark Ormrod and Phillip G. Lindley, eds., *The Black Death in England*, Stamford.

Harrison, David (2004), *The bridges of medieval England: transport and society 400–1800*, Oxford.

Harvey, Barbara (1991), 'Introduction: the "crisis" of the early fourteenth century', 1–24 in Bruce M. S. Campbell, ed., *Before the Black Death: studies in the 'crisis' of the early fourteenth century*, Manchester.

Harvey, Barbara (1993), *Living and dying in England 1100–1540: the monastic experience*, Oxford.

Harvey, Barbara (2001), 'Conclusion', 243–64 in Barbara Harvey, ed., *The twelfth and thirteenth centuries*, Oxford.

Harvey, P. D. A. (1965), *A medieval Oxfordshire village: Cuxham 1240–1400*, London.

Harvey, P. D. A. (1973), 'The English inflation of 1180–1220', *P&P* 61, 3–30.

Harvey, P. D. A. (1984a), 'Introduction', 1–28 in P. D. A. Harvey, ed., *The peasant land market in medieval England*, Oxford.

Harvey, P. D. A., ed. (1984b), *The peasant land market in medieval England*, Oxford.

Harvey, P. D. A. (1996), 'The peasant land market in medieval England – and beyond', 392–407 in Zvi Razi and Richard M. Smith, eds., *Medieval society and the manor court*, Oxford.

Hassan, Fekri A. (2007), 'Extreme Nile floods and famines in medieval Egypt (AD 930–1500) and their climatic implications', *Quaternary International* 173, 101–12.

Hassan, Fekri A. (2011), 'Nile flood discharge during the Medieval Climate Anomaly', *PAGES news* 19, 30–1.

Hatcher, John (1973), *English tin production and trade before 1550*, Oxford.

Hatcher, John (1977), *Plague, population and the English economy 1348–1530*, London and Basingstoke.

Hatcher, John (1981), 'English serfdom and villeinage: towards a reassessment', *P&P* 90, 3–39. Reprinted as 247–84 in T. H. Aston, ed. (1987), *Landlords, peasants and politics in medieval England*, Cambridge.

Hatcher, John (1996), 'The great slump of the mid-fifteenth century', 237–72 in R. H. Britnell and J. Hatcher, eds., *Progress and problems in medieval England: essays in honour of Edward Miller*, Cambridge.

Hatcher, John (2003), 'Understanding the population history of England 1450–1750', *P&P* 180, 83–130.

Hatcher, John (2008), *The Black Death: an intimate history*, London.

Hatcher, John (2011), 'Unreal wages: long run living standards and the "golden age" of the fifteenth century?', 1–24 in Ben Dodds and Christian Drummond Liddy, eds., *Commercial activity, markets and entrepreneurs in the Middle Ages: essays in honour of Richard Britnell*, Woodbridge.

Hatcher, John; Bailey, Mark (2001), *Modelling the Middle Ages: the history and theory of England's economic development*, Oxford.

Hatcher, John; Piper, A. J.; Stone, David (2006), 'Monastic mortality: Durham Priory, 1395–1529', *EcHR* 59 (4), 667–87.

Hays, J. N. (2005), *Epidemics and pandemics: their impacts on human history*, Santa Barbara.

Hecker, Justus Friedrich Carl (1832), *Der schwarze Tod im vierzehnten Jahrhundert: Nach den Quellen für Ärzte und gebildete Nichtärzte bearbeitet* (The Black Death in the fourteenth century: from the sources by physicians and non-physicians), Berlin.

Heier, Lise; Storvik, Geir O.; Davis, Stephen A.; Viljugrein, Hildegunn; Ageyev, Vladimir S.; Klassovskaya, Evgeniya; Stenseth, Nils Chr. (2011), 'Emergence, spread, persistence and fade-out of sylvatic plague in Kazakhstan', *Proceedings of the Royal Soc. B: Biological Sciences* 278 (1720), 2915–23.

Henderson, John (2010), 'Public health, pollution and the problem of waste disposal in early modern Tuscany', 373–82 in Simonetta Cavaciocchi, ed., *Le interazioni fra economia e ambiente biologico nell'Europe preindustriale secc. XIII–XVIII*, Istituto Internazionale di Storia Economica 'F. Datini', Prato.

Henriques, António (2015), 'Plenty of land, land of plenty: the agrarian output of Portugal (1311–20)', *EREH* 19 (2), 149–70.

Herlihy, David (1967), *Medieval and Renaissance Pistoia: the social history of an Italian town, 1200–1430*, New Haven.

Herlihy, David (1997), *The Black Death and the transformation of the West*, ed. and intro. Samuel K. Cohn, Jr, Cambridge, Mass., and London.

Herweijer, Celine; Seager, Richard; Cook, Edward R.; Emile-Geay, Julien (2007), 'North American droughts of the last millennium from a gridded network of tree-ring data', *Journal of Climate* 20 (7), 1353–76.

Hessl, A. E.; Pederson, N.; Baatarbileg, N.; Anchukaitis, K. J. (2013), 'Pluvials, droughts, the Mongol Empire, and modern Mongolia', *American Geophysical Union's Fall Meeting Abstracts* 1, 6.

Hewitt, H. J. (1966), *The organization of war under Edward III, 1338–62*, Manchester.

Hilton, R. H. (1985), 'Medieval market towns and simple commodity production', *P&P* 109, 3–23.

Hinde, Andrew (2003), *England's population: a history since the Domesday Survey*, London.

Hoffmann, Richard C. (2014), *An environmental history of medieval Europe*, Cambridge.

Hollingsworth, T. H. (1969), *Historical demography*, London.

Holt, Richard (1988), *The mills of medieval England*, Oxford.

Horrox, Rosemary, trans. & ed. (1994), *The Black Death*, Manchester.

Hoskins, W. G. (1964), 'Harvest fluctuations and English economic history, 1480–1619', *AHR* 12 (1), 28–46.

Houhamdi, Linda; Lepidi, Hubert; Drancourt, Michel; Raoult, Didier (2006), 'Experimental model to evaluate the human body louse as a vector of plague', *Journal of Infectious Diseases* 194 (11), 1589–96.

Howell, Cicely (1983), *Land, family and inheritance in transition: Kibworth Harcourt 1280–1700*, Cambridge.

Hoyt, Robert S. (1950), *The royal demesne in English constitutional history: 1066–1272*, New York.

Hudson, R. W. (1921), 'The prior of Norwich's manor of Hindolveston: its early organisation and rights of the customary tenants to alienate their strips of land', *Norfolk Archaeology* 20, 179–214.

Hufthammer, Anne Karin; Walløe, Lars (2013), 'Rats cannot have been intermediate hosts for *Yersinia pestis* during medieval plague epidemics in Northern Europe', *Journal of Archaeological Science* 40, 1752–9.

Humphries, Jane; Weisdorf, Jacob (2015), 'The wages of women in England, 1260–1850', *JEH* 75 (2), 405–47.

Hunt, Edwin S. (1990), 'A new look at the dealings of the Bardi and Peruzzi with Edward III', *JEH* 50 (1), 149–62.

Hunt, Edwin S. (1994), *The medieval super-companies: a study of the Peruzzi Company of Florence*, Cambridge.

Hunt, Edwin S.; Murray, James M. (1999), *A history of business in medieval Europe, 1200–1550*, Cambridge.

Hurst, J. G. (1988), 'Rural building in England and Wales: England', 888–98 in H. E. Hallam, ed., *The agrarian history of England and Wales, II, 1042–1350*, Cambridge.

Hyams, Paul R. (1970), 'The origins of a peasant land market in England', *EcHR* 23 (1), 18–31.

Hyams, Paul R. (1980), *Kings, lords and peasants in medieval England: the Common Law of Villeinage in the twelfth and thirteenth centuries*, Oxford.

Hybel, Nils (1989), *Crisis or change: the concept of crisis in the light of agrarian structural reorganization in late medieval England*, Aarhus.

Hybel, Nils (2002), 'Klima og hungersnød I middelalderen', *Historisk tidsskrift (Kopenhagen)* 102, 265–81.

Hymes, Robert (2014), 'Epilogue: a hypothesis on the East Asian beginnings of the *Yersinia pestis* polytomy', 285–307 in Monica Green, ed., *Pandemic disease in the medieval world: rethinking the Black Death, The Medieval Globe* 1, special issue, www.arc-humanities.org/the-medieval-globe.html.

Inglesby, Thomas V.; Dennis, David T; Henderson, Donald A.; Bartlett, John G.; Ascher, Michael S.; Eitzen, Edward; Fine, Anne D.; Friedlander, Arthur M.; Hauer, Jerome; Koerner, John F.; Layton, Marcelle; McDade, Joseph; Osterholm, Michael T.; O'Toole, Tara; Parker, Gerald; Perl, Trish M.; Russell, Philip K.; Schoch-Spana, Monica; Tonat, Kevin (2000), 'Plague as a biological weapon: medical and public health management', *Journal of the American Medical Association* 283 (17), 20pp.

Jacoby, G. C.; D'Arrigo, R. D.; Buckley, B.; Pederson, N. (no date), 'Mongolia (*Larix Sibirica*): Solongotyn Davaa (Tarvagatay Pass)', NOAA Paleoclimatology Tree Ring Data Sets, http://hurricane.ncdc.noaa.gov/pls/paleo/ftpsearch.treering.

James, Margery Kirkbride (1971), *Studies in the medieval wine trade*, Oxford.

Jamroziak, E. M. (2005), 'Networks of markets and networks of patronage in thirteenth-century England', 41–9 in Michael Prestwich, Richard H. Britnell and Robin Frame, eds., *Thirteenth-century England X*, Woodbridge.

Jansen, Katherine L. (2009), 'Giovanni Villani on food shortages and famine in central Italy (1329–30, 1347–48)', 20–3 in Katherine L. Jansen, Joanna Drell and Frances Andrews, eds., *Medieval Italy: texts in translation*, Philadelphia.

Jenks, S. (1998), 'The lay subsidies and the state of the English economy (1275–1334)', *Vierteljahrschrift für Sozial- und Wirtschaftsgeschichte*, 85, 1–39.

Jiang, Hui; Eiríksson, Jón; Schulz, Michael; Knudsen, Karen-Luise; Seidenkrantz, Marit-Solveig (2005), 'Evidence for solar forcing of sea-surface temperature on the North Icelandic Shelf during the late Holocene', *Geology* 33 (1), 73–6.

Jiang, J.; Mendelssohn, R.; Schwing, F.; Fraedrich, K. (2002), 'Coherency detection of multiscale abrupt changes in historic Nile flood levels, *GRL* 29 (8), 112 (1–4).

Jones, E. D. (1996), 'Medieval merchets as demographic data: some evidence from the Spalding Priory estates, Lincolnshire', *C&C* 11 (3), 459–70.

Jordan, William Chester (1996), *The Great Famine: Northern Europe in the early fourteenth century*, Princeton.

Kadens, Emily (2011), 'Myth of the customary law merchant', *Texas Law Review* 90, 1153.

Kander, Astrid; Malanima, Paolo; Warde, Paul (2014), *Power to the people: energy in Europe over the last five centuries*. Princeton.

Kanzaka, Junichi (2002), 'Villein rents in thirteenth-century England: an analysis of the Hundred Rolls of 1279–80', *EcHR* 55 (4), 593–618.

Kaplan, Jed O.; Krumhardt, Kristen M.; Zimmermann, Niklaus (2009), 'The prehistoric and preindustrial deforestation of Europe', *QSR* 28 (27), 3016–34.

Karpov, Sergej P. (2007), *History of the Empire of Trebizond* (in Russian), St Petersburg.

Kausrud, Kyrre Linné; Begon, Mike; Ari, Tamara Ben; Viljugrein, Hildegunn; Esper, Jan; Büntgen, Ulf; Leirs, Herwig; Junge, Claudia; Yang, Bao; Yang, Meixue; Xu, Lei; Stenseth, Nils Chr. (2010), 'Modeling the epidemiological history of plague in Central Asia: palaeoclimatic forcing on a disease system over the past millennium', *BMC Biology* 8 (112), 14pp.

Kedar, B. Z. (1976), *Merchants in crisis: Genoese and Venetian men of affairs and the fourteenth-century depression*, New Haven and London.

Keene, Derek (1984a), 'A new study of London before the Great Fire', *Urban History* 11 (1), 11–21.

Keene, Derek (1984b), 'Social and economic study of medieval London: summary report 1979–84', unpublished report to the Economic and Social Research Council, London.

Keene, Derek J. (1985), *Cheapside before the Great Fire*, London.

Keene, Derek J. (2000a), 'Changes in London's economic hinterland as indicated by debt cases in the Court of Common Pleas', 59–81 in J. A. Galloway, ed., *Trade, urban hinterlands and market integration, c.1300–1600: a collection of working papers given at a conference organised by the Centre for Metropolitan History and supported by the Economic and Social Research Council, 7 July 1999*, Centre for Metropolitan History, Working Papers 3, London.

Keene, Derek J. (2000b), 'London from the post-Roman period to 1300', 187–216 in D. M. Palliser, ed., *The Cambridge urban history of Britain, I, 600–1540*, Cambridge.

Keene, Derek J. (2011), 'Crisis management in London's food supply, 1250–1500', 45–62 in Ben Dodds and Christian D. Liddy, eds., *Commercial activity, markets and entrepreneurs in the Middle Ages: essays in honour of Richard Britnell*, Woodbridge.

Keil, Ian (1964), 'The estates of Glastonbury Abbey in the later Middle Ages: a study in administration and economic change', unpublished PhD thesis, University of Bristol.

Kelly, Morgan; Ó Gráda, Cormac (2014), 'The waning of the Little Ice Age: climate change in early modern Europe', *JIH* 44 (3), 301–25.

Kermode, Jenny (1998), *Medieval merchants: York, Beverley and Hull in the later Middle Ages*, Cambridge.

Kermode, Jenny (2000), 'The greater towns 1300–1540', 441–65 in D. M. Palliser, ed., *The Cambridge urban history of Britain*, Cambridge.

Kershaw, Ian (1973a), 'The great famine and agrarian crisis in England 1315–1322', *P&P* 59, 3–50.

Kershaw, Ian (1973b), *Bolton Priory: the economy of a northern monastery 1286–1325*, Oxford.

Kershaw, Ian (1976), 'The Great Famine and agrarian crisis in England 1315–22', 85–132 in R. H. Hilton, ed., *Peasants, knights and heretics*, Cambridge (reprinted from *P&P* 59 (1973a), 3–50).

Kershaw, Ian; Smith, David M., eds (2001), *The Bolton Priory compotus, 1286–1325: together with a priory account roll for 1377–1378*, Yorkshire Archaeological Society Record Series, Woodbridge.

Kitsikopoulos, Harry (2000), 'Standards of living and capital formation in pre-plague England: a peasant budget model', *EcHR* 53 (2), 237–61.

Kitsikopoulos, Harry, ed. (2012), *Agrarian change and crisis in Europe, 1200–1500*, London.

Knowles, David; Hadcock, R. N. (1971), *Medieval religious houses: England and Wales*, 2nd edn, London.

Kobashi, T.; Severinghaus, J. P.; Barnola, J.-M.; Kawamura, K.; Carter, T.; Nakaegawa, T. (2010a), 'Persistent multi-decadal Greenland temperature fluctuation through the last millennium', *Climatic Change* 100, 733–56.
Data: Kobashi, T.; Severinghaus, J. P.; Barnola, J.-M.; Kawamura, K.; Carter, T.; Nakaegawa, T. (2010b), 'GISP2 ice core 1000 year A^r-N^2 isotope temperature reconstruction', IGBP # 2010-057.

Kool, Jacob L. (2005), 'Risk of person-to-person transmission of pneumonic plague', *Healthcare Epidemiology* 40, 1166–72.

Kowaleski, Maryanne (2000), 'The western fisheries', 23–8 in David J. Starkey, Chris Reid and Neil Ashcroft, eds., *England's sea fisheries: the commercial sea fisheries of England and Wales since 1300*, London.

Kowaleski, Maryanne (2014), 'Medieval people in town and country: new perspectives from demography and bioarchaeology', *Speculum* 89 (3), 573–600.

Kundzewicz, Zbigniew W. (2005), 'Intense precipitation and high river flows in Europe – observations and projections', *Acta Geophysica Polonica* 53 (4), 385–400.

Kuznets, Simon (1966), *Modern economic growth, rate, structure, and spread*, New Haven.

Laayouni, H.; Oosting, M.; Luisi, P.; Ioana, M.; Alonso, S.; Ricaño-Ponce, I.; Trynka, G.; Zhernakova, A.; Plantinga, T. S.; Cheng, S. C.; Meer, J. W. van der; Popp, R.; Sood, A.; Thelma, B. K.; Wijmenga, C.; Joosten, L. A.; Bertranpetit, J.; Netea, M. G. (2014), 'Convergent evolution in European and Roma populations reveals pressure exerted by plague on toll-like receptors', *PNAS* 111 (7), 2668–73.

Lagerås, Per (2007), *The ecology of expansion and abandonment: medieval and post-medieval land-use and settlement dynamics in a landscape perspective*, Stockholm.

Lamb, Hubert Horace (1965), 'The early medieval warm epoch and its sequel', *Palaeogeography, Palaeoclimatology, Palaeoecology* 1, 13–37.

Landers, John (2003), *The field and the forge: population, production, and power in the pre-industrial West*, Oxford.

Langdon, John L. (1983), 'Horses, oxen, and technological innovation: the use of draught animals in English farming from 1066 to 1500', unpublished PhD thesis, University of Birmingham.

Langdon, John L. (1986), *Horses, oxen and technological innovation: the use of draught animals in English farming from 1066–1500*, Cambridge.

Langdon, John L. (1991), 'Water-mills and windmills in the west midlands, 1086–1500', *EcHR* 44 (3), 424–44.

Langdon, John L. (2004), *Mills in the medieval economy: England 1300–1540*, Oxford.

Langdon, John L.; Claridge, Jordan (2014), 'Women and children in the medieval English labour force before the Black Death: the examples of building and agriculture', unpublished paper.

Langdon, John L.; Masschaele, James (2006), 'Commercial activity and population growth in medieval England', *P&P* 190, 35–81.

Latimer, Paul (1997), 'Wages in late twelfth- and early thirteenth-century England', *Haskins Soc. Journal* 9, 185–205.

Latimer, Paul (1999), 'Early thirteenth-century prices', 41–73 in S. D. Church, ed., *King John: new interpretations*, Woodbridge.

Latimer, Paul (2011), 'Money and the English economy in the twelfth and thirteenth centuries', *History Compass* 9 (4), 246–56.

Laudisoit, Anne; Leirs, Herwig; Makundi, Rhodes H.; Van Dongen, Stefan; Davis, Stephen; Neerinckx, Simon; Deckers, Jozef; Libois, Roland (2007), 'Plague and the human flea, Tanzania', *EID* 13 (5), 687–93.

Lavigne, Franck; Degeai, Jean-Philippe; Komorowski, Jean-Christophe; Guillet, Sébastien; Robert, Vincent; Lahitte, Pierre; Oppenheimer, Clive; Stoffel, Markus; Vidal, Céline M.; Surono; Pratomo, Indyo; Wassmer, Patrick; Hajdas, Irka; Hadmoko, Danang Sri; Belizal, Edouard de (2013), 'Source of the great AD 1257 mystery eruption unveiled, Samalas volcano, Rinjani Volcanic Complex, Indonesia', *PNAS* 110 (42), 16742–7.

Lee, John S. (2003), 'Feeding the colleges: Cambridge's food and fuel supplies, 1450–1560', *EcHR* 56 (2), 243–64.

Le Roy Ladurie, Emmanuel (1971), *Times of feast and times of famine: a history of climate since the year 1000*, trans. Barbara Bray, New York.

Lepine, David (2003), 'England: Church and clergy', 359–80 in S. H. Rigby, ed., *A companion to Britain in the later Middle Ages*, Oxford.

Letters, Samantha (2010), *Online gazetteer of markets and fairs in England and Wales to 1516* www.history.ac.uk/cmh/gaz/gazweb2.html (updated 15 July 2010).

Letters, Samantha; Fernandes, Mario; Keene, Derek; Myhill, Owen (2003), *Gazetteer of markets and fairs in England and Wales to 1516*, List & Index Society, Special series 32 and 33.

Leulmi, Hamza; Socolovschi, Cristina; Laudisoit, Anne; Houemenou, Gualbert; Davoust, Bernard; Bitam, Idir; Raoult, Didier; Parola, Philipe (2014), 'Detection of *Rickettsia felis*, *Rickettsia typhi*, *Bartonella* species and *Yersinia pestis* in fleas (Siphonaptera) from Africa', *PLoS Neglected Tropical Diseases* 8 (10), e3152.

Levett, Ada Elizabeth (1916), *The Black Death on the estates of the see of Winchester; with a chapter on the manors of Witney, Brightwell, and Downton by A. Ballard*, Oxford Studies in Social and Legal History 5, Oxford.

Lieberman, Victor (2009), *Strange parallels: Southeast Asia in global context, c. 800–1830, 2, Mainland Mirrors: Europe, Japan, China, South Asia, and the Islands*, Cambridge.

Lieberman, Victor; Buckley, Brendan (2012), 'The impact of climate on Southeast Asia, circa 950–1820: new findings', *Modern Asian Studies* 46, 1049–96.

Limberger, Michael (2008), *Sixteenth-century Antwerp and its rural surroundings: social and economic changes in the hinterland of a commercial metropolis (ca. 1450–ca. 1570)*, Turnhout.

Lindert, Peter H.; Williamson, Jeffrey Gale (1982), 'Revising England's social tables, 1688–1812', *EEH* 19, 385–408.

Little, Lester K., ed. (2007), *Plague and the end of Antiquity: the pandemic of 541–750*, Cambridge.

Little, Lester K. (2011), 'Plague historians in lab coats', *P&P* 213, 267–90.

Livi-Bacci, Massimo (1991), *Population and nutrition: an essay on European demographic history*, trans. T. Croft-Murray and Carl Ipsen, Cambridge.

Livi-Bacci, Massimo (2000), *The population of Europe*, trans. Cynthia De Nardi Ipsen and Carl Ipsen, Oxford.

Livi-Bacci, Massimo (2001), *A concise history of world population*, 3rd edn, Oxford.

Livingstone, Marilyn Ruth (2003), 'The *Nonae*: the records of the taxation of the ninth in England 1340–41', 2 vols., unpublished PhD thesis, The Queen's University of Belfast.

Ljungqvist, F. C. (2009), 'Temperature proxy records covering the last two millennia: a tabular and visual overview', IGBP # 2009-017.

Lloyd, T. H. (1977), *The English wool trade in the Middle Ages*, Cambridge.

Lloyd, T. H. (1982), *Alien merchants in England in the high Middle Ages*, Brighton.

Lo Cascio, Elio; Malanima, Paolo (2009), 'GDP in pre-modern agrarian economies (1–1820 AD), a revision of the estimates', *Rivista di Storia Economica* 25, 391–419.

Loehle, Craig; McCulloch, J. Huston (2008), 'Correction to: "A 2000-year global temperature reconstruction based on non-tree ring proxies"', *Energy & Environment* 19 (1), 93–100, www.econ.ohio-state.edu/jhm/AGW/Loehle/.

Longden, J. (1959), 'Statistical notes on Winchester heriots', *EcHR* 11 (3), 412–17.

Lopez, Robert S. (1971), *The commercial revolution of the Middle Ages, 950–1350*, Englewood Cliffs.

Lopez, Robert S. (1987), 'The trade of medieval Europe: the South', 306–401 in M. M. Postan and Edward Miller, eds., *The Cambridge economic history of Europe, II, Trade and industry in the Middle Ages*, 2nd edn, Cambridge.

Lorange, Ellen A.; Race, Brent L.; Sebbane, Florent; Hinnebusch, B. Joseph (2005), 'Poor vector competence of fleas and the evolution of hypervirulence in *Yersinia pestis*', *Journal of Infectious Diseases* 191 (11), 1907–12.

Ludlow, Francis; Stine, Alexander R.; Leahy, Paul; Murphy, Enda; Mayewski, Paul A.; Taylor, David; Killen, James; Baillie, Michael G. L.; Hennessy, Mark; Kiely, Gerard (2013) 'Medieval Irish chronicles reveal persistent volcanic forcing of severe winter cold events, 431–1649 CE', *Environmental Research Letters* 8 (2), L024035.

Lyons, Mary (1989), 'Weather, famine, pestilence and plague in Ireland, 900–1500', 321–74 in E. Margaret Crawford, ed., *Famine: the Irish experience, 900–1900: subsistence crises and famine in Ireland*, Edinburgh.

MacMillan, Katherine; Enscore, Russell E.; Ogen-Odoi, Asaph; Borchert, Jeff N.; Babi, Nackson; Amatre, Gerald; Atiku, Linda A.; Mead, Paul S.; Gage, Kenneth L.; Eisen, Rebecca J. (2011), 'Landscape and residential variables associated with plague-endemic villages in the West Nile region of Uganda', *American Journal of Tropical Medicine & Hygiene* 84 (3), 435–42.

Maddicott, John Robert (1987), 'The English peasantry and the demands of the Crown, 1294–1341', 285–359 in T. H. Aston, ed., *Landlords, peasants and politics in medieval England*, Cambridge. Reprinted from (1975), *P&P*, Supplement 1.

Maddison, Angus (2007), *Contours of the world economy, 1–2030 AD: essays in macro-economic history*, Oxford.

Magilligan, Francis J.; Goldstein, Paul S. (2001), 'El Niño floods and culture change: a late Holocene flood history for the Rio Moquegua, southern Peru', *Geology* 29 (5), 431–4.

Maitland, F. W., ed. (1889), *Select pleas in manorial and other seigniorial courts: reigns of Henry III and Edward I*, Selden Society 2, London.

Malanima, Paolo (1998), 'Italian cities 1300–1800: a quantitative approach', *Rivista di storia economica* 14 (2), 91–126.

Malanima, Paolo (2002), *L'economia italiana: dalla crescita medievale alla crescita contemporanea*, Bologna.

Malanima, Paolo (2003), 'Measuring the Italian economy, 1300–1861', *Rivista di storia economica* 19 (3), 265–96.

Malanima, Paolo (2005), 'Urbanisation and the Italian economy during the last millennium', *EREH* 9 (1), 97–122.

Malanima, Paolo (2008), 'The Italian Renaissance economy (1250–1600)', unpublished paper available at: www.paolomalanima.it/default_file/.../RENAISSANCE_ITALY.doc.pdf.

Malanima, Paolo (2011), 'The long decline of a leading economy: GDP in central and northern Italy, 1300–1913', *EREH* 15 (2), 169–219.

Malanima, Paolo (2012), 'Italy', 93–127 in Harry Kitsikopoulos, ed., *Agrarian change and crisis in Europe, 1200–1500*, London ['Statistical appendix: consumer price indices and wages in Central-Northern Italy and Southern England 1300–1850', www.paolomalanima.it/default_file/Italian%20Economy/StatisticalAppendix.pdf].

Malanima, Paolo (no date a), 'Italian GDP 1300–1913', Institute of Studies on Mediterranean Societies (ISSM), Italian National Research Council (CNR), www.cepr.org/meets/wkcn/1/1714/papers/Malanima.pdf.

Malanima, Paolo (no date b), 'Wheat prices in Tuscany', Institute of Studies on Mediterranean Societies, Italian National Research Council.

Malowist, Marian (1987), 'The trade of Eastern Europe in the later Middle Ages', 525–612 in M. M. Postan and Edward Miller, eds., *The Cambridge economic history of Europe, II, Trade and industry in the Middle Ages*, 2nd edn, Cambridge.

Maltas, Joan Montoro (2013), 'Mortality crises in Catalonia between 1285 and 1350: famines, shortages, disease and pestilence', unpublished paper presented at the workshop, *Mortality crises between the plagues, c. 800–c. 1300 CE*, University of Stirling, November 2013.

Mann, Michael (1986), *The sources of social power, I, A history of power from the beginning to A.D. 1760*, Cambridge.

Mann, Michael E.; Cane, Mark A.; Zebiak, Stephen E.; Clement, Amy (2005), 'Volcanic and solar forcing of the tropical Pacific over the past 1000 years', *Journal of Climate* 18, 447–56.

Mann, Michael E., Fuentes, Jose D.; Rutherford; Scott (2012), 'Underestimation of volcanic cooling in tree-ring based reconstructions of hemispheric temperatures', *Nature Geoscience*, 5 February.

Mann, Michael E.; Zhang, Zhihua; Hughes, Malcolm K.; Bradley, Raymond S.; Miller, Sonya K.; Rutherford, Scott; Ni, Fenbiao (2008), 'Proxy-based reconstructions of hemispheric and global surface temperature variations over the past two millennia', *PNAS* 105 (36), 13252–7. *Data*: www.ncdc .noaa.gov/paleo/metadata/noaa-recon-6252.html.

Mann, Michael E.; Zhang, Zhihua; Rutherford, Scott; Bradley, Raymond S.; Hughes, Malcolm K.; Shindell, Drew; Ammann, Caspar; Faluvegi, Greg; Ni, Fenbiao (2009), 'Global signatures and dynamical origins of the Little Ice Age and Medieval Climate Anomaly', *Science* 326 (5957), 1256–60.

Marcus, G. J. (1980), *The conquest of the North Atlantic*, Woodbridge.

Martin, Janet (2012), 'Russia', 292–329 in Harry Kitsikopoulos, ed., *Agrarian change and crisis in Europe, 1200–1500*, London.

Masschaele, James (1994), 'The multiplicity of medieval markets reconsidered', *JHG* 20 (3), 255–71.

Masschaele, James (1997), *Peasants, merchants and markets: inland trade in medieval England, 1150–1350*, New York.

Massé, Guillaume; Rowland, Steven J.; Sicre, Marie-Alexandrine; Jacob, Jeremy; Jansen, Eystein; Belt, Simon T. (2008), 'Abrupt climatic changes for Iceland during the last millennium: evidence from high resolution sea ice reconstructions', *Earth & Planetary Science Letters* 269, 565–9.

Mayhew, Nicholas (1999), *Sterling: the history of a currency*, London.

McCormick, Michael (2001), *Origins of the European economy: communications and commerce AD 300–900*, Cambridge.

McEvedy, Colin (1992), *The new Penguin atlas of medieval history*, Harmondsworth.

McEvedy, Colin; Jones, Richard (1978), *Atlas of world population history*, Harmondsworth.

McFarlane, Kenneth Bruce (1973), *The nobility of later medieval England: the Ford Lectures for 1953 and related studies*, Oxford.

McIntosh, Marjorie Keniston (2012), *Poor relief in England, 1350–1600*, Cambridge.

McMichael, Anthony J. (2010), 'Paleoclimate and bubonic plague: a forewarning of future risk?', *BMC Biology* 8 (108), 3pp.

McNamee, Colm (1997), *The wars of the Bruces: Scotland, England and Ireland, 1306–1328*, East Linton.

McNeill, T. E. (1980), *Anglo-Norman Ulster: the history and archaeology of an Irish barony, 1177–1400*, Edinburgh.

McNeill, William H. (1977), *Plagues and peoples*, New York.

Meeker, Loren D.; Mayewski Paul A. (2001), 'A 1400-year high-resolution record of atmospheric circulation over the North Atlantic and Asia', *The Holocene* 12 (3), 257–66.

Milgrom, Paul R.; North, Douglass C.; Weingast, Barry R. (1990), 'The role of institutions in the revival of trade: the law merchant, private judges, and the Champagne fairs', *Economics & Politics* 2 (1), 1–23.

Miller, Edward; Hatcher, John (1995), *Medieval England: towns, commerce and crafts, 1086–1348*, Harlow.

Miller, Gifford H.; Geirsdóttir, Áslaug; Zhong, Yafang; Larsen, Darren J.; Otto-Bliesner, Bette L.; Holland, Marika M.; Bailey, David A.; Refsnider, Kurt A.; Lehman, Scott J.; Southon, John R.; Anderson, Chance; Björnsson, Helgi; Thordarson, Thorvaldur (2012), 'Abrupt onset of the Little Ice Age triggered by volcanism and sustained by sea-ice/ocean feedbacks', *GRL* 39 (2), 5pp.

Mills, James N.; Gage, Kenneth L.; Khan, Ali S. (2010), 'Potential influence of climate change on vector-borne and zoonotic diseases: a review and proposed research plan', *Environmental Health Perspectives* 118 (1), 1507–14.

Mitchell, B. R. (1988), *British historical statistics*, Cambridge.

Moberg, Anders; Sonechkin, Dmitry M.; Holmgren, Karin; Datsenko, Nina M.; Karlén, Wibjörn (2005), 'Highly variable northern hemisphere temperatures reconstructed from low- and high-resolution proxy data', *Nature* 3265, 5pp.

Mohtadi, Mahyar; Romero, Oscar E.; Kaiser, Jérôme: Hebbeln, Dierk (2007), 'Cooling of the southern high latitudes during the medieval period and its effect on ENSO', *QSR* 26, 1055–66.

Mokyr, Joel (1992), *The lever of riches: technological creativity and economic progress*, Oxford.

Monecke, Stefan; Monecke, Hannelore; Monecke, Jochen (2009), 'Modelling the Black Death: a historical case study and implications for the epidemiology of bubonic plague', *International Journal of Medical Microbiology* 299, 582–93.

Moore, Ellen Wedemeyer (1985), *The fairs of medieval England: an introductory study*, Toronto.

Moore, Robert Ian (1987), *The formation of a persecuting society: power and deviance in Western Europe 950–1250*, Oxford.

Moreda, Vicente Pérez (1988), 'La población española', 345–431 in Miguel Artola, ed., *Enciclopedia de Historia de España, 1, Economía y sociedad*, Madrid.

Morelli, Giovanna; Song, Yajun; Mazzoni, Camila J.; Eppinger, Mark; Roumagnac, Philippe; Wagner, David M.; Feldkamp, Mirjam; Kusecek, Barica; Vogler, Amy J.; Li, Yanjun; Cui, Yujun; Thomson, Nicholas R.; Jombart, Thibaut; Leblois, Raphael; Lichter, Peter; Rahalison, Lila; Petersen,

Jeannine M.; Balloux, François; Keim, Paul; Wirth, Thierry; Ravel, Jacques; Yang, Ruifu; Carniel, Elisabeth; Achtman, Mark (2010), '*Yersinia pestis* genome sequencing identifies patterns of global phylogenetic diversity', *Nature Genetics* 42 (12), 1140–3.

Moreno, Ana; Pérez, Ana; Frigola, Jaime; Nieto-Moreno, Vanesa; Rodrigo-Gámiz, Marta; Martrat, Belén; González-Sampériz, Penélope; Morellón, Mario; Martín-Puertas, Celia; Corella, Juan Pablo; Belmonte, Ánchel; Sancho, Carlos; Cacho, Isabel; Herrera, Gemma; Canals, Miquel; Grimalt, Joan O.; Jiménez-Espejo, Francisco; Martínez-Ruiz, Francisca; Vegas-Vilarrúbia, Teresa; Valero-Garcés, Blas L. (2012), 'The Medieval Climate Anomaly in the Iberian Peninsula reconstructed from marine and lake records', *Quaternary Science Reviews* 43, 16–32.

Morris, Christopher (1971), '1. The plague in Britain', *Historical Journal* 14 (1), 205–15.

Morris, Marc (2005), *The Bigod earls of Norfolk in the thirteenth century*, Woodbridge.

Morris, Richard (1979), *Cathedrals and abbeys of England and Wales: the building Church, 600–1540*, London.

Mullan, John (2007/8), 'Mortality, gender, and the plague of 1361–2 on the estate of the bishop of Winchester', Cardiff Historical Papers, Cardiff, www.cardiff.ac.uk/hisar/research/projectreports/historicalpapers/index.html.

Mundill, Robin R. (2002), 'Christian and Jewish lending patterns and financial dealings during the twelfth and thirteenth centuries', 42–67 in Phillipp Schofield and N. J. Mayhew, eds., *Credit and debt in medieval England, c.1180–c.1350*, Oxford.

Mundill, Robin R. (2010), *The king's Jews: money, massacre and exodus in medieval England*, London.

Munro, John H. (1991), 'Industrial transformations in the north-west European textile trades, c.1290–c.1340: economic progress or economic crisis?', 110–48 in Bruce M. S. Campbell, ed., *Before the Black Death: studies in the 'crisis' of the early fourteenth century*, Manchester.

Munro, John H. (1998), 'The "industrial crisis" of the English textile towns, c.1290–c.1330', University of Toronto, Department of Economics Working Paper 68 (MUNRO 98-02: [1998-06-18]). Published as Munro (1999c).

Munro, John H. (1999a), 'The symbiosis of towns and textiles: urban institutions and the changing fortunes of cloth manufacturing in the Low Countries and England, 1270–1570', *Journal of Early Modern History* 3 (3), 1–74.

Munro, John H. (1999b), 'The Low Countries' export trade in textiles with the Mediterranean basin, 1200–1600: a cost–benefit analysis of comparative advantages in overland and maritime trade routes', *International Journal of Maritime History* 11 (2), 1–30.

Munro, John H. (1999c), 'The "industrial crisis" of the English textile towns, 1290–1330', 103–41 in Michael Prestwich, Richard Britnell and Robin Frame, eds., *Thirteenth-Century England VII*, Woodbridge.

Munro, John H. (2001), 'The "new institutional economics" and the changing fortunes of fairs in medieval and early modern Europe: the textile trades, warfare, and transaction costs', 405–51 in Simonetta Cavaciocchi, ed., *Fiere e mercati nella integrazione delle economie Europee secc. XIII–XVIII, Istituto internazionale di storia economica 'F. Datini'*, Prato.

Munro, John H. (2003a), 'Medieval woollens: the western European woollen industries and their struggles for international markets, c.1000–1500', 228–324 in D. Jenkins, ed., *The Cambridge history of western textiles, 1*, Cambridge.

Munro, John H. (2003b), 'Wage-stickiness, monetary changes, and real incomes in late-medieval England and the Low Countries 1300–1500: did money matter?', *Research in Economic History* 21, 185–297.

Munro, John H. (2007), 'The anti-red shift – to the "dark side": colour changes in Flemish luxury woollens, 1300–1550', 55–96 in Robin Netherton and Gale R. Owen-Crocker, eds., *Medieval clothing and textiles, 3*, Woodbridge.

Munro, John H. (2009), 'Before and after the Black Death: money, prices, and wages in fourteenth-century England', 335–64 in Troels Dahlerup and Per Ingesman, eds., *New approaches to the history of late medieval and early modern Europe: selected proceedings of two international conferences at the Royal Danish Academy of Sciences and Letters in Copenhagen in 1997 and 1999*, Copenhagen.

Munro, John H. (no date), 'The Phelps Brown and Hopkins "basket of consumables" commodity price series and craftsmen's wage series, 1264–1700: revised by John H. Munro', www.economics.utoronto.ca/munro5/ResearchData.html.

Myrdal, Janken (2006), 'The forgotten plague: the Black Death in Sweden', 141–86 in Pekka Hämäläinen, ed., *When disease makes history: epidemics and great historical turning points*, Helsinki.

Myrdal, Janken (2012), 'Scandinavia', 204–49 in Harry Kitsikopoulos, ed., *Agrarian change and crisis in Europe, 1200–1500*, London.

Myśliwski, Grzegorz (2012), 'Central Europe', 250–91 in Harry Kitsikopoulos, ed., *Agrarian change and crisis in Europe, 1200–1500*, London.

National Academy of Sciences (2008), *Global climate change and extreme weather events: understanding the contributions to infectious disease emergence: workshop summary*, Washington D.C.

Newfield, Timothy P. (2009), 'A cattle panzootic in early fourteenth-century Europe', *AHR* 57 (2), 155–90.

Newfield, Timothy P. (2012), 'A great Carolingian panzootic: the probable extent, diagnosis and impact of an early ninth-century cattle pestilence', *Argos* 46, 200–10.

Nicholas, David M. (1968), 'Town and countryside: social and economic tensions in fourteenth-century Flanders', *Comparative Studies in Society and History* 10 (4), 458–85.

Nicholas, David M. (1976), 'Economic reorientation and social change in fourteenth-century Flanders', *P&P* 70, 3–29.

Nicholas, David M. (1987), *The metamorphosis of a medieval city: Ghent in the age of the Arteveldes, 1302–1390*, Lincoln (Nebraska) and London.

Nicholas, David M. (1992), *Medieval Flanders*, London and New York.

Nightingale, Pamela (1990), 'Monetary contraction and mercantile credit in later medieval England', *EcHR* 43 (4), 560–75.

Nightingale, Pamela (1995), *A medieval mercantile community: the Grocers' Company and the politics and trade of London, 1000–1485*, New Haven.

Nightingale, Pamela (1996), 'The growth of London in the medieval English economy', 89–106 in Richard H. Britnell and John Hatcher, eds., *Progress and problems in medieval England: essays in honour of Edward Miller*, Cambridge.

Nightingale, Pamela (1997), 'England and the European depression of the mid-fifteenth century', *Journal of European Economic History* 26 (3), 631–56.

Nightingale, Pamela (2004a), 'Money and credit in the economy of late medieval England', 51–71 in Diana Wood, ed., *Medieval money matters*, Oxford.

Nightingale, Pamela (2004b), 'The lay subsidies and the distribution of wealth in medieval England, 1275–1334', *EcHR* 57 (1), 1–32.

Nightingale, Pamela (2005), 'Some new evidence of crises and trends of mortality in late medieval England', *P&P* 187, 33–68.

Nightingale, Pamela (2010), 'The rise and decline of medieval York: a reassessment', *P&P* 206, 3–42.

Norris, John (1977), 'East or west? The geographic origin of the Black Death', *BHM* 51 (1), 1–24.

Norris, John (1978), 'Geographical origin of the Black Death: response', *BHM* 52 (1), 114–20.

Noymer, Andrew (2007), 'Contesting the cause and severity of the Black Death: a review essay', *Population & Development Review* 33 (3), 616–27.

Nutton, Vivian, ed. (2008a), 'Pestilential complexities: understanding medieval plague', *Medical History*, Supplement 27, London.

Nutton, Vivian (2008b), 'Introduction', *Medical History*, Supplement 27, 1–16.

Ó Cróinín, Dáibhí (1995), *Early medieval Ireland 400–1200*, London and New York.

O'Rourke, K. H.; Williamson, J. G. (2002), 'After Columbus: explaining Europe's overseas trade boom, 1500–1800', *JEH* 62 (2), 417–56.

O'Sullivan, M. D. (1962), *Italian merchant bankers in Ireland in the thirteenth century: a study in the social and economic history of medieval Ireland*, Dublin.

Olea, Ricardo A.; Christakos, George (2005), 'Duration of urban mortality for the fourteenth-century Black Death epidemic', *Human Biology* 77 (3), 291–303.

Oosthuizen, Susan (2010), 'Medieval field systems and settlement nucleation: common or separate origins?', 107–32 in Nicholas J. Higham and Martin J. Ryan, eds., *Landcape archaeology of Anglo-Saxon England*, Woodbridge.

Oppenheimer, Clive (2003), 'Ice core and palaeoclimatic evidence for the timing and nature of the great mid-thirteenth century volcanic eruption', *International Journal of Climatology* 23, 417–26.

Oram, Richard D.; Adderley, W. Paul (2008a), 'Lordship and environmental change in central highland Scotland, c.1300–c.1400', *Journal of the North Atlantic* 1, 74–84.

Oram, Richard D.; Adderley, W. Paul (2008b),'Lordship, land and environmental change in west Highland and Hebridean Scotland, c.1300 to c.1450', 257–67 in Simonetta Cavaciocchi, ed., *Le interazioni fra economia e ambiente biologico nell'Europe preindustriale, secc. XIII–XVIII, Istituto Internazionale di Storia Economica 'F. Datini'*, Prato.

Ormrod, W. Mark (1990), *The reign of Edward III: Crown and political society in England, 1327–1377*, New Haven.

Ormrod, W. Mark (1991), 'The Crown and the English economy, 1290–1348', 149–83 in Bruce M. S. Campbell, ed., *Before the Black Death: studies in the 'crisis' of the early fourteenth century*, Manchester.

Ormrod, W. Mark (1996), 'The politics of pestilence: government in England after the Black Death', 147–81 in W. Mark Ormrod and Phillip G. Lindley, eds., *The Black Death in England*, Stamford.

Ormrod, W. Mark (2010), 'The relative income from direct and indirect taxation in England, 1295–1454', in *European State Finances Database*: www.esfdb .org/table.aspx?resourceid=11762.

Overton, Mark; Campbell, Bruce M. S. (1991), 'Productivity change in European agricultural development', 1–50 in Bruce M. S. Campbell and Mark Overton, eds., *Land, labour and livestock: historical studies in European agricultural productivity*, Manchester.

Overton, Mark; Campbell, Bruce M. S. (1992), 'Norfolk livestock farming 1250–1740: a comparative study of manorial accounts and probate inventories', *JHG* 18 (4), 377–96.

Page, Mark (2001), 'Peasant land market in southern England,1260–1350' [computer file]. Raw Access database deposited at ESRC data archive Colchester, Essex, ref. no. SN: 4086.

Page, Mark (2003), 'The peasant land market on the estate of the bishopric of Winchester before the Black Death', 61–80 in Richard H. Britnell, ed., *The Winchester Pipe Rolls and medieval English society*, Woodbridge.

Page, Mark (2012), 'The smallholders of Southampton Water: the peasant land market on a Hampshire manor before the Black Death', 181–97 in Sam Turner and Bob Silvester, eds., *Life in medieval landscapes: people and places in the Middle Ages*, Oxford.

Palma, Nuno; Reis, Jaime (2014), 'Portuguese demography and economic growth, 1500–1850', unpublished working paper presented at the Hi-Pod Workshop *Accounting for the Great Divergence*, University of Warwick in Venice, Palazzo Pesaro Papafava, May 2014: www2.warwick.ac.uk/fac/ soc/economics/research/centres/cage/events/conferences/greatdivergence14/ portuguese_demography_and_economic_growth_1500--1850_-_may_19th_ 2014.pdf.

Palmer, Robert C. (1985a), 'The origins of property in England', *Law & History Review* 3, 1–50.

Palmer, Robert C. (1985b), 'The economic and cultural impact of the origins of property: 1180–1220', *Law & History Review* 3 (2), 375–96.

Palmer, Robert C. (2003), 'England: law, society and the state', 242–60 in S. H. Rigby, ed., *A companion to Britain in the later Middle Ages*, Oxford.

Parker, Geoffrey (2013), *Global crisis: war, climate change and catastrophe in the seventeenth century*, New Haven and London.

Parry, Martin L. (1978), *Climatic change, agriculture and settlement*. Folkestone.

Patterson, William P.; Dietrich, Kristin A.; Holmden, Chris; Andrews, John T. (2010), 'Two millennia of North Atlantic seasonality and implications for Norse colonies', *PNAS* 107 (12), 5306–10.

Patz, Jonathan A.; Campbell-Lendrum, Diarmid; Holloway, Tracey; Foley, Jonathan A. (2005), 'Impact of regional climate change on human health', *Nature* 438, 310–17.

Pedersen, Kathrine Vestergard; Nosch, Marie-Louise, eds. (2009), *The medieval broadcloth: changing trends in fashions, manufacturing and consumption*, Oxford.

Pederson, Neil; Hessl, Amy E.; Baatarbileg, Nachin; Anchukaitis, Kevin J.; Cosmo, Nicola Di (2014), 'Pluvials, droughts, the Mongol Empire, and modern Mongolia', *PNAS* 111 (12), 4375–9.

Pegolotti, Francesco Balducci (*c.*1340 and 1936), *La pratica della mercatura*, ed. Allan Evans, Cambridge, Mass.

Persson, Karl Gunnar (1988), *Pre-industrial economic growth: social organization and technological progress in Europe*, Oxford and New York.

Pfister, C.; Schwarz-Zanetti, G.; Wegmann, M. (1996), 'Winter severity in Europe: the fourteenth century', *Climatic Change* 34, 91–108.

Phelps Brown, E. Henry; Hopkins, Sheila V. (1956), 'Seven centuries of the prices of consumables, compared with builders' wage rates', *Economica* new series 23 (92), 296–314. Reprinted in E. Henry Phelps Brown and Sheila V. Hopkins (1981), *A perspective of prices and wages*, London.

Phillips, J. R. S. (1988), *The medieval expansion of Europe*, Oxford and New York.

Phythian-Adams, Charles (2002), *Desolation of a city: Coventry and the urban crisis of the late Middle Ages*, Cambridge.

Piarroux, Renaud; Abedi, Aaron Aruna; Shako, Jean-Christophe; Kebela, Benoit; Karhemere, Stomy; Diatta, Georges; Davoust, Bernard; Raoult, Didier; Drancourt, Michel (2013), 'Plague epidemics and lice, Democratic Republic of the Congo', [letter] *EID* 19 (3), 505–6.

Piponnier, Françoise; Mane, Perrine (1997), *Dress in the Middle Ages*, New Haven, Conn.

Pomeranz, Ken (2000), *The Great Divergence: China, Europe, and the making of the modern world economy*, Princeton.

Poos, Lawrence R. (1985), 'The rural population of Essex in the later Middle Ages', *EcHR* 38 (4), 515–30.

Popper, William (1951), *The Cairo Nilometer: studies in Ibn Taghrī Birdī's chronicles of Egypt I*, Berkeley and Los Angeles.

Postan, Michael Moïssey (1954), *The* famulus*: the estate labourer in the XIIth and XIIIth centuries*, EcHR Supplement 2, Cambridge.

Postan, Michael Moïssey (1966), 'Medieval agrarian society in its prime: England', 549–632 in M. M. Postan, ed., *The Cambridge economic history of Europe, I, The agrarian life of the Middle Ages*, 2nd edn, Cambridge.

Postan, Michael Moïssey; Titow, Jan Z. (1959), 'Heriots and prices on Winchester manors', *EcHR* 11 (3), 392–411. Reprinted as 150–85 in M. M.

Postan (1973), *Essays on medieval agriculture and general problems of the medieval economy*, Cambridge.

Postles, David (1986), 'The perception of profit before the leasing of demesnes', *AHR* 34 (1), 12–28.

Pounds, Norman J. G. (1973), *An historical geography of Europe 450 B.C.–A.D. 1330*, Cambridge.

Pounds, Norman J. G. (1974), *An economic history of medieval Europe*, London.

Power, Eileen (1941), *The wool trade in English medieval history*, Oxford.

Power, John P.; Campbell, Bruce M. S. (1992), 'Cluster analysis and the classification of medieval demesne-farming systems', *Trans. Institute British Geographers* 17, 227–45. Reprinted in Bruce M. S. Campbell (2008), *Field systems and farming systems in late medieval England*, Aldershot.

Prentice, Michael B.; Rahalison, Lila (2007), 'Plague', *The Lancet* 369, 1196–207.

Prestwich, Michael (1980), *The three Edwards: war and the state in England 1272–1377*, London.

Prestwich, Michael (1988), *Edward I*, London.

Pretty, Jules (1990), 'Sustainable agriculture in the Middle Ages: the English manor', *AHR* 38 (1), 1–19.

Proctor, C. J.; Baker, A.; Barnes, W. L. (2002a), 'A three thousand year record of North Atlantic climate', *Climate Dynamics* 19 (5–6), 449–54.

Data: Proctor, C. J.; Baker, A.; Barnes, W. L. (2002b), 'Northwest Scotland stalagmite data to 3600 BP', IGBP # 2002-028.

Rackham, Oliver (1986), *The history of the countryside*, London.

Rad, Ulrich von; Schaaf, M.; Michels, Klaus; Schulz, Hartmut; Berger, Wolfgang H.; Sirocko, Frank (1999), 'A 5000-year record of climate change in varved sediments from the oxygen minimum zone off Pakistan, northeastern Arabian Sea', *Quaternary Research* 51 (1), 39–53.

Raftis, J. Ambrose (1974), *Warboys: two hundred years in the life of an English mediaeval village*, Toronto.

Raftis, J. Ambrose (1996), *Peasant economic development within the English manorial system*, Stroud.

Raoult, Didier; Aboudharam, Gérard; Crubézy, Eric; Larrouy, Georges; Ludes, Bertrand; Drancourt, Michel (2000), 'Molecular identification by "suicide PCR" of *Yersinia pestis* as the agent of medieval Black Death', *PNAS* 97 (23), 12800–3.

Raoult, Didier; Woodward, Theodore; Dumler, J. Stephen (2004), 'The history of epidemic typhus', *Infectious Disease Clinics of North America* 18 (1), 127–40.

Ratovonjato, Jocelyn; Rajerison, Minoarisoa; Rahelinirina, Soanandrasana; Boyer, Sébastien (2014), '*Yersinia pestis* in *Pulex irritans* fleas during plague outbreak, Madagascar', *EID* 20 (8), 1414.

Razi, Zvi (1980), *Life, marriage and death in a medieval parish: economy, society and demography in Halesowen, 1270–1400*, Cambridge.

Razi, Zvi; Smith, Richard M. (1996a), 'The origin of the English manorial court rolls as a written record: a puzzle', 36–68 in Zvi Razi and Richard M. Smith, eds., *Medieval society and the manor court*, Oxford.

Razi, Zvi; Smith, Richard M., eds. (1996b), *Medieval society and the manor court*, Oxford.

Reeves, Albert Compton (1995), *Pleasures and pastimes in medieval England*, Stroud.

Rein, Bert; Lückge, Andreas; Sirocko, Frank (2004), 'A major Holocene ENSO anomaly during the medieval period', *GRL* 31, L17211, 4pp. Data: www .klimaundsedimente.geowiss.uni-mainz.de/128.php.

Richard, J. M. (1892), 'Thierry d'Hireçon, agriculteur artésien', *Bibliothèque de l'école des chartes* 53, 383–416, 571–604.

Rigby, S. H. (2010), 'Urban population in late medieval England: the evidence of the lay subsidies', *EcHR* 63 (2), 393–417.

Robo, Etienne (1929), 'The Black Death in the Hundred of Farnham', *English Historical Review*, 44 (176), 560–72.

Rodríguez, Ana (2012), 'Spain', 167–203 in Harry Kitsikopoulos, ed., *Agrarian change and crisis in Europe, 1200–1500*, London.

Rogers, J. E. Thorold (1866–1902), *A history of agriculture and prices in England from the year after the Oxford parliament (1259) to the commencement of the continental war (1793)*, Oxford.

Rogers, K. H. (1969), 'Salisbury', 1–9 in Mary D. Lobel, ed., *Historic towns: maps and plans of towns and cities in the British Isles, I*, London and Oxford. www.historictownsatlas.org.uk/atlas/volume-i/historic-towns/salisbury.

Rogozo, N. R.; Echer, E.; Vieira, L. E. A.; Nordemann, D. J. R. (2001), 'Reconstruction of Wolf sunspot numbers on the basis of spectral characteristics and estimates of associated radio flux and solar wind parameters for the last millennium', *Solar Physics* 203, 179–91.

Rohr, Christian (2007), 'Writing a catastrophe: describing and constructing disaster perception in narrative sources from the late Middle Ages', *Historical Social Research* 32 (3), 88–102.

Royer, Katherine (2014), 'The blind men and the elephant: imperial medicine, medieval historians and the role of rats in the historiography of plague', 99–110 in Poonam Bala, ed., *Medicine and colonialism: historical perspectives in India and South Africa*, London.

Russell, Ephraim (1918), 'The societies of the Bardi and the Peruzzi and their dealings with Edward III', 93–135 in George Unwin, ed., *Finance and trade under Edward III*, London.

Russell, Josiah Cox (1948), *British medieval population*, Albuquerque.

Russell, Josiah Cox (1958), 'Late ancient and medieval population', *Trans. American Philosophical Soc.* 48 (3), 1–152.

Russill, Chris (2015), 'Climate change tipping points: origins, precursors, and debates', *WIREs Climate Change*.

Rutledge, Elizabeth (1988), 'Immigration and population growth in early fourteenth-century Norwich: evidence from the tithing roll', *Urban History* 15 (1), 15–30.

Rutledge, Elizabeth (1995), 'Landlord and tenants: housing and the rented property market in early fourteenth-century Norwich', *Urban History* 22 (1), 7–24.

Rutledge, Elizabeth (2004), 'Norwich before the Black Death/Economic life', 157–88 in Carole Rawcliffe and Richard Wilson, eds., *Medieval Norwich*, London.

Sachs, Stephen E. (2002), 'The "law merchant" and the fair court of St. Ives, 1270–1324', PhD dissertation, Harvard University, Cambridge, Mass.

Sachs, Stephen E. (2006), 'From St. Ives to cyberspace: the modern distortion of the medieval "law merchant"', *American University International Law Review* 21 (5), 685–812.

Salzer, Matthew W.; Hughes, Malcolm K. (2007), 'Bristlecone pine tree rings and volcanic eruptions over the last 5000 yr', *Quaternary Research* 67 (1), 57–68.

Sapoznik, Alexandra (2013), 'The productivity of peasant agriculture: Oakington, Cambridgeshire, 1360–91', *EcHR* 66 (2), 518–44.

Sarris, Peter (2002), 'The Justinianic Plague: origins and effects', *C&C* 17 (2), 169–82.

Saul, A. (1979), 'Great Yarmouth and the Hundred Years War in the fourteenth century', *Historical Research* 52 (126), 105–15.

Schamiloglu, Uli (1993), 'Preliminary remarks on the role of disease in the history of the Golden Horde', *Central Asian Survey* 12 (4), 447–57.

Scheffer, Marten (2009), *Critical transitions in nature and society*, Princeton.

Schmid, Boris V.; Büntgen, Ulf; Easterday, W. Ryan; Ginzler, Christian; Walløe, Lars; Bramanti, Barbara; Stenseth, Nils Chr. (2015), 'Climate-driven introduction of the Black Death and successive plague reintroductions into Europe', *PNAS*, 23 February.

Schofield, John; Allen, Patrick; Taylor, Colin (1990), 'Medieval buildings and property development in the area of Cheapside', *Trans. London & Middlesex Archaeological Soc.* 41, 39–238.

Schofield, Phillipp R. (1997), 'Dearth, debt and the local land market in a late thirteenth-century village community'. *AHR* 45 (1), 1–17.

Schofield, Phillipp R. (2008), 'The social economy of the medieval village in the early fourteenth century', *EcHR* 61, special issue 1, 38–63.

Schofield, Phillipp; Mayhew, N. J., eds. (2002), *Credit and debt in medieval England, c.1180–c.1350*, Oxford.

Schön, Lennart; Krantz, Olle (2012), 'The Swedish economy in the early modern period: constructing historical national accounts', *EREH* 16 (4), 529–49.

Schuenemann, Verena J.; Bos, Kirsten; DeWitte, Sharon; Schmedes, Sarah; Jamieson, Joslyn; Mittnik, Alissa; Forrest, Stephen; Coombes, Brian K.; Wood, James W.; Earn, David J. D.; White, William; Krause, Johannes; Poinar, Hendrik N. (2011), 'Targeted enrichment of ancient pathogens yielding the pPCP1 plasmid of *Yersinia pestis* from victims of the Black Death', *PNAS* 108 (38), e746–e752.

Scott, Susan; Duncan, Christopher J. (2001), *Biology of plagues: evidence from historical populations*, Cambridge.

Scott, Susan; Duncan, Christopher J.; Duncan, S. R. (1996), 'The plague in Penrith, Cumbria, 1597/8: its causes, biology and consequences', *Annals of Human Biology* 23 (1), 1–21.

Scott, Tom (2002), *Society and economy in Germany 1300–1600*, Basingstoke and New York.

Seager, Richard; Graham, Nicholas; Herweifer, Celine; Gordon, Arnold L.; Kushnir, Yochanan; Cook, Ed (2007), 'Blueprints for medieval hydroclimate', *QSR* 26, 2322–36.

Seebohm, Frederic (1890), *The English village community: examined in its relations to the manorial and tribal systems and to the common or open field system of husbandry*, London.

Semenza, Jan C.; Menne, Bettina (2009), 'Climate change and infectious diseases in Europe', *Lancet Infectious Diseases* 9 (6), 365–75.

Sen, Amartya Kumar (1981), *Poverty and famines: an essay on entitlement and deprivation*, Oxford.

Sharp, Buchanan (2000), 'The food riots of 1347 and the medieval moral economy', 35–54 in A. Randall and A. Charlesworth, eds., *Moral economy and popular protest: crowds, conflict and authority*, London.

Sharp, Buchanan (2013), 'Royal paternalism and the moral economy in the reign of Edward II: the response to the Great Famine', *EcHR* 66 (2), 628–47.

Shi, Feng; Yang, Bao; Gunten, Lucien von (2012), 'Preliminary multiproxy surface air temperature field reconstruction for China over the past millennium', *Science China Earth Sciences* 55 (12), 2058–67.

Shrewsbury, J. F. D. (1971), *A history of bubonic plague in the British Isles*, Cambridge.

Simmons, I. G. (1974), *The ecology of natural resources*, London.

Sinha, A.; Cannariato, K. G.; Stott, L. D.; Cheng, H.; Edwards, R. L.; Yadava, M. G.; Ramesh, R.; Singh, I. B. (2007), 'A 900-year (600 to 1500 A.D.) record of the Indian summer monsoon precipitation from the core monsoon zone of India', *GRL* 34, L16707.

Sinha, Ashish; Stott, Lowell; Berkelhammer, Max; Cheng, Hai; Edwards, R. Lawrence; Buckley, Brendan; Aldenderfer, Mark; Mudelsee, Manfred (2011), 'A global context for megadrought in Monsoon Asia during the past millennium', *QSR* 30, 47–62.

Slack, Paul (1989), 'The Black Death past and present. 2. Some historical problems', *Trans. Royal Soc. Tropical Medicine & Hygiene* 83, 461–3.

Slavin, Philip (2009), 'Chicken husbandry in late-medieval eastern England: c.1250–1400', *Anthropozoologica* 44 (2), 35–56.

Slavin, Philip (2010), 'The fifth rider of the apocalypse: the great cattle plague in England and Wales and its economic consequences, 1319–1350', 165–79 in Simonetta Cavaciocchi, ed., *Le interazioni fra economia e ambiente biologico nell'Europe preindustriale secc. XIII–XVIII, Istituto Internazionale di Storia Economica 'F. Datini'*, Prato.

Slavin, Philip (2012), 'The great bovine pestilence and its economic and environmental consequences in England and Wales, 1318–50', *EcHR* 65 (4), 1239–66.

Slavin, Philip (2014), 'Warfare and ecological destruction in early fourteenth-century British Isles', *Environmental History* 19 (3), 528–50.

Smith, R. A. L. (1943), *Canterbury Cathedral Priory: a study in monastic administration*, Cambridge.

Smith, Richard M. (1984a), 'Families and their land in an area of partible inheritance: Redgrave, Suffolk 1260–1320', 135–95 in Richard M. Smith, ed., *Land, kinship and life-cycle*, Cambridge.

Smith, Richard M., ed. (1984b), *Land, kinship and life-cycle*, Cambridge.

Smith, Richard M. (1996), 'A periodic market and its impact upon a manorial community: Botesdale, Suffolk, and the manor of Redgrave, 1280–1300', 450–81 in Zvi Razi and Richard M. Smith, eds., *Medieval society and the manor court*, Oxford.

Smith, Richard M.; Razi, Zvi (1996), 'Origins of the English manorial court rolls as a written record: a puzzle', 36–68 in Zvi Razi and Richard M. Smith, eds., *Medieval society and the manor court*, Oxford.

Smyrlis, Kostis (2012), 'Byzantium', 128–66 in Harry Kitsikopoulos, ed., *Agrarian change and crisis in Europe, 1200–1500*, London.

Soens, Tim (2011), 'Floods and money. Funding drainage and flood control in coastal Flanders (13th–16th centuries)', *C&C* 26 (3), 333–65.

Soens, Tim (2013), 'The social distribution of land and flood risk along the North Sea Coast: Flanders, Holland and Romney Marsh compared (c.1200–1750)', 147–79 in Bas van Bavel and Erik Thoen, eds., *Rural societies and environments at risk. Ecology, property rights and social organisation in fragile areas (Middle Ages–twentieth century)*, Turnhout.

Soens, Tim; Thoen, Erik (2008), 'The origins of leasehold in the former county of Flanders', 31–56 in Bas van Bavel and Phillipp Schofield, eds., *The development of leasehold in northwestern Europe, c.1200–1600*, Turnhout.

Solanki, S. K.; Usoskin, I. G.; Kromer, B.; Schüssler, M.; Beer, J. (2004), 'An unusually active Sun during recent decades compared to the previous 11,000 years', *Nature* 431 (7012), 1084–7.
  Data: Solanki, S. K.; Usoskin, I. G.; Kromer, B.; Schüssler, M.; Beer, J. (2005), '11,000 year sunspot number reconstruction', IGBP # 2005-015.

Spinage, C. A. (2003), *Cattle plague: a history*, New York, Boston, Dordrecht, London and Moscow.

Spufford, Peter (1988), *Money and its use in medieval Europe*, Cambridge.

Stacey, R. C. (1995), 'Jewish lending and the medieval English economy', 78–101 in Richard H. Britnell and Bruce M. S. Campbell, eds., *A commercialising economy: England 1086 to c.1300*, Manchester.

Stapp, Paul; Antolin, Michael F.; Ball, Mark (2004), 'Patterns of extinction in prairie dog metapopulations: plague outbreaks follow El Niño events', *Frontiers in Ecology & the Environment* 2 (5), 235–40.

Stenseth, Nils Chr.; Atshabar, Bakyt B.; Begon, Mike; Belmain, Steven R.; Bertherat, Eric; Carniel, Elisabeth; Gage, Kenneth L.; Leirs, Herwig; Rahalison, Lila (2008), 'Plague: past, present, and future', *PLoS Medicine* 5 (1), 009–13.

Stenseth, Nils Chr.; Samia, Noelle I.; Viljugrein, Hildegunn; Kausrud, Kyrre Linné; Begon, Mike; Davis, Stephen; Leirs, Herwig; Dubyanskiy, V. M.; Esper, Jan; Ageyev, Vladimir S.; Klassovskiy, Nikolay L.; Pole, Sergey B.; Chan, Kung-Sik (2006), 'Plague dynamics are driven by climate variation', *PNAS* 103 (35), 13110–15.

Stephenson, Martin J. (1988), 'Wool yields in the medieval economy', *EcHR* 41 (3), 368–91.

Stern, Derek Vincent (2000), *A Hertfordshire demesne of Westminster Abbey: profits, productivity and weather*, ed. and intro. Christopher Thornton, Hatfield.

Stocks, Katharine (2003), 'Payments to manorial courts in the early Winchester accounts', 45–59 in Richard H. Britnell, ed., *The Winchester Pipe Rolls and medieval English society*, Woodbridge.

Stoffel, Markus; Khodri, Myriam; Corona, Christophe; Guillet, Sébastien; Poulain, Virginie; Bekki, Slimane; Guiot, Joël; Luckman, Brian H.; Oppenheimer, Clive; Lebas, Nicolas; Beniston, Martin; Masson-Delmotte, Valérie (2015), 'Estimates of volcanic-induced cooling in the northern hemisphere over the past 1,500 years', *Nature Geoscience advance online*.

Stone, David (1997), 'The productivity of hired and customary labour: evidence from Wisbech Barton in the fourteenth century', *EcHR* 50 (4), 640–56.

Stone, David (2005), *Decision-making in medieval agriculture*, Oxford.

Stone, David (2011), 'The Black Death and its immediate aftermath: crisis and change in the Fenland economy, 1346–1353', 213–44 in Mark Bailey and Stephen Henry Rigby, eds., *Town and countryside in the age of the Black Death: essays in honour of John Hatcher*, Turnhout.

Stone, David (2014), 'The impact of drought in early fourteenth-century England', *EcHR* 67 (2), 435–62.

Stone, Eric (1962), 'Profit and loss accountancy at Norwich Cathedral Priory', *Trans. Royal Historical Soc.*, 5th series, 12, 25–48.

Stothers, Richard B. (1999), 'Volcanic dry fogs, climate cooling, and plague pandemics in Europe and the Middle East', *Climatic Change* 42, 713–23.

Stothers, Richard B. (2000), 'Climatic and demographic consequences of the massive volcanic eruption of 1258', *Climatic Change* 45, 361–74.

Stuiver, Minze; Quay, Paul D. (1980), 'Changes in atmospheric Carbon-14 attributed to a variable Sun', *Science* 207 (4426), 11–19.

Sun, Junyan; Liu, Yu (2012), 'Tree ring based precipitation reconstruction in the south slope of the middle Qilian Mountains, northeastern Tibetan Plateau, over the last millennium', *Journal of Geophysical Research* 117, D08108.

Sun, Yi-Cheng; Jarrett, Clayton O.; Bosio, Christopher F.; Hinnebusch, B. Joseph (2014), 'Retracing the evolutionary path that led to flea-borne transmission of *Yersinia pestis*', *Cell Host & Microbe* 15 (5), 578–86.

Suntsov, V. V. (2014), 'Ecological aspects of the origin of *Yersinia pestis*, causative agent of the plague: concept of intermediate environment', *Contemporary Problems of Ecology* 7 (1), 1–11.

Sussman, George D. (2011), 'Was the Black Death in India and China?', *BHM* 85 (3), 319–55.

Tana, Li (2014), 'Towards an environmental history of the eastern Red River Delta, Vietnam, c.900–1400', *Journal of Southeast Asian Studies* 45, 315–37.

Tetzlaff, Gerd; Börngen, Michael; Mudelsee, Manfred: Raabe, Armin (2002), 'Das Jahrtausendhochwasser von 1342 am Main aus meteorologisch-hydrologischer Sicht', *Wasser und Boden* 54, 41–9.

Theilmann, John; Cate, Frances (2007), 'A plague of plagues: the problem of plague diagnosis in medieval England', *JIH* 37 (3), 371–93.

Thirsk, Joan (1961), 'Industries in the countryside', 70–88 in F. J. Fisher, ed., *Essays in the economic and social history of Tudor and Stuart England in honour of R. H. Tawney*, London.

Thirsk, Joan (1973), 'Roots of industrial England', 93–108 in Alan R. H. Baker and J. B. Harley, eds., *Man made the land: essays in English historical geography*, Newton Abbot.

Thoen, Erik (1997), 'The birth of "the Flemish husbandry": agricultural technology in medieval Flanders', 69–88 in Grenville Astill and John Langdon, eds., *Medieval farming and technology: the impact of agricultural change in northwest Europe*, Leiden and New York.

Thompson, L. G.; Mosley-Thompson, E.; Davis, M. E.; Zagorodnov, V. S.; Howat, I. M.; Mikhalenko, V. N.; Lin, P.-N. (2013), 'Annually resolved ice core records of tropical climate variability over the past ~1800 years', *Science* 340 (6135), 945–50.

Thornton, Christopher (1991), 'The determinants of land productivity on the bishop of Winchester's demesne of Rimpton, 1208 to 1403', 183–210 in Bruce M. S. Campbell and Mark Overton, eds., *Land, labour and livestock: historical studies in European agricultural productivity*, Manchester.

Thrupp, Sylvia L. (1962), *The merchant class of medieval London*, Ann Arbor.

Thrupp, Sylvia L. (1965), 'The problem of replacement rates in late medieval English population', *EcHR* 18 (1), 101–19.

Thünen, Johann Heinrich von (1826 and 1966), *Der isolierte staat (Von Thünen's isolated state)* (ed. Peter Hall, trans. C. M. Wartenberg, Oxford), Hamburg.

Timmreck, Claudia; Lorenz, Stephan J.; Crowley, Thomas J.; Kinne, Stefan; Raddatz, Thomas J.; Thomas, Manu A.; Jungclaus, Johann H. (2009), 'Limited temperature response to the very large AD 1258 volcanic eruption', *GRL* 36, L21708, 5pp.

Titow, Jan Z. (1960), 'Evidence of weather in the account rolls of the bishopric of Winchester 1209–1350', *EcHR* 12 (3), 360–407.

Titow, Jan Z. (1962a), 'Land and population on the bishop of Winchester's estates 1209–1350', unpublished PhD thesis, University of Cambridge.

Titow, Jan Z. (1962b), 'Some differences between manors and their effects on the condition of the peasant in the thirteenth century', *AHR* 10 (1), 1–13.

Titow, Jan Z. (1969), *English rural society, 1200–1350*, London.

Titow, Jan Z. (1987), 'The decline of the Fair of St Giles, Winchester, in the thirteenth and fourteenth centuries', *Nottingham Medieval Studies* 31 (1), 58–75.

Tran, Thi-Nguyen-Ny; Signoli, Michel; Fozzati, Luigi; Aboudharam, Gérard; Raoult, Didier; Drancourt, Didier (2011), 'High throughput, multiplexed pathogen detection authenticates plague waves in medieval Venice, Italy', *PLoS One* 6 (3), e16735.

Trenholme, Norman Maclaren (1901), 'The risings in the English monastic towns in 1327', *American Historical Review* 6 (4), 650–70.

Trouet, V.; Esper, J.; Graham, N. E.; Baker, A.; Scourse, J. D.; Frank, D. C. (2009a), 'Persistent positive North Atlantic Oscillation mode dominated the Medieval Climate Anomaly', *Science* 324, 78–80.

Data: Trouet, V.; Esper, J.; Graham, N. E.; Baker, A.; Scourse, J. D.; Frank, D. C. (2009b), 'Multi-decadal winter North Atlantic Oscillation reconstruction', IGBP # 2009-033.

Tuchman, Barbara Wertheim (1978), *A distant mirror: the calamitous fourteenth century*, New York.

Tupling, G. H. (1933), 'The origins of markets and fairs in medieval Lancashire', *Trans. Lancashire & Cheshire Antiquarian Soc.* 49, 75–94.

Twigg, Graham (1984), *The Black Death: a biological reappraisal*, London.

Unger, Richard W. (1980), *The ship in the medieval economy 600–1600*, London.

Unwin, Tim (1981), 'Rural marketing in medieval Nottinghamshire', *JHG* 7 (3), 231–51.

Vanhaute Erik (2001), 'Rich agriculture and poor farmers: land, landlords and farmers in Flanders, 18th–19th centuries', *Rural History: Economy, Society, Culture* 12, 19–40.

Veale, Elspeth M. (1966), *The English fur trade in the later Middle Ages*, London.

Velisevich, S. N.; Kozlov, D. S. (2006), 'Effects of temperature and precipitation on radial growth of Siberian larch in ecotopes with optimal, insufficient, and excessive soil moistening', *Russian Journal of Ecology* 37 (4), 241–6.

Victoria County History (1973), *A history of the County of Hampshire*, 2, ed. H. Arthur Doubleday and William Page, London.

Vieira, L. E. A.; Solanki, S. K.; Krivova, N. A.; Usoskin, I. (2011), 'Evolution of the solar irradiance during the Holocene', *Astronomy & Astrophysics* 531, 20pp.

Vogler, Amy J.; Chan, Fabien; Wagner, David M.; Roumagnac, Philippe; Lee, Judy; Nera, Roxanne; Eppinger, Mark; Ravel, Jacques; Rahalison, Lila; Rasoamanana, Bruno W.; Beckstrom-Sternberg, Stephen M.; Achtman, Mark; Chanteau, Suzanne; Keim, Paul (2011), 'Phylogeography and molecular epidemiology of *Yersinia pestis* in Madagascar', *PLoS Neglected Tropical Diseases* 5 (9), e1319.

Wagner, David M.; Klunk, Jennifer; Harbeck, Michaela; Devault, Alison; Waglechner, Nicholas; Sahl, Jason W.; Enk, Jacob; Birdsell, Dawn N.; Kuch, Melanie; Lumibao, Candice; Poinar, Debi; Pearson, Talima; Fourment, Mathieu; Golding, Brian; Riehm, Julia M.; Earn, David J. D.; DeWitte, Sharon; Rouillard, Jean-Marie; Grupe, Gisela; Wiechmann, Ingrid; Bliska, James B.; Keim, Paul S.; Scholz, Holger C.; Holmes, Edward C.; Poinar, Hendrik (2014), '*Yersinia pestis* and the Plague of Justinian 541–543 AD: a genomic analysis', *Lancet Infectious Diseases* 14 (4), 319–26.

Walker, James T. (2009), 'National income in Domesday England', unpublished paper presented at the Hi-Pod conference *Reconstructing the national income of Europe before 1850: estimates and implications for long run growth and development*, University of Warwick in Venice, Palazzo Pesaro Papafava, April 2009.

Wallerstein, Immanuel (1980), *The modern world system, II, Mercantilism and the consolidation of the European world economy, 1600–1750*, New York.

Walløe, Lars (2008), 'Medieval and modern bubonic plague: some clinical continuities', *Medical History*, Supplement 27, 59–73.

Wang, Yongjin; Cheng, Hai; Edwards, R. Lawrence; He, Yaoqi; Kong, Xinggong; An, Zhisheng; Wu, Jiangying; Kelly, Megan J.; Dykoski, Carolyn A.; Li,

Xiangdong (2005), 'The Holocene Asian monsoon: links to solar changes and North Atlantic climate', *Science* 308 (5723), 854–7.

Data: Wang, Yongjin; Cheng, Hai; Edwards, R. Lawrence; He, Yaoqi; Kong, Xinggong; An, Zhisheng; Wu, Jiangying; Kelly, Megan J.; Dykoski, Carolyn A.; Li, Xiangdong (2006), 'Dongge Cave stalagmite high-resolution Holocene d18O data', IGBP # 2006-096.

Warren, W. L. (1973), *Henry II*, London.

Webb, Colleen T.; Brooks, Christopher P.; Gage, Kenneth L.; Antolin, Michael F. (2006), 'Classic flea-borne transmission does not drive plague epizootics in prairie dogs', *PNAS* 103 (16), 6236–41.

Welford, Mark R.; Bossak, Brian H. (2010a), 'Revisiting the medieval Black Death of 1347–1351: spatiotemporal dynamics suggestive of an alternate causation', *Geography Compass* 4 (6), 561–75.

Welford, Mark R.; Bossak, Brian H. (2010b), 'Body lice, *Yersinia pestis orientalis*, and Black Death', *EID* 16 (10), 1649.

Wheelis, Mark (2002), 'Biological warfare at the 1346 siege of Caffa', *EID* 8 (9), 971–5.

White Jr, Lynn T. (1962), *Medieval technology and social change*, Oxford.

White Jr, Lynn T. (1967), 'The historical roots of our ecologic crisis', *Science* 155 (3767), 1,203–7.

Whittle, Jane (2000), *The development of agrarian capitalism: land and labour in Norfolk 1440–1580*, Oxford.

Wicksteed, Philip H. (1906), *Villani's chronicle: being selections from the first nine books of the* Croniche Fiorentine *of Giovanni Villani*, trans. Rose E. Selfe, London.

Wiechmann, Ingrid; Grupe, Gisela (2005), 'Detection of *Yersinia pestis* DNA in two early medieval skeletal finds from Aschheim (Upper Bavaria, 6th century AD)', *American Journal of Physical Anthropology* 126 (1), 48–55.

Wiles, Gregory C.; D'Arrigo, Rosanne D.; Villalba, Ricardo; Calkin, Parker E.; Barclay, David J. (2004), 'Century-scale solar variability and Alaskan temperature change over the past millennium', *GRL* 31, L15203.

Williams, Michael (2000), 'Dark ages and dark areas: global deforestation in the deep past', *JHG* 26 (1), 28–46.

Williams, Shanna K.; Schotthoefer, Anna M.; Montenieri, John A.; Holmes, Jennifer L.; Vetter, Sara M.; Gage, Kenneth L.; Bearden, Scott W. (2013), 'Effects of low-temperature flea maintenance on the transmission of *Yersinia pestis* by *Oropsylla montana*', *Vector-Borne & Zoonotic Diseases* 13 (7), 468–78.

Williamson, Janet (1984), 'Norfolk: thirteenth century', 31–105 in P. D. A. Harvey, ed., *The peasant land market in medieval England*, Oxford.

Williamson, Oliver E. (1989), 'Transaction cost economics', *Handbook of Industrial Organization* 1, 135–82.

Witney, Kenneth P. (1990), 'The woodland economy of Kent, 1066–1348', *AHR* 38 (1), 20–39.

Witney, Kenneth P., trans. & ed. (2000), *The survey of Archbishop Pecham's Kentish manors 1283–85*, Kent Records 28, Maidstone.

Witze, Alexandra (2012), '13th century volcano mystery may be solved', *Science News* 182 (1), 14 July, p. 12.

Wolffe, Bertram Percy (1971), *The royal demesne in English history: the Crown estate in the governance of the realm from the Conquest to 1509*, London.

Wood, James W.; Ferrell, Rebecca J.; Dewitte-Avina, Sharon N. (2003), 'The temporal dynamics of the fourteenth-century Black Death: new evidence from English ecclesiastical records', *Human Biology* 75 (4), 427–49.

Woodruff, Rosalie; Guest, Charles (2000), 'Teleconnections of the El Niño phenomenon: public health and epidemiological prospects', 89–108 in Richard H. Grove and John Chappell, eds., *El Niño – history and crisis: studies from the Asia-Pacific region*, Cambridge.

Woolgar, Christopher Michael (1999), *The great household in late medieval England*, London.

Woolgar, Christopher Michael (2010), 'Food and the Middle Ages', *Journal of Medieval History* 36 (1), 1–19.

Wrigley, E. Anthony (1962), 'The supply of raw materials in the industrial revolution', *EcHR* 15 (1), 1–16.

Wrigley, E. Anthony (1966), 'Family limitation in pre-industrial England', *EcHR* 19 (1), 82–109.

Wrigley, E. Anthony (1985), 'Urban growth and agricultural change: England and the Continent in the early modern period', *JIH* 15 (4), 683–728.

Yang, B., Braeuning, A.; Johnson, K. R.; Yafeng, S. (2002), 'Temperature variation in China during the last two millennia', IGBP # 2002-061.

Yang, Bao; Qin, Chun; Wang, Jianglin; He, Minhui; Melvin, Thomas M.; Osborn, Timothy J.; Briffa, Keith R. (2014), 'A 3,500-year tree-ring record of annual precipitation on the north-eastern Tibetan Plateau', *PNAS* 111 (8), 2903–8.

Yates, Margaret (2007), *Town and countryside in western Berkshire, c.1327–c.1600: social and economic change*, Woodbridge.

Yates, Margaret (2013), 'The market in freehold land, 1300–1509: the evidence of feet of fines', *EcHR* 66 (2), 579–600.

Yoshinobu, S. (1988), *Sodai Konan keizaishi no kenkyu [A study of the economic history of Song-dynasty Jiangnan]*, Tokyo.

Yule, Sir Henry, trans. & ed. (1875), *The book of Marco Polo, the Venetian, concerning the kingdoms and marvels of the East*, 2 vols., revised 2nd edn, London.

Yule, Sir Henry; Cordier, Henri, trans. & ed. (1916), *Cathay and the way thither, being a collection of medieval notices of China, III*, London.

Zanden, Jan Luiten van (2009), *The long road to the industrial revolution: the European economy in a global perspective, 1000–1800*, Leiden and Boston.

Zanden, Jan Luiten van; Leeuwen, Bas van (2012), 'Persistent but not consistent: the growth of national income in Holland 1347–1807', *EEH* 49 (2), 119–30.

Zhang, David D.; Lee, Harry F.; Wang, Cong; Li, Baosheng; Pei, Qing; Zhang, Jane; An, Yulun (2011), 'The causality analysis of climate change and large-scale human crisis', *PNAS* 108 (42), 17296–301.

Zhang, Pingzhong; Cheng, Hai; Edwards, R. Lawrence; Chen, Fahu; Wang, Yongjin; Yang, Xunlin; Liu, Jian; Tan, Ming; Wang, Xianfeng; Liu, Jingua; An, Chunlei; Dai, Zhibo; Zhou, Jing; Zhang, Dezhong; Jia, Jihong; Jin, Liya; Johnson, Kathleen R. (2008), 'A test of climate, sun, and culture relationships from an 1810-year Chinese cave record', *Science* 322 (5903), 940–2.

Zhang, Zhibin; Li, Zhenqing; Tao, Yi; Chen, Min; Wen, Xinyu; Xu, Lei; Tian, Huidong; Stenseth, Nils Chr. (2007), 'Relationship between increase rate of human plague in China and global climate index as revealed by cross-spectral and cross-wavelet analyses', *Integrative Zoology* 2 (3), 144–53.

Zhao, Cheng; Liu, Zhonghui; Rohling, Eelco J.; Yu, Zicheng; Liu, Weiguo; He, Yuxin; Zhao, Yan; Chen, Fahu (2013), 'Holocene temperature fluctuations in the northern Tibetan Plateau', *Quaternary Research* 80 (1), 55–65.

Ziegler, Philip (1969), *The Black Death*, London.

Zielinski, G. A. (1995), 'Stratospheric loading and optical depth estimates of explosive volcanism over the last 2100 years derived from the Greenland Ice Sheet Project 2 ice core', *Journal of Geophysical Research* 100, 20,937–55.

Index

Places within England are identified by their pre-1973 counties; places outside England are identified by the countries/territories to which they currently belong.